The Arbitrator's Role as a Settlement Facilitator in International Commercial Arbitration

The Arbitrator's Role as a Settlement Facilitator in International Commercial Arbitration

Toward Harmonized Transnational Standards

Carmel Wahby

Wolters Kluwer

Published by:
Kluwer Law International B.V.
PO Box 316
2400 AH Alphen aan den Rijn
The Netherlands
E-mail: lrs-sales@wolterskluwer.com
Website: www.wolterskluwer.com/en/solutions/kluwerlawinternational

Sold and distributed by:
Wolters Kluwer Legal & Regulatory U.S.
920 Links Avenue
Landisville, PA 17538
United States of America
E-mail: customer.service@wolterskluwer.com

ISBN 978-94-035-3809-9

e-Book: ISBN 978-94-035-3819-8
web-PDF: ISBN 978-94-035-3829-7

About the Author

Dr. Carmel Wahby is an international lawyer with more than 25 years of experience, specializing in cross-border negotiation, mediation, and arbitration. Since 2021, he has led a European firm dedicated to international dispute resolution and a broad range of legal services, spanning economic, commercial, and public law, as well as advising on government relations and peace processes. From 2005 to 2021, he served as judge and president of a district court, where he pioneered the integration of mediation into judicial proceedings. Fluent in English, Arabic, and Hebrew, with professional proficiency in German, he holds a PhD in Law (Leiden University), an LL.M. (Haifa University), an MBA in Strategy and Entrepreneurship (Tel Aviv University), and is admitted to the Berlin and Tel Aviv bars.

"Discourage litigation. Persuade your neighbors to compromise whenever you can. Point out to them how the nominal winner is often a real loser—in fees, expenses, and waste of time. As a peacemaker, the lawyer has a superior opportunity of being a good man. There will still be business enough."

Abraham Lincoln[1]

1. Lincoln, 2008, p. 81.

Table of Contents

List of Abbreviations

AAA	American Arbitration Association
ABA	American Bar Association
ACICA	Australian Centre for International Commercial Arbitration
ADR	Alternative Dispute Resolution
ADRIC	ADR Institute of Canada
AMA Protocol	Arb-Med-Arb Protocol (of SIAC-SIMC, Singapore)
Arb-Med	Arbitration-Mediation
Arb-Med-Arb	Arbitration-Mediation-Arbitration
ASA	*Association Suisse de l'Arbitrage* (Swiss Arbitration Association)
BAC	Beijing Arbitration Commission
BRI	Belt and Road Initiative
CCA	College of Commercial Arbitrators
CEDR	Centre for Effective Dispute Resolution
CETA	Comprehensive Economic and Trade Agreement
CIArb	Chartered Institute of Arbitrators
CICC	China International Commercial Court
CIETAC	China International Economic and Trade Arbitration Commission
CPR	International Institute for Conflict Prevention and Resolution
DIS	*Deutsche Institution für Schiedsgerichtsbarkeit* (German Arbitration Institute)
ECHR	European Convention on Human Rights
ECtHR	European Court of Human Rights
EU	European Union
FDRC	(Hong Kong) Financial Dispute Resolution Centre
FOA	Final Offer Arbitration
GPC	Global Pound Conference (Series)

HKIAC	Hong Kong International Arbitration Centre
HKMC	Hong Kong Mediation Centre
IAMA	Institute of Arbitrators and Mediators Australia (i.e., Resolution Institute)
IBA	International Bar Association
ICA	International Commercial Arbitration
ICC	International Chamber of Commerce
ICDR	International Centre for Dispute Resolution
ICM	International Commercial Mediation
ICSID	International Centre for Settlement of Investment Disputes
IMI	International Mediation Institute
JAMS	Judicial Arbitration and Mediation Services
LCIA	London Court for International Arbitration
LMAA	London Maritime Arbitrators Association
Med-Arb	Mediation-Arbitration
MEDALOA	Mediation followed by Last-Offer Arbitration
NAI	Netherlands Arbitration Institute
PCA	Permanent Court of Arbitration
RCAP	(UNCITRAL) Regional Centre for Asia and the Pacific
SCC	Stockholm Chamber of Commerce
SCIA	Shenzhen Court of International Arbitration
SIAC	Singapore International Arbitration Centre
SIMC	Singapore International Mediation Centre
SPEDR	(UNCITRAL's Model Clauses on) specialized express dispute resolution
UK	United Kingdom
UN	United Nations
UNCITRAL	UN Commission on International Trade Law
UNCTAD	UN Conference on Trade and Development
UNIDROIT	International Institute for the Unification of Private Law
US	United States
WAC	Wuhan Arbitration Commission
WTO	World Trade Organization

Preface

International commercial arbitration (ICA), a time-honored instrument of peaceful dispute resolution, has established itself as the preferred method for resolving cross-border commercial conflicts. This rise is grounded in a combination of attributes that have set it apart from traditional litigation and other forms of alternative dispute resolution. Among its most valued features are the impartiality of the tribunal, procedural flexibility, confidentiality, and, crucially, the emphasis on party autonomy—allowing disputing parties to define the seat of arbitration, the applicable legal framework, and the composition of the tribunal. ICA's effectiveness is further enhanced by the broad international enforceability of arbitral awards, primarily under the 1958 New York Convention.

However, despite its strengths, ICA has not remained immune to criticism. In recent decades, users and scholars have raised concerns about the growing "judicialization" of the field—marked by the assimilation of court-like procedures, increased complexity, delays, and rising costs. These developments have shifted the focus of arbitration away from its pragmatic, business-driven origins and toward more formal, rights-based processes. Consequently, ICA is facing increasing competition from other dispute resolution methods, particularly international mediation, and from the growing network of international commercial courts that aim to provide streamlined, transnationally relevant alternatives to arbitration.

In light of these trends, a broader recalibration of global dispute resolution is underway—one that seeks to balance adjudicative authority with flexibility, efficiency, and early settlement. Among the most innovative developments in this evolving landscape is the role of the arbitrator as a settlement facilitator. This dual role challenges traditional boundaries by enabling arbitrators, in appropriate circumstances, to take an active part in fostering amicable resolution alongside their adjudicative duties.

While this role has drawn increasing attention from scholars, arbitral institutions, and regulators, it remains one of the least harmonized and most debated areas in the field. Jurisdictions differ in their acceptance of the arbitrator's dual function; some embrace it as a natural evolution of party autonomy and procedural innovation, while others view it with caution or skepticism, citing risks to impartiality and enforceability. Despite this divergence, recent empirical studies, institutional rules, and legislative developments suggest that the role is gaining traction across legal traditions, prompting calls for a clearer normative framework.

This book responds to that need. It offers a comprehensive and systematic exploration of the arbitrator's role as a settlement facilitator in ICA, addressing both theoretical and practical dimensions. The research is driven by the conviction that, while arbitration must remain a reliable forum for enforceable adjudication, it should also respond more effectively to the evolving needs of users—especially in an era marked by globalization, increasing case complexity, and growing emphasis on efficiency and relational outcomes.

The book maps a wide spectrum of facilitation methods that arbitrators may use, whether as part of a standalone arbitration or within hybrid arbitration-mediation processes. These methods are critically evaluated in light of their potential benefits and risks, including concerns related to due process, party consent, and award enforceability. A key feature of the book is its comparative analysis of how different jurisdictions and legal traditions regulate, accept, or reject the arbitrator's involvement in settlement efforts. It also examines institutional rules, past harmonization efforts, and emerging regulatory trends to identify commonalities and challenges.

Importantly, the book aims not only to inform but also to support practical implementation. It proposes concrete contractual safeguards and procedural mechanisms that parties may adopt to employ the arbitrator as a settlement facilitator without compromising the integrity of the proceedings. It also offers broader policy recommendations for advancing global recognition and harmonization of this role.

Although rooted in academic research and supported by extensive comparative and empirical analysis, the book is ultimately practice-oriented. It draws on my own professional experience as a judge, mediator, and arbitrator—roles in which I have witnessed firsthand the value of integrating adjudication and facilitation to resolve disputes more effectively. This background informs the book's focus on accessibility, usability, and practical application.

The book is intended for a diverse audience: arbitrators, practitioners, arbitral institutions, students, academics, and policymakers engaged in dispute resolution at both the international and domestic levels. Given that many of the settlement-facilitation mechanisms discussed here are equally applicable to domestic arbitration, national-level professionals will also find practical insights. Additionally, the book's institutional and normative recommendations will be of particular interest to regulators and lawmakers shaping the future of cross-border dispute resolution.

I am deeply grateful to Leiden Law School, and especially to my esteemed supervisors, Prof. dr. H.J. Snijders and Prof. dr. M.E. Koppenol-Laforce, for their expert guidance and encouragement throughout this research journey. Their unwavering support, intellectual generosity, and belief in this project have shaped every chapter of this work.

I am equally thankful to my family, whose love, understanding, and support made this endeavor possible. Their motivation has carried me through each stage, and it is to them that I dedicate this book—with deepest gratitude and affection.

I hope this work contributes meaningfully to the evolving field of international arbitration and that it sparks further discussion and innovation in the role arbitrators can play in facilitating just, efficient, and collaborative resolutions.

Carmel Wahby
June 2025

Part I Setting the Stage

CHAPTER 1

Introduction

1.1 INTRODUCTION

Arbitration is considered one of the world's oldest peaceful dispute resolution methods.[1] It has existed in different variations since the beginning of recorded time, long before the law was established and courts were organized.[2] Throughout history, including in the ancient civilizations of Greece, Rome, Ptolemaic Egypt, and Asia, whenever commerce developed significantly, arbitration—which originally relied on mediation elements as its primary component—was resorted to as an important mechanism for dispute resolution between traders.[3] During the Middle Ages, when transactions between merchants expanded considerably beyond states' political, cultural, and geographical boundaries, arbitration flourished as an autonomous mode of dispute resolution for cross-border transactions. Hence, members of particular industries and guilds outside the purview of the local court operated arbitration according to the standards and customs of trade as well as the principles of flexibility, informality, expedition, party autonomy, and equal treatment of the parties.[4] This self-regulated and extra-judicial normative system, known as *lex mercatoria*,[5] paved the way for modern international commercial arbitration (ICA),[6] which, in the current globalized world, "has become a very important, if not the most important, method of resolving disputes between companies involved in cross-border business."[7] Contributing to this

1. Kun, 2013b, p. 182; Horvath, 2011, p. 252; Lew, 2007, p. 457.
2. Horvath, 2011, p. 252; Kun, 2013b, pp. 182-183; Kellor & Angell, 1948, p. 3.
3. Blackaby et al., 2022, §1.05; Born, 2021, §1.01[B][1]; Roebuck, 2007, p. 106; Kun, 2013b, p. 183; Horvath, 2011, p. 252; Lew, 2007, p. 457; Böckstiegel, 2009, p. 294; Ross, 2013, p. 353.
4. Gaillard, 2023, p. 36; Blackaby et al., 2022, §1.05; Horvath, 2011, pp. 252-253; Lew, 2007, p. 459; Kun, 2013b, p. 183; Böckstiegel, 2009, p. 294.
5. Burdick, 1902, pp. 472-475; Gaillard, 2023, p. 36; Kun, 2013b, pp. 183-184, 203; Kun & Jemielniak, 2016, p. 569.
6. Trakman, 2006, p. 6; Kun, 2013b, pp. 183-184.
7. Ruckteschler & Wendelstein, 2021, p. 761. *See also* Lew, 2007, p. 463; Horvath, 2011, p. 254; Cremades, 1998, p. 157.

leading position of ICA are the following initial advantages it offers, the combination of which cannot arguably be found in national court proceedings or any other alternative dispute-resolution (ADR) method: (a) *neutrality* that allows parties to avoid fear of bias resulting from litigation in front of the "home" courts of their co-contractors; (b) *flexibility* and *party autonomy* that derive from the contractual foundation of the process, which allow parties to design the dispute-resolution mechanism according to their needs by deciding on the seat of arbitration, applicable law, arbitration institution, procedural rules, and arbitrators; (c) the *confidentiality* of the process and its outcome; (d) the *preservation of business relationships* due to confidentiality and flexibility that allow parties to keep the arbitral process informal, pragmatic and business-oriented; (e) the *cost-effectiveness* of the process resulting from potential saving of time and costs; and (f) the *finality* of the dispute alongside the *safe and worldwide enforcement mechanism* of the arbitral award under the 1958 United Nations (UN) Convention on the Recognition and Enforcement of Foreign Arbitral Awards (New York Convention).[8]

1.2 HARMONIZATION TRENDS IN ICA

The continuous process of globalization has triggered a constant and considerable increase in the number, scope, and complexity of international business relations,[9] which has resulted in a manifold regulatory regime for the cross-border economic system. Unlike the traditional legal regime of the domain, based mainly on binding norms designed through a top-down process such as conventions and state laws,[10] this regime has undergone a process of "legal globalization" or "transnational legal ordering"[11] to accommodate a wide variety of legal sources,[12] many of which have

8. Born, 2021, §1.02[B][1]-[8]; Blackaby et al., 2022, §1.122-1.128; Nobles, 2012, pp. 79-83; Kun, 2013b, pp. 184-185; Bermann, 2017, p. 22; Berger & Jensen, 2016, pp. 4-5; Horvath, 2011, pp. 255-256; Hrnčiříková, 2016, p. 98; Jemielniak, 2014, pp. 319, 332, 329; Lew, 2007, p. 463; Jemielniak, 2017, pp. 166-167; Lopez-Rodriguez, 2003, p. 67; Dasser, 2021, pp. 56-57; Kaufmann-Kohler, 2010, p. 285; Pate, 2010, p. 162; Najar, 2009, pp. 515-517; Lalive, 1998, p. 487; Smit, 1986, pp. 9-12; McLean, 2009, pp. 1088-1089; Queen Mary University of London and White & Case LLP, 2018, p. 7; New York Convention, 1958, Article III.
9. Strong, 2014a, pp. 19-21; Brekoulakis, 2016b, p. 5; Cremades, 1998, p. 157; Horvath, 2011, pp. 258-259.
10. Mistelis, 2001, p. 15; Tietje & Nowrot, 2006, p. 22.
11. Jemielniak, 2017, pp. 156-157; Kun, 2016a, p. 245; Twining, 2009, p. 39; Glenn, 2009, p. 25; Scheuerman, 1999, p. 243; Ali, 2021, p. 24; Kun & Jemielniak, 2016, p. 581; Kaufmann-Kohler, 2003, p. 1333.
12. Including national law, private and public international law, as well as innovative soft norms to be discussed below. *See* Jessup, 1956, pp. 1-3; Ali, 2021, pp. 21-22; Michaels, 2007, p. 451; Tietje & Nowrot, 2006, pp. 28-29; Levit, 2005, p. 125; Tietje & Nowrot, 2004, p. 342; Koh, 1996, p. 184; Anders, 2004, p. 51, stating that "transnational law includes conventional public international law, human rights law, environmental regulation, economic law and lex mercatoria." Some scholars, however, still conceptualize transnational law as distinct from national and international law, since it mainly origins from and targets private actors involved in transnational activities, not nation-states or international organs founded on conventions or treaties. *See* Cotterrell, 2012, p. 501; Calliess, 2007, p. 476.

been designed through a bottom-up process by actors below the state level.[13] The resulting transnational law of commerce has triggered a broad harmonization process across all normative levels of the international business landscape.[14] It has also weakened the traditional authority of the domestic court system over cross-border commercial disputes and accelerated a shift toward ADR mechanisms, particularly international arbitration, for their resolution.[15]

As an "enterprise" of the legal regime that governs the international business system[16] and therefore strives to meet the global challenges of the domain[17] and the unified need of merchants and business institutes worldwide in an international dispute resolution mechanism that offers the abovementioned advantages,[18] ICA has undergone a similar process toward the transnationalization and harmonization of its practice and legal regime worldwide:

> There has been a powerful wave of harmonisation of the law and practice of international arbitration in the last decades. The beauty of this harmonisation process is that it merges very different procedural cultures. This comes as no surprise. International arbitration is a place where arbitrators and counsel trained in different legal systems (along with the parties they represent) meet and work

---

13. Tietje & Nowrot, 2006, pp. 18, 22, 29; Koh, 1996, pp. 183-184; Berman, 2005, p. 492; Vesting, 2004, pp. 247-252; Kaufmann-Kohler, 2010, p. 285; Kaufmann-Kohler, 2003, p. 1333; Ali, 2021, pp. 24-25; Tietje & Nowrot, 2004, p. 346; Beviglia-Zampetti, 2003, p. 121; Levit, 2005, p. 125.
14. This process of harmonization is exemplified by the establishment of the World Trade Organization (WTO) that its global rules and agreements aim to ensure that trade between nations "flows as smoothly, predictably and freely as possible," *see WTO: Overview*, n.d. It is also demonstrated by the establishment of the International Institute for the Unification of Private Law (UNIDROIT), an independent intergovernmental organization with 63 Member States, dedicated to "study needs and methods for modernising, harmonising and co-ordinating private and in particular commercial law as between states and groups of states and to formulate uniform law instruments, principles and rules to achieve those objectives," *see UNIDROIT: Overview*, 2023. For further discussion about the impact of globalization on the harmonization process of cross-border commercial relations, *see* Dasser, 2021, p. 91; Kaufmann-Kohler, 2010, pp. 285-286; Kun, 2016a, p. 245; Kun, 2013b, pp. 177, 182; Kaufmann-Kohler, 2003, p. 1333; Tietje & Nowrot, 2006, p. 18; Cremades, 1998, pp. 157-158.
15. Hrnčiříková, 2016, p. 98; Jemielniak, 2014, pp. 319, 332, 329; Lew, 2007, p. 463; Jemielniak, 2017, pp. 166-167; Lopez-Rodriguez, 2003, p. 67; Dasser, 2021, pp. 56-57; Kaufmann-Kohler, 2010, p. 285; Pate, 2010, p. 162.
16. Since ICA is based on domestic and international law, it may not fit into the orthodox categories of the law or modes of dispute resolution, despite its close association with private international law. Therefore, the literature views international arbitration from different prisms of the law, including public international law, private international law, national law, and cosmopolitan non-state norms to be discussed below. Such mixture of legal sources creates that "enterprise" of ICA. From a broader view arbitration may be defined as an interdisciplinary domain where the law constitutes only one dimension among others, such as economy, culture, and psychology. *See* Gaillard, 2023, p. 27; Bermann, 2017, pp. 17-72; Paulsson, 2008, p. 2; Bantekas, 2015, pp. 33-35.
17. Ali, 2021, p. 26; Bermann, 2017, p. 66; Strong, 2014a, pp. 18-24; Pate, 2010, pp. 144, 164; Brekoulakis, 2016a, p. 120, stating that "the unprecedented scale of sophistication of international commerce presents crucial challenges for international arbitration today and tests its traditional role and bilateral nature to its limits."
18. Bermann, 2017, p. 22; Born, 2021, §1.02[B][1]-[8]; Pate, 2010, p. 146; Ginsburg, 2011, p. 55; Kun, 2013b, pp. 181-182; Michaels, 2013, p. 37; Kun, 2016a, p. 246; Karton, 2014, pp. 14-15; Calliess & Renner, 2009, p. 1342.

> together to achieve a result—the resolution of a dispute. They have no choice but to find some common ground.[19]

This strong movement toward harmonization in ICA has been carried out through various normative levels,[20] starting with binding norms such as conventions and domestic arbitration laws—referred to in the literature as hard law norms[21]—and ending with non-binding rules and guidelines, classified by the literature as soft law norms.[22] The primary contribution to this process of harmonization is attributed to the UN Commission on International Trade Law (UNCITRAL), which through its legal instruments has influenced commercial arbitration at the global and local levels.[23] The *first milestone* of UNCITRAL is the New York Convention;[24] its worldwide accepted standards regarding recognition and enforcement of arbitral awards among all signed jurisdictions[25] are referred to as "transnational substantive norms or rules" of commercial arbitration,[26] which has created "the uniform standard for the practice of international arbitration."[27] Already signed by 172 countries,[28] the convention is considered "the most successful multilateral instrument in the field of international trade law" since it grants "additional measure of commercial security for parties entering into cross-border transactions."[29] The *second milestone* of UNCITRAL is the Model Law on International Commercial Arbitration (Model Law on ICA),[30] which despite lacking the binding characteristics of the convention, still constitutes a significant accelerator toward harmonization since many jurisdictions have followed

19. Kaufmann-Kohler, 2009, p. 189. *See also* Gaillard, 2023, pp. 42-44; Kun, 2016a, pp. 246-247; Ali, 2021, p. 24; Jemielniak, 2017, p. 156; Karton, 2014, p. 3; Ruggie, 2014, pp. 8-9; McLean, 2009, p. 1087; Kaufmann-Kohler, 2003, p. 1320; Kun, 2013b, pp. 182-185; Garnett, 2002, p. 400; Draetta, 2015, p. 329; Tschanz, 2016, pp. 82-83; Bantekas, 2015, pp. 37-38. For a general discussion about efforts to reconcile between different procedural attitudes in ICA, *see* Baum, 2001, pp. 21-30.
20. Ali, 2021, p. 27; Ruggie, 2014, pp. 8-9.
21. Ali, 2021, pp. 12, 30; Pate, 2010, pp. 146-147; Tietje & Nowrot, 2006, p. 22; Kaufmann-Kohler, 2010, p. 285.
22. Soft law refers generally to legal instruments that are not binding unless contractually agreed or signed/ratified. In international arbitration, such instruments include arbitration rules, model laws and clauses, and various guidelines on legal, practical and ethical issues connected with the domain. *See* Ali, 2021, pp. 13, 20-21; Tschanz, 2016, pp. 82-83; Draetta, 2015, p. 331; Bantekas, 2015, pp. 63-66; Cordero-Moss, 2012, p. 113; Kaufmann-Kohler, 2010, pp. 284, 288, 298-299; Pate, 2010, p. 147; Seidl-Hohenveldern, 1979, p. 194.
23. Herrmann, 1998, pp. 49-52; Von Schlabrendorff, 2009, pp. 92-93; Berger, 2019, p. 301; Ali, 2021, p. 8; Dasser, 2021, p. 123; Kaufmann-Kohler, 2003, 1321; Kun, 2013b, p. 185; Kaufmann-Kohler, 2010, p. 291; Kun, 2016a, pp. 247-248. According to the UN General Assembly, Resolution 2205, 1966, Article I, the mandate of UNCITRAL is to allow "the promotion of the progressive harmonization and unification of the law of international trade."
24. New York Convention, 1958. *See also* Blackaby et al., 2022, §1.103-1.106; Born, 2021, §1.04[A][1].
25. New York Convention, 1958, Articles II & V; Jemielniak, 2014, p. 329.
26. Brekoulakis, 2016b, p. 8. *See also* Bantekas, 2015, p. 5.
27. Cremades, 1998, p. 170. *See also* Kaufmann-Kohler, 2003, p. 1321; Kun, 2016a, p. 247; Von Schlabrendorff, 2009, p. 93; Garnett, 2002, pp. 403-405.
28. *Status: New York Convention*, n.d.
29. Kaplan, 2011, p. xi. *See also* Pate, 2010, p. 146; Helmer, 2003, pp. 65-66; Kaufmann-Kohler, 2003, p. 1321; Kun, 2016a, p. 247; Kun, 2013b, p. 185; Kun & Jemielniak, 2016, p. 570; Bernardini, 2004, p. 116.
30. Model Law on ICA, 2006. *See also* Dasser, 2021, pp. 67-72; Born, 2021, §1.04[B][1][a].

the recommendation of the General Assembly of the UN[31] and adopted its text as a ready-made legislation or alternatively based or amended their laws according to its principles.[32] This process has reduced "legal obstacles to the flow of international trade" caused by inconsistencies in domestic laws regulating international arbitration.[33] The fact that the Model Law on ICA has also been adopted by countries lacking "a strong arbitration tradition and culture" has been observed by some commentators as its true success since harmonization was primarily needed in those jurisdictions.[34] In addition, even countries that have not followed the Model Law on ICA have still moved increasingly toward harmonization due to the expanding global acceptance of its principles that have influenced lawmakers worldwide.[35] The *third milestone* of UNCITRAL is the UNCITRAL Arbitration Rules.[36] Their high acceptance and wide adoption by practitioners, arbitration institutes, and legislatures,[37] including those from developing countries, has contributed to the harmonization of standards and rules for conducting commercial arbitration globally.[38] These rules were followed by the UNCITRAL Notes on Organizing Arbitral Proceedings (UNCITRAL Notes on Arbitration), an explanatory text focused on international arbitration,[39] which, by announcing and restating common and innovative practices in international arbitration, has been pivotal in the harmonization of the domain.[40] The Notes' contribution to harmonization has also been attributed to the consultation process that has preceded their setting and publishing, including with "governments, interested

31. UN General Assembly, Resolution 40/72, 1985, recommending that "all States give due consideration to the Model Law on International Commercial Arbitration, in view of the desirability of uniformity of the law of arbitral procedures and the specific needs of international commercial arbitration practice." *See also* Berger, 2019, p. 300; Fouchard et al., 1999, p. 109.
32. Legislation based on the Model Law on ICA has been adopted in 93 states. *See Status: Model Law on ICA*, n.d. *See also* Born, 2021, §1.04[B][1][a]; Bantekas, 2015, p. 63; Von Schlabrendorff, 2009, p. 93; Kun, 2016a, p. 248; Kaufmann-Kohler, 2003, p. 1321; Kaplan, 2011, p. xi; Kaufmann-Kohler, 2010, p. 291; Holtzmann & Neuhaus, 1989, p. 10; Abou Youssef, 2012, p. 113; Helmer, 2003, pp. 63-65; Garnett, 2002, p. 408; Karton, 2014, pp. 31-32.
33. UN General Assembly, Resolution 2205, 1966, Introduction. *See also* Karton, 2014, p. 39; Holtzmann & Neuhaus, 1989, p. 10; Honka, 1996, p. 117; Kaufmann-Kohler, 2010, p. 291.
34. Brekoulakis, 2016b, p. 8. This attitude is supported by the 2016-2017 GPC Survey, to be presented in section 1.3 below, where the majority of respondents selected the harmonization of international laws and standards for dispute resolution systems as one of the most influential trends on the future of commercial dispute resolution. *See* GPC Series, 2016-2017, Question 4(5).
35. Kaufmann-Kohler, 2003, p. 1321; Bantekas, 2015, p. 63; Berger, 2019, p. 301, stating that "even countries like England, France, Sweden, or Switzerland, which have decided not to adopt the Model Law ... have sought inspiration and guidance from the text and systematic structure of the Model Law for their own reform projects in the past years."
36. UNCITRAL Arbitration Rules, 2021. *See also* Dasser, 2021, pp. 72-76; Born, 2021, §1.04[C][4].
37. UNCITRAL lists 60 leading arbitration institutions worldwide that base their rules on or were inspired by UNCITRAL Arbitration Rules, including the Swiss Arbitration Association (ASA) and the Permanent Court of Arbitration (PCA). *See Status: UNCITRAL Arbitration Rules*, n.d.; Swiss Arbitration Rules, 2021; PCA Arbitration Rules, 2012, Introduction; Dasser, 2021, p. 74.
38. Berger, 2019, p. 304; Kaufmann-Kohler, 2003, p. 1324; Dasser, 2021, pp. 74-75; Helmer, 2003, pp. 58-59; Kun, 2016a, p. 248; Von Schlabrendorff, 2009, p. 93.
39. UNCITRAL Notes on Arbitration, 2023, Article 1; Born, 2021, §1.04[D][5].
40. Ali, 2021, p. 13; Sussman & Berger, 2021b, p. 15; Helmer, 2003, pp. 60-61; Uzelac, 1997, p. 154.

intergovernmental and international non-governmental organizations active in the field of arbitration, including arbitral institutions, as well as individual experts."[41]

Apart from UNCITRAL, contribution to the harmonization of ICA is also attributed to the International Centre for Settlement of Investment Disputes (ICSID); its globally recognized and detailed instruments—the Convention on the Settlement of Investment Disputes between States and Nationals of Other States (ICSID Convention)[42] and the ICSID Arbitration Rules[43]—have contributed to the standardization of the practice and normative regime of ICA, despite their unique characteristics relating to investor-state interactions.[44] Other significant forces behind the harmonization process of ICA are national forces, mainly legislatures and judiciary systems in various jurisdictions, as well as non-governmental and private actors in the domain,[45] including leading arbitral institutions, professional arbitral organizations, and leading practitioners and scholars, generally referred to as the "global arbitration community" or the "global epistemic community" of arbitration.[46] Although this community lacks legislative authority and focuses on promoting soft norms,[47] it is crucial as a fundamental vehicle for the global standardization of ICA. Organized within globalized "legal social networks,"[48] it actively contributes to the academic development of the field.[49] Additionally, it addresses a wide range of substantive, procedural, and ethical issues connected with its practice while introducing arbitral rules, guidelines, and

41. UN General Assembly, Resolution 71/137, 2016. *See also* Ali, 2021, pp. 27-28, 32; Bantekas, 2015, p. 64.
42. ICSID Convention, 1966. For a general discussion about the convention, *see* Born, 2021, §1.04[A][4].
43. ICSID Arbitration Rules, 2022.
44. Kaufmann-Kohler, 2003, pp. 1324-1325.
45. Berger, 2019, pp. 303-304; Ali, 2021, p. 20; Kaufmann-Kohler, 2010, p. 285; Park, 2006, p. 141; Karrer, 2011; Bermann, 2017, p. 58, stating that "no contemporary architectural representation of international arbitration would be complete or accurate without reference to the numerous non-state actors engaged importantly in the international arbitration world."
46. Ali, 2021, p. 14; Sussman & Berger, 2021a, p. 28; Karton, 2014, p. 20; Kun, 2016a, p. 259; Jemielniak, 2014, p. 333; Lynch, 2003, pp. 94-100; Teubner et al., 1997, p. 158; Kerr, 1997, p. 124; Kaufmann-Kohler, 2010, p. 295, stating that "legal theorists would call the global arbitration community an epistemic community, a community that shares a particular interest and expertise. The actors within this community are well-known: arbitral institutions and organizations, the legal profession, and academia. Through a process of intellectual cross-fertilization, these actors play a dominant role in shaping the transnational consensus on arbitration law and practice."
47. Bantekas, 2015, pp. 65-66; Tschanz, 2016, p. 82; Park, 2017, pp. 1-2; Kaufmann-Kohler, 2010, pp. 298-299; Ali, 2021, pp. 20-21. It should, however, be mentioned that soft norms may emanate also from government-related domestic and international actors especially in highly contested subjects that are less likely to produce a hard-norm consensus or when the instrument is originally designed as a set of recommendations. *See* Ali, 2021, p. 30; Abbott & Snidal, 2000, p. 421; Kaufmann-Kohler, 2010, p. 284. For example, the WTO resorts to soft law instruments in highly controversial matters and the Swiss Code of Best Practice for Corporate Governance was designed from the outset as a set of recommended practices. *See* Footer, 2010, p. 248; Swiss Code of Best Practice for Corporate Governance, 2002.
48. Kaufmann-Kohler, 2010, p. 285. *See also* Ali, 2021, p. 14.
49. For example, the Swiss Arbitration Academy is a private institution founded and directed by arbitration practitioners which provides academic studies and professional training in arbitration, in cooperation with some Swiss universities. *See ASA: Swiss Arbitration Academy*, 2024.

"best practices" across various subjects that offer practical solutions for accommodating the diverse approaches stemming from different legal cultures.[50]

Following the abovementioned harmonization efforts invested by the different forces behind ICA, an established transnational consensus has been achieved on numerous areas of the domain:

> This procedural Esperanto comprises of transnational rules and practices, which exhibit considerable convergence on many aspects of the arbitration process, such as the commencement of arbitration, the constitution of an arbitral tribunal, the method which tribunals adopt to determine the applicable substantive law, the requirements for a valid award, the production of documents, the presentation of witnesses of fact and expert witnesses, inspections as well as the conduct of evidentiary hearings. Standard practices and norms gradually have emerged with regard to advocacy and ethical conduct before international tribunals too.[51]

Additionally, transnational unanimity has been achieved concerning the overriding principles of due process[52] and party autonomy,[53] with a consensus emerging on a third principle of procedural efficiency.[54]

1.3 CHALLENGES OF ICA

During the last decades, ICA users have repeatedly complained about significant delays and increasing costs of the process,[55] as reflected in the results of the 2015 and 2018 International Arbitration Surveys of Queen Mary University of London and White &

50. Ali, 2021, p. 14; Dasser, 2021, pp. 57, 86; Berger, 2019, pp. 303-304; Bermann, 2017, pp. 59-66; Berger, 2018b, p. 516; Jemielniak, 2017, pp. 167, 170; Berger & Jensen, 2017, p. 916; Vilaça, 2016, pp. 502-503; Kun, 2016a, p. 287; Bantekas, 2015, p. 66; Draetta, 2015, p. 331; Jemielniak, 2014, p. 333; Karton, 2014, p. 22; Kaufmann-Kohler, 2010, p. 295; Rau, 2005, p. 450; Helmer, 2003, p. 60; Lynch, 2003, pp. 96-100; Kaufmann-Kohler, 2003, pp. 1323-1325; Nariman, 2000, p. 267; Craig et al., 2000, §23.04. One of the most influential efforts towards harmonization of ICA are the International Bar Association (IBA) Rules on the Taking of Evidence in International Arbitration, which are intended to balance the conflicting approaches between the adversarial Common Law and the inquisitorial Civil Law traditions and present enhanced standardization regarding the methodology of the arbitral process. *See* IBA Rules on Evidence in International Arbitration, 2020; Bantekas, 2015, p. 66; Draetta, 2015, p. 334.
51. Brekoulakis, 2016b, p. 9. *See also* Kun, 2016a, p. 249; Kaufmann-Kohler, 2003, pp. 1325-1330; Kaufmann-Kohler, 2009, p. 189; Kun, 2013b, p. 185.
52. The term "due process" is commonly used as an umbrella term to express several basic rights of the parties during the arbitral process, including the right to natural justice, procedural fairness, the right to self-determination, the right to be heard, and the right to equal treatment by the tribunal. *See* Kaufmann-Kohler, 2003, p. 1321; Bernardini, 2004, p. 117.
53. Kun, 2016a, p. 249; Von Schlabrendorff, 2009, pp. 92-93; Kun, 2013b, p. 185; Bantekas, 2015, pp. 4-5; Bernardini, 2004, p. 115; Kaufmann-Kohler, 2003, p. 1321; Garnett, 2002, p. 402.
54. Kaufmann-Kohler, 2003, p. 1321; Kaufmann-Kohler, 2009, p. 193; Nigmatullina, 2019, p. 9; Prague Rules, 2018. Empirical data supports the emerging status of the efficiency principle. In the 2016-2017 GPC Survey, presented in section 1.3 below, efficiency was chosen as the key priority of parties when selecting dispute resolution processes. *See* GPC Series, 2018, pp. 3, 10.
55. Blackaby et al., 2022, §1.144-1.147; Stipanowich, 2023, p. 691; Ruckteschler & Wendelstein, 2021, p. 761; Chua, 2018, p. 8; Nigmatullina, 2018, p. 3; Berger & Jensen, 2016, pp. 1-2; Berger, 2016b; Pappas, 2015, p. 159; Mayer, 2016, p. 4; Ross, 2013, p. 353; Kun, 2011b, p. 549; Greenwood, 2011a, pp. 199-200; Najar, 2009, pp. 517-520; Rivkin, 2008, p. 376; Marriott, 2005, p. 546.

Case LLP (Queen Mary International Arbitration Survey), where hundreds of ICA users cited costs and lack of speed as its worst characteristics.[56] In addition, user discontent has been raised against the "judicialization"[57] process of the domain, which has resulted from incorporating judicial-style regulations, procedures, and behaviors that increase costs and delays while shifting its original focus on business considerations, including the preservation of business relationships, toward a new arbitral paradigm emphasizing formal and narrow legal-rights-based considerations similar to national court proceedings.[58] As a result, ICA has been increasingly referred to as the "new litigation."[59] More voices have lately questioned its ability to meet the needs of its users[60] and, consequently, maintain its status as the leading dispute resolution mechanism for cross-border commercial disputes.[61]

Indeed, following its growing formalization with increasing costs and duration that constitute important factors for choosing arbitration over litigation,[62] ICA has been subject to expanding competition with other ADR methods, particularly international mediation.[63] Empirical data confirms that the use of international mediation, considered by some scholars as the "new arbitration,"[64] has been growing globally.[65] Many practitioners and scholars believe that its attractiveness will grow further following the introduction of the UN Convention on International Settlement Agreements Resulting

56. Queen Mary University of London and White & Case LLP, 2018, p. 8; Queen Mary University of London and White & Case LLP, 2015, p. 7. For further empirical data about the escalated costs and protracted proceedings in ICA, *see* Nigmatullina, 2018, p. 4; Respondek, 2014, pp. 507-508; Najar, 2009, pp. 517-518.
57. Blackaby et al., 2022, §1.191; Trakman & Montgomery, 2017, p. 405; Bermann, 2017, p. 71; Berger, 2016b; Kun, 2011b, p. 549; Horvath, 2011, p. 251; Stipanowich, 2010, p. 8; Park, 2006, pp. 146-147; Cremades, 1998, p. 162.
58. Stipanowich, 2021a, p. 306; Kun & Jemielniak, 2016, pp. 582-583; Strong, 2013, pp. 117-118; Bernini, 2007, p. 52; Lalive, 1998, p. 484; Draetta, 2015, p. 342; Hrnčiříková, 2016, p. 109; Park, 2009, p. 693; Berger, 2019, p. 306; Nigmatullina, 2018, p. 4; Berger, 2003, p. 390; Stipanowich, 2023, p. 693; ICC Guide on Effective Management of Arbitration, 2018, p. 3.
59. Benzidi, 2017, p. 7; Pappas, 2015, p. 159; Stipanowich, 2010, p. 8; Ross, 2013, p. 353; Stipanowich, 2023, p. 692.
60. Stipanowich, 2023, pp. 692-693; Risse, 2013, p. 453; Brekoulakis, 2016b, p. 12; Strong, 2014a, pp. 19-21; Horvath, 2011, p. 271.
61. Berger, 2016b; Horvath, 2011, p. 271; Najar, 2009, p. 518; Marriott, 2005, p. 546.
62. Strong, 2014b, p. 22; Nigmatullina, 2018, p. 6; Guo, 2020, p. 228; Ross, 2013, p. 353. In a survey conducted in 2011 by Cornell University, the Straus Institute and the CPR International Institute among counsels in the 1,000 major U.S. corporations about current trends in the use of arbitration, mediation, and other ADR mechanisms (2011 Cornell University Survey), the most cited reasons by respondents for choosing ADR methods, including arbitration, over litigation were the saving of time (70.9% of the respondents) and the saving of costs (68.7%). *See* Stipanowich & Lamare, 2014, pp. 24, 37; Stipanowich & Ulrich, 2014b, p. 8.
63. Stipanowich, 2023, p. 691; Strong, 2014a, pp. 18-24; Berger & Jensen, 2016, p. 2; Berger, 2016b; Stipanowich & Ulrich, 2014a, p. 462; Ross, 2013, p. 353.
64. Nigmatullina, 2018, p. 6; Ross, 2013, p. 353.
65. Stipanowich, 2023, pp. 687, 691; Stipanowich, 2021a, pp. 270-271. In the aforementioned 2011 Cornell University Survey, 98% of respondents reported that their company had utilized mediation at least once during the three-year period preceding the survey, while only 83% reported the use of arbitration at least once during the same time frame. *See* Stipanowich & Lamare, 2014, pp. 41, 44-54. For further empirical studies that supports the expanding use of mediation for cross-border commercial disputes, *see* Born, 2021, §1.02[B][9]; Guo, 2020, p. 228; Strong, 2014b, pp. 15-18; Najar, 2009, p. 518.

from Mediation (Singapore Convention), which entered into force in September 2020 to establish a worldwide enforcement mechanism for settlement agreements resulting from international commercial mediation (ICM).[66] In addition, ICA has been subject to an evolving competition with litigation in front of national courts,[67] especially following the expansion of international commercial courts that strive to operate according to transnational standards despite their seat in specific jurisdictions to provide an alternative to international arbitral tribunals.[68] According to the literature, the attractiveness of court litigation for cross-border commercial disputes may increase further following the introduction in 2019 of the Convention on the Recognition and Enforcement of Foreign Judgments in Civil or Commercial Matters (Hague Judgments Convention), aimed at establishing an easier and safer international enforcement mechanism for national civil and commercial judgments.[69]

Alongside this competition with standalone methods of ICM and cross-border litigation, ICA has been challenged by wider changes in the transnational dispute-resolution landscape, with various approaches to dispute resolution offered and reshaped to decrease costs, delays, and the formalization of the dispute-resolution process while opening the door for additional opportunities for settlement and early resolution of the dispute.[70] Explicit empirical data shows that as part of this trend, parties to cross-border commercial relations worldwide have expressed clear and growing interest in dispute-resolution processes that combine arbitration with other ADR methods and prefer them over pure arbitration, litigation, and ADR mechanisms. A survey conducted by the International Mediation Institute (IMI) during the 2016-2017 Global Pound Conference (GPC) Series, which included 28 conferences across 24 countries and focused on ADR tools and techniques,[71] gathered responses

66. Ortolani, 2025, §21.6; Sussman & Berger, 2021b, p. 12; Stipanowich, 2023, p. 691; Born, 2021, §1.02[B][9]; Guo, 2020, p. 238; Nigmatullina, 2018, p. 6; Berger, 2016b; Stipanowich & Ulrich, 2014a, p. 462; Stipanowich & Lamare, 2014, p. 6; Singapore Convention, 2018.
67. Berger, 2016b; Rivkin, 2008, p. 376, relating to a survey conducted among in-house counsel at leading corporations worldwide, in which nearly two-thirds of the respondents believed that international arbitration was more expensive than transnational litigation. *See also* Najar, 2009, pp. 517-520, relating to additional empirical data supporting this position.
68. Such as the London Commercial Court, the Singapore International Commercial Court, and the Dubai International Financial Centre Courts that offer to convert their court judgments into arbitration awards. *See* Guo, 2020, pp. 226-227, 233; Hwang, 2015, p. 203; Berger, 2016b, stating that "the competition arbitration is facing today is not limited to 'alternative' forms of dispute resolution. Rather, national legal systems are also setting up to be more competitive by trying to eliminate the reasons for parties to choose alternative dispute resolution methods in the first place. Indeed, some jurisdictions work on re-establishing state court litigation as the favoured means of resolving international business disputes, thus trying to reverse the development away from state courts."
69. Sussman & Berger, 2021b, p. 12; Guo, 2020, p. 238; Berger, 2016b; Hague Judgments Convention, 2019. *See also* Guo, 2020, p. 225, claiming that despite the dominance of ICA in the resolution of cross-border commercial disputes, the introduction of the Singapore and the Hague Conventions "completes the institutional development of a cross-border enforcement regime for international commercial disputes and reflects the clear potential for normative shifts in the IDR [International Dispute Resolution] landscape." However, the Hague Judgments Convention has entered into force only in the European Union (EU) Member States, the UK, Ukraine, Uruguay, Albania, Andorra, and Montenegro. *See Status: Hague Judgments Convention*, n.d.
70. Stipanowich, 2021a, p. 268; Guo, 2020, p. 225; Berger, 2016b.
71. Masucci, 2018, pp. 6-8; *Global Pound Conference Series: Overview*, n.d.; GPC Series, 2018.

from over 4,000 ADR users, including commercial parties, counsels, mediators, and arbitrators, about their preferences regarding the resolution of disputes resulting from international commercial contracts (2016-2017 GPC Survey).[72] When requested to describe the most effective commercial dispute-resolution process, most respondents stated that it should usually combine adjudicative and non-adjudicative methods, such as arbitration and mediation.[73] The increasing inclination of parties engaged in cross-border business transactions to combine ICA with other ADR methods was further supported by findings from the Queen Mary International Arbitration Surveys. According to the 2021 survey, among respondents who specified arbitration as their favored method for resolving cross-border commercial disputes, 59% preferred conducting arbitration in conjunction with other ADR methods, while only 31% preferred it as a standalone method. Notably, in the 2018 survey, only 49% indicated a preference for such a combination, highlighting a marked increase in interest over time.[74] In addition, when respondents in the 2015 and 2018 surveys were asked to highlight the "most valuable characteristics of international arbitration" that affected their decision to resort to ICA, the flexibility of the process was ranked as one of the leading features.[75]

Several scholars and practitioners have argued that the outlined developments—which, according to legal anthropology, reflect typical phases in the continuous evolutionary trajectory of every dispute resolution mechanism[76]—are unlikely, at least for the foreseeable future, to undermine the established status of ICA as the primary method for resolving cross-border commercial disputes.[77] Empirical data supports this position. In the 2015, 2018, and 2021 Queen Mary International Arbitration Surveys, at least 90% of the respondents described ICA as their preferred method for resolving cross-border business disputes, while mediation, cross-border litigation, and litigation combined with other ADR methods collectively accounted for a maximum of 10% of

72. GPC Series, 2016-2017; GPC Series, 2018, p. 2; Lack, 2021, p. 12; Chua, 2018, p. 1.
73. GPC Series, 2016-2017, Question 2(5). *See also* Lack, 2021, p. 12; Stipanowich, 2021a, p. 271; Chua, 2018, p. 1.
74. Queen Mary University of London and White & Case LLP, 2021, p. 5; Queen Mary University of London and White & Case LLP, 2018, p. 5. *See also* Yip, 2021, p. 183; Stipanowich, 2021a, p. 271; Chua, 2018, p. 2.
75. Flexibility of the process was selected by 38-40% of the respondents as the most valuable characteristic of ICA, even above "speed" that was selected by 10-12% of the respondents and "cost" that was selected only by 2-3%. *See* Queen Mary University of London and White & Case LLP, 2018, p. 7; Queen Mary University of London and White & Case LLP, 2015, p. 6.
76. Kaufmann-Kohler, 2009, p. 203, claiming that "on the basis of the history of dispute settlement in all regions of the world, legal anthropologists observe a constant alternation between formal and informal dispute resolution methods. At the beginning, a method of dispute resolution is always informal. The human search for predictability then generates more and more rules relating to that method of dispute resolution. In the end, there are too many rules and the mechanism becomes too slow and cumbersome. It no longer meets the needs of its users, so the users turn to other methods of dispute resolution that are less formal, and the cycle starts anew"; Horvath, 2011, p. 261, relating to the formalization process of ICA as unavoidable due to the legitimate search for "a degree of certainty and foreseeability in uncertain circumstances." *See also* Berger & Jensen, 2016, p. 3; Stipanowich, 2010, pp. 24-29; Kaufmann-Kohler, 2010, p. 298; Park, 2006, p. 149.
77. Born, 2021, §1.03; Yip, 2021, p. 190; Nigmatullina, 2018, p. 4; Berger, 2016b; Cheng, 2011, pp. 434-435; McLean, 2009, p. 1087.

respondents' preferences.[78] Further empirical evidence indicates that, given the increasing complexity of cross-border business relations, neither international mediation nor transnational litigation necessarily offers a faster, less expensive, or less complex alternative to ICA.[79] Moreover, their enforcement mechanisms at the international level—including the recently introduced frameworks—lag far behind the well-established enforcement regime of ICA under the New York Convention.[80]

Nonetheless, given the undeniable current challenges to ICA, which, as supported by the aforementioned empirical data, have led to increased dissatisfaction with certain aspects of the arbitral process, competition with other mechanisms of dispute resolution, and an expanding trend that favors comprehensive processes combining adjudicative and non-adjudicative approaches, a growing chorus has advocated for fundamental enhancements to ICA to ensure its continued prominence in resolving international commercial disputes:

> The risk is that a highly effective and successful dispute resolution mechanism will be lost to the international business community. In order to prevent this, international arbitration must be taken back to its foundations. The judicialization of international arbitration must cease and, indeed, a process of de-judicialization should be carried out. ... Provided that these measures are taken, there is no reason why the simple and idealistic dispute resolution mechanism of international arbitration should not continue to serve the international business community for many years to come.[81]

Aware of the challenges facing ICA and users' anticipation of essential reforms in the domain, various stakeholders—including states, arbitral institutions, practitioners, and scholars—have promoted various initiatives to meet user needs and adapt ICA practices to the evolving landscape of cross-border dispute resolution.[82] These initiatives encompass amendments to arbitration laws, rules, and guidelines, introducing tailored arbitration clauses, submission restrictions, and strict control over document exchange. They also include midstream conferences and hearings, and the promotion of technological methods for hearings, including teleconferencing and videoconferencing.[83] Several leading arbitral institutions, including UNCITRAL, the International Chamber of Commerce (ICC), and the Netherlands Arbitration Institute (NAI), have also developed expedited arbitration procedures. These procedures allow parties to opt for simplified and rapid dispute resolution, particularly for cases involving low to

78. Queen Mary University of London and White & Case LLP, 2021, p. 5; Queen Mary University of London and White & Case LLP, 2018, p. 5; Queen Mary University of London and White & Case LLP, 2015, p. 5.
79. ICC Guide on Effective Management of Arbitration, 2018, p. 3, exhibiting empirical data indicating that like in mediation processes, the vast majority of costs in arbitration are party costs, including lawyers' fees and expenses. *See also* Nigmatullina, 2018, pp. 7-8; Nolan-Haley, 2012, p. 91; Strong, 2014a, p. 16; Cheng, 2011, p. 438.
80. Stipanowich, 2021a, p. 270; Chua, 2018, pp. 6-7; Nigmatullina, 2018, pp. 36-39; Sussman, 2010a, p. 393. *See also* the discussion in sections 3.6.1 & 3.6.2.
81. Horvath, 2011, p. 271. *See also* Blackaby et al., 2022, §1.191; Berger, 2016b; Stipanowich, 2010, pp. 1-2; Kaufmann-Kohler, 2009, p. 203; Najar, 2009, p. 518; Marriott, 2005, p. 546.
82. Dasser, 2021, pp. 57-58; Berger, 2016b; Draetta, 2015, p. 328; Bermann, 2015, p. 76; Karton, 2014, p. 39; Kaufmann-Kohler, 2010, p. 299.
83. Sussman & Berger, 2021a, p. 25.

medium monetary amounts. Features of expedited procedures include the appointment of a sole arbitrator through an accelerated process, limitations on submissions, restrictions on the number of hearings typically conducted electronically, reliance on documents and written statements rather than witness testimony, and shortened timelines, including for the rendering of awards.[84]

Within this framework, UNCITRAL Working Group II (WGII) —focused on dispute settlement, including international arbitration and mediation[85]—recently introduced the UNCITRAL Model Clauses on Specialized Express Dispute Resolution (SPEDR). These clauses provide customized mechanisms for the expedited resolution of international disputes, particularly in sectors where speed and technical expertise are critical.[86] Among the SPEDR's provisions is the Highly Expedited Arbitration clause, designed for industries such as technology, construction, and finance, where delayed resolution can cause significant harm or project failure.[87] Another notable provision is the Model Clause on Adjudication, which is suitable for long-term projects such as major construction ventures. This mechanism enables disputes to be provisionally resolved by adjudicators who are experts in the relevant subject matter. Adjudicators' decisions are binding until referred to arbitration for final determination, and parties are required to comply with these decisions unless and until the arbitral tribunal overturns them.[88] Additionally, the SPEDR includes the Model Clause on Technical Advisors, which is intended to enhance the resolution of highly specialized or technical disputes by allowing technical advisors to support arbitral tribunals in understanding complex issues without replacing experts appointed by the parties or the tribunal.[89]

Despite the impressive scope of these initiatives, most efforts have focused on improving the efficiency, cost-effectiveness, and timeliness of ICA as a standalone adversarial process.[90] Few initiatives have specifically addressed the growing trend of combining arbitration with other ADR methods or integrating ADR elements into ICA frameworks.

84. UNCITRAL Arbitration Rules, 2021, Article 1(5); UNCITRAL Expedited Arbitration Rules, 2021; ICC Arbitration Rules, 2021, Article 30 & Appendix VI; NAI Arbitration Rules, 2024, Article 42 & Appendix D. For further discussion about expedited procedures in ICA, *see* Blackaby et al., 2022, §6.25-6.39.
85. *See UNCITRAL WGII*, n.d.
86. UNCITRAL Model Clauses on SPEDR, 2024, Introduction. *See also UNCITRAL WGII*, n.d., at Report of Working Group on the work of its eightieth session (A/CN.9/1193).
87. UNCITRAL Model Clauses on SPEDR, 2024, pp. 7-12; *UNCITRAL WGII*, n.d., at Report of Working Group on the work of its eightieth session (A/CN.9/1193), p. 5.
88. UNCITRAL Model Clauses on SPEDR, 2024, pp. 13-25; *UNCITRAL WGII*, n.d., at Report of Working Group on the work of its eightieth session (A/CN.9/1193), pp. 5-8.
89. UNCITRAL Model Clauses on SPEDR, 2024, pp. 27-29; *UNCITRAL WGII*, n.d., at Report of Working Group on the work of its eightieth session (A/CN.9/1193), pp. 8-9.
90. Stipanowich, 2021a, pp. 306-307; Nigmatullina, 2018, p. 5; Stipanowich & Ulrich, 2014b, pp. 5-6, 8; Najar, 2009, pp. 519, 527; Rivkin, 2008, p. 378; Ehle, 2010, p. 94; McLean, 2009, pp. 1096-1097; ICC Guide on Effective Management of Arbitration, 2018.

1.4 THE ARBITRATOR AS A SETTLEMENT FACILITATOR IN ICA

Several ICA stakeholders have focused on promoting initiatives that foster an interplay between ICA and other ADR mechanisms in response to the growing demand from parties engaged in cross-border business relations for effective dispute resolution processes integrating adjudicative and non-adjudicative methods while opening the door for early settlements in adversarial proceedings with adjudicator assistance and prioritizing flexibility, party autonomy, enhanced efficiency, and business considerations over formalized and rigid procedures.[91] Some of those initiatives have implemented "linear" combinations, where each process ends before the beginning of the following, as customary in multi-tiered or stepped dispute resolution processes. They usually start with negotiations, continue with mediation, and end with binding arbitration.[92] Thus, these combinations have gained increasing popularity and are routinely implemented in contracts relating to cross-border commercial relations[93] and bilateral and multilateral investment treaties.[94] Other initiatives have implemented more innovative approaches in which ICA and ADR methods or elements are carried out in full or partial overlap. One pattern of such "non-linear"[95] arrangements is hybrid processes that combine arbitration with mediation or conciliation,[96] while assigning

91. Lack, 2021, p. 12; Yip, 2021, p. 183; Chua, 2018, pp. 1-2; Stipanowich, 2021a, p. 271; Ross, 2013, p. 353; Kun, 2011b, p. 549; Cremades, 1998, pp. 162-163. *See also* Gomez, 2015, p. 154, asserting that, given the complex nature of transnational disputes, parties involved in ICA are likely to increasingly rely on combinations of "as many dispute-processing mechanisms as they deem necessary to obtain leverage toward a favorable outcome."
92. Blackaby et al., 2022, §1.119-1.121; Born, 2021, §2.02[C][2][f]; Stipanowich & Ulrich, 2014b, p. 8; Ruckteschler & Wendelstein, 2021, p. 762; Chua, 2018, p. 1. For further discussion about multi-tier commercial dispute resolution processes, *see* Stipanowich, 2021b.
93. *See*, for example, Chua, 2018, p. 1, relating to an empirical study in the US, where 82% of the respondents indicated that they "use multiple steps in their alternative dispute resolution (ADR) clauses, with 73% incorporating negotiation as one of the steps, 46% using mediation, and 58% finishing with arbitration." On the other hand, *see* Ruckteschler & Wendelstein, 2021, p. 762, criticizing such clauses for delaying the dispute resolution process and potentially triggering new controversies, particularly concerning the duration of the negotiation stage and its implications for limitation periods.
94. Kun, 2020b, pp. 331-337; Nitschke, 2019, p. 143.
95. Stipanowich & Ulrich, 2014b, p. 9.
96. In this book, the terms conciliation and mediation are used interchangeably to describe non-adjudicative processes in which a neutral third party engages with disputing parties in joint or separate sessions (i.e., caucuses) and employs evaluative or non-evaluative techniques to facilitate an amicable resolution, which remains non-binding in nature. Nevertheless, in some jurisdictions, conciliation refers to evaluative processes in which neutrals only express their views about the dispute, such as an assessment of the outcome and strengths and weaknesses of legal positions or the evidential base of the case. In these jurisdictions, conciliation is equivalent to evaluative mediation, as distinguished from other sorts of mediation, such as facilitative (where neutrals seek to promote amicable outcome without expressing any evaluative views) and transformative (where neutrals focus on encouraging the disputants to resolve their conflict while recognizing their opponents' interests and needs). In practice, however, the distinction between facilitative and evaluative techniques is not always clear, as neutrals often tend to apply those methods simultaneously or other techniques that overlap with part of their components, such as directive techniques (where neutrals seek to promote settlement by asking questions intended to allow the disputants to understand the strengths and weaknesses of their legal positions, the consequences of non-settlement, and the possible outcomes of the adjudicative process, without expressing their views on these issues). Moreover, in few jurisdictions,

different neutrals for each role to distinguish between adjudication and the efforts to settle.[97] Another model—the focus of this book—is to cast the arbitrator in ICA[98] as a settlement facilitator,[99] so that, in addition to their adjudicative mandate, they are authorized to promote an amicable outcome of the dispute by carrying out various possible initiatives, whether during the arbitration or within a hybrid process that involves arbitration and mediation:

> The arbitrator's role in settlement processes ... [ranges] from simply taking steps in the course of a hearing which are designed to provide an opportunity for the parties to reach a settlement, to taking an active role as a mediator. Within this spectrum the arbitrator might simply encourage the parties to agree particular issues, or might suggest but not participate in settlement discussions. Alternatively the arbitrator might provide an advisory opinion (or early neutral evaluation) on a non-binding basis.[100]

---

such as France, conciliation refers to legal non-adjudicative processes as distinguished from non-legal mediation, while in others (e.g., Canada and Brazil), conciliation describes judicial non-adjudicative processes as different from other non-judicial mediation. *See* Stipanowich, 2021a, p. 268; Fraser & Kun, 2021, p. 21; CIArb Practice Guideline on the Use of Mediation in Arbitration, 2021, Article 3(5); Benzidi, 2017, p. 25; Stipanowich & Fraser, 2017, pp. 868, 872-874; Hopt & Steffek, 2013, pp. 11-15; Kun, 2020a, p. 163; Thevenin, 2013, p. 367; Nigmatullina, 2018, p. 15; Stipanowich & Kaskell, 2001, pp. 15-16.

97. Such as a mediation window (where the arbitration process is stayed to enable a mediation process carried out by a different neutral); shadow mediation (where a different mediator takes passive part in arbitration and during a later stage attempts to mediate the dispute on the basis of legal issues and positions expressed during arbitration); Co-Med-Arb (where the mediator and the arbitrator are present at the information exchange between the parties, but from that point the mediator works solely with the disputants, including in private meetings, and if mediation fails the dispute is decided by a binding award rendered by the arbitrator); Med-Arb-diff (where following failed mediation arbitration is carried out by a different neutral); Arb-Med-diff (where arbitration is followed by mediation carried out by a different neutral whether after or before issuing the arbitral award); Arb-Med-Arb-diff (where mediation is carried out by a different neutral during the course of arbitration). *See* Ruckteschler & Wendelstein, 2021, p. 762; Gu, 2019, p. 121; Nigmatullina, 2018, pp. 281-282; De Gramont et al., 2017, p. 965; Wolski, 2013, pp. 258-260; Ross, 2013, p. 358; Dendorfer & Lack, 2007; Schneider, 1998, p. 73; Peter, 1997, p. 102; Bartel, 1991, pp. 665-668; Fullerton, 2009, pp. 34-36.
98. Given the differences between domestic arbitration and ICA, which has a transnational legal regime that heavily relies on norms and considerations exceeding the domestic level, this book focuses on the arbitrator's role as a settlement facilitator in ICA. Nevertheless, part of the discussion, including the suggested initiatives for settlement facilitation by the arbitrator and the solutions recommended in Part IV, may *mutatis mutandis* also apply to this role in domestic arbitration. For further discussion about the differences between domestic and cross-border arbitration, including in relation to the arbitrator's role in settlement, *see* Abramson, 1999, p. 1; Paulsson, 2008.
99. Stipanowich, 2021a, p. 279; Born, 2021, §13.04[D]; Berger, 2018b, p. 507; Berger & Jensen, 2017, p. 888; Stipanowich & Ulrich, 2014b, p. 8; Kaufmann-Kohler, 2009, p. 188, defining this role of the arbitrator as follows: "It does not deal with separate proceedings of mediation or conciliation and arbitration, nor does it deal with other mechanisms in which different individuals act as arbitrator and as mediator or conciliator. ... It is concerned with cases in which the same person acts as both arbitrator and settlement facilitator."
100. Gill, 2006, p. 158. *See also* Sachs, 2020, p. 232; Marzolini, 2016, pp. 110-111; Stipanowich & Ulrich, 2014b, p. 10; Kaufmann-Kohler, 2009, p. 188; Plant, 2000, p. 143; Abramson, 1999, pp. 5-6.

1.5 WHY THIS BOOK?

The role of the arbitrator as a facilitator of settlement has gained traction among ICA users worldwide, including in jurisdictions where this role was not traditionally recognized.[101] Recent empirical data, as presented in this book,[102] and past efforts toward harmonization by different ICA stakeholders regarding the arbitrator's authority to promote amicable dispute resolution[103] indicate an emerging transnational trend encouraging neutrals, practitioners, and users of ICA to view the arbitrator's mandate more broadly and recognize settlement facilitation as an integral aspect of their professional toolkit.[104] However, despite the general harmonization trend in the practice and legal regime of ICA, the question of "whether arbitrators can facilitate settlement is one of the few issues in modern arbitration that has not yet reached a transnational consensus."[105] The literature identifies the following reasons contributing to this state of affairs. *First*, despite its increasing acceptance among users from various jurisdictions, since this role of the arbitrator has only been a recent focus in academia and practice,[106] no clear understanding exists regarding its components and boundaries:

> The debate regarding the arbitrator's role in parties' settlement efforts can be traced back to inconsistent terminology and fundamental misunderstandings. The terms "to encourage," "to promote," and "to facilitate" settlement are often used interchangeably. At other times, they are used to indicate differing degrees of arbitral involvement in the parties' settlement discussions. Such terminological ambiguity acts as a catalyst for the ongoing controversial debate. If there is no uniform understanding of what settlement facilitation is and means, there is a

101. Sussman & Berger, 2021b, p. 37; Ruckteschler & Wendelstein, 2021, p. 771; Stipanowich, 2021a, p. 271; Sachs, 2020, p. 232; Berger, 2019, p. 313; Born, 2021, §13.04[D]; Jemielniak, 2014, p. 331; Kun, 2013b, p. 216; Berger, 2018b, pp. 507, 511, 516; Berger & Jensen, 2017, pp. 898-899; Berger, 2016b; Kaufmann-Kohler, 2009, p. 188; Marriott, 2005, p. 546; Plant, 2000, p. 143; Lew & Shore, 1999, p. 38.
102. *See* the discussion in section 6.2 regarding current empirical data demonstrating a clear and growing acceptance of the arbitrator's role as a settlement facilitator in ICA. In addition, *see* the extensive empirical data presented in Chapter 5, which demonstrates an increasing acknowledgement of this role in various jurisdictions with different legal cultures.
103. *See* the discussion in section 6.3.
104. Sussman & Berger, 2021a, p. 26; Lack, 2021, p. 12; Ruckteschler & Wendelstein, 2021, p. 771; Sussman & Berger, 2021b, p. 37; ICC Report on Facilitating Settlement in ICA, 2023, p. 6; Chua, 2018, p. 2; Berger & Jensen, 2017, p. 889; Marzolini, 2016, pp. 99, 117; Berger, 2018b, p. 509; Nigmatullina, 2019, pp. 13, 21; Najar, 2009, pp. 522-526; Wenger, 2006, p. 147; Marriott, 2005, p. 546; Collins, 2003, p. 343; Mayer, 2016, p. 4, arguing that currently "in international arbitration, it is generally accepted, and even expected, that arbitrators enjoy at least some power of initiative; the parties do not wish them to remain passive." Interestingly, this trend has not evolved in investor-state arbitrations. Therefore, section 4.4.2 discusses the suitability of settlement facilitation for this category of arbitration.
105. Kun, 2013b, p. 213. *See also* Stipanowich, 2021a, p. 272; Berger, 2018b, pp. 501-502; Kun & Jemielniak, 2016, p. 557; Kun, 2016a, p. 261; Kaufmann-Kohler, 2009, p. 189; Kaufmann-Kohler, 2004, p. 72.
106. Stipanowich, 2021a, p. 269; Stipanowich & Fraser, 2017, p. 858.

> danger that any discussion about this issue results in little more than two ships passing in the night.[107]

Following this lack of clarity, the normative instruments regulating the arbitrator's role as a settlement facilitator, including national statutes and international arbitration rules and guidelines, provide little guidance about its practice, limits, and ethics.[108] Moreover, when attempts were made to do so, the results were "inconsistent, unclear, and incomplete."[109] As a result, the ambiguity surrounding this role of the arbitrator relates to the steps the arbitrator may take to facilitate a settlement and fundamental issues connected with its practice, such as the essential requirements for allowing an arbitrator to act as a settlement facilitator, the necessary conditions for permitting the arbitrator to resume their adjudicative role following failed efforts to settle, how confidential information disclosed during the settlement negotiations should be treated, and whether and under what conditions ex parte communication should be allowed during the settlement phase.[110] Scholars and practitioners commonly agree that enhancing the transnational regulation of the arbitrator's role as a settlement facilitator in ICA first requires "develop[ing] a clear understanding of the differing degrees of arbitrator involvement in the parties' settlement efforts,"[111] including the merits, challenges, and boundaries of such involvement:

> It is time to reevaluate med-arb, arb-med, and arbitrator roles in negotiated settlement in light of their potential utility as creative alternatives for problem-solving in appropriate situations and to propound more systematic guidance for their use, including effective options for avoiding or managing attendant risks.[112]

Second, even when there is an agreement about the role of the arbitrator as a settlement facilitator and its components, due to the influence of legal traditions and professional backgrounds, ICA practitioners and users may have different expectations regarding the exact objective of the role[113] and the specific procedures connected with its practice:

107. Berger & Jensen, 2017, p. 891. *See also* Stipanowich, 2021a, p. 268, arguing that "we still have far to go in understanding and addressing the dynamics of ... the combination and interplay of settlement-focused activities and third-party adjudication. This is especially true of situations where it is agreed that ... an arbitrator mediates or engages directly in efforts to help parties reach a negotiated settlement of substantive issues in dispute."; Sachs, 2020, p. 232, stating that "settlement facilitation is not a defined term."; Gill, 2006, p. 158, arguing that "it is important when contemplating the arbitrator's role in settlement processes to recognise that there are a number of different approaches that might be undertaken."; Ruckteschler & Wendelstein, 2021, p. 771; Berger, 2016a, pp. 46-47; Ehle, 2010, pp. 79, 83; Draetta, 2009, pp. 487-491; Hwang, 2005, p. 572; Plant, 2000, p. 143.
108. Stipanowich, 2021a, p. 273; Ruckteschler & Wendelstein, 2021, pp. 768-769; Berger & Jensen, 2017, p. 891; Plant, 2000, p. 143.
109. Ruckteschler & Wendelstein, 2021, p. 771. These efforts are discussed in Chapter 6.
110. Ruckteschler & Wendelstein, 2021, p. 771; Stipanowich, 2021a, pp. 352-361; Plant, 2000, p. 145.
111. Berger & Jensen, 2017, p. 891.
112. Stipanowich, 2021a, p. 269.
113. These differing expectations stem, among other things, from conflicting views on the relationship between arbitration and other ADR mechanisms. When arbitration is viewed as a subset of ADR, implying that the arbitrator is responsible for *resolving* the dispute, settlement

> In International Commercial Arbitration more than just the legal issues are issues. Whether procedure is agreed upon ad hoc, or institutional rules are used, expectations of the process may well differ from participant to participant. Why? Divergence in cultural backgrounds. ... Despite harmonization of procedural rules in International Commercial Arbitration, expectations of the process differ based on cultural background of parties or arbitrators. In order to overcome cultural barriers of this and other sorts, one should understand the differences and use them creatively.[114]

Indeed, the comparative and empirical data presented and debated in this book demonstrate that despite the evolving transnational trend connected with the arbitrator's role in the settlement, different legal cultures dissimilarly relate to the role of adjudicators—including judges and arbitrators—as settlement facilitators.[115] In general (certainly not exhaustive) terms, while Common Law jurisdictions have traditionally observed adjudicators as *decision-makers* and therefore expressed hesitant positions about their involvement in the settlement process, Civil Law jurisdictions have traditionally considered adjudicators as *dispute-resolvers* and hence expressed more tolerant attitudes toward their role as settlement facilitators.[116] In addition, jurisdictions from Eastern legal cultures, particularly East Asian, Arabic, and Islamic jurisdictions, have traditionally applied conciliatory approaches that allow adjudicators to facilitate settlements by acting as mediators in the same dispute.[117]

---

facilitation may be seen as a legitimate part of the mandate. However, if arbitration is distinguished from ADR and defined as a subcategory of litigation, which implies that the arbitrator is responsible for *deciding* the dispute, then the mandate may be perceived as excluding the role of settlement facilitator. *See* Kaufmann-Kohler, 2009, pp. 188-189; Berger & Jensen, 2017, p. 889; Stipanowich & Ulrich, 2014a, pp. 459-460; Kun, 2011b, pp. 536-537; Collins, 2003, p. 343; Berger, 2003, pp. 387-388; Wang, 2000, p. 192; Brown & Marriott, 1999, at No. 2-002; Fouchard et al., 1999, p. 14; Sanders, 1996, p. 173. For further discussion about the relationship between ICA and ADR, *see* Nottage, 2002.

114. Pair, 2002, p. 58. *See also* Mayer, 2016, p. 4; Kaufmann-Kohler, 2003, p. 1322; Jemielniak, 2017, p. 169; Kun, 2016a, pp. 254-255; Kaufmann-Kohler, 2009, pp. 188-189; Berger, 2018b, pp. 501-502, stating that "the view that an individual arbitrator takes with respect to his or her role in the promotion of an amicable settlement of the dispute is strongly influenced by the legal background of the arbitrator."
115. *See* the discussion in Chapter 5. *See also* Born, 2021, §13.04[D]; Stipanowich, 2021a, pp. 282-283, stating that "in some parts of the world, arbitrators may be expected to engage in activities that help promote settlement or even mediate the dispute. In other places, settlement facilitation is normally not a part of the arbitral role. In the former situation, it may be expected that the arbitrator brings up the subject of engaging in settlement-oriented activities. In the latter case, however, an arbitrator's request to the parties to permit the arbitrator to change roles may present a dilemma for the disputants and even undermine their autonomy."; Kun, 2013b, p. 213, claiming that the controversy regarding the arbitrator's role as a settlement facilitator results from "the divergent perceptions on the mission of arbitrators in different legal traditions."; Berger, 2018b, p. 502, stating that "different jurisdictions ... have different views as to whether the courts' role includes the facilitation of a settlement."
116. Born, 2021, §13.04[D]; Ortolani, 2025, §21.3; Stipanowich, 2021a, p. 271; Chua, 2018, pp. 1-2; Berger, 2018b, pp. 502-506; Nigmatullina, 2018, pp. 64-65; Berger & Jensen, 2017, p. 889; De Gramont et al., 2017, pp. 964-972; Mayer, 2016, p. 3; Nottage & Garnett, 2010, pp. 35-36; Ehle, 2010, pp. 79-80; Cheng, 2010, pp. 424-426; Kaufmann-Kohler, 2009, pp. 190-192; Lew, 2005, p. 427; Burr, 2005, p. 63; Schneider, 1998, p. 78; Kun, 2013b, pp. 213-214.
117. Gu, 2019, p. 151; Nigmatullina, 2018, pp. 68-70; Chua, 2018, pp. 1-2; Stipanowich, 2021a, p. 271; Deekshitha & Saha, 2014, pp. 84-85; Ehle, 2010, pp. 79-80; De Vera, 2004, p. 183;

Third, following the influence of the legal culture while considering the individual preferences and approaches of arbitrators, practitioners, and users,[118] the role of the arbitrator as a settlement facilitator has sparked a heated discussion about its adherence to fundamental principles of the arbitral process. Its supporters usually emphasize the contractual foundation of the arbitral process, which grants the parties the autonomy to design the proceedings according to their preferences and interests, with the contribution of settlement facilitation to the efficiency of the dispute-resolution process and the administration of justice.[119] Conversely, its opponents commonly highlight its potential risk to due process and natural justice and, consequently, to enforcing the arbitration's outcome.[120]

The working premise is that the absence of clarity regarding the components of the arbitrator's role in the settlement, the diverse approaches of different legal traditions regarding it, and the controversy surrounding its adherence to the fundamental principles of ICA constitute restraining factors for its harmonization,[121] which seems vital and needed considering its rising status among practitioners and users worldwide alongside the transnational nature of the domain and its general harmonization process:

> In this vast movement of convergence, there remain a few trouble spots. The role of the arbitrator as settlement facilitator in international arbitration appears to be one of those remaining differences. ... In domestic arbitration, ... national laws show many differences. However, in international arbitration, where the activities giving rise to disputes are transnational or global in nature and where the participants come from different national and legal backgrounds or cultures, divergences are not desirable.[122]

Therefore, the time is ripe to explore and propose avenues for enhancing the harmonization and effective implementation of the arbitrator's role as a settlement facilitator in ICA.[123] Accordingly, this book comprehensively addresses the following key questions:

Cremades, 1998, pp. 158-159; Kun, 2016a, p. 251; Kun, 2016b, pp. 482-483; Kun, 2013a, p. 137; El-Ahdab & El-Ahdab, 2011, pp. 8-11; Cheng, 2010, pp. 424-426; Najar, 2009, p. 520.

118. Stipanowich, 2021a, pp. 276, 289, 345; Stipanowich & Fraser, 2017, p. 882; Stipanowich & Ulrich, 2014b, pp. 25-26; Kaufmann-Kohler, 2003, p. 1331.

119. Stipanowich, 2021a, p. 280; Nigmatullina, 2018, p. 142; Berger & Jensen, 2017, pp. 901, 904; Karton, 2013, pp. 106-107; Kun, 2011b, p. 537; Marriott, 2005, p. 533; Dezalay & Garth, 1996, p. 40; Sachs, 2020, p. 232; Kaufmann-Kohler, 2009, p. 188.

120. Stipanowich, 2021a, pp. 290-291; Nigmatullina, 2018, pp. 54-57; Ludington, 2017, pp. 317-320; Berger & Jensen, 2017, pp. 914-915; Stipanowich & Fraser, 2017, pp. 855; Kun, 2011b, pp. 537-538; Sussman, 2010a, p. 384; Rosoff, 2009, pp. 92-93; Kaufmann-Kohler, 2009, pp. 198-199; Sussman, 2009a, p. 71; Blankenship, 2006, pp. 35-36; Stipanowich & Kaskell, 2001, p. 22; Abramson, 1999, pp. 3-4.

121. Kaufmann-Kohler, 2009, p. 189; Berger, 2018b, p. 502, arguing that the absence of transnational consensus in the matter results from "these cultural and legal differences concerning the involvement of international arbitrators in the facilitation of a settlement of a dispute."

122. Kaufmann-Kohler, 2009, p. 189.

123. Stipanowich, 2021a, p. 339; Berger, 2018b, p. 502; Stipanowich & Fraser, 2017, p. 858; Sussman & Berger, 2021b, pp. 37-38; Kaufmann-Kohler, 2009, pp. 204-205; Stipanowich & Ulrich, 2014b, pp. 29-31; Nigmatullina, 2019, p. 45.

Question 1: What does the arbitrator's role entail as an ICA settlement facilitator? What initiatives can the arbitrator take to facilitate a settlement, and when are these initiatives likely to be implemented? Are these initiatives limited to indirect actions, or can they involve active and direct engagement in the settlement process?
Question 2: What are the advantages of the arbitrator's role as an ICA settlement facilitator? Do these advantages adequately address concerns and criticism about increased costs, delays, and formalization in ICA proceedings?
Question 3: What are the concerns associated with the arbitrator's role as an ICA settlement facilitator? How fundamental are these concerns? Can they be categorized to better address them? Is settlement facilitation suitable for all categories of disputes related to cross-border commercial or economic activities, such as investor-state disputes?
Question 4: How do different jurisdictions approach the role of the arbitrator as a settlement facilitator in domestic and international arbitral proceedings? How and to what extent does legal tradition influence attitudes toward this role? What components of this role are considered most controversial, how have they been addressed, and what can be learned from these experiences? Is there mutual influence between different legal cultures regarding the arbitrator's role in the settlement process?
Question 5: What are the current perspectives of ICA users regarding the arbitrator's role as a settlement facilitator? What initiatives have been taken at the transnational level to promote the harmonization of this role, and who have been the forces behind them? What have these initiatives achieved, and what gaps remain?
Question 6: How can the harmonization process of the arbitrator's role as a settlement facilitator be enhanced? What solutions can be offered under the current normative regime of ICA to improve the regulation and safe utilization of this role and enhance its global acceptance? Which external solutions to the arbitral process can be offered to harmonize the perspectives toward the arbitrator's dual role worldwide, and which stakeholders should be involved? Is it feasible to reach homogenized standards regarding this role of the arbitrator across all legal traditions, practitioners, and users?

While previous scholarship on the arbitrator's role in settlement facilitation has provided valuable insights into practitioner and user attitudes—as well as jurisdictional practices—much of this work has been *quantitative*, focusing on empirical data to highlight regional differences and converging trends.[124] In light of the questions outlined above, this book employs both (a) *comparative methods* to examine the treatment of this role across jurisdictions and legal traditions, and (b) *qualitative methods* to gain a deeper understanding of its components, advantages, and limitations. Such understanding is essential for any meaningful harmonization efforts:

124. Kun, 2020a, p. 137; Kun, 2014, p. 785.

> More qualitative research is needed to understand how the process is typically conducted and what common techniques are used by the arbitrators in settlement facilitation. Qualitative illustrations on the actual practice would be most useful to generalize some good practices so as to provide some guidance for arbitrators, to maximize the benefits ... and to minimize the disadvantages.[125]

Accordingly, this book draws extensively on both primary and secondary legal sources, including books, scholarly articles, online resources, legal databases, domestic court decisions, reports on arbitral awards, national legislation, and international legal instruments—ranging from conventions and treaties to soft law norms. In addition, it integrates a wide range of empirical data, including recent local and international surveys and experimental studies, to support and contextualize the discussion of the arbitrator's dual role.

1.6 BOOK STRUCTURE

The book is divided into four parts. Part I includes this introductory chapter and Chapter 2, which presents the range of settlement facilitation initiatives available for the ICA arbitrator. These initiatives start with minimal or indirect involvement aimed at setting the stage for settlement to be concluded through direct negotiations between the disputants, continue with direct participation in the settlement efforts while implementing mediation elements, and end with hybrid processes where the arbitrator "switches hats" between the roles of arbitrator and mediator. Part II consists of Chapters 3 and 4. Chapter 3 discusses the advantages of the arbitrator's role as an ICA settlement facilitator, while Chapter 4 addresses the concerns associated with this role, including the suitability of settlement facilitation within investor-state arbitral proceedings.

Part III displays the transition from domestic legal traditions connected with the arbitrator's role as a settlement facilitator toward transnational standards connected with its practice in ICA. It consists of Chapters 5 and 6. Chapter 5 introduces traditional and current approaches to this role in various legal systems, including Islamic and Arab jurisdictions, East Asian jurisdictions with Civil Law (China) and Common Law (Hong Kong and Singapore) legal traditions, and Western Common Law (the US, the UK, and Australia) and Civil Law (Germany and Brazil) jurisdictions. Furthermore, this chapter explores the impact of legal traditions on this role, the resolution of practice-related concerns, and the interplay between different legal cultures in its regard. Chapter 6 presents current perspectives of ICA users regarding the arbitrator's role as a settlement facilitator and critically discusses former attempts to codify and harmonize practices and norms related to that role at the transnational level.

Part IV suggests ways to enhance the global harmonization of the arbitrator's role as an ICA settlement facilitator. It consists of Chapters 7 and 8. Chapter 7 focuses on

125. Kun, 2020a, p. 137. *See also* Kun, 2014, p. 785; Ali, 2010, p. 251; Kun & Jemielniak, 2016, pp. 556, 563, relating to the weakness of the quantitative research regarding the role of arbitrators as settlement facilitators due to the impact of the cultural factors on its implementation, and the need to focus on qualitative research with an "anthropological frame of mind."

internal solutions to the arbitral process and recommends various safeguards for ICA parties willing to employ the arbitrator as a settlement facilitator to enhance its regulation and safe utilization under the domain's existing legal regime while contributing to its global recognition. Chapter 8 recommends external solutions to the arbitral process to harmonize perspectives toward the arbitrator's dual role in ICA worldwide. While addressing these solutions according to their responsible stakeholders, it highlights their limitations and recommends future research regarding the arbitrator's dual role in ICA.

CHAPTER 2
The Arbitrator as a Settlement Facilitator in ICA: The Range of Initiatives

2.1 INTRODUCTION

The international arbitrator can take various initiatives to promote a settlement in the dispute before them:

> He or she can simply ask a few well-targeted questions at the right time, which may shed light on the weaknesses of a party's case and trigger settlement discussions between the parties. He or she can suggest to the parties to settle their dispute in direct negotiations. The arbitrator can also become more involved, and these are the situations of interest here. ... The arbitrator can offer to provide his or her own assessment of the dispute, which will serve as a basis for the parties' direct negotiations, or even offer to assist them in their settlement discussions. He or she can do so either on his or her own motion or at the request of one or both parties.[1]

Settlement facilitation initiatives can be placed on a continuum,[2] starting with minimal or indirect involvement in the settlement efforts, continuing with direct participation in the settlement negotiations while implementing mediation or conciliation elements, and ending with a dual role as an arbitrator and a mediator at the same time or sequentially.[3] While indirect involvement of the arbitrator in the settlement

1. Kaufmann-Kohler, 2009, p. 188. *See also* Sachs, 2020, p. 232; Marzolini, 2016, pp. 110-111; Gill, 2006, p. 158; Plant, 2000, p. 143; Abramson, 1999, pp. 5-6; Stipanowich, 2021a, pp. 278-284, relating to various scenarios that bring the arbitrator to facilitate a settlement, including prior agreement between the parties, expectations stimming from their cultures or legal traditions, and spontaneous proposal of the arbitrator or the parties.
2. Sussman & Berger, 2021a, p. 26; Berger & Jensen, 2017, p. 892; Berger, 2003, p. 402; Fraser & Kun, 2021, p. 21.
3. Stipanowich, 2021a, pp. 278-284; Sachs, 2020, p. 232; Berger, 2018b, p. 512; Berger & Jensen, 2017, pp. 913-916; Marzolini, 2016, pp. 110-111, 117-118; Kun, 2011b, pp. 552; Kaufmann-Kohler, 2009, p. 188; Gill, 2006, p. 158; Raeschke-Kessler, 2005, p. 531; Berger, 2003, p. 402.

process is less likely to create a challenge to the arbitrator or the outcome of the arbitration and may even be viewed as part of their inherent duty to manage the proceedings efficiently,[4] direct involvement in the process and fulfilling the dual role as an arbitrator and a mediator may raise significant concerns,[5] especially when those direct initiatives are taken on the arbitrator's motion, not following the parties' request or consent.[6]

This chapter introduces the range of initiatives the arbitrator can take to facilitate a comprehensive or partial settlement of the dispute. This presentation is needed to frame the discussion about the components of the arbitrator's role as a settlement facilitator and enable a critical examination of it in the following chapters. Since a wide range of possible initiatives exists on the continuum, addressing each is unfeasible. Therefore, this chapter practically focuses on scenarios falling into three main categories that reflect the degree of the arbitrator's involvement in the settlement efforts.[7] One category relates to the indirect involvement of the arbitrator in the settlement process, mainly by "setting the stage for settlement."[8] The second category relates to scenarios comprising the direct involvement of the arbitrator in the settlement discussions intended to promote an amicable outcome of the dispute. The third category relates to scenarios where the arbitrator "switches hats"[9] between the adjudicator and mediator roles in the same dispute. Although these dual roles can be observed as a subgroup of the second category relating to direct involvement in the settlement process, they still justify a distinguished discussion due to the special challenges they raise, as discussed in Chapters 4 and 5.

2.2 SETTING THE STAGE FOR SETTLEMENT

Within the boundaries of the arbitral agreement, the arbitrator has a continued responsibility and authority over the procedural and managerial aspects of the arbitration.[10] The empirical data presented below indicates that handling these aspects proactively, particularly at the pre-hearing stage, constitutes a significant catalyst for settling the dispute amicably, although the arbitrator is not directly involved in the

4. Sachs, 2020, p. 232; Carrara, 2019, p. 43; Marzolini, 2016, p. 112; Ehle, 2010, p. 85; Stipanowich & Ulrich, 2014b, p. 29; Kaufmann-Kohler, 2009, p. 197. The duty to conduct the arbitration in a cost-effective way is anchored in various arbitration rules, including IBA Rules on Evidence in International Arbitration, 2020, Article 2; UNCITRAL Arbitration Rules, 2021, Article 17; ICC Arbitration Rules, 2021, Article 22; NAI Arbitration Rules, 2024, Article 25(3).
5. Abramson, 1999, p. 6; Stipanowich, 2021a, p. 268.
6. Kaufmann-Kohler, 2009, p. 188; Berger, 2018b, pp. 511, 513-514; Berger & Jensen, 2017, p. 904.
7. For the importance of categorizations in critical analysis and in developing understanding about the dual role of the arbitrator, *see* Stipanowich & Ulrich, 2014b, pp. 16-19; Stipanowich & Fraser, 2017, pp. 846-847; Kun, 2016b, p. 482; Donahey, 1995, p. 74; Nigmatullina, 2018, p. 64.
8. Stipanowich, 2021a, p. 331; Stipanowich & Fraser, 2017, pp. 856-860. *See also* Lurie & Lack, 2014, pp. 175-177.
9. Stipanowich & Mironi, 2021, p. 29; Stipanowich, 2021a, p. 276; Gu, 2019, p. 133; Stipanowich & Fraser, 2017, pp. 850-856; Stipanowich & Kaskell, 2001, pp. 39-45.
10. Berger & Jensen, 2017, pp. 904-905; Stipanowich, 2021a, p. 289; Marzolini, 2016, p. 112; Stipanowich & Ulrich, 2014a, pp. 452-454; Bernardini, 2004, p. 120; Stipanowich & Ulrich, 2014b, p. 29. For further discussion, *see* Blackaby et al., 2022, §6.01-6.06.

settlement's negotiations or substance.[11] Nevertheless, a very recent survey of arbitration practitioners from jurisdictions worldwide revealed that many of the procedural and managerial methods available for the arbitrator are not widely used within ICA,[12] which constitutes a missed opportunity for arbitrators to enrich the toolbox that enables the promotion of settlements in these processes.[13] This section introduces the following indirect initiatives the arbitrator may take to promote an amicable outcome of the dispute: managing the first organizational conference proactively, asking the parties targeted questions on procedural and substantive issues related to the dispute, raising abstract proposals to settle and designing mediation windows throughout the proceedings, bifurcating the arbitral process, deciding preliminary issues, providing an early neutral evaluation of the case, initiating a mid-term arbitration review to promote a settlement, encouraging the use of sealed offers to allocate costs and legal fees, encouraging the parties to authorize the arbitrator to decide the case in whole or in part as an *amiable compositeur*, and offering to render a consent award if the parties settle.

2.2.1 Proactive Case Management Conference

The pre-hearing stage constitutes an important opportunity for the arbitrator to exercise their responsibility to tailor the procedural framework of the arbitration and handle key procedural issues to better match the parties' needs and the nature of the dispute.[14] This prospect is especially true regarding the case management conference,[15] as this first organizational meeting allows the arbitrator to become acquainted with the parties to explore and develop the most appropriate process to resolve their dispute:

> [It] presents an opportunity for the Tribunal to get a real sense of the parties and what they view as important, both in terms of the merits and process. The Tribunal can start developing a relationship with counsel as well as getting a sense of

11. *See* the discussion in section 2.2.1 below. *See also* Stipanowich & Ulrich, 2014a, pp. 445-451, 458-461; Stipanowich, 2021a, p. 345.
12. This survey of the International Task Force on Mixed Mode Dispute Resolution is discussed in sections 2.2.3 & 2.2.5-2.2.8 below. *See also* Sussman & Berger, 2021b, pp. 17-20, 26-32, 36-42.
13. Sussman & Berger, 2021b, p. 15; Sussman & Berger, 2021a, p. 28.
14. Stipanowich, 2021a, p. 345; Harris, 2016, p. 96; Stipanowich & Ulrich, 2014a, p. 445; Bernardini, 2004, p. 120. This procedural discretion of the arbitrator becomes extremely wide in the absence of a detailed agreement between the parties about the procedural rules of the arbitration, as according to various laws and arbitration rules the arbitrator is then authorized to determine those procedural rules. Even when there are agreed procedural rules, the arbitrator is still free to manage the arbitration in a way they consider as suitable, so long as it does not contradict the agreed procedural rules. *See*, for example, Model Law on ICA, 2006, Article 19(2); Swiss International Arbitration Law, 1987, Article 182(2); U.K. Arbitration Act, 1996, sections 33-34(1); German Arbitration Law, 2005, section 1042(4); UNCITRAL Arbitration Rules, 2021, Article 17; NAI Arbitration Rules, 2024, Article 25(1); Swiss Arbitration Rules, 2021, Article 19; ICC Arbitration Rules, 2021, Article 22; ADRIC Arbitration Rules, 2025, Article 4(7)(1). For further discussion, *see* Nater-Bass, 2016, p. 10; Rivkin, 2008, p. 385, stating that "there is an age-old debate about who is in charge of the arbitration: the parties or the arbitrators. Recently, the view has become more common that it is the arbitrators."
15. Also known as the procedural conference, the first organizational meeting, or the preliminary hearing. *See* Nater-Bass, 2016, p. 13; Stipanowich & Ulrich, 2014a, p. 444; Sussman & Berger, 2021b, p. 14; Harris, 2016, p. 96.

> counsel and how they work together. The Tribunal can address any cultural differences and develop common expectations as to the conduct of the arbitration. The Tribunal can invite party representatives to attend the session, thereby encouraging a more active client engagement and participation in decision-making. Discussion and guidance by the Tribunal can lead to consensus as to the framework of the proceeding.[16]

Instead of technical and routine discussions with the parties about timetables for submissions, disclosures, and hearings that stem from the presumed assumption that the arbitral process will simply proceed,[17] the arbitrator can designate the first organizational meeting for proactive and thorough discussions with the disputants about efficient procedural measures and other strategies that may promote partial or full settlement of the disputed issues.[18] For instance, the arbitrator can attempt to establish detailed procedural timetables and schedules, narrow the issues to be addressed, limit the submissions and the discovery processes, and examine the possibility of earlier submissions and initial merits to assist in framing the arbitration procedures.[19] Additionally, during this procedural conference, the arbitrator can discuss with the parties the feasibility of designated mediation windows and a pre-hearing conference to be scheduled in advance as part of the arbitration timetable, alongside other initiatives to set the stage for settlement, such as the early resolution of issues, the bifurcation of the proceedings, the early neutral evaluation of the case, and other strategies discussed below.[20] Although the arbitrator can introduce such initiatives in the later stage of the arbitral process, they may be more complicated to

16. Sussman & Berger, 2021b, p. 14. *See also* Carrara, 2019, p. 43; Nater-Bass, 2016, pp. 13-14; Bernardini, 2004, p. 120.
17. Carrara, 2019, p. 43; Sussman & Berger, 2021b, p. 14; Sussman & Berger, 2021a, p. 25.
18. Harris, 2016, p. 96; Nater-Bass, 2016, p. 17; ICC Guide on Effective Conflict Management, 2023, p. 36; Sussman & Berger, 2021b, p. 14, stating that "this first meeting [is] the preliminary and essential first step to an engaged tribunal that can helpfully promote settlement."
19. The procedural measures the arbitrator can introduce to promote efficiency are very wide and may relate to every aspect of the arbitration. For example, the arbitrator can establish an appropriate order of proof, establish and maintain a realistic daily hearing schedule, require submission of organized core exhibits prior to hearing, urge the parties to focus on the probativeness of evidence rather than its admissibility, discourage traditional objections, limit the presentation of cumulative testimony, accept affidavits or pre-recorded testimony regarding less critical matters, encourage the use of written direct testimony for witnesses, establish procedures to narrow and highlight matters on which opposing experts agree, and encourage the parties to limit the time for examination and arguments. *See* Blackaby et al., 2022, §6.40-6.46; Carrara, 2019, pp. 43-44; Nater-Bass, 2016, pp. 15-17; Stipanowich & Ulrich, 2014a, pp. 444-454; Stipanowich et al., 2010, pp. 75-76; Raviv, 2012, p. 488; Sussman & Berger, 2021b, p. 14; Marriott, 2005, p. 542; Bernardini, 2004, p. 121; UNCITRAL Notes on Arbitration, 2023, Article 1(b)(i); ADRIC Arbitration Rules, 2025, Article 4(6)(2) & Appendix R1.
20. Harris, 2016, pp. 96-97; Sussman & Berger, 2021b, pp. 14-15; ICC Guide on Effective Conflict Management, 2023, p. 36; Nater-Bass, 2016, p. 17, stating that "the arbitrators may want to take the opportunity at the organizational conference to inquire about the need for any settlement discussions. Depending on such need and the will of the parties to cooperate and work towards reaching of an amicable settlement, the arbitrators can decide whether or not they want to offer any settlement facilitation. This decision must then also be factored into the procedural timetable and the structuring of the proceedings."

implement after the schedule of the proceedings has been established and the parties have prepared accordingly.[21]

Many arbitration rules have recognized the magnitude of the first procedural conference in ICA as a mandatory phase within the arbitral process.[22] This significance is also reflected in various guidelines for ICA, such as the UNCITRAL Notes on Arbitration, which emphasize the necessity of creating common ground regarding the arbitral procedure, especially among parties from different legal backgrounds who are often accustomed to differing procedural styles or lack experience with certain aspects of the arbitral process.[23] Similarly, the ICC Guide on Effective Management of Arbitration considers the case management conference as an important catalyst for settlement since it allows the arbitrator to handle the procedural aspects of the arbitration while agreeing with the parties on strategies aimed at maintaining their relationship and mitigating the risk of loss, such as the bifurcation of the proceedings, the early determination of issues, and settlement procedures undertaken during the arbitral process.[24]

The impact of conducting a comprehensive case management conference on the prospects of amicably settling the dispute is also supported by empirical data. In 2013, the College of Commercial Arbitrators (CCA) and the Straus Institute for Dispute Resolution of Pepperdine Law School in the US (The Straus Institute) surveyed 134 U.S. arbitrators experienced with domestic and international arbitration about arbitration practices and the future of arbitration (2013 Straus Institute Survey).[25] According to the survey's results, among 59 respondents who affirmed their engagement with the informal settlement of their cases, most saw "a connection between their process management activities, particularly at the pre-hearing stage, and the possible settlement of the underlying dispute."[26] In addition, arbitrators who identified and addressed key procedural matters and important issues to be decided during the arbitration contributed to the initiation of productive negotiations between the parties and enhanced the likelihood of an amicable settlement of the dispute.[27]

2.2.2 Targeted Questions by the Arbitrator

Beyond initiatives best introduced during the first procedural conference, other initiatives connected to settlement can only be promoted later in the arbitral process,

21. Sussman & Berger, 2021b, p. 14; Sussman, 2020, p. 22; Harris, 2016, p. 96.
22. Such as ICC Arbitration Rules, 2021, Article 24; Swiss Arbitration Rules, 2021, Article 19; NAI Arbitration Rules, 2024, Article 26; SCC Arbitration Rules, 2023, Article 28; ADRIC Arbitration Rules, 2025, Article 4(6)(1). For further discussion, *see* Sussman & Berger, 2021b, p. 15.
23. UNCITRAL Notes on Arbitration, 2023, Article 1(b)(i). These differences in the arbitral process, especially concerning the role of the arbitrator as a settlement facilitator, are discussed in detail in Chapter 5. *See also* Sussman & Berger, 2021b, p. 15; Carrara, 2019, pp. 43-44; Nater-Bass, 2016, p. 14.
24. ICC Guide on Effective Management of Arbitration, 2018, pp. 13-14. *See also*: ICC Report on Facilitating Settlement in ICA, 2023, p. 6.
25. Stipanowich & Ulrich, 2014a, p. 398; Stipanowich & Ulrich, 2014b, p. 2.
26. Stipanowich & Fraser, 2017, p. 859.
27. Stipanowich & Ulrich, 2014b, pp. 16-19; Stipanowich & Ulrich, 2014a, pp. 445-451, 458-461; Stipanowich & Fraser, 2017, pp. 858-859.

mainly after the first round of submissions.[28] The working assumption is that the arbitrator at this stage has already become familiar with the disputed issues and the arguments and positions of the parties[29] and, therefore, is in a better position to focus the discussion with them on key procedural, legal, and factual issues that may be relevant to the outcome of the arbitration.[30] An effective technique the arbitrator can implement at this point is questioning the parties on procedural and substantial aspects of the dispute to test their understanding of the case and informally examine whether the dispute is suitable for settlement and whether the parties are willing to explore settlement possibilities.[31] This proactive intervention of the arbitrator, viewed as an integral component of their role as a "process manager,"[32] may help in setting the stage for settlement:

> The parties may benefit from those questions as they will become aware of the arbitrator's approach to their dispute. The parties may also realise that the strengths and weaknesses of their respective case need to be reassessed. The parties may ultimately decide to re-shape their case and possibly even drop some allegations, arguments or procedural requests. In some instances, the questions put by the arbitrator may provide the main impetus for the parties' decision to start settlement negotiations.[33]

According to some commentators, the questions posted by the arbitrator, after reviewing the written pleadings and all attached statements and documents, also have a psychological effect on the parties' willingness to settle, as they signal that the arbitrator has a good understanding of their positions, which "is most important for [the] willingness to re-open settlement negotiations which had failed prior to the arbitration."[34]

2.2.3 Abstract Proposals to Settle and Designing of Mediation Windows

The arbitrator can encourage the parties to negotiate directly with each other, sometimes while excluding their counsels, to settle the dispute amicably.[35] This indirect method to promote settlement is mentioned in various arbitration rules and guidelines, such as the UNCITRAL Notes on Arbitration, which authorize the arbitrator

28. Sussman & Berger, 2021b, p. 18; Raeschke-Kessler, 2005, p. 528.
29. Marzolini, 2016, p. 112; Raeschke-Kessler, 2005, p. 530; Harris, 2016, p. 97.
30. Harris, 2016, p. 97; Marzolini, 2016, p. 113; Raeschke-Kessler, 2005, p. 528.
31. Marzolini, 2016, pp. 111-113; Harris, 2016, p. 97; Gill, 2006, p. 162.
32. Stipanowich et al., 2010, p. 43; Stipanowich & Ulrich, 2014a, p. 445; Stipanowich, 2014, pp. 341-342. The authority to raise these questions derives from the general duty of the arbitrator to discuss with the parties any issue that is material to the dispute and its outcome. *See* IBA Rules on Evidence in International Arbitration, 2020, Article 2(3); Sussman & Berger, 2021b, pp. 22-23; Raeschke-Kessler, 2005, pp. 524-525.
33. Marzolini, 2016, p. 113. *See also* Schneider, 1998, pp. 72, 76; Raeschke-Kessler, 2005, p. 531.
34. Raeschke-Kessler, 2005, p. 531. For further discussion on the psychological impact of procedural measures on the incentive to settle, *see* Sussman & Berger, 2021b, pp. 9-10; Sussman & Berger, 2021a, p. 27.
35. Gill, 2006, p. 162; Raeschke-Kessler, 2005, p. 533; Bernardini, 2004, p. 122; Stipanowich & Kaskell, 2001, pp. 28-29.

"in appropriate circumstances ... [to] raise the prospect of a settlement that would not involve the arbitral tribunal,"[36] and the ICC Arbitration Rules that empower the arbitrator to encourage "the parties to consider settlement of all or part of the dispute either by negotiation or through any form of amicable dispute resolution methods."[37] Despite the prevailing view among scholars and international practitioners that such initiative is an integral part of the arbitrator's "managerial role" over the proceedings,[38] its use by international arbitrators is not extensive. A very recent survey conducted by the International Task Force on Mixed Mode Dispute Resolution[39] examined the position of 75 arbitration practitioners from jurisdictions worldwide regarding the role of arbitrators in settlements and the various techniques they used to promote ICA settlements (2020 Mixed Mode Task Force Survey).[40] When asked if they raised the possibility of a settlement at the first organizational conference, 56% of participants responded affirmatively, while the rest answered negatively. When asked if they raised the possibility of a settlement in the later stages of the arbitral process, 62% responded positively, and the rest negatively.[41]

In addition to abstract proposals to settle, the arbitrator can allow—and when agreed on, enforce—"cooling-off periods" during the arbitration (i.e., mediation windows) to create better conditions for the parties to explore settlement possibilities,[42] including mediation conducted by a different neutral.[43] Although mediation windows may occur spontaneously without previous agreement between the parties or discussion with the arbitrator,[44] it may be more effective to agree about them sufficiently in advance[45] due to schedule considerations as mentioned above and to overcome one of the main barriers to settlement: the parties' concern that suggesting or agreeing to mediation or settlement discussions during the arbitration may show

36. UNCITRAL Notes on Arbitration, 2023, Article 12.
37. ICC Arbitration Rules, 2021, Appendix IV, section h(i).
38. Pitkowitz & Richter, 2009, p. 227; Berger, 2018b, pp. 506-509; Draetta, 2009, p. 493; Kaufmann-Kohler, 2009, p. 188.
39. The initiative of this task force is discussed in section 6.3.3.4.
40. Sussman & Berger, 2021b, p. 7.
41. Sussman & Berger, 2021b, p. 19; Sussman, 2020, p. 22. Although the results of this survey were not presented according to the legal background of the surveyed practitioners, they might have been influenced by this factor. As discussed in Chapter 5, some of the arbitrators with Common Law backgrounds refuse to mention the possibility of settlement to the parties because they considered their options prior to initiating the arbitral proceedings, so no need exists for further assistance from the arbitrator's side in this matter. *See also* Berger & Jensen, 2017, p. 892; Stipanowich & Ulrich, 2014a, pp. 459-460.
42. Stipanowich, 2021a, pp. 345-346; Stipanowich, 2021b, p. 286; Sussman, 2020, p. 20; Sussman & Berger, 2021a, p. 25; Faleck, 2021, p. 52; Greenwood, 2011a, pp. 209-210; Gill, 2006, p. 162; Bernardini, 2004, p. 122; ICC Report on Facilitating Settlement in ICA, 2023, p. 7; ICC Guide on Effective Conflict Management, 2023, p. 37.
43. Faleck, 2021, p. 53; Stipanowich, 2021a, pp. 345-346; Sussman & Berger, 2021b, p. 18; Sussman, 2020, p. 21; Nigmatullina, 2018, p. 222; Blankenship, 2006, p. 32; Marriott, 2005, p. 543; Stipanowich & Kaskell, 2001, p. 29.
44. Faleck, 2021, p. 52; Blankenship, 2006, p. 32.
45. Whether through discussions with the arbitrator during the case management conference or as part of the parties' dispute resolution clauses. In addition, when parties agree on institutional arbitration rules, they may adopt arrangements suggested by those rules for carrying out mediation windows. *See* Faleck, 2021, p. 53; Sussman & Berger, 2021b, pp. 19-20; Sussman, 2020, p. 21.

weakness or damage their negotiation position.[46] In most cases, mediation windows are scheduled after the first round of submissions to allow the parties to "realistically assess the relevant facts and legal principles, the likely outcome and what a reasonable compromise might be, as well as the likely expense in terms of legal costs and damage to reputation, commercial relationships, and other non-monetary factors."[47] However, these windows may also fit at earlier or later phases of the arbitration process, depending on various considerations, including the nature of the dispute, the scope of controversies, and the interests at stake.[48] Normally, during these windows, the arbitral proceedings are stayed to allow undisturbed and sincere attempts to settle. However, the mediation or settlement discussions sometimes run simultaneously with the arbitration, particularly when the mediation window is set early in the process or when the allocated period is over.[49] Although the arbitrator is not directly involved in the settlement negotiations or the mediation, they may still have partial responsibilities over these efforts, such as deciding the number and the exact timing of the mediation windows, choosing the mediator, and determining the issues to be mediated, subject to the parties' requests.[50]

The authority of the arbitrator to establish mediation windows is articulated in various arbitration rules and guidelines.[51] For example, the ICC Arbitration Rules authorize the arbitrator to encourage "the parties to consider settlement ... through any form of amicable dispute resolution methods such as ... mediation under the ICC Mediation Rules"[52] when the ICC Mediation Guidance Notes explicitly address mediation windows during arbitration. They recommend staying the arbitral proceedings by default during this period to allow the parties to focus on settlement efforts and avoid incurring arbitration costs that may become redundant if a settlement is reached.[53] Moreover, the Rules for the Facilitation of Settlement in International Arbitration of the Centre for Effective Dispute Resolution (CEDR) even oblige the arbitrator to "insert a mediation window in the arbitral proceedings when requested to do so by all parties in order to enable settlement discussions, through mediation or otherwise, to take place."[54] In addition, the Swiss Arbitration Rules enable the parties "at any time during the arbitration proceedings ... to resolve their dispute, or any portion of it, by

46. Sussman & Berger, 2021b, p. 17; Faleck, 2021, p. 52; Sussman, 2020, pp. 20-21; Sussman & Berger, 2021a, p. 25; Greenwood, 2011a, p. 209.
47. Sussman & Berger, 2021b, p. 18. *See also* ICC Guide on Effective Conflict Management, 2023, p. 37; Sussman, 2020, p. 21; Nigmatullina, 2018, p. 222; Greenwood, 2011a, p. 209.
48. ICC Report on Facilitating Settlement in ICA, 2023, pp. 11-13; Harris, 2016, p. 96; Sussman, 2020, p. 21; Greenwood, 2011a, pp. 209-210; Faleck, 2021, p. 52, suggesting allowing more than one mediation window during the arbitral process.
49. Faleck, 2021, p. 52; Sussman & Berger, 2021b, p. 18; ICC Mediation Guidance Notes, 2014, section 29; ICC Report on Facilitating Settlement in ICA, 2023, p. 13; ICC Guide on Effective Conflict Management, 2023, p. 38.
50. Sussman & Berger, 2021b, p. 18; Greenwood, 2011a, pp. 209-210; Myers, 1996, p. 28; Abramson, 1999, p. 2.
51. Sussman & Berger, 2021b, p. 19; Sussman, 2020, pp. 21-22.
52. ICC Arbitration Rules, 2021, Appendix IV, section h(i).
53. ICC Mediation Guidance Notes, 2014, section 29.
54. CEDR Rules for Settlement Facilitation, 2009, Article 5(3)(1). *See also* Berger & Jensen, 2017, p. 895; Stipanowich & Ulrich, 2014b, p. 14.

mediation" when, by default, "the arbitration proceedings will be stayed during that period."[55] Similarly, the Arbitration Rules of the ADR Institute of Canada (ADRIC) authorize the arbitrator to "encourage settlement of the dispute and recommend that the parties use mediation, conciliation, or other dispute resolution procedures at any time during the arbitration proceedings."[56] Furthermore, these rules empower the arbitrator to establish timeframes for such settlement efforts as early as the preliminary meeting with the parties.[57] Another notable arrangement regarding the mediation window is anchored in the Arbitration Rules of the American Arbitration Association (AAA), which state that, unless otherwise agreed, parties involved in arbitrations with claims exceeding USD 100,000 are required to mediate their dispute during the arbitral process. However, the arbitration cannot be stayed for this purpose.[58]

Despite this growing regulative trend, based on the 2020 Mixed Mode Task Force Survey, it seems that, in practice, the use of mediation windows in ICA is minimal. Although several respondents from diverse jurisdictions agreed that a mediation window "would be a good idea," when the respondents were asked if they "set a mediation window at the first conference that requires the parties to consider mediation at a set time in the schedule," only 24% answered positively, and the rest negatively. When asked whether they "schedule a mediation window at the first conference that builds a pause into the arbitration to allow the parties to try to mediate," only 12% responded affirmatively, and the remaining answered negatively.[59]

2.2.4 Bifurcation of the Arbitral Process

The bifurcation of the arbitral process is another method the arbitrator can use to promote complete or partial dispute settlement.[60] In international arbitration, where monetary damages constitute the primary way to compensate violated rights,[61] bifurcation relates primarily to the division of the proceedings between the liability and the quantum of damages to allow a decision on one of these issues before litigating the second.[62] In most cases, the tribunal decides the liability first to allow the parties during the quantum phase, which usually requires more extensive and markedly different evidence, to focus their discussions only on issues that bear liability.[63] However, the nature of the dispute may justify the implementation of a reverse bifurcation by

55. Swiss Arbitration Rules, 2021, Article 19(6). A similar arrangement is anchored in the AMA Protocol of the Singapore Centres for International Arbitration and International Mediation, as discussed in section 5.2.2.3.
56. ADRIC Arbitration Rules, 2025, Article 4(20).
57. ADRIC Arbitration Rules, 2025, Article 4(6)(2) & Appendix R1(n).
58. AAA Arbitration Rules, 2022, Article R-10.
59. Sussman & Berger, 2021b, p. 19; Sussman, 2020, p. 22.
60. Rivkin, 2008, p. 381; Greenwood, 2011b, p. 107; Sussman & Berger, 2021a, p. 25; Sussman & Berger, 2021b, pp. 23-24; ICC Report on Facilitating Settlement in ICA, 2023, p. 7.
61. Sussman & Berger, 2021b, p. 21.
62. Blackaby et al., 2022, §6.53-6.58; Greenwood, 2019, p. 421; Rivkin, 2008, p. 381; Sussman & Berger, 2021b, pp. 21-22; Benedettelli, 2013, p. 495.
63. Rivkin, 2008, p. 381; Sussman & Berger, 2021b, p. 24.

deciding the damage issues first and then narrowing the liability phase only to issues where damages can be proven.[64] In addition, given the growing complexity of international arbitration, bifurcation can be implemented in other creative ways, such as addressing the jurisdiction before the merits, as customary in investment treaty arbitrations, or when the arbitration groups a large number of identical disputes, as frequently the case in construction arbitrations, deciding the highest monetary-value claim first, possibly through a partial or interim award,[65] to save discussions on overlapping facts and issues while discussing the others.[66] Although the decision about the appropriate type of bifurcation can only be made after a clear understanding of the parties' arguments and positions (i.e., not before the first round of submissions), it may be useful if the arbitrator introduces this initiative at the first organizational conference to obtain the parties' cooperation and promote other techniques, such as the determination of preliminary issues and the pre-hearing conference to be discussed below, to support bifurcated proceedings.[67]

The authority to bifurcate the arbitral process is expressed explicitly or implicitly in multiple arbitration rules and guidelines that relate to it as a case management technique contributing to the efficient resolution of the dispute.[68] In practice, however, empirical data shows that bifurcation has not been widely used in ICA,[69] despite scholars' and practitioners' common opinion that bifurcation saves time and expenses, regardless of its exact implementation.[70] It also increases the likelihood of a settlement, as it puts the parties who wish to mitigate the risk of loss and possibly preserve their business relationship in a better position to resolve undecided issues between them or through settlement procedures during the remaining part of the arbitration:

> In appropriate cases, a partial award on jurisdiction or liability may facilitate settlement. For example, if the arbitral tribunal decides that it has jurisdiction, the parties will know that the arbitration will go forward. This could prompt them to discuss settlement. Similarly, if the tribunal finds a party to be liable, the parties

64. Sussman & Berger, 2021b, p. 24; Rivkin, 2008, p. 381.
65. Benedettelli, 2013, p. 496; ICC Guide on Effective Management of Arbitration, 2018, p. 11.
66. Greenwood, 2019, pp. 421-422; Stipanowich & Ulrich, 2014a, p. 448; Sussman & Berger, 2021b, pp. 22, 24; Rivkin, 2008, p. 381; Benedettelli, 2013, p. 495.
67. Raeschke-Kessler, 2005, pp. 528-529; Rivkin, 2008, p. 381; Sussman & Berger, 2021b, p. 21; ICC Guide on Effective Management of Arbitration, 2018, p. 14.
68. Such as ICC Arbitration Rules, 2021, Articles 22(2) & 24(3) and Appendix IV(a); UNCITRAL Arbitration Rules, 2021, Article 17(1); LCIA Arbitration Rules, 2020, Article 14(1); HKIAC Arbitration Rules, 2024, Article 13(1); CIArb Arbitration Rules, 2015, Appendix II(15); IBA Rules on Evidence in International Arbitration, 2020, Article 2; ICSID Arbitration Rules, 2022, Article 42; SIAC Investment Arbitration Rules, 2017, Article 16(4); ICDR International Arbitration Rules, 2021, Article 23.
69. In the aforementioned 2013 Straus Institute survey, although 124 of 134 respondents confirmed that they tailored the arbitration procedures according to the parties' needs and the nature of the dispute, only 15 respondents (13.2%) confirmed the use of bifurcation. *See* Stipanowich & Ulrich, 2014a, pp. 446-448.
70. Sussman & Berger, 2021a, p. 25; Greenwood, 2011b, p. 107; Benedettelli, 2013, p. 497; ICSID Arbitration Rules, 2022, Article 42.

may prefer to settle the issue of damages rather than incur the time and expense of completing the arbitration.[71]

2.2.5 Determination of Preliminary Issues

Deciding preliminary issues in the arbitration constitutes another initiative the arbitrator can take to set the stage for settlement.[72] Compared to litigation, ICA traditionally has had fewer procedures available to allow for the preliminary determination of issues.[73] Interestingly, even when the arbitration rules have granted explicit authorization to decide preliminary issues, arbitrators—particularly from Civil Law jurisdictions—have been traditionally reluctant to do so, except on issues of jurisdiction and discovery, despite the common understanding that an early decision might contribute to the efficiency of the process.[74] This attitude was taken for various reasons, including (a) concerns that preliminary decisions might expose the resulting award to challenges before courts, particularly when they led to the termination of the process, entirely or partly, at an early stage without any right of appeal as customary in arbitration; (b) concerns that preliminary decisions might harm the appearance of justice because, unlike preliminary views on the merits, as discussed below, these decisions are final; and (c) the attitudes of arbitrators according to which, in international arbitration, the parties should be granted the full opportunity to be heard by presenting the evidence they feel is relevant, regardless its impact on the ultimate determination of the case.[75]

Nevertheless, in recent years, this reality has changed, as multiple arbitration rules and guidelines have been updated to grant procedural tools that authorize and encourage arbitrators to deliver preliminary determinations, either in the form of an award or an order, on issues expected to narrow the dispute and enhance the efficiency of the process. These determinations include decisions declaring that one or more issues of law or fact are manifestly inadmissible, legally unfounded, or beyond the

71. ICC Guide on Effective Management of Arbitration, 2018, p. 11. *See also* Greenwood, 2011b, p. 107; Sussman & Berger, 2021a, p. 25; Rivkin, 2008, p. 381; Sussman & Berger, 2021b, pp. 23-24; Benedettelli, 2013, pp. 497, 503.
72. Sussman & Berger, 2021b, p. 26; Harris, 2016, p. 96; Sussman & Berger, 2021a, p. 25; Rivkin, 2008, p. 380; ICC Guide on Effective Management of Arbitration, 2018, p. 14; Howes & Stowell, 2020, p. 52; Raviv, 2012, p. 495; Gill, 2006, pp. 161-162.
73. In particular, arbitration rules used to lack clear authorization to hear and grant dispositive motions, which if granted, would have resulted in early termination of the case, entirely or in part, without hearing all the evidence first. Examples for such motions are a motion to dismiss that is granted when there is no merit and summary judgment that is granted when the case or its relevant part is meritorious. *See* Harris, 2016, p. 96; Sussman & Berger, 2021b, p. 26; Rivkin, 2008, p. 379.
74. Howes & Stowell, 2020, p. 52; Harris, 2016, p. 96; Rivkin, 2008, pp. 380-381; Sussman & Berger, 2021b, p. 26; Raviv, 2012, p. 499; Sperow, 2020.
75. Berger & Jensen, 2016, p. 6; Rivkin, 2008, p. 380; Sussman & Berger, 2021b, p. 26; Harris, 2016, pp. 96-97; Howes & Stowell, 2020, p. 52. For a comprehensive discussion about the reluctancy of arbitrators to allow dispositive motions, *see* Raviv, 2012, pp. 500-507.

tribunal's jurisdiction.[76] Indeed, following this regulatory backup, decisions on preliminary issues have gained popularity in international arbitration on matters of jurisdiction and other controlling issues, including key legal points, dispositive motions, and limitations on the discovery process,[77] which have presented new challenges for international arbitrators as "process managers."[78] Empirical data supports the growing popularity of decisions on preliminary issues in international arbitration. In the 2020 Mixed Mode Task Force Survey, 84% of the respondents confirmed that they "isolate and decide preliminary issues (other than jurisdiction)" at an early stage of the proceedings.[79] Importantly, 80% suggested that arbitrators should introduce this initiative to the parties during the first organizational conference since preliminary motions impact the prospects of settling the case amicably.[80] This clear result aligns with the conclusions of the 2013 Straus Institute Survey, according to which arbitrators who decide key preliminary issues and grant dispositive motions set the stage for productive negotiations between the parties and enhance the chances for comprehensive or partial settlement of the underlying dispute.[81] These results are also consistent with the views expressed in the literature about the connection between preliminary decisions and settlement:

> The determination of a specific issue may well unlock the dispute from a settlement perspective, whether by knocking out a claim which was of a value disproportionate to the other claims at issue, or by determining a point of law which is central to a defence, for example. Naturally, such determinations will not be possible or appropriate in every case, but where they are, arbitrators should perhaps be more willing to grasp the nettle and to decide points which are likely to have a significant impact on the parties' dispute without waiting for a full merits hearing on all issues. The importance of ensuring both parties have a proper opportunity to state their case and to be heard should not allow an obstructive party to prevent such determinations for tactical reasons.[82]

76. Stipanowich, 2021a, p. 306; Sussman & Berger, 2021b, pp. 27-28; Sperow, 2020; Rivkin, 2008, p. 380; Raviv, 2012, pp. 490-494. *See,* for example, IBA Rules on Evidence in International Arbitration, 2020, Article 2(3)(b); UNCITRAL Notes on Arbitration, 2023, Article 21; ICC Arbitration Rules, 2021, Appendix IV(a); NAI Arbitration Rules, 2024, Article 45; LCIA Arbitration Rules, 2020, Article 22(1)(viii); AAA Arbitration Rules, 2022, Rule R-34; ICSID Arbitration Rules, 2022, Article 41; SIAC Arbitration Rules, 2025, Articles 46-47; ICDR International Arbitration Rules, 2021, Articles 22(4) & 23. However, according to the prevailing approach, in the absence of authorization by the arbitration rules, a prior consent by the parties constitutes a prerequisite for delivering early determinations by the arbitrator, *see* Berger, 2003, p. 400; Sanders, 1999, p. 373.
77. Eiseman et al., 2013, p. 701; Stipanowich, 2010, p. 12; Stipanowich & Ulrich, 2014a, p. 444; Sperow, 2020. For various examples on issues that may be subject to preliminary decisions, *see* Rivkin, 2008, pp. 380-381.
78. Stipanowich et al., 2010, p. 43; Stipanowich & Ulrich, 2014a, p. 445; Stipanowich, 2014, pp. 341-342; Sperow, 2020.
79. Sussman & Berger, 2021b, p. 26.
80. Sussman & Berger, 2021b, pp. 28-29.
81. Stipanowich & Ulrich, 2014b, pp. 16-19; Stipanowich & Ulrich, 2014a, pp. 445-451, 458-461; Stipanowich & Fraser, 2017, pp. 858-859.
82. Harris, 2016, p. 96. *See also* ICC Guide on Effective Management of Arbitration, 2018, p. 14, suggesting that "when parties wish to settle the case, ... they may use the case management conference to seek ... an early determination of controlling issues, the resolution of which might facilitate settlement."; Howes & Stowell, 2020, p. 52, stating that "even when a summary

2.2.6 Early Neutral Evaluation of the Case

An early neutral evaluation of the case constitutes another initiative the arbitrator can take to promote settlement without direct involvement in its details.[83] This technique, also known as preliminary evaluation or preliminary view, relates to oral or written[84] statements made by the arbitrator about their current thoughts and views on one or more disputed issues or the entire case.[85] Unlike the determination of preliminary issues, characterized by its final and binding nature, early neutral evaluation is intended to grant the parties an objective outside "snapshot" view of the case or particular issues as the arbitrator perceives them at the time when they are provided and, therefore, are inherently non-final and non-binding.[86] Despite its "early" nature, preliminary evaluation may, in principle, be delivered by the arbitrator at different stages of the proceedings. While some practitioners and scholars maintain that such evaluation should be provided early, mainly after the first round of the written submissions,[87] others hold that the arbitrator should choose the appropriate timing to take this initiative, depending on considerations connected with the specific dispute.[88] In any case, it is widely accepted that the arbitrator should be familiar with all key legal and factual aspects of the case before providing preliminary views,[89] as normally, such evaluations relate to the preliminary findings of facts, the conclusions of law, and the level of proof required to establish the issues in dispute.[90]

---

disposition application is unsuccessful, it nonetheless encourages settlement by focusing the parties and the tribunal on potentially dispositive issues, or at least on factually or legally specious claims."; Sussman & Berger, 2021a, p. 25, suggesting that "dispositive motions which resolve certain aspects of the case at an early stage" may grant the needed guidance for parties "to assess their settlement options."; Sussman & Berger, 2021b, p. 26; Raviv, 2012, p. 495.

83. De Gramont et al., 2017, p. 966; Sussman & Berger, 2021b, pp. 36, 39; Baysal & Cevik, 2021; Berger, 2018b, p. 509; Berger & Jensen, 2017, p. 893; Marzolini, 2016, p. 114; Harris, 2016, p. 90; Gill, 2006, p. 162; Raeschke-Kessler, 2005, p. 531; ICC Report on Facilitating Settlement in ICA, 2023, pp. 14-16.
84. Some scholars hold that arbitrators should avoid providing preliminary views in writing to underline the non-binding and preliminary nature of these considerations and prevent the disputants from referring to recorded statements made by the arbitrator in this regard if the arbitration continues. On the other hand, recorded preliminary views emphasis the transparency of the process. *See* Sussman & Berger, 2021b, pp. 36, 39; Berger, 2018b, p. 512; Harris, 2016, pp. 90-91; ICC Report on Facilitating Settlement in ICA, 2023, p. 15.
85. Harris, 2016, p. 90; Berger, 2018b, p. 510; Gill, 2006, p. 162; Baysal & Cevik, 2021; Marriott, 2005, p. 540.
86. Sussman & Berger, 2021b, p. 39; ICC Guide on Effective Management of Arbitration, 2018, p. 6; Berger, 2018b, p. 510; Harris, 2016, pp. 90, 97; Gill, 2006, p. 162; ICC Report on Facilitating Settlement in ICA, 2023, p. 15.
87. Harris, 2016, p. 90; Berger, 2018b, p. 511; Stipanowich & Fraser, 2017, p. 857; Stipanowich & Ulrich, 2014a, pp. 444-451.
88. Marzolini, 2016, p. 115; Kaufmann-Kohler, 2009, p. 197; Harris, 2016, p. 90; ICC Guide on Effective Management of Arbitration, 2018, p. 6.
89. Sussman & Berger, 2021b, p. 40; Berger, 2018b, p. 515; Marzolini, 2016, pp. 113-114; Harris, 2016, p. 90; De Gramont et al., 2017, p. 966; ICC Report on Facilitating Settlement in ICA, 2023, p. 15.
90. Stipanowich & Fraser, 2017, p. 857; Raeschke-Kessler, 2005, pp. 534-536.

Preliminary evaluation, particularly when supported by "decision-tree analysis or other means of visualization,"[91] enables the arbitrator to function as an "agent of reality"[92] and help the parties to see the "big picture" related to the dispute.[93] This interaction may contribute to the efficiency of the arbitration by encouraging the parties to narrow the disputed issues and focus on the legal and factual points the arbitrator considers as core to the case,[94] while enhancing the chances for settlement since it projects the parties' strengths and weaknesses and their correlating chances to succeed in the arbitration.[95] Some scholars even hold that an early evaluation is the most effective initiative to promote settlement in ICA:

> Preliminary evaluation of the case by the tribunal pursuant to a request by both sides frequently proves to be the most powerful means of facilitating a settlement between the parties during the arbitration process. It may also reduce the parties' "judgmental over-confidence" with which they have entered the proceedings and may lead them to adopt a more realistic evaluation of their case.[96]

The authority of the arbitrator to provide an early neutral evaluation of the case is anchored in an increasing number of arbitration rules and guidelines. For instance, the CEDR Rules for the Facilitation of Settlement in International Arbitration authorize the tribunal to "provide all parties with the ... preliminary views on the issues in dispute ... and what the arbitral tribunal considers will be necessary in terms of evidence from each party in order to prevail on those issues," as well as to "provide all parties with preliminary non-binding findings on law or fact on key issues in the arbitration."[97] Despite this growing regularity support and the impact of early neutral evaluation on settlement, the 2020 Mixed Mode Task Force Survey indicated that, in

91. Berger, 2018b, pp. 511-512. *See also* ICC Report on Facilitating Settlement in ICA, 2023, p. 15; Berger, 2015, vol. II, No. 10-33-10-36. Sometimes early evaluation is combined with an active promotion of mediation window and in jurisdictions that commonly use mediation, even with ordering one. *See* Stipanowich & Fraser, 2017, p. 857.
92. Berger, 2018b, p. 509. *See also* Harris, 2016, p. 90; Sussman & Berger, 2021b, p. 36.
93. Karton, 2013, p. 107.
94. Baysal & Cevik, 2021; Schneider, 2010, p. 318; Berger, 2018b, p. 506; Sussman & Berger, 2021b, p. 36; Harris, 2016, p. 90; Marriott, 2005, p. 540.
95. Berger & Jensen, 2017, p. 893; Sussman & Berger, 2021b, pp. 36, 39; De Gramont et al., 2017, p. 966; Harris, 2016, p. 90; Raeschke-Kessler, 2005, p. 531; ICC Guide on Effective Management of Arbitration, 2018, p. 6, considering early neutral evaluation as one of the settlement procedures.
96. Berger, 2018b, p. 509. *See also* Raeschke-Kessler, 2005, p. 531, holding that preliminary evaluations grant the parties a new risk assessment that may bring their positions closer and allow an easier path toward settlement. From a settlement facilitation perspective, preliminary assessments are typically not overly categorical. This approach prevents scenarios in which any party may lose its incentive to settle due to the expectation of receiving a more favorable final award based on these assessments. As discussed in Chapter 4, avoiding categorical assessments is also essential to prevent arguments questioning the arbitrator's impartiality. *See* in this regard Berger, 2003, p. 400.
97. CEDR Rules for Settlement Facilitation, 2009, Article 5(1)(1)-(2). Other arbitration rules and guidelines that empower the arbitrator to express preliminary evaluation are the Prague Rules, 2018, Article 2(4)(e); DIS Arbitration Rules, 2018, Article 27(4)(i) referring to Annex 3(f); LMAA Early Neutral Evaluation Guidance Note, 2022. *See also* IBA Rules on Evidence in International Arbitration, 2020, Article 2(3)(a), authorizing the tribunal "to identify to the parties, as soon as it considers it to be appropriate, any issues ... that the arbitral tribunal may regard as relevant to the case and material to its outcome."

practice, the use of neutral preliminary evaluation may be less widespread than expected. Indeed, almost 80% of the respondents answered negatively when asked if they offered preliminary views to the parties.[98] This figure is consistent with the survey responses to the proposition that "arbitrators should suggest the possibility of offering preliminary views," where only 38% expressed strong support or support to this proposition, while the rest were undecided or against it.[99] While commentators usually tend to address the arbitrator's attitude toward early neutral evaluation through the prism of the Common Law-Civil Law divide regarding the engagement of adjudicators in settlement facilitation,[100] it seems that these explicit results exceed this often cited—and definitely inaccurate—explanation.[101] Another possible explanation for such pervasive hesitation to express preliminary views may be connected, as some scholars have argued, to the confusion of arbitrators and practitioners alike between early neutral evaluation and evaluative mediation or conciliation—usually implemented within hybrid procedures—that empowers the arbitrator to mediate the dispute while exploring with the parties a broader range of interests aimed at facilitating an amicable outcome.[102]

2.2.7 Mid-Term Arbitration Review

Another indirect initiative the arbitrator can take to set the stage for settlement is to hold a mid-term arbitration review conference.[103] This innovative technique, widely known as the Kaplan Opening—named after the arbitrator Neil Kaplan, who introduced it[104]—is primarily aimed at saving time and reducing costs in complex disputes involving extensive evidence and numerous witnesses[105] by bringing parties and counsel together in front of the tribunal to identify key factual and legal issues in dispute.[106] However, unlike the traditional pre-hearing conference, which usually occurs after the final round of briefs and shortly before the main hearing and tends to

98. Sussman & Berger, 2021b, p. 36.
99. Sussman & Berger, 2021b, p. 37.
100. Berger, 2018b, p. 502; Sussman & Berger, 2021b, pp. 36-37; Harris, 2016, p. 91.
101. As broadly discussed in Chapter 5, in practice, the approaches toward preliminary evaluation are more complex, as not all Civil Law jurisdictions welcome this initiative but mainly countries with a Germanic legal tradition and, to some extent, the Netherlands and Austria. In addition, Chinese arbitrators tend to be very proactive during the arbitration and mediate their cases but consider any evaluative opinion as improper and counter to their duty to remain impartial. *See* Kaufmann-Kohler, 2009, p. 197; Stipanowich & Fraser, 2017, p. 859; Stipanowich & Ulrich, 2014a, pp. 445-451, 459-461; Sussman & Berger, 2021b, pp. 36-37.
102. Berger, 2018b, p. 512; Sussman & Berger, 2021b, p. 40.
103. Kaplan, 2014, p. 174; De Gramont, 2017, p. 56; Sussman & Berger, 2021b, p. 31.
104. Kaplan, 2014, p. 172; De Gramont, 2017, p. 56; Sussman & Berger, 2021a, p. 26; Sussman & Berger, 2021b, p. 31.
105. Sussman & Berger, 2021b, p. 31; Kaplan, 2014, p. 173. At the same time, *see* De Gramont, 2017, p. 57, suggesting that "even in smaller cases, some type of early opening argument can help the parties and the tribunal productively grapple with the issues in the case early on."
106. Sussman & Berger, 2021a, p. 26; Sussman & Berger, 2021b, pp. 31-32; Kaplan, 2014, p. 174; De Gramont, 2017, p. 56.

focus on preparations for the hearing stage,[107] the Kaplan Opening is conducted during an earlier stage of the proceedings and enables a broader dialogue between the arbitrator and the parties than is usually possible through preliminary evaluation:

> At a convenient time in the arbitration, probably after the first round of written submissions and witness statements but well before the main hearing, the Tribunal should fix a hearing at which both counsel will open their respective cases before the Tribunal. They may be required to serve skeleton arguments in advance. After the openings any expert witness should make a presentation of his or her evidence and explain the areas of difference from the expert of like discipline on the other side.[108]

Following these presentations, the arbitrator can discuss with the parties various subjects, such as key issues that may require further submissions or evidence, limitations on reply written submissions, the identification of issues suitable for accelerated determination, document disclosure and the relevancy of requested documents, proceedings to narrow disputed issues between the experts, the organization of documents for the main hearing, and issues related to damages.[109] Although the primary purpose of this initiative is not to actively promote settlement but rather to enhance the cost-effectiveness and efficiency of the process,[110] bringing the disputants together before the tribunal well in advance of the hearing may nevertheless increase the likelihood of a full or partial settlement.[111] Contributing to this likelihood is the comprehensive nature of this conference, which encourages the parties to "think outside the box,"[112] triggers direct settlement discussions either between them or with the tribunal,[113] and bears a psychological effect that helps mitigate the aggressive tone often found in the parties' direct communications or written submissions.[114]

A variation of this initiative, which mandates its application during the arbitral process, grants the tribunal broader discretion regarding its timing and explicitly empowers it to explore the possibility of settlement, was recently incorporated into the NAI Arbitration Rules:

> The arbitral tribunal may at any stage of the proceedings, and will in any case after the submission of the statement of defence, order a midstream conference, taking place electronically or otherwise, for the purpose of providing information, consultation on the further course of the arbitration or for exploring the possibility of a settlement. The arbitral tribunal may also re-address the points of [the case management conference]. Having heard the parties, the arbitral tribunal may

107. De Gramont, 2017, p. 56; Sussman & Berger, 2021b, p. 33; ICC Arbitration Rules, 2021, Appendix IV(g).
108. Kaplan, 2014, p. 174. *See also* De Gramont, 2017, p. 56; Sussman & Berger, 2021b, p. 32.
109. Kaplan, 2014, p. 175; Sussman & Berger, 2021b, pp. 34-35.
110. Kaplan, 2014, p. 174; De Gramont, 2017, pp. 56-57; Sussman & Berger, 2021b, pp. 32-33.
111. Kaplan, 2014, p. 174; De Gramont, 2017, p. 56; Sussman & Berger, 2021b, p. 31; ICC Report on Facilitating Settlement in ICA, 2023, p. 6.
112. Sussman & Berger, 2021b, pp. 32-33.
113. Sussman & Berger, 2021b, p. 31.
114. Kaplan, 2014, p. 174; Sussman & Berger, 2021b, pp. 33-34.

designate its chair to conduct the midstream conference, unless the parties have agreed otherwise.[115]

Although most arbitration acts and rules do not explicitly address this initiative, the authority to implement it can generally be inferred from most arbitration rules and various arbitration acts, which typically grant arbitrators discretion to adopt procedures appropriate for the specific dispute.[116] Nonetheless, in practice, the use of this initiative within ICA has been limited. In the 2020 Mixed Mode Task Force Survey, only 35% of the respondents indicated conducting mid-term arbitration review conference. More encouraging results, however, were obtained about the prospects of this method in the future, as 60% of the respondents agreed that it should be offered sometimes, while 30% agreed that it should be offered depending on the circumstances of the dispute.[117]

2.2.8 Sealed Offers for Allocation of Costs

As part of their responsibility to manage the arbitral process efficiently and reduce unnecessary costs, the arbitrator can encourage the parties to use "sealed offers"[118] for the allocation of costs and legal fees.[119] This tool, recognized and implemented in some Common Law jurisdictions,[120] relates to a written settlement offer (or offers) made by one or more parties to the arbitration on a "without prejudice save as to costs" basis. These are revealed to the arbitrator only after the decision on liability and quantum has been delivered to guarantee that they do not influence the decision on the merits. At that point, instead of deciding the costs according to the basic rule of "costs follow the event,"[121] the arbitrator can consider the parties' response to these offers to allocate the costs and the legal fees. If, following a rejected offer, the party achieved a more

115. NAI Arbitration Rules, 2024, Article 30. The NAI's midstream conference is relevant also in the context of the tribunal's direct involvement in the settlement process through a settlement conference with the parties, as explored in section 2.3.2 below.
116. For example, *see* the following arbitration rules and acts, which state that as long as the parties' agreement is not contradicted and they are treated equally, the tribunal is authorized to adopt suitable procedures for the particular case and to conduct the arbitration in a manner it considers appropriate to ensure an expeditious and cost-effective resolution of the dispute: LCIA Arbitration Rules, 2020, Article 14(1)(ii); ICDR International Arbitration Rules, 2021, Article 22(1); NAI Arbitration Rules, 2024, Article 25(1) & (3); SIAC Arbitration Rules, 2025, Article 32(2); ICC Arbitration Rules, 2021, Article 22(2); Model Law on ICA, 2006, Article 19(2); Hong Kong Arbitration Ordinance, 2011, Article 46(3)(c); U.K. Arbitration Act, 1996, Article 33(1)(b). *See also* Kaplan, 2014, p. 174.
117. Sussman & Berger, 2021b, p. 31.
118. Also known as the "Calderbank Offer," as this mechanism was originally developed by the U.K. Court of Appeal in the case of *Jacqueline Anne Calderbank v. John Thomas Calderbank*, 1975, and later anchored in the U.K. Civil Procedure Rules, 1998, Part 36. *See* Emmerson, 2016; Samberg, 2018; Sussman & Berger, 2021b, p. 41.
119. Stipanowich, 2021a, p. 346; Emmerson, 2016; Sussman & Berger, 2021b, p. 41; Sussman & Berger, 2021a, p. 26.
120. Such as the UK, Singapore, Hong Kong, Australia, and New Zealand. *See* Sussman & Berger, 2021b, p. 41; CEDR Report on Settlement in ICA, 2009, p. 21; Emmerson, 2016.
121. This rule, which stipulates that arbitration costs are, in principle, imposed on the losing party, is embedded in many arbitration rules and guidelines, including UNCITRAL Arbitration Rules,

favorable outcome in the final award, this refusal would be considered legitimate and would not justify a deviation from the basic rule. Otherwise, the arbitrator could impose arbitration costs on that party from the date the offer is available to accept.[122]

This initiative was adopted by two influential ICA guidelines. The ICC Note on the Conduct of the Arbitration under the ICC Rules provides detailed instructions for implementing sealed offers in ICC arbitrations.[123] According to the Note, the tribunal is encouraged to introduce this tool early in the proceedings, preferably during the case management conference, and invite the parties to agree on a specific procedure for its use.[124] The Note states that when the mechanism is agreed on and a party wishes to rely on any rejected settlement offer made to other parties in the arbitration, it should send that offer, sealed and marked "without prejudice save as to costs," to the Secretariat. The Secretariat shall treat that offer as confidential and only inform the tribunal of its submission. The offer will be transmitted to the tribunal only after all issues related to liability and quantum have been decided. If the tribunal agrees to receive the sealed offer, it has the discretion to decide what weight, if any, to give to the offer in allocating the arbitration costs.[125] A similar arrangement regarding the implementation of sealed offers in ICA is detailed in the Final Report of the CEDR Commission on Settlement in International Arbitration, which recognizes this mechanism as a method for enhancing the efficiency of the arbitral process and promoting settlements.[126] Although other arbitration rules and guidelines do not explicitly suggest or regulate this initiative,[127] the discretion typically granted to arbitrators in deciding arbitration costs—allowing them to consider the parties' relative success in the arbitration and their contribution to the process's cost-effectiveness—may provide indirect support for its use within ICA.[128]

2021, Article 42(1); Swiss Arbitration Rules, 2021, Article 40; UNCITRAL Notes on Arbitration, 2023, para. 48; NAI Arbitration Rules, 2024, Article 59(2)-(3). *See also* Sussman & Berger, 2021b, p. 42.

122. Emmerson, 2016; Stipanowich, 2021a, p. 346; Sussman & Berger, 2021b, pp. 41-42; Samberg, 2018.
123. ICC Note on the Conduct of Arbitration, 2021, paras. 267-270; Samberg, 2018; Sussman & Berger, 2021b, pp. 41, 43.
124. ICC Note on the Conduct of Arbitration, 2021, para. 268.
125. ICC Note on the Conduct of Arbitration, 2021, paras. 269 & 270(a)-(h). For further discussion on the implementation of the Sealed Offers initiative under the ICC Rules, *see* ICC Guide on Effective Conflict Management, 2023, pp. 39-40.
126. CEDR Report on Settlement in ICA, 2009, section 4(2)(6), as well as Appendix 3 that provides a detailed regulation of this tool in a manner analogous to that discussed above in the ICC Note.
127. Sussman & Berger, 2021b, p. 41; Samberg, 2018. An exception in this context is found in the ADRIC Arbitration Rules, 2025, which, under Article 1(3), may apply to ICA proceedings. Articles 4(15) & 5(3)(2) of these rules provide a general framework allowing parties, at any stage of the arbitration, to submit "without prejudice" settlement offers to other parties. However, these offers may only be disclosed to the tribunal after all substantive issues, except for costs, have been resolved. At that point, the tribunal may take such offers into account when determining the allocation of arbitration costs.
128. The tribunal's discretion to consider the parties' relative success, conduct during the process, and contribution to the cost-effectiveness of the arbitration when determining arbitration and legal costs is embedded in various arbitration rules, including LCIA Arbitration Rules, 2020, Article 28(4); Prague Rules, 2018, Article 11; Swiss Arbitration Rules, 2021, Article 40; ICC Arbitration Rules, 2021, Article 38(5); NAI Arbitration Rules, 2024, Article 59(4); HKIAC Arbitration Rules, 2024, Article 34(3); SIAC Arbitration Rules, 2025, Articles 57-58. *See also*

The views expressed in the CEDR Report regarding the effect of sealed offers on the ability to promote an amicable outcome of the dispute are supported in the academic literature:

> Sealed offers can have a direct effect on the parties' willingness to settle. If a party runs the risk of bearing the costs of the arbitration, a party has an increased incentive to accept a settlement offer. At the same time, if a party sees a chance that it could avoid to bear the costs of the arbitration, a party has an incentive to make a reasonable settlement offer. It has been reported that in some arbitrations the recoverable costs of both parties may come to represent 30 to 40% or more of the amount in dispute. Thus, the amount in question can be considerable and likely to be taken seriously into account in deciding whether to accept or reject the offer. Therefore, sealed offers may provide a strong incentive for settlement.[129]

Despite its sensible contribution to achieving a settlement, this initiative is not widely used in ICA. When the respondents of the 2020 Mixed Mode Task Force Survey were asked whether they use sealed offers, only 27.5% answered positively, and the rest negatively. Notably, the results showed no division between East and West regarding the use of sealed offers. Furthermore, arbitrators who employ this initiative have enthusiastically endorsed it, recognizing that such offers "often play a critical role in creating the right conditions for settlement."[130]

2.2.9 *Ex aequo et bono* Decision

Furthermore, the arbitrator can encourage the parties to authorize them to decide the case, or part of it, based on equitable grounds, essentially fairness, justice, and good conscience, rather than on principles of law.[131] Although many commentators consider this decision-making process (usually referred to as *ex aequo et bono*) as vague,[132] equitable determinations by arbitrators are recognized by the vast majority of domestic arbitration laws and various international arbitration rules, which generally accept them as final awards, similar to those based on standards of law.[133] Furthermore, according to most of these rules, including the UNCITRAL Arbitration Rules, when the

Emmerson, 2016, claiming that the absence of legislative regulation in Civil Law and most of Common Law jurisdictions regarding sealed offers "does not mean that a similar mechanism ... cannot be used in international arbitrations" as parties to those processes tend to have specific agreements about costs to be awarded by the tribunal or to rely on institutional rules that grant "the tribunal a discretion or an obligation to award legal and other costs."

129. Sussman & Berger, 2021b, p. 42. *See also* Samberg, 2018; Stipanowich, 2021a, p. 346; Emmerson, 2016.
130. Sussman & Berger, 2021b, p. 41.
131. Blackaby et al., 2022, §3.216-3.217; Born, 2021, §2.02[C][3]; Teramura, 2020, p. 49; Bantekas, 2015, p. 48; Nottage, 2012, p. 5; Trakman, 2007, p. 622; Berger, 2003, p. 397.
132. Teramura, 2020, p. 68; Trakman, 2007, pp. 639-641. Despite the lack of guidance regarding decisions based on equitable considerations, it is widely accepted that such determinations must always consider the applicable trade usages. *See* in this regard Bantekas, 2015, pp. 49-50; Model Law on ICA, 2006, Article 28(4), stating that "in all cases, the arbitral tribunal ... shall take into account the usages of the trade applicable to the transaction."
133. Bantekas, 2015, p. 49. *See*, for example, Model Law on ICA, 2006, Article 28(3); German Arbitration Law, 2005, section 1051(3); UNCITRAL Arbitration Rules, 2021, Article 35(2); NAI Arbitration Rules, 2024, Article 48(3); Swiss Arbitration Rules, 2021, Article 35(2); SIAC

parties request the tribunal to decide the dispute *ex aequo et bono* or as *amiable compositeur,*[134] it is obliged to do so.[135] At the same time, unlike most of the above-discussed initiatives, which arguably fall into the arbitrator's managerial authority over the process and can therefore be promoted according to their discretion, deciding the case on equity principles cannot be imposed as default and is allowed only subject to the express authorization of the parties.[136] In addition, despite the parties' authorization to dispense with the legal rules, the arbitrator's decisions should still adhere to fundamental procedural maxims, including the parties' due process rights and public policy[137] considerations, and may not "create a new set of relationships that were not originally intended by the parties,"[138] and as abovementioned should usually consider the applicable trade usages.[139]

Since parties to international arbitration are required to subject their agreement to applicable law or "rules of law,"[140] and as arbitrators normally feel bound by the imperative rules of the applicable law,[141] authorizing the arbitrator to decide on an equity basis may practically be suitable for cases or issues where the relevant law is vague or indeterminate or when the question is simply a matter of fact.[142]

Apart from saving costs and time,[143] this initiative fosters settlements in international arbitration, especially when an equitable decision resolves "stumbling block" issues that can clear the path for the parties to reach agreements on other matters.[144] Moreover, by moving beyond narrow legal positions, this decision-making process

---

Arbitration Rules, 2025, Article 35(3); HKIAC Arbitration Rules, 2024, Article 36(2); ICC Arbitration Rules, 2021, Article 21(3).

134. Despite some differences in their legislative evolution, these terms are now regularly used interchangeably to describe arbitral decisions based on principles of equity. For further discussion, *see* Berger, 2003, p. 397; Teramura, 2020, pp. 51-54, relating to the legislative history of these terms and their equal treatment by various arbitration laws, rules and decisions, including the Model Law on ICA, the English Arbitration Act, the UNCITRAL Arbitration Rules, and decisions of the ICC.
135. UNCITRAL Arbitration Rules, 2021, Article 35(2). *See also* Bantekas, 2015, p. 49, relating to court decisions that have set aside arbitral awards that, contrary to the parties' request to decide the case according to principles of equity, were based on formal law and strict application of the contract.
136. Blackaby et al., 2022, §3.222; Teramura, 2020, p. 51; Bantekas, 2015, p. 49; Berger, 2003, p. 397.
137. Although the term "public policy" under the New York Convention and the Model Law on ICA is confined to the jurisdictions connected to the arbitral process—such as the seat of arbitration, the substantive law, and the place of enforcement—many jurisdictions define this term more broadly to include transnational public policy, which refers to principles of morality and universal justice accepted by all civilized nations. *See* New York Convention, 1958, Article V(2)(b); Model Law on ICA, 2006, Article 36(1)(b)(ii); Kryvoi & Davydenko, 2015, pp. 859-860.
138. Bantekas, 2015, p. 49. *See also* New York Convention, 1958, Article V(1)(c), authorizing the court to refuse recognition or enforcement of arbitral awards relating to disputes beyond those submitted to arbitration. However, *see* the discussion in section 3.6.3 regarding the possibility of doing so in consent awards.
139. Blackaby et al., 2022, §3.218; Trakman, 2007, p. 638; Bantekas, 2015, pp. 49-50; Berger, 2003, p. 398.
140. For a discussion about the differences between "law" and "rules of law," *see* section 8.3.
141. Berger, 2003, p. 397; Nigmatullina, 2018, p. 58.
142. Bantekas, 2015, p. 48.
143. Teramura, 2020, pp. 68-69; Nottage, 2012, p. 5.
144. Trakman, 2007, pp. 634, 642; Teramura, 2020, p. 68.

enables the parties to prioritize their actual interests and, potentially, preserve or enhance their future business relationships.[145]

2.2.10 Consent Award as a Catalysator for Settlement

Arbitrators in ICA are frequently asked by parties to incorporate or convert their negotiated settlement agreements into consent awards to leverage the enforcement mechanism under the New York Convention.[146] While this option is acknowledged by the majority of arbitration laws and rules,[147] it is subject to certain prerequisites.[148] To fulfill their obligation to render an enforceable award,[149] arbitrators must thoroughly assess these conditions before recording any settlement as a consent award.[150] Arbitrators can leverage this authority—and the obligation it involves—to set the stage for settlement by reminding the parties of the possibility of converting settlement agreements into enforceable awards[151] and offering guidance on the process to ensure enforceability.[152] This guidance, which excludes direct involvement in the settlement process itself, may bolster the parties' confidence in their ability to enforce the

145. Berger, 2003, p. 398. At the same time, this decision-making process is not mediation or conciliation, as it still results with an arbitral award that is enforceable under the New York Convention. *See* Brown & Marriott, 1999, at No. 4-062.
146. Paisley & Player, 2021, p. 34; Sussman & Berger, 2021b, p. 39; Stipanowich & Fraser, 2017, p. 881; Berger & Jensen, 2017, p. 899; Kaufmann-Kohler, 2009, p. 197; Steele, 2007, p. 1397; ICC Guide on Effective Conflict Management, 2023, p. 35. In addition, *see* the discussion in section 3.6.3 about the admissibility of consent awards for enforcement under the New York Convention.
147. *See*, for example, Model Law on ICA, 2006, Article 30(1); UNCITRAL Arbitration Rules, 2021, Article 36(1); NAI Arbitration Rules, 2024, Article 51; LCIA Arbitration Rules, 2020, Article 26(9); ICC Arbitration Rules, 2021, Article 33; Swiss Arbitration Rules, 2021, Article 36(1); ICDR International Arbitration Rules, 2021, Article 35(1); SIAC Arbitration Rules, 2025, Article 43(2); HKIAC Arbitration Rules, 2024, Article 37(2)(a); SCC Arbitration Rules, 2023, Article 45. *See also* Paisley & Player, 2021, p. 35; Nigmatullina, 2018, p. 40; Gill, 2006, p. 163.
148. For example, the consent award must not exceed the tribunal's jurisdiction, contradict public policy at the seat or place of enforcement, or raise concerns connected with fraud or illegality, such as bribery, money laundering, or violations of competition law. *See* Ortolani, 2025, §21.3 & §21.5(g); Paisley & Player, 2021, p. 36; Kryvoi & Davydenko, 2015, pp. 856, 860; Stipanowich & Fraser, 2017, pp. 861-862; Horvath, 2001, pp. 143-144.
149. Ortolani, 2025, §21.3; Stipanowich, 2021a, p. 344; Horvath, 2001, p. 135; Nigmatullina, 2018, p. 67; Marzolini, 2016, p. 117; Lew, 2005, p. 425. This obligation to render an enforceable award is anchored in various arbitration rules and guidelines, including CEDR Report on Settlement in ICA, 2009, section 2(4)(1); ICC Arbitration Rules, 2021, Appendix IV(h)(ii); CEDR Rules for Settlement Facilitation, 2009, Article 3(1).
150. Almost all arbitration rules authorize the arbitrator to decline recording a settlement agreement as an award on agreed terms when there is a good reason to believe that such agreement violates public policy or intends to allow illegal activity. *See*, for example, Model Law on ICA, 2006, Article 30(1); UNCITRAL Arbitration Rules, 2021, Article 36(1); ICC Arbitration Rules, 2021, Article 33; HKIAC Arbitration Rules, 2024, Article 37(2)(a); Swiss Arbitration Rules, 2021, Article 36(1). *See also* Ortolani, 2025, §21.5(g); Paisley & Player, 2021, p. 36; Kryvoi & Davydenko, 2015, pp. 856, 860.
151. Gill, 2006, p. 163.
152. Stipanowich, 2021a, p. 287.

agreement under the New York Convention, thereby increasing the likelihood of reaching a settlement.[153]

2.3 DIRECT INVOLVEMENT IN ACHIEVING A SETTLEMENT

Unlike the first category on the continuum of settlement facilitation (i.e., indirect initiatives the arbitrator can take to set the stage for a settlement through direct negotiations between the parties), the next category comprises scenarios in which the arbitrator is directly involved in the settlement discussions,[154] usually while integrating mediation or conciliation elements.[155] This section presents the main available initiatives belonging to this group, starting from suggesting general settlement proposals, continuing with a settlement conference with the disputants, and ending with separate meetings with the parties (i.e., caucusing) to promote an amicable settlement of the dispute. These direct initiatives, which include discussions of actual possible settlements, are separate and distinguished from evaluative views on the case and normally constitute a step further on the continuum of settlement facilitation.[156] According to the 2020 Mixed Mode Task Force Survey, ICA arbitrators approach direct engagement in settlement efforts more cautiously than indirect initiatives discussed in the previous section, as only 31 % of those surveyed reported involvement in settlement discussions with the parties.[157]

2.3.1 Settlement Proposals by the Arbitrator

A direct initiative the arbitrator can take is to offer the parties settlement proposals; their scope and nature may depend on the characteristics of the dispute, the arbitrator's attitude, and the parties' request.[158] Compared to preliminary views on the merits, settlement proposals are typically suggested by the arbitrator at a more advanced stage of the proceedings, usually after the parties have presented substantial legal and evidentiary parts of the case, which enables the arbitrator to form opinions about the dispute and discuss and suggest settlement possibilities.[159] Hence:

> Arbitrators can ask if they can give some preliminary thoughts. They may say they think one side will have a tough time demonstrating what it needs on one issue or the other has not yet presented evidence to prove something else. Or arbitrators

153. This guidance may be particularly necessary when the arbitrator is directly involved in the settlement process. In addition to the general conditions for recognition and enforcement, such direct intervention—which is introduced in the sections below—can create additional challenges for enforcement discussed in Chapter 4. *See also* Stipanowich, 2021a, p. 287; Nigmatullina, 2018, pp. 106-111.
154. Stipanowich, 2021a, p. 285; Berger, 2018b, pp. 501; Kaufmann-Kohler, 2009, p. 188; Rivkin, 2008, p. 382.
155. Berger, 2018b, pp. 512; Stipanowich, 2021a, p. 282; Berger, 2003, p. 397.
156. Sussman & Berger, 2021b, p. 39; Berger, 2018b, p. 510.
157. Sussman & Berger, 2021b, p. 37.
158. Rivkin, 2008, p. 382; Raeschke-Kessler, 2005, p. 534; Berger, 2018b, pp. 509, 511; Stipanowich, 2021a, p. 285.
159. Stipanowich, 2021a, p. 285; Raeschke-Kessler, 2005, p. 534; Rivkin, 2008, p. 382.

can ask if they can propose a general solution, or if it would be helpful to discuss with the parties where they stand on settlement and to offer their perspectives to help accelerate that process.[160]

Settlement proposals, which the parties can equally request,[161] may take several forms, such as general outlines for a settlement, a range of possibilities, amounts that the parties may use as a starting point for direct negotiations that no longer involve the arbitrator, or detailed and comprehensive settlement offers related to concrete actions and definite payments, including the allocation of costs.[162] In disputes resulting from ongoing or long-term contractual relations, settlement proposals may also relate to redrafting the disputed clauses to avoid future differences between the parties on those issues.[163]

This initiative, which normally does not involve separate meetings with the parties and, in most cases, is subject to the parties' consent,[164] is recognized by several arbitration rules and guidelines. For example, the CEDR Rules for the Facilitation of Settlement in International Arbitration state that following a written request of the parties, if the tribunal considers it a helpful step in settling part or all disputed issues, the arbitrator is authorized to "offer suggested terms of settlement as a basis for further negotiation" between the parties.[165] Other arbitration rules and guidelines, including the ICC Arbitration Rules, the Swiss Arbitration Rules, the IBA Guidelines on Conflicts of Interest in International Arbitration (IBA Guidelines on Conflicts of Interest), and the Rules on the Efficient Conduct of Proceedings in International Arbitration (the Prague Rules), lack explicit reference to settlement proposals by the arbitrator during standalone arbitrations. However, they still empower the arbitrator to assist the parties, subject to their consent, in reaching an amicable settlement of the dispute, and therefore seem to recognize this initiative, even if indirectly.[166]

160. Rivkin, 2008, p. 382. *See also* Berger, 2003, pp. 399-400, suggesting that "the tribunal can ask if the parties would like a settlement suggestion from the tribunal. ... For this purpose the tribunal can summarize the disputed issues between the parties and clearly indicate the alternative decisions open to it and the associated time, cost and decision risks which will be incurred by both parties if the procedure continues. The parties can then negotiate a settlement on this basis and if necessary, take advantage of further assistance by the tribunal."
161. Stipanowich, 2021a, p. 280; Kaufmann-Kohler, 2009, p. 188; Berger, 2018b, p. 511; Raeschke-Kessler, 2005, p. 534. At the same time, *see* Berger, 2003, p. 399, suggesting that usually the arbitrator needs to take the initiative and propose settlement options, as the disputants might be hesitant to make the first move to avoid showing weakness. *See* in this regard the discussion in section 3.2.
162. Sachs, 2020, p. 232; Berger, 2003, p. 400; Stipanowich, 2021a, p. 343; Raeschke-Kessler, 2005, p. 534.
163. Raeschke-Kessler, 2005, p. 534.
164. Rivkin, 2008, p. 382; Raeschke-Kessler, 2005, pp. 534-535; Berger, 2018b, pp. 512-513.
165. CEDR Rules for Settlement Facilitation, 2009, Article 5(1)(3). *See also* Stipanowich, 2021a, pp. 334; Stipanowich & Ulrich, 2014b, pp. 14-15.
166. ICC Arbitration Rules, 2021, Appendix IV(h)(ii); Swiss Arbitration Rules, 2021, Article 19(5); IBA Guidelines on Conflicts of Interest in International Arbitration, 2024, General Standard 4(d); Prague Rules, 2018, Article 9(1). *See also* Stipanowich & Ulrich, 2014b, p. 10. These rules, along with other international arbitration rules and guidelines, are discussed in Chapter 6.

2.3.2 Settlement Conferences with the Parties

The arbitrator's efforts to promote an amicable outcome of the dispute are not limited to settlement proposals that are merely offered to the parties but usually involve a dialogue between the arbitrator and the disputants, which may culminate in a designated settlement conference intended to allow thorough discussions regarding the settlement options:

> In that conference, the Tribunal and the parties openly discuss the chances of reaching a settlement agreement and its possible content. During such a meeting, the Tribunal will ... present a proposal of possible settlement terms to the parties. ... A settlement agreement may then be concluded by the parties during or subsequent to the meeting. That agreement may then be converted by the Tribunal into an award on agreed terms if all parties so wish.[167]

The settlement conference is characterized by interactive discussions between the arbitrator and the parties, during which the arbitrator may rationally indicate how the dispute may best be resolved and address specific contents of the settlement.[168] It can conclude with a detailed settlement proposal by the arbitrator[169] or, ideally, with a finalized settlement agreement.[170] Although enriched with mediative elements, this setting remains integral to the arbitral process and is distinguished from pure mediation.[171] For this reason, the settlement conference is subject to due process considerations, particularly the parties' right to be heard.[172] It typically excludes caucusing[173] and requires the prior consent of the disputants.[174] Nevertheless, the "careful relaxation of the trial-like atmosphere"[175] during the settlement conference enables the arbitrator, who still retains an adjudicative role, to focus on setting the dispute while creating an intuitive connection between the parties' legal rights and interest-focused considerations. This approach paves the way for solutions that address the immediate dispute and the parties' future business relationships and interests.[176]

---

167. Sussman & Berger, 2021b, p. 39. *See also* ICC Report on Facilitating Settlement in ICA, 2023, p. 16; Berger, 2018b, pp. 509-510; Stipanovich & Ulrich, 2014a, p. 16. For a general discussion about the role of settlement conferences in adjudicative proceedings, *see* Menkel-Meadow, 1985.
168. Berger & Jensen, 2017, pp. 893-894, 910.
169. Rivkin, 2008, p. 382; Schneider, 1998, p. 87; Berger, 2018b, pp. 509-510.
170. Berger & Jensen, 2017, p. 911.
171. Berger, 2003, p. 397. To distinguish the settlement conference from pure mediation, some scholars define this process as "quasi-mediation" or a "low-intensity form of mediation," *see* Abramson, 1999, pp. 6-7; Bühring-Uhle, 1996, pp. 201-203. This differentiation is also emphasized in the CEDR Rules for Settlement Facilitation, 2009, Article 5(3), which calls for separating purely mediative activities from the arbitral proceedings.
172. Berger, 2018b, p. 513.
173. Raeschke-Kessler, 2005, p. 534; Berger, 2018b, p. 513; Berger, 2003, p. 397; ICC Report on Facilitating Settlement in ICA, 2023, pp. 16-17.
174. Sussman & Berger, 2021b, p. 39; Stipanowich, 2021a, p. 332; Berger, 2018b, p. 509; Berger, 2003, pp. 399-400; ICC Report on Facilitating Settlement in ICA, 2023, p. 16.
175. Berger, 2003, p. 402.
176. Stipanowich, 2021a, p. 285; Chua, 2018, p. 11; Rivkin, 2008, p. 382; Schneider, 1998, p. 61; Koch & Schäfer, 1999, p. 180; Berger, 2003, pp. 400, 403.

The CEDR Rules for the Facilitation of Settlement in International Arbitration recognizes this direct involvement of the arbitrator in the settlement efforts, which, subject to the parties' written request, authorize the arbitrator to "chair one or more settlement meetings attended by representatives of the parties at which possible terms of settlement may be negotiated."[177] The arbitrator's direct involvement is further acknowledged by the NAI Arbitration Rules, which, as noted earlier, empower the tribunal to conduct a midstream conference with the parties at any stage of the proceedings to explore the possibility of a settlement.[178] Additionally, this initiative appears to be supported by the ICC and Swiss Arbitration Rules, the IBA Guidelines on Conflicts of Interest, and the Prague Rules,[179] which, despite lacking explicit reference to the term "settlement conference," grant arbitrators wide discretion regarding the procedures and actions taken in facilitating a settlement, which may endorse conducting settlement conferences with the parties.[180] Such conferences are also supported by the Arbitration Rules of the German Arbitration Institute (DIS)[181] and the arbitration laws in several jurisdictions, including the Netherlands and Canada.[182]

2.3.3 Caucusing

The most venturesome direct intervention of the arbitrator in the settlement efforts is holding separate meetings with the parties throughout the arbitration.[183] In various jurisdictions, this practice of caucusing constitutes a fundamental component of mediation procedures[184] aimed at increasing the chances for settlement by understanding the dispute's background and the parties' underlying interests:

177. CEDR Rules for Settlement Facilitation, 2009, Article 5(1)(4). *See also* Stipanowich, 2021a, pp. 332-333.
178. NAI Arbitration Rules, 2024, Article 30. For additional discussion, *see* section 2.2.7 above.
179. ICC Arbitration Rules, 2021, Appendix IV(h)(ii); Swiss Arbitration Rules, 2021, Article 19(5); IBA Guidelines on Conflicts of Interest in International Arbitration, 2024, General Standard 4(d); Prague Rules, 2018, Article 9(1).
180. For example, the IBA Guidelines on Conflicts of Interest in International Arbitration, 2024, General Standard 4(d), authorizes the arbitrator to "assist the parties in reaching a settlement of the dispute, through conciliation, mediation, or otherwise, at any stage of the proceedings." Similarly, the ICC Arbitration Rules, 2021, Appendix IV(h)(ii), empowers the arbitrator to "take steps to facilitate settlement of the dispute."
181. DIS Arbitration Rules, 2018, Article 26. However, performing settlement conferences is subject to prior consent of the parties. *See*: Berger & Jensen, 2017, p. 910; Elsing, 2015, pp. 690-692.
182. Dutch Arbitration Act, 2015, Article 1043; British Columbia International Commercial Arbitration Act, 1996, section 30.
183. Berger & Jensen, 2017, pp. 894-895. These meetings can be held in the presence of each party and its counsel, or alternatively, in the presence of only one of them. For a discussion on the advantages of having both parties and their counsel present during caucusing, *see* Marzolini, 2016, p. 118; Abramson, 1999, pp. 9-10; Menkel-Meadow, 1985, pp. 510-511.
184. Kaufmann-Kohler, 2009, p. 199; Berger, 2018b, p. 513; Goldberg et al., 1992, p. 109; Alexander, 2017, p. 6; Dendorfer & Lack, 2007, pp. 82-83; Raeschke-Kessler, 2005, p. 525; Berger, 2003, p. 392. As an integral part of mediation procedures in many jurisdictions, caucusing should intuitively be discussed in the next section, which relates to neutrals who facilitate settlements through hybrid processes by switching roles between arbitrators and mediators. However, as presented in the next section and in Chapter 5, some arbitrators, particularly those from Civil Law jurisdictions, participate in hybrid procedures without caucusing. In contrast, others, primarily in China, tend to caucus during arbitration without labelling the process as hybrid.

> Caucuses are confidential private settings where the mediator can explore the parties' true interests and assist in the negotiation of a possible settlement of the dispute. The mediator in caucusing does this especially through a variety of mechanisms, such as (a) a reality check, where the mediator helps the parties think through the potential ramifications of failing to resolve the dispute; (b) a facilitative role where the mediator assists the parties' efforts to formulate a settlement without expressing a view on the merits or on the appropriate terms of settlement; and (c) an evaluative role where the mediator takes an active and interventionist role, making suggestions or putting forward views on the merits of the case.[185]

During ex parte communications with the arbitrator, parties may potentially reveal confidential information that they would not typically disclose in the presence of their counterparties[186] for fear that their opponents may misuse it.[187] Therefore, caucusing is generally expected to foster a more candid and open dialogue between the arbitrator and each disputant that allows the arbitrator to explore the parties' real underlying interests and engage in "reality testing."[188] This process helps the parties overcome the "negotiator's dilemma" while assisting them in achieving an efficient and value-creating resolution for their dispute.[189] However, as discussed in Chapter 4, when caucusing is conducted by an arbitrator who retains the authority to decide the dispute, it can raise fundamental concerns regarding the parties' due process rights.[190] Hence, in most jurisdictions, particularly in the West, caucusing is not usually conducted within arbitral proceedings.[191] The same approach has traditionally been taken in ICA, as reflected in the CEDR Rules for the Facilitation of Settlement in International Arbitration, which, despite acknowledging a wide range of initiatives for settlement facilitation by the arbitrator, clearly state that "the arbitral tribunal shall not ... meet with any party without all other parties being present ... or obtain information from any party which is not shared with the other parties."[192]

Nevertheless, as presented in Chapters 5 and 6, in recent years, caucusing within arbitral proceedings has been subject to fewer objections in various jurisdictions as well as in ICA, particularly when the arbitral rules or the arbitral agreement address concerns connected with its practice. The most telling evidence for this change is the

For further discussion, *see* Thevenin, 2013, p. 367; Blankley, 2011, p. 335; Sussman, 2010a, p. 384; Kaufmann-Kohler, 2009, pp. 196-197; Stipanowich, 2021a, pp. 268-269.

185. Thevenin, 2013, pp. 367-368. *See also* Stipanowich, 2021a, pp. 288-289; Benzidi, 2017, pp. 12-13; Nigmatullina, 2018, pp. 57-58; Berger & Jensen, 2017, p. 894; Stipanowich & Kaskell, 2001, pp. 15-16; Abramson, 1999, p. 4; Schneider, 1998, p. 90.
186. Raeschke-Kessler, 2005, p. 525; Stipanowich, 2021a, pp. 288-289.
187. Berger, 2015, pp. 12-13.
188. Lew, 2005, p. 425; Thevenin, 2013, p. 367; Abramson, 1999, p. 4; Nigmatullina, 2018, pp. 57-58.
189. Nigmatullina, 2018, pp. 57-58; Berger & Jensen, 2017, p. 894; Berger, 2015, pp. 12-13; Bühring-Uhle et al., 2006, p. 248.
190. *See* the discussion in section 4.2. *See also* Berger & Jensen, 2017, p. 913; Nigmatullina, 2018, p. 60; Stipanowich, 2021a, pp. 347, 349; Abramson, 1999, p. 7.
191. Schneider, 1998, pp. 90-95; Berger, 2003, pp. 401-402.
192. CEDR Rules for Settlement Facilitation, 2009, Article 5(2). *See also* CEDR Report on Settlement in ICA, 2009, sections 2(4)(3) & 2(5); Stipanowich, 2021a, p. 333; Berger & Jensen, 2017, p. 916; Stipanowich & Ulrich, 2014b, p. 15.

IBA Guidelines on Conflicts of Interest, which empower the arbitrator to "assist the parties in reaching a settlement of the dispute, through conciliation, mediation, or otherwise, at any stage of the proceedings."[193] Although this authorization does not relate specifically to caucusing, the arbitrator's authority to do so under the IBA Guidelines can be learned from the fact that the current version of the guidelines abandoned a provision that appeared in the previous version and prohibited the arbitrator from caucusing with the parties during the arbitration.[194] Empirical data also supports the growing openness to caucusing within arbitral proceedings. In 2007, a survey was conducted among 115 highly experienced arbitration practitioners from over 18 Eastern and Western jurisdictions about the role of arbitrators in the settlement process of ICA and the particular elements that constitute roadblocks and facilitators of settlement in those proceedings (2007 Ali Survey).[195] When asked whether it is "appropriate for the arbitrator to meet with parties separately to discuss settlement options (with both parties request),"[196] 38% of respondents from the West (i.e., North America and Europe) and 43% from East Asia answered positively, which resulted in no significant differences between the respondents' attitudes based on geography or legal culture.[197] These results align with the increasingly prevalent view among commentators that ex parte communications can play a pivotal role in promoting settlements within ICA processes. Such communications may enable arbitrators to address the cross-cultural complexities inherent in international commercial disputes, which often hinder their ability to elicit the parties' true interests during bilateral meetings. By mitigating these challenges, ex parte communications can enhance the likelihood of facilitating an amicable resolution.[198]

2.4 ARBITRATORS "SWITCHING HATS"

Another far-reaching initiative of the arbitrator on the continuum of settlement facilitation is fulfilling a dual role as an arbitrator and a mediator in the same dispute. Some commentators relate to all scenarios in which the arbitrator "switches hats" between these roles as one category of hybrid processes represented by the umbrella

193. IBA Guidelines on Conflicts of Interest in International Arbitration, 2024, General Standard 4(d). *See also* Sussman & Berger, 2021a, p. 26; Berger, 2019, p. 309; Berger & Jensen, 2017, p. 904; Nigmatullina, 2018, p. 178; Von Schlabrendorff, 2009, p. 98.
194. IBA Rules of Ethics for International Arbitrators, 1987, Article 8, stating that "the arbitral tribunal should point out to the parties that it is undesirable that any arbitrator should discuss settlement terms with a party in the absence of the other parties" due to its possible implication on the arbitrator's qualification to handle the continuing arbitration. *See also* Marriott, 2005, p. 539.
195. Ali, 2011b, pp. 6-8. For further discussion about this survey, *see* Ali, 2010; Ali, 2011a; section 5.2.2.
196. This question related to caucusing as part of a standalone arbitration. *See* Stipanowich & Ulrich, 2014b, p. 21. A different survey, which explored opinions about caucusing within hybrid processes involving arbitration and mediation, is discussed in the next section.
197. Ali, 2011b, p. 18.
198. Thevenin, 2013, p. 368.

term of "Med-Arb."[199] According to this approach, all processes that involve arbitration and mediation conducted by the same neutral enjoy a "blended mechanism" and full flexibility that enable the arbitrator to start the process with either mediation or arbitration, move back and forth between the mechanisms as needed, and even arbitrate and mediate simultaneously.[200] However, most scholars hold that although arbitration and mediation are conducted by the same neutral, their inherent differences limit their combination into one process. Therefore, they should be conducted separately, with attention paid to the specific sequence in which the arbitrator performs them[201] to avoid confusion between the variants of such a hybrid process[202] and, most importantly, address particular issues related to the implementation of each variant.[203] Nevertheless, scholars who subscribe to this dominant approach are divided on the number of mediation attempts an arbitrator may take throughout the process. While some argue that the arbitrator should mediate only once, others hold that as long as the separation between the arbitration and mediation parts is maintained, the arbitrator may resort to mediation multiple times, depending on the parties' needs and the developments during settlement negotiations.[204]

Additional fundamental deviation between practitioners and scholars, regardless of their attitudes toward the importance of the exact sequence between the components of the process and the possible number of mediation attempts, relates to the question of whether the mediation stage of the hybrid process should include separate communications between the arbitrator and each of the parties.[205] The controversy regarding this matter stems from three main reasons. *First*, although in many jurisdictions, caucusing is considered an inherent part of the mediation process,[206] in others, mainly with Civil Law tradition, mediation is considered a limited form of settlement facilitation that explores the parties' interests without implementing evaluative techniques and, therefore, excludes ex parte communications.[207] As a result, in these jurisdictions, the mediation stage of the hybrid process usually does not include

199. Gu, 2019, pp. 120-121; Chua, 2018, p. 3; Nigmatullina, 2018, p. 17; Ludington, 2017, p. 314; Pappas, 2015, p. 204; Stipanowich & Ulrich, 2014b, p. 9; Blankenship, 2006, p. 30; Stipanowich & Kaskell, 2001, p. 20.
200. Nigmatullina, 2018, pp. 19-20; Stipanowich & Ulrich, 2014b, p. 10; Blankenship, 2006, p. 30; Lew, 2005, p. 422; Brewer & Mills, 1999, p. 34; Sawada, 2003, p. 29.
201. Chua, 2018, p. 3; Gu, 2019, p. 120; Nigmatullina, 2018, p. 20; Berger & Jensen, 2017, pp. 894-895; Blankenship, 2006, p. 30; Brewer & Mills, 1999, p. 34; Peter, 1997, p. 91; Bartel, 1991, pp. 678-679.
202. Including by the disputants themselves, who legitimately want to understand at any given stage of the process whether they are arbitrating or mediating the dispute.
203. Gu, 2019, p. 121; Chua, 2018, p. 3; Brewer & Mills, 1999, p. 34.
204. Nigmatullina, 2018, pp. 23-25; Marzolini, 2016, p. 117; Ross, 2013, p. 361; Wolski, 2013, p. 260; Mason, 2011, p. 541; Blankenship, 2006, p. 30; Peter, 2005, p. 167; Sawada, 2003, p. 29; Bühring-Uhle, 1996, p. 370; Peter, 1997, p. 103.
205. Stipanowich, 2021a, p. 288; Marzolini, 2016, p. 118; Blankley, 2011, pp. 334-335; Sussman, 2010a, p. 384; Kaufmann-Kohler, 2009, pp. 199-200; Blankenship, 2006, p. 30.
206. Stulberg & Montgomery, 1986, p. 531; Kaufmann-Kohler, 2009, pp. 199-200; Berger, 2018b, p. 513; Goldberg et al., 1992, p. 109; Alexander, 2017, p. 6; Dendorfer & Lack, 2007, pp. 82-83; Raeschke-Kessler, 2005, p. 525; Berger, 2003, p. 392.
207. Thevenin, 2013, p. 367; Kaufmann-Kohler, 2009, pp. 196-197; Hopt & Steffek, 2013, p. 58, relating to different legal traditions that disfavor evaluative techniques in mediation.

caucusing.[208] *Second*, as discussed in Chapter 5, even in jurisdictions that accept the practice of caucusing during standalone mediation, including Common Law jurisdictions, concerns have been expressed regarding its admissibility within hybrid processes, in which the arbitrator, unlike the mediator in standalone mediation, retains the power to decide the dispute after futile settlement efforts. Consequently, in most of these jurisdictions, concerns relating to due process considerations, particularly the parties' right to be heard,[209] have resulted in imposing several limitations on the practice of caucusing within hybrid processes. In some cases, jurisdictions have gone further by either completely prohibiting caucusing in such contexts or banning hybrid processes altogether.[210] *Third*, sometimes the objection to caucusing during hybrid processes does not necessarily derive from the principled approaches in its regard but merely from practical considerations connected with the particular dispute, for example, when there is considerable distrust between the disputants or when the arbitrator believes that it is better for the parties to work directly together to resolve their disputed issues.[211] For these reasons, the mediation part may typically involve two types of settings in hybrid processes. The first includes joint sessions of the arbitrator with all parties and caucuses in which the arbitrator assembles with one or with part of the disputants.[212] The second includes merely joint sessions due to legal limitations on caucusing or deliberate choice of the arbitrator or the parties to avoid those private communications.[213]

Nonetheless, empirical data supports that most hybrid processes in international commercial disputes involve caucusing. In 2014, an empirical study was conducted among 81 leading international dispute-resolution practitioners from 28 countries worldwide[214] to gather data about the combined use of mediation and arbitration in the resolution process of international commercial disputes (2014 Nigmatullina Study).[215] According to the results, mediation was conducted by the sole arbitrator in only 11.5% of these disputes, with an additional 19.2% conducted by a member of the arbitral tribunal (mostly from Common Law jurisdictions).[216] Notwithstanding the identity of the neutral involved in the mediation phase, 88.9% of the respondents indicated that caucuses were used "always" or "in the majority of cases" during mediation, while only 7.4% confirmed their use "in the minority of cases," with 3.7% claimed they were never used.[217]

208. Stipanowich, 2021a, p. 288; Blankley, 2011, pp. 334-335; Sussman, 2010a, p. 384; Kaufmann-Kohler, 2009, pp. 199-200.
209. Berger & Jensen, 2017, p. 913.
210. Stipanowich, 2021a, p. 288; Nolan-Haley, 2020, pp. 299-300; Berger, 2018b, p. 513; Nigmatullina, 2018, p. 60; Gill, 2006, p. 164; Kaufmann-Kohler, 2004, p. 72; Berger, 2003, pp. 401-402; Stipanowich & Kaskell, 2001, p. 22; Schneider, 1998, pp. 90-95; Abramson, 1999, p. 7.
211. Kaufmann-Kohler, 2009, pp. 199-200; Abramson, 1999, p. 11.
212. Blankley, 2011, p. 334; Menkel-Meadow, 1985, pp. 510-511.
213. Blankley, 2011, p. 335; Sussman, 2010a, p. 384.
214. One-third of them from Continental Europe, another third from Common Law Asia-Pacific countries, approximately one-sixth from other Civil Law jurisdictions, and the same number from other Common Law jurisdictions.
215. Nigmatullina, 2018, pp. 84-86.
216. Nigmatullina, 2018, pp. 98-99.
217. Nigmatullina, 2018, pp. 103-104.

The following sections introduce the main variants of the hybrid process. Consistent with the dominant approach discussed above, which attributes importance to the timing and sequence in which the arbitrator performs the arbitration and mediation stages to avoid confusion between these variants, the presentation below uses terminology that implies the literal order in which mediation and arbitration occur during the hybrid process.

2.4.1 Med-Arb

Mediation-Arbitration (Med-Arb) refers to a process where a neutral is appointed first as a mediator who assists the parties in settling the dispute amicably before arbitration commences. After the mediation phase, the parties appoint the same neutral as an arbitrator for the same dispute.[218] If, during mediation, a comprehensive settlement agreement is concluded, the mediator-turned-arbitrator records that agreement as a consent arbitral award, and the process ends. If, during mediation, no settlement or only a partial agreement is concluded, the mediator-turned-arbitrator proceeds to hear the case on the disputed issues and, at the end of the arbitration phase, delivers an award that includes a binding decision on disputed issues and a consent decision on issues that were agreed upon during the mediation phase.[219] This form of Med-Arb, usually referred to by scholars and practitioners as the "most common," "pure," "original," and "traditional" Med-Arb process,[220] is recognized by the 2018 UNCITRAL Model Law on International Commercial Mediation and International Settlement Agreements from Mediation (Model Law on ICM),[221] as well as by several institutional rules relating to mediation.[222] In this common version of Med-Arb, which, as mentioned, may include or exclude caucusing during the mediation phase and contain one

218. According to some commentators, in hybrid processes that involve mediation and arbitration, the parties should agree in advance that the same neutral will conduct a dual role as an arbitrator and a mediator. Other scholars, however, reject this requirement for practical considerations, as parties may prefer not to commit in advance for the dual role of the neutral or may even agree ad hoc during or after the first phase of the hybrid process that the neutral will conduct the second phase. *See* Stipanowich & Fraser, 2017, p. 854; Limbury, 2009b, p. 5; Bartel, 1991, p. 665; Blankenship, 2006, p. 30; Phillips, G. F., 2009, p. 77; Rosoff, 2009, p. 89; Nigmatullina, 2018, p. 18, along with the references listed therein.

219. Stipanowich, 2021a, p. 277; Tezuka, 2020, p. 279; Gu, 2019, p. 121; Chua, 2018, pp. 3-4; Nigmatullina, 2018, pp. 17-20; Benzidi, 2017, p. 3; Ludington, 2017, p. 314; Berger & Jensen, 2017, pp. 894-895; Stipanowich & Fraser, 2017, pp. 852-853; Stipanowich & Ulrich, 2014b, p. 10; Ross, 2013, p. 359; Weisman, 2013, p. 40; Blankley, 2011, p. 318; Sussman, 2010a, p. 383; Limbury, 2009b, p. 5; Fullerton, 2009, pp. 31-32; Sussman, 2009a, p. 71; Mironi, 2007, p. 56; Dendorfer & Lack, 2007, p. 82; Blankenship, 2006, p. 30; Burr, 2005, p. 61; De Vera, 2004, p. 156.

220. Nigmatullina, 2018, p. 21; Pappas, 2015, p. 159; Blankenship, 2006, p. 30; Peter, 2005, p. 159; Oghigian, 2003, p. 76; Sawada, 2003, p. 29; Peter, 1997, p. 88; Elliott, 1995, p. 163; Bartel, 1991, p. 665; Landry, 1996, p. 264.

221. Model Law on ICM, 2018, Article 13. Although according to this article, as discussed in section 6.3.2.5, a mediator should not by default act as an arbitrator in the same dispute, the parties are free to agree otherwise. *See also* Stipanowich, 2021a, p. 289.

222. *See*, for example, ADRIC Med-Arb Rules, 2020, Article 1(1); BAC Mediation Rules, 2011, Article 26, allowing parties to mediation to opt-out for this arrangement, similar to the outlined provision in the Model Law on ICM.

or more mediation attempts by the arbitrator, the arbitration phase—in particular, the fact-finding and arguments parts—is expected to be shorter than standalone arbitration:

> The arbitration phase in Med-Arb is like any traditional arbitration, except that fact-finding and the education of the neutral have usually already been accomplished. The parties will normally have been able to explore key events that occurred (often in a "witness conference" setting, in a joint session) and will have reached consensus wherever possible on issues of fact. ... Before the arbitration phase actually gets under way, the disputants can reiterate the precise issues to be considered during arbitration and try to resolve any issues that may arise as a result of caucuses having been used. ... The Med-Arbitrator hears arguments on all remaining issues and renders a binding decision.[223]

Alongside this traditional version, other variations of Med-Arb relate differently to the arbitration phase of the process. One variant is Mediation followed by Last-Offer Arbitration (MEDALOA), also known as "baseball arbitration," where after failed mediation, each party submits a final offer to the mediator-turned-arbitrator. The arbitrator is limited to basing the award on one of these offers according to equity considerations or other agreed terms, including commercial practices or customs, without the ability to modify it.[224] This method, recognized by several arbitration rules and court decisions in the US,[225] can, in principle, apply to all aspects of the dispute. However, it may be more effective in the context of claim value or where liability has been clarified while quantum remains to be decided, particularly where the gaps between the parties are insignificant, which justifies the risk of avoiding full-fledged arbitration.[226] Another similar variant of Med-Arb is mediation followed by High-Low Arbitration, in which, after a futile mediation, the parties exchange written last offers or agree on a range for the arbitral award. The mediator-turned-arbitrator is informed of the offers or the agreed range and is obliged to issue an award between those limits. Alternatively, the parties can agree not to disclose the agreed range or the exchanged

223. Dendorfer & Lack, 2007, p. 84. *See also* Flake, 2016, p. 4.
224. Born, 2021, §2.02[C][2][h]; Sussman & Gleason, 2019, pp. 19-20; Chua, 2018, p. 4; Stipanowich & Mironi, 2021, p. 32; Benzidi, 2017, p. 27; Nigmatullina, 2018, p. 26; Stipanowich & Fraser, 2017, p. 853; Stipanowich & Ulrich, 2014b, p. 10; Ross, 2013, pp. 361-362; Sussman, 2010a, p. 383; Limbury, 2009b, p. 5; Rivkin, 2008, p. 383; Blankenship, 2006, pp. 31-32; Stipanowich & Kaskell, 2001, p. 25; Elliott, 1995, p. 164; ICDR Final Offer Arbitration Rules, 2015, Introduction (pp. 3-5).
225. Sussman & Gleason, 2019, p. 20; Nigmatullina, 2018, p. 150. *See*, for example, the ICDR Final Offer Arbitration Rules, 2015, that regulate all aspects of this method, including the way final offers are exchanged, the scope of the offers, the ability to amend them, and the arbitral award that according to Article 6 "shall be limited to choosing only one of the final offers submitted by the parties." Additionally, *see* the discussion in section 5.3.1.1 about the U.S. court's decision in *U.S. Steel Mining Company v. Wilson Downhole Services* that recognized this method even when parties authorized the arbitrator to rely on confidential information disclosed during the settlement process, including through caucusing, while selecting between the parties' final offers.
226. Stipanowich, 2021a, pp. 357-358; Sussman & Gleason, 2019, p. 20; Nigmatullina, 2018, p. 152; Flake, 2016, p. 9; Rivkin, 2008, p. 383; Stipanowich & Kaskell, 2001, pp. 25-26; Peter, 1997, p. 102. *See* in this regard the ICDR Final Offer Arbitration Rules, 2015, Article 5, stating that "each party's final offer shall be a single monetary amount."

final offers to the arbitrator. In this case, the arbitrator delivers a decision following a short hearing. If the decision falls between the parties' offers or within the agreed range, it becomes a final and binding award. Otherwise, the arbitrator's decision is adjusted (i.e., reduced or increased) to the closer offer or limit of the agreed range and becomes a final and binding award.[227] An additional variant of the Med-Arb process conducted by the same neutral is Med-Arb Show Cause, where, following failed mediation, the mediator-turned-arbitrator delivers a tentative award, and the parties are granted the opportunity to convince the arbitrator that the differences should not be resolved according to the suggested award.[228] Another notable variant of Med-Arb is Med-Arb-Opt-Out, where, following futile efforts to fully resolve the dispute during the mediation phase, each party has a veto on the decision whether to proceed to arbitration and whether arbitration will be conducted by the mediator or by a different neutral.[229]

2.4.2 Arb-Med

Arbitration-Mediation (Arb-Med) relates to a process where the neutral initially functions as an arbitrator, conducts a complete arbitration, and records an arbitral award without revealing it to the disputants. At this stage, the arbitrator shifts to the role of a mediator to assist the parties in resolving their dispute amicably.[230] If mediation is successful, the arbitrator issues a new arbitral award based on the parties' agreement without disclosing the sealed award. If mediation fails, the arbitrator renders the sealed award, which becomes automatically binding.[231] In another variant of Arb-Med, the arbitrator does not compose an award before the mediation phase but at the end of the process after the conclusion of the arbitration and mediation stages.[232]

Many scholars and practitioners argue that Arb-Med, in its literal sense, is less likely to occur in practice, as a final arbitration stage is necessary following mediation, whether to convert the mediated agreement into a consent award or to allow the arbitrator to render a final decision on the dispute—either the sealed award written before the mediation or an award composed at the end of the whole process.[233] According to this perspective, if the parties decide not to revert to arbitration following mediation, the process should not be viewed as a hybrid process from the outset but rather as a post-arbitration mediation whose outcome is a settlement agreement rather

227. Stipanowich, 2021a, p. 358; Born, 2021, §2.02[C][2][h]; Sussman & Gleason, 2019, p. 19; Stipanowich & Kaskell, 2001, p. 25.
228. Chua, 2018, p. 4; Limbury, 2009b, p. 5.
229. Nigmatullina, 2018, p. 27; Blankenship, 2006, p. 31; Berger, 2003, p. 394; Peter, 2005, p. 164; Peter, 1997, pp. 98-99; Bartel, 1991, p. 666.
230. As mentioned above, the mediation stage may include or exclude caucusing, and variations exist regarding the number of mediation attempts by the arbitrator.
231. Chua, 2018, p. 4; Stipanowich, 2021a, p. 359; Stipanowich & Fraser, 2017, p. 853; Nigmatullina, 2018, pp. 22-23; Deekshitha & Saha, 2014, p. 80; Ross, 2013, p. 359; Fullerton, 2009, p. 36; Limbury, 2009b, p. 5; Dendorfer & Lack, 2007, pp. 87-88; Blankenship, 2006, p. 31; Telford, 2000, p. 2; Peter, 1997, p. 99.
232. Roth et al., 2021, §37:9; Nigmatullina, 2018, p. 23.
233. Gu, 2019, p. 122; Nigmatullina, 2018, p. 24; Wolski, 2013, p. 260.

than an arbitral award.[234] For these reasons, many scholars and practitioners consider Arb-Med in its literal sense a variant of the Arbitration-Mediation-Arbitration (Arb-Med-Arb) process discussed below. Thus, they use the terms Arb-Med and Arb-Med-Arb interchangeably.[235]

2.4.3 Arb-Med-Arb

Arb-Med-Arb relates to a process where, after the commencement of arbitration, the arbitrator attempts to settle the dispute by acting as a mediator.[236] If mediation is entirely successful, arbitration is renewed only to render a consent award based on the settlement agreement between the parties. If mediation fails to resolve all issues in dispute, substantive arbitration hearings resume for the unsettled matters, followed by an award based on the partially settled outcome and the resumed arbitral proceedings.[237] Arb-Med-Arb seems to embody the most flexible hybrid approach since, in addition to the abovementioned general variations regarding caucusing and the number of possible mediation attempts, this process allows mediation to take place at various points of time throughout the arbitral process, depending on the parties' request or agreement, the arbitrator's proposal, or the applicable arbitration rules.[238] The flexibility of this process is also demonstrated by its interesting variant, referred to as Arb-Med-Arb-Opt-Out, according to which, if the mediation phase is unsuccessful in resolving the whole dispute, each party maintains a veto on the decision of whether the renewed arbitration will be conducted by the same arbitrator or by a different neutral.[239] As discussed in Chapters 5 and 6, almost all domestic legislation and international arbitration rules and guidelines that authorize the arbitrator to act as a mediator relate de facto to the Arb-Med-Arb process,[240] although these laws and rules do not often use this specific term.[241]

---

234. Berger & Jensen, 2017, p. 895; Gu, 2019, p. 122; Nigmatullina, 2018, pp. 23-24.
235. Chua, 2018, p. 4; Stipanowich, 2021a, pp. 277-278; Tezuka, 2020, p. 280; Gu, 2019, p. 122; Nigmatullina, 2018, p. 24; Stipanowich & Fraser, 2017, p. 853; Sussman, 2010a, p. 383; Rosoff, 2009, p. 89; Sussman, 2009a, p. 71.
236. Scholars who differentiate between mediation and conciliation refer to this process as Arb-Conciliation-Arb to emphasize the evaluative nature of the arbitrator's involvement in the settlement, which includes views about the disputed issues, assessments regarding their outcome, and settlement proposals, but excludes caucusing. At the same time, other scholars who perceive the arbitrator's role in the settlement in a broader meaning, including but not limited to mediation, refer to this process as Arb-settlement-Arb. *See* Nigmatullina, 2018, pp. 24-25; Lack, 2010, pp. 350, 359; Abramson, 1999, pp. 2-3.
237. Ruckteschler & Wendelstein, 2021, p. 762; Stipanowich, 2021a, pp. 277-278; Tezuka, 2020, p. 280; Gu, 2019, p. 122; Chua, 2018, pp. 4-5; Ludington, 2017, p. 314; Ross, 2013, p. 361; Sussman, 2010a, p. 383; Stipanowich & Fraser, 2017, p. 853; Nottage & Garnett, 2010, p. 179; Sussman, 2009a, p. 71; Rosoff, 2009, p. 89.
238. Chua, 2018, p. 5; Stipanowich, 2021a, p. 277; Nigmatullina, 2018, p. 44; Ross, 2013, p. 361.
239. Nigmatullina, 2018, p. 142; Sussman, 2009a, p. 71; Blankenship, 2006, p. 31; Bühring-Uhle et al., 2006, p. 253; Peter, 2005, p. 164; Berger, 2003, p. 394; Peter, 1997, p. 99.
240. Examples for such laws are British Columbia International Commercial Arbitration Act, 1996, section 30; Quebec Arbitration Act, 2014, section 620; Singapore International Arbitration Act, 1994, Articles 16-17; Hong Kong Arbitration Ordinance, 2011, Article 33; Australia Commercial Arbitration Act, 2010, Part 5, section 27D; India Arbitration and Conciliation Act, 1996, Article

2.5 CONCLUSIONS

The arbitrator can take various initiatives to facilitate a settlement in ICA. As presented in this chapter, these initiatives can be placed on a continuum, starting with minimal or indirect intervention that may set the stage for a settlement to be concluded independently by the disputants, continuing with direct participation in the settlement efforts while implementing mediation elements, and ending with a dual role as an arbitrator and a mediator at the same time or sequentially. While very often, the opinions regarding the arbitrator's role as a settlement facilitator are expressed through the prism of direct involvement in the settlement efforts, particularly within hybrid procedures where the arbitrator is authorized to act as a mediator, the discussion in this chapter demonstrates many indirect initiatives the arbitrator can take to promote an amicable outcome of the dispute without being directly involved in the settlement negotiations. Most of these indirect initiatives (e.g., proactively managing the first organizational conference, designing mediation windows, bifurcating the arbitral process, deciding preliminary issues, delivering an early neutral evaluation of the case, offering to decide the case as an *amiable compositeur*, and suggesting to deliver a consent award if the parties settle) are recognized by various international arbitration rules and guidelines and have been increasingly observed as an integral part of the arbitrator's managerial role over the proceedings. According to empirical data, these initiatives, part of which are not subject to the disputants' consent but to the arbitrator's discretion, may catalyze achieving a settlement when properly handled by the arbitrator. At the same time, very recent empirical data reveals that some of these procedural and managerial methods are not widely used within ICA, which results in missed opportunities for arbitrators to enrich their toolbox to promote settlements in these proceedings.

Unlike indirect initiatives that only set the stage for settlement, the direct involvement of the arbitrator in the settlement process seems more challenging. When permitted by arbitration laws and rules, direct involvement is usually subject to the parties' consent. As presented in this chapter, this direct involvement can be carried out with varying intensity. One group of such initiatives relates to the promotion of a settlement by integrating mediation elements "without changing the process into something else,"[242] which includes settlement proposals by the arbitrator, settlement conferences with the disputants intended to detail the contents of the settlement, and caucusing with the parties to understand the dispute's background and the parties'

30(1). Examples for such arbitral rules and guidelines are CIETAC Arbitration Rules, 2024, Article 47; BAC Arbitration Rules, 2022, Article 43; SCIA Arbitration Rules, 2022, Article 48; JAMS Comprehensive Arbitration Rules and Procedures, 2021, Rule 28(a)-(b); IBA Guidelines on Conflicts of Interest in International Arbitration, 2024, General Standard 4(d); CIArb Practice Guideline on the Use of Mediation in Arbitration, 2021, Articles 8-9; Prague Rules, 2018, Article 9.

241. The CIArb Practice Guideline on the Use of Mediation in Arbitration, 2021, is one of the very few guidelines and rules that explicitly use this term. Another guideline is the AMA Protocol of the SIAC-SIMC in Singapore. However, it uses this term primarily to relate to a process conducted by different neutrals (*see* the discussion in section 5.2.2.3).

242. Berger & Jensen, 2017, p. 895.

underlying interests. Indeed, the direct involvement of the arbitrator in settlement efforts has generally garnered greater acceptance among practitioners and scholars. This growing recognition has also been reflected in recent arbitral rules and guidelines. However, due to the various concerns discussed in Chapters 4 and 5, caucusing remains one of the most controversial practices. In many jurisdictions, particularly in the West, it is not commonly employed within arbitral proceedings. Nonetheless, empirical data indicates that in recent years, caucusing has faced fewer objections in various jurisdictions and within ICA, particularly when arbitral rules or agreements explicitly address the concerns associated with its implementation.

The second group of direct initiatives relates to hybrid processes in which the arbitrator maintains a dual role as an arbitrator and a mediator in the same dispute. The prevailing approach among scholars and practitioners emphasizes that hybrid processes—whether they include caucusing or involve one or more mediation attempts by the arbitrator—should be categorized based on the sequence in which the arbitration and mediation stages are conducted. This categorization minimizes confusion between the different variants of the hybrid process and addresses specific issues associated with their implementation. Accordingly, this book adopts terminology that reflects the literal order in which mediation and arbitration occur during the hybrid process. Hence, Med-Arb refers to processes in which the arbitrator tries first to mediate the dispute, and only if mediation is unable to resolve all disputed issues, arbitration is commenced, whether in its full format or other limited variations, such as MEDALOA or mediation followed by High-Low Arbitration. In contrast, Arb-Med refers, in its literal sense, to procedures where the arbitrator initiates the arbitral proceedings first. Therefore, only after the hearings are concluded, and according to the primary variation, the arbitral award is written but not disclosed, the arbitrator attempts to mediate the dispute. If mediation proves successful, the arbitrator converts the agreed terms into a new consent award; otherwise, the concealed award is delivered as the final and binding decision of the arbitration. However, most scholars and practitioners hold that Arb-Med, in its literal form, is less likely to occur in practice, as, following the mediation part, arbitration should resume, whether to conclude the mediated agreement in a consent award or to allow the arbitrator to render a binding decision based on the arbitral proceedings. Therefore, Arb-Med is commonly viewed as a sub-category of Arb-Med-Arb, which relates to processes where, after arbitration is commenced, the arbitrator attempts to mediate the dispute at an agreed-upon time. If mediation proves successful, the renewal of arbitration solely serves to record a consent award based on the parties' agreement; otherwise, it recommences to address the unresolved issues to be decided in the final award. Whether initiated with arbitration or mediation, hybrid processes have interesting variants that allow the parties to opt out of the process after completing the first stage. Hence, the parties can change their minds during the ongoing proceedings about the possibility that the arbitrator fulfills a dual role in the same dispute.

Having presented the range of initiatives that enable the arbitrator to facilitate a settlement in a dispute before them, the next part of the book discusses the advantages and drawbacks of the arbitrator's dual role.

Part II Settlement Facilitation by the Arbitrator in ICA: Advantages and Concerns

CHAPTER 3

Advantages of Facilitating a Settlement by the Arbitrator in ICA

3.1 INTRODUCTION

The opinions regarding the arbitrator's role as a settlement facilitator often relate to its advantages and drawbacks from different perspectives: the arbitration process, the ADR process, the interests and rights of the disputants, and general considerations such as public policy and legal culture diversity.[1] Identifying and discussing those advantages and drawbacks are important both for shaping the role of the arbitrator as well as for examining whether harmonized standards are likely in its regard:

> What are the advantages and drawbacks of the judge or arbitrator promoting settlement? The pros and cons are important because they ideally should shape the type of activity in which the arbitrator may engage in support of settlement. ... Having determined where we stand by setting out the current law and practice, and the advantages and drawbacks, the next step is to examine where we are going from here and whether we are moving towards a transnational rule.[2]

Supporters of the arbitrator's role in settlement facilitation usually relate to the contractual foundation of the arbitral process and the parties' autonomy to design the proceedings according to their preferences and needs.[3] As part of this attitude, the arbitrator's mandate is not limited to *deciding* the dispute as customary in adjudicative proceedings but rather viewed in broader terms as aimed at *resolving* the dispute, which leaves the promotion of settlement as an integral and legitimate component of

1. Stipanowich, 2021a, pp. 284, 287; Berger, 2018b, pp. 501-502; Nigmatullina, 2018, pp. 29-30; Kun, 2011b, p. 537; Berger, 2009, p. 217; Kaufmann-Kohler, 2009, p. 197; Blankenship, 2006, p. 33; Stipanowich & Kaskell, 2001, pp. 20-22.
2. Kaufmann-Kohler, 2009, pp. 197, 203-205.
3. Stipanowich, 2021a, p. 280; Nigmatullina, 2018, p. 142; Berger & Jensen, 2017, pp. 901, 904; Karton, 2013, pp. 106-107; Dezalay & Garth, 1996, p. 40.

the arbitrator's mandate.[4] While debating the role of the arbitrator, the literature usually highlights the following advantages it may bring to the dispute-resolution process: flexibility, efficiency, an enhanced commitment of the parties to the process and increased incentive to settle, improved quality and a wider variety of solutions, as well as the finality and international enforceability of the amicable outcome under the New York Convention.[5] Advocates of this role of the arbitrator argue that these advantages improve the administration of justice[6] since their combination cannot be found in any standalone arbitration, mediation, or other ADR mechanism.[7] This chapter discusses the abovementioned advantages of the arbitrator's role as a settlement facilitator. Moreover, it examines whether these advantages apply to every arbitrator's initiative on the continuum of settlement facilitation or whether they may not always exist.

3.2 FLEXIBILITY OF THE PROCESS

Compared to pure arbitration, a process endorsing the arbitrator's role as a settlement facilitator grants parties and arbitrators greater procedural flexibility and improved control over the process.[8] Instead of being bound to full adversarial proceedings, as offered in standalone arbitration or non-binding ADR processes, the parties can shape a more flexible and adaptable process that employs elements from both dispute-resolution mechanisms to meet their needs and interests.[9] According to some commentators, this procedural richness, which arguably cannot be found in independent arbitration or any other ADR process, is responsible for the combined advantages connected with the arbitrator's role as a settlement facilitator, including the quality and variety of the solutions, as well as the increased chances to settle the dispute amicably.[10] These magnified chances to settle are partially attributed to the timing flexibility of the process, which grants the experienced arbitrator the ability to select the right—and sometimes the crucial—moment to initiate the settlement efforts:

4. Berger, 2018b, p. 504; Berger & Jensen, 2017, pp. 889, 904; Kun, 2011b, p. 537; Kaufmann-Kohler, 2009, pp. 188-189; Raeschke-Kessler, 2005, p. 530; Sanders, 1996, p. 173.
5. Ortolani, 2025, §21.2; Yip, 2021, p. 192; Stipanowich, 2021a, pp. 284-287; Chua, 2018, p. 6; Nigmatullina, 2018, p. 32; Ludington, 2017, p. 315; Blankley, 2011, p. 326; Kun, 2011b, p. 537; Kaufmann-Kohler, 2009, p. 197; Blankenship, 2006, pp. 33-35; Stipanowich & Kaskell, 2001, pp. 20-21.
6. Kun, 2011b, p. 537; Kaufmann-Kohler, 2009, p. 188; Marriott, 2005, p. 533.
7. Nigmatullina, 2018, p. 32; Leon & Peterson, 2009, p. 92; McLaren & Sanderson, 1994, at 6-1; Bartel, 1991, p. 665; Phillips, G. F., 2009, p. 77; Wolski, 2013, p. 258.
8. Benzidi, 2017, p. 7; Ludington, 2017, p. 315; Chua, 2018, p. 8; Nigmatullina, 2018, pp. 43-44; Berger & Jensen, 2017, p. 904; Stipanowich, 2021a, p. 340; Ross, 2013, p. 357; Weisman, 2013, p. 41; Blankley, 2011, pp. 328, 337; Abramson, 1999, p. 3; Kaufmann-Kohler, 2009, p. 197; Blankenship, 2006, pp. 33-34; Schneider, 1998, p. 77; Phillips, G. F., 2009, p. 76; Pappas, 2015, p. 159; Condliffe & Zeleznikow, 2014, p. 333.
9. Berger & Jensen, 2017, p. 904; Berger, 2018b, p. 516; Karton, 2013, pp. 106-107; Blankenship, 2006, pp. 39-40; Blankley, 2011, pp. 329, 337.
10. Nigmatullina, 2018, p. 44; Blankley, 2011, pp. 325, 329; Blankenship, 2006, p. 33; Schneider, 1998, p. 77.

> The arbitrator is the master of the timing of the proceedings, and is in the best position to choose the appropriate moment to offer the tribunal's services for settlement purposes. This may often be after the exchange of written briefs and before the hearing. It may also be after a partial award. It should not be too early in the proceedings, when the arbitrators (and sometimes the parties as well) do not have a sufficient understanding of the issues. It should not be too late either; it should not be at a time when the parties have already spent too much on the arbitration and may no longer be willing to settle. Identifying the right moment is a question of judgment, and experienced arbitrators will generally know when the time is ripe.[11]

Additionally, a flexible process, which by definition allows the arbitrator to facilitate a settlement, may help the parties overcome a significant barrier to settlement: the hesitation to suggest negotiations or make the first move toward a settlement to avoid showing weakness or damaging the initial negotiation position.[12] Empirical data supports the impact of this concern on the chances of amicably settling the dispute. In the 2007 Ali Survey,[13] over 60% of the respondents from Eastern and Western countries considered the "parties hesitating to make the first move toward settlement" as a "highly relevant" or "significant" barrier to achieving an amicable outcome of the dispute.[14] Therefore, the arbitrator appears as the right delegate to bring up the settlement option and carry it out.[15] Nevertheless, the intensity of the arbitrator's intervention in the settlement efforts largely depends on the flexibility of the process. In general terms, while less flexible or full adversarial processes only enable minimal or indirect involvement in the settlement negotiations, flexible processes—particularly the hybrid ones—allow more intensive participation of the arbitrator in the settlement efforts, including by fulfilling a dual role as an arbitrator and a mediator in the same dispute.[16] As discussed in Chapter 2, Arb-Med-Arb seems to be the most flexible of all hybrid processes, as it usually allows the arbitrator to engage with mediation at various points in time throughout the arbitral process, and subject to the parties' consent, even several times.[17]

3.3 EFFICIENCY: SAVING TIME AND COSTS

Given the increased costs and delays in ICA,[18] empowering the arbitrator to act as a settlement facilitator may improve the efficiency of the arbitral process.[19] *First*, the

11. Kaufmann-Kohler, 2009, p. 197. *See also* Berger, 2018b, pp. 515-516; Nigmatullina, 2018, p. 44; Berger & Jensen, 2017, p. 899; Ehle, 2010, pp. 85-86; Phillips, G. F., 2009, p. 76; Kun, 2011b, p. 537.
12. Sussman & Berger, 2021b, p. 17; Faleck, 2021, p. 52; Sussman, 2020, pp. 20-21; Sussman & Berger, 2021a, p. 25; Berger & Jensen, 2017, p. 899; Greenwood, 2011a, p. 209.
13. *See* the discussion in section 2.3.3.
14. Ali, 2010, pp. 266-267; Sussman & Berger, 2021b, p. 17; Sussman, 2020, p. 21.
15. Berger & Jensen, 2017, p. 899.
16. Chua, 2018, p. 5; Nigmatullina, 2018, p. 43; Blankley, 2011, p. 337; Blankenship, 2006, p. 34; Schneider, 1998, p. 77.
17. Stipanowich, 2021a, p. 277; Chua, 2018, p. 5; Nigmatullina, 2018, p. 44.
18. Ruckteschler & Wendelstein, 2021, p. 761; Chua, 2018, p. 8; Nigmatullina, 2018, p. 3; Pappas, 2015, p. 159; Mayer, 2016, p. 4; Greenwood, 2011a, pp. 199-200.
19. Stipanowich, 2021a, pp. 284-285; Ruckteschler & Wendelstein, 2021, p. 762; Chua, 2018, p. 8; Ludington, 2017, p. 315; Berger & Jensen, 2017, p. 900; Benzidi, 2017, p. 7; Harris, 2016, p. 94;

arbitrator, who has already been educated with the commercial background of the dispute, the important facts and legal issues, and possibly the parties' interests and needs, can assist the disputants in solving their differences at an earlier stage of the proceedings while saving costs and time.[20] This outcome is particularly important in international arbitration, where participants in the arbitral process, including arbitrators, parties, counsel, and witnesses, usually arrive from different countries, which makes the scheduling of the proceedings more difficult and the general expenses higher.[21] These benefits of saving time and costs may not be achieved when resorting to a third-party neutral to promote a settlement, as the disputants need to invest additional time and expenses to educate that neutral with the abovementioned knowledge,[22] let alone the process of their selection, that may by itself be expensive and time-consuming.[23] *Second*, if the arbitrator's efforts are successful, the amicable outcome can be converted immediately into an arbitral award on agreed terms, without the need to initiate other proceedings as required when parties to a non-binding ADR process are willing to anchor their agreement within an arbitral award.[24] *Third*, even when the settlement efforts fail to comprehensively resolve the dispute, they will most likely help narrow factual and legal controversies, including the possibility of anchoring agreed issues in a partial consent award.[25] As a result, the remaining part of the arbitration may include fewer issues to decide on, while leaving the hearing and arguments parts shorter, the binding award more concise, and the whole process less costly and lengthy.[26] Given these advantages, efficiency has repeatedly been cited as the main advantage of the arbitrator's role as a settlement facilitator.[27]

Nevertheless, the benefit of efficiency mainly depends on the stage at which the arbitrator attempts the settlement efforts, leaving late-stage efforts with a reduced contribution to the cost-effectiveness of the whole process.[28] This consideration is especially true concerning hybrid processes involving arbitration and mediation. Of all these processes, Med-Arb, on its various variants, but predominantly those which limit

---

Pappas, 2015, p. 159; Ross, 2013, p. 357; Weisman, 2013, pp. 40-41; Kun, 2011b, p. 537; Blankley, 2011, p. 326; Kaufmann-Kohler, 2009, p. 197; Blankenship, 2006, p. 34; Abramson, 1999, p. 3.

20. Ortolani, 2025, §21.2; Stipanowich, 2021a, p. 284; Berger, 2018b, p. 505; Berger & Jensen, 2017, p. 899; Harris, 2016, p. 94; Kun, 2011b, p. 537; Kaufmann-Kohler, 2009, p. 197.
21. Abramson, 1999, p. 3.
22. Stipanowich, 2021a, p. 284; Benzidi, 2017, p. 18; Kaufmann-Kohler, 2009, p. 197; Berger & Jensen, 2017, p. 899; Abramson, 1999, p. 3; Kun & Kaufmann-Kohler, 2008, p. 490; Blankenship, 2006, p. 34; De Vera, 2004, p. 149; Stipanowich & Kaskell, 2001, p. 20.
23. Nigmatullina, 2018, p. 33; Phillips, G. F., 2009, p. 76.
24. Chua, 2018, p. 8; Nigmatullina, 2018, p. 33; Blankenship, 2006, p. 34.
25. Stipanowich, 2021a, p. 286; Dendorfer & Lack, 2007, p. 84; Benzidi, 2017, p. 9; CIArb Practice Guideline on the Use of Mediation in Arbitration, 2021, Article 10(1).
26. Benzidi, 2017, pp. 7-9; Ludington, 2017, p. 315; Nigmatullina, 2018, p. 33; Kun, 2011b, p. 537; Phillips, G. F., 2009, p. 76; Kun & Kaufmann-Kohler, 2008, pp. 490-491; Dendorfer & Lack, 2007, p. 84; Blankenship, 2006, p. 34; Brewer & Mills, 1999, p. 35.
27. Gu, 2019, p. 127; Nigmatullina, 2018, p. 32; Sussman, 2009a, p. 73; Blankenship, 2006, p. 34; Houzhi, 2005, p. 555; Sawada, 2003, p. 33; Leon & Peterson, 2009, 92. Empirical data supports the primacy of the efficiency consideration. In the 2016-2017 GPC Survey, efficiency was selected as the parties' key factor when considering a dispute resolution process. *See* GPC Series, 2016-2017, Question 1(2); GPC Series, 2018, pp. 3, 10.
28. Chua, 2018, pp. 9-10.

the arbitration stage, such as MEDALOA or mediation followed by High-Low Arbitration, can potentially offer a greater degree of efficiency since the arbitration stage is expected to be shorter and focus on converting the mediated dispute into a consent award or handling the remaining issues in dispute.[29] On the other hand, in its literal form, Arb-Med seems to suggest the least efficient hybrid process since a full-fledged arbitration would have been completed before mediation commenced.[30] The efficiency of the Arb-Med-Arb process is more challenging to assess because parties usually invest time and costs in the initial arbitration regardless of the success of the following mediation phase. However, when mediation is attempted early in the process, costs and time may be reduced.[31]

3.4 PARTIES' APPROACH AND INCENTIVE TO SETTLE

The arbitrator's role as a settlement facilitator can enhance the parties' approaches to the settlement process and increase their incentive to settle[32] for three main reasons related to the arbitrator's authority to decide the dispute. *First*, knowing that the process is moving toward a final and binding decision will arguably encourage the parties to approach the settlement process in honesty, good faith, and with reasonable demands. Otherwise, the settlement efforts may fail, and the arbitral process may resume with limited control from their side over its duration and outcome.[33] The fear of losing control, exacerbated due to very limited grounds to review an arbitral award by the courts,[34] may motivate the parties to moderate their tactics and aspirations, engage in problem solving, and develop creative ideas to settle the differences amicably.[35] *Second*, detached from the parties' fear of losing control over the process, the authority of the settlement facilitator to decide the dispute may alone put additional pressure to settle due to the imminence of the approaching award to be imposed by the arbitrator.[36] Although legitimate fears exist that this "muscle" of the arbitrator may be

29. Nigmatullina, 2018, p. 35; Chua, 2018, pp. 9-10; Ross, 2013, p. 360; Dendorfer & Lack, 2007, p. 85.
30. Chua, 2018, p. 9; Deason, 2013, p. 222; Ross, 2013, p. 359; Blankenship, 2006, p. 31. This assertion is supported by an empirical study conducted among students that engaged in simulated Arb-Med (with sealed awards) and Med-Arb, both conducted by the same neutral (2002 Conlon Study). The results show that, compared to Med-Arb, Arb-Med was more time-consuming and less successful in reducing the pre-disputed issues. *See* Conlon et al., 2002, p. 983.
31. Nigmatullina, 2018, p. 35; Chua, 2018, pp. 9-10.
32. Stipanowich, 2021a, pp. 286-287; Nigmatullina, 2018, pp. 44-47; Benzidi, 2017, p. 8; Weisman, 2013, p. 40; Blankenship, 2006, p. 34; Phillips, G. F., 2009, p. 77; Sawada, 2003, p. 33; Bartel, 1991, pp. 681-683; Weisman, 2011, p. 4.
33. Ortolani, 2025, §21.2; Nigmatullina, 2018, p. 46; Benzidi, 2017, p. 8; Pappas, 2015, p. 159; Blankenship, 2006, p. 34; Phillips, G. F., 2009, p. 76; Kagel, 1973, p. 62. *See also* Bartel, 1991, p. 683, holding that even "the stronger party will be induced to be reasonable and fair by the realization that the neutral facilitating the process ultimately will decide the issue."
34. Nigmatullina, 2018, p. 46; Bantekas, 2015, p. 52; Jemielniak, 2014, p. 319; Goode et al., 2007, pp. 663-665; Pate, 2010, p. 162; New York Convention, 1958, Article III.
35. Stipanowich, 2021a, p. 287; Weisman, 2013, p. 40; Bartel, 1991, p. 682; Pruitt et al., 1989, p. 374.
36. Stipanowich, 2021a, p. 286; Nigmatullina, 2018, p. 45; Blankenship, 2006, p. 34; Phillips, G. F., 2009, p. 77.

used to coerce the parties to settle,[37] when used decently, it can also constitute "a healthy incentive to reasonableness."[38] Nevertheless, when the arbitrator functions as a settlement facilitator, the pressure on the disputants to reach an amicable outcome seems higher.[39] *Third*, the incentive of the parties to settle can equally be influenced by their trust in the arbitrator and respect for their professionalism throughout the arbitral proceedings that anticipated the settlement stage:

> In addition to being a convenient choice, the sitting arbitrator may also have extensive familiarity with the issues and the evidence. Having had an opportunity to observe the arbitrator manage arbitration proceedings, including supervising aspects of the pre-hearing process and hearings, the parties may have developed a level of rapport with and trust in that person. This may permit them to feel comfortable with that person playing a more direct role in negotiations, including perhaps their offering of preliminary views or serving as a facilitator/mediator going forward.[40]

Since the abovementioned aspects related to the arbitrator's authority do not exist in standalone mediation or any other independent non-binding ADR mechanism,[41] it would be reasonable to expect that when the arbitrator is authorized to act as a settlement facilitator, the parties are more encouraged to settle than in a standalone ADR process or when a different neutral is involved in the settlement efforts during the arbitration.[42] This determination was confirmed in a field experiment aimed at comparing the parties' approach to settlement during three mediation types: standalone mediation, mediation conducted during arbitral proceedings by the same neutral, and mediation conducted during arbitration by a different neutral (1987 McGillicuddy Field Experiment).[43] According to the experiment's results, when the arbitrator mediated the dispute, the parties were more conciliatory, less hostile, more involved in the settlement efforts, more motivated to settle, and more creative than they were in standalone mediation or when a different neutral was involved in the mediation phase.[44] The experimenters explained this behavior of the disputants due to the fear of losing control if arbitration resumed following failed mediation, and the respect granted to the neutral, given their authority to decide the dispute.[45] Not less interesting, when different neutrals conducted the mediation during the arbitral proceedings, they were less involved in the settlement process than mediators in standalone mediation or arbitrators who conducted the mediation. In addition, these different neutrals made

37. *See* the discussion in section 4.2.2. *See also* Kun, 2011b, p. 552; Nigmatullina, 2018, p. 52; Kaufmann-Kohler, 2009, p. 200; Blankenship, 2006, p. 34.
38. Kaufmann-Kohler, 2009, p. 200. *See also* Pappas, 2015, p. 159.
39. Nigmatullina, 2018, p. 44; Blankenship, 2006, p. 34; Phillips, G. F., 2009, p. 77.
40. Stipanowich, 2021a, p. 286. *See also* Benzidi, 2017, p. 9; Brewer & Mills, 1999, p. 35.
41. Blankenship, 2006, p. 34; Henry, 1988, p. 390.
42. Nigmatullina, 2018, pp. 44-45; Kun, 2011b, p. 537; Blankenship, 2006, p. 34; Phillips, G. F., 2009, p. 77.
43. McGillicuddy et al., 1987. Also discussed in Blankenship, 2006, p. 34; Nigmatullina, 2018, pp. 45-46.
44. McGillicuddy et al., 1987, pp. 104, 110; Stipanowich, 2021a, p. 287; Nigmatullina, 2018, p. 45; Blankenship, 2006, p. 34.
45. McGillicuddy et al., 1987, p. 110; Nigmatullina, 2018, p. 45.

less effort to reach an amicable outcome and even ended the mediation earlier.[46] Three possible explanations were suggested by the experimenters for the attitudes of the different neutrals: lower commitment to and responsibility for the case because other neutrals could be relied on to take it over, a lack of motivation knowing they were low-power neutrals compared to the high-power arbitrators, and the possibility that the disputants would see these neutrals as weak figures compared to the arbitrators waiting in the wings.[47]

Hence, as long as the arbitrator takes the settlement efforts before deciding the case, the parties should have one incentive or another to settle the dispute amicably. When considering hybrid processes involving arbitration and mediation, Med-Arb and Arb-Med-Arb provide the incentive to settle, as the subsequent and binding arbitration process puts psychological pressure on them and constitutes "the motor that makes mediation run" by enhancing the chances to produce a settlement.[48] Although this pressure can be moderated when the parties choose to employ variants that enable them to opt out of these processes following failed mediation,[49] the parties' incentives to settle may nevertheless be influenced by their desire to keep control over the process, which may not always be achieved by opting out from the hybrid process to initiate other proceedings in front of a new neutral. Empirical data supports the importance of this consideration for users of hybrid processes. In an experimental study conducted in 2010 among 252 potential users of hybrid processes, the participants engaged in structured simulations and were asked to express their preferences for different processes involving mediation and arbitration (2010 Condliffe and Zeleznikow Study).[50] The findings demonstrated that Med-Arb conducted by the same neutral was by far the most preferred process by the participants, as it answered "their need for control" over the process, which was ranked even above considerations connected with fairness and justice.[51] Although the study did not relate to Arb-Med-Arb, in terms of control over the process when mediation is launched at an early stage of the Arb-Med-Arb process, Med-Arb and Arb-Med-Arb can be assumed to employ similar considerations.[52] Another process that was not inspected by that study was Arb-Med, conducted by the same neutral. Arguably, in this process, the parties would have less incentive to settle during mediation, with the arbitral phase fully conducted. Nonetheless, a distinction should be made between a situation in which the award is delivered to the disputants at the end of the arbitration phase and a situation where it is kept sealed until the end of the consecutive mediation stage. In the latter setting, the parties may have a strong incentive to settle as the sealed award creates psychological

46. McGillicuddy et al., 1987, p. 111; Nigmatullina, 2018, pp. 45-46; Blankenship, 2006, p. 34.
47. McGillicuddy et al., 1987, p. 111; Nigmatullina, 2018, p. 46.
48. Dendorfer & Lack, 2007, p. 85. *See also* Javits, 2017, p. 171; Telford, 2000, p. 3.
49. Blankenship, 2006, p. 31.
50. Condliffe & Zeleznikow, 2014, pp. 313-314.
51. Condliffe & Zeleznikow, 2014, pp. 305, 317.
52. Chua, 2018, p. 12.

pressure that may encourage them to work together to achieve an amicable arrangement.[53] Some scholars hold that even when the award is published following the arbitration stage of the Arb-Med process, parties still have an incentive to settle during mediation, as they may feel more open, candid, and willing to exchange information that cannot impact the award anymore, which increases the chances of an amicable outcome.[54]

3.5 QUALITY AND VARIETY OF THE SOLUTIONS

The arbitrator's role as a settlement facilitator may also help achieve better and more diverse solutions that cannot arguably be obtained in a standalone arbitration or a separate ADR process.[55] Several reasons underline this logic. *First*, when the arbitrator is responsible for promoting a settlement between the parties, they are incentivized to formulate a decent and just solution to the dispute. Otherwise, the parties may dismiss their suggestions and ask to end the dispute with an arbitral award. This incentive does not necessarily apply to neutrals in standalone ADR processes, as in many cases, they are only responsible for walking the parties through their negotiations with less responsibility for ending the conflict or for the appropriateness or fairness of the settlement terms.[56] Alternatively, arbitrators in standalone arbitration are usually restricted to legal and formal standards that do not necessarily overlap with considerations of fairness, justice, and the parties' real interests.[57] *Second*, while facilitating a settlement, the arbitrator can encourage the parties to focus on their interests and needs rather than their legal rights.[58] Under the guidance of the arbitrator, this dialogue paves the way for "out of the box"[59] solutions that prioritize their business interests and the preservation of the relationship over limited outcomes that only relate to the pathological dispute.[60] These solutions, which may include the redrafting of the disputed clauses to avoid future controversies and, in some cases, the rewriting of the

53. Chua, 2018, p. 9; Dendorfer & Lack, 2007, pp. 87-88. This position is supported by the above-discussed 2002 Conlon Study conducted among students that engaged in simulated Arb-Med (with sealed awards) and Med-Arb, both conducted by the same neutral. The results demonstrated that Arb-Med produced a significantly greater number of settlements in the mediation phase than did Med-Arb. In addition, Arb-Med achieved settlements of higher joint benefit than Med-Arb. *See* Conlon et al., 2002, pp. 982-983.
54. Blankenship, 2006, p. 31; Chua, 2018, p. 13.
55. Chaisse & Shang, 2021, p. 97; Stipanowich, 2021a, p. 285; Nigmatullina, 2018, p. 42; Rivkin, 2008, p. 382; De Vera, 2004, pp. 156-157; Elliott, 1995, p. 171.
56. Gu, 2019, p. 133; Nigmatullina, 2018, p. 42; Bartel, 1991, p. 682; Stulberg, 1998, p. 911; Stulberg, 1989, p. 42.
57. Nigmatullina, 2018, p. 42; Phillips, G. F., 2009, p. 76; Rivkin, 2008, p. 382.
58. Berger & Jensen, 2017, pp. 901, 904; Mayer, 2016, p. 4; Raeschke-Kessler, 2005, 534; Berger, 2003, pp. 400, 403; Stipanowich & Kaskell, 2001, p. 16; Koch & Schäfer, 1999, p. 180; Schneider, 1998, p. 61; Dezalay & Garth, 1996, p. 40; Elliott, 1995, pp. 164-171.
59. Sussman & Berger, 2021b, pp. 32-33.
60. Ortolani, 2025, §21.2; Stipanowich, 2021a, p. 285; Chua, 2018, p. 11; Rivkin, 2008, p. 382; Schneider, 1998, p. 61; Koch & Schäfer, 1999, p. 180; Berger, 2003, pp. 400, 403; Plant, 2000, p. 145.

business arrangement or the initiation of a new one,[61] are not always possible through standalone arbitration, as they may exceed the arbitrator's adjudicative mandate.[62] Although these solutions can potentially be obtained through a standalone ADR process, as demonstrated in the next section, they may lack the enforcement mechanism of the New York Convention, which grants an extra layer of security for negotiated or facilitated settlements through arbitral proceedings. Empirical data clearly reflects the significance of business relationship preservation to users of cross-border dispute-resolution mechanisms. In the 2016-2017 GPC Survey,[63] when asked "what outcomes do parties most often want before starting a process in commercial civil dispute resolution?," respondents who identified as users/parties ranked the preservation of the business relationship as the third most important outcome, immediately after financial and action-focused results.[64] Additionally, in the 2014 Nigmatullina Study,[65] preserving the business relationship was ranked as the main benefit of combining mediation with arbitration, slightly above the faster resolution of the dispute and lower costs.[66] However, other empirical data reveals that, in terms of maintaining business relationships, Med-Arb and Arb-Med-Arb—where mediation occurs early in the process—are clearly more effective than Arb-Med. In these scenarios, parties encounter fewer opportunities for their relationship to deteriorate compared to the aftermath of a full-blown arbitration, as is typical in Arb-Med.[67] *Third*, even when the settlement discussions fail to bring a comprehensive resolution of the substantive dispute, the fact that they enable the arbitrator to gain a better understanding of the parties' business backgrounds and needs, as well as narrow the differences and generate partial agreements on factual and legal issues, can make the binding award more predictable, informed, and acceptable, which contributes to its quality.[68]

3.6 FINALITY AND ENFORCEABILITY

Other main advantages of the arbitrator's role as a settlement facilitator are the dispute's finality and its outcome's international enforceability under the New York Convention.[69] By engaging in a process that empowers the arbitrator to facilitate a

61. Blankenship, 2006, p. 33; Nigmatullina, 2018, pp. 42-43; Raeschke-Kessler, 2005, 534. *See* in this regard the discussion in section 3.6.3 below about the arbitrator's authority to include in the facilitated settlement solutions that are not connected to issues in dispute and the possibility of enforcing these kinds of settlements under the New York Convention.
62. Nigmatullina, 2018, p. 42; Phillips, G. F., 2009, p. 76.
63. *See* the discussion in section 1.3.
64. GPC Series, 2016-2017, Question 1(1). *See also* Chua, 2018, p. 11.
65. *See* the discussion in section 2.4.
66. Nigmatullina, 2018, pp. 111-112.
67. Chua, 2018, p. 12, relating to three different empirical studies that have reached this conclusion. *See also* Blankenship, 2006, p. 33.
68. Stipanowich, 2021a, p. 286; Nigmatullina, 2018, p. 42; Kun & Kaufmann-Kohler, 2008, pp. 490-491; Kun, 2011b, p. 537; Dendorfer & Lack, 2007, p. 85; Blankenship, 2006, p. 34.
69. Stipanowich, 2021a, pp. 286-287; Chua, 2018, p. 6; Nigmatullina, 2018, p. 35; Kaufmann-Kohler, 2009, p. 197; Kun & Kaufmann-Kohler, 2008, pp. 490-491; Ross, 2013, p. 362; Kun, 2011b, p. 537; Blankenship, 2006, pp. 34-35.

settlement, the parties know that their dispute will be resolved in one way or another —if not during the settlement stage, then by a binding and final award.[70] Standalone ADR mechanisms cannot offer this prospect of finality since their non-binding nature prevents the neutral from imposing a decision that ends the conflict.[71] Hence, some scholars view finality as the main justification for the arbitrator's dual role and as the source of its additional benefits:

> The attribute of finality is, indeed, hard to overstate. Knowing the dispute will be resolved brings tremendous tangible and intangible benefits to the parties and the process. This attribute provides advantages not only over mediation, but arbitration as well. ... Finality is the advantage that is largely responsible for the existence of many of the other advantages. The savings of time and money, and the manner in which the parties approach the process are due in large part to the finality.[72]

In addition to finality, facilitated settlements during arbitration can be incorporated into arbitral awards on agreed terms and enjoy worldwide enforceability under the New York Convention.[73] Many scholars and practitioners hold that this benefit of enhanced global enforceability, which arguably is unavailable to such an extent for mediated international settlement agreements or national judgments,[74] is the ultimate reason why parties to international commercial disputes resort to arbitration in general and arbitral processes that allow the arbitrator to act as a settlement facilitator in particular.[75] This clear advantage of worldwide enforcement under the New York Convention is demonstrated below while examining two main alternative instruments for enforcing negotiated settlement agreements in foreign jurisdictions: court judgments and international settlement agreements resulting from mediation.

3.6.1 Court Judgments

One alternative is to formalize the negotiated settlement as a judgment of a national court[76] or an international commercial court seated in a specific jurisdiction.[77] This judgment can then be enforced in other jurisdictions as a foreign decision pursuant to bilateral or multilateral agreements,[78] or under regional treaties such as the EU

70. Stipanowich, 2021a, p. 286; Benzidi, 2017, p. 7; Nigmatullina, 2018, p. 35; Blankley, 2011, p. 331; Blankenship, 2006, pp. 34-35.
71. Nigmatullina, 2018, p. 35; Benzidi, 2017, p. 7; Harris, 2016, pp. 94-95; Ross, 2013, p. 362; Bartel, 1991, p. 665. *See also* Model Law on ICM, 2018, Article 1(3), stating explicitly that "the mediator does not have the authority to impose upon the parties a solution to the dispute."
72. Blankenship, 2006, pp. 33-34. *See also* Nigmatullina, 2018, p. 35; Rewald & Jachimek, 2014, pp. 1-2.
73. *See* the discussion in section 3.6.3 below, which demonstrates that consent awards are enforceable under the New York Convention like any other award.
74. Chua, 2018, pp. 6-7; Nigmatullina, 2018, pp. 36-39; Sussman, 2010a, p. 393.
75. Nigmatullina, 2018, p. 39; Chua, 2018, p. 7; Ross, 2013, p. 362; Wolski, 2013, p. 249; Almoguera, 2010, p. 130.
76. Chua, 2018, pp. 6-7; Sussman, 2010a, p. 393; Nigmatullina, 2018, p. 39.
77. Such as the Dubai International Financial Centre Courts, the London Commercial Court, and the Singapore International Commercial Court. For a general discussion about the evolving trend of international commercial courts, *see* Hwang, 2015; Guo, 2020, pp. 226-227.
78. Nigmatullina, 2018, p. 39; Sussman, 2010a, p. 393.

Regulation on the Recognition and Enforcement of Judgments in Civil and Commercial Matters. This regulation ensures that any judgment rendered in a Member State is enforceable in other Member States without the need for a declaration of enforceability, provided that it is enforceable in the issuing state.[79] However, this option does not seem as appealing to international parties. First, regardless of the enforcement consideration, resorting to national courts, even to enter a settlement agreement into a judgment, is usually subject to jurisdiction over the dispute, which may undermine the parties' interest in conducting the process in a neutral forum while applying different substantive law and tailor-made procedures:

> Companies choose international arbitration over pursuing judgment in domestic courts for a variety of reasons such as the elimination of perceived bias by domestic courts. However, a primary and perhaps underappreciated advantage is the flexibility offered by international arbitration. Parties can choose the applicable law, the seat of arbitration, the arbitration institution, the arbitrators, the jurisdictional scope, and the general procedure and conduct of the arbitration, all of which can provide efficiency advantages over domestic courts as well as important legal and tactical advantages customized to the subject matter of the dispute.[80]

Additionally, the possibility to enter a negotiated settlement as a foreign judgment without formal court proceedings is not available in every jurisdiction,[81] let alone the inherent difficulties resulting from enforcement relating to international business matters.[82] Although an important step toward enhancing the international recognition and enforcement of civil judgments of national courts was made in 2019 with the introduction of the Hague Judgments Convention,[83] its progress has been limited. The convention is in force only in EU Member States, the UK, Ukraine, Uruguay, Albania, Andorra, and Montenegro. Beyond these jurisdictions, it has been signed by only six additional states, which have yet to ratify it.[84] Noting this limited response to joining the convention, scholars and practitioners have expressed concerns about its ability to

---

79. EU Regulation on Jurisdiction and the Recognition and Enforcement of Judgments in Civil and Commercial Matters, 2012, Article 39.
80. Nobles, 2012, p. 79. *See also* Berger & Jensen, 2016, pp. 4-5; Kun, 2013b, p. 185; Guo, 2020, p. 227, holding that these considerations are also relevant when deciding whether to resort to international commercial courts, as these courts continue to struggle with ensuring "an appellate process, strong powers of joinder and consolidation, a reduced possibility of bias (since judges are not appointed by the parties), the support of the court's administrative apparatus and the publication of judgements."
81. For instance, this option is provided under Article 6 of the EU Mediation Directive, 2008, which stipulates that, with the consent of all parties to a mediation, EU Member States shall allow the conversion of a written settlement agreement into a judgment or court decision and enforce it accordingly. *See also* Chua, 2018, pp. 6-7, relating to several jurisdictions that allow mediated settlement agreements to be entered as judgments.
82. Sussman, 2010a, p. 393; Nigmatullina, 2018, p. 39; Smit, 1986, p. 10; Chua, 2018, p. 7, arguing that relying on this kind of enforcement avenues "may be effective in a domestic context but may be more challenging on an international plane."
83. Hague Judgments Convention, 2019, Article 4(1), stipulating that "a judgment given by a court of a Contracting State (State of origin) shall be recognised and enforced in another Contracting State (requested State) in accordance with the provisions of this Chapter. Recognition or enforcement may be refused only on the grounds specified in this Convention." *See also* Sussman & Berger, 2021b, p. 12; Guo, 2020, p. 225; Sachs & Weiler, 2020, pp. 764-765.
84. *Status: Hague Judgments Convention*, n.d.

significantly transform the enforcement landscape for private international commercial disputes.[85] Furthermore, unlike the New York Convention, which does not permit its Member States to make reservations regarding awards originating from other Member States, the Hague Judgments Convention is based on a bilateral concept that allows a Member State to notify the depositary that the convention shall not apply to another Member State.[86] According to some commentators, this opt-out approach contradicts the convention's initial objective of promoting a globally uniform mechanism for recognizing and enforcing civil national judgments while exacerbating the segmentation of international law.[87] Additionally, the Hague Convention explicitly states that its provisions shall not apply to arbitral proceedings, which effectively prevents the possibility of undermining the provisions of the New York Convention by resorting to the Hague Convention.[88]

3.6.2 International Settlement Agreements Resulting from Mediation

Another alternative is incorporating a negotiated settlement as an international settlement agreement resulting from mediation to enforce its outcome under the Singapore Convention.[89] Introduced in 2018 alongside its supplementary Model Law on ICM,[90] the convention, which entered into force in September 2020, states that all signed parties shall enforce international settlement agreements according to the mechanism anchored in the convention,[91] while defining an international settlement agreement as follows:

> An agreement resulting from mediation and concluded in writing by parties to resolve a commercial dispute, ... which, at the time of its conclusion, is international in that: (a) at least two parties to the settlement agreement have their places of business in different states; or (b) the state in which the parties to the settlement agreement have their places of business is different from either: (i) the state in which a substantial part of the obligations under the settlement agreement is performed; or (ii) the state with which the subject matter of the settlement agreement is most closely connected.[92]

The Model Law on ICM, which anchors the enforcement of international settlement agreements according to the convention's principles,[93] defines those agreements

85. Burgsdorff & Burkert, 2020; Guo, 2020, p. 227; Sachs & Weiler, 2020, p. 779, arguing that "whether the Judgments Convention will become a serious competitor to the New York Convention ... will depend significantly on how many members will accede to the convention which is not least a political question."
86. Hague Judgments Convention, 2019, Article 29; Sachs & Weiler, 2020, p. 768; Burgsdorff & Burkert, 2020.
87. Sachs & Weiler, 2020, p. 769; Burgsdorff & Burkert, 2020.
88. Hague Judgments Convention, 2019, Article 2(3); Sachs & Weiler, 2020, p. 778.
89. Singapore Convention, 2018. For a general discussion about the convention, *see* Hioureas, 2019.
90. Model Law on ICM, 2018.
91. Singapore Convention, 2018, Article 3.
92. Singapore Convention, 2018, Article 1.
93. Model Law on ICM, 2018, Articles 15 & 17.

in the same way as the convention.[94] However, interestingly, it also allows parties to "an agreement to mediate" to apply the Model Law provisions on their mediation process on an opt-in basis, even when the aforementioned conditions for defining mediation as "international" were not met.[95] Undeniably, the Singapore Convention and its supplementary Model Law can enhance the international enforceability of settlement agreements resulting from international mediation[96] while also increasing the attractiveness of this dispute-resolution mechanism as an effective alternative to international arbitration.[97] However, this result is not guaranteed for the following reasons. *First*, an examination of the convention's status reveals that although 61 states have signed, only 18 states have ratified its provisions in their domestic legal systems to become full members.[98] In addition, only one jurisdiction has based its legislation on the text of the Model Law on ICM.[99] Since securing enforcement under the convention requires its ratification by all jurisdictions where enforcement is sought,[100] the initial status of the convention leaves significant uncertainties regarding its effectiveness as an enforcement mechanism for international settlement agreements.[101] *Second*, unlike the New York Convention, the Singapore Convention does not permit a reciprocity reservation, under which a contracting state would commit to enforcing mediated settlement agreements only if they originate from other contracting states.[102] This broad obligation of Member States to enforce all international settlement agreements, regardless of the convention's applicability in the jurisdiction where the mediation was conducted or the settlement agreement was concluded, may create an incentive for states not to join the Singapore Convention, which will further weaken its effectivity:

> Given the lack of a reciprocity requirement, a state seeking an asymmetric advantage for its nationals could simply not join the Convention at all, because it could still obtain the benefits of the Singapore Convention, which admits enforcement of settlement agreements made in such non-contracting states, in other contracting states.[103]

94. Model Law on ICM, 2018, Articles 3(2) & 16.
95. Model Law on ICM, 2018, Article 3(4), stating that "this section also applies to commercial mediation when the parties agree that the mediation is international or agree to the applicability of this section."
96. Guo, 2020, pp. 229-230; Sussman & Berger, 2021b, p. 12; Schnabel, 2019, p. 60.
97. Ortolani, 2025, §21.6; Tezuka, 2020, p. 287; Schnabel, 2019, p. 60; Guo, 2020, p. 230.
98. *Status: Singapore Convention*, n.d.
99. *Status: Model Law on ICM*, n.d. That is the state of Georgia in the US.
100. Singapore Convention, 2018, Article 14.
101. *The Singapore Mediation Convention: An update on developments in enforcing mediated settlement agreements*, 2019; Schnabel, 2019, p. 60, stating that "whether the Convention will live up to this promise will depend on whether a critical mass of states choose to join the Convention."
102. Singapore Convention, 2018, Article 8(2); Tezuka, 2020, p. 286.
103. Tezuka, 2020, p. 286. Notably, even Member States can limit the applicability of the convention. According to Article 8(1)(b), a Member State can make a reservation that replaces the automatic applicability of the convention on all settlement agreements with an opt-in mechanism in which the convention will be applicable only for parties that have explicitly agreed to its application. *See* Schnabel, 2019, p. 58, stating that "hopefully, few states will make such a declaration, as doing so would significantly limit the application of the Convention."

For these reasons, in the context of worldwide enforcement, international mediation remains, at least for the time being, an inferior substitute to international arbitration. In this reality, it seems much safer to settle international commercial disputes within the framework of arbitral proceedings:

> It remains to be seen how popular this instrument will be going forward and whether the uncertainties can be satisfactorily resolved in the near future. Accordingly, it may still be prudent and sensible to combine mediation with arbitration in the dispute resolution clause, as opposed to relying on mediation alone, for some time to come. Relying on adversarial forms of dispute resolution alone (such as arbitration and litigation), on the other hand, ensures that an outcome would be reached in every case, but it does not facilitate the preservation of the parties' commercial relationship.[104]

This conclusion aligns with the findings of the aforementioned 2016-2017 GPC Survey, where a significant majority of respondents (i.e., parties involved in cross-border commercial contracts) expressed that the most effective commercial dispute-resolution process typically involved combined adjudicative and non-adjudicative methods (e.g., arbitration and mediation).[105] It is further supported by the results of the above-presented 2021 Queen Mary International Arbitration Survey, where among the 90% of respondents who specified arbitration as their prioritized method for resolving cross-border commercial disputes, 59% preferred combining it with other ADR methods.[106] Thus, an overwhelming majority of parties to international commercial relations prefer to settle disputes through arbitration. Moreover, for current ICA users, mediation does not seem to provide an independent alternative but mainly a supplementary mechanism to be combined with arbitration as part of the dispute resolution process.[107] In this reality, ICA users have few reasons to resort to the Singapore Convention to enforce settlements facilitated during processes that involve arbitration with mediation when they can guarantee safe and worldwide enforcement under the New York Convention.

Furthermore, the reluctance to resort to standalone mediation to settle cross-border commercial disputes does not entirely stem from the initial status of the Singapore Convention. According to some commentators, the growing complexity of these disputes and the increasing number of participants involved in the process challenge the ability of international mediation as the adequate dispute-resolution

104. Yip, 2021, p. 190. *See also* Ortolani, 2025, §21.6, holding that "the Singapore Convention should be understood as a safety net for settlements that have been recorded into an arbitral award, to be used whenever the courts of the state of enforcement conclude that such a consent award is not enforceable under the New York Convention or any other international or domestic legal instrument regulating the recognition and enforcement of foreign awards."
105. *See* the discussion in section 1.3.
106. *See* the discussion in section 1.3.
107. Strong, 2014a, p. 16; Nigmatullina, 2018, p. 8. *See also* Nolan-Haley, 2012, p. 90, suggesting to approach this phenomenon "based on [the] assimilation theory where the dominant model swallows the marginal one;" consequently, "mediation is no longer a separate 'alternative' to the judicial system, but a part of it." In the context of arbitration, this theory implies that mediation is not an independent alternative to arbitration but part of the arbitral process.

method,[108] let alone the repeated arguments about its increasing costs and duration,[109] as well as its transition into a "less interest-based, less problem-solving-oriented, more rights-based and more adversarial" mechanism.[110] For these reasons, some scholars argue that even if the enforcement mechanism of international mediation gains worldwide acceptance, its use may only expand in small- and medium-sized disputes, which are not the main focus of international arbitration:

> While international arbitration is currently experiencing some transformative trends from other sources in the international dispute resolution landscape, the growth of cross-border mediation anticipated as a result of the new enforcement regime is unlikely to result in reduced reliance on international arbitration as a primary means of dispute resolution for current users. Instead, the new Convention will expand the suite of services available to international dispute resolution users and providers and expand access to dispute resolution for micro, small and medium enterprises conducting cross-border and transnational commerce in the new enforcement regime.[111]

Hence, beyond the general advantages that ICA brings to the resolution of cross-border commercial disputes, it offers a safer and more efficient mechanism for the worldwide enforcement of facilitated and mediated settlements compared to national judgments or settlements resulting from standalone mediation. However, for such settlements to qualify for enforcement under the New York Convention, they must be recognized as "arbitral awards."[112] This raises the critical question of whether facilitated or mediated settlements reached during the arbitral process can meet the criteria for "arbitral awards" under the New York Convention, as explored in the discussion below.

3.6.3 Consent Awards as Arbitral Awards

The New York Convention does not define "arbitral awards" or reference consent awards.[113] It merely states that "the term 'arbitral awards' shall include not only awards made by arbitrators appointed for each case but also those made by permanent arbitral bodies to which the parties have submitted."[114] This silence of the convention regarding the possibility of recording mediated or facilitated settlements as arbitral awards on agreed terms has resulted in a controversy regarding the admissibility of these awards for recognition and enforcement under the convention.[115] It seems, however, that this disagreement has been decided. While some commentators explain the silence of the convention as a signal to disqualify the enforcement of consent

108. Strong, 2014a, pp. 18-24; Nigmatullina, 2018, p. 7.
109. Nigmatullina, 2018, p. 7; Cheng, 2011, p. 438; Strong, 2014a, p. 16. In addition, *see* the empirical data presented in this regard in section 1.3.
110. Nolan-Haley, 2012, p. 91.
111. Checkley, 2020, p. 23.
112. New York Convention, 1958, Article I(1)-(2).
113. Blackaby et al., 2022, §9.05-9.06; Kryvoi & Davydenko, 2015, p. 850.
114. New York Convention, 1958, Article I(2).
115. Paisley & Player, 2021, p. 35; Nigmatullina, 2018, p. 40; Stipanowich & Fraser, 2017, p. 861; Kryvoi & Davydenko, 2015, p. 850.

awards according to its provisions,[116] the common opinion holds that consent awards should not be distinguished from other awards:

> The New York Convention ... continues to allow for broad enforcement of arbitral awards including consent awards falling within its scope. ... With respect to whether a consent award is properly considered to be an award, the prevailing view is that a consent award is an award within the meaning of the New York Convention, and neither the language of the New York Convention itself nor that of the major international arbitration's rules would argue against a consent award being considered an award.[117]

This approach is supported by Article 30(2) of the Model Law on ICA, which asserts that "an award on agreed terms ... has the same status and effect as any other award on the merits of the case."[118] This notion is further reinforced by court decisions,[119] as well as by most international arbitration rules and many domestic arbitration laws that expressly provide for recording a settlement as a consent award.[120] Additionally, this interpretation finds support in Article 3(b) of the Singapore Convention, which excludes the convention's applicability to "settlement agreements that have been recorded and are enforceable as an arbitral award."[121] Hence, the Singapore Convention considers settlement agreements concluded during arbitral proceedings as enforceable under the New York Convention.[122]

Nevertheless, the language of the New York Convention stipulates that its provisions relating to recognition and enforcement apply to arbitral awards "arising out of *differences* between persons, whether physical or legal."[123] According to several scholars and practitioners, if a settlement intended to be recorded as a consent award was facilitated or mediated before the arbitration commenced, questions may arise regarding its enforceability under the convention. This is because, after concluding the settlement, there may no longer be a "difference" to submit to arbitration, potentially

116. Kryvoi & Davydenko, 2015, p. 850; Nigmatullina, 2018, p. 40; Steele, 2007, pp. 1397-1398.
117. Paisley & Player, 2021, pp. 34-35. *See also* Blackaby et al., 2022, §9.35-9.39; Stipanowich, 2021a, p. 287; Kaster, 2018, p. 48; Chua, 2018, p. 6; Ludington, 2017, p. 315; Stipanowich & Fraser, 2017, p. 861; Nigmatullina, 2018, pp. 35, 40; Ross, 2013, p. 362; Sussman, 2010a, pp. 391-398; Kaufmann-Kohler, 2009, p. 197; Steele, 2007, pp. 1387, 1397; Blankenship, 2006, p. 35; Bartel, 1991, pp. 681-683.
118. Model Law on ICA, 2006, Article 30(2). *See also* Ortolani, 2025, §21.4-21.5(a); Paisley & Player, 2021, p. 35.
119. Such as recent ruling of the U.S. court in *Transocean Offshore Gulf of Guinea Vii v. Erin Energy Corp.*, 2018, §4, stating that excluding consent awards from the applicability of the New York Convention "would dissuade parties from seeking arbitration in the first place or benefitting from the efficiencies it is meant to provide." For further discussion and court decisions in other jurisdictions, *see* Ortolani, 2025, §21.4-21.5(a); Kaster, 2018, pp. 48-49; Borrasso, 2018. In addition, *see* Nigmatullina, 2018, p. 40, referencing a study by Kaufmann-Kohler that found no court decision worldwide refusing enforcement solely because an award is a consent award.
120. Paisley & Player, 2021, p. 35; Kaster, 2018, p. 49; Nigmatullina, 2018, p. 40. For examples of such international rules, *see* the discussion in section 2.2.10.
121. Singapore Convention, 2018, Article 3(b).
122. Ortolani, 2025, §21.6.
123. New York Convention, 1958, Article I(1).

leaving the tribunal without jurisdiction to act.[124] Although other commentators reject this approach, arguing that the convention does not explicitly require the "difference" to exist at the time the arbitrator is appointed,[125] to avoid uncertainties regarding the enforcement of the settlement, it seems much safer to initiate the settlement efforts only after the commencement of the arbitration.[126] Since settlement facilitation by the arbitrator during the arbitration should not raise concerns regarding this issue, the question is most pertinent to hybrid processes involving arbitration and mediation. In practice, only these hybrid processes can include scenarios where a neutral facilitates a settlement before arbitration is formally initiated or before being nominated as an arbitrator. Consequently, in terms of enforceability under the New York Convention, Arb-Med and Arb-Med-Arb processes are considered safer than Med-Arb, as they confine the mediation phase to periods following the initiation of arbitration.[127]

Furthermore, some commentators hold that independent of concerns regarding the timing of arbitration's commencement, certain Med-Arb processes that limit the arbitrator's decision-making authority during the arbitration phase, particularly MED-ALOA, raise additional enforceability challenges under the New York Convention. These concerns arise because, in such instances, "the Med-Arbitrator had no real authority to provide a final judgment, and had to compromise when selecting between two imperfect offers."[128] However, these concerns may be adequately addressed by ensuring that the arbitrator delivers a detailed award that outlines and justifies the reasons underpinning the choice between the available alternatives and corresponds with fundamental principles of the law.[129]

Another issue arguably affected by these "differences" relates to the possibility of including in the facilitated or mediated settlement solutions not connected to issues in dispute, such as a remedy in the form of a new business relationship as part of a

124. Ortolani, 2025, §21.4-21.5(a); Yip, 2021, p. 195; Born, 2021, §5.09; Hioureas, 2019, p. 69; Kaster, 2018, pp. 49-50; Nigmatullina, 2018, p. 41; Kryvoi & Davydenko, 2015, p. 866; Kryvoi, 2015; Boog, 2015, pp. 91-96; Alexander, 2009, p. 28. This approach was applied in *Castro v. Tri Marine Fish Co. LLC*, 2019, where a U.S. federal court refused to enforce a settlement agreement under the New York Convention because it was concluded before the tribunal's constitution. The approach is also reflected in the Model Law on ICA, 2006, Article 30(1), which provides that a consent award may be issued if the settlement is reached "during arbitral proceedings."
125. Sussman, 2009b, p. 12; Kaster, 2018, p. 50.
126. Paisley & Player, 2021, p. 33; Yip, 2021, p. 196; Kaster, 2018, p. 50; Kryvoi & Davydenko, 2015, p. 867. *See also* CIArb Practice Guideline on the Use of Mediation in Arbitration, 2021, Article 9(3), suggesting to attempt mediation only during the course of the arbitral proceedings.
127. Stipanowich, 2021a, p. 287; Ortolani, 2025, §21.4-21.5(a),(f); Kaster, 2018, p. 50; Paisley & Player, 2021, p. 33; Nigmatullina, 2018, p. 41; Ross, 2013, pp. 360, 362-363; Nottage & Garnett, 2010, p. 35.
128. Dendorfer & Lack, 2007, pp. 92-94. *See also* Benzidi, 2017, p. 27; Nigmatullina, 2018, p. 152; Stipanowich & Kaskell, 2001, p. 26.
129. Sussman & Gleason, 2019, pp. 20-21, holding that since "awards based on an *ex aequo et bono* equitable decision ... [are] accepted as an alternative arbitration decision-making process, it would seem that there would be no enforcement issue with a reasoned award that adopted an FOA [Final Offer Arbitration] process. In a reasoned award, the arbitrator's discussion would not only include standard elements—history of the case, recitation of facts, and discussion of the applicable law, etc.—but also an explanation of the FOA process within the procedural section and the arbitrator's analysis of why the winning final offer was selected." *See also* Ortolani, 2025, §21.5(c); Benzidi, 2017, p. 27.

comprehensive dispute resolution. Based on the above-presented approach while relying on Article V(1)(c) to the convention,[130] some commentators hold that promoting these kinds of solutions may also challenge the enforceability of the consent award, as in the absence of "differences" in their regard, the tribunal exceeds its jurisdiction.[131] While the general duty of the arbitrator to grant remedies that relate to issues in dispute cannot be denied, a distinction should exist between arbitral awards of a compelling nature, even when based on equitable grounds, and consent awards that reflect mediated or facilitated settlements considered by all parties to the dispute as binding. This differentiation, which reflects the consensual nature of the arbitral process, can also rely on the New York Convention itself, as Articles I and V(1)(e) do not require for enforcement in other jurisdictions that the award "be jurisdictional in nature in the legal system in which it was rendered, but rather that it be binding on the parties, which the contractual arbitral award clearly is."[132] According to this logic, so long as the consent award reflects an agreement between all relevant parties, it may include solutions that fall out of the original differences submitted to arbitration. To avoid uncertainties in this matter, the parties may also petition jointly to expand the disputed issues before the arbitrator formally renders the consent award.[133]

3.7 CONCLUSIONS

Standalone arbitration, mediation, or any other ADR mechanism cannot offer the combination of benefits that the arbitrator's role as a settlement facilitator brings to the resolution process of cross-border commercial disputes. Alongside flexibility and saving costs and time, this role enhances the parties' commitment to the dispute-resolution process. It helps them overcome significant barriers to settlement, including the hesitation to suggest negotiations or to make the first move toward a settlement, while increasing their incentive to settle, whether to retain control over the process, to avoid uncertainties resulting from an arbitral award to be imposed by the arbitrator, or due to their trust in the arbitrator and respect for their authority. In addition, the role of the arbitrator can improve the quality and variety of the solutions, as it encourages the parties to focus on their interests and needs rather than their legal rights, which opens the door for more creative, decent, and just solutions that prioritize their business relationship. Even when the settlement efforts fail to bring a comprehensive resolution, the dual-role arbitrator can help the parties narrow the disputed issues to

130. New York Convention, 1958, Article V(1)(c), authorizing the court to refuse recognition or enforcement if the award "deals with a difference not contemplated by or not falling within the terms of the submission to arbitration, or it contains decisions on matters beyond the scope of the submission to arbitration."
131. Ortolani, 2025, §21.5(d); Bantekas, 2015, p. 49.
132. Morresi, 2009, p. 108. *See also* New York Convention, 1958, Articles I & V(1)(e).
133. This outline is recognized by Article 33(1) of the NAI Arbitration Rules, 2024, which permits parties to amend their claims prior to the commencement of the final hearing and, in exceptional circumstances, even at a later stage, subject to the tribunal's discretion. For further discussion on the possibility of extending the scope of the original arbitration agreement to include a consent award based on a settlement involving rights not originally in dispute, *see* Ortolani, 2025, §21.5(d).

make the binding award more predictable, informed, and acceptable. Other main benefits connected with this role are the finality it offers to the dispute and the international enforceability of the outcome (i.e., the consent award) under the New York Convention, which, compared to the alternatives saved for national judgments and settlements resulting from international mediation, grants a much safer and more effective enforcement mechanism.

Nevertheless, the advantages reviewed in this chapter are not absolute, as they do not exist in all scenarios where the arbitrator acts as a settlement facilitator. This relativity is best exemplified by hybrid processes that involve arbitration and mediation. While Med-Arb bears the best potential of saving time and costs while preserving the parties' business relationships, it may raise enforcement concerns as the settlement concludes before arbitration commences. Arb-Med, which attempts mediation only after the commencement of arbitration, does not raise such enforcement concerns. However, conducting a full arbitration before the mediation stage reduces the process's attractiveness in terms of efficiency and business relationship preservation. Therefore, Arb-Med-Arb seems to be the most balanced process since it holds the potential to bring the combined benefits of the arbitration and mediation processes while mitigating their shortfalls. Since Arb-Med-Arb opens with arbitration, it removes the enforceability concerns related to mediated or facilitated settlements under the New York Convention. Furthermore, this process seems to allow for excessive flexibility and adaptability, which enables the arbitrator to mediate the dispute at various stages throughout the arbitration process when early mediation offers significant opportunities to reduce costs and time and preserve the parties' business relationships.

Alongside its virtues, the arbitrator's role as a settlement facilitator raises various concerns that, if not addressed properly, may overshadow its benefits and risk the outcome of processes employing it. The next chapter discusses these concerns.

CHAPTER 4

Concerns Associated with Facilitating a Settlement by the Arbitrator in ICA

4.1 INTRODUCTION

Opponents of the arbitrator's role as a settlement facilitator argue that arbitration should be kept as a fully adjudicative process aimed at *deciding* the dispute by a binding award. Thus, the arbitrator's mandate is unsuitable for any involvement in settlement efforts, even when the disputants explicitly request it.[1] This attitude, which emphasizes the differences between arbitration and other ADR methods, usually refers to the concerns associated with the arbitrator's dual role, particularly its potential risk to due process and natural justice.[2] However, these concerns are not ignored by supporters of the arbitrator's dual role, as most scholars, practitioners, and jurisdictions accepting this role agree it should be implemented within certain boundaries according to particular safeguards to guarantee the integrity of the process and the enforceability of the arbitration's outcome.[3] As demonstrated in Chapter 2, when assessing the arbitrator's involvement in the settlement process, a distinction should principally be made between *indirect* initiatives intended to set the stage for settlement—usually observed as an integral part of the arbitrator's managerial role—and *direct* involvement in the settlement efforts that is more likely to raise concerns. Therefore, addressing the concerns connected with the arbitrator's role as a

1. Berger, 2018b, p. 503; Berger & Jensen, 2017, p. 889; Stipanowich & Ulrich, 2014b, p. 6; Kun, 2011b, p. 537; Kaufmann-Kohler, 2009, pp. 188-189; Fiechter, 2008, p. 261; Hwang, 2005, p. 571; Collins, 2003, p. 343; Abramson, 1999, p. 2; Costa Braga de Oliveira, 2009, p. 89; Lang, 2009, p. 102; Masood, 2010, p. 276.
2. Stipanowich, 2021a, pp. 290-291; Nigmatullina, 2018, p. 56; Ludington, 2017, pp. 317-320; Berger & Jensen, 2017, p. 914; Stipanowich & Fraser, 2017, pp. 855; Kun, 2011b, p. 537; Sussman, 2010a, p. 384; Kaufmann-Kohler, 2009, pp. 198-199; Rosoff, 2009, pp. 92-93; Sussman, 2009a, p. 71; Blankenship, 2006, p. 36.
3. Stipanowich, 2021a, p. 335; Harris, 2016, p. 98; Kun, 2011b, p. 552; Berger, 2018b, pp. 511-513; Marzolini, 2016, pp. 117-118; Newmark, 2008, p. 89; Abramson, 1999, pp. 7-15.

settlement facilitator is vital for identifying its controversial components and challenges, exploring possible ways to address them, and eventually suggesting solutions to enhance its harmonization within ICA.[4]

The concerns associated with the role of the arbitrator are nonhomogeneous and can be divided into three different groups. One group of concerns is fundamental and relates to the risk of the parties' due process rights—including their right to self-determination, impartial tribunal, and the right to be heard—as a result of the arbitrator's involvement in the settlement negotiations.[5] These concerns, the realization of which may be at the root of the procedure and affect the admissibility of its outcome, are usually raised in relation to caucusing[6] and the coercive behavior of the arbitrator.[7] The second group of concerns relates to the hesitant attitude of the participants toward the settlement process, in particular, the parties' tactical use of the settlement negotiations and lack of transparency, as well as the arbitrator's inhibited conduct.[8] Although such concerns represent opposite behavioral expectations from those presented in the previous chapter[9] and are less likely to challenge the outcome of the arbitration, they may still influence the chances of settling the case amicably during the settlement phase.[10] The third group relates to external concerns, such as the incompatibility of the arbitrator with the dual role[11] or the incompatibility of the dispute for settlement due to public interests at stake, as may arguably be the case in investment treaty disputes.[12] This chapter discusses these concerns, starting with those fundamental to the threat of impartiality and breach of due process.

4. Kaufmann-Kohler, 2009, pp. 197, 203-205; Stipanowich & Ulrich, 2014b, p. 30.
5. Stipanowich, 2021a, pp. 290-291; Benzidi, 2017, p. 10; Nigmatullina, 2018, pp. 54-57; Berger & Jensen, 2017, pp. 914-915; Ludington, 2017, pp. 317-320; Kun, 2011b, pp. 537-538; Sussman, 2010a, p. 384; Kaufmann-Kohler, 2009, pp. 198-199; Blankenship, 2006, pp. 35-36; Stipanowich & Kaskell, 2001, p. 22; Abramson, 1999, pp. 3-4.
6. Gu, 2019, pp. 135-136; Nigmatullina, 2018, p. 48; Ross, 2013, p. 360; Kun, 2011b, pp. 552-554; Leon & Peterson, 2009, p. 93; Kaufmann-Kohler, 2009, pp. 198-200.
7. Stipanowich, 2021a, p. 328; Rombach & Shalbanava, 2019, p. 59; Berger, 2018b, p. 513; Stipanowich & Ulrich, 2014b, pp. 25-26; Blankenship, 2006, p. 36; Nigmatullina, 2018, pp. 52-53; Kun, 2011b, pp. 551-552; Kaufmann-Kohler, 2009, p. 200; Stipanowich & Kaskell, 2001, p. 22; Abramson, 1999, pp. 8-9.
8. Stipanowich, 2021a, pp. 290-291; Benzidi, 2017, p. 10; Nigmatullina, 2018, pp. 49-51; Stipanowich & Ulrich, 2014b, p. 26; Kaufmann-Kohler, 2009, p. 200; Blankenship, 2006, pp. 36-37; Stipanowich & Kaskell, 2001, pp. 21-22; Abramson, 1999, p. 4.
9. *See* the discussion in sections 3.4-3.5 about the parties' approach and their incentive to settle, as well as the arbitrator's incentive to promote a decent and just solution that focuses on the parties' needs and future relations. *See also* Blankenship, 2006, p. 37, arguing that the advantages and disadvantages of the arbitrator' dual role "are interrelated. ... One could argue they are all different variations of a fundamental flaw—the same neutral taking off a mediator's hat and putting on an arbitrator's hat."
10. Stipanowich, 2021a, p. 290; Kun, 2011b, p. 538; Kaufmann-Kohler, 2009, p. 200.
11. Yip, 2021, pp. 192-194; Stipanowich, 2021a, pp. 288-289; Gu, 2019, p. 133; Ludington, 2017, p. 316; Benzidi, 2017, pp. 9-10; Stipanowich & Ulrich, 2014b, p. 26; Stipanowich & Kaskell, 2001, p. 21.
12. Kun, 2020b, pp. 329-330; Kaufmann-Kohler, 2009, pp. 200-202, 204; Sussman, 2010b, pp. 333-337; Bantekas, 2015, pp. 29-32.

4.2 FUNDAMENTAL CONCERNS

Arguments about a breach of the parties' due process rights are raised in relation to different scenarios during the settlement process. Most arguments are directed toward the practice of caucusing, considered "the most controversial settlement facilitation technique on the arbitrator role continuum."[13] In particular, concerns have been raised about the confidential information shared with the arbitrator during caucusing and its potential influence on the arbitral award if the settlement efforts fail and the arbitration resumes.[14] However, as discussed below, not all concerns connected with caucusing relate to the disclosure of confidential information, and not all fundamental concerns derive from the practice of caucusing. Such fundamental concerns are also raised about the coercive behavior of the arbitrator during the settlement process[15] and, in some jurisdictions, regarding the practice of expressing evaluative views about the disputed issues and the outcome of the case.[16] The common ground of these concerns is their potential to challenge the outcome of the process[17] and, consequently, eliminate one of the main advantages of the arbitrator's dual role: saving time and costs.[18] This section discusses these fundamental concerns.

4.2.1 Threat to Impartiality

Concerns about the arbitrator's impartiality may be raised even when the arbitrator refrains from caucusing with the parties. Following joint settlement sessions, the arbitrator is exposed to more information than any "pure arbitrator" can receive based solely on the formal record of the case, including the underlying conflict, the history of the parties' business relationship, and possibly their personal relations.[19] If the settlement efforts fail and arbitration resumes, the risk exists that the arbitrator, consciously or unconsciously, relies on the off-record information while deciding the dispute.[20] Similar concerns can arise related to evaluative views expressed by the

---

13. Berger & Jensen, 2017, p. 913. *See also* Baysal & Cevik, 2021; Stipanowich, 2021a, pp. 347, 349; Nigmatullina, 2018, p. 60; Ross, 2013, p. 360; Abramson, 1999, p. 7.
14. Ruckteschler & Wendelstein, 2021, p. 763; Stipanowich, 2021a, p. 291; Baysal & Cevik, 2021; Benzidi, 2017, p. 13; Nigmatullina, 2018, p. 54; Ludington, 2017, p. 320; Weisman, 2013, p. 41; Kun, 2011b, p. 538; Blankley, 2011, p. 321.
15. Stipanowich, 2021a, p. 290; Rombach & Shalbanava, 2019, p. 59; Berger, 2018b, p. 513; Stipanowich & Ulrich, 2014b, pp. 25-26; Blankenship, 2006, p. 36; Nigmatullina, 2018, pp. 52-53; Kun, 2011b, pp. 551-552; Fullerton, 2009, p. 34; Kaufmann-Kohler, 2009, p. 200; Stipanowich & Kaskell, 2001, p. 22; Abramson, 1999, pp. 8-9.
16. Stipanowich, 2021a, pp. 290, 335; Nigmatullina, 2018, p. 54; Peter, 1997, p. 94; Hwang, 2005, p. 572; Stipanowich & Kaskell, 2001, pp. 30-32.
17. Yip, 2021, p. 192; Berger & Jensen, 2017, p. 914; Karton, 2013, p. 106; Nigmatullina, 2018, p. 55; Stipanowich, 2021a, pp. 293-294; Gill, 2006, p. 160; Stipanowich & Kaskell, 2001, p. 22.
18. Nigmatullina, 2018, p. 55; Stipanowich, 2021a, p. 284; Ross, 2013, p. 360; Deekshitha & Saha, 2014, p. 89; Lew, 2005, pp. 422-23; Rosoff, 2009, p. 90.
19. Benzidi, 2017, pp. 17-18; Nigmatullina, 2018, p. 54; Kaufmann-Kohler, 2009, p. 198; Blankenship, 2006, p. 35; Kun & Kaufmann-Kohler, 2008, p. 491; Bartel, 1991, p. 679.
20. Gu, 2019, pp. 135-136; Gill, 2006, pp. 158-159; Elliott, 1995, p. 167; Nigmatullina, 2018, pp. 54-55; Benzidi, 2017, p. 18.

arbitrator on the disputed issues and their possible outcomes,[21] as, despite their provisional and non-binding nature, the arbitrator may arguably feel obliged to adhere to these views in the resumed arbitration, thus undermining their neutrality.[22] In addition, unlike in standalone mediation that allows free-flowing communications between the neutral and the disputants, in the settlement stage of the arbitration, the parties and the arbitrator may communicate more carefully and vaguely since the arbitrator will decide the dispute if settlement efforts fail. This dialogue may create gaps between the intention of the arbitrator while expressing evaluative views about the dispute and the disputants' understanding of these views, which results in different expectations regarding the future award.[23] If the award is incompatible with these expectations, arguments can be raised against the arbitrator's impartiality relating to the communications during the settlement stage.[24]

When the arbitrator caucuses with the parties as part of the settlement attempts, impartiality concerns are obviously exacerbated. In addition to exposure to "private and perhaps intimate, emotional and other legally irrelevant information"[25] during these ex parte sessions, the arbitrator can gain access to confidential information, including negotiated positions and highly sensitive details that may significantly influence the outcome of the arbitration,[26] without allowing other parties to respond or provide counterarguments.[27] The fear that the arbitrator cannot disregard such information while deciding the dispute may raise significant concerns about their impartiality:

> How, some ask, can a mediator-turned-arbitrator purge his mind of acts and positions learned in confidence, and what is to prevent the neutral from relying on information vouchsafed confidentially in mediation in making an award? And how, if at all, might a party not privy to the confidential communication effectively respond and counteract its potential impact?[28]

---

21. Stipanowich, 2021a, pp. 349, 352-354; Nigmatullina, 2018, p. 54; Gu, 2019, p. 136; Marzolini, 2016, p. 114; Karton, 2013, p. 106; Stipanowich & Kaskell, 2001, pp. 30-32; Abramson, 1999, p. 7.
22. Rombach & Shalbanava, 2019, pp. 55-56; Benzidi, 2017, pp. 25-26; Nigmatullina, 2018, p. 54; Marzolini, 2016, pp. 114-115; Gill, 2006, p. 159; Peter, 1997, p. 94; Hwang, 2005, p. 572; Harris, 2016, p. 90, relating to a risk of pre-judgment that can influence the final award.
23. Stipanowich, 2021a, p. 292; Ludington, 2017, p. 323; Stipanowich & Ulrich, 2014b, p. 15; Blankley, 2011, pp. 325, 334.
24. Benzidi, 2017, pp. 25-26; Nigmatullina, 2018, p. 55; Stipanowich & Ulrich, 2014b, p. 15; Karton, 2013, p. 106; Nappert & Flader, 2011, p. 461.
25. Nigmatullina, 2018, p. 54. *See also* Gu, 2019, p. 136; Lang, 2009, p. 100; Peter, 1997, pp. 92-93.
26. Ruckteschler & Wendelstein, 2021, p. 763; Stipanowich, 2021a, pp. 291, 302; Baysal & Cevik, 2021; Ludington, 2017, p. 318; Gu, 2019, p. 136; Benzidi, 2017, p. 13; Berger & Jensen, 2017, p. 915; Blankley, 2011, p. 325; Gill, 2006, p. 159; Blankenship, 2006, p. 35; Peter, 1997, pp. 92-93.
27. Yip, 2021, p. 192; Gu, 2019, p. 136; Ludington, 2017, p. 319; Benzidi, 2017, p. 23; Kun, 2011b, pp. 537-538; Nigmatullina, 2018, pp. 54-55; Kaufmann-Kohler, 2009, p. 198; Gill, 2006, p. 159; Blankenship, 2006, p. 35; Elliott, 1995, p. 167.
28. Stipanowich, 2021a, p. 291. *See also* Yip, 2021, p. 192; Nolan-Haley, 2020, p. 382; Gu, 2019, p. 136; Ludington, 2017, p. 320; Benzidi, 2017, pp. 14-15, 26-27; Berger & Jensen, 2017, p. 915; Harris, 2016, pp. 93-94; Lang, 2009, p. 98; Gill, 2006, p. 159; Stipanowich & Kaskell, 2001, p. 22; Wistrich et al., 2005, p. 1323; Sussman, 2009a, p. 71; Sussman, 2010a, pp. 384-385; Blankley, 2011, p. 325; Baysal & Cevik, 2021; Rosoff, 2009, pp. 90, 92.

One can argue that even in standalone arbitration, neutrals may be affected by irrelevant information or misleading impressions,[29] similar to the influence that judges can experience in judicial proceedings.[30] Nevertheless, it seems that arguments regarding bias are more likely when the neutral fulfills a dual role:

> Dual role neutrals undoubtedly become privy to much more than arbitrators in standalone arbitration would. This exposes dual role neutrals much more to the danger of bias than arbitrators. Even if parties limit the decision-making to only certain facts, a dual role neutral might still struggle to block out information gained in mediation. ... It may be even more difficult for the losing party to believe that the neutral did so. Counsel might fear that the mediator who has become the arbitrator has developed a skewed view of their client's position that is not possible to set right anymore.[31]

Two empirical studies confirmed these concerns. One study, conducted between 2002 and 2004 among 265 U.S. judges who facilitated settlements (2002-2004 Andrew Study),[32] found that judges, like laypersons and other expert decision-makers, were subject to bias since most of the time they were unwittingly influenced by inadmissible information and could not disregard it when making substantive decisions in their cases.[33] In another survey conducted in 2008 among Ohio lawyers about their experiences with mediation and settlement conferences in federal courts (2008 Wissler Survey), most participants supported the opinion that judges assigned to the cases could not fully explore settlements without risking ongoing litigation if the settlement efforts failed. The vast majority of the surveyed lawyers expressed an opposite position about the effect of failed settlement efforts on ongoing litigation when different neutrals carried out the efforts.[34] Nevertheless, a large study identified only one case in which a court refused enforcement of an arbitral award following the arbitrator's involvement in the settlement efforts.[35] Hence, some scholars hold that the fear of impartiality seems to be more perceived than real.[36]

4.2.2 Threat to Other Aspects of Due Process

The risk to impartiality resulting from the arbitrator's involvement in the settlement process represents only one aspect of due process concerns.[37] Another fundamental

29. Nigmatullina, 2018, p. 55.
30. Kun, 2020a, p. 156; Kaufmann-Kohler, 2009, pp. 197-198; Kun & Kaufmann-Kohler, 2008, p. 491; Blankenship, 2006, pp. 35-36.
31. Nigmatullina, 2018, p. 55. *See also* Gu, 2019, p. 136; Deekshitha & Saha, 2014, p. 89; Gu, 2016, pp. 89-90; Ross, 2013, p. 360; De Vera, 2004, p. 159; Bartel, 1991, p. 685; Oghigian, 2003, p. 77.
32. Andrew et al., 2005, pp. 1279-1281.
33. Andrew et al., 2005, p. 1323. Due to this conclusion, the experimenters even suggested (p. 1325) that "courts should separate judges' 'managerial' functions from their 'adjudicative' functions as a way of reducing the likelihood that judges will be influenced by inadmissible evidence they encounter during pretrial proceedings when making merits-based decisions on motions or at trial." *See also* Benzidi, 2017, p. 15.
34. Wissler, 2011, pp. 286-287, also discussed in Nigmatullina, 2018, p. 55.
35. Kaufmann-Kohler, 2009, p. 198.
36. Kaufmann-Kohler, 2009, p. 198; Nigmatullina, 2018, pp. 55-56; Rosoff, 2009, p. 91.
37. Kun, 2011b, pp. 537-538; Oghigian, 2003, pp. 75-76; Sawada, 2003, p. 29; Berger, 2003, p. 393; Hwang, 2005, p. 575; Schneider, 2007, pp. 25-26.

aspect of due process, related primarily to caucusing, is the parties' right to be heard and answer their opponents' claims or defense to guarantee the fairness of the dispute-resolution process.[38] This practice may underline the principle of due process because disputants can make allegations and relate to confidential information without allowing their opponents to respond during the caucusing.[39] This risk is exacerbated when disputants take advantage of ex parte meetings to deliberately and inappropriately influence the arbitrator by relating to information that should have been proven or rebutted during the formal hearing in hopes of easily converting the information into "evidence" that later leaks into the binding award.[40] Arguably, identical due process concerns may arise in standalone mediation as the mediator also meets privately with the disputants and can potentially be exposed to confidential information and arguments without receiving the response of the other parties. However, unlike in arbitration, if mediation fails, the mediator has no mandate to decide the case, which is the main difference related to due process concerns:

> Mediation is a different proceeding than arbitration with different sets of obligations between the parties and the mediator to the dispute. A party does not have an inalienable right to defend all accusations in mediation. The arbitrator-mediator is not ruling on the dispute during mediation. Hybrid procedures become problematic when mediation fails and the arbitrator-mediator resumes his role as a biased arbitrator.[41]

Other important aspects of due process, connected to both caucusing and joint settlement sessions, are party autonomy and the right to self-determination during the dispute resolution process.[42] One can argue that the arbitrator's authority to decide the case may, by definition, compel the parties to agree to the arbitrator's engagement in the settlement negotiations and create a coercive atmosphere during their course.[43] Therefore, any agreement reached through this process should not be considered voluntary but a violation of party autonomy.[44] While this approach may be viewed as extreme,[45] it is undeniable that if an arbitrator uses their "muscle,"[46] which initially

38. Stipanowich, 2021a, p. 291; Benzidi, 2017, pp. 21-24; Berger & Jensen, 2017, p. 913; Harris, 2016, p. 93; Ross, 2013, p. 361; Kun, 2011b, pp. 537; Kaufmann-Kohler, 2009, p. 198; Nigmatullina, 2018, p. 56; Rosoff, 2009, pp. 92-93; Blankenship, 2006, p. 36; Bernardini, 2004, p. 117.
39. Berger & Jensen, 2017, pp. 913-914; Harris, 2016, p. 93; Ross, 2013, p. 361; Kun, 2011b, pp. 537-538; Gill, 2006, p. 159; Blankenship, 2006, p. 36; Rosoff, 2009, pp. 92-93; Sussman, 2009a, p. 71; Nigmatullina, 2018, p. 56; Jordaan, 2009, p. 117; Limbury, 2010a, p. 454; Kaufmann-Kohler, 2009, p. 198; Kun & Kaufmann-Kohler, 2008, p. 491; Elliott, 1995, pp. 166-167; Xu & Wilson, 2000, p. 68; Baysal & Cevik, 2021.
40. Stipanowich, 2021a, p. 291; Nigmatullina, 2018, p. 56; Gu, 2019, p. 136; Phillips, G. F., 2009, p. 76. Blankenship, 2006, p. 36; Peter, 1997, p. 94; Gregory, 2001, p. 29.
41. Rosoff, 2009, pp. 92-93. *See also* Nigmatullina, 2018, p. 56; Schneider, 2007, p. 27.
42. Stipanowich, 2021a, p. 290; Stipanowich & Kaskell, 2001, p. 21; Blankenship, 2006, p. 34.
43. Rombach & Shalbanava, 2019, p. 59; Ross, 2013, p. 360; Kun, 2011b, p. 552; Kaufmann-Kohler, 2009, p. 200; Abramson, 1999, p. 9; Stipanowich, 2021a, p. 338.
44. Blankenship, 2006, p. 36; Nigmatullina, 2018, p. 52; Landry, 1996, p. 265; Deekshitha & Saha, 2014, p. 93.
45. Gu, 2019, p. 134.
46. *See* the discussion in section 3.4 about the impact of the arbitrator's adjudicative authority on the incentive of the parties to settle.

was intended to *encourage* compromise, as a "big stick" that *compels* the parties to settle, the arbitration's outcome may be challenged based on the allegation of depriving the parties of their right for self-determination while breaching their due process rights.[47] This fear of coercion may also occur when the arbitrator "telegraphs" their personal perspective on the disputed issues or expresses highly decisive evaluations about the dispute and its outcome,[48] as the parties, who have no interest in upsetting the arbitrator, may feel their only choice is to settle according to the arbitrator's views.[49] In this case, the parties' right to self-determination is deprived, while the essence of the settlement may be compromised because instead of focusing on their real interests and best options, the parties become limited to the alternatives presented by the arbitrator.[50] Although the arbitrator can also behave coercively in a standalone arbitration, the adversarial nature of the process and its usual exclusion of ex parte communications diminish the likelihood of such issues arising.[51]

4.3 HESITANT ATTITUDE TOWARD SETTLEMENT EFFORTS

The fact that, following failed efforts to settle, the arbitrator will retain the power to deliver a binding and final decision regarding the dispute may deter the parties from full, honest, and transparent involvement in the settlement negotiations. For the same reason, the arbitrator may also approach the settlement stage hesitantly and thus further weaken the chances of promoting an amicable outcome of the dispute.[52] This section discusses the effect of these hesitant approaches on the prospect of achieving a settlement while focusing on the parties' reluctance to disclose, their tactical use of the settlement stage, and the arbitrator's hesitancy to facilitate a settlement.

4.3.1 Parties' Reluctance to Disclose

The dual role of the arbitrator may arguably reduce the effectiveness of the settlement negotiations since, unlike in standalone mediation, the parties may be less candid and open knowing that the arbitrator will render a binding decision following failed

47. Baysal & Cevik, 2021; Stipanowich, 2021a, p. 290; Nigmatullina, 2018, p. 52; Deekshitha & Saha, 2014, p. 93; Stipanowich & Ulrich, 2014b, pp. 25-26; Ross, 2013, p. 360; Phillips, G. F., 2009, p. 76; Kichaven, 2009, p. 82; Fullerton, 2009, p. 34; Blankenship, 2006, p. 36; Peter, 1997, p. 94.
48. Stipanowich, 2021a, pp. 290, 301; Gu, 2019, p. 136; Stipanowich & Kaskell, 2001, p. 21; Abramson, 1999, pp. 10-11; Love, 1997, pp. 940, 942.
49. Berger & Jensen, 2017, p. 903; Nigmatullina, 2018, p. 52; Marzolini, 2016, p. 115; Ross, 2013, p. 360; Blankenship, 2006, p. 34; Stipanowich & Kaskell, 2001, p. 21; Peter, 1997, p. 94; Bartel, 1991, p. 679.
50. Nigmatullina, 2018, p. 52; Fullerton, 2009, p. 34; Pappas, 2015, p. 179.
51. Nigmatullina, 2018, p. 52; Rosoff, 2009, pp. 92-93.
52. Stipanowich, 2021a, pp. 290-291; Nigmatullina, 2018, pp. 49-51; Stipanowich & Ulrich, 2014b, p. 26; Kaufmann-Kohler, 2009, p. 200; Blankenship, 2006, pp. 36-37; Gill, 2006, pp. 160-161; Stipanowich & Kaskell, 2001, pp. 21-22; Abramson, 1999, p. 4.

settlement efforts.[53] According to this view, expressing real interests and positions in front of the arbitrator shows weakness and may risk the desired outcome of the arbitration.[54] For the same reasons, this reluctance to disclose may also extend to ex parte meetings with the arbitrator, which are intended to foster free-flowing communication with the neutral and the exposure of confidential information that can assist in promoting the settlement without being revealed to the opposing party.[55] Consequently, instead of equipping the arbitrator with the necessary information for facilitating a settlement, such as the disputants' intentions, underlying commercial interests, and compromise positions, the parties may focus their discussions during the settlement stage on legal rather than commercial issues and attempts to persuade the arbitrator of the correctness of their formal arguments and positions,[56] which may undermine the arbitrator's ability to serve them effectively and reduce the chances of promoting an amicable solution to the dispute.[57]

Empirical data supports the reluctance of the parties to approach the settlement stage with candor when the settlement facilitator is the same person who decides the dispute. In the 2008 Wissler Survey,[58] most participants supported the opinion that during the settlement negotiations, "parties could be much less candid with judges assigned to the case than with judges not assigned to the case, court staff mediators, volunteer mediators, and private mediators."[59] However, opposite results were obtained in the 1987 McGillicuddy Field Experiment.[60] According to the collected data, when the arbitrator was the mediator, disputants were more honest, open, conciliatory, involved, creative, and motivated to settle versus during standalone mediation or when a different neutral mediated the dispute.[61] Some commentators have explained these contradicting views about the parties' approach to a process that allows the decision-maker to facilitate a settlement due to the dichotomic points of view that observe the process, whether through the lens of standalone mediation or traditional arbitration, when, in reality, it is "a different process."[62] Even if the reference point is a standalone mediation, parties may still not be open to sharing their real interests and positions or revealing confidential information to the mediator, whether to end the mediation or to influence its outcome.[63] In any case, when the arbitrator facilitates the

53. Stipanowich, 2021a, p. 290; Yip, 2021, pp. 192-193; Harris, 2016, p. 93; Ross, 2013, p. 360; Kun, 2011b, p. 538; Blankley, 2011, pp. 333, 335; Kaufmann-Kohler, 2009, p. 200; Gill, 2006, p. 160; Blankenship, 2006, p. 37; Marriott, 2005, p. 541; Stipanowich & Kaskell, 2001, pp. 21-22.
54. Benzidi, 2017, p. 10; Stipanowich & Ulrich, 2014b, p. 26; Nigmatullina, 2018, p. 49; Gill, 2006, p. 160; Abramson, 1999, p. 4.
55. Nigmatullina, 2018, p. 49; Flake, 2016, p. 8; Ross, 2013, p. 360; Blankley, 2011, p. 335; Phillips, G. F., 2009, p. 76; Peter, 1997, p. 98.
56. Gill, 2006, pp. 160-161; Nigmatullina, 2018, p. 49; Kaufmann-Kohler, 2009, p. 200.
57. Stipanowich, 2021a, p. 290; Nigmatullina, 2018, p. 49; Stipanowich & Ulrich, 2014b, p. 26; Gill, 2006, pp. 160-161.
58. *See* the discussion in section 4.2.1 above.
59. Nigmatullina, 2018, p. 50, relating to the survey discussed is Wissler, 2011, p. 286.
60. *See* the discussion in section 3.4.
61. McGillicuddy et al., 1987, pp. 104, 110; Nigmatullina, 2018, p. 50; Blankenship, 2006, pp. 36-37; Stipanowich, 2021a, p. 287.
62. Blankenship, 2006, p. 37.
63. Blankenship, 2006, p. 37.

settlement, the possible shortage of information resulting from the parties' reluctance to disclose can partly be compensated by the knowledge the arbitrator gained during the earlier part of the arbitration regarding the dispute's background and possibly the parties' business interests.[64]

4.3.2 Manipulation of the Process

As refusal or reluctance to cooperate and open during the settlement negotiations can force the transition of the process toward a binding and final decision,[65] parties or counsel who are unwilling to compromise may use the settlement phase to "spin" the arbitrator and "score points" toward the desired arbitral award.[66] In addition, knowing that ex parte meetings are confidential, parties may misuse them to influence the arbitrator's discretion by glorifying their position, discrediting the opposing party's arguments, or even trying to create new "evidence" to hopefully affect the arbitral award.[67]

Nevertheless, tactical behavior and attempts to influence the outcome of the process may happen in all types of dispute resolution, including in standalone mediation, so a process that accepts the dual role of the arbitrator is no exception.[68] The aforementioned 2008 Wissler Survey supports this conclusion. According to its results, there are "marginal differences between dual role and separate neutrals in their ability to ensure parties' good behaviour in settlement conferences."[69] Moreover, according to the results of the 1987 McGillicuddy Field Experiment,[70] when the arbitrator was in charge of facilitating a settlement, the parties were more honest and open than during other processes.[71]

4.3.3 Arbitrator's Reluctance to Facilitate a Settlement

For several reasons, the arbitrator may approach the settlement negotiations hesitantly or refrain from promoting an amicable solution to the dispute, even when explicitly asked by the parties to do so. *First*, the arbitrator can legitimately worry that a facilitated or mediated arbitral award may be subject to enforceability challenges,

64. Nigmatullina, 2018, p. 50; Schneider, 1998, p. 93.
65. Kichaven, 2009, p. 80; Blankenship, 2006, p. 37; Bartel, 1991, p. 683.
66. Yip, 2021, p. 194; Stipanowich, 2021a, pp. 290-291; Rosoff, 2009, p. 92; Nigmatullina, 2018, p. 51; Benzidi, 2017, p. 10; Deason, 2013, p. 224; Sussman, 2009a, p. 71; Phillips, G. F., 2009, p. 76; Ross, 2013, p. 360; Elliott, 1995, p. 179; Greenwood, 2011a, p. 201.
67. Stipanowich, 2021a, p. 291; Yip, 2021, p. 194; Nigmatullina, 2018, p. 51; Benzidi, 2017, p. 10; Blankley, 2011, p. 336; Kichaven, 2009, p. 80; Blankenship, 2006, p. 36. *See also* Deason, 2013, p. 224, relating to the tactical use of the settlement phase as an attempt to "shape the views of the person who will become the ultimate fact finder."
68. Nigmatullina, 2018, p. 51; Blankenship, 2006, p. 37; Ross, 2013, p. 360.
69. Nigmatullina, 2018, p. 51, relating to the survey discussed in Wissler, 2011, p. 295.
70. *See* the discussion in section 3.4.
71. McGillicuddy et al., 1987, pp. 104, 110; Nigmatullina, 2018, p. 50; Blankenship, 2006, pp. 36-37; Stipanowich, 2021a, p. 287.

particularly an award rendered following failed settlement efforts.[72] Since many jurisdictions develop and regulate the legal frameworks for arbitration and mediation separately and independently, a single neutral fulfilling a dual role in the same process may raise questions about the nature of the process and the relevant legal framework for its enforcement in that jurisdiction. Indeed, enforceability may become particularly acute in jurisdictions that impose essential or procedural strictures on the dual role.[73] Aware of these uncertainties and eager to avoid scrutiny regarding their primary duty as a decision-maker to render an enforceable award,[74] the arbitrator may opt to avoid the dual role altogether or engage in the settlement more passively while excluding evaluations and ex parte communications with the disputants.[75] *Second*, the arbitrator may be reluctant to facilitate a settlement to avoid casting doubts regarding their integrity. According to some critics, the dual role creates significant ethical conflicts between its adjudicative and mediative components,[76] with the potential to corrupt the arbitrator.[77] Even when the arbitrator strives to perform the dual role with maximum integrity and fairness and has no doubts regarding the ability to switch between the roles, the disputants, particularly the losing party, may still be skeptical about the arbitrator's ability.[78] To avoid arguments against the process or its outcome on this ground, the arbitrator may refrain from fulfilling the dual role or engaging in settlement negotiations under suspicion. *Third*, some commentators explain the arbitrator's reluctance to facilitate a settlement due to fee considerations. According to this view, since the settlement is expected to end the dispute earlier and reduce the arbitrator's fees, the dual-role arbitrator may be "placed under a conflict of personal interest (of receiving more remuneration) and duty."[79] Even when the arbitrator disregards financial considerations while implementing a dual role, they may still "come under attack for not working as hard to bring both parties to a consensual settlement of their dispute out of the self-interest of wanting to receive more remuneration for his/her subsequent role as the arbitrator."[80] *Fourth*, reluctance to facilitate settlements may stem from the arbitrator's legal background,[81] personal preferences, and characteristics

72. Yip, 2021, p. 192; Stipanowich, 2021a, pp. 293-294; Berger & Jensen, 2017, p. 914; Sussman, 2009a, p. 73; Gill, 2006, p. 160; Stipanowich & Kaskell, 2001, p. 22.
73. Stipanowich, 2021a, p. 293; Folberg, 2016, pp. 794-795.
74. Lew, 2005, p. 425; Horvath, 2001, p. 135; Stipanowich, 2021a, p. 344.
75. Stipanowich, 2021a, p. 290; Nigmatullina, 2018, pp. 50-51; Flake, 2016, p. 7; Kaufmann-Kohler, 2009, p. 200.
76. Blankenship, 2006, p. 37; Anderson, 2003, pp. 195, 196; Bühring-Uhle et al., 2006, p. 248; Nigmatullina, 2018, p. 59.
77. Blankenship, 2006, p. 37.
78. Nigmatullina, 2018, p. 55; Oghigian, 2003, p. 77; Bartel, 1991, p. 686.
79. Yip, 2021, p. 192. It should, however, be mentioned that no empirical data supports this argument. Some scholars have suggested addressing this possible conflict by creating a financial incentive for the dual role to settle the dispute amicably, whether by an arrangement that pays the arbitrator a premium if the settlement stage is successful or other means that provide a discounted rate for neutrals who engage in the dual role. *See* Nigmatullina, 2018, p. 33; Blankley, 2011, p. 328.
80. Yip, 2021, p. 192.
81. The influence of the arbitrator's legal background on their attitude toward the dual role is discussed in detail in Chapter 5.

that create discomfort with the dual role.[82] Some arbitrators may lack the professional capacity to fulfill the dual role, given its unique requirements, as discussed in the next section.

4.4 INCOMPATIBILITY OF THE NEUTRAL OR THE DISPUTE

Concerns regarding the arbitrator's role as a settlement facilitator may derive from external considerations of the arbitral process. One concern relates to uncertainties about the arbitrator's compatibility with the dual role since it may require the neutral to demonstrate a combination of characteristics and abilities not necessarily required from a neutral in traditional arbitration or a standalone ADR process. This incompatibility may deter the specific disputants from agreeing on a process that allows the arbitrator to assume the role while affecting the general approach of parties to international business disputes toward the dual role.[83] Another concern relates to the nature of the dispute, particularly the effect of facilitating a settlement within its framework on public interests or rights of third parties that may not be fully represented in the dispute resolution process. Since this concern is mainly raised in relation to investor-state disputes, the discussion focuses on this type of arbitration.[84]

4.4.1 The Incompatibility of the Arbitrator with the Dual Role

The dual role of the arbitrator requires different competencies to be employed during the adjudicative and settlement-oriented parts of the process, which are often diametrically opposed.[85] This issue is particularly true when the arbitrator becomes extensively involved in the settlement efforts while implementing mediation elements such as caucusing or engaging in hybrid arbitration and mediation processes.[86] The adjudicative role of the arbitrator is mostly confined to adversary hearings during which evidence and arguments are presented, and the arbitrator delivers a binding decision.[87] Throughout the proceedings, the arbitrator should be capable of rendering decisions based on the differences between the parties while basing the final and binding award on legal grounds and the presented facts.[88] In addition, the adjudicative role requires

82. Stipanowich, 2021a, pp. 276, 289, 345; Stipanowich & Fraser, 2017, p. 882. Empirical data presented in the next section supports this reasoning.
83. Yip, 2021, pp. 192-194; Stipanowich, 2021a, pp. 288-289; Gu, 2019, p. 133; Ludington, 2017, p. 316; Stipanowich & Ulrich, 2014b, p. 26; Stipanowich & Kaskell, 2001, p. 21.
84. Kun, 2020b, pp. 329-330; Kaufmann-Kohler, 2009, pp. 200-202, 204; Sussman, 2010b, pp. 333-337; Bantekas, 2015, pp. 29-32.
85. Ortolani, 2025, §21.4; Stipanowich, 2021a, p. 288; Stipanowich & Mironi, 2021, p. 31; Gu, 2019, p. 133; Nigmatullina, 2018, pp. 57-58; Ludington, 2017, p. 316; Harris, 2016, p. 94; Blankley, 2011, p. 319; Kun, 2011b, p. 550; Sussman, 2010a, pp. 381-382; Stipanowich & Kaskell, 2001, pp. 23-24, 32; Bartel, 1991, pp. 688-689; Pitkowitz & Richter, 2009, p. 226; De Vera, 2004, p. 159.
86. Gu, 2019, p. 133; Nigmatullina, 2018, p. 59; Bühring-Uhle et al., 2006, pp. 248-250.
87. Stipanowich, 2021a, p. 288; Gu, 2019, p. 133; Harris, 2016, p. 94; Sussman, 2010a, p. 391; Stipanowich & Kaskell, 2001, p. 21; CIArb Practice Guideline on the Use of Mediation in Arbitration, 2021, Article 3(1).
88. Ortolani, 2025, §21.4; Nigmatullina, 2018, p. 58; Lew, 2005, p. 425; Gu, 2019, p. 133.

the arbitrator to keep a distance from the parties to maintain strict impartiality and neutrality, which usually removes ex parte communications from their professional toolbox.[89] To a large extent, the arbitrator's adjudicative role resembles a judicial role. It requires good knowledge of the law, the skills of a decision-maker, the ability to manage the proceedings effectively, and, above all, judicial etiquette.[90]

In contrast, the role of a settlement facilitator is to find a consensual, efficient, and value-creating resolution of the dispute.[91] For this purpose, the neutral needs to understand the underlying interests and the real preferences of the disputants, mainly through a reality-testing process that works particularly well during caucuses and exposure to confidential information.[92] This role of the neutral requires mastery of many psychological skills, including an awareness of interpersonal dynamics and building trust between adversaries, as well as developed negotiation skills and creativity.[93] Furthermore, the role requires a developed understanding of cultural differences fundamental to the settlement process in cross-border disputes.[94] Accordingly, facilitating a settlement requires the neutral to maintain a well-developed, sometimes close personal relationship with the disputants.[95]

These different skills required for each of the adversarial and settlement-facilitating components of the dual role may lead to legitimate questions about the qualifications and suitability of the arbitrator to conduct both roles in the same process:

> Since the essential functions of mediators and arbitrators are often perceived as fundamentally different, experience and competence as a mediator does not automatically qualify an individual to perform the role of arbitrator. Some excellent mediators may not have the temperament, managerial skills or procedural knowledge to be effective arbitrators. Similarly, many arbitrators lack the ability to be effective mediators.[96]

89. Bühring-Uhle et al., 2006, pp. 248-250; Gu, 2019, p. 133; Nigmatullina, 2018, p. 58; Stipanowich, 2021a, p. 288; CIArb Practice Guideline on the Use of Mediation in Arbitration, 2021, Article 3(2).
90. Ludington, 2017, p. 316; Nigmatullina, 2018, p. 58; Gu, 2019, p. 133; Mason, 2011, p. 543; Kun, 2011b, p. 551; Sussman, 2010a, p. 391.
91. Stipanowich, 2021a, pp. 288-289; Kun, 2011b, p. 551; Sussman, 2010a, p. 391; Nigmatullina, 2018, p. 57; Stipanowich & Kaskell, 2001, p. 21; CIArb Practice Guideline on the Use of Mediation in Arbitration, 2021, Article 3(4).
92. Ortolani, 2025, §21.4; Gu, 2019, p. 133; Bühring-Uhle et al., 2006, p. 248; Sussman, 2010a, p. 391; Stipanowich, 2021a, p. 289; Nigmatullina, 2018, pp. 57-58; Lew, 2005, p. 425; Stipanowich & Kaskell, 2001, p. 21; Stipanowich & Ulrich, 2014b, pp. 25-26; Harris, 2016, p. 95; CIArb Practice Guideline on the Use of Mediation in Arbitration, 2021, Article 3(4).
93. Ludington, 2017, p. 316; Kun, 2011b, p. 551; Sussman, 2010a, p. 391; Nigmatullina, 2018, p. 58; Mason, 2011, p. 543. For further discussion of the arbitrator's role as a settlement facilitator from a psychological perspective, *see* Nappert & Flader, 2011.
94. Thevenin, 2013, p. 374; Barker, 1996, pp. 17-19; Cheng, 2010; Dress, 1988, pp. 570-571; Pair, 2002, p. 58.
95. Gu, 2019, p. 133; Nigmatullina, 2018, p. 58; Bühring-Uhle et al., 2006, p. 248.
96. Stipanowich, 2021a, p. 289. *See also* Yip, 2021, p. 194; Benzidi, 2017, p. 9; Deason, 2013, pp. 224, 228-229; Sussman, 2010a, pp. 390-391; Mason, 2011, p. 542; Stipanowich & Ulrich, 2014b, p. 26; Stipanowich & Kaskell, 2001, p. 23; Nigmatullina, 2018, p. 58; Ludington, 2017, p. 316; Blankley, 2011, p. 336.

Consequently, many neutrals prefer to avoid the dual role.[97] Contributing to this attitude is that the qualifications of arbitrators and ADR neutrals usually have little in common and are, in many cases, local in nature.[98] Nevertheless, even if the neutral is trained and experienced in both roles, fulfilling the dual role in the same process may still present unique challenges that do not necessarily arise when the processes are conducted separately.[99] For instance, a dual-role neutral can find it difficult to switch between serving as a problem-solver and a decision-maker, or exhaust their entire energy to settle the dispute amicably when the parties may eventually ask them to formally decide the dispute.[100]

Empirical data supports the impact of the aforementioned challenges on the willingness of neutrals to engage with the dual role in resolving business disputes. The Straus Institute conducted a 2014 survey among members of the International Academy of Mediators regarding their experience playing dual roles as arbitrators and mediators in the same disputes (2014 Straus Institute Survey).[101] According to the collected data, 36% of respondents expressed hesitancy to play a dual role in the same dispute for reasons including a lack of interest or comfort in serving as an arbitrator and inadequate training or qualifications for this adjudicative role.[102] These results align with the findings of the 2013 Straus Institute Survey,[103] where the arbitrators' reluctance to serve in the dual role was explained, among other reasons, by insufficient qualifications for both roles and the fundamental disjunction between the nature of arbitration and mediation processes.[104]

Hence, selecting the right neutral for the dual role is crucial to overcoming its challenges and increasing the chances of settling the dispute amicably.[105] Additionally, the neutral should possess skills, qualifications, and experience in each role to implement this mandate successfully and effectively,[106] with a significant understanding of the cross-cultural context of international business disputes.[107] Equally important is that the neutral enjoys the trust of parties and their counsel,[108] as "the success

97. Stipanowich, 2021a, p. 349; Nigmatullina, 2018, p. 59; Bühring-Uhle et al., 2006, p. 250; Pappas, 2015, p. 201.
98. Born, 2021, §2.02[C][2][c]; Sussman, 2010a, p. 391; Nigmatullina, 2018, p. 58; Sussman, 2009a, p. 73.
99. Stipanowich, 2021a, p. 289; Nigmatullina, 2018, p. 59.
100. Nigmatullina, 2018, p. 59; Stipanowich, 2021a, pp. 348-349; Mason, 2011, p. 545; Bartel, 1991, p. 689; Phillips, G. F., 2009, p. 76.
101. Stipanowich, 2021a, pp. 287-289.
102. Stipanowich, 2021a, p. 289.
103. *See* the discussion in section 2.2.1.
104. Stipanowich & Ulrich, 2014b, pp. 25-26.
105. Yip, 2021, p. 194; Stipanowich & Mironi, 2021, p. 30; Stipanowich, 2021a, p. 349; Costa Braga de Oliveira, 2009, p. 90; Blankenship, 2006, p. 36; Bartel, 1991, pp. 687-688; Nigmatullina, 2018, p. 57; Blankley, 2011, p. 337; Najar, 2009, pp. 523-524.
106. Stipanowich, 2021a, pp. 348-349; Stipanowich & Mironi, 2021, p. 31; Benzidi, 2017, p. 31; Ludington, 2017, p. 316; Nigmatullina, 2018, p. 57; Stipanowich & Ulrich, 2014b, p. 26; Weisman, 2013, p. 41; Ross, 2013, p. 366; Kun, 2011b, pp. 550-551; Weisman, 2011, p. 4; Rosoff, 2009, p. 97; Phillips, G. F., 2009, p. 78; Bühring-Uhle et al., 2006, p. 265; De Vera, 2004, p. 159; Bartel, 1991, pp. 679, 688-689; Leon & Peterson, 2009, p. 92; Abramson, 1999, p. 8.
107. Thevenin, 2013, p. 374.
108. Sussman, 2010a, p. 391; Stipanowich & Mironi, 2021, p. 30; Stipanowich, 2021a, p. 349; Weisman, 2013, p. 41; Ross, 2013, p. 366; Blankenship, 2006, p. 34; Nigmatullina, 2018, p. 60; Phillips, G. F., 2009, p. 78; Marriott, 2005, p. 544.

of any dispute resolution method often depends on the quality of the neutral"[109] and "arbitration is only as good as its arbitrators."[110] Thus, arbitral processes allowing the arbitrator to act as a settlement facilitator should not be an exception.

4.4.2 The Nature of the Dispute

According to some scholars and practitioners, certain categories of disputes are unsuitable for settlement, which omits the arbitrator's role as a settlement facilitator from the resolution process.[111] One category not necessarily related to commercial disputes is the arbitration of sports disputes involving doping and disciplinary matters. The argument is that facilitating a settlement in such disputes is incompatible with public interests due to the need to treat the athletes equally.[112] Another category highly connected to ICA is the arbitration of investor-state disputes. The argument is that, unlike private commercial disputes, where the incentive to settle is mainly due to the negotiators since any compensation imposed would "come out of their pocket,"[113] the settlement of investor-state disputes may undermine strong public interests and rights of third parties that are insufficiently represented, if at all, in the arbitral process:

> A significant number of investment arbitration cases involve investment in public service sectors and public utilities; investment claims arising out of emergency economic measures or civil unrest; and cases that revolve around issues of public health, environmental regulation, and human rights, in general. Moreover, investor-state cases often involve allegations of state misconduct and corruption, ... and the payment of compensation in connection with any arising arbitration awards is borne by the taxpayers of the host state. All these factors are to the interest of the local population as the objectives of foreign investors, governments, and local populations are oftentimes conflicting.[114]

This section discusses the arbitrator's role as a settlement facilitator in investor-state disputes to examine whether this arbitration type should exclude the role of the arbitrator and whether it is justified to distinguish between the settlement of "regular" commercial versus investor-state disputes.

---

109. Nigmatullina, 2018, p. 57. *See also* Bartel, 1991, p. 688.
110. Hacking, 2011, p. 224. *See also* Ross, 2013, p. 366; Kun, 2011b, p. 550; Cremades, 1998, p. 157.
111. Kun, 2020b, pp. 329-330; Kaufmann-Kohler, 2009, pp. 200-202, 204; Sussman, 2010b, pp. 333-337; Bantekas, 2015, pp. 29-32.
112. These matters are normally excluded from negotiated settlements since they are considered more similar to criminal sanctions that can affect the interests of other competitors and the sport community in general. However, according to the Code of Sports-Related Arbitration, when the dispute relates to commercial issues, the arbitral tribunal may conciliate that dispute. *See* Kaufmann-Kohler, 2009, pp. 193-194, 204; Newmark, 2002, p. 82; Code of Sports-Related Arbitration, 2023, Article 42.
113. Sussman, 2010b, p. 337.
114. Ali & Repousis, 2017, p. 227. *See also* Kun, 2020b, pp. 329-330; Kaufmann-Kohler, 2009, p. 200; Blackaby & Richard, 2010, pp. 253-255; Brower & Blanchard, 2014, pp. 719-720; Boisson de Chazoumes, 2005, pp. 105-108.

4.4.2.1 *Barriers to Settlement Facilitation in Investor-State Disputes*

The literature lists the following barriers to settlement in investor-state disputes, which affect the ability and, in some cases, the legitimacy of the arbitrator to facilitate a settlement. *First*, settlements in investment disputes may not be practical because, unlike the private sector, a clear decision-maker does not always exist due to multiple stakeholders across the bureaucratic and political levels who may need to approve or relate to the settlement, let alone possible conflicting perspectives and priorities between them.[115] *Second*, the involvement of manifold governmental and political levels, alongside the complexity of the disputes, cannot guarantee a shorter or less expensive process, especially when arbitration is placed on hold to facilitate or mediate a settlement.[116] *Third*, since parties to investor-state disputes may have a mutual interest in keeping their business relationship, they likely initiate arbitral proceedings only after exhausting the "cooling-off period" provided under many investment treaties to allow preliminary—and under many treaties also obligatory—steps to resolve the dispute, including direct negotiations, settlement committees, conciliation, and mediation.[117] The chances of amicably resolving the dispute are low following such efforts. Therefore, the arbitrator should avoid facilitating a settlement to avoid additional delays and costs.[118] *Fourth*, host states may view investors' claims as a direct attack on their sovereignty and right to regulate their affairs and, as a result, should refrain from settlement.[119] *Fifth*, facilitating a settlement, which usually maintains confidentiality as an inherent part of the process, may not be consistent with the growing trend of transparency and participation of third parties in investor-state arbitration to better protect public interests.[120] *Sixth*, compromise on the part of host states may encourage other investors to pursue remedies or demand similar compensation and treatment from those states without having to prove their cases to a tribunal, which sets a bad precedent at the expense of the public purse.[121] *Seventh*, settlements in investor-state disputes may encourage a "regulatory chill" toward foreign investors instead of implementing a higher degree of regulation while stating the law in this domain.[122] *Eighth*, implementing a settlement by host states may require legislative amendments or specific budgetary authorizations, often making it easier for these states to have the

115. Kun, 2020b, p. 329; Sussman, 2010b, pp. 333-334; Kaufmann-Kohler, 2009, p. 202; Harvard Law Review, 2014, pp. 2547-2548.
116. Sussman, 2010b, p. 335.
117. Hioureas, 2019, p. 68; Ali & Repousis, 2017, pp. 229-237; Kun, 2020b, p. 331; Harvard Law Review, 2014, p. 2545; Thomas, 1999, pp. 115-119; Lee, 2001, p. 2669.
118. Kaufmann-Kohler, 2009, p. 201; Sussman, 2010b, p. 335.
119. Lopez-Rodriguez, 2017, p. 148; Johnson & Sachs, 2016, p. 11; Sussman, 2010b, p. 333; Choudhury, 2008, pp. 786-787.
120. Coe, 2010, p. 349, relating to recent trends in investor-state arbitration "in which hearings have sometimes been opened to the public, amicus participation has been allowed, and awards and other informative documents have been widely published."; Harvard Law Review, 2014, p. 2547. *See* further discussion on this subject in section 4.4.2.3 below.
121. Kun, 2020b, p. 329; Sussman, 2010b, p. 336; Kaufmann-Kohler, 2009, p. 202.
122. Ali & Repousis, 2017, p. 227; Tienhaara, 2011, p. 607; Miller et al., 2015; Kaufmann-Kohler, 2009, p. 200; Menkel-Meadow, 1985, pp. 500-502.

arbitral tribunal decide the dispute.[123] *Ninth*, host states may be subject to adverse public reactions or allegations of corruption regarding the investments in dispute. Hence, they can find it simpler to blame the tribunal for "imposing" a binding decision than voluntarily agreeing to the investor's demands, even partially, through settlement negotiations while increasing public or political criticism.[124] *Tenth*, as opposed to commercial arbitration, investor-state arbitration arguably has a more formal setting and fewer avenues for settlement, such as conciliation and mediation.[125]

Empirical data supports the impact of most of the aforementioned barriers to facilitating a settlement in investor-state disputes. A 2016 survey, conducted by the Centre for International Law of the National University of Singapore (2016 National University of Singapore Survey), asked 47 practitioners and scholars worldwide with substantial experience in investor-state arbitration to rank 29 possible obstacles to settling investor-state disputes.[126] Interestingly, 70% of the respondents thought the state party was more hesitant to settle these disputes.[127] The main barriers to settlement in descending order of influence were as follows: it is easier for the state to defer the responsibility of decision making to a third-party adjudicator; the dispute may become a political concern because of media coverage that pressures the state to take a firmer stance; the fear of public criticism; officials' struggling in obtaining budgetary approval for a settlement, as opposed to any sum awarded; disputes involving highly regulated, politicized, or sensitive industries and issues, such as extractive industries and civil aviation; the hierarchical nature of governmental decision making and the fact that various ministries and agencies may have different and even conflicting perspectives and priorities; the fear of possible prosecution for either alleged corruption or sacrificing the state's interests by negotiating a settlement; and the fear of setting a precedent for future demands and claims.[128] Consequently, it is no surprise that collected data from investor-state arbitration cases of the ICSID shows that arbitrators do not engage in the settlement facilitation of the disputes before them.[129]

4.4.2.2 *Settlements in Investor-State Disputes and the Rise of Mediation*

Other important aspects connected to settlement should be considered when examining the arbitrator's role as a settlement facilitator in investor-state disputes. *First*, although arbitrators in these disputes tend not to engage in settlement facilitation, according to recent data from the ICSID, approximately 36% of such arbitration cases

123. Kun, 2020b, p. 329; Sussman, 2010b, p. 335.
124. Hioureas, 2019, p. 68; Sussman, 2010b, pp. 323, 335; Kaufmann-Kohler, 2009, pp. 201-202; Coe, 2007; Kun, 2020b, pp. 329-330.
125. Kaufmann-Kohler, 2009, p. 202; Hioureas, 2019, p. 68; Coe, 2007; De Brabandere, 2014, p. 73.
126. Chew et al., 2018, pp. 1, 4; Kun, 2020b, p. 329.
127. Chew et al., 2018, pp. 1, 11; Kun, 2020b, p. 329.
128. Chew et al., 2018, pp. 28-29; Kun, 2020b, p. 329.
129. *ICSID: Caseload Statistics*, 2022, p. 14, indicating that none of the undecided disputes resulted from a settlement facilitated by the tribunal (contrary to settlement agreements concluded by the parties and embodied in arbitral awards following the parties' request). *See also* Nitschke, 2019, p. 140; Kaufmann-Kohler, 2009, p. 201.

are settled or discontinued due to direct negotiations between the parties.[130] This significant portion of settled disputes, let alone disputes settled before initiating arbitral proceedings, confirms that settlements constitute an integral part of investment disputes as in other international commercial disputes.[131] *Second*, investor-state arbitration has struggled to maintain its legitimacy and effectiveness.[132] Similar to concerns raised related to commercial arbitration, investor-state arbitration is currently referred to as a more confrontational, judicialized, lengthy, and costly mechanism for resolving disputes among parties,[133] with empirical data showing significant increases in costs and delays.[134] Consequently, more practitioners and scholars have offered mediation as a relatively more efficient alternative mechanism to resolve investor-state disputes, especially following the introduction of the Singapore Convention that potentially extends its international enforcement framework for mediated settlements resulting from investment disputes if they relate to commercial matters.[135] Mediation has also been praised as particularly beneficial in investment disputes with cross-cultural characteristics,[136] as well as in "cases where adjudication has reached its 'limits' such as in 'polycentric disputes' where there are no clear issues subject to proofs and contentions,"[137] which may create "jurisdictional chaos."[138]

A clear indication of the change in attitude by governments, institutions, and investors toward mediation as a settlement mechanism for investor-state disputes is its growing integration into bilateral and multilateral investment treaties.[139] A recent study of 2,572 bilateral investment treaties collected by the Investment Policy Hub's

130. *ICSID: Caseload Statistics*, 2022, p. 13. *See also* Ortolani, 2025, §21.3; Harvard Law Review, 2014, p. 2546.
131. Kaufmann-Kohler, 2009, p. 201.
132. Langford et al., 2020, p. 184; Scheu & Nikolov, 2021, p. 171.
133. Kun, 2020b, p. 327; Hioureas, 2019, pp. 67-68; Ali & Repousis, 2017, p. 233; Harvard Law Review, 2014, p. 2552.
134. UN Conference on Trade and Development, 2014, pp. 28-29, stating that "on average, costs, including legal fees (which on average amount to approximately 82% of total costs) and tribunal expenses, have exceeded $8 million per party per case" and that most arbitrations "take several years to conclude."; Kun, 2020b, p. 330, arguing, based on collected data about costs and duration of investor-state arbitration, that "the median length of arbitration proceedings is four years and four months and median costs are just over four-million dollars for claimants and almost three-and-a-half million for respondents." *See also* Ali & Repousis, 2017, pp. 233-234; Coe, 2010, pp. 343-344.
135. Schnabel, 2019, p. 22; Hioureas, 2019, p. 68; Ali & Repousis, 2017, pp. 234-235, 240-241; Ali, 2015, p. 137; Harvard Law Review, 2014, pp. 2543, 2554-2556. *See also* Kun, 2020b, p. 328, holding that considering "increasing distrust of investor-state arbitration, mediation regained its momentum as a method of resolving investor-state disputes." Although the Singapore Convention does not define the term "commercial," Article 1(1) of the Model Law on ICM, 2018, defines this term widely to cover various investor-state business relations, including factoring, construction of works, investments, business and industrial joint ventures, and different kinds of transportation industries.
136. Coe, 2010, p. 347; UNCITRAL Guidelines on Mediation of Investment Disputes, 2024, section H, paras. 17(g) & 20.
137. Ali & Repousis, 2017, p. 234; Ali, 2015, p. 137; Fuller, 1970, pp. 329-330.
138. Hyman & Kovacic, 2019, pp. 1460-1463.
139. Nitschke, 2019, p. 143; Kun, 2020b, pp. 331-337, reviewing many bilateral and multilateral investment treaties and agreements, including model ones, that refer to mediation as an alternative mechanism to arbitration or a supplementary method to implement during the

database of the UN Conference on Trade and Development (UNCTAD) found that almost 25% (624) of the treaties provided for mediation or conciliation as a primary mechanism to settle disputes or within an escalating mechanism of dispute resolution ending with arbitration (2020 UNCTAD Study).[140] More evidence of the increasing popularity of mediation in investor-state disputes is the 2012 IBA Rules for Investor-State Mediation,[141] which apply when parties to those disputes agree to mediate according to their terms or when the mediator or the mediation institute has adapted them in whole or in part following the authorization of the parties.[142] The rules were designed to allow mediation of investor-state disputes to be conducted as standalone processes or in conjunction with arbitration, mainly conducted under the ICSID or the UNCITRAL Arbitration Rules.[143] According to the IBA rules, the mediator may communicate or meet with the parties together or individually at any point throughout the proceedings. If, during a separate meeting, any information was provided only for the mediator's review, they cannot disclose it to the other party.[144] In addition, the mediation is confidential, and unless otherwise agreed upon by the disputants, no third parties are allowed to participate in its course or be exposed to its content.[145] Hence, documents and communications related to the mediation are confidential unless their disclosure is necessary for compliance with the legal duty of disclosure or a pre-existing legal disclosure obligation between the parties.[146] The IBA concept of mediating investor-state disputes has been implemented in a growing number of bilateral and multilateral trade agreements that specifically refer to mediation as an alternative or additional means of resolving investment disputes.[147] It was also assimilated in the current EU Model regarding investor-state disputes[148] and in the emerging model of the EU's investment and trade agreements that establish dedicated investment tribunals as part of their framework to replace the current investor-state dispute settlement mechanism.[149]

"cooling-off period" of the investment arbitration. *See* in this regard the recommendations detailed in sections D & M of the UNCITRAL Guidelines on Mediation of Investment Disputes, 2024.

140. Kun, 2020b, p. 331.
141. IBA Rules for Investor-State Mediation, 2012; Kun, 2020b, p. 338; Hioureas, 2019, pp. 68-69; Ali & Repousis, 2017, p. 238; Maniruzzaman, 2013.
142. IBA Rules for Investor-State Mediation, 2012, Article 1.
143. Nitschke, 2014, p. 128; Kun, 2020b, p. 338.
144. IBA Rules for Investor-State Mediation, 2012, Article 8(3)-(4).
145. IBA Rules for Investor-State Mediation, 2012, Article 10(1).
146. IBA Rules for Investor-State Mediation, 2012, Article 10(2)-(3).
147. Nitschke, 2019, p. 143, and the treaties listed there, including the EU-Canada Comprehensive Economic and Trade Agreement (CETA), the Trans-Pacific Partnership Trade Agreement, and the EU-Vietnam Free Trade Agreement.
148. Ali & Repousis, 2017, pp. 238-240; Hioureas, 2019, p. 69.
149. The CETA EU-Canada, for example, provides for mediation despite the establishment of an investment tribunal under the agreement. *See* CETA EU-Canada, 2017, Articles 8.20 & 8.27-8.29; Hioureas, 2019, p. 69; Winnington-Ingram & Kim, 2021, relating to similar arrangement under the investment and trade agreements between the EU and Singapore, Vietnam and Mexico.

An additional signal of the growing status of mediation as a legitimate mechanism to resolve investment disputes is the ICSID Mediation Rules introduced in 2022.[150] Similar to the IBA Rules for Investor-State Mediation, the ICSID rules are designed to "complement ICSID's existing rules for arbitration, conciliation, and fact-finding, and may be used either independently of, or in conjunction with, arbitration proceedings."[151] According to the rules, unless otherwise agreed or required by law, mediation and all related documents are confidential, including the fact that the mediation occurred.[152] Furthermore, unless otherwise agreed, the content of the mediation cannot be used by the parties in other proceedings.[153] The rules also stipulate that during mediation, the neutral is authorized to caucus with the disputants but is obliged to keep any information received ex parte confidential unless the relevant party agrees to its disclosure.[154]

Amid the ongoing global debate over the declining attractiveness of investor-state arbitration driven by increasing costs and delays,[155] UNCITRAL Working Group III (WGIII) initiated a reform of the investor-state dispute resolution regime to enhance its efficiency.[156] The UNCITRAL Guidelines on Mediation of Investment Disputes and the Model Provisions on Mediation of Investment Disputes were recently introduced as part of this initiative.[157] These instruments promote mediation as a cost-effective alternative for resolving investment disputes by enabling parties to retain control over the process and preserve their business relationships.[158] The Guidelines and Model Provisions refer to the mediation rules of the ICSID, the IBA, and UNCITRAL to facilitate investor-state mediation.[159] Additionally, they recommend the Singapore Convention as a suitable mechanism for enforcing mediated settlements and encourage parties to ensure that their settlement agreements comply with the enforcement requirements outlined in the Convention and the Model Law on ICM.[160] Consistent

150. ICSID Mediation Rules, 2022; Kun, 2020b, pp. 339-340; Nitschke, 2019, p. 143.
151. *ICSID rules and regulations: Mediation*, n.d. *See also* Kun, 2020b, p. 340.
152. ICSID Mediation Rules, 2022, Article 10.
153. ICSID Mediation Rules, 2022, Article 11.
154. ICSID Mediation Rules, 2022, Article 17(4).
155. Scheu & Nikolov, 2021, p. 171; Langford et al., 2020, p. 184; Harvard Law Review, 2014, p. 2549.
156. *UNCITRAL WGIII*, n.d., at Investor-State Dispute Settlement Reform.
157. UNCITRAL Guidelines on Mediation of Investment Disputes, 2024; UNCITRAL Model Provisions on Mediation of Investment Disputes, 2024.
158. UNCITRAL Guidelines on Mediation of Investment Disputes, 2024, sections B-C. Interestingly, initial draft of the text considered the possibility of promoting mandatory mediation for investor-state disputes, however this option was later abandoned. *See UNCITRAL WGIII*, n.d., at Initial Drafts on Reform Options—Initial draft on mediation and other forms of alternative dispute resolution (ADR), p. 9.
159. UNCITRAL Guidelines on Mediation of Investment Disputes, 2024, section F; UNCITRAL Model Provisions on Mediation of Investment Disputes, 2024, Provision 1(6). Like the ICSID and IBA investment mediation rules, the UNCITRAL Mediation Rules state that the mediation process is confidential, ex parte communications are allowed, and the mediator cannot disclose to other parties any confidential information delivered by one party during caucusing without its prior consent. Furthermore, unless otherwise agreed, the mediation's content cannot be used in other proceedings. *See* UNCITRAL Mediation Rules, 2021, Articles 5-7.
160. UNCITRAL Guidelines on Mediation of Investment Disputes, 2024, sections L-M; UNCITRAL Model Provisions on Mediation of Investment Disputes, 2024, Provision 5.

with the mediation rules they reference, the Model Provisions adopt a comprehensive confidentiality framework for investment mediation procedures.[161] While the Guidelines advise parties to consider whether third parties should be allowed to participate in the process to address public interest concerns or to enhance transparency for greater public acceptance and legitimacy of mediation outcomes,[162] these aspects remain subject to the parties' discretion unless such transparency and participation requirements are mandated, either partially or fully, by international agreements, domestic legislation, or the court systems of relevant jurisdictions.[163]

Thus, the mediation of investor-state disputes is already a *fait accompli*. According to some commentators, its popularity within such disputes will continue to increase, similar to international commercial disputes.[164] This important development in the settlement regime of investor-state disputes, alongside the aforementioned data regarding the significant portion of investment arbitrations settled through direct negotiations, should raise the question of whether categorically excluding investment disputes from settlement facilitation by arbitrators is warranted, as indeed happens in practice. As discussed in the next section, the involvement of arbitrators in the settlement process of investor-state disputes may bring significant advantages that cannot be offered by standalone mediation, including enhanced international enforceability of the settlement and better representation of public interests through the established arrangements under arbitration and transparency rules, which allow third parties to express their positions regarding the dispute and a wider disclosure and publication about the process.

4.4.2.3 The Arbitrator's Role in the Settlement of Investor-State Disputes

Investment arbitration has unique characteristics that distinguish it from commercial arbitration. To a large extent, it is an "arbitration without privity,"[165] so the dispute resolution is conducted according to an international treaty or agreement governed by public international law and based on principles intended to protect the investor, such as the principle of fair and equal treatment.[166] Moreover, arbitrators are more prominent in interpreting these principles according to the treaty's wording and possibly according to precedents in the matter.[167] Furthermore, monetary damages are the primary remedy for breach.[168] Nevertheless, most aspects of investor-state arbitral proceedings, including the tribunal's constitution, the applicable principles, and how

161. UNCITRAL Model Provisions on Mediation of Investment Disputes, 2024, Provision 4.
162. For example, this could include disclosing the fact that mediation is taking place, sharing part or all of the information presented or obtained during the process, and implementing protocols to provide public updates on the mediation's progress, including any settlements reached or its failure.
163. UNCITRAL Guidelines on Mediation of Investment Disputes, 2024, sections I (at para. 30) & K.
164. Kun, 2020b, p. 341; Hioureas, 2019, p. 68.
165. Paulsson, 1995, p. 232. *See also* Lopez-Rodriguez, 2017, pp. 146-147.
166. Lopez-Rodriguez, 2017, p. 147; Schill, 2011, pp. 59, 62, 87-88.
167. Schill, 2011, pp. 66-67, 80-83.
168. Lopez-Rodriguez, 2017, p. 147; Van Harten & Loughlin, 2006, pp. 131, 134; Baldwin et al., 2006, p. 1.

awards are rendered, are similar to those of ICA proceedings.[169] In addition, the role of the arbitrators in both procedures is quite similar:

> The role, function and qualifications of the arbitrator in investment treaty arbitration differ to a certain extent from those of the arbitrator in international commercial arbitration, and in fact resemble more those of the arbitrator in interstate disputes or even of judges in international judicial procedures. At the same time, to say that arbitrators in investment treaty arbitration have an entirely different role and function than arbitrators in international commercial arbitration would be an overstatement. The arbitral function and the qualifications of arbitrators generally have many common features in investment treaty arbitration, interstate arbitration, international commercial arbitration or even national arbitration, because of the common principles applicable to any arbitral procedure. One should also keep in mind that the powers and duties of arbitrators differ substantially from judges in national judicial proceedings, since an arbitral tribunal, contrary to judges in national courts, derives its powers and duties from the consent of the parties.[170]

When assessing the arbitrator's role as a settlement facilitator in investor-state disputes, the above-discussed barriers to settlement cannot be ignored. Indeed, considerations relating to the complexity of the disputes, failed previous attempts to settle, political involvement in the process, the multiplicity of decision-makers, public criticism, fear of bad precedents, and the possible need for legislative amendments or specific budgetary authorizations may burden the ability to facilitate a settlement in investment disputes more than in commercial disputes.[171] However, the fact that parties to investor-state disputes settle a significant portion of arbitral proceedings through direct negotiations and engage in standalone mediation processes that an increasing number of investment treaties have promoted demonstrates that these considerations cannot alone justify the restraint of arbitrators in facilitating settlements in investor-state arbitral proceedings. In addition, some barriers to settlement, such as the complexity of the disputes, the fact that preceding attempts to settle have failed, and the fear of bad precedents, also apply to ICA. However, arbitrators in those proceedings facilitate settlements. Even if the arbitrator's role in investment arbitration resembles judges in national courts or international judicial tribunals, as discussed in the next chapter, the growing attitude in many jurisdictions with Common and Civil Law systems allows and encourages judges to facilitate settlements in their cases for reasons of efficiency.[172]

A careful examination of arbitration and mediation rules connected with investor-state disputes reveals that arbitrators are authorized to facilitate settlements during arbitration and participate in hybrid processes involving arbitration and mediation. First, since a sizable portion of investor-state arbitrations are carried out under the UNCITRAL Arbitration Rules,[173] the arbitrator's recognized "proactive approach"

169. Lopez-Rodriguez, 2017, p. 147.
170. De Brabandere, 2014, p. 73.
171. Kaufmann-Kohler, 2009, p. 202.
172. Berger, 2018b, pp. 502-506; Kaufmann-Kohler, 2009, pp. 189-193.
173. De Brabandere, 2014, pp. 112-113; Scheu & Nikolov, 2021, p. 181, stating that in "intra-EU investment arbitration practice, ... about 55 percent of the cases are arbitrated under the ICSID

under those rules should equally apply to investor-state disputes. Similarly, the ICSID Arbitration Rules empower the tribunal to proactively handle all procedural matters, make the necessary orders for the proceeding, encourage partial agreements on key issues and facts to narrow the differences, and promote a dispute settlement.[174] Hence, the tribunal should order at least one case management conference to narrow the disputed issues and address substantive or procedural matters related to resolving the differences.[175] In addition, the tribunal is authorized to bifurcate the arbitral process[176] and, when a settlement is concluded, to record its terms as an award.[177] Analogous powers are conferred to the tribunal under the Investment Arbitration Rules of the Singapore International Arbitration Centre (SIAC), including the duty to conduct case management conferences throughout the proceedings to discuss the most efficient procedures to resolve the dispute in a fair, expeditious, economical and final way.[178] Furthermore, the tribunal is authorized to direct the order of the proceedings, bifurcate the disputed matters, and order presentations on issues; its decision may resolve the case in full or in part.[179] According to the SIAC rules, subject to the parties' request, the tribunal may also decide the case on equitable grounds[180] and record a settlement as a consent award.[181]

In addition to encouraging the proactive role of the arbitrator, the ICSID Arbitration Rules allow the arbitrator to act as a mediator in the same dispute:

> A person previously involved in the resolution of the dispute as a conciliator, judge, mediator or in a similar capacity may be appointed as an arbitrator only by agreement of the parties.[182]

This recognition of the arbitrator's role as a mediator, viewed by some commentators as corresponding with the mandate originally intended for the ICSID,[183] can also be inferred from the ICSID Mediation Rules, although they implement an opposite

Convention, whereas the other 45 percent are conducted within the framework of the NYC [New York Convention] under the arbitration rules of UNCITRAL." The Permanent Court of Arbitration (PCA), for example, relies heavily on UNCITRAL Arbitration Rules in investment arbitration. *See PCA: Application of UNCITRAL Rules*, n.d. (stating that UNCITRAL Arbitration Rules, as well as UNCITRAL Rules on Transparency in Investor-State Arbitration, should by default apply to investor-state arbitrations).

174. Obadia, 1999, p. 10, holding that so long as the parties' autonomy is maintained the tribunal in investment arbitrations is entitled to "take an active role in helping the parties to reach an amicable settlement." *See also* Stevens & Love, 2010, pp. 408-409; Braun, 2010, p. 388; Shihata, 1986, p. 10.
175. ICSID Arbitration Rules, 2022, Article 31.
176. ICSID Arbitration Rules, 2022, Article 42.
177. ICSID Arbitration Rules, 2022, Article 55(2).
178. SIAC Investment Arbitration Rules, 2017, Article 16.
179. SIAC Investment Arbitration Rules, 2017, Article 16(4).
180. SIAC Investment Arbitration Rules, 2017, Article 28(2).
181. SIAC Investment Arbitration Rules, 2017, Article 30(10).
182. ICSID Arbitration Rules, 2022, Article 13(4).
183. Stevens & Love, 2010, p. 408, claiming that "ICSID itself has acknowledged and shown in the past that it was minded to fulfil a more active role in promoting amicable settlements."; Shihata, 1995, p. 449, holding that helping the parties to reach an agreed settlements would help the ICSID to fulfil its broad mandate optimally as those settlements bring the confidence needed "to increasing the flow of international investment."

default standard stipulating that "unless the parties and the mediator agree otherwise, a mediator may not act as arbitrator ... in any proceeding relating to the issues in dispute in the mediation."[184] Identical arrangements are also anchored in the IBA Rules for Investor-State Mediation and the UNCITRAL Mediation Rules.[185] Furthermore, the recently introduced UNCITRAL Code of Conduct for Arbitrators in Investment Arbitration does not prohibit arbitrators from acting as mediators in the same dispute. Instead, it imposes default periodic limitations on arbitrators acting as legal representatives or expert witnesses in matters related to the same dispute—limitations the parties can entirely waive.[186] While the Code prohibits arbitrators from engaging in private communications with the parties on procedural or substantive issues related to the dispute—a provision that may be interpreted as an effective ban on ex parte communications for settlement facilitation—this prohibition applies exclusively to the arbitration process.[187] Since the Code does not prevent neutrals from acting as both arbitrators and mediators, there appears to be no obstacle to substantive ex parte communications conducted during clearly distinct and separate settlement efforts, as customary in scenarios involving a segregated settlement phase within a standalone arbitration or during the mediation stage of an Arb-Med-Arb process.[188] In addition, in most investor-state arbitrations, the tribunal is composed of three arbitrators, enabling the employment of only a subset of the arbitrators in settlement efforts involving caucusing to mitigate some concerns connected with this practice.[189]

Hence, the rules and guidelines governing investor-state arbitration and mediation acknowledge the arbitrator's role as a settlement facilitator. Similar to ICA, settlement initiatives of arbitrators in investor-state proceedings can be placed on a continuum, starting with minimal or indirect involvement intended to set the stage for a settlement to be concluded through negotiations between the parties and ending with direct involvement in the settlement efforts, including through hybrid processes that permit ex parte communications with the disputants. Consequently, there are no compelling reasons to categorically exclude the arbitrator's role as a settlement facilitator in investment arbitration. This dual role can deliver many of the benefits typically associated with the mediation of investor-state disputes, such as preserving business relationships, exploring innovative and flexible solutions beyond rigid legal remedies, maintaining control over the process, narrowing the scope of disputes,

184. ICSID Mediation Rules, 2022, Article 14(7).
185. IBA Rules for Investor-State Mediation, 2012, Article 7(5); UNCITRAL Mediation Rules, 2021, Article 12. Similar provision is anchored also in Article 13 of the Model Law on ICM, 2018, discussed in section 6.3.2.5.
186. UNCITRAL Code of Conduct for Arbitrators in Investment Arbitration, 2024, Article 4 & paras. 29-37 of the commentary to the code.
187. UNCITRAL Code of Conduct for Arbitrators in Investment Arbitration, 2024, Article 7(3) & paras. 49-55 to the commentary to the code.
188. *See* in this regard the recommendation in section 7.3.1.3 to establish a clear demarcation between the formal arbitration and the settlement phases.
189. *See* the discussion and proposals in section 7.4.5.

improving compliance rates with arbitral awards, and fostering an increased awareness of the cross-cultural dimensions of international disputes.[190]

The arbitrator's role as a settlement facilitator in investment disputes offers additional significant advantages that are not achievable through standalone investor-state mediation, relegating mediation to a "supplementary gap-filling mechanism" in investment arbitration, as is the case in ICA disputes.[191] *First*, the enforcement mechanisms provided under the ICSID and the New York Conventions offer established and reliable routes for facilitated or mediated investment disputes that are converted into arbitral awards.[192] In contrast, the initial status of the enforcement mechanism under the Singapore Convention[193] may render it particularly challenging to enforce mediated settlements against sovereign states,[194] let alone its limited applicability to commercial disputes, which, despite their wide definition under the Model Law on ICM, may not cover all aspects of investor-state relations.[195] However, as noted by many scholars and practitioners, to guarantee enforceability under the ICSID and the New York Conventions, settlement efforts should commence only after the arbitral tribunal has been constituted, as in other forms of commercial arbitration. Otherwise, courts may decide "that such consent awards are not enforceable because there was no 'dispute' before the tribunal for the purposes of jurisdiction."[196] *Second*, unlike standalone investment mediation, which is highly retrogressive in terms of transparency in favor of strict confidentiality,[197] an arbitral process that authorizes arbitrators to facilitate or mediate settlements can better balance confidentiality with the growing duty of the tribunal to consider public interests when deciding investment disputes, as required by the Convention on Transparency in Treaty-based Investor-State Arbitration, the UNCITRAL Rules on Transparency in Investor-State Arbitration, the ICSID Arbitration Rules, and other institutional rules and guidelines, all of which apply mandatory arrangements regarding transparency and participation of third parties in investment arbitrations.[198] An effective equilibrium point between these

---

190. Kun, 2020b, pp. 330-331; Ali & Repousis, 2017, p. 234; Sussman, 2010b, pp. 323, 329-332; Coe, 2010, pp. 345-347.
191. Ali & Repousis, 2017, p. 248. *See also* Timothy, 2015; Coe, 2010, p. 342; the discussion in section 3.6.2 regarding the suitability of mediation for large-size disputes.
192. New York Convention, 1958, Article III; ICSID Convention, 1966, Article 54; ICSID Arbitration Rules, 2022, Article 55.
193. *See* the discussion in section 3.6.2.
194. Ali & Repousis, 2017, p. 248; Sussman, 2010b, p. 336; Harvard Law Review, 2014, pp. 2545-2546.
195. *See* the discussion in section 4.4.2.2 above.
196. Hioureas, 2019, p. 69. *See also* Kun, 2020b, p. 340, suggesting recording a mediated investor-state settlement as an arbitral award only if that settlement was reached "through mediation during an arbitration," leaving Med-Arb processes vulnerable to enforcement objections. In addition, *see* the discussion in section 3.6.3 about the need to constitute the tribunal before concluding the settlement as an arbitral award to guarantee its safe enforcement.
197. Coe, 2010, p. 349.
198. Convention on Transparency in Investor-State Arbitration, 2014, Articles 1-2 (applying the UNCITRAL Rules on Transparency in Investor-State Arbitration to all investor-state arbitrations under any bilateral or multilateral treaty, regardless the application of the UNCITRAL Arbitration Rules on those arbitrations); UNCITRAL Rules on Transparency in Investor-State Arbitration, 2014, Article 1 (stating that due to public interests "the disputing parties may not derogate from these Rules, by agreement or otherwise, unless permitted to do so by the treaty"), Articles

opposing values, which can increase the confidence of all concerned parties in the settlement process, may be achieved when confidentiality is applied to all parts of the settlement stage, while limited to that stage.[199] By implementing this proposed procedural safeguard, the disputants can approach the settlement negotiations candidly without third-party involvement or exposure of their discussions. Additionally, during caucusing, the disputants can share further information and positions with the tribunal that they prefer not to disclose to the opposing side. Simultaneously, third parties representing public interests may participate in the broader arbitral process or submit relevant observations to the tribunal, ensuring that public concerns are acknowledged and considered. The trust of third parties in the settlement process can be further enhanced when only a subset of the tribunal members conducts the settlement negotiations, thereby reinforcing the separation between the settlement phase and the formal arbitral proceedings. Moreover, since the settlement facilitator is aware of the tribunal's duty to render an enforceable award,[200] they are incentivized to promote a balanced and fair resolution that considers public interests. Otherwise, third parties may challenge the published award's enforceability.[201] The settlement facilitator can also highlight the importance of public interests during joint and separate meetings with the parties, encouraging them to consider these interests as integral to the resolution of the dispute.

2-3 (allowing comprehensive publication of information and documents from the arbitral proceedings, including all written statements and submissions, written submissions by third parties, a table listing all exhibits, transcripts of hearings, decisions and awards of the arbitral tribunal), and Articles 4-5 (allowing submissions by third persons and non-disputing parties to the bilateral or multilateral investment treaty); ICSID Arbitration Rules, 2022, Articles 62-65 (allowing publication of awards, decisions and documents, as well as observation of the hearings) and Articles 67-68 (allowing submissions by and participation of non-disputing parties in the arbitral process); SCC Arbitration Rules, 2023, Appendix III, Article 3(1), stating that "any person that is neither a disputing party nor a non-disputing treaty party ... may apply to the Arbitral Tribunal for permission to make a written submission in the arbitration." *See also* Born, 2021, §1.04[C][5] & §20.11[A]; Kun, 2020b, pp. 329-330; Ali & Repousis, 2017, pp. 241-246; Calamita, 2014, pp. 650-653; Sussman, 2010b, p. 336; Schill, 2015, pp. 201-204; Schill, 2014, pp. 369-372; Johnson, 2014, pp. 1-3; Coe, 2010, p. 349; Atik, 2004, pp. 149-150.

199. From a formal point of view, this arrangement can be justified on two grounds. *First*, according to the UNCITRAL Rules on Transparency in Investor-State Arbitration, 2014, Article 6(1), transparency applies to "hearings for the presentation of evidence or for oral argument." As the settlement process does not include formal presentation of evidence or formal oral argument, especially when carried out by part of the tribunal's members, it can be argued that it is not a "hearing" for the purpose of the duty of transparency. *Second*, even if the settlement process qualifies as a "hearing," according to Articles 6(2) & 7 of the rules, the tribunal is authorized to apply confidentiality to protect "confidential business information." As settlement negotiations relate regularly to confidential business information, which may be interpreted in wide terms, it is possible to argue that the settlement process justifies full confidentiality.

200. Stipanowich, 2021a, p. 344; Horvath, 2001, p. 135; Nigmatullina, 2018, p. 67; Marzolini, 2016, p. 117; Lew, 2005, p. 425.

201. *See* in this regard SCIA Arbitration Rules, 2022, Article 49(3), which authorizes the tribunal to refuse recording a settlement agreement as an arbitral award if it may harm public interests, including interests of third parties to the dispute.

4.5 CONCLUSIONS

Alongside the significant advantages discussed in the previous chapter, the arbitrator's role as a settlement facilitator raises several concerns, primarily stemming from the dual mandate to *decide* the dispute and *facilitate* an amicable resolution. These concerns can be categorized into three main groups. The first group involves fundamental issues related to due process rights, including party autonomy, impartiality, and the right to be heard. These concerns, often associated with caucusing, exposure to confidential information, coercive behavior by the arbitrator, and, in some jurisdictions, the expression of evaluative views, can undermine the procedure's integrity and jeopardize the enforceability of its outcomes. The second group relates to participants' hesitance toward the settlement process, which includes parties' tactical use of the settlement stage, reluctance to negotiate openly, and arbitrators' hesitation to facilitate settlement due to various factors such as personal preferences, professional considerations, and the influence of their legal background. While these reservations may not directly challenge enforceability, they can inhibit the likelihood of achieving an amicable resolution. The third group encompasses external concerns affecting the process and its outcomes. A critical issue within this group is the arbitrator's suitability for the dual role, which demands a unique combination of skills not typically required when adjudicative and facilitative functions are performed separately. Selecting a skilled, trusted, and experienced neutral is thus critical for ensuring both efficacy and enforceability. Another external concern, particularly relevant to investor-state disputes, is the appropriateness of settlement given public interest considerations. Although empirical data shows arbitrators rarely facilitate settlements in these disputes, this chapter argues against categorically excluding the dual role in such cases. Various rules and guidelines recognize the arbitrator's dual role in investment arbitration. This role offers significant advantages, including enhanced enforceability and better protection of public interests, which the current investment mediation framework cannot guarantee. However, from an enforceability perspective, it is generally safer to initiate settlement efforts only after the tribunal is constituted, as is customary in other ICA processes. Consequently, Med-Arb outcomes are often more vulnerable to enforcement challenges than arbitral awards.

Based on this discussion and those in previous chapters, in principle, there should be no objections to arbitrators' settlement efforts when implemented within the procedural framework of arbitration or while exercising their managerial authority over the process. Concerns arise primarily when arbitrators engage directly in settlement efforts—particularly through caucusing, exposure to confidential information, or the expression of evaluative views—or when they coerce disputants into a settlement, thereby undermining party autonomy. As such concerns are most prominent in hybrid processes combining arbitration with mediation, critics of the dual role are usually raised in their regard. A possible approach to address these concerns is to limit the arbitrator's role to procedural authority while excluding direct involvement in the settlement efforts. However, this restrictive approach may disregard parties' needs and preferences. A more moderate solution is to permit settlement facilitation only after arbitration has concluded, as is customary in the basic setting of Arb-Med, to avoid the effect of caucusing, confidential information, and evaluative opinions on the subsequent award.[202] Nonetheless, as discussed in the previous chapter, this option is unattractive in terms of efficiency, let alone the coercive effect of the sealed award on the subsequent settlement efforts.[203] Consequently, Arb-Med remains one of the least favored hybrid processes.[204] A more attractive solution is to conduct settlement efforts during arbitration or within an Arb-Med-Arb hybrid framework. This flexible approach addresses enforceability concerns by initiating settlement efforts only after the arbitration process has commenced. Early settlement efforts can reduce costs and time while preserving business relationships. Furthermore, this approach can mitigate concerns regarding the arbitrator's dual role by incorporating procedural safeguards, such as measures to handle confidential information disclosed during settlement negotiations and providing opt-out options for parties following unsuccessful settlement attempts. This outline may not eliminate all risks resulting from the arbitrator's dual role.[205] Nevertheless, it is important to recognize that no dispute-resolution method is entirely risk-free,[206] particularly when designating potentially conflicting responsibilities to the neutral. Therefore, the focus should shift from attempting to eliminate risks to effectively mitigating and managing them.

The next chapter examines how various legal systems perceive and regulate the arbitrator's dual role, addressing the aforementioned concerns associated with its practice. By drawing insights from these experiences, this analysis aims to support a comprehensive exploration of the potential for unified standards governing the arbitrator's role as a settlement facilitator.

202. Dendorfer & Lack, 2007, p. 82; Deason, 2013, 222; Fullerton, 2009, p. 59.
203. Dendorfer & Lack, 2007, pp. 87-88.
204. Deason, 2013, p. 222.
205. Kaufmann-Kohler, 2009, p. 200; Nigmatullina, 2018, p. 183; CIArb Practice Guideline on the Use of Mediation in Arbitration, 2021, Article 8(3).
206. Marriott, 2005, p. 546.

Part III The Arbitrator's Role as a Settlement Facilitator in ICA: The Transition from Domestic Legal Traditions Toward Transnational Standards

CHAPTER 5

Diverse Domestic Approaches to the Arbitrator's Role as a Settlement Facilitator

5.1 INTRODUCTION

Whether arbitrators in ICA should be directly involved in facilitating an amicable settlement in a pending dispute, and if so, how far their involvement can go, has not yet reached a transnational consensus.[1] Apart from individual approaches and preferences of arbitration practitioners and users in this matter,[2] the empirical data below confirms that the views about this involvement are influenced by the legal culture[3] of those practitioners and users, as well as by the practice of the judiciary and of arbitral tribunals in their home jurisdictions.[4] Therefore, before addressing the subject from an international perspective, it may be essential to examine it from the perspective of

1. Kun, 2020a, p. 130; Berger, 2018b, p. 501; Berger & Jensen, 2017, pp. 888-889; Kaufmann-Kohler, 2009, p. 189; Hwang, 2005, pp. 571-581; Nariman, 2005, pp. 531-532; Harris, 2016, p. 89.
2. Stipanowich, 2021a, pp. 276, 289, 345; Stipanowich & Fraser, 2017, p. 882; Stipanowich & Ulrich, 2014b, pp. 25-26; Kaufmann-Kohler, 2003, p. 1331.
3. In this context, legal culture expresses the values held in a geographical or ethnical boundaries regarding the legal system. It points to "differences in the way features of law are themselves embedded in larger frameworks of social structure and culture which constitute and reveal the place of law in society" (Nelken, 2011, p. 25) or to "those parts of general culture—customs, opinions, ways of doing and thinking—that bend social forces toward or away from the law" (Friedman, 1975, p. 15). *See also* Mitchell & Powell, 2011, pp. 20-21; Kun, 2016a, pp. 257-259; Nigmatullina, 2018, pp. 62-63; Ginsburg, 2003, p. 1336. The next chapter will relate to the cross-national aspects of legal culture, shaped by external forces such as the international community of professionals.
4. Born, 2021, §13.04[D]; Ortolani, 2025, §21.3; Stipanowich, 2021a, p. 276; Nigmatullina, 2018, pp. 62-64; Berger, 2018b, pp. 501-502; Stipanowich & Fraser, 2017, pp. 850-851; Marzolini, 2016, p. 108; Kun & Jemielniak, 2016, p. 557; Goodrich, 2012, p. 4; Kun, 2011b, pp. 536, 538-539; Ehle, 2010, pp. 79-80; Ali, 2020, §6.01-6.08; Kaufmann-Kohler, 2009, p. 189; Kaufmann-Kohler & Bonnin, 2007, pp. 79-85; Kaufmann-Kohler, 2003, p. 1331; Cremades, 1998, p. 164; Schneider, 1998, p. 78; Cohen, 1991, pp. 11-14; Baysal & Cevik, 2021; Chase & Bruner, 2005, pp. 62-65; Abramson, 1999, pp. 4-5.

different legal cultures and legal systems. This inquiry is of double importance since, in the era of globalization, local rules and norms may transform into transnational or influence internationally recognized norms,[5] while at the same time, "our own legal cultures remain, for the time being, in certain areas, an important limiting factor to harmonization."[6] In addition, despite their decreasing influence over international arbitration, national laws still govern most parts of those proceedings and are notably relevant for enforcing their outcomes.[7]

The arbitrator's role as a settlement facilitator has been approached by the academic literature, in particular legal theory, comparative law, and the study of globalization, mainly by comparing *Common Law systems*, which traditionally have not granted judges the power to facilitate settlements, and *Civil Law systems*, which traditionally have enabled judges to be involved in this role and observed it as an integral component of their professional duties.[8] When relating to non-Western legal experience regarding that role, a binary differentiation has normally been presented between *Western legal cultures*—introduced as traditionally litigious cultures that prefer individualism and legal certainty, and *Eastern legal cultures*—familiarized as traditionally conciliatory cultures that apply communitarian approaches to avoid social conflicts.[9] While this binary comparison may hold some truths regarding the role of judges and arbitrators in the "Eastern World," it may also transgress due to generalization and stereotyping that ignore the complex reality deriving from sub-Eastern cultures and differences between regions and jurisdictions,[10] as well as from the aforementioned individual approaches and preferences of practitioners and arbitration users. In fact, this transgression may also hold in the main comparison of the literature between Common Law and Civil Law systems in the West, as variations regarding the roles of judges and arbitrators can be observed among jurisdictions belonging to each of these legal systems.[11] Furthermore, this dichotomic approach may ignore that some

5. Kun, 2016a, pp. 250-251; Kun, 2013b, pp. 180, 215-218.
6. Lazareff, 1999, p. 1. *See also* Kun, 2016a, p. 251; Chase & Bruner, 2005, p. 49; Stipanowich, 2021a, p. 298.
7. Blackaby et al., 2022, §1.91 & §7.04-7.06; Brekoulakis, 2016b, p. 19; Kaufmann-Kohler, 2003, pp. 1315-1320. For further discussion about current influence of domestic law on international arbitral proceedings, *see* sections 8.3-8.4.
8. Born, 2021, §13.04[D]; Ortolani, 2025, §21.3; Berger, 2018b, pp. 502-506; Nigmatullina, 2018, pp. 64-65; Berger & Jensen, 2017, p. 889; De Gramont et al., 2017, pp. 964-972; Mayer, 2016, p. 3; Nottage & Garnett, 2010, pp. 35-36; Ehle, 2010, pp. 79-80; Cheng, 2010, pp. 424-426; Kaufmann-Kohler, 2009, pp. 190-192; Lew, 2005, p. 427; Burr, 2005, p. 63; Schneider, 1998, p. 78; Kun, 2013b, pp. 213-214.
9. Nigmatullina, 2018, pp. 68-70; Gu, 2019, p. 151; Deekshitha & Saha, 2014, pp. 84-85; Ehle, 2010, pp. 79-80; De Vera, 2004, p. 183; Cremades, 1998, pp. 158-159; Kun, 2016a, p. 251; Kun, 2016b, pp. 482-483; Kun, 2013a, p. 137; El-Ahdab & El-Ahdab, 2011, pp. 8-11; Ross, 2013, p. 354.
10. Gu, 2019, pp. 128, 151; Kun & Jemielniak, 2016, pp. 576-577; Nigmatullina, 2018, p. 64. *See also* Kun, 2016a, p. 251, arguing that East-West or Tradition-Modernity binaries derives from the West's legal orientalism that frames the East as lawless by virtue of its differences from the West. According to the author "such perception is based upon a misunderstanding of world history, which draws essentially on European history" and reflects "a misunderstanding of earlier societies, and a misunderstanding of our current situation."
11. Kun, 2020a, pp. 132-133; Born, 2021, §13.04[D]; Bühring-Uhle et al., 2006, pp. 110-111; Nigmatullina, 2018, pp. 64-69; Gu, 2019, pp. 152-160; Marzolini, 2016, pp. 108-110; Mitchell & Powell, 2011, pp. 20-21.

legal systems in the East, such as Singapore and Hong Kong, apply more than one comparison and division due to being influenced by different legal cultures.[12]

Due to practical constraints, this chapter does not attempt to provide an exhaustive review of every jurisdiction's approach to the arbitrator's role as a settlement facilitator. Instead, it employs a comparative legal methodology that emphasizes both cultural and legal diversity by examining representative jurisdictions from distinct legal traditions—namely, Civil Law, Common Law, and Eastern legal systems, including Arab-Islamic and East Asian jurisdictions. This approach enables a structured yet wide-ranging analysis of how this role is conceptualized, regulated, and practiced across varied normative, procedural, and cultural contexts. While a degree of generalization remains necessary for academic purposes,[13] the jurisdictions selected for closer examination were deliberately chosen to yield valuable insights into both established and emerging practices. These jurisdictions serve two complementary purposes. First, certain jurisdictions—such as China, Germany, Australia, Brazil, and those influenced by Islamic legal traditions—exhibit particularly notable or innovative approaches to regulating or applying the arbitrator's role in settlement facilitation.[14] These cases offer both instructive models and cautionary lessons that enrich the discussion of associated risks, safeguards, and implementation challenges. Second, jurisdictions such as the US, the UK, Hong Kong, and Singapore serve as leading international arbitration hubs. Their institutional practices and evolving regulatory trends exert significant influence on global standards and are thus especially relevant for evaluating the potential for transnational harmonization.[15]

This chapter begins by exploring how Eastern legal cultures conceptualize the roles of judges and arbitrators in facilitating settlement, focusing first on the legal

12. Singapore, for example, belongs to East Asian cultures but adopted the Common Law system. Additionally, legal systems in most Arab countries can apply for both divisions as they belong to the Eastern and Islamic legal culture, while at the same time they were influenced by Civil Law systems during the colonialism period. Malaysia can also be mentioned in this context since it has two different legal systems: Common law and Islamic law. For further discussion, *see* Mitchell & Powell, 2011, p. 22; Nigmatullina, 2018, pp. 69, 75-76; Chung, 2016, p. 165; Kun & Jemielniak, 2016, pp. 572-576; Stipanowich, 2021a, pp. 320-321; Gu, 2019, pp. 152-156.
13. Kun, 2016b, p. 482, arguing (in footnote 222), that "this symbolic dichotomy is used for the sake of illustrations of cultural trends. The reality is more complex"; Donahey, 1995, p. 74; Nigmatullina, 2018, pp. 64, 68.
14. In China and countries with Islamic law culture, court and arbitral proceedings are traditionally combined with mediation and the boundaries between the adjudicative and mediative roles are somehow blurred. In Germany, judges and arbitrators have been traditionally involved in settlement facilitating. Singapore, Hong Kong, and Australia recognize the role of arbitrators as settlement facilitators, but impose different safeguards aimed to maintain due process. Brazil, on the other hand, imposed some restrictions on that role of arbitrators.
15. According to 2021 Queen Mary International Arbitration Survey, Singapore and Hong Kong are part of the five most preferred seats for ICA, alongside with London, Paris, and Geneva (when New York, Beijing, Shanghai, Dubai, and Stockholm close the list of the ten most preferred seats). Comparison with the results of the 2015 and 2018 Queen Mary International Arbitration Surveys indicates that year-by-year key Asian arbitral hubs, particularly Singapore and Hong Kong, are climbing towards the top of the most preferred seats. Hence, these seats have cemented a longstanding and dominant position "as a 'safe seat' for international arbitration." The 2021 Survey concludes that the growth in popularity of these Asian seats reflects "an increasing willingness by parties with commercial interests linked to that locale to also resolve disputes 'locally.'" *See* Queen Mary University of London and White & Case LLP, 2021, pp. 5-7.

frameworks and practices in Islamic and Arab jurisdictions, followed by an analysis of East Asian jurisdictions, including China, Hong Kong, and Singapore. The discussion then shifts to Western legal systems, with particular attention to the approaches taken in the US, the UK, Australia, Germany, and Brazil. Beyond illustrating the cultural diversity surrounding the arbitrator's dual role and evaluating the prospects for its global acceptance and regulatory development, this selection of jurisdictions also serves to highlight the national forces shaping the legal globalization of this role[16]—alongside other transnational influences discussed in the next chapter.

5.2 LEGAL CULTURES IN THE EAST

Compared to Western cultures, traditionally characterized by their litigious traditions, Eastern cultures, especially in East Asia and the Arabic and Islamic world, are generally referred to as conciliatory cultures.[17] In these Eastern communitarian cultures, characterized by stable and long-lasting relationships between individuals due to strong feelings of belonging to their families, society, and business groups, procedures that allow for compromises (e.g., mediation) are well-rooted in dispute settlement regimes and have been historically preferred over court proceedings as a method to resolve disputes.[18] Relating to East Asian legal cultures seems quite natural when discussing the role of the arbitrators as settlement facilitators since this mandate is well-accepted in East Asian jurisdictions,[19] particularly in China, where its legal culture emphasizes mediation.[20] Nevertheless, this acceptance is also true regarding Islamic and Arab jurisdictions since their legal culture, which stems from Islamic law, supports and encourages arbitrators to facilitate settlements and to engage in mediation during arbitral proceedings.[21] Therefore, the practice in these jurisdictions contributes to the discussion on the role of arbitrators, particularly for the following reasons. *First*, according to some legal theory scholars, Islamic law is considered one of the world's three major domestic legal traditions, alongside Civil Law and Common Law.[22] This view can indeed be confirmed by the fact that Islamic law is currently the main legal source in 26 Arab and Islamic jurisdictions[23] and has influenced quite a few additional

16. Kun, 2016a, p. 260.
17. Nigmatullina, 2018, pp. 68-69; Kun, 2016b, pp. 482-483; Deekshitha & Saha, 2014, pp. 84-85; Ross, 2013, pp. 354-356; Ehle, 2010, pp. 79-80; Cheng, 2010, pp. 424-426; De Vera, 2004, p. 183; Cremades, 1998, pp. 158-159; Najar, 2009, p. 520.
18. Rashid, 2004, pp. 96-99; Link & Haftel, 2021, pp. 561-563; Kun, 2020a, p. 138; Almoguera, 2010, pp. 112-113; Antaki, 2009, p. 113; Chung, 2016, pp. 159-160; Nigmatullina, 2018, p. 69; Kun, 2016b, pp. 463-465, 482-483; Kun & Kaufmann-Kohler, 2008, pp. 480-481; Bühring-Uhle et al., 2006, p. 131.
19. Kun, 2013c, p. 12; Nigmatullina, 2018, pp. 69-70; Kun, 2020a, p. 138.
20. Kun, 2020a, p. 131; Nigmatullina, 2018, pp. 70-74; Kun & Kaufmann-Kohler, 2008, pp. 482-485; Kaufmann-Kohler, 2009, pp. 196-197.
21. Antaki, 2009, p. 113, stating: "Arabs and Muslims traditionally do not distinguish arbitration and mediation, they have an integrated approach to disputes"; Pair, 2002, pp. 71-73; Abu Sadah & Norton, 2008, pp. 219-223; El-Ahdab & El-Ahdab, 2011, p. 11.
22. Mitchell & Powell, 2011, pp. 21-22, 29-30; Badr, 1978, p. 187.
23. Mitchell & Powell, 2011, p. 26, providing a detailed listing of Arab and Islamic jurisdictions where Islamic law serves as the primary source of the legal system.

jurisdictions in Africa and Asia, including Indonesia, Malaysia, North and East India, and North-West China.[24] As a result, the debate regarding the arbitrators' mandate to facilitate settlements cannot be comprehensive without exploring their position on the matter. *Second*, analyzing the current preferred seats of international arbitration reveals an evolving trend that favors arbitral institutions in the Gulf area.[25] This trend can be explained by the establishment of national, regional, and international arbitration centers in that area, intended to encourage the practice of arbitration and attract international users.[26] Although domestic law in this region, which relies on Islamic law, may not directly affect arbitral proceedings conducted within international institutions,[27] it may still influence these proceedings at the regulative and enforcement levels,[28] not to mention its effect on the attitude of local practitioners participating in these arbitrations. Therefore, exploring the attitude of Islamic and Arab jurisdictions concerning the role of arbitrators is vital from a transnational point of view, especially if the abovementioned trend regarding the preferred seats of international arbitration continues.

5.2.1 Islamic and Arab Jurisdictions

Compared to Common Law and Civil Law systems, Islamic and Arab legal systems are characterized by greater informality, including in the dispute resolution process,[29] due to their shared communitarian culture and reliance on Islamic law, regardless of differences in their political and legal structures.[30] The cornerstone of these systems is the *Shari'a*: the religious law for Muslims bound to the Islamic faith. The *Shari'a* embodies all aspects of law, including commercial and international law, as well as ethical guidelines and standards for proper conduct in every sphere of life.[31] Islamic law is incorporated into all levels of Islamic and Arab domestic legal systems, starting with personal status and commercial laws and ending with constitutions and other

24. Mitchell & Powell, 2011, pp. 29-30; Badr, 1978, p. 188; Kun, 2016a, pp. 250-261; Chung, 2016, p. 165.
25. Almutawa & Maniruzzaman, 2014, p. 195. According to the 2021 Queen Mary International Arbitration Survey, Dubai was chosen for the first time as one of the ten most preferred seats for international arbitration. *See* Queen Mary University of London and White & Case LLP, 2021, pp. 5-7.
26. Chaisse & Shang, 2021, p. 93; Almutawa & Maniruzzaman, 2014, pp. 195-196; Najar, 2009, p. 520; Tannous & Omran, 2018; Kadhim, 2021; Al Houti, 2018.
27. Almutawa & Maniruzzaman, 2014, pp. 232, 243; Pair, 2002, p. 71.
28. Nurmohamed, 2020, pp. 467-469; Qouteshat, 2017, pp. 3-9; Almutawa & Maniruzzaman, 2014, pp. 229-232.
29. Link & Haftel, 2021, pp. 561-563; Iqbal, 2001, pp. 1035-1045; Najar, 2009, p. 520. *See also* Othman, 2007.
30. Antaki, 2009, p. 113; Ross, 2013, p. 356.
31. Blackaby et al., 2022, §3.209; Badr, 1978, pp. 188-189; Sanders, 1999, pp. 50-54; Link & Haftel, 2021, pp. 561-563; Nurmohamed, 2020, pp. 445-448; Mitchell & Powell, 2011, pp. 36-37, stating: "In Islamic legal culture, there exists no sharp division between morals, religion, and legal obligations. ... Even though both of the Western legal traditions extracted many important legal principles from religious sources, such as the Bible, the legal systems themselves are separate from religion. In contrast, Islamic law is intrinsic to Islamic faith and life in Islamic countries."

basic laws relating to it as a binding source of legislation or interpretation.[32] In these jurisdictions, there is an "inherent bond between *Shari'a*, or Islamic law, and state rule," with the *Shari'a* "above all man-made laws."[33] Islamic law dictates that disputes should mainly be settled amicably, more flexibly, and informally.[34] Accordingly:

> Procedural law is least formalized in Islamic law. Western-style formality of dispute resolution is replaced in Islamic law by the emphasis on acknowledgment, apology, and forgiveness. During a trial, reaching a consensus (reconciliation) between the parties is given a priority. During a typical Islamic trial, oral proceedings constitute the main element, and the parties simply present their statements in front of the *qadi* (judge). The in-court proceedings comprise a simple common-sense mechanism, without any documentation, formal procedure, or rules of evidence.[35]

The aversion of Islamic law to formal venues to settle disputes is based on the conception that these proceedings are not the ultimate truth-finding mechanism, as they are "shaped and concluded by men and not by god" and can favor "the more eloquent or resourceful disputant" while keeping substantive justice away from those who deserve it.[36] Therefore, the preferable mechanism for dispute settlement is the *Sulh* (conciliation), through which the adjudicator should "guide the parties in the process of finding a common understanding and restoring their fellowship" or business partnership.[37] According to the Islamic faith, while formal adjudication may "breed hatred between parties," reconciliation can "bring them together" with a true compromise.[38]

The Islamic equivalent to arbitration is *Tahkim*,[39] described as a "spontaneous and ... improvised move by two or more parties in dispute to submit their case to a third party neutral for settlement based on the provision of Islamic law."[40] The favored "third party" for the role is an "unbiased insider with strong connections to the aggrieved parties as well as a good sense of the common good and standing within the community."[41] Despite its informal characteristics, an arbitral award based on *Tahkim* is binding, and as long as no legal error is found in the award, it is enforceable.[42] The impact of *Tahkim* is well reflected in arbitration laws and procedures in Arab and Islamic states. Even though most of these countries were influenced by Civil Law legal

32. Lombardi, 2006, p. 1; Link & Haftel, 2021, p. 563.
33. Mitchell & Powell, 2011, p. 38.
34. Link & Haftel, 2021, pp. 561-562; Othman, 2007, p. 65; Iqbal, 2001, pp. 1035-1045.
35. Mitchell & Powell, 2011, p. 50. *See also* Antaki, 2009, p. 114.
36. Link & Haftel, 2021, p. 562. *See also* Mitchell & Powell, 2011, p. 50.
37. Mitchell & Powell, 2011, p. 50. *See also* Antaki, 2009, p. 114; Othman, 2007, p. 68, defining *sulh* as "settlement grounded upon compromise negotiated by the disputants themselves or with the help of a third party."
38. Iqbal, 2001, p. 1040. *See also* Mitchell & Powell, 2011, p. 50; Othman, 2007, p. 69.
39. The *Tahkim* as a process of dispute resolution originated in the pre-Islamic Arabia and is acceptable on the four major Sunni Islamic schools: *Maliki, Hanafi, Hanbali,* and *Shafi'i. See* Hanis, 2015, p. 73; Nadar, 2009, p. 187.
40. Chung, 2016, p. 160.
41. Irani & Funk, 1998, p. 63. *See also* Antaki, 2009, p. 114.
42. Chung, 2016, p. 160.

traditions during colonialism,[43] with their arbitration laws inspired by the UNCITRAL Model Law on ICA,[44] these jurisdictions have traditionally combined many conciliation features with commercial arbitral proceedings. The procedural flexibility of arbitration expresses this combination, with the focus of the arbitrator on "the spiritual and the relationships not on an allocation of blame" and the expectation that "the *Shari'a* and its procedural requirements apply regardless of what the contract states."[45] Therefore, commercial arbitration in Islamic and Arab jurisdictions is highly similar to hybrid procedures combining arbitration with mediation:

> This is a flexible process that requires the agreement of both parties to the dispute. As part of the process of dispute settlement, the preferred conciliator or arbitrator in [Islamic Legal Tradition] is an insider, who maintains good relations with both parties. This can be contrasted with the ideal arbitrator in Western approaches, who is often portrayed as a neutral, unaffiliated, outsider.[46]

In principle, Islamic law should also apply to international arbitration proceedings since it has an element of international law applicable based on the religion of the disputants, regardless of their jurisdictional origin.[47] However, the influence of Islamic law over ICA has declined over time, particularly in cases involving international parties.[48] Additionally, in the Arab region, a modernization process of arbitral legislation has been carried out, mainly in the spirit of regional and international conventions, such as the New York Convention,[49] as well as following the increased use of ICA and the establishment of the abovementioned international arbitration institutes.[50]

5.2.2 East Asian Legal Cultures

Despite differences in cultural backgrounds, languages, ethnicities, and religions,[51] the literature identifies important common cultural dimensions in East Asian jurisdictions

43. Pair, 2002, p. 71; Sanders, 1999, p. 50; Majid & Lenzen, 2011.
44. Bantekas, 2015, p. 60; Pair, 2002, pp. 72-73; Abu Sadah & Norton, 2008, pp. 219-223; El-Ahdab & El-Ahdab, 2011, pp. 155-156.
45. Pair, 2002, p. 71. *See also* Bantekas, 2015, p. 60; Rayner, 1991, p. 96, stating that in these jurisdictions "all kinds of contract would be acceptable providing that they do not contradict the ... *Shari'a*."
46. Link & Haftel, 2021, pp. 561-562. *See also* Irani & Funk, 1998, pp. 63-64; Chung, 2016, pp. 162-163; Antaki, 2009, p. 114, describing the arbitration process as follows: "The parties do not ask themselves whether they are in the presence of a mediator or of an arbitrator. They place themselves entirely in the hands of a person whom they know, respect and believe to be capable of helping them out of the deadlock."
47. Pair, 2002, p. 71; Bantekas, 2015, pp. 59-60; Riyadh Arab Agreement for Judicial Cooperation, 1983, Article 37(e), requiring the courts of Arab Member States to deny recognition or enforcement of arbitral awards that contradict the *Shari'a*.
48. Almutawa & Maniruzzaman, 2014, pp. 232, 243; El-Ahdab & El-Ahdab, 2011, p. 49; Pair, 2002, p. 71.
49. El-Ahdab & Stackpool-Moore, 2008, pp. 279-280.
50. Chaisse & Shang, 2021, p. 93; Almutawa & Maniruzzaman, 2014, pp. 195-196; Tannous & Omran, 2018; Kadhim, 2021; Al Houti, 2018.
51. Kun, 2016b, p. 455.

directly connected to dispute-resolution preferences:[52] collectivism, long-term orientation, and high-power distance.[53] *Collectivism* describes how people live together in groups (e.g., nuclear families, extended families, and tribes) or are organized in guilds according to their crafts.[54] It also reflects the prevailing values and behaviors of a given group or society and its relationship with the individuals.[55] Cultures with a high level of collectivism, like most East Asian countries, do not share Western values of privacy and individualism and prefer to handle disputes diplomatically within the community.[56] These cultures highlight relationships between people to a greater degree and emphasize the commitment and loyalty of the individual to the group, even at the expense of sacrificing their personal interests.[57] Additionally, in collectivist cultures, communications between people are characterized by a less direct and confrontational style, so "the wants, needs and goals of the speaker are not obvious in the spoken message."[58] The *long-term orientation* dimension, reflecting society's search for virtue, was introduced to address the Confucian values that dominate East Asian cultures and states, including China, Japan, Hong Kong, Singapore, and South Korea.[59] Confucian morality is based on social harmony and peace that can only be achieved by avoiding disputes or settlements.[60] According to the Confucian philosophy, resorting to the law to settle disputes may end with the social sanction of losing face, as the law "can convict and execute people, but it cannot teach humanity, kindness, benevolence and compassion."[61] Furthermore, due to the variety and complexity of human relations, a deep mistrust should be expressed in preset rules of law or absolute resolution of controversies.[62] As a result, disputes can be settled respectably only through the "parties' willingness to compromise and meet with each other halfway."[63] *High-power distance* is another frequent cultural dimension in East Asia that reflects the hierarchical order of society, the central position of authority, and the acceptance of its power and legitimacy.[64] In high-power distance cultures, disputants are less likely to conduct

52. Kun & Jemielniak, 2016, p. 572.
53. Those cultural dimensions were first introduced by the Geert Hofstede's model, designed to measure cultural differences between compatible samples from different regions and countries. *See* Kun & Jemielniak, 2016, pp. 571-577; Hofstede et al., 2010, pp. 53-134, 235-276.
54. Hofstede, 2001, p. 209; Kun, 2013b, pp. 197-205; Kun & Jemielniak, 2016, p. 573.
55. Kun & Jemielniak, 2016, p. 573.
56. Stallard, 2002, p. 476; De Vera, 2004, p. 183; Cheng, 2010, p. 424; Deekshitha & Saha, 2014, pp. 84-85; Nigmatullina, 2018, p. 69; Kun, 2016a, pp. 265-266.
57. Kun & Jemielniak, 2016, pp. 573, 576.
58. Kun & Jemielniak, 2016, p. 573. *See also* Jandt, 2013, p. 172. In contrast to collectivist societies, in individualistic societies, relationships between individuals are less binding while the communication tend to be more direct.
59. Hofstede et al., 2010, pp. 235-276; Kun & Jemielniak, 2016, pp. 574-575.
60. Kaufmann-Kohler, 2009, p. 196; Chung, 2016, pp. 152-155; Donahey, 1995, pp. 74-75; Peter, 1997, p. 107; Stipanowich, 2021a, p. 311; Nigmatullina, 2018, pp. 69-70; Ames & Rosemont, 1999, p. 51; Kun, 2013b, pp. 188-189; Huang, 1990, p. 139.
61. De Vera, 2004, p. 166. *See also* Stipanowich, 2021a, pp. 311-312; Kun & Kaufmann-Kohler, 2008, pp. 480-481; Kun, 2016b, p. 463; Cohen, 1966, p. 1206; Kun, 2013b, p. 189; Nigmatullina, 2018, p. 69.
62. Taniguchi, 1998, p. 36; Kun & Jemielniak, 2016, p. 576; Kim, 2007, p. 27.
63. De Vera, 2004, p. 168. *See also* Kun & Kaufmann-Kohler, 2008, p. 480; Chung, 2016, p. 154; Kun, 2013b, p. 189; Kun & Jemielniak, 2016, p. 575.
64. Kun, 2020a, p. 138; Donahey, 1995, p. 74; Kun & Jemielniak, 2016, p. 576.

the dispute resolution process independently. They expect the decision-maker to help them design a decent settlement or render a fair decision that ends the dispute.[65] Consequently, procedural justice in these cultures gains less weight than the distribution of justice, and efficiency considerations often override due process and natural justice concerns.[66]

The above-discussed cultural dimensions can explain why the conciliation culture is deeply rooted in East Asian jurisdictions. A conciliatory process can maintain collectivist values due to its non-confrontational style and the ability to suggest socially and individually accepted solutions. It helps to maintain long and lasting relations within the community, as well as social harmony and peace. The conciliatory process is also consistent with the disputants' expectation that the neutral would be actively involved in formulating an amicable resolution.[67] Consequently, contrary to the litigious culture often attributed to the West, initiating legal proceedings is not socially tolerable before exhausting all available options for reaching a suitable settlement.[68] The conciliation culture in East Asia has affected all aspects of dispute resolution in the region. It has paved the way for the expansion and flourishing of mediation, considered a "hand-in-glove" with the ideals deriving from the above cultural dimensions.[69] It has also influenced the arbitrator's role as a settlement facilitator and the wide acceptance of hybrid proceedings combining arbitration and mediation:

> Influenced by the local culture emphasizing conciliation to maintain harmony, arbitrators are generally viewed as individuals, familiar with the parties and their dispute, who will not only end their dispute, but also assist them in reaching a mutually agreeable solution and restore harmony. Thus, the role of a settlement facilitator and that of a decision-maker is not clearly distinguished and can be combined in Asian minds ... in both common law and civil law jurisdictions.[70]

The detailed discussion below demonstrates how China, Hong Kong, and Singapore recognize the arbitrator's role as a settlement facilitator, including through the combined use of mediation and arbitration,[71] similar to the approach of almost all other jurisdictions in the region, including Japan, India, and South Korea.[72] Empirical data

65. Stipanowich, 2021a, p. 311.
66. Kun, 2020a, p. 138; Kun & Jemielniak, 2016, pp. 576-577.
67. Kun & Jemielniak, 2016, pp. 576-577; Nigmatullina, 2018, pp. 69-70; De Vera, 2004, p. 183; Donahey, 1995, p. 74; Deekshitha & Saha, 2014, pp. 84-85.
68. Kun & Jemielniak, 2016, p. 576; Stipanowich, 2021a, pp. 311-312; Taniguchi, 1998, p. 36.
69. Kun, 2013b, p. 189; Goh, 2002, pp. 75-78; Gu, 2019, p. 127; Kun & Jemielniak, 2016, p. 575; Nigmatullina, 2018, pp. 69-70.
70. Kun, 2016b, p. 483. *See also* Taniguchi, 1998, p. 36; Kun, 2013a.
71. Kun, 2013c, p. 12; Nigmatullina, 2018, pp. 69-70; Kun, 2020a, p. 138.
72. For example, Japan Arbitration Law, 2003, Article 38(4)-(5), applicable for both national and international arbitrations, allows the arbitral tribunal to attempt settlement of civil disputes, subject to a written consent of the parties and so long as they have not withdrawn their consent in writing; India Arbitration and Conciliation Act, 1996, Article 30(1), authorizes the arbitrator to encourage settlement, including through mediation and conciliation; Republic of Korea Arbitration Act, 2016, Article 20(2), empowers arbitrators to conduct the arbitration in a way they consider appropriate, subject to maintaining due process. *See also* Ruckteschler & Wendelstein, 2021, p. 766; Nottage, 2004, p. 57; Kun, 2016b, pp. 481-482; Gu, 2019, p. 129; Ross, 2013, pp. 355-356.

confirms the general acceptance of this role. The 2007 Ali Survey, conducted among 115 highly experienced arbitration practitioners from over 18 Eastern and Western jurisdictions,[73] confirmed that compared to their Western colleagues, East Asian arbitrators fulfilled a more significant role in settlement facilitation within ICA proceedings.[74] According to the collected data, 82 % of practitioners working in East Asia considered settlement facilitation one of the arbitration's objectives, compared to only 62 % of Western practitioners.[75] Additionally, over 40 % of practitioners working in the East reported that arbitrators were regularly involved in the settlement process by suggesting settlement negotiations, compared to only 16 % of their Western colleagues.[76] The data further revealed that over 30 % of practitioners operating in the East confirmed the regular engagement of arbitrators with the settlement process, compared to only 16 % of their Western counterparts.[77] Furthermore, 26 % of practitioners in East Asia reported that during the settlement negotiations, arbitrators frequently met separately with the parties to discuss and promote settlements, compared to only 8 % of practitioners in the West.[78] Interviews conducted in the survey with East Asian arbitrators revealed that they considered settlement facilitation an integral part of their mandate due to their social and ethical responsibility to the disputants.[79]

Despite mutual cultural dimensions, due to several factors such as "former colonial influence, voluntary borrowing, and contemporary religious or ideological influences," variations still exist between East Asian jurisdictions related to the role of arbitrators as settlement facilitators, particularly when arbitration is combined with mediation.[80] These variations are presented below while discussing the mandate of arbitrators in China, Hong Kong, and Singapore.

5.2.2.1 China

Influenced by the Confucian doctrines of social order, governance, and dispute resolution,[81] informal dispute settlement procedures, primarily mediation, have dominated the legal culture in China for decades and gained priority over adjudicative proceedings.[82] Those non-adversarial methods, favoring amicable solutions, have been based on collectivist conceptions that prefer harmony and peace in society over the

73. *See* the discussion in section 2.3.3. This survey focused on practitioners from East Asia as 75 % of the respondents were from East Asian jurisdictions and only 25 % from the US and Europe. *See* Ali, 2011b; Ali, 2010; Ali, 2011a.
74. Ali, 2011b, pp. 6-8, 16-17; Ali, 2010, pp. 251-252.
75. Ali, 2011a, p. 102, Appendix B.
76. Ali, 2011b, p. 25.
77. Ali, 2011b, p. 26.
78. Ali, 2011b, pp. 26-27.
79. Ali, 2011b, p. 25.
80. Kun, 2016b, pp. 455-456.
81. Kun, 2016b, p. 463; Kaufmann-Kohler, 2009, p. 196; Farina, 1989, p. 142.
82. Gu, 2019, p. 127; Kun, 2016a, p. 260; Kun, 2011b, p. 539; Kun & Kaufmann-Kohler, 2008, p. 480; Ross, 2013, p. 354; Zweigert & Koötz, 1987, pp. 362-365.

interests of the individual, long-term relationships over confrontation, and compromise over adherence to legal rights.[83] Despite introducing Western civilization into China during the 18th and 19th centuries, these traditional values have continued to lead its legal culture and have not been undermined.[84] Interestingly, the status of mediation as a dispute-resolution mechanism became even more dominant after the Communist Party came into power in the mid-19th century and initiated a new legal system to serve the needs of a socialist country.[85] According to some scholars, the Communist Party promoted mediation as the key mechanism for resolving all kinds of disputes to achieve better governability of civil society, channel social grievances about the regime, and reduce publicized conflicts that may affect its legitimacy.[86] Therefore, the hostility of the Communist ideology to litigation,[87] alongside the promotion of mediation through a "top-down" political design,[88] did not necessarily reflect traditional Confucian values but socialist political doctrines under the guise of tradition.[89] Whatever the reason for promoting mediation by the Communist regime, different mediation committees were established under its rule to reduce the pressure on courts.[90] Hence, this mechanism became the cornerstone of dispute resolution in China, whether alone or combined with other procedures.[91]

5.2.2.1.1 Mediation Within Judicial Proceedings

The dominant role of mediation in the contemporary legal regime in China has seeped into the courts that "shifted towards conciliation and mediation as a primary objective, with adjudication being secondary."[92] The primary reliance on mediation within judicial proceedings was formalized in 1962 through various Opinions on the Civil Judicial Work issued by the Supreme Court in the country, as later affirmed in the Chinese Civil Procedure Law in 1982 and 1991.[93] As a result, in civil cases, the court is obliged to first mediate the case and render a judgment only following failed attempts

83. Chung, 2016, p. 150; Stipanowich, 2021a, pp. 311-312; Kun, 2013b, pp. 187-192; Kun, 2016b, pp. 463-465; Kaufmann-Kohler, 2009, pp. 196-197; Kun & Kaufmann-Kohler, 2008, pp. 480-482; Wong, 2000, p. 307; Huang, 1990, p. 139; De Vera, 2004, p. 164; Farina, 1989, p. 139.
84. Kun, 2016b, pp. 463-464; Xingzhong, 1989, pp. 32-33.
85. Kun, 2016b, pp. 464-465; Xingzhong, 1989, p. 29.
86. Gu, 2021, p. 72; Gu, 2019, p. 127; Kun, 2016a, pp. 269-270; Lu, 2011, p. 232; Minzner, 2011, p. 939.
87. Cohen, 1966, p. 1226; Kun & Kaufmann-Kohler, 2008, pp. 482-483.
88. Gu, 2019, p. 129; Kun, 2016a, p. 269.
89. Fu, 2003, p. 122; Gu, 2021, p. 86; Gu, 2019, pp. 127, 131; Kun, 2016a, pp. 269-270; Palmer, 2010, p. 251.
90. Kun & Kaufmann-Kohler, 2008, pp. 483-485.
91. Kun, 2011b, p. 539; Kun & Kaufmann-Kohler, 2008, p. 483.
92. Kaufmann-Kohler, 2009, p. 196. *See also* Kun & Kaufmann-Kohler, 2008, pp. 484-485; Kun, 2011b, pp. 539-540.
93. Kun & Kaufmann-Kohler, 2008, pp. 484-485; Kun, 2011b, p. 539; Kun, 2016b, p. 478. According to the Civil Procedure Law of the People's Republic of China, 1991, Articles 9, "In trying civil cases, the people's courts shall conduct conciliation for the parties on a voluntary and lawful basis; if conciliation fails, judgments shall be rendered without delay." Additionally, Article 85 further stipulates that "In the trial of civil cases, the people's court shall ... conduct conciliation between the parties on a voluntary basis."

to settle.[94] The expansion of mediation within judicial proceedings in China is further attributed to the 2004 Supreme Court Provisions on Court's Civil Mediation Work, requiring the court to conduct mediation in every possible case.[95] Consequently:

> Courts have revised their incentive mechanisms to encourage court-mediation; many have established a target settlement rate for civil litigation. As a result, an increasing number of cases are settled rather than adjudicated. The percentage of civil cases resolved through mediation in China increased from 31% in 2004 to 65.29% in 2010, doubling within six years.[96]

Judicial mediation and mediation by governmental committees in China are noticeably different from their Western counterparts and considered more "adjudicatory, aggressive, and interventionist."[97] Neutrals in these proceedings are highly active and usually apply pressure to lead to a particular outcome.[98] In judicial mediation, judges, who, according to the law and governmental policy, are encouraged to mediate their cases, usually force parties to negotiate and settle their disputes amicably.[99]

5.2.2.1.2 Mediation Within Arbitral Proceedings

A frequent reliance on mediation constitutes a main feature of contemporary arbitration in China.[100] Based on existing statistics, between 2014 and 2018, approximately 47% of all arbitration cases in the country were concluded through successful mediation carried out by the tribunal.[101] The literature attributes this extensive use of mediation within arbitral proceedings to different reasons. According to one attitude, the practices of the Chinese courts, which regularly combine mediation with adjudication due to governmental policies, have influenced arbitral proceedings significantly and explain why Chinese arbitrators often promote settlements in their cases while integrating mediation with arbitration.[102] Another approach holds that while "top-down" design may explain the political incentive of judges to engage in mediation, such governmental interference cannot rationalize the arbitrators' tendency to mediate their cases:

> Arbitrators are not hired by the states, but are selected by the parties, either by direct nomination, or by indirect appointment through one of the arbitration institutions that the parties have chosen on an ad hoc basis. The arbitrators' mandate will terminate once an arbitral award is rendered. The arbitrators' fees

94. Gu, 2019, p. 127; Zhang, 2015, p. 45; Kun & Kaufmann-Kohler, 2008, pp. 484-485.
95. Kun, 2011b, pp. 539-540.
96. Kun, 2011b, pp. 539-540.
97. Fu & Cullen, 2011, p. 33. *See also* Gu, 2021, pp. 70-71.
98. Nolan-Haley, 2012, p. 63; Gu, 2019, pp. 125-126.
99. Fu & Cullen, 2011, p. 33; Gu, 2021, p. 71.
100. Kun & Kaufmann-Kohler, 2008, p. 485; Kaufmann-Kohler, 2009, pp. 196-197; Kun, 2016a, p. 261; Nigmatullina, 2018, pp. 70-72; Stipanowich, 2021a, pp. 308-309.
101. Gu, 2019, pp. 123-124.
102. Stipanowich, 2021a, pp. 308-309; Gu, 2019, p. 125; Nigmatullina, 2018, p. 70; Kun, 2011b, p. 540; Ehle, 2010, p. 82; Kaufmann-Kohler, 2009, p. 196; Kun & Kaufmann-Kohler, 2008, p. 485; Bühring-Uhle, 1996, p. 272.

are generally determined according to the fee scale of a chosen arbitration institution. Different from judges, arbitrators do not have any salary or career rewards linked to the mediation ratio. Indeed, the arbitrators are generally paid less if the parties reach a settlement and withdraw the arbitration proceeding than if the matter results in a final award. Nevertheless, Chinese arbitrators still tend to play an active role in promoting mediation in arbitration proceedings.[103]

Hence, the tendency of Chinese arbitrators can only be explained by the influence of cultural values and local traditions that blurred the line between arbitration and mediation and enabled the "old man arbitrator" in the community to become involved in settlement facilitation.[104] In other words, according to this approach, the imported concept of modern arbitration was given "a Chinese face—the combination of mediation and arbitration."[105] A third attitude suggests that the paucity of laws applied to commercial disputes left Chinese arbitrators no choice but to base their decisions on principles of fairness or actively facilitate settlements in their disputes, including through mediation.[106]

While more than one reason could affect the practice of Chinese arbitrators, including cultural and political reasons,[107] it is undisputed that until the Chinese Arbitration Law was announced in 1994, the role of arbitrators as settlement facilitators was not regulated by the legislator.[108] Article 51 of the Arbitration Law, applicable for both local and international arbitration in China,[109] provides the following:

> The arbitration tribunal may carry out conciliation prior to giving an arbitration award. The arbitration tribunal shall conduct conciliation if both parties voluntarily seek conciliation. If conciliation is unsuccessful, an arbitration award shall be made promptly. If conciliation leads to a settlement agreement, the arbitration tribunal shall make a written conciliation statement or make an arbitration award in accordance with the result of the settlement agreement. A written conciliation statement and an arbitration award shall have equal legal effect.[110]

Although in practice, the combination of mediation and arbitration in China was acknowledged and widely implemented by arbitration institutes long before,[111] the introduction of the Arbitration Law made this combination, for the first time, officially recognized, regulated, and actively encouraged.[112] According to Article 51, detached from the tribunal's discretion to resort to mediation even when the parties decide against that attempt, when the disputants jointly request for that involvement, the

103. Kun, 2016a, p. 270.
104. Kun, 2013b, pp. 193-197; Kun, 2016a, p. 271. *See also* Stipanowich, 2021a, pp. 308, 311; De Vera, 2004, pp. 185-186.
105. Kun, 2016a, p. 271.
106. Kun & Kaufmann-Kohler, 2008, p. 485.
107. Gu, 2021, p. 84.
108. Kun, 2016b, p. 465.
109. Gu, 2019, pp. 140, 143; Gu, 2021, p. 79; Kun, 2013b, p. 209.
110. Arbitration Law of the People's Republic of China, 1994, Article 51.
111. Kun & Kaufmann-Kohler, 2008, p. 485; Stipanowich, 2021a, p. 309; Nigmatullina, 2018, p. 71; Cheng & Kohtio, 2009, p. 95.
112. Nigmatullina, 2018, p. 70; Kun & Kaufmann-Kohler, 2008, p. 486; Kun, 2011b, p. 540; Ehle, 2010, p. 82.

tribunal is obliged to conduct mediation.[113] Following this legislation, most arbitral institutes in China amended their rules in line with its directive to explicitly allow a combination of mediation and arbitration.[114] Article 47 of the Arbitration Rules of the China International Economic and Trade Arbitration Commission (CIETAC), for example, states that, subject to the parties' consent, during the arbitration, the tribunal is authorized to conciliate the dispute in a way it considers appropriate.[115] Similar provisions appear in Article 43 of the Arbitration Rules of the Beijing Arbitration Commission (BAC) and Article 48(1) of the Rules of Shenzhen Court of International Arbitration (SCIA).[116]

Despite these normative acknowledgments, neither the Chinese arbitration law nor the institutional arbitration rules particularize the procedures and methods to be used during the mediation phase nor include any guidance regarding the timing of conducting mediation by the tribunal.[117] In addition, the law does not apply any safeguards to address due process concerns resulting from the dual role of arbitrators, such as apparent or real bias or the use of confidential information disclosed during mediation.[118] As discussed below, these concerns have been partially addressed by only a handful of leading arbitration institutes that host most international arbitrations in China.[119]

Valuable data about the actual practice of Chinese arbitrators as settlement facilitators was collected through two connected studies. The first study of a qualitative nature was conducted in 2007 and included in-depth personal interviews with 20 leading Chinese arbitrators with extensive experience in ICA proceedings in China, who are frequently appointed by the CIETAC and BAC arbitration institutions, as well as the Wuhan Arbitration Commission (WAC) institution (2007 Kun and Kaufmann-Kohler Study).[120] According to the interview data, Chinese arbitrators systematically inquire about the possibility of assisting the disputants in settling the case. Parties respond positively to this initiative in approximately 50% of the cases.[121] In domestic arbitrations, where parties are generally familiar with this practice and often propose mediation themselves,[122] arbitrators experience a significantly higher rate of positive responses to their initiative compared to cases involving international parties.[123] Additionally, Chinese arbitrators tend to propose mediation only after the parties have submitted their written submissions and presented their oral statements. They consider

113. Gu, 2021, p. 80; Gu, 2019, p. 140.
114. Kun, 2016b, pp. 478-479; Harpole, 2007, p. 624; Nigmatullina, 2018, p. 71; Gu, 2021, pp. 73-74.
115. CIETAC Arbitration Rules, 2024, Article 47. *See also* Ruckteschler & Wendelstein, 2021, pp. 765-766; Ross, 2013, p. 354.
116. BAC Arbitration Rules, 2022, Article 43; SCIA Arbitration Rules, 2022, Article 48(1).
117. Nigmatullina, 2018, p. 71.
118. Gu, 2021, p. 79.
119. Gu, 2019, pp. 132-143, 168; Gu, 2021, p. 78.
120. Kun & Kaufmann-Kohler, 2008; Kun, 2020a; Kaufmann-Kohler, 2009, pp. 196-197.
121. Kun & Kaufmann-Kohler, 2008, p. 487; Kaufmann-Kohler, 2009, p. 196; Kun, 2011b, p. 540. *See also* Kun, 2020a, p. 139, references another empirical study conducted in 2000 by CIETAC among Chinese arbitrators, which yielded very similar results.
122. Kun & Kaufmann-Kohler, 2008, p. 486; Gu, 2016, p. 89; Gu, 2019, p. 135.
123. Gu, 2021, p. 75; Kun & Kaufmann-Kohler, 2008, p. 487; Kun, 2020a, p. 145; Kun, 2016b, p. 480; Kun, 2014, p. 792.

this timing to be the most effective for facilitating settlement, as the parties are already familiar with the weaknesses of their arguments and positions.[124] Nevertheless, since in the Chinese combined model, "mediation occurs during the ongoing process of arbitration" without a clear distinction between each of the phases,[125] deciding the best moment is subject to the case's specific circumstances. So long as an arbitral award has not yet been rendered, the proposal to mediate can be raised anytime, even several times, during the proceedings.[126] The interview data further revealed that during mediation, and subject to the parties' consent, Chinese arbitrators do not hesitate to caucus with the disputants and engage in "back-to-back" diplomacy.[127] In their view, these private meetings are essential for facilitating an amicable outcome of the dispute:

> During the caucusing, the arbitrators ask for each party's bottom line separately, so as to have a better understanding of the real interests at stake. If the difference between the parties' bottom line is considerable, then the arbitrators terminate the mediation and render an award; if the difference is less important, then they may try to narrow the gap in an effort to reach settlement. Meeting parties separately also allows the arbitrators to conduct a so-called 'reality check' that can encourage a party with an overly optimistic view of its chances of success to reconsider its case on its merits, and thereby increase the possibility that the parties reach a settlement.[128]

The Chinese arbitrators are confident that their discretion remains uncontaminated following exposure to confidential information during ex parte meetings since the parties are not expected to fully disclose damaging information that cannot already be discerned from the formal record.[129] Additionally, other scenarios exist where arbitrators need to reject or disregard information after being exposed to its content, such as improperly submitted arguments or documents, so confidential information revealed during caucusing is no exception.[130] Furthermore, even judges are obliged by law to disregard improperly submitted documents, and jurors have to decide after hearing the witnesses' inadmissible statements.[131] Since, like judges, arbitrators are well-trained adjudicators, there is no justification for questioning their impartiality following exposure to confidential information during the settlement negotiations.[132]

124. Kun & Kaufmann-Kohler, 2008, p. 487.
125. Kun & Kaufmann-Kohler, 2008, p. 487. *See also* Kun, 2013a, p. 166; Nigmatullina, 2018, p. 71.
126. Kun & Kaufmann-Kohler, 2008, p. 487; Kun, 2013a, p. 166; Nigmatullina, 2018, p. 71; Donahey, 1995, p. 76.
127. This technique, also referred to as "shuttle diplomacy," relates to private meetings of the arbitrator with the disputants, back and forth, to better understand their respective expectations and estimate the gaps between their positions. *See* Alexander, 2017, p. 6; Kaufmann-Kohler, 2009, pp. 196-197; Kun, 2020a, pp. 149-152, 164; Nigmatullina, 2018, p. 72; Kun & Kaufmann-Kohler, 2008, p. 488; Kun, 2013a, p. 167; Kun, 2011b, pp. 552-554.
128. Kun & Kaufmann-Kohler, 2008, p. 488. *See also* Kun, 2020a, pp. 149-150; Gu, 2021, p. 69; Stipanowich, 2021a, p. 309.
129. Kun & Kaufmann-Kohler, 2008, pp. 491.
130. Kun & Kaufmann-Kohler, 2008, p. 491; Ruckteschler & Wendelstein, 2021, pp. 772-773; Schneider, 1998, p. 94. *See*, for example, CIETAC Guidelines on Evidence, 2024, Article 19(1), authorizing the tribunal to reject submitted evidence that contains confidential information or communications.
131. Kun, 2020a, p. 156; Kun & Kaufmann-Kohler, 2008, p. 491.
132. Kun & Kaufmann-Kohler, 2008, p. 491; Kun, 2020a, p. 156.

Moreover, contrary to court litigation, arbitral proceedings are voluntary. If the parties who nominated the arbitrator to the case trust them to decide the controversies despite exposure to confidential information, their desire should be respected.[133]

Unlike their favorable attitude toward caucusing, the Chinese arbitrators consider expressing evaluative views on the parties' positions or the outcome of the dispute as improper and a threat to their impartiality and independence. Therefore, they tend to refrain from these assessments during mediation,[134] although evidence exists for occasional use by arbitrators to reduce the gaps between the parties' positions.[135] Additionally, the Chinese arbitrators disagree about the appropriateness of making settlement proposals to the parties. While some arbitrators rarely deliver such proposals, others believe these proposals may increase the chances of settling the dispute amicably, especially when the gaps between the parties are not considerable.[136] Arbitrators who do offer settlement proposals usually wait until the facts of the dispute are entirely clear, the parties understand their relative positions, and the gaps between them have been narrowed.[137] At this stage, the settlement proposals may state an exact amount or a range to be paid, actions to be taken, and, in some cases, a business arrangement intended to maintain the parties' business relationship. Despite their direct involvement in the settlement attempts, the Chinese arbitrators refrain from compelling the parties into a settlement,[138] although this conduct is reflected in the literature, particularly in domestic cases.[139]

According to the interview data, although Article 51 of the Chinese Arbitration Law allows the parties to conclude a mediated settlement agreement either as a mediation statement or a consent award, to guarantee enforcement under the New York Convention, settlements are usually incorporated as arbitral awards.[140] If arbitration resumes following failed efforts to settle, the arbitrators disregard the confidential information obtained during mediation, and the parties are not allowed to use it.[141] Nevertheless, according to the literature, whether arbitrators—unlike the parties—can use confidential information within the renewed arbitration lacks legal clarity, as most arbitration rules only prohibit the parties from doing so but are silent about the tribunal's duty to disregard this information.[142] Additionally, the literature shows evidence of the broad reliance of Chinese arbitrators on confidential information in their awards, especially in domestic cases.[143] Based on the collected interview data, the

133. Kun & Kaufmann-Kohler, 2008, p. 492; Gu, 2021, p. 75; Gu, 2019, p. 135; Kun, 2020a, p. 154.
134. Kun, 2020a, p. 150; Kaufmann-Kohler, 2009, p. 197; Nigmatullina, 2018, p. 72; Kun & Kaufmann-Kohler, 2008, p. 488; Kun, 2013a, p. 167; Kun, 2011b, pp. 554-555.
135. Kun & Kaufmann-Kohler, 2008, p. 488; Kun, 2020a, pp. 150, 152, 163-165; Stipanowich, 2021a, pp. 352-354; Nigmatullina, 2018, p. 72.
136. Kun & Kaufmann-Kohler, 2008, p. 488; Kun, 2011b, p. 555.
137. Kun, 2020a, p. 151; Kun & Kaufmann-Kohler, 2008, pp. 488-489.
138. Kun, 2020a, p. 151; Kun & Kaufmann-Kohler, 2008, p. 489.
139. Gu, 2021, p. 71; Stipanowich, 2021a, pp. 308-309; Gu, 2019, p. 126; Stipanowich, 2009, pp. 395-396.
140. Kun & Kaufmann-Kohler, 2008, p. 489; Cao, 2006, p. 91.
141. Kun & Kaufmann-Kohler, 2008, pp. 490-491.
142. Stipanowich, 2021a, pp. 309-310; Gu, 2019, p. 138; Gu & Zhang, 2012, p. 1021. This uncertainty is exemplified below by several rules of leading arbitration institutes in China.
143. Gu & Zhang, 2012, p. 1021.

2007 Kun and Kaufmann-Kohler Study concluded that the combined use of mediation and arbitration in China remains strongly influenced by the traditional role of mediation in the country and its integration into civil court proceedings. However, greater emphasis has been placed on party autonomy in arbitration compared to judicial mediation or mediation conducted by governmental committees.[144]

The second study about the practice of the Chinese combined model was conducted between 2011 and 2012 and relied on an online survey that gathered empirical data from 36 arbitrators affiliated with the CIETAC and the BAC (2011-2012 Kun and Kaufmann-Kohler Survey).[145] Interestingly, the vast majority of surveyed arbitrators considered the combined use of mediation and arbitration as reflective of traditional culture.[146] According to 89.9% of the respondents, settlement facilitation is an adequate duty of the arbitrator.[147] Moreover, 91.7% agreed that it is appropriate for arbitrators to offer mediation, with 80.6% considering it suitable to hold ex parte communications during the mediation phase.[148] However, the respondents expressed more hesitant positions regarding case evaluations and the initiation of settlement proposals. While 27.8% considered it appropriate for arbitrators to propose settlements on their own initiative, 63.9% believed such proposals should only occur at the parties' request.[149] Similarly, 19.5% found it acceptable for arbitrators to deliver case evaluations on their own initiative, while 47.2% believed such evaluations should only be given upon the disputants' request, and 33.3% deemed them always inappropriate.[150]

When asked about applying the combined model in practice, the data revealed that 77.8% of the respondents conduct mediation on their own initiative, with 50% proposing mediation in over 90% of their cases. Notably, when all disputants are Chinese, the positive response rate to mediation is 59.5%, whereas this rate drops to 19.5% when foreign parties are involved.[151] Regarding the timing of suggesting mediation, most respondents indicated they make suggestions not earlier than the first hearing (i.e., 38.9% propose mediation during the first hearing, while 52.8% only after the main hearing).[152] As to the timing of settlements, 30.6% stated that settlements occur mostly during the first hearing, while 61.1% asserted that settlements are most likely to occur after the main hearing.[153] The data further revealed that 97.3% of the respondents "rarely" or "never" express evaluative views during mediation, even when asked by the parties.[154] Additionally, 63.9% "almost always" or "often" caucus with the disputants during mediation and employ "back-to-back" diplomacy and "reality check" techniques to narrow the gaps between the parties.[155] At the same time,

144. Kun & Kaufmann-Kohler, 2008, p. 486.
145. Kun, 2020a; Kun, 2014; Kun, 2016b, p. 479.
146. Kun, 2014, p. 811; Kun, 2020a, p. 169.
147. Kun, 2020a, pp. 142, 159; Kun, 2014, p. 805.
148. Kun, 2020a, pp. 143, 161.
149. Kun, 2020a, pp. 143, 161.
150. Kun, 2020a, pp. 143, 161.
151. Kun, 2014, pp. 791-792; Kun, 2020a, pp. 143, 161-163; Kun, 2016b, p. 480.
152. Kun, 2020a, pp. 147-148, 162.
153. Kun, 2020a, pp. 148, 162.
154. Kun, 2020a, pp. 150-151.
155. Kun, 2020a, pp. 149-150, 164.

only 25% of the respondents "almost always" or "often" raise settlement proposals at the parties' request, whereas 75% "rarely" or "never" do so despite explicit requests.[156] Hence, the 2011-2012 Kun and Kaufmann-Kohler Survey results aligned with the collected interview data and the conclusions of the 2007 Kun and Kaufmann-Kohler Study regarding the Chinese combined model.

5.2.2.1.3 Addressing Due Process Concerns Resulting from the Dual Role

Alongside confirming the actual practice of the combined use of arbitration and mediation by Chinese arbitrators, the 2011-2012 Kun and Kaufmann-Kohler Survey reflected a heated debate in China regarding the excessive use of mediation within arbitral proceedings and the need to implement necessary safeguards during the mediation phase aimed to address due process concerns.[157] The surveyed participants suggested implementing the following safeguards in these combined procedures: (a) prohibiting the use of any confidential information, opinions, views, statements, or proposals expressed during the mediation in the formal arbitration; (b) informing the parties about the typical conduct of the combined procedure and the risks associated with its implementation, particularly during caucusing; and (c) allowing the disputants to replace the arbitrator following futile efforts to settle if they raise concerns about possible influence of the mediation on the final award.[158] When asked to suggest ways to improve the use of the combined model in China, the participants proposed the following: (a) focusing on more conciliatory skills within the training process of arbitrators to enhance their ability to handle barriers for settlements; and (b) encouraging arbitrators to respect the voluntariness of the combined process while always seeking the parties' consent before its implementation.[159] Interestingly, some participants even suggested establishing more independent mediation institutions to significantly reduce the application of the combined model and focus more on standalone mediation.[160]

According to the literature, the debate regarding the need to implement necessary safeguards to enhance the combined model in China broke out in 2011 after a decision of the Hong Kong court in the *Gao Haiyan* case, refusing for the first time to enforce an arbitration award rendered in Mainland China under the New York Convention following private communications of the tribunal with one of the parties. During the agreed mediation conducted by the tribunal throughout the arbitral proceedings, a party-appointed arbitrator met privately with a shareholder of the other party and asked him to "work on" their party to agree to a suggested settlement proposal. After the shareholder's party declined the proposal, the tribunal rendered a considerably lower award less favorable to the shareholder's party, who later challenged the final

156. Kun, 2020a, pp. 151-152, 164.
157. Kun, 2020a, pp. 153-156. *See also* Gu, 2019, pp. 138-139; Kun & Kaufmann-Kohler, 2008, p. 486; Phillips, F. P., 2009, pp. 320-321.
158. Kun, 2020a, pp. 154-155.
159. Kun, 2020a, pp. 145-147, 168-169.
160. Kun, 2020a, pp. 168-169.

award in front of the Chinese court on the grounds of favoritism and malpractice by the tribunal. The shareholder's party argued that the unfavorable award reflected a "punishment" for its refusal to accept the settlement offer. The Chinese court dismissed these arguments, ruling that the ex parte meeting, being part of the agreed mediation process and permitted under the rules of the arbitration institute, rendered the award enforceable. However, when the award was submitted for enforcement in Hong Kong, the shareholder's party objected to enforcement due to the same arguments raised in front of the Chinese court. The Hong Kong Court of First Instance accepted these arguments and refused to enforce the award.[161] According to the court's reasoning, the arbitrator's conduct during the ex parte meeting could cause a "fair-minded observer" to comprehend an actual probability of bias, so the enforcement contradicted public policy in Hong Kong.[162] Eventually, the decision was reversed by the Court of Appeal in Hong Kong for the following reasons: the respondents waived their right of objection to enforceability since they failed to raise claims regarding the arbitrator's behavior during the arbitration process; the claimed apparent bias did not establish any public policy issue; and since the examined process allowing the combination of mediation with arbitration was tolerated in Mainland China, it would "not amount to a breach of public policy in Hong Kong unless it was so serious as to be contrary to fundamental conceptions of morality and justice."[163]

Despite the prevailing opinion in the literature, holding that the arbitrator's behavior in the *Gao Haiyan* case does not reflect the normal practice of Chinese arbitrators,[164] several important implications of this case should still be considered. *First*, it emphasizes the risks associated with ex parte communications by the arbitrator and the need to set clear safeguards for their use to impede actual or apparent bias.[165] *Second*, it demonstrates a possible direct link between caucusing during the mediation stage and the enforceability of the award. It seems that by enforcing the award, the Hong Kong appellate court applied a narrow interpretation of public policy considerations since it mainly relied on the acceptability of the caucus practice in the seat of arbitration without relating to public policy considerations applicable in Hong Kong.[166] However, it cannot be guaranteed that while examining similar award courts in other jurisdictions would not reach a different conclusion and refuse enforcement for public policy considerations applicable in their legal systems.[167] Therefore, the Court of

161. *Gao Haiyan and Xie Heping v. Keeneye Holdings Ltd and New Purple Golden Resources Development Ltd,* HKEC (CFI) 514, 2011; Gu, 2014, p. 99; Kun, 2011b, pp. 536, 538-542; Gu, 2019, pp. 136-138; Stipanowich, 2021a, pp. 310-311; Chaisse & Shang, 2021, pp. 97-99.
162. Kun, 2011b, pp. 540-542; Kun, 2011a, pp. 11-14. *See also* Hong Kong Arbitration Ordinance, 2011, section 95(3), allowing the court to refuse enforcement of an award from Mainland China due to public policy considerations.
163. Kun, 2011b, pp. 546-549. *See also Gao Haiyan and Xie Heping v. Keeneye Holdings Ltd and New Purple Golden Resources Development Ltd,* CACV (CA) 79, 2011; Chaisse & Shang, 2021, pp. 98-99; Yan & Woo, 2014; Croft, 2014, pp. 10-12.
164. As demonstrated above, Chinese arbitrators rarely provide settlement proposals to disputants, especially when such proposals have not been specifically requested by the parties. *See* Stipanowich, 2021a, p. 310.
165. Gu, 2021, p. 76; Gu, 2019, pp. 136-139.
166. Kun, 2011b, p. 549; Gu, 2021, p. 77.
167. Ortolani, 2025, §21.5(g); Sussman, 2013, p. 13; Gu, 2021, pp. 77, 89.

Appeal's decision in the *Gao Haiyan* case may grant Chinese arbitrators a feigned sense of security regarding ex parte communications during the arbitral process when, in practice, it is still necessary to address enforceability concerns deriving from them.[168] *Third*, due process concerns connected to the combined model should be addressed from a wider perspective since they may arise in situations other than caucusing, such as coercive behavior of the arbitrator, violation of the parties' autonomy, and the use of confidential information received while caucusing or otherwise:

> Labelling a process as either 'arb-med' or 'med-arb' does not mean that anything goes. There are appropriate and inappropriate ways of conducting such a proceeding. The discussions on appropriateness of conduct in the so-called arb-med procedure in Gao Haiyan ... have garnered a lot of discussion regarding the boundary between the role of an arbitrator and the role of a mediator. It highlights the importance of ensuring that any mediation conducted by arbitrators is done in an appropriate manner to ensure that, if the mediation does not end in a settlement and the arbitration proceedings resume, an award will be enforceable. It warns mediators (who might later become arbitrators) to avoid, wherever possible, conduct which might give rise to allegations of procedural irregularities or other grounds to challenge an award or its enforcement.[169]

Fourth, beyond procedures that combine arbitration with mediation, due process concerns also arise in scenarios where the arbitrator is directly involved in settlement facilitation, even within standalone arbitration.[170] In this context, while the implications of the *Gao Haiyan* case are particularly relevant for China, whose legal culture encourages mediation during arbitral proceedings, they hold even greater significance for jurisdictions that discourage such practice or implement stricter safeguards to ensure procedural fairness.[171]

As part of the debate regarding the need to introduce safeguards to the dual role of arbitrators in China,[172] the literature offers several solutions: separating mediation and arbitration procedures,[173] enhancing the judicial supervision on the combined model while restraining the "pro-arbitration" attitude of the Chinese courts to better address due process concerns and avoid coerced settlements,[174] ensuring the parties' informed consent to participate in combined processes while demanding them to waive their right to challenge the arbitrator or the award following their fulfillment,[175] and choosing the right neutrals who are qualified for the dual role.[176] However, neither the Chinese Arbitration Law nor the Supreme Court's judicial interpretations and guidelines suggest safeguards for the dual role, which leaves concerns connected with its

168. Gu, 2019, p. 156; Gu, 2014, p. 109.
169. Kun, 2011b, pp. 549-550. *See also* Sussman, 2013, pp. 12-13.
170. Berger, 2018b, pp. 513-515.
171. Kun, 2020a, p. 154.
172. Kun, 2011b, p. 536.
173. Gu, 2019, p. 171.
174. Kun, 2011b, pp. 551-552; Gu, 2019, pp. 161, 171; Gu, 2021, pp. 89-90.
175. Kun, 2011b, p. 551; Sussman, 2009a, pp. 71-73; Sussman, 2013, pp. 10-11.
176. Sussman, 2013, p. 9; Kun, 2011b, pp. 550-551; Blankenship, 2006, p. 36; Bartel, 1991, pp. 687-688; Nigmatullina, 2018, p. 57; Blankley, 2011, p. 337.

practice without proper regulation.[177] Recent judicial policy introduced in 2018 has further complicated the refusal of award enforcement on public policy grounds, requiring prior approval from the High People's Court in China before such a decision can be rendered.[178] According to some scholars, the reluctance of the Chinese legislator and judiciary to regulate due process concerns indicates that China has delegated the regulation of due process standards to the market's responsibility through a bottom-up approach, which potentially may result in inconsistent safeguards among the hundreds of arbitration institutions in the country.[179] However, only a handful of leading institutes in China, which host the vast majority of ICA processes, have partly addressed due process concerns, mainly to meet the expectations of international parties instead of exercising local obligation and responsibility.[180] Nevertheless, these initiatives, introduced as amendments to the institutions' rules, are crucial steps in line with the proposals above. An example relates to the parties' consent. Even though the Chinese Arbitration Law explicitly authorizes arbitrators to conduct mediation even when the parties oppose that attempt, the BAC, CIETAC, and SCIA Rules stipulate this initiative of arbitrators with the parties' consent.[181] The CIETAC and SCIA Rules even clearly state that arbitrators shall terminate the mediation when parties withdraw their consent.[182] Another example relates to the possibility of replacing the arbitrator should the mediation fail to produce an amicable solution. While the Chinese Arbitration Law provides that arbitration shall resume under the same arbitrator in such circumstances, the BAC Rules enable the parties to replace the arbitrator if failed mediation efforts may affect the final award.[183] Although this arrangement is embedded only in the BAC Rules,[184] the CIETAC Rules enable international parties to arbitrate under the UNCITRAL Arbitration Rules,[185] and the SCIA Rules use the UNCITRAL Arbitration Rules as a default for international disputes.[186] Since under the UNCITRAL Arbitration Rules, parties can challenge the arbitrator if justifiable doubts arise regarding their impartiality or independence,[187] then, potentially, also according to the CIETAC and SCIA Rules, it is possible to replace arbitrators who have earlier engaged in mediation.[188] An additional example relates to the possibility of conducting the mediation by a separate neutral. Although the arbitration law is silent about this possibility, according to the CIETAC, BAC, and SCIA Rules, subject to the parties' request, mediation can be conducted separately—within their mediation centers or other partner institutes—when mediated settlement agreements can later be converted into arbitral

177. Gu, 2019, p. 140; Gu, 2021, pp. 72, 78-79.
178. Gu, 2021, pp. 82-83; Gu, 2019, pp. 150-151.
179. Gu, 2021, pp. 80-81; Gu, 2019, p. 141.
180. Gu, 2017, pp. 826-829; Gu, 2019, pp. 141-142; Gu, 2021, p. 78.
181. CIETAC Arbitration Rules, 2024, Article 47(1)-(2); BAC Arbitration Rules, 2022, Article 43(1); SCIA Arbitration Rules, 2022, Article 48(1)-(3); Gu, 2021, p. 80.
182. CIETAC Arbitration Rules, 2024, Article 47(3); SCIA Arbitration Rules, 2022, Article 48(4).
183. BAC Arbitration Rules, 2022, Article 67(2).
184. Gu, 2019, p. 135; Gu, 2021, p. 74.
185. CIETAC Arbitration Rules, 2024, Article 4(3).
186. SCIA Arbitration Rules, 2022, Article 3(4)-(5).
187. UNCITRAL Arbitration Rules, 2021, Article 12(1); Gu, 2019, p. 143.
188. Gu, 2019, p. 143; Gu, 2021, pp. 81-82.

awards.[189] However, since these developments are quite recent, insufficient data is available regarding their attractiveness in terms of saving time and costs while improving enforceability, given that such settlements are reached completely outside the arbitral process.[190] Another example relates to confidential information disclosed during the mediation phase. Although the arbitration law does not regulate this issue, the CIETAC, BAC, and SCIA Rules prohibit parties from using that information in subsequent arbitration.[191] However, the rules do not address the aforementioned legal uncertainty related to the arbitrator's alleged authority to use confidential information in the renewed arbitration, as they only prohibit the parties from doing so. Better protection of confidential information may also require applying that prohibition to the arbitrator.[192]

The impact of these institutional initiatives, as a foundation for better regulation of the combined model, is well reflected in the recent "top-down" design[193] of the dispute-resolution mechanism under the Belt and Road Initiative (BRI).[194] As part of this initiative, in mid-2018, China announced the establishment of the China International Commercial Court (CICC), annexed to the Chinese Supreme Court and comprising senior judges familiar with international law.[195] Since participating BRI jurisdictions have various legal cultures, the dispute-resolution mechanisms offered under the CICC are diversified and include mediation, arbitration, and litigation.[196] Within this framework, in 2019, China signed the Singapore Convention to encourage using ICM to resolve disputes arising from the BRI.[197] One of the most interesting features of this "one-stop" platform of the CICC is conducting the mediation and arbitration parts of Med-Arb processes within separate leading mediation and arbitration institutions in the country[198] and, consequently, by separate neutrals.[199] Arbitral awards under this platform can be recognized and directly enforced by the CICC, and mediated settlements can be converted into judgments by the CICC.[200]

189. CIETAC Arbitration Rules, 2024, Article 47(8); BAC Arbitration Rules, 2022, Article 44; SCIA Arbitration Rules, 2022, Article 49(1)-(2). *See also* Harpole, 2007, pp. 627-628; Gu, 2019, p. 144; Gu, 2021, pp. 74, 82.
190. Gu, 2019, p. 155; Alexander et al., 2018, pp. 85-87.
191. CIETAC Arbitration Rules, 2024, Article 47(9); BAC Arbitration Rules, 2022, Article 43(5); SCIA Arbitration Rules, 2022, Article 48(6).
192. Gu, 2016, p. 101.
193. Gu, 2021, p. 84.
194. The BRI is a global infrastructure development strategy adopted by the Chinese government in 2013 to invest in nearly 70 countries and international organizations and to create new trade routes connecting China with the rest of the world. *See* World Bank Group, 2018; Tang, 2019.
195. Sun, 2020, pp. 48-49; Gu, 2019, pp. 162-169; Wang et al., 2020, pp. 11-12.
196. Gu, 2021, p. 86; Gu, 2019, p. 162; Sun, 2020, p. 49; Wang et al., 2020, pp. 11-16.
197. Chaisse & Shang, 2021, p. 108; Gu, 2021, p. 91; *Status: Singapore Convention*, n.d. Notably, China has yet to enact or amend its relevant domestic legislation to implement the provisions of the Convention. *See* Gu, 2021, pp. 85, 91; Gu, 2019, p. 154.
198. Gu, 2019, pp. 166-167, relating to the participating mediation and arbitration institutions.
199. Wang et al., 2020, Appendix 1—The Dispute Resolution Mechanism for the Belt and Road Initiative, p. 87, and Appendix 4, p. 128; Gu, 2019, p. 166; Sun, 2020, p. 49; Gu, 2021, p. 88.
200. Sun, 2020, p. 49; Gu, 2019, p. 167.

Intended to meet international rather than local needs,[201] separating arbitration and mediation proceedings under the CICC is inconsistent with the rooted attitude in China that favors hybrid procedures, prioritizing efficiency over high standards of due process.[202] This development signals that when international users are involved, China is willing to enhance the quality of the arbitral process:

> Judging from the most recent efforts of leading Chinese arbitration institutions, such as CIETAC, BAC, and SCIA, it is evident that regulation of arb-med detaching the two processes has become the trend when faced with international clients and the need to compete with international arbitration institutions in the BRI dispute resolution market. ... The CICC's most recent actions show that leading international arbitration norms and attracting foreign parties, in addition to BRI-dispute-resolution-market pressures, are the main factors driving Chinese regulators to look beyond sociopolitical imperatives and cultural boundaries.[203]

Apart from the above-discussed developments designated to meet the expectations of international users, the traditional combined model in China seems to represent "the most complete integration of mediation into arbitration"[204] with a "level of fluidity" that cannot be found in other jurisdictions, including in the region of East Asia.[205] As a leading economy and a jurisdiction that traditionally combined arbitration with mediation, China may still play an important role in developing transnational standards regarding the arbitrator's role as a settlement facilitator,[206] as recent surveys have indicated that parties to international commercial relations prefer dispute-resolution processes combining arbitration with other ADR methods over standalone arbitration or ADR mechanisms.[207] According to these surveys, when selecting an arbitration seat, the most important factors considered by international parties are the increased neutrality and impartiality of the local courts and clear support for arbitration by the local legislator and court system, expressed by a high enforcement record of agreements to arbitrate and arbitral awards.[208] These preferences may explain why the Chinese arbitration institutions and government have recently adjusted arbitral procedures according to "Western trends" in international user processes. Nevertheless, if China is willing to be a more attractive jurisdiction for foreign parties, better emphasis must be placed on safeguards intended to ensure the parties' due process rights and guarantee the arbitrator's impartiality in processes involving arbitration and mediation to diminish enforcement risks in other jurisdictions.[209] The question remains whether

201. Gu, 2021, p. 85.
202. Gu, 2021, p. 90.
203. Gu, 2019, pp. 170-171.
204. Kun & Kaufmann-Kohler, 2008, p. 487. *See also* Donahey, 1995, p. 76.
205. Nigmatullina, 2018, p. 71; Kun, 2013a, p. 166; Kun & Kaufmann-Kohler, 2008, p. 487.
206. Kun, 2016b, p. 456; Kun, 2013b, p. 184; Kun, 2020a, p. 137; Ali, 2011a, p. 68; Ross, 2013, p. 353.
207. Queen Mary University of London and White & Case LLP, 2021, p. 5; Queen Mary University of London and White & Case LLP, 2018, p. 5; GPC Series, 2016-2017, Question 2(5). For further discussion about these surveys, *see* the discussion in section 1.3. *See also* Lack, 2021, p. 12; Yip, 2021, p. 183; Stipanowich, 2021a, p. 271; Chua, 2018, p. 1.
208. Queen Mary University of London and White & Case LLP, 2021, p. 8. *See also* Guo, 2020, p. 227, relating to similar considerations while selecting international commercial courts.
209. Gu, 2021, p. 89.

the aforementioned initiatives will eventually penetrate domestic arbitration in China or whether different legal regimes will continue to separate foreign and local arbitration in the country.[210] Thus far, there are no indications that these procedures will be embedded into Chinese Arbitration Law or the rules of other arbitral institutes in China.[211]

5.2.2.2 Hong Kong

Unlike Mainland China, where the rules of specific arbitration institutes serve as the primary regulatory framework for the arbitrator's dual role, Hong Kong, similar to Singapore and Japan, has relied on legislation to better regulate the arbitrator's mandate and establish procedural standards intended to address due process concerns.[212] Following the 2009 Civil Justice Reform in Hong Kong,[213] courts have engaged in settlement facilitation and "court-directed mediation" to hold the settlement rate at approximately 60 %.[214] To strengthen the role of mediation within judicial proceedings, the Practice Direction on Mediation, intended for Courts of First Instance and District Courts, states that in allocating the trial costs, courts may "depart from the common law practice that a losing party pays the winning side's litigation costs" and instead "penalise the winning party if it unreasonably fails to engage in mediation."[215] In line with civil justice reform, the 2011 Arbitration Ordinance, based on the UNCITRAL Model Law on ICA and applicable to local and international arbitrations,[216] deliberately empowers the arbitrator to conduct the role of a mediator to facilitate a settlement in pending arbitral proceedings.[217] However, this mandate of the arbitrator is subject to the following procedural safeguards. *First*, the arbitration proceedings have commenced, and all parties have given their written consent to mediation. *Second*, during mediation, the arbitral proceedings must be stayed to increase the chances for a successful settlement process. *Third*, the arbitrator can mediate as long as none of the parties has canceled its consent in writing; otherwise, mediation terminates and arbitration resumes. *Fourth*, if mediation fails, the arbitrator must disclose to all parties

210. Gu, 2019, pp. 151, 156; Gu, 2021, p. 85.
211. Gu, 2019, p. 154; Gu, 2021, pp. 85, 91. This separation between domestic proceedings—implementing traditional "Chinese-styled Arb-Med," and proceedings under leading arbitral institutions—applying Western standards to attract international users, has been criticized by leading Chinese scholars and practitioners who call for reforms in domestic arbitration to comply with international standards of due process. *See* the discussion in section 6.3.4; Gu, 2019, pp. 142, 169-170; Kun, 2011b, pp. 552-555.
212. Taylor & Pryles, 2006, pp. 15-17; Gu, 2021, p. 69; Stipanowich, 2021a, pp. 320-323; Gu, 2019, pp. 152-154.
213. Kun, 2011b, pp. 540-541; Chaisse & Shang, 2021, p. 95.
214. McFadden, 2013, p. 222; Chaisse & Shang, 2021, p. 95; Kun, 2011b, p. 540; *Mediation statistics for Civil Justice Reform related cases*, n.d.
215. Chaisse & Shang, 2021, pp. 95-96. *See also* McFadden, 2013, p. 225; Kun, 2011a, pp. 11-14; Hong Kong Judiciary Practice Direction on Mediation, 2010, Article 2(5).
216. Kun, 2012, p. 717; Gu, 2021, p. 78; Gu, 2019, p. 139.
217. Hong Kong Arbitration Ordinance, 2011, Article 33; D'Agostino, 2011b; Chaisse & Shang, 2021, p. 97; Kun, 2011b, p. 541; Stipanowich, 2021a, pp. 321-322; Nigmatullina, 2018, p. 96; Ruckteschler & Wendelstein, 2021, pp. 766-767.

any confidential information shared during mediation that the arbitrator considers material to the arbitral proceedings before reverting to arbitration.[218] According to the Arbitration Ordinance, the arbitrator may engage with the disputants collectively or separately during mediation. Additionally, parties may not challenge the arbitrator on the mere ground of mediating the dispute.[219]

Despite settlement facilitation's express permission by law and contrary to its success within judicial proceedings, it has not enjoyed actual recognition within arbitral proceedings in Hong Kong.[220] As reflected in the *Gao Haiyan* case, compared to their counterparts in Mainland China, arbitrators in Hong Kong have expressed deep distrust in the dual role of arbitrators.[221] This attitude is exemplified by the Hong Kong International Arbitration Centre (HKIAC), which implements a "watertight approach to mediation and arbitration, securing separate rules that do not appear to provide for any mixing or blending."[222] Parties to arbitral proceedings under the HKIAC who seek to amicably settle their dispute are referred to the Hong Kong Mediation Centre (HKMC) when a successful mediation is recorded as a settlement agreement and not a consent award.[223] Although the HKIAC Arbitration Rules are silent regarding the arbitrator's authority to facilitate a settlement, the HKIAC Mediation Rules explicitly forbid the mediator from arbitrating the dispute subsequently.[224] Since these rules are indispensable, parties cannot agree on a contradictory arrangement that allows the arbitrator to maintain the dual role.[225]

The separation between arbitration and mediation has also been implemented by Hong Kong's Financial Dispute Resolution Centre (FDRC), a governmental body that resolves monetary disputes between customers and financial institutions.[226] Although the FDRC focuses on affordable and amicable solutions to these disputes,[227] it implements a "mediation first and arbitration next" process,[228] under which disputes are first referred to mediation. If it fails to settle the dispute amicably, the FDRC appoints a different neutral to act as an arbitrator.[229] According to some scholars, this schematic design under the FDRC, which does not allow the same neutral to conduct the entire proceeding while "switching hats" between the mediator and arbitrator

218. Hong Kong Arbitration Ordinance, 2011, Article 33(1)-(4); Kun, 2011b, p. 541; Chaisse & Shang, 2021, p. 97; Gu, 2019, pp. 139, 153; Ross, 2013, p. 356; Kun, 2012, pp. 715-722; Rosoff, 2009, pp. 98-100; Marriott, 2005, p. 545.
219. Hong Kong Arbitration Ordinance, 2011, Article 33(3) & (5); Stipanowich, 2021a, pp. 322-323; Kun, 2011b, p. 541; Chaisse & Shang, 2021, p. 97; Ruckteschler & Wendelstein, 2021, pp. 766-767; Rosoff, 2009, pp. 98-99.
220. Kun, 2011b, p. 541; Nigmatullina, 2018, pp. 95-96, 100; Chaisse & Shang, 2021, p. 97; Kun, 2012, p. 720; Wilson, 2012; Georgiou & Seow, 2014.
221. Kun, 2011b, p. 541; Chaisse & Shang, 2021, pp. 98-99.
222. De Vera, 2004, p. 191. *See also* Nigmatullina, 2018, pp. 132-133; HKIAC Arbitration Rules, 2024.
223. HKIAC Mediation Rules, 1999, Introduction Chapter and Article 11(a).
224. HKIAC Mediation Rules, 1999, Article 14.
225. Nigmatullina, 2018, p. 132.
226. *FDRC: Objectives*, n.d.; Chaisse & Shang, 2021, pp. 99-106.
227. *FDRC: Objectives*, n.d.
228. *FDRC: Dispute resolution process*, n.d.; Chaisse & Shang, 2021, p. 103.
229. Chaisse & Shang, 2021, pp. 104, 106.

roles, is unnecessary for this kind of disputes and is inconsistent with the dual role authority of financial ombudsmen in many other jurisdictions, including in the UK.[230]

Possible explanations for the hesitant attitude in Hong Kong toward the dual role of arbitrators are suggested below after presenting the Singaporean model of the role.

5.2.2.3 Singapore

Singapore is another East Asian jurisdiction that has relied on legislation to regulate the dual role of arbitrators. The Arbitration Act, which addresses domestic arbitrations, and the International Arbitration Act authorize arbitrators to facilitate settlements and act as mediators in the same arbitral proceedings.[231] Similar to Hong Kong, this mandate of the arbitrators is subject to the following safeguards: (a) all parties must consent in writing before mediation is initiated; (b) parties can withdraw their consent any time in writing, then the arbitrator shall terminate the mediation and resume the arbitral proceedings; and (c) if mediation fails to achieve an amicable outcome, before reverting to arbitration, the arbitrator must disclose to all parties any confidential information shared during mediation that the arbitrator considers material to the arbitral proceedings.[232] Additionally, during mediation, the arbitrator can meet with the parties collectively or separately and cannot be challenged solely on the grounds of mediating the dispute.[233] However, unlike the arrangement in Hong Kong, no explicit requirement exists to stay the arbitration during mediation.

Similar to Hong Kong, the dual role of arbitrators has not gained actual recognition within arbitral proceedings in Singapore despite explicit law authorization.[234] The SIAC, the leading arbitration institute in the country, designates a clear separation between arbitration and mediation proceedings.[235] Although the SIAC Arbitration Rules are silent about the arbitrator's mandate to act as a mediator or settlement facilitator,[236] parties willing to settle their disputes are referred to the Arb-Med-Arb Protocol (AMA Protocol) launched in 2014 through cooperation between the SIAC and the Singapore International Mediation Centre (SIMC).[237] According to the Protocol, arbitration and mediation are carried out separately by these institutes.[238] After arbitration commences under the SIAC, arbitral proceedings are stayed for several weeks, during which the SIMC mediates the case. Although the AMA Protocol does not prohibit the arbitrator from mediating the dispute if the parties so wish, it encourages

230. Chaisse & Shang, 2021, pp. 104, 106, 109; James & Morris, 2003, pp. 169-171.
231. Singapore International Arbitration Act, 1994, Articles 16 & 17; Singapore Arbitration Act, 2001, Article 63; Stipanowich, 2021a, p. 320; Yip, 2021, p. 191; Nigmatullina, 2018, p. 96.
232. Singapore International Arbitration Act, 1994, Article 17(1) & (3); Singapore Arbitration Act, 2001, Article 63(1) & (3); Gu, 2019, pp. 139, 152-153; Stipanowich, 2021a, pp. 320-321; Gu, 2021, pp. 78-79; Yip, 2021, p. 193; Ross, 2013, p. 356; Rosoff, 2009, pp. 99-100.
233. Singapore International Arbitration Act, 1994, Articles 16(3), 17(2) & (4); Singapore Arbitration Act, 2001, Article 63(2) & (4); Rosoff, 2009, pp. 99-100.
234. Nigmatullina, 2018, pp. 76, 95-96, 100; Nottage, 2014, p. 227; Hwang, 2005, pp. 574-575.
235. Gu, 2019, p. 155; Yip, 2021, pp. 194-201.
236. SIAC Arbitration Rules, 2025.
237. SIAC-SIMC AMA Protocol, 2014; Boog, 2015, pp. 91-96; Henderson & Chua, 2014.
238. SIAC-SIMC AMA Protocol, 2014, Article 5; Gu, 2019, p. 155; Nigmatullina, 2018, p. 132.

the nomination of different neutrals for each process to eliminate the possibility of structural bias.[239] According to the Protocol, a successfully mediated settlement is considered a consent award by the SIAC to ensure worldwide enforcement under the New York Convention. If mediation fails to bring a settlement, arbitral proceedings resume under the SIAC to eventually render an arbitral award.[240] According to recent data, the settlement rate under the AMA Protocol is 85%.[241] However, as of 2021, the protocol has been adopted only in 14 cases.[242] Scholars and users criticized the AMA protocol for the additional allocation of time and expenses resulting from the institutional partitioning of mediation and arbitration[243] and for its rigid structure that does not necessarily allow a deviation from its standard process if the parties seek to exercise their party autonomy and tailor a more flexible process that meets their needs.[244] Particular criticism was raised against the early stage of mediation under the protocol—immediately after the commencement of arbitration—when the gaps between the parties may still be significant, and they have not yet examined their possibilities or reconsidered their preliminary positions.[245]

The literature suggests several explanations for the infrequent use of the dual role in Hong Kong and Singapore. *First*, the arbitrator's obligation to disclose confidential information material to arbitration has been widely criticized by academics and practitioners, who consider it the main obstacle to fulfilling the dual role.[246] Although designed to safeguard the parties' due process rights and encourage transparency during the resumed arbitration,[247] this obligation creates uncertainty regarding the disclosure of confidential information, which many practitioners consider crucial to a successful mediation.[248] As a result, parties may be discouraged from participating in mediation or behaving candidly and openly during the settlement negotiations.[249] According to some commentators, this uncertainty regarding confidential information may even force parties to settle while knowing that full disclosure may follow in the resumed arbitral process.[250] Even from a practical point of view, this obligation may be challenging for the arbitrator to fulfill:

239. Stipanowich, 2021a, pp. 277, 287; Yip, 2021, p. 196; Alexander et al., 2018, pp. 85-87; Alexander, 2017, p. 14; Nigmatullina, 2018, p. 132; *SIMC: Arb-Med-Arb*, n.d., clarifying that the intention of the AMA protocol is to assign different neutrals for arbitration and mediation.
240. SIAC-SIMC AMA Protocol, 2014, Articles 5-9; Yip, 2021, pp. 194-195; Alexander et al., 2018, pp. 85-87; Gu, 2019, p. 155; Alexander, 2017, p. 14.
241. Alexander et al., 2018, pp. 85-87.
242. Yip, 2021, p. 201.
243. Yip, 2021, p. 196; Gu, 2019, p. 155.
244. Yip, 2021, pp. 199-200.
245. Yip, 2021, p. 199; Wolski, 2013, p. 267.
246. Nigmatullina, 2018, pp. 96, 131; Harris, 2016, p. 94; Ma & Brock, 2017, p. 12; Ross, 2013, p. 361; Wilson, 2012; D'Agostino, 2011a; Kun, 2012, p. 720; Donahey, 1995, p. 77; Hwang, 2005, p. 574.
247. Yip, 2021, pp. 193-194; Stipanowich, 2021a, p. 321; Rosoff, 2009, p. 100.
248. Stipanowich, 2021a, p. 321; Rosoff, 2009, p. 100.
249. Chaisse & Shang, 2021, p. 97; Yip, 2021, pp. 193-194; Nigmatullina, 2018, p. 96; Harris, 2016, p. 94; Kun, 2012, p. 720; Stipanowich, 2021a, pp. 321, 355; Rosoff, 2009, p. 100; Deason, 2001, pp. 84-85; Wolski, 2013, p. 263; Hwang, 2005, p. 575; CIArb Practice Guideline on the Use of Mediation in Arbitration, 2021, Article 8(5).
250. Yip, 2021, p. 194.

> It puts the dual role neutral in a difficult position by requiring the neutral to take a view about what information is 'material' and how exactly to disclose it. Furthermore, mediations usually take place in an informal fashion with few notes taken, which makes it difficult for the neutral to record everything accurately. It might happen that one party will object to the disclosure made by the neutral as not reflecting an accurate summary of what was said. Also, it would seem to open up the neutral to subsequent challenges as to what should have been disclosed.[251]

Consequently, arbitrators may be hesitant to act as settlement facilitators or, according to some scholars, may simply disclose everything to the parties, even unnecessary information, to avoid challenges.[252] This disclosure obligation, which cannot be waived by the parties, is observed by practitioners as a limiting factor of their party autonomy and their right to design the process according to their wishes and needs.[253] *Second*, the unconditional right of the parties to withdraw their consent to mediation at any stage of the process has been criticized by scholars and practitioners for granting a veto power to each party over the arbitrator's efforts to settle the dispute amicably.[254] The concern is that parties may tactically use this right to replace an undesired arbitrator, end the mediation to take advantage of the arbitrator's obligation to disclose information and improve their position, or simply to delay the proceedings.[255] *Third*, the rare use of the dual role in Hong Kong and Singapore, despite explicit authorization by the law, may be attributed to the difficulty of practitioners, who are trained in Common Law that traditionally involve separate neutrals as arbitrators and settlement facilitators, to accept attitudes of other legal cultures in the matter, including in neighboring jurisdictions such as Civil Law China.[256] This attitude can also explain why legislation supporting and regulating the arbitrator's dual role has been more endorsed in Common Law jurisdictions and less in Civil Law systems, which are traditionally more accustomed to the involvement of adjudicators in the settlement process.[257] Other scholars, however, have argued that these legislative provisions in Hong Kong and Singapore have been influenced by East Asian cultures, including the Chinese traditional way of dispute settlement, but could not in practice prevail over the established Common Law legal tradition in these jurisdictions.[258] *Fourth*, the rare use of the dual role may result from the comparatively novel exposure to mediation procedures in Hong Kong and Singapore and the fact that the dual role of the arbitrator

251. Nigmatullina, 2018, p. 200. *See also* Ruckteschler & Wendelstein, 2021, p. 773; Goodrich, 2012, pp. 6-7; Deekshitha & Saha, 2014, p. 92; Wolski, 2013, p. 263.
252. Ross, 2013, p. 361. According to some scholars, full disclosure after failed settlement attempts may be mandatory in jurisdictions that adapted Article 24(3) to the Model Law on ICA, 2006, which mandates the arbitrator to communicate to all parties any information received from one party to the arbitration. *See*, in this regard, the discussion in section 8.3.2.
253. Gojkovic, 2021, p. 71; Ludington, 2017, pp. 320-321; Nigmatullina, 2018, p. 202; Goodrich, 2012, p. 6; Rosoff, 2009, p. 100.
254. Goodrich, 2012, p. 7; Nigmatullina, 2018, p. 201.
255. Nigmatullina, 2018, p. 201; Goodrich, 2012, p. 7.
256. Nigmatullina, 2018, pp. 97, 100; Nottage & Garnett, 2010, p. 36.
257. Chaisse & Shang, 2021, p. 96; Nigmatullina, 2018, p. 97; Menkel-Meadow, 2013, p. 424; Wissler, 2011, pp. 297-298; Ehle, 2010, p. 83; Jones, 2005, p. 406.
258. Kaufmann-Kohler, 2009, p. 193; Nigmatullina, 2018, p. 97; Donahey, 1995, pp. 74, 77.

has not been developed enough by courts and practitioners.[259] As a result, excess weight is given to due process concerns, particularly the risk of losing impartiality, which may jeopardize the legitimacy of the whole proceedings.[260] According to some commentators, the 2009 Civil Justice Reform in Hong Kong, under which parties may feel compelled to mediate their disputes, affects practitioners' attitudes about mediation unfavorably and may contribute to the infrequent use of the dual role by arbitrators in that jurisdiction.[261] *Fifth*, Singapore and Hong Kong host most international arbitrations in Asia and belong to the three most preferred seats for international arbitration worldwide.[262] Even under the BRI initiative, international parties prefer to arbitrate their disputes in these jurisdictions over Chinese arbitral institutes, which have been criticized for their arbitral procedures that need improvement.[263] It appears that to attract Western parties, arbitral institutes in Singapore and Hong Kong have integrated more predictable Western standards into their rules that are inconsistent with the provisions of their domestic laws.[264] According to some views in the literature, this level of due process protection implemented by arbitral institutions in Singapore and Hong Kong may indicate that legal culture has only limited influence when cross-border arbitration rules are at stake.[265]

5.3 LEGAL CULTURES IN THE WEST

Western legal systems are disunified regarding the role of judges and arbitrators as settlement facilitators.[266] While Western Common Law systems have not traditionally permitted the active involvement of adjudicators in settlement facilitation, some of their Civil Law counterparts in the West have enabled this involvement and regarded it as part of the adjudicators' professional duties.[267] This controversy stems from fundamentally differing attitudes toward the role of adjudicators in general. While Common Law systems traditionally limited the adjudicator's role in *deciding* the dispute by rendering a binding decision, Civil Law systems implemented a more liberal approach that considered the adjudicator a *dispute-resolver* and tolerated their proactive involvement in settlement efforts.[268] However, the picture is more complicated in

259. Nigmatullina, 2018, pp. 96-97; Wilson, 2012; Hwang, 2005, p. 577.
260. Kun, 2012, p. 720; Chaisse & Shang, 2021, pp. 98-99; Kun, 2011b, p. 541; De Vera, 2004, p. 192.
261. Nigmatullina, 2018, p. 96; D'Agostino, 2011a.
262. Queen Mary University of London and White & Case LLP, 2021, pp. 5-7; Gu, 2019, pp. 152, 168.
263. Gu, 2021, p. 89; Gu, 2019, pp. 161, 168.
264. Nigmatullina, 2018, p. 133; De Vera, 2004, p. 192.
265. Cheng, 2010, pp. 424-426; Gu, 2019, pp. 128-129.
266. De Gramont et al., 2017, p. 955; Raeschke-Kessler, 2005, p. 525; Kaufmann-Kohler, 2009, pp. 190-191; Ehle, 2010, pp. 79-80; Berger & Jensen, 2017, p. 889; Nigmatullina, 2018, p. 64; Berger, 2018b, p. 502; Born, 2021, §13.04[D].
267. Berger, 2018b, pp. 502-506; Ortolani, 2025, §21.3; Nigmatullina, 2018, pp. 64-65; Berger & Jensen, 2017, p. 889; De Gramont et al., 2017, pp. 964-972; Mayer, 2016, p. 3; Nottage & Garnett, 2010, pp. 35-36; Ehle, 2010, pp. 79-80, 83; Cheng, 2010, pp. 424-426; Kaufmann-Kohler, 2009, pp. 190-192; Lew, 2005, p. 427; Burr, 2005, p. 63; Schneider, 1998, p. 78; Kun, 2013b, pp. 213-214.
268. Berger & Jensen, 2017, p. 889; De Gramont et al., 2017, p. 955; Nigmatullina, 2018, p. 65; Mayer, 2016, p. 3; Stipanowich & Ulrich, 2014b, p. 6; Elsing, 2011, p. 117; Abramson, 1999, p.

practice since various approaches are observed within Common Law jurisdictions and among Civil Law states.[269] For example, in some Western Common Law jurisdictions, such as the UK, a clear distinction is observed between the role of judges in facilitating settlements versus the role of arbitrators.[270] Additionally, other Common Law jurisdictions, such as Australia and Canada, authorize arbitrators to act as mediators in pending proceedings and regulate the mandate of arbitrators through legislation.[271]

This reality, where divergent approaches toward the dual role of arbitrators exceed the traditional binary division between Common Law and Civil Law, was reflected in an empirical study conducted between 2001 and 2004, which examined the general attitude of arbitrators in settlement facilitation according to their legal background. The study collected data from 53 practitioners who served as in-house counsels, advocates, and arbitrators: 20 from the US, eight from Germany, 11 from other continental European countries, 11 from other Common Law countries, and the remaining three from other jurisdictions (2001-2004 Bühring-Uhle Study).[272] While 86% of the respondents agreed that settlement facilitation is one of the arbitration's goals, the distribution of the answers according to the respondents' legal background was interesting: 100% of German and non-American respondents with a Common Law background (including the UK, Canada, Hong Kong, and Australia) thought that facilitating a settlement is one of arbitration's goals, whereas only 74% of the American respondents and 85% of non-German Civil Law practitioners concurred.[273] The collected data regarding the settlement rates after the initiation of the arbitration revealed more notable differences depending on the legal background of the practitioners. While 43% of all cases were settled before an arbitral decision, German and non-American respondents from Common Law jurisdictions reported that settlement was achieved in 69% of cases. In contrast, American practitioners reported that a settlement was concluded in only 33% of the cases, with non-German Civil Law practitioners in only 24%.[274] The study concluded that the considerable divergence in experience among the participating practitioners could be explained only by the differing practices and traditions of their respective legal systems, particularly regarding the judiciary's function and the role of judges.[275]

Nonetheless, a closer and updated look at the attitude of Common and Civil Law jurisdictions in the West regarding the role of arbitrators as settlement facilitators

2; Kaufmann-Kohler, 2009, p. 190; Berger, 2018b, p. 503; Karton, 2013, p. 196; Collins, 2003, p. 343; McIlwrath & Alvarez, 2020, §2.01, §2.03 & §2.09; Baysal & Cevik, 2021; Chase & Bruner, 2005, pp. 62-65.

269. Kun, 2020a, pp. 132-133; Bühring-Uhle et al., 2006, pp. 110-111; Nigmatullina, 2018, pp. 64-69; Gu, 2019, pp. 152-160.

270. Ehle, 2006; Harris, 2016, p. 92; Lang, 2009, p. 98.

271. Stipanowich, 2021a, pp. 323-327; Born, 2021, §13.04[D]; Gu, 2019, pp. 159-160; Nigmatullina, 2018, pp. 75-76; Marriott, 2005, pp. 537-538; Australia Commercial Arbitration Act, 2010, Part 5, section 27D; British Columbia International Commercial Arbitration Act, 1996, section 30; Quebec Arbitration Act, 2014, section 620.

272. Bühring-Uhle et al., 2006, pp. 105-128; Stipanowich, 2021a, pp. 316-317; Bühring-Uhle et al., 2003.

273. Bühring-Uhle et al., 2006, pp. 110-111.

274. Bühring-Uhle et al., 2006, p. 112.

275. Bühring-Uhle et al., 2006, p. 112. *See also* Kun, 2020a, pp. 132-133.

reveals a more accepting approach to the mandate, particularly in international arbitral proceedings.[276] According to some commentators, this increasing acceptance of the arbitrator's dual role is attributed to inter-influence between Common and Civil Law systems as well as between Eastern and Western legal cultures,[277] which has resulted in more unified trends in ICA that favor the mandate of the arbitrator while blurring the traditional binary division between Common Law and Civil Law.[278]

This section presents traditional attitudes of Western Common Law and Civil Law traditions toward the mandate of judges and arbitrators as settlement facilitators, alongside recent developments regarding the role in specific jurisdictions, including the US, the UK, Australia, Germany, and Brazil. It shows that, despite different approaches among these jurisdictions, the dual role of the arbitrator has increasingly gained recognition and acceptance in the West, even in Common Law jurisdictions that have traditionally opposed it. At the same time, compared to the practice of this role in most Eastern jurisdictions, Western countries have implemented more procedural safeguards to address due process concerns resulting from its utilization.

5.3.1 Western Common Law Legal Systems

The traditional aversion of Common Law systems to the role of judges and arbitrators as settlement facilitators rests mainly in the risk of losing impartiality and prejudging the dispute before receiving all the evidence and hearing the full arguments of the parties.[279] This traditional position is also based on the perception that for a successful engagement in settlement facilitation, the adjudicator must hold ex parte meetings and discussions with the parties, as customary in standalone mediation. Therefore, judges and arbitrators should completely refrain from the dual role.[280] Additionally, the traditional Common Law approach considers the adjudicator's preliminary views of the merits problematic since, if the settlement efforts fail, the disputants may challenge the neutral for being intentionally or unintentionally influenced by their own assessments.[281] Hence, according to the traditional Common Law approach, if the disputants are willing to settle, they should do so outside the hearing room without involving the adjudicator in the settlement process.[282] As aforementioned, the separation between these roles in Common Law systems can explain why, historically, ADR procedures,

276. Berger, 2018b, pp. 506-507; Berger & Jensen, 2017, p. 896; Ross, 2013, p. 354; Ehle, 2010, p. 84; Böckstiegel, 2010; Favalli & Hasenclever, 2008, p. 2; Baysal & Cevik, 2021; Marriott, 2005, pp. 537-538; Sussman & Berger, 2021b, p. 37, relating to data collected during the 2016 Fordham International Arbitration and Mediation Conference indicating that almost 70% of practitioners with Common Law background acknowledged this role of arbitrators in ICA proceedings.
277. Nigmatullina, 2018, pp. 74-79; Cremades, 1998, pp. 159-160; Kun & Kaufmann-Kohler, 2008, p. 492.
278. Berger, 2019, pp. 311-312; Nigmatullina, 2018, p. 78; Berger & Jensen, 2017, p. 916; Kun & Kaufmann-Kohler, 2008, p. 492.
279. Nigmatullina, 2018, p. 64; Ehle, 2010, p. 83; Baysal & Cevik, 2021; Gill, 2006, pp. 158-159.
280. Raeschke-Kessler, 2005, p. 525; Ehle, 2010, p. 83; Baysal & Cevik, 2021; Gill, 2006, p. 159.
281. Berger, 2018b, p. 503; Gill, 2006, pp. 159-160; Ehle, 2010, pp. 83-84; Pitkowitz & Richter, 2009, p. 227; Baysal & Cevik, 2021.
282. Stipanowich, 2021a, p. 288; Berger, 2018b, p. 503; Baysal & Cevik, 2021; Böckstiegel, 2009, pp. 293-302; Resnik, 1982, p. 376; Gill, 2006, p. 165.

particularly mediation, have evolved and expanded in these jurisdictions.[283] Nevertheless, the literature suggests other explanations for their expansion, including the relatively costly and lengthy court proceedings in Common Law jurisdictions compared to those in Civil Law systems.[284]

Despite the traditional reluctance of Common Law systems to involve adjudicators in settlement facilitation, an increasing number of jurisdictions are now adopting this practice.[285] Following significant reforms in their judiciary framework, many Common Law jurisdictions have embraced the proactive role of judges in facilitating settlements, mainly to overcome caseloads.[286] This shift has also influenced arbitral proceedings in these jurisdictions at both the legislative and practice levels. Consequently:

> The idea that arbitrators may act as settlement facilitators is increasingly accepted even in common law jurisdictions. US courts have held that an arbitrator is not precluded from developing views regarding the merits of a dispute early in the proceedings, and an award will not be vacated because he expresses those views. Even in England, where the idea of the arbitral tribunal's mandate to facilitate a settlement has always been met with strong resistance, the role of the arbitrator under the English Arbitration Act 1996 includes encouraging settlements.[287]

The literature suggests that the growing acceptance of the arbitrator's role as a settlement facilitator in Common Law jurisdictions is also influenced by the increasing number of cross-border business disputes submitted to arbitration. These proceedings often involve practitioners and users from diverse jurisdictions and legal traditions, who encourage their Common Law counterparts to adopt innovative methods for resolving arbitral disputes, even if such methods are less frequently employed in domestic contexts.[288] As demonstrated in Chapter 6, some of these methods have been incorporated into international arbitral guidelines and rules, reflecting a shift away from the traditional adversarial approach in ICA proceedings toward more pragmatic practices. These practices acknowledge the role of arbitrators as settlement facilitators and, in some instances, as mediators.[289] Moreover, these international rules and guidelines, which reinforce the transnational character of ICA, further diminish the influence of domestic legal cultures on its practice.[290]

283. Ehle, 2010, p. 83; Jones, 2005, p. 406; Gill, 2006, pp. 157-178; Nigmatullina, 2018, pp. 68, 97.
284. Arguably, compared to Civil Law jurisdictions, which primarily rely on documentary evidence and exclude pretrial procedures and discovery from their court proceedings, adversarial proceedings in Common Law systems place greater emphasis on witness testimony and pretrial procedures, making them longer and more costly. *See* Stipanowich, 2021a, pp. 312-313; Hazard, 1998, p. 1020; McIlwrath & Alvarez, 2020, §2.07-2.08.
285. Baysal & Cevik, 2021; Schneider, 1998, p. 80.
286. Kaufmann-Kohler, 2009, pp. 192-193; Nigmatullina, 2018, pp. 75-76; De Gramont et al., 2017, p. 958; Mayer, 2016, p. 3.
287. Berger, 2018b, p. 507. *See also* Favalli & Hasenclever, 2008, p. 2; Power, 2007, p. 254; Dezalay & Garth, 1996, p. 168; Baysal & Cevik, 2021; Born, 2021, §13.04[D].
288. Power, 2007, p. 254; Nigmatullina, 2018, pp. 75, 77-78; Cremades, 1998, p. 164; Schneider, 1998, p. 80; Newmark, 2008, p. 90; Kaufmann-Kohler, 2009, pp. 191-192; Berger, 2019, pp. 311-312; *Guide to international arbitration law and rules in England and Wales*, 2022.
289. Berger & Jensen, 2017, p. 890; Berger, 2018b, p. 507; Berger, 2019, p. 312.
290. Berger, 2019, p. 312.

The following sections discuss the adjudicator's role as a settlement facilitator in the following Common Law jurisdictions: the US, the UK, and Australia.

5.3.1.1 The United States

Until four decades ago, the legal culture in the US dictated a classical Common Law view of the judicial role, under which judges were entrusted merely with adjudicating disputes before them fairly and impartially, not settling them or assisting the parties to reach amicable outcomes.[291] Evidence of this approach can be found in the original version of the 1938 Federal Rules of Civil Procedure, which empowered the court to hold a discretionary pretrial conference but did not include a settlement as a matter to be considered by judges.[292] This omission reflected the legislator's attitude that, during this conference, judges were limited to issues related to trial preparations.[293] In the early 1980s, following a debate launched by influential commentators regarding the increasing costs, delays, and formalism of adjudication in the US, practitioners and scholars introduced more efficient alternatives to the traditional adversarial court proceedings, such as "judicial management" methods and the intervention of third parties (e.g., mediators) in the resolution of court disputes.[294] Following this process, known as the "Quiet Revolution,"[295] in 1983, the aforementioned federal rules were amended to authorize judges to discuss and facilitate settlements during the pretrial conference.[296] The later amendment of the rules explicitly acknowledged judges' mandate to actively engage in settlement facilitation by taking the appropriate action during any conference conducted under the rules.[297] Further legislation, such as the 1990 Civil Justice Reform Act and the 1998 Alternative Dispute Resolution Act, required the courts to adopt and implement ADR programs while assigning judicial officers to supervise ADR procedures conducted within court proceedings.[298]

Despite the explicit authorization of judges to actively promote settlements in their cases, the legislator has not specified the extent of the permissible actions they can take to fulfill this mandate.[299] Even the Model Code of Judicial Conduct, which presents

291. De Gramont et al., 2017, p. 957; Kaufmann-Kohler, 2009, pp. 190-191; Resnik, 1982, p. 376.
292. U.S. Federal Rules of Civil Procedure, 1938, Rule 16.
293. De Gramont et al., 2017, pp. 957-958; Kaufmann-Kohler, 2009, p. 191; Brunet, 2003, pp. 242-243.
294. Kaufmann-Kohler, 2009, p. 191; De Gramont et al., 2017, p. 958; Resnik, 1982, p. 376; Chase & Bruner, 2005, p. 63.
295. Stipanowich, 2023, p. 686; Stipanowich, 2021a, p. 298.
296. U.S. Federal Rules of Civil Procedure, 1983, Rules 16(a)(5) & 16(c)(7). *See also* Dezalay & Garth, 1996, p. 168; Miller, 1984, p. 20; De Gramont et al., 2017, p. 958, relating to the Notes of the advisory committee to the 1983 amendments of the U.S. Federal Rules of Civil Procedure, which state that given the advantages of early settlement in terms of saving time and costs while reducing the burden on the courts, it is appropriate to discuss and facilitate settlements during the pretrial conference. For further discussion, *see* Galanter, 1985.
297. U.S. Federal Rules of Civil Procedure, 1993, Rule 16(c)(9). *See also* Kaufmann-Kohler, 2009, p. 191; Dezalay & Garth, 1996, p. 168.
298. U.S. Civil Justice Reform Act, 1990, Article 476; U.S. Alternative Dispute Resolution Act, 1998, Articles 651-658. *See also* Baer, 2001, pp. 133-134; De Gramont et al., 2017, pp. 958-959.
299. De Gramont et al., 2017, p. 959.

an authoritative and practical analysis of rules and opinions relating to judicial ethics, includes little guidance on the matter. It states that judges may encourage settlements of disputes before them but shall not coerce the parties into a settlement.[300] Consequently, U.S. judges are significantly divided regarding their role as settlement facilitators in their cases:

> Some judges, for example, will not adjudicate a case on the merits if they have previously participated in an unsuccessful form of ADR. Some judges routinely have Magistrate Judges handle settlement conferences and ADR processes to avoid any appearance of bias should the settlement efforts fail. Other judges, however, will participate in the ADR process and also adjudicate the dispute if settlement efforts fail. Beyond those differences, some judges will meet separately with the parties (while others will only address all parties together), while others will separate clients from attorneys for individual discussions.[301]

Despite these differing approaches among U.S. judges regarding the proper scope of involvement in settlement negotiations, court rulings generally view this participation—in and of itself—as appropriate.[302] Empirical data supports this view. In a 2006 survey of California judges who served in the capacity of trial and settlement judges (2006 Robinson Survey), 80% of the respondents thought that conducting a settlement conference before the trial to mediate the dispute and avoid litigation was appropriate and unproblematic, provided the parties agreed to the initiative.[303] Additionally, 95% of the respondents expressed no concern about being exposed to inadmissible or confidential information if the case did not settle during the pretrial conference. Similarly, 90% rejected fears that predicting an outcome of the case during settlement conferences would bias their decisions during the trial.[304] However, only one-third of the respondents confirmed regularly organizing settlement conferences. Additionally, an overwhelming majority admitted that their dual role as trial judges following failed settlement efforts led them to adopt a less evaluative approach and refrain from predicting case outcomes during the settlement process.[305]

Although limited evidence in the literature suggests that certain U.S. judges caucus with parties during settlement negotiations or provide case evaluation,[306] the general view among scholars and practitioners disfavors these methods because they are considered inconsistent with the dominant adversarial values of the U.S. legal

300. ABA Model Code of Judicial Conduct, 2020, Rule 2.6(b). *See also* Cratsley, 2011, p. 4, criticizing this rule for being very general, thus recognizing almost every initiative to facilitate a settlement as legitimate and ethically acceptable.
301. De Gramont et al., 2017, p. 961. *See also* Cratsley, 2011, pp. 4-6; Kaufmann-Kohler, 2009, p. 192.
302. Kaufmann-Kohler, 2009, p. 192; Floyd, 1994, pp. 70-72; *Wiley v. United Parcel Service Inc.*, 2001, at 182; *Bell v. Johnson*, 2005, at 1005; *Johnson v. Shaker Heights City School District*, 2007, at 5-10.
303. Stipanowich, 2009, pp. 402-403. *See also* Gu, 2019, p. 152.
304. Stipanowich, 2009, p. 403.
305. Stipanowich, 2009, p. 402.
306. Kaufmann-Kohler, 2009, p. 192; Berger & Jensen, 2017, p. 903; Floyd, 1994, pp. 53-56; Galanter, 1985, p. 7.

tradition, potentially undermining party autonomy and self-determination, compromising judicial impartiality, and jeopardizing the overall fairness of the process.[307] For similar reasons, hybrid procedures that fully integrate judicial functions with mediation have generally faced skepticism, despite the widespread recognition of judges' managerial roles and their mandate as settlement facilitators following the Quiet Revolution.[308]

The abovementioned evolution in dispute processing within the courts has influenced the practice of commercial arbitration in the US.[309] Regarding the promotion of settlements, until these developments, the academic literature and legal practice largely viewed arbitration as a direct substitute for litigation and advocated for a clear separation between the arbitrator's adjudicative role and roles aimed at assisting the parties in reaching an amicable resolution.[310] The main concern centered on ex parte communications by arbitrators, driven by fears that exposure to confidential information shared during caucusing could risk their impartiality in the consequent proceedings.[311] Additionally, concerns were raised about case evaluation by arbitrators, as it was perceived to potentially undermine party autonomy and self-determination.[312]

Despite these concerns, the debate among scholars and practitioners about the increasing formalism, costs, and delays of adjudication in the US has also extended to arbitral proceedings that have faced criticism for incorporating litigation-like features, resulting in heightened expenses and prolonged timelines.[313] The reality:

> has prompted user demands for speed and cost-efficiency in arbitration practice, as well as rising rates of settlement prior to award, even during the pre-hearing process. The phenomenon of "arbi-gotiation" has sometimes led, among other things, to experienced arbitrators strategically handling key procedural or substantive issues to stimulate the early settlement of the dispute. Paradoxically, it has also opened the door for mediated negotiation prior to or during the course of arbitration and, occasionally, triggered the use of med-arb or arb-med.[314]

This expanding trend among U.S. arbitrators taking active role in settlement facilitation and even "switching hats" during arbitral proceedings was confirmed in the 2013 Straus Institute Survey conducted among 134 U.S. arbitrators with experience in domestic and international arbitration.[315] The survey's results indicated that the number of settled cases during arbitral proceedings in the US, including ICA cases, had

307. Stipanowich, 2021a, pp. 299-301; Kaufmann-Kohler, 2009, p. 192.
308. Stipanowich, 2021a, pp. 299, 301; Berger & Jensen, 2017, p. 903; Dezalay & Garth, 1996, p. 168.
309. Stipanowich, 2021a, p. 306.
310. Blankley, 2011, p. 337; Donahey, 1995, pp. 76-77; Favalli & Hasenclever, 2008, p. 2; Ehle, 2010, p. 79; Stipanowich, 2021a, p. 302; Favalli & Hasenclever, 2008, p. 2.
311. Pappas, 2015, pp. 177-178; Donahey, 1995, pp. 76-77; De Vera, 2004, pp. 192-194; Blankley, 2011, pp. 332-337; Deason, 2013, pp. 228-229; Stipanowich, 2021a, p. 302.
312. Stipanowich & Lamare, 2014, pp. 60-66; Stipanowich, 2021a, p. 301.
313. Von Kann, 2009, p. 500; Stipanowich, 2010, p. 5; Wolf, 2006, pp. 306-307.
314. Stipanowich, 2021a, pp. 306-307. *See also* Stipanowich & Ulrich, 2014b, pp. 17, 21-28; Stipanowich & Ulrich, 2014a, p. 458; Stipanowich et al., 2010; Stipanowich, 2004, pp. 848-850; Sussman, 2013, pp. 10-11.
315. *See* the discussion in section 2.2.1.

increased considerably during the last decade.[316] According to the collected data, over 88% of the respondents confirmed being "never" or "only sometimes" concerned about their involvement in the settlement process of cases before them.[317] More than 80% of the respondents indicated that in practice, they "usually," "about half the time," or at least "sometimes" promoted settlement by either managing the pre-hearing process, issuing summary dispositions, or ruling on discovery matters.[318] Interestingly, among 59 respondents who indicated some level of informal engagement in the settlement process of their cases, approximately 50% confirmed that they "switched hats" between the roles of arbitrators and mediators in the same case.[319] This figure aligns with the findings of the 2014 Straus Institute Survey conducted among members of the International Academy of Mediators,[320] where over 60% of the respondents reported having at least some experience serving as both arbitrators and mediators in the same dispute, with two-thirds describing that experience as "generally satisfactory."[321] Similarly, a 2013 survey of 400 U.S. arbitrators (2013 Sussman Survey) found that 51.6% expressed willingness to mediate a case with the parties' informed consent during arbitration.[322]

Growing support for hybrid procedures that combine arbitration and mediation conducted by the same neutral has also been expressed in the academic literature, which relies on the principle of party autonomy to justify their use:

> Combining mediation and arbitration in a hybrid process with the same neutral can be an effective mechanism for reducing costs, increasing efficiency and maximizing the possibility of achieving the win-win result that optimizes the position of all parties and arrives at the best resolution of a dispute. If the parties are fully informed and consent knowingly to same neutral mediation and arbitration, party autonomy should be respected and the resolution derived from the process should be honored.[323]

Some scholars have even suggested allowing ex parte communications of arbitrators with the parties as part of the disputants' right to design their own dispute resolution process. Being aware of due process concerns deriving from confidential information disclosed during these communications and used later by the arbitrator, these academics have suggested the following alternatives to address such concerns: (a) following the Hong Kong model, which requires the arbitrator to disclose any confidential information material to arbitration after unsuccessful settlement attempts; (b) adopting the Chinese disregard concept, which prohibits disputants from using opinions, views, or statements made during mediation in the arbitral process, while applying this prohibition to arbitrators as well; or (c) including an "opt-out clause" in

316. Stipanowich & Ulrich, 2014b, pp. 16-19; Berger & Jensen, 2017, p. 898.
317. Stipanowich & Ulrich, 2014b, pp. 19-21.
318. Stipanowich & Ulrich, 2014b, pp. 21-22.
319. Stipanowich & Ulrich, 2014b, pp. 25-26; Stipanowich, 2021a, pp. 307-308.
320. *See* the discussion in section 4.4.1.
321. Stipanowich, 2021a, p. 287.
322. Sussman, 2013, p. 13.
323. Sussman, 2009a, p. 73. *See also* Blankenship, 2006, pp. 39-41; De Gramont et al., 2017, p. 972.

the arbitration agreement, allowing for the replacement of the neutral in the event of failed settlement efforts.[324]

Although the U.S. Supreme Court has not yet related to the arbitrator's role as a settlement facilitator, lower courts have had opportunities to address hybrid proceedings conducted by the same neutrals and ex parte communications of arbitrators with the parties.[325] Despite the concerns raised, the courts have uniformly recognized this emerging trend of neutrals "switching hats" as a derivative of party autonomy that allows arbitration parties to design the dispute resolution process according to their wishes and interests.[326] The courts' main concern was associated with the confidential nature of the mediation process and the legal prohibition, as established in mediation laws and court decisions, against using any private or joint communication made during mediation in other legal proceedings, including subsequent arbitration.[327] Other concerns were related to conducting hybrid processes or caucusing with the parties without their prior informed consent, which may later prejudice the enforceability of the arbitral award.[328] Due to these concerns, in *Bowden v. Weickert*, the Ohio Court of Appeals set several conditions as mandatory requirements for recognizing an arbitral award resulting from a hybrid process:

> At a minimum, the record must include clear evidence that the parties have agreed to engage in a med-arb process, by allowing ... [the] arbitrator to function as the mediator of their dispute. The record must also contain: (1) evidence that the parties are aware that the mediator will function as an arbitrator if the mediation attempt fails; (2) a written stipulation as to the agreed method of submitting their disputed factual issues to an arbitrator if the mediation fails; and (3) evidence of whether the parties agree to waive the confidentiality requirements imposed on the mediation process ... in the event that their disputes are later arbitrated.[329]

In this case, following a failed attempt to mediate the dispute, the arbitrator returned to their role as an arbitrator. Determining that the arbitrator had relied on information received during the mediation, in violation of the statutory confidentiality of mediation, and without explicit agreement allowing its use in arbitration, the court found the award arbitrary and capricious and set it aside.[330] A similar decision was rendered in *Gaskin v. Gaskin*, in which the Texas Court of Appeals emphasized that

324. Silberberg & Badaracco, 2019, pp. 34-35; Sussman, 2013, p. 8.
325. Sussman, 2010a, p. 387; Sussman, 2009a, p. 71.
326. Sussman, 2010a, p. 387; Stipanowich, 2021a, p. 303; Nigmatullina, 2018, p. 203; Sussman, 2009a, p. 71; Chaisse & Shang, 2021, p. 96; Menkel-Meadow, 2013, p. 424.
327. The U.S. Uniform Mediation Act, 2010, adopted by most U.S. states, determines in sections 4-5 & 7A that all communications in mediation are privileged and are not subject to discovery nor admissible as evidence in other proceedings, unless privilege is expressly waived by all parties to the mediation. *See also* Benzidi, 2017, pp. 11-12; Nigmatullina, 2018, p. 203; Blankley, 2011, pp. 338-339; Deason, 2013, p. 227.
328. Sussman, 2010a, pp. 387; Nigmatullina, 2018, p. 205.
329. *Bowden v. Weickert*, 2003, §6. *See also* Stipanowich, 2021a, pp. 303-304; Benzidi, 2017, pp. 19-20; Nigmatullina, 2018, pp. 205-206; Sussman, 2009a, pp. 71-73; Sussman, 2010a, pp. 387-388.
330. *Bowden v. Weickert*, 2003, §7. *See also* Benzidi, 2017, p. 19; Sussman, 2010a, pp. 387-388; Nigmatullina, 2018, pp. 203-204; Blankley, 2011, pp. 346-351, 358-359.

since mediation requires candid dialogue, including disclosure of confidential information to the neutral, the arbitrator should not conduct the dual role without the parties' express consent.[331] In *Town of Clinton v. Geological Services Corp.*, the Massachusetts Superior Court clarified that in hybrid procedures, the mediation privilege must be explicitly waived, as consent to a process conducted by the same neutral does not inherently constitute consent to waive the confidentiality of the mediation.[332] Other judgments have shown that when the courts were convinced that the disputants had granted express and documented consent allowing the arbitrator to rely on confidential information delivered during the mediation phase, arbitral awards were not vacated for relying on such information by the arbitrator.[333] For example, in *U.S. Steel Mining Company v. Wilson Downhole Services*, the parties empowered the arbitrator to mediate the dispute and select between the parties' final offers if mediation failed. To that end, the parties expressly allowed the arbitrator to rely on confidential information disclosed during the mediation phase, including in ex parte meetings. The losing party challenged the award, claiming fraud due to the presentation of information during the mediation session. In dismissing this claim and approving the award, the court held that, based on the facts presented, which showed express consent to the process and the reliance on confidential information, the claim of fraud had to be clear and substantiated by convincing evidence.[334] A similar decision was made in *Conkle and Olesten v. Goodrich Goodyear and Hinds*, where a party waived confidentiality and later challenged the award on the grounds that the arbitrator's previous involvement as a mediator in a closely related case was not disclosed. Despite these circumstances, the California Court of Appeals refused to set aside the award after finding the waiver explicit and unequivocal.[335] Even when express consent regarding the possibility of relying on confidential information was absent, the courts did not automatically rule to set aside awards resulting from hybrid proceedings. For instance, in *Logan v. Logan*, the losing party claimed that the arbitral award relied on confidential information revealed within the mediation stage without the parties' express consent and, therefore, asked to set aside the award. The court ruled that although unlawful reference to confidential information received during mediation could essentially result in vacating the award, the remedy was likely to be granted only if the reference had materially affected the substantial rights of the concerned party. Finding no evidence that the reference to such information in this case had materially affected substantial rights, the California Court of Appeals refused to set aside the award.[336] In contrast, in *Lindsay v.*

331. *Gaskin v. Gaskin*, 2006, §2. *See also* Sussman, 2010a, p. 388.
332. *Town of Clinton v. Geological Services Corp.*, 2006, §1, as discussed in Nigmatullina, 2018, pp. 205-206; Deekshitha & Saha, 2014, p. 90; Blankley, 2011, pp. 350-353. For similar decisions of the U.S. court in other cases, *see* Benzidi, 2017, p. 20.
333. Sussman, 2010a, p. 388.
334. *U.S. Steel Mining Company v. Wilson Downhole Services*, 2006, §5; Nigmatullina, 2018, p. 205; Kryvoi & Davydenko, 2015, p. 849; Sussman, 2010a, p. 388.
335. *Conkle and Olesten v. Goodrich Goodyear and Hinds*, 2006, §12. *See also* Sussman, 2010a, p. 389.
336. *Logan v. Logan*, 2007, §§1-3. However, in *John Eisendrath v. Superior Court*, 2003, the California's Second District Court of Appeals held that waiver of the mediation privilege must be expressed, not implied. *See also* Nigmatullina, 2018, pp. 204-205; Sussman, 2010a, p. 389.

Lewandowski, while expressly recognizing the parties' right to develop hybrid processes to settle their disputes, the court stated that such processes must be anchored in clear and written agreements that adhere to terminology and legal principles with which the law is familiar since allowing "a 'create your own alternate dispute resolution' regime would impose a significant burden on appellate courts to create a body of law on what can and cannot be done, injecting more complexity and litigation into a process aimed at less."[337]

As demonstrated by the above-discussed series of judgments, the U.S. courts seem to honor hybrid procedures conducted by the same neutral and fundament them on the disputants' right to design the dispute resolution process according to their needs. Nevertheless, this recognition is subject to specific conditions, including the express and documented consent of all parties to engage in such procedures, a waiver of the right to challenge the arbitration's outcome following failed attempts to settle, and an explicit arrangement regarding the possibility of using confidential information disclosed during the settlement negotiations in the renewed arbitration.[338] The endorsement of these hybrid procedures by the courts should validate *per a fortiori* any other active participation of the arbitrator on the continuum of settlement facilitation, as hybrid procedures are considered the most far-reaching, and hence controversial, involvement of the arbitrator in the efforts to resolve the dispute amicably.[339] Further consolidation of the arbitrator's role as a settlement facilitator is apparent in very recent rulings of U.S. courts, which have confirmed the enforcement of consent awards under the New York Convention, despite the absence of specific guidance on this matter in the Federal Arbitration Act.[340] This recognition has permeated state legislation in the US, as exemplified in the New Jersey International Arbitration Mediation and Conciliation Act, which provides that consent awards, including those resulting from mediation, conciliation, or other ADR forms involving the assistance of a neutral, are enforceable under the New York Convention and the Federal Arbitration Act.[341] An additional establishment of the arbitrator's dual role in the US is demonstrated by court rulings that recognize case evaluation as a legitimate component of the arbitrator's mandate, leading courts to refrain from setting aside arbitral awards when, during the process, the arbitrator expressed views on the merits of the dispute.[342]

337. *Lindsay v. Lewandowski*, 2006, §18.
338. Nigmatullina, 2018, p. 205; Sussman, 2010a, p. 390; Blankley, 2011, p. 366.
339. Berger & Jensen, 2017, p. 913; Nigmatullina, 2018, p. 29; Ross, 2013, p. 352; Berger, 2016a, p. 48; Abramson, 1999, p. 6.
340. *Actors' Equity Ass'n v. Paradise Square Prod. Servs. Inc.*, 2023; *McGuire v. Safeguard Metals, LLC*, 2023; *Teamsters Loc. 630 v. W. Cent. Produce*, 2022; *Trustees for Mason Tenders Dist. Council Welfare Fund v. Golden Dev. & Constr. Corp.*, 2018; *New York City & Vicinity Dist. Council of Carpenters v. J.M.R. Concrete Corp.*, 2018; *Transocean Offshore Gulf of Guinea Vii v. Erin Energy Corp.*, 2018, §4; *Albtelecom SH.A v. UNIFI Communs. Inc.*, 2017, determining that any prohibition on the enforcement of a settlement concluded in the course of arbitration is counter to public policy. *See also* Ortolani, 2025, §21.3 & §21.5(a); Paisley & Player, 2021, p. 35; Kaster, 2018, pp. 48-49; Nigmatullina, 2018, p. 41; Borrasso, 2018.
341. New Jersey International Arbitration Mediation and Conciliation Act, 2017, Articles 23E-3 & 23E-8. *See also* Lauren, 2019; Nigmatullina, 2018, p. 41.
342. *Spector v. Torenberg*, 1994, p. 209; *Ballantine Books Inc. v. Capital Distributing Co.*, 1962, p. 21. *See also* Berger, 2018b, p. 507; Baysal & Cevik, 2021; Favalli & Hasenclever, 2008, pp. 7-8,

Given the growing recognition of the arbitrator's mandate to facilitate settlement, leading arbitral institutions in the U.S. have amended their rules to permit the active involvement of arbitrators in settlement facilitation, including hybrid procedures that combine arbitration and mediation.[343] A representative example of such rules is the 2021 Comprehensive Arbitration Rules and Procedures of the Judicial Arbitration and Mediation Services (JAMS), which stipulate that:

> The parties may agree to seek the assistance of the arbitrator in reaching settlement. By their written agreement to submit the matter to the arbitrator for settlement assistance, the parties will be deemed to have agreed that the assistance of the arbitrator in such settlement efforts will not disqualify the arbitrator from continuing to serve as arbitrator if settlement is not reached; nor shall such assistance be argued to a reviewing court as the basis for vacating or modifying an award.[344]

The JAMS rules further provide that, subject to the parties' agreement, the arbitrator can act as the mediator in the same dispute.[345] This authorization is consistent with the JAMS Arbitrators Ethics Guidelines, which allow the arbitrator, subject to the parties' request and written waiver of the right to challenge the neutral or the arbitration's outcome, to engage with the settlement discussions and combine arbitration with other dispute resolution processes.[346]

At the legislative level, while the Federal Arbitration Act is silent regarding the arbitrator's role in the settlement process,[347] the evolving trend has led several U.S. jurisdictions to incorporate the following provision authorizing arbitrators to facilitate settlements in disputes before them and act as mediators (California, North Carolina, and Texas—into their international arbitration acts, and Oregon—into its general arbitration act),[348] borrowed from the British Columbia International Commercial Arbitration Act:

> It is not incompatible with an arbitration agreement for an arbitral tribunal to encourage settlement of the dispute and, with the agreement of the parties, the

holding that given the similarities between arbitral and judicial proceedings, the authority of the arbitral tribunal to express evaluative views should be learned, *mutatis mutandis*, from the U.S. Federal Rules of Civil Procedure that grant the court broad discretion regarding the actions and techniques for settlement facilitation.

343. Stipanowich, 2021a, p. 303.
344. JAMS Comprehensive Arbitration Rules and Procedures, 2021, Rule 28(b). Interestingly, the JAMS rules for international arbitral proceedings are silent about the involvement of the arbitrator in the settlement process. *See* JAMS International Arbitration Rules and Procedures, 2021.
345. JAMS Comprehensive Arbitration Rules and Procedures, 2021, Rule 28(a).
346. JAMS Arbitrators Ethics Guidelines, 2021, Article III(B).
347. U.S. Federal Arbitration Act, 1925. *See also* Aragaki, 2021, p. 58; Gu, 2019, p. 158; Favalli & Hasenclever, 2008, p. 7.
348. California International Commercial Arbitration and Conciliation Act, 2016, section 1297.301; North Carolina International Commercial Arbitration and Conciliation Act, 2013, section 1-567.60; Texas International Commercial Arbitration and Conciliation Act, 2008, section 172.117; Oregon Mediation and Arbitration Act, 2021, section 36.512. According to the provisions in these jurisdictions, mediated settlements can be recorded in the form of arbitral awards on agreed terms.

arbitral tribunal may use mediation, conciliation, or other procedures at any time during the arbitral proceedings to encourage settlement.[349]

The Oregon legislator added to the above provision a supplementary clause that allows the parties to agree explicitly that the arbitrator would not be disqualified from retaining their adjudicative role following their participation in the settlement process.[350] On the other hand, the Ohio legislator adopted a reverse arrangement into its International Commercial Arbitration and Conciliation Act, which prohibits the arbitrator from resuming their arbitral role after serving as a conciliator in the same dispute unless the parties agree otherwise.[351] Apart from the aforementioned legislative arrangements, neither the federal legislation nor the legislation in the remaining U.S. jurisdictions regulate or relate to the arbitrator's role as a settlement facilitator or to hybrid procedures that combine arbitration with mediation.[352]

Despite the noticeable developments indicating a growing acceptance of the arbitrator's dual role, skepticism remains prevalent among U.S. practitioners and scholars regarding hybrid procedures that combine arbitration with mediation.[353] In light of the legal tradition, the same position is still taken against ex parte communications,[354] despite attempts to address associated concerns and proposed solutions, such as replacing the arbitrator in the resumed arbitration process after unsuccessful settlement efforts.[355] This cautious stance toward hybrid procedures and ex parte communications is reflected in several arbitral rules and codes of ethics that prohibit arbitrators from engaging separately with parties or "switching hats" during arbitral proceedings.[356] It is also evident in current court rulings that review arbitral proceedings primarily through the lens of justice distribution while focusing on the arbitrator's independence and impartiality, similar to how judicial proceedings are evaluated.[357] The lack of federal legislation and the limited presence of state laws regulating hybrid procedures further contribute to the mistrust prevalent in U.S. legal practice toward hybrid procedures and ex parte communications.[358] This doubtful attitude is highlighted in the Final Report of the Commission on the Future of Arbitration, established

349. British Columbia International Commercial Arbitration Act, 1996, section 30. Additional Canadian legislation recognizing the arbitrator's dual role is anchored in section 620 of Quebec Arbitration Act, 2014, stating that "the arbitrator's mission also includes attempting to reconcile the parties, if they so request and circumstances permit, and continuing the arbitration process, with the parties' express consent, if the conciliation attempt fails." For further discussion, *see* Aragaki, 2021, p. 58; Antaki, 2009, p. 113.
350. Oregon Mediation and Arbitration Act, 2021, section 36.512.
351. Ohio International Commercial Arbitration and Conciliation Act, 2015, section 2712.85.
352. Aragaki, 2021, p. 58; Gu, 2019, p. 158; Bühring-Uhle et al., 2006, p. 122.
353. Ruckteschler & Wendelstein, 2021, p. 765; Ehle, 2010, p. 79; Favalli & Hasenclever, 2008, p. 6; Donahey, 1995, pp. 76-77; Stipanowich, 2021a, pp. 299, 302; Lemley, 2004, pp. 307-309.
354. Pappas, 2015, pp. 177-178; Stipanowich, 2021a, p. 302; Deason, 2013, pp. 228-229; Blankley, 2011, pp. 332-337; De Vera, 2004, pp. 192-194; Donahey, 1995, pp. 76-77.
355. Stipanowich, 2021a, p. 304; Silberberg & Badaracco, 2019, pp. 34-35; Sussman, 2013, p. 8.
356. *See*, for example, AAA Code of Ethics, 2004, Canons III(B) & IV(F); CPR Rules for International Arbitration, 2019, Rule 21; CPR Rules for Non-Administered Arbitration, 2018, Rule 19. These rules and guidelines are discussed in the next chapter.
357. Stipanowich, 2021a, p. 303, along with the cases listed therein.
358. Gu, 2019, p. 158; Bühring-Uhle et al., 2006, p. 122; Aragaki, 2021, p. 58; Favalli & Hasenclever, 2008, p. 7.

by the International Institute for Conflict Prevention and Resolution (CPR), as discussed in the next chapter.[359]

5.3.1.2 The United Kingdom

The traditional legal attitude in the UK disfavored and even banned judges and arbitrators from taking an active role in settlement efforts and certainly from hybrid procedures combining adjudication with mediation:

> In England, ... the tradition is firmly one of separation of the roles of decision-maker and active settlement facilitator. This perhaps reflects the adversarial system where the role of the judge or arbitrator is perceived to be to decide the case on the material before them; it is not usual for the decision-maker to investigate the facts or to seek to discover the full truth, still less to become involved in settlement of the case through, for example, acting as mediator.[360]

The reasons for such opposition were outlined above when presenting the Common Law's traditional aversion to adjudicators' dual role.[361] However, like in the US, following the 1996 reform in the U.K. civil justice system, known as the "Woolf Reform,"[362] courts are currently required to promote the use of ADR methods within judicial proceedings. They are also expected to actively assist litigants before them to settle their dispute amicably,[363] including by encouraging settlement discussions and expressing evaluative views on the merits of the dispute.[364] This attitude is reflected in the Civil Procedure Rules, which state that as part of their active case management responsibilities, judges should encourage parties to revert to ADR mechanisms to settle their disputes and assist them to fully or partly settle the case.[365] However, despite the judiciary's strong movement in favor of settlement to reduce lengthy adjudication proceedings, the active role of U.K. judges does not extend to "switching hats" between the roles of adjudicator and mediator, nor does it involve holding separate meetings with the disputants.[366]

359. *See* the discussion in section 6.3.3.1.
360. Harris, 2016, p. 92. *See also* Ehle, 2010, p. 83; Gill, 2006, p. 155; Berger, 2018b, p. 507; Favalli & Hasenclever, 2008, p. 2; Böckstiegel, 2009, pp. 293-302.
361. *See* the discussion in section 5.3.1 above. *See also* Nigmatullina, 2018, p. 64; Berger, 2018b, p. 503; Ehle, 2010, pp. 83-84; Raeschke-Kessler, 2005, p. 525; Pitkowitz & Richter, 2009, p. 227; Gill, 2006, pp. 159-160.
362. Woolf, 1996; Kaufmann-Kohler, 2009, p. 192.
363. Woolf, 1996, Chapter 1, paras. 7(d) & 16(b)-(c); Karton, 2013, p. 105; Brown & Marriott, 1999, pp. 28-29; Gill, 2006, pp. 156-157; Mayer, 2016, p. 3; Kaufmann-Kohler, 2009, p. 192; Harris, 2016, p. 89; Ehle, 2006; Naughton, 2007, p. 32; Marriott, 2005, pp. 536-537. As part of this trend, in *Halsey v. Milton Keynes General NHS Trust*, 2004, the Court of Appeal held that despite the basic rule in England that costs follow the event, to encourage litigants to mediate, courts are intitled to impose costs sanctions on winning parties for unreasonable decision to take part of mediation.
364. Woolf, 2008, p. 169; Ehle, 2010, p. 84; Gill, 2006, pp. 156, 161-162.
365. U.K. Civil Procedure Rules, 1998, Rule 1.4(1)-(2). *See also* Berger & Jensen, 2017, p. 903; Chase & Bruner, 2005, p. 64.
366. Harris, 2016, pp. 92, 95; Gill, 2006, pp. 157-158; Nariman, 2005, pp. 531-532; Houzhi, 2005, pp. 550-551; Raeschke-Kessler, 2005, p. 525; Ehle, 2010, p. 83; Berger, 2018b, p. 503; Stipanowich, 2021a, p. 288.

Affected by the civil justice reform, the 1996 U.K. Arbitration Act[367] abandoned the traditional resistance to the arbitrator's involvement in the settlement process and empowered them with the mandate to facilitate settlement.[368] This view was supported by Lord Woolf, who stated that following the introduction of the amended Arbitration Act, arbitrators are encouraged to assist the parties in resolving the dispute as early in the arbitral process as possible, when, for that end, they are empowered to fulfill the role of settlement facilitators.[369] The arbitrator's proactive role in the settlement stems from their authority under the Arbitration Act to decide on suitable procedures for resolving the dispute, including the way facts and legal issues will be ascertained to avoid unnecessary delays and costs.[370] According to some scholars, this authority of the arbitrator, alongside the parties' right under the Arbitration Act "to agree how their disputes are resolved, subject only to such safeguards as are necessary in the public interest,"[371] even allows the arbitrator to mediate the dispute subject to the parties' consent.[372]

Unlike the active role of the courts in the settlement efforts following the civil justice reform, in practice, the arbitrator's mandate as a settlement facilitator is still subject to objections and has not gained significant success in the UK.[373] Concerns have been raised against any direct involvement of the arbitrator in the settlement negotiations, particularly when delivering preliminary views on the merits of the case, perceived as an unfair intervention that may affect the arbitrator's impartiality, undermine the disputants' confidence in the process, and increase the risk to challenge the award.[374] Opponents of the arbitrator's involvement in settlement argue that, unlike in many Civil Law systems, in the tension between their independence and impartiality, the drafters of the Arbitration Act granted clear priority to the arbitrator's impartiality, so they should refrain from any involvement in the settlement efforts.[375] Furthermore, while a budget shortage in the national justice system can justify the promotion of settlements by the courts to reduce their dockets, this consideration does not apply to the private justice system, including arbitration, so these procedures are expected to take place in full.[376] More significant concerns have been raised against hybrid procedures that combine arbitration with mediation by the same neutral:

367. U.K. Arbitration Act, 1996.
368. Berger, 2018b, p. 507; *Guide to international arbitration law and rules in England and Wales*, 2022; Baysal & Cevik, 2021.
369. Woolf, 2008, p. 172.
370. U.K. Arbitration Act, 1996, sections 33(1)(b) & 34(2)(g); Bernardini, 2004, p. 118. Interestingly, this authority under the Arbitration Act is viewed by some scholars as allowing the arbitrator to abandon the adversarial approach in favor of an inquisitorial one. *See* in this regard Marriott, 1997, p. 31; Bernardini, 2004, p. 118; *Guide to international arbitration law and rules in England and Wales*, 2022.
371. U.K. Arbitration Act, 1996, section 1(b).
372. Aragaki, 2021, p. 31; Scherpe & Marten, 2013, p. 375; Houzhi, 2005, p. 549.
373. Ehle, 2006; Gill, 2006, pp. 158-159.
374. Harris, 2016, pp. 90-91; Ehle, 2006; Gill, 2006, p. 159.
375. Hodges & Greenaway, 2013, pp. 297-298; Foster & Barratt, 2013, pp. 321-322; Saville, 1997, para. 102.
376. Harris, 2016, p. 89.

> From an English perspective, the temporary transition from arbitrator to mediator presents a number of serious risks to the arbitrator, and thus also to the arbitral process. Perhaps the two most obvious risks are to be found in the communications that take place between the mediator and each of the parties privately and the acquisition by the mediator of confidential information.[377]

Reflecting that fear of apparent or real bias caused by caucusing and exposure to confidential information, the English courts have ruled that arbitrators should only collectively engage with the parties except for purely procedural matters.[378] In one reported case, an application was made to remove the arbitrator for conducting an ex parte meeting to discuss the dispute's merits. Even though a transcript of the meeting was made available to the other party, the London Court for International Arbitration (LCIA) ruled that this meeting violated the arbitrator's mandatory, nonwaivable duty under the Arbitration Act to conduct the proceedings fairly and impartially while granting each party a reasonable opportunity to respond to the opponents' claims.[379] Therefore, the LCIA ordered the arbitrator to be replaced.[380] Given the strong opposition raised against hybrid processes, their rare use in the UK comes as no surprise,[381] which may also explain why the legislator has not enacted a provision to regulate them,[382] unlike other Common Law jurisdictions, including Singapore, Hong Kong, Australia, Canada, and some U.S. states.[383]

The aversion of the legal practice from the arbitrator's involvement in the settlement negotiations is well reflected in the rules of leading arbitral institutes in the UK. The arbitration rules of the LCIA, the most sought-after arbitral institute for ICA in the UK and one of the four most preferred institutions worldwide,[384] do not empower the arbitrator to act as a settlement facilitator[385] but only to deliver consent awards based on settlements between the disputants.[386] Additionally, the LCIA offers a separate mediation process to resolve disputes amicably.[387] Although its mediation rules do not explicitly prohibit the mediator from acting as an arbitrator in the same dispute, the fact that its provisions relating to confidentiality set a nonwaivable

377. Harris, 2016, p. 92. *See also* Gill, 2006, pp. 159-160, arguing that in the UK concerns connected with hybrid procedures conducted by the same arbitrator "are not simply academic musings. There is a real risk that an arbitrator who engages in the role of mediator in the course of arbitration proceedings could have either his continued involvement or his award challenged."
378. Hodges & Greenaway, 2013, p. 295; Nariman, 2005, p. 531; Rawding et al., 2013, p. 383.
379. U.K. Arbitration Act, 1996, section 33(1)(a), which according to Schedule 1 is a mandatory provision. *See also* Harris, 2016, pp. 93-95; Gill, 2006, p. 159.
380. Nicholas & Partasides, 2007, pp. 39-40, relating to Decision 10 of the LCIA Court (dated February 13, 2002).
381. Lang, 2009, p. 98; Harris, 2016, p. 95; Gill, 2006, p. 161.
382. Interestingly, also domestic mediation legislation is not available in the UK, with the exception relating to cross-border mediation legislation enacted to comply with the EU Directive. *See* Aragaki, 2021, pp. 33, 58.
383. Stipanowich, 2021a, pp. 323-327; Gu, 2019, pp. 159-160; Nigmatullina, 2018, pp. 75-76.
384. Queen Mary University of London and White & Case LLP, 2021, p. 10.
385. LCIA Arbitration Rules, 2020; Marzolini, 2016, p. 105.
386. LCIA Arbitration Rules, 2020, Article 26(9). This provision aligns with the U.K. Arbitration Act, 1996, section 51, which empowers the tribunal to issue consent awards and accords them the same status as any other award. *See also* Rawding et al., 2013, p. 397.
387. LCIA Mediation Rules, 2020.

prohibition on the use of documents or information obtained during mediation in any other proceedings, including litigation or arbitration, indicates that the arbitrator is not entitled to conduct hybrid procedures involving arbitration and mediation.[388] Similarly, the London Maritime Arbitrators Association (LMAA), the second most preferred arbitral institute in the UK for international arbitration whose rules are the fourth most adopted in ad hoc arbitrations worldwide,[389] does not authorize the arbitrator to take active part in the settlement efforts[390] but alternatively suggests a separate Early Neutral Evaluation procedure,[391] as well as independent mediation rules that impose a clear and nonwaivable prohibition on mediators to act as arbitrators in the same dispute.[392]

Nevertheless, arbitrators in the UK still engage in settlement facilitation, even in hybrid processes. The literature indicates that English arbitrators "find ways to encourage the parties to enter into settlement negotiations."[393] Some arbitrators, for example, exhaust their procedural power to enable designated windows for settlement negotiations or mediation and hold conferences to handle key legal and factual issues to reduce controversies.[394] Others guide the parties by asking "subtle questions which indicate their provisional view on the merits."[395] Subject to the disputants' consent, some even provide preliminary views on the merits and express clear views about particular issues arising during arbitration.[396] In addition, evidence exists regarding the use of procedures that combine arbitration with mediation. The main case in the UK addressing the consequences of a decision made by an arbitrator who had earlier futilely mediated the dispute is *Glencot Development & Design Ltd v. Ben Barrett & Son Ltd*.[397] The losing party challenged the adjudicator's[398] decision on the basis that, after engaging in mediation, which, according to the parties' consent, included a private meeting with the parties and exposure to confidential information, the adjudicator lost their ability to make an impartial decision and therefore should not have reverted to the adjudicator's role after the failed mediation. These arguments were brought before the adjudicator immediately after the mediation stage, but the adjudicator rejected them because the process was conducted according to the parties' request, who also agreed that the adjudicator would resume their initial role regardless of the mediation's outcome. Consequently, the adjudicator proceeded to render a decision in the controversy. Based on a former precedent of the House of Lords in *R v. Cough*,[399] the High

388. LCIA Mediation Rules, 2020, Article 12.
389. Queen Mary University of London and White & Case LLP, 2021, pp. 9-10.
390. LMAA Arbitration Rules, 2021, Article 19.
391. LMAA Early Neutral Evaluation Guidance Note, 2022. *See also* Harris, 2016, p. 91.
392. LMAA Mediation Rules, 2002, Article 14.
393. Ehle, 2006.
394. Harris, 2016, pp. 96-97; Gill, 2006, pp. 161-162.
395. Ehle, 2006. *See also* Gill, 2006, p. 162.
396. Harris, 2016, p. 91; Gill, 2006, p. 162.
397. *Glencot Development & Design Ltd v. Ben Barrett & Son Ltd*, 2001.
398. As accepted in the construction sector, the decision-maker in this case was referred to as an adjudicator, although their role was functionally equivalent to that of an arbitrator. *See* Harris, 2016, p. 95.
399. *R v. Gough*, 1993, p. 15, setting the test of "apparent bias" or "a real danger of bias" to examine whether a court or an arbitral tribunal acted impartially. *See also* Lang, 2009, p. 99.

Court set out an objective test for apparent bias that seeks to ascertain whether the "circumstances would lead a fair-minded and informed observer to conclude that there was a real possibility or a real danger ... that the tribunal was biased."[400] Upon examining the particulars of the case, the court ruled that from an objective standpoint, the mediation phase had created a real danger of bias on the adjudicator's part, which affected the validity of their decision. This determination was based on the heated discussions between the parties, the adjudicator's caucuses with the parties that might have revealed positions or information potentially influencing their decision, and the adjudicator's reliance on matters where "there was no documentary evidence."[401] While the court acknowledged the parties' consent to the hybrid process, it held that such consent, even when anchored in an advance and formal agreement, could not preclude a successful challenge to the adjudicator's final decision when allegations of apparent or actual bias were established.[402]

Scholars opposing hybrid processes in the UK relate to the *Glencot* case as "a salutary tale for English arbitrators, demonstrating that the best of intentions can result in a vulnerable award" and argue that its analysis "is strongly in favour of using an independent mediator and keeping arbitrators away from that process."[403] Nonetheless, a profound examination of the *Glencot* decision and the related literature should lead to a different conclusion regarding the acceptability of hybrid processes in the UK. *First*, the court did not state at any stage of the judgment that hybrid proceedings are prohibited.[404] *Second*, while referring to prior rulings that explored the implications of waiving the right to object based on apparent bias, the court did not declare such a waiver as prohibited but, in fact, related to it as one of the circumstances to consider.[405]

400. *Glencot Development & Design Ltd v. Ben Barrett & Son Ltd*, 2001, para. 21. *See also* Nigmatullina, 2018, pp. 171-172; Lang, 2009, p. 99; Foster & Barratt, 2013, pp. 323-325; Gu, 2019, pp. 158-159. Very recent ruling of the UK Supreme Court confirmed the applicability of this objective test to all institutional and ad hoc arbitrations in the UK, including equal application to wing arbitrators and chairs. Interestingly, this ruling suggests that the objective test may be enforced more strictly in ICA compared to court proceedings because arbitral processes are private and confidential, awards undergo limited review, neutrals are directly compensated by the parties, and they comprise of various legal backgrounds and ethical norms that result in differing perspectives regarding independence and impartiality. *See Halliburton Company v. Chubb Bermuda Insurance Ltd*, 2020, paras. 56-63 & 144; Gojkovic, 2021, pp. 69-70.

401. *Glencot Development & Design Ltd v. Ben Barrett & Son Ltd*, 2001, para. 24. *See also* Nigmatullina, 2018, pp. 171-172; Rosoff, 2009, pp. 90-91; Freehills, 2001; Gu, 2019, pp. 158-159.

402. *Glencot Development & Design Ltd v. Ben Barrett & Son Ltd*, 2001, para. 23.

403. Harris, 2016, pp. 95-96. *See also* Gill, 2006, p. 160; Lang, 2009, p. 102; Freehills, 2001; Hwang, 2005, pp. 573-574.

404. Freehills, 2001, arguing that the validity of agreed hybrid procedures between disputants "is clear from [the court] remarks in *Glencot*, although strictly it was not what happened in that case."

405. According to some court decisions in the UK, the waiver of the right to due process and an impartial tribunal is deemed to contradict the Human Rights Act, which implements the European Convention on Human Rights (ECHR), and is therefore precluded. However, other court decisions, have clarified that such a prohibition may apply only to court proceedings, as parties to arbitration can waive their rights under the convention in favor of privacy and finality. *See* European Convention on Human Rights, 1950, Article 6; U.K. Human Rights Act, 1998, Article 1; *Halsey v. Milton Keynes General NHS Trust*, 2004; *North Range Shipping Ltd v.*

One of the cases discussed in the *Glencot* decision was *Smith v. Kvaerner Cementation*, where the Court of Appeal noted that for a waiver of the right to object based on apparent bias to be recognized, it must be clear, unequivocal, and indicate an evident understanding of the consequences.[406] Another case discussed in the *Glencot* decision was *ASM Shipping Ltd of India v. TTMI Ltd of England*, where the High Court ruled that claims related to bias should be raised without any delay; therefore, a party cannot withhold such claims until the end of the arbitral process and raise them only in the event of an unfavorable award.[407] This position of the court aligns with a provision in the U.K. Arbitration Act, which stipulates that the right to object to procedural irregularities or issues concerning the tribunal may be forfeited if not raised promptly or within the specified time frame.[408] The above discussion in the *Glencot* case should, therefore, lead to a conclusion that also in the UK, if parties grant informed and clear consent to participate in a hybrid process, as well as a clear and unequivocal waiver of the right to object based on apparent bias, they can be held as committed to such agreement without an automatic ability to be released from its consequences, certainly when claims in the matter were not raised in time. In this context, the *Glencot* case can be observed as a "marker" for the risks associated with hybrid processes rather than an absolute prohibition on their use.[409]

In conclusion, despite the aversion of legal practitioners and scholars in the UK toward the arbitrator's mandate as a settlement facilitator, particularly within hybrid procedures involving arbitration and mediation, such practices are utilized in the UK and have not been prohibited by the courts. However, according to the 2001-2004 Bühring-Uhle Study, which examined the general attitude of arbitrators in settlement facilitation based on their legal background,[410] it appears that UK practitioners are more receptive to the arbitrator's dual role in international arbitrations than in domestic ones.[411] This finding aligns with contemporary calls from commentators advocating for a more accepting attitude toward this role in ICA proceedings conducted in the UK:

> One of the advantages of arbitration over litigation as a means of settling international commercial disputes is that, because of its flexibility, arbitration can transcend the confines of national legal systems and the parties can tailor a procedure to suit their particular needs and to ensure that the arbitration progresses efficiently, proportionately and in the interests of the parties.[412]

Seatrans Shipping Corp., 2002; Seatzu & Vargiu, 2022, pp. 209-211; Nigmatullina, 2018, p. 189; Hodges & Greenaway, 2013, pp. 297-298; Kaufmann-Kohler, 2009, p. 198; Limbury, 2009b, p. 13; Freehills, 2001. For further discussion about the ability of ICA parties to waive their procedural rights, *see* section 7.3.2.

406. *Smith v. Kvaerner Cementation*, 2006, discussed in Lang, 2009, pp. 100-101.
407. *ASM Shipping Ltd of India v. TTMI Ltd of England*, 2006, discussed in Lang, 2009, p. 101. *See also* Nigmatullina, 2018, p. 184; Foster & Barratt, 2013, p. 320.
408. U.K. Arbitration Act, 1996, section 73(1); Lang, 2009, p. 98; Nigmatullina, 2018, p. 184.
409. Lang, 2009, p. 99; Freehills, 2001; Hodges & Greenaway, 2013, p. 300.
410. *See* the discussion in section 5.3 above.
411. Bühring-Uhle et al., 2006, pp. 110-112.
412. *Guide to international arbitration law and rules in England and Wales*, 2022. *See also* Berger, 2019, pp. 311-312; Berger & Jensen, 2016, pp. 4-5; Nigmatullina, 2018, pp. 75, 78.

Nevertheless, similar demands have been expressed regarding domestic arbitrations in the UK, as opponents to the arbitrator's dual role have admitted that many objections to its utilization could be alleviated if ex parte communications were excluded from the arbitrator's toolkit.[413] In addition, more practitioners have begun to realize the positive influence of preliminary views expressed by the arbitrator on cutting "the Gordian knot" and achieving a settlement. Therefore, they have suggested assimilating it in arbitral proceedings when "all relevant parties have given their express written consent."[414] Supporters of the arbitrator's active role in the settlement argue that "continuing to conduct arbitrations in the manner of English court proceedings is wasteful of time and costs, is certainly old-fashioned and ... not very imaginative."[415] Some of them even call for expanding the use of hybrid procedures within arbitration in the UK, especially in disputes concerning large transactions:

> It is not practical to artificially distinguish the function of the arbitrator and the mediator, particularly in the resolution of disputes of big business transactions. The distinction may delay the final resolution of the dispute and increase unnecessary expenses, because if mediation fails, the case will be heard anew by another person who is not familiar with the dispute. Therefore, the parties may freely abandon such distinction provisions set forth in the mediation and arbitration rules. If mediation is not successful, the parties should be allowed to reach an agreement that the mediator may continue to participate in the resolution of the dispute, but he must appear as an arbitrator.[416]

5.3.1.3 Australia

Australia serves as an example of a Western Common Law jurisdiction that moved to regulate the arbitrator's role in the settlement process as early as 1984.[417] The original version of the Commercial Arbitration Act, applicable to domestic arbitrations and adopted uniformly by all states and territories in the country,[418] authorized arbitrators, subject to the parties' consent, to facilitate settlements in disputes before them, whether during the arbitration process or through dedicated conferences. Furthermore, the Act permitted arbitrators to act as mediators, stipulating that no objections could be raised against their resumption of the arbitral role solely because of their prior involvement in settlement efforts.[419] The provision even expressly authorized disputants to waive their due process rights during the settlement phase, effectively enabling

413. Gill, 2006, p. 164.
414. Harris, 2016, pp. 91, 98.
415. Rees, 2007, pp. 506, 510. *See also* Saville, 1997, para. 153.
416. Houzhi, 2005, p. 548. *See also* Marriott, 2005, p. 533, expressing firm position in favor of active involvement of arbitrators in the settlement process, including in hybrid procedures combining arbitration and mediation.
417. Limbury, 2010b, p. 4; Monichino, 2010, p. 45; Limbury, 2009a, p. 85; Nigmatullina, 2018, pp. 75-76.
418. Nigmatullina, 2018, p. 189; Limbury, 2010b, p. 4.
419. Australia Commercial Arbitration Act, 1984, section 27; Monichino, 2010, p. 45; Limbury, 2009a, p. 85; Limbury, 2010b, p. 4.

arbitrators to caucus with the parties.[420] However, this regulatory framework was confined to domestic arbitrations,[421] as the Australian legislature intentionally excluded its application, and that of its 2010 successor, from the International Arbitration Act.[422] This omission reflected concerns that courts in foreign jurisdictions might refuse to enforce Australian awards influenced by the arbitrator's direct involvement in the settlement negotiations.[423]

The court approved the explicit authorization for arbitrators to facilitate settlements in domestic arbitrations, including the disputants' right to waive their due process rights during the settlement phase. In *The Duke Group Ltd v. Alamain Investments Ltd*, a judge disqualified themselves from hearing a case in which they had previously mediated between the parties' officers several years before being appointed to the bench. The court ruled that, while ex parte communications with the parties might conflict with basic notions of fairness, such communications could be approved subject to "previous knowledge or consent of the other party."[424] According to this decision, which was also applied to arbitral proceedings,[425] in the balance between procedural fairness and party autonomy, the latter should take precedence, especially when the parties are fully aware of the potential consequences of their choices.[426]

In practice, however, the main attitude in Australia toward the role of arbitrators remained skeptical, particularly in hybrid proceedings,[427] which resulted in limited application of the aforementioned provision in the Domestic Arbitration Act.[428] Similar to reservations raised in other Common Law jurisdictions, Australian scholars and practitioners have expressed concerns that this mandate may breach the principles of natural justice, mainly when arbitrators express definite opinions regarding the appropriate outcome of the process or caucus with the disputants and rely on confidential information while deciding the case.[429] In hybrid processes, particular concerns have also arisen regarding the vagueness of the arbitration act on whether the parties can "opt out after the mediation phase, should the dispute be unresolved."[430]

Subsequently, in 2010, while amending the Domestic Arbitration Act according to the Model Law on ICA,[431] the Australian legislator addressed due process concerns connected with the original provision to make the mandate of arbitrators clearer and

420. Australia Commercial Arbitration Act, 1984, section 27(3); Nigmatullina, 2018, p. 189; Limbury, 2009a, p. 85; Limbury, 2010b, p. 4.
421. Gu, 2019, p. 159; Monichino, 2010, p. 40; Stipanowich, 2021a, p. 324; Firth, 2018.
422. Australia International Arbitration Act, 1974; Monichino, 2010, p. 40; Gu, 2019, p. 160; Nigmatullina, 2018, p. 217.
423. Gu, 2019, p. 160; Garnett, 2015, p. 21; Limbury, 2009a, pp. 84-85; Limbury, 2010b, p. 2.
424. *The Duke Group Ltd v. Alamain Investments Ltd*, 2003, cited in Limbury, 2010b, pp. 3-4. *See also* Croft, 2014, pp. 3-4; Limbury, 2009a, p. 85; Nigmatullina, 2018, pp. 188-189.
425. Croft, 2014, p. 4; Nigmatullina, 2018, pp. 188-189.
426. Limbury, 2009b, p. 9; Nigmatullina, 2018, p. 188; Lack, 2010, p. 374; Talbot, 2001, p. 228; Elliott, 1995, p. 169.
427. Limbury, 2009a, p. 84; Limbury, 2010b, p. 4; Nigmatullina, 2018, p. 76; Stipanowich, 2021a, p. 323.
428. Limbury, 2009a, p. 84; Limbury, 2010b, p. 4.
429. Croft, 2014, pp. 2-4; Limbury, 2010b, pp. 2-4; Limbury, 2009a, pp. 84-85; Astor & Chinkin, 2002, pp. 145-146.
430. Limbury, 2009a, p. 84. *See also* Limbury, 2010b, p. 4.
431. Monichino, 2010, p. 42; Gu, 2019, p. 159; Nigmatullina, 2018, p. 211.

more attractive to users.[432] However, for the same reasons mentioned above, the International Arbitration Act was deliberately left again without any provision granting arbitrators the mandate to facilitate settlements in cases before them.[433] The 2010 Domestic Arbitration Act, which, as of 2017, was adopted by all states and territories in the country,[434] empowers the arbitrator to mediate, conciliate, or conduct any other non-arbitral intermediary between the parties.[435] However, this mandate is subject to the following conditions. *First*, the arbitration agreement provides for the arbitrator's involvement in the settlement, or all parties have consented in writing to that involvement. *Second*, the settlement phase terminates if the disputants agree to terminate it, if any party withdraws consent to the role of the arbitrator, or if the arbitrator decides to terminate it. *Third*, following terminated settlement negotiations, the arbitrator may not resume their initial role as an arbitrator without a renewed written consent of all parties, after which no objections can be raised against the arbitrator in the renewed arbitration merely based on their prior involvement in the settlement process. Without such written consent, the arbitrator's mandate terminates, necessitating the appointment of a replacement arbitrator. *Fourth*, during the settlement phase, the arbitrator can meet with the disputants jointly or separately but must keep information obtained through caucuses confidential unless otherwise agreed or provided in the arbitral agreement. *Fifth*, if the settlement stage concludes and the arbitrator has acquired confidential information in its course, they must disclose any information deemed relevant to the arbitration before resuming their role as an arbitrator.[436]

The new provision of the domestic arbitration law, which resembles those of Singapore and Hong Kong,[437] includes an innovative requirement for renewed written consent to allow arbitrators to resume their initial role following failed settlement negotiations. This exclusive requirement, not adopted by any other jurisdiction that followed the UNCITRAL Model Law, has been praised for its enhanced protection of due process when arbitrators perform dual roles.[438] Recently, this requirement was tested by the New South Wales Supreme Court in *Ku-ring-gai Council v. Ichor*

432. Limbury, 2010b, p. 4.
433. Garnett, 2015, p. 21; Gu, 2019, p. 160; Monichino, 2010, p. 40; Nigmatullina, 2018, p. 217.
434. Gu, 2019, p. 159; Monichino, 2010, p. 40; Stipanowich, 2021a, p. 324; Firth, 2018; Nigmatullina, 2018, p. 216.
435. Australia Commercial Arbitration Act, 2010, Part 5, section 27D.
436. Australia Commercial Arbitration Act, 2010, Part 5, section 27D; Stipanowich, 2021a, pp. 324-326; Gu, 2019, p. 159; Monichino, 2010, p. 45; Ruckteschler & Wendelstein, 2021, p. 767. To accommodate the specific arrangement outlined in the revised Domestic Arbitration Act regarding confidential information obtained during caucusing, the Australian legislature opted not to include Article 24(3) of the Model Law on ICA, 2006, in the Domestic Arbitration Act. As previously mentioned, including this provision can prohibit arbitrators from maintaining any level of confidentiality over information obtained during ex parte communications. However, this provision was incorporated into the Australian International Arbitration Act. For further discussion, *see* section 8.3.2.
437. Gu, 2019, p. 159; Stipanowich, 2021a, p. 324.
438. Stipanowich, 2021a, p. 325; Gu, 2019, p. 159; Gu, 2014, p. 119. Similar arrangement was added lately to the Georgian mediation law, which stipulate that arbitrators and mediators who shift roles need to obtain renewed consent from the parties after one process is concluded and prior to the commencement of the other. *See* Law of Georgia on Mediation, 2019, Article 6.

Constructions Pty Ltd,[439] which related to arbitral proceedings where the arbitrator proposed assisting the parties with the settlement efforts while acting as a mediator. The parties granted written consent for this purpose; however, after the settlement efforts proved unsuccessful, arbitration recommenced without obtaining renewed written consent.[440] The court ruled that, although the parties voluntarily continued to participate in the arbitration after the failed settlement stage, implied consent could not substitute for the explicit requirement of renewed written consent mandated by law. This consent had to be granted after the termination of the settlement phase and before arbitration could resume. Consequently, the court terminated the arbitrator's mandate and revoked the award.[441] The literature suggests that this decision underscores the Australian courts' strict application of the procedural requirement for renewed written consent. Without such consent, the "arbitral award will be vulnerable to challenge on the basis that the arbitrator lacks a mandate to give the award."[442] This strict approach can be justified by the absence in the new provision of a central feature present in the original one: the parties' explicit authority to waive their due process rights. Some commentators argue, however, that the new provision's comprehensive framework—allowing parties to compromise these rights under specific conditions designed to uphold the integrity of the arbitral process—may render this feature unnecessary.[443] Accordingly, the court's decision in *Ku-ring-gai Council v. Ichor Constructions Pty Ltd* does not deviate from previous court rulings in Australia, including *The Duke Group Ltd v. Alamain Investments Ltd*, which recognized the parties' authority to waive due process rights provided appropriate safeguards are in place. Instead, it highlights the importance of precise implementation of those safeguards, whether established by law or contractually agreed upon.

Despite efforts to improve the procedural fairness of the arbitrator's role as a settlement facilitator, the new legislative provision appears to be infrequently utilized in practice.[444] This limited application is reflected in the arbitration rules of leading arbitral institutes in Australia, such as the Institute of Arbitrators and Mediators Australia (IAMA, also known as the Resolution Institute) and the Australian Centre for International Commercial Arbitration (ACICA), neither of which authorizes arbitrators to facilitate settlements or engage in hybrid procedures.[445] While the ACICA rules instruct arbitrators to raise before the disputants the possibility of using other ADR techniques to promote the "timely, cost effective and fair" settlement of disputes, they

439. *Ku-ring-gai Council v. Ichor Constructions Pty Ltd*, 2018.
440. *Ku-ring-gai Council v. Ichor Constructions Pty Ltd*, 2018, §§3-6.
441. *Ku-ring-gai Council v. Ichor Constructions Pty Ltd*, 2018, §§13-23.
442. Firth, 2018. *See also* Gu, 2019, p. 159; Stipanowich, 2021a, p. 326. This interpretation is supported by Australia Commercial Arbitration Act, 2010, Part 1, section 4, which stipulates that the loss of the right to object—whether due to delays in raising the objection or deviations from fixed schedules—is restricted to provisions from which the parties are permitted to derogate. The new provision concerning written renewed consent does not fall within the scope of such derogable provisions.
443. Croft, 2014, p. 4; Monichino, 2010, p. 45.
444. Nigmatullina, 2018, p. 216; Croft, 2014, p. 5; Garnett & Nottage, 2011, p. 43; Stipanowich, 2021a, p. 323; Limbury, 2010b, p. 4.
445. ACICA Arbitration Rules, 2021; IAMA Arbitration Rules, 2014; Croft, 2014, p. 5.

stipulate that such procedures must be conducted by other neutrals, which leaves arbitrators with the mere authority to suspend arbitration to allow their utilization.[446] This divergence, wherein the Australian legislature encourages arbitrators' involvement in settlement efforts while practitioners and arbitral institutions maintain a skeptical stance toward this role, underscores how legal culture can act as a limiting factor in implementing external dispute resolution models.[447] Moreover, the deliberate exclusion of this mandate from Australia's International Arbitration Act suggests an acknowledgment that the arbitrator's dual role remains controversial at the international level and lacks consensus. These considerations should be carefully weighed when proposing solutions to enhance the transnational harmonization of the arbitrator's role as a settlement facilitator.

Despite the hesitant attitude in Australia toward the active involvement of arbitrators in settlement negotiations, an increasing number of scholars and practitioners have advocated for broader recognition of this role, particularly given the supportive legal framework.[448] Concerned with the growing delays and costs of arbitral proceedings in the country,[449] these commentators argue that "unless arbitrators willingly facilitate settlement, arbitration will become less attractive than litigation,"[450] especially when courts continue to streamline their processes and emphasize cost-effective conduct of proceedings.[451] Similar to suggestions raised in the US and the UK, Australian commentators have suggested applying the "managerial role" of judges to arbitral proceedings, developing the "proactive mandate" of arbitrators, and promoting the use of hybrid processes.[452] Additionally, some scholars have criticized the requirement for arbitrators to disclose confidential information before resuming their arbitral role, raising concerns similar to those expressed regarding the obligations of arbitrators in Hong Kong and Singapore.[453] However, most criticism has been directed at the legislator's choice to exclude the arbitrator's settlement facilitation mandate from the International Arbitration Act. While acknowledging enforcement concerns, critics contend that there are no compelling reasons to exclude this role from ICA proceedings conducted in Australia:

> The international arbitration legislation of nearly all of Australia's Asia-Pacific neighbours (especially our major competitors, Hong Kong and Singapore) provides for an arbitrator to encourage amicable settlement of a dispute by engaging the parties in negotiation, as opposed to determination. Resolution through a process of conciliated negotiation is not only legislated in Asian countries but is

446. ACICA Arbitration Rules, 2021, Articles 25(3) & 55.
447. Lazareff, 1999, p. 1; Kun, 2016a, p. 251; Chase & Bruner, 2005, p. 49; Link & Haftel, 2021, pp. 562-563.
448. Stipanowich, 2021a, p. 324; Limbury, 2010b, pp. 1-2; Croft, 2014, pp. 2-4; Limbury, 2009a, pp. 85-86.
449. Limbury, 2009a, p. 84; Croft, 2014, p. 1.
450. Limbury, 2010b, p. 1. *See also* Croft, 2014, p. 1.
451. Croft, 2014, p. 1; Limbury, 2010b, p. 1.
452. Croft, 2014, pp. 6-9; Stipanowich, 2021a, p. 324; Monichino, 2010, p. 45.
453. Ruckteschler & Wendelstein, 2021, p. 773; Monichino, 2010, p. 46; Stipanowich, 2021a, pp. 326-327. For the discussion about this obligation in Hong Kong's and Singapore's arbitration laws, *see* section 5.2.2.3 above.

> part of a cultural ethos which prefers a face-saving resolution to a contest in which there is a winner and a loser. Moreover, the promotion of amicable settlement by international arbitrators is now touted as *"international best practice."* It is therefore disappointing that a [settlement facilitation] provision was not contained in the IAA Amending Act.[454]

Aimed at moderating the opposition to applying this mandate in international arbitrations in Australia, some scholars have proposed a compromise. Rather than fully adopting the domestic framework—which permits ex parte communications but requires the disclosure of confidential information—they recommend amending the International Arbitration Act to formally recognize the active and direct role of arbitrators in settlement facilitation while prohibiting caucusing.[455]

5.3.2 Western Civil Law Legal Systems

Western Civil Law systems, although generally more tolerant toward the adjudicator's mandate as a settlement facilitator,[456] still present diverse positions.[457] While jurisdictions with Germanic legal tradition allow and expect adjudicators to engage proactively in settlement negotiations,[458] some Civil Law jurisdictions, such as France, Italy, Belgium, and Brazil, are highly hesitant toward the role of adjudicators, even when it is recognized in their legislation.[459] In comparison, other Civil Law jurisdictions implement a middle way between these opposing positions.[460] Despite this division, almost all Western Civil Law jurisdictions express concerns regarding hybrid procedures, particularly when they include ex parte communications and exposure to confidential information.[461] Consequently, adjudicators in Western Civil Law jurisdictions are usually reluctant to participate in hybrid procedures even when they are not explicitly prohibited by the law or even legally recognized.[462] Nevertheless, when they do, they generally refrain from caucusing due to its potential influence on the subsequent adjudicative process.[463] In certain Western Civil Law jurisdictions, such as

454. Monichino, 2010, p. 40. *See also* Hatzistergos, 2010, p. 33.
455. Nottage, 2013, p. 489; Nottage, 2014, p. 227; Nigmatullina, 2018, p. 217.
456. Born, 2021, §13.04[D]; Ehle, 2010, p. 80; Nigmatullina, 2018, p. 65; Mayer, 2016, p. 3; Favalli & Hasenclever, 2008, p. 2; Berger, 2018b, p. 504.
457. Schneider, 1998, p. 78; Marzolini, 2016, p. 108.
458. Berger, 2018b, p. 504; Marzolini, 2016, p. 108; Harris, 2016, pp. 91-92; Karton, 2013, p. 107; Ross, 2013, p. 355; Ehle, 2010, pp. 80-83; Berger & Kellerhals, 2015, pp. 56, 171.
459. Berger & Jensen, 2017, p. 902; Marzolini, 2016, pp. 109-110; Nigmatullina, 2018, p. 65; Ross, 2013, p. 355; Kaufmann-Kohler, 2009, p. 190; Morresi, 2009, pp. 106-108; Ehle, 2010, pp. 80-83; Schneider, 1998, pp. 78-80; Sussman & Berger, 2021b, pp. 36-37.
460. Nigmatullina, 2018, p. 65; Schneider, 1998, p. 80. For example, the Dutch Code of Civil Procedure, 2011, Article 87(1), empowers the court to attempt a settlement, regardless the stage of the proceedings, whether following the parties' request or ex officio. Similar authority is granted to arbitrators according to Article 1043 of the Dutch Arbitration Act, 2015.
461. Stipanowich, 2021a, p. 288; Raeschke-Kessler, 2005, p. 535; Ehle, 2010, pp. 92-93.
462. Kaufmann-Kohler, 2009, p. 190; Morresi, 2009, p. 108; Marzolini, 2016, pp. 109, 117; Ehle, 2010, p. 82.
463. Berger & Jensen, 2017, p. 915; Stipanowich, 2021a, p. 288; Berger, 2009, p. 224; Ehle, 2010, p. 82; Raeschke-Kessler, 2005, p. 535; Morresi, 2009, p. 108.

Austria, Liechtenstein, and Brazil, concerns about hybrid procedures have resulted in legal limitations on their use, mainly when arbitration is involved.[464]

In Germanic legal systems, applicable in Germany, Austria, and parts of Switzerland,[465] the proactive role of judges and arbitrators in assisting the disputants to reach a settlement during the proceedings is deeply rooted in the legal tradition.[466] In these jurisdictions, judges and arbitrators are perceived as dispute-resolvers rather than dispute-deciders. Therefore, parties expect them to encourage settlements and express preliminary views on the case when requested and ex officio.[467] This involvement in the settlement efforts, perceived as a *noble officium* of the adjudicators to manage the dispute most cost-effectively,[468] does not constitute grounds for disqualifying them from resuming their adjudicative role should those efforts fail,[469] particularly when their mandate excludes ex parte communications.[470] Interestingly, an exception to this approach regarding caucusing is observed in Canton Zurich in Switzerland, where judges of the Commercial Court, unlike Swiss arbitrators,[471] may engage in ex parte communications to facilitate settlements, subject to the parties' consent.[472] The Germanic legal tradition's influence on arbitrators' approaches toward settlement facilitation was confirmed in a study that reviewed 63 consent awards delivered between 2002 and 2005 under the ICC Rules (2002-2005 Kaufmann-Kohler and Bonnin Study).[473] The results showed that of 13 awards rendered after the active involvement of the tribunal in the settlement efforts, six tribunals were presided over by German or Swiss arbitrators, and seven other tribunals included at least one party-appointed arbitrator from these two jurisdictions. The remaining tribunals were exclusively composed of arbitrators from Latin American jurisdictions where the courts were allowed to facilitate settlements.[474] The study concluded that, despite the limited data reviewed, it is noteworthy that in all cases where the tribunal actively participated in settlement efforts, the arbitrators (or at least some of them) were from jurisdictions that recognized the role of adjudicators as facilitators of settlements.[475] As presented in the

464. Stipanowich, 2021a, p. 288; Aragaki, 2021, pp. 49-50, 62-63. For example, the Austrian Law on Mediation in Civil Law Matters, 2003, section 16(1), stipulates that the decision-maker in a conflict may not serve as a mediator. The Brazilian framework is addressed in section 5.3.2.2 below.
465. Kaufmann-Kohler, 2009, p. 190; Berger, 2018b, p. 504; Wenger, 2006, p. 139; Ehle, 2010, p. 81.
466. Berger, 2018b, p. 504; Karton, 2013, p. 107; Ehle, 2010, p. 80; Favalli & Hasenclever, 2008, p. 2; Marzolini, 2016, pp. 108-109; Ross, 2013, p. 355.
467. Ehle, 2010, p. 80; Stipanowich, 2021a, pp. 312-317; Berger, 2018b, pp. 504-505; Berger & Jensen, 2017, pp. 899-900; Böckstiegel, 2009, pp. 293-302; Raeschke-Kessler, 2005, p. 525; Elsing, 2015, pp. 690-692; Baysal & Cevik, 2021; Stutzer, 2017, pp. 598-600.
468. Marzolini, 2016, pp. 108-109; Favalli & Hasenclever, 2008, p. 2; Raeschke-Kessler, 2005, 527.
469. Giovannini, 2010, pp. 515-516; Ehle, 2010, p. 82.
470. Stipanowich, 2021a, p. 317; Raeschke-Kessler, 2005, p. 535; Ehle, 2010, p. 82.
471. Although the Swiss Arbitration Rules explicitly permit arbitrators to adopt a proactive role in settlement negotiations, they do not address the possibility of caucusing. In practice, Swiss arbitrators avoid caucusing while facilitating settlements. *See* Swiss Arbitration Rules, 2021, Article 19(5); Stutzer, 2017, pp. 605-606; Kozmenko & Groselj, 2021.
472. Stutzer, 2017, pp. 600-601; Baysal & Cevik, 2021.
473. Kaufmann-Kohler & Bonnin, 2007, pp. 79-85; Kaufmann-Kohler, 2009, pp. 195-196.
474. Kaufmann-Kohler & Bonnin, 2007, p. 82.
475. Kaufmann-Kohler, 2009, p. 196; De Gramont et al., 2017, p. 955.

next chapter, the arbitration practice in jurisdictions with Germanic legal culture underlines the CEDR guidelines regarding settlements in ICA proceedings and the Prague Rules that promote the efficient conduct of international arbitration.[476]

Non-Germanic Civil Law jurisdictions in the West, although accepting the adjudicators' role as dispute-resolvers, are still more hesitant toward their mandate to facilitate settlements.[477] Consequently, when adjudicators from these jurisdictions engage in settlement negotiations, they usually limit their role to the bare minimum necessary to avoid jeopardizing their adjudicative role.[478] In France, for example, although the Code of Civil Procedure clearly defines conciliation as an integral part of the adjudicators' mandate,[479] in practice, French judges and arbitrators are hesitant to promote settlements in their cases without the parties' explicit consent.[480] In court proceedings, when parties are willing to settle, French judges usually refer them to other judges, who assist them in reaching an amicable outcome to avoid risking their judicial power.[481] In arbitral proceedings, when parties seek amicable solutions, they are referred to independent mediation. French courts instruct arbitrators to avoid ex parte communications and extend their obligation to maintain confidentiality to hybrid procedures. As a result, arbitration and mediation must be conducted by different neutrals.[482] Italian judges implemented a similar approach despite an amended provision introduced in 2013 to handle the caseloads, which empowered judges to actively engage in the settlement efforts and make concrete settlement proposals without jeopardizing their independence or impartiality.[483] In arbitration, the skeptical approach toward settlement facilitation also stems from the dichotomic separation under the Italian Arbitration Law between "procedural arbitration," which is practically identical to litigation and is enforceable as a court judgment even though the adjudicator is not a judge, and "contractual arbitration," which despite its similarity to a hybrid procedure, is enforced merely as a settlement agreement and may be easily revoked or require further litigation.[484]

As demonstrated, similar to Common Law jurisdictions, practices related to the arbitrator's role as a settlement facilitator in Civil Law countries are profoundly influenced by the judiciary's attitude toward settlement facilitation, irrespective of

---

476. Berger & Jensen, 2017, p. 911; Stipanowich, 2021a, p. 312; CEDR Report on Settlement in ICA, 2009, pp. 4-5; Prague Rules, 2018. *See* the discussion of these guidelines and rules in sections 6.3.3.2-6.3.3.3.
477. Hwang, 2005, p. 571; Berger & Jensen, 2017, p. 901; Collins, 2003, p. 343.
478. Berger & Jensen, 2017, pp. 901-902; Stipanowich & Ulrich, 2014b, p. 6; Collins, 2003, p. 343; Rogers & Jeng, 2014, pp. 204-205.
479. French Code of Civil Procedure, 2011, Article 21. This power to act as a conciliator is applicable to arbitrators according to Article 1460 of the French Arbitration Act, 2011.
480. Kaufmann-Kohler, 2009, p. 190; Ross, 2013, p. 355; Ehle, 2010, p. 82; Nigmatullina, 2018, p. 65; Gu, 2019, p. 158; Bühring-Uhle et al., 2006, p. 122; Schneider, 1998, p. 78.
481. Marzolini, 2016, p. 109; Kaufmann-Kohler, 2009, p. 190.
482. Morresi, 2009, p. 108.
483. Italian Code of Civil Procedures, 2013, Article 185-*bis*; Marzolini, 2016, pp. 109-110; Ferrari, 2014, contending that the amended provision has failed to achieve its intended purpose and has instead led to numerous interpretative challenges.
484. Italian Arbitration Law, 2013, Article 808-*ter*; Morresi, 2009, pp. 106-107.

whether the legislature explicitly regulates such a mandate.[485] The following sections examine Germany and Brazil, which, as previously highlighted, represent distinctive approaches to the arbitrator's involvement in settlement processes. These jurisdictions provide valuable perspectives for the ongoing discussion and contribute to identifying potential solutions for enhancing the transnational harmonization of practices and legal frameworks related to this role. Germany is analyzed as a jurisdiction where judges and arbitrators have traditionally played an active role in settlement facilitation and gained extensive experience in this capacity. Conversely, Brazil is explored as a jurisdiction where the legislature adopts a dual approach to hybrid procedures involving arbitration and mediation by explicitly endorsing Arb-Med processes while prohibiting Med-Arb ones.

5.3.2.1 Germany

In Germany, the proactive role judges play in settlement negotiations is statutory.[486] According to the German Code of Civil Procedure, the court "shall, at any stage of the proceedings, seek to promote an amicable settlement of the dispute or of individual disputed issues."[487] This mandate, which extends the judges' basic role as "decision-makers" to a broader one as "dispute-resolvers" and "managerial judges,"[488] is intended to serve several purposes: avoiding lengthy and costly court proceedings, maximizing transparency and minimizing uncertainties in the dispute-resolution process, emphasizing the result of the legal proceedings rather than how it is reached, and improving the chances to bring "legal peace in general" and "lasting relationship between the parties," which arguably cannot equally be achieved through *ex cathedra* decision of the court.[489] As part of this mandate, before the trial's opening, German judges usually hold pre-hearing settlement sessions to deliver preliminary opinions on the merits and direct questions to the parties to reveal their strengths and weaknesses.[490] Additionally, during the proceedings, German judges explore the most efficient ways to resolve the dispute, indicate provisional assessments and views of the expected outcome to help the parties evaluate their chances, encourage the parties to compromise, and, when needed, suggest concrete alternatives to the settlement.[491] Despite its mediative elements,[492] this involvement in settlement negotiations differs

485. Schneider, 1998, p. 79.
486. Berger, 2018b, p. 504; Jones, 2005, p. 406.
487. German Code of Civil Procedure, 2005, section 278(1). *See also* Berger, 2003, p. 398.
488. Nigmatullina, 2018, p. 66; Berger, 2018b, p. 504; Ehle, 2010, p. 82.
489. Stipanowich, 2021a, p. 314; Hofstede & McRae, 2004, p. 74; Langbein, 1985, p. 826; Berger, 2018b, p. 504, relating to the ruling of the German Federal Constitutional Court in *BVerfG, 1 BvR 1351/01*, 2007, p. 1073, emphasizing that even though Germany is governed by the rule of law, amicable and interest-oriented resolution of disputes should still be preferred over win-lose court decisions based purely on legal considerations.
490. Baysal & Cevik, 2021; Ehle, 2010, p. 80; Berger & Jensen, 2017, pp. 909-910; Harris, 2016, pp. 91-92.
491. Stipanowich, 2021a, pp. 313-314; Nigmatullina, 2018, p. 67; Langbein, 1985, pp. 828-830; Peter, 2005, p. 175.
492. Berger, 2003, pp. 401-402; Stipanowich, 2021a, p. 314; Ehle, 2010, p. 80.

from standalone mediation or other hybrid procedures,[493] as it usually excludes caucusing and tends to focus more on legal opinions and less on interest-based views regarding the dispute.[494] In addition, German judges consider the obligation of promoting a settlement as an additional task to their main adjudicative one.[495] Given these restraining characteristics of the additional role, German courts have held that it is almost impossible to challenge German judges merely for their involvement in promoting settlements.[496]

Strongly influenced by the pro-settlement approach of the courts, German arbitral proceedings are traditionally characterized by the active involvement of arbitrators in settlement efforts.[497] The DIS Arbitration Rules mandate the tribunal to encourage full or partial settlement of the dispute during arbitration.[498] However, this duty, which resembles that of judges according to the Code of Civil Procedure, is subject to a veto right of the parties who can object to its utilization.[499] According to the DIS rules, shortly after the constitution of the tribunal, arbitrators must hold a case management conference to promote procedural efficiency, including by referring the parties to mediation or any other ADR mechanism,[500] and, subject to the consent of all parties, to provide a preliminary non-binding assessment of the disputed issues.[501] According to the German approach, these preliminary views on the merits allow the parties to efficiently use their fundamental right to be heard, as they can gain a deeper understanding of the tribunal's thoughts about the strengths and weaknesses of their positions and improve submissions on weak arguments.[502] They also help the parties to avoid an unexpected final and binding award in proceedings where the tribunal remains silent, allowing them to make a fully informed decision regarding settlement possibilities.[503] In addition to promoting the use of mediation and providing preliminary views on legal and factual issues, during arbitration, German arbitrators tend to provide evaluations and assessments regarding possible outcomes of the case, hold settlement conferences whenever needed, and render partial awards on agreed issues.[504] Moreover, subject to the parties' request, they directly engage in the settlement negotiations:

493. Nigmatullina, 2018, pp. 66-67; Berger, 2003, p. 401; Berger, 2018b, p. 512; Ehle, 2010, p. 82.
494. Nigmatullina, 2018, p. 67; Newmark, 2008, p. 88; Ehle, 2010, p. 82; Peter, 2005, p. 174.
495. Ehle, 2010, pp. 81-82; Nigmatullina, 2018, p. 67; Peter, 2005, p. 174.
496. *Oberlandesgericht Bremen, 1 U 35/12, NJW-RR 2013*, 2012, 573. *See also* Berger, 2018b, p. 504.
497. Marzolini, 2016, p. 104; Ehle, 2010, p. 81; Stipanowich, 2021a, p. 314; Berger, 2018b, p. 505. For a general discussion, *see* Berger, 2016a.
498. DIS Arbitration Rules, 2018, Article 26.
499. DIS Arbitration Rules, 2018, Article 26, stipulating that the tribunal shall facilitate settlement "unless any party objects thereto." *See also* Berger, 2018b, p. 505; Nigmatullina, 2018, p. 67; Berger & Jensen, 2017, p. 910.
500. DIS Arbitration Rules, 2018, Article 27(4)(iii).
501. DIS Arbitration Rules, 2018, Article 27(4)(i) referring to Annex 3(f). *See also* Nigmatullina, 2018, p. 66; Stipanowich, 2021a, pp. 314-315; Marzolini, 2016, p. 104.
502. Schneider, 2010, p. 318; Berger, 2018b, p. 506.
503. Stipanowich, 2021a, p. 315; Raeschke-Kessler, 2005, p. 534; Berger, 2018b, p. 506.
504. DIS Arbitration Rules, 2018, Article 27(6) & Annex 3(d); Nigmatullina, 2018, p. 72; Berger & Jensen, 2017, p. 910.

> They may ask [the tribunal] to propose a range containing a minimum and maximum amount, which they may then use as a starting point for their own final settlement negotiations, in which the arbitral tribunal no longer participates. Or they may ask for a proposal of a definite figure that one side should pay to the other, including the allocation of costs. If, in an ongoing contractual relationship between the parties, one of the issues of the arbitration had been the interpretation of a particular clause in the agreement, the parties may ask the arbitral tribunal to make a proposal for the redrafting of the disputed clause in order to avoid new disputes in the future.[505]

Despite this proactive role in settlement negotiations, arbitrators rarely practice caucusing to avoid risking the tribunal's impartiality.[506] The attitude of German arbitrators regarding caucusing and providing assessments on the merits seems completely opposite to that of Chinese arbitrators. While German arbitrators provide preliminary views and assessments about possible outcomes of the case but refrain from caucusing to maintain due process, Chinese arbitrators caucus with the parties but refrain from providing evaluations or assessments regarding the dispute to keep their impartiality.[507]

The practice of German arbitrators as settlement facilitators was confirmed in the aforementioned 2001-2004 Bühring-Uhle Study that examined the general attitude of arbitrators in settlement negotiations according to their legal background.[508] All German respondents in that study agreed that facilitating a settlement was a goal of arbitration.[509] In addition, German respondents reported a notable settlement rate of 69% of the cases after initiating the proceedings and before delivering the arbitral award.[510] According to the collected data, German arbitrators were likelier to suggest settlement proposals during the proceedings or discuss possible arbitration outcomes with the parties,[511] while rarely holding ex parte communications with them during settlement negotiations.[512]

In Germany, the arbitrators' obligation to facilitate settlements serves both the private interests of the disputing parties and the public interest, as amicable solutions allow parties to save legal costs and preserve business relationships while contributing to economic stability and legal peace in general.[513] German courts have held that proactive arbitrators cannot be challenged merely for fulfilling their obligation to facilitate settlement.[514] According to these rulings, the arbitrators' statements and

505. Raeschke-Kessler, 2005, p. 534. *See also* Stipanowich, 2021a, p. 315; Nigmatullina, 2018, p. 66; Berger & Jensen, 2017, pp. 910-911.
506. Raeschke-Kessler, 2005, pp. 534-535; Nigmatullina, 2018, p. 67; Newmark, 2008, p. 88; Ehle, 2010, p. 82.
507. Nigmatullina, 2018, p. 72; Kun, 2020a, p. 150; Kaufmann-Kohler, 2009, p. 197; Kun & Kaufmann-Kohler, 2008, p. 488; Kun, 2013a, p. 167; Kun, 2011b, pp. 554-555.
508. *See* the discussion in section 5.3 above.
509. Bühring-Uhle et al., 2006, pp. 110-111.
510. Bühring-Uhle et al., 2006, p. 112.
511. Bühring-Uhle et al., 2006, p. 120.
512. Bühring-Uhle et al., 2006, pp. 120-121.
513. Ehle, 2010, p. 81; Marriott, 2005, p. 537; Bühring-Uhle et al., 2003, p. 82; Berger, 2018b, p. 505.
514. *Bayerisches Oberstes Landesgericht, 102 SchH 135/24e*, 2024; *Oberlandesgericht Dresden, 3 Sch 3/12*, 2012; *Oberlandesgericht Köln, 9 Sch (H) 22/03*, 2004.

assessments during settlement negotiations are not final and, therefore, should not affect their impartiality and independence:

> The fact that an arbitrator has participated in settlement negotiations with the parties and has supported a settlement proposal which is far away from the expectations of the party that challenges him, does not justify, in and of itself, doubts as to his independence and impartiality. ... From the perspective of a reasonable party, this would only be the case if that party could have the legitimate impression that the conduct of the arbitrator is based on bias or arbitrariness. If a settlement shall be reached in the course of settlement negotiations, the arbitrator must be granted a wide latitude for own proposals. The considerations which the arbitrator makes in such a context must not be regarded as final determinations [of the legal issues at stake], but as mere thought-provoking impulses for the parties' settlement negotiations. If one of the parties discovers errors in the tribunal's arguments and proposals, it may always argue against them and reject a settlement based on those arguments or proposals and may, through further submissions and motions for the taking of evidence, try to make the arbitrators change their minds.[515]

German courts have also ruled that parties' consent to participate in settlement conferences is sufficient to preclude any challenge to the arbitrators based on their involvement in settlement negotiations, so an explicit waiver of the right to challenge the arbitral tribunal is unnecessary.[516] According to some commentators, this waiver is also clearly dispensable according to the DIS Arbitration Rules, as arbitrators' duty to facilitate settlements under these rules protects them against challenge based on the mere fact that they have fulfilled the obligation.[517]

Although most scholars differentiate the role of German arbitrators in settlement negotiations from hybrid processes or independent mediation,[518] some commentators contend that this practice effectively implements a same-neutral Arb-Med-Arb process, albeit without caucusing.[519] Notably, under the DIS Conciliation Rules, "parties in conciliation proceedings may, at any stage in the proceedings, agree in writing that the conciliators continue with their mandate in the function of arbitrators" with the

515. Berger, 2018b, pp. 505-506, citing from the decision of the Higher Regional Court of Munich in *Oberlandesgericht Munich, 34 SchH 3/07, SchiedsVZ*, 2008, 102, 104. *See also* Berger & Jensen, 2017, pp. 911-912. A similar position has been taken by German courts in the following cases: *Bayerisches Oberstes Landesgericht, 102 SchH 135/24e*, 2024; *Oberlandesgericht Berlin, 13 SchH 2/17, MDR 2018*, 2018, 885, 886; *Oberlandesgericht Munich, 34 SchH 5/15, NJW 2016*, 2015, 881, 882; *Oberlandesgericht Frankfurt, 26 SchH 1/06, SchiedsVZ 2006*, 2006, 329, 331; *Oberlandesgericht Dresden, 3 Sch 3/12*, 2012; *Oberlandesgericht Köln, 9 Sch (H) 22/03*, 2004.

516. *Oberlandesgericht Munich, 34 SchH 3/07, SchiedsVZ*, 2008, 102, 104; *Oberlandesgericht Frankfurt, 26 SchH 1/06, SchiedsVZ 2006*, 2006, 329, 331. *See also* Berger & Jensen, 2017, p. 912; *Oberlandesgericht Köln, 9 Sch (H) 22/03*, 2004, where the Higher Regional Court of Köln held that, under German law, an arbitral tribunal may provide preliminary assessments and propose settlements even without the parties' explicit consent.

517. Elsing, 2015, pp. 690-692; Berger & Jensen, 2017, pp. 910, 912; Favalli & Hasenclever, 2008, pp. 3-4.

518. Nigmatullina, 2018, pp. 66-67; Ehle, 2010, p. 82; Berger, 2003, p. 401; Berger, 2018b, p. 512.

519. Aragaki, 2021, p. 53; Bühring-Uhle et al., 2006, p. 110; Stipanowich & Fraser, 2017, pp. 854-855.

conciliators' duty to maintain confidentiality not applying in the subsequent arbitration.[520] While the DIS Mediation Rules do not explicitly address this possibility within mediation proceedings,[521] in practice, parties to arbitration under the DIS Rules who wish to employ the arbitrator in a de facto Arb-Med-Arb process—including caucusing and applying the aforementioned confidentiality-release rule—may refer the case to conciliation after constituting the arbitral tribunal while empowering the arbitrator to act as the conciliator. Since the conciliation rules allow the conciliator to determine "the particulars of the proceedings ... in consultation with the parties,"[522] thereby permitting ex parte communication during conciliation, and since these rules also allow the conciliator to subsequently serve as an arbitrator in the same dispute, a full Arb-Med-Arb process that includes ex parte communications is effectively possible under the DIS Rules. Given the skeptical attitude of German arbitrators and practitioners toward caucusing[523] and the relatively limited development of commercial mediation in the country compared to other jurisdictions,[524] the practical feasibility of implementing such hybrid procedures in Germany remains low. Nevertheless, this framework may still be considered by parties involved in ICA processes conducted in Germany.

5.3.2.2 Brazil

A basic principle of Brazil's civil procedures is the obligation of judges to encourage the use of conciliation, mediation, and other ADR methods throughout the proceedings.[525] Alongside the duty to refer disputes to independent conciliation and mediation,[526] judges are required to urge and assist the parties to settle amicably at all stages of the court proceedings, regardless of the trial initiation or any prior efforts to settle through ADR methods.[527] In practice, however, Brazilian judges seldom assist litigants in reaching amicable settlements and usually express a skeptical attitude toward conciliation.[528] Nevertheless, when they engage in conciliation, they meet the disputants

520. DIS Conciliation Rules, 2002, Article 14. *See also* Ruckteschler & Wendelstein, 2021, p. 765; Stipanowich, 2021a, pp. 315-316.
521. DIS Mediation Rules, 2010.
522. DIS Conciliation Rules, 2002, Article 11(2).
523. Bühring-Uhle et al., 2006, pp. 120-121; Raeschke-Kessler, 2005, pp. 534-535; Nigmatullina, 2018, p. 67; Ehle, 2010, p. 82; Stipanowich, 2021a, p. 317.
524. Stipanowich, 2021a, p. 316; Hess & Pelzer, 2015, pp. 291-294.
525. Brazil Code of Civil Procedure, 2015, Article 3§3; Netto, 2005, p. 582.
526. Brazil Code of Civil Procedure, 2015, Articles 165-175 & 334. Until the Mediation Act was introduced in 2015, conciliation was the only recognized method by the Brazilian civil procedures for settlements driven by courts. Interestingly, current civil procedures still differentiate between these methods, as conciliation is intended for disputes between parties without any previous relationship and mediation for parties with prior interactions. In practice, however, both methods are conducted in a typical manner, mostly by a neutral different than the judge. *See* Stipanowich, 2015, p. 1208; Stipanowich, 2021a, p. 318.
527. Brazil Code of Civil Procedure, 2015, Articles 139§V & 359; Costa Braga de Oliveira, 2009, p. 89; Netto, 2005, p. 582.
528. Costa Braga de Oliveira, 2009, p. 89; Stipanowich, 2021a, p. 318.

collectively and refrain from ex parte communications.[529] Interestingly, this attitude toward settlement facilitation within court proceedings stems from the belief, among judges and lawyers alike, that the state owns the monopoly on the delivery of justice, so court disputes should principally be decided.[530]

Although this principle does not apply to arbitration being a private mechanism of dispute resolution, Brazilian arbitrators still adopt a formal approach in the course of arbitral proceedings, similar to what judges do within court proceedings: they are reticent to facilitate settlements or rarely engage in conciliation or other hybrid procedures. When they do, they principally refrain from caucuses.[531] This attitude of Brazilian arbitrators seems to contradict their duty, as stipulated in the Brazil Arbitration Act, to encourage settlement and attempt to reconcile the parties already at the commencement of the procedure, when, for that purpose, they are not required to obtain prior consent from the parties.[532]

Quite exceptionally, the Brazilian legislator has a dual approach concerning hybrid procedures that involve arbitration. While provisions empowering arbitrators to conciliate the dispute during the arbitration, including the possibility of basing their awards on settlements reached within their framework,[533] appear to establish recognition of Arb-Med processes in Brazil,[534] an opposite attitude has been taken regarding Med-Arb processes.[535] According to the 2015 Mediation Act, a mediator may not act as an arbitrator in the same dispute,[536] which effectively prohibits the use of Med-Arb.[537] Consequently, mediated agreements cannot be enforced as arbitral awards in Brazil, and when recorded in the form of an award, they would be null and void.[538] However, settlements concluded after the commencement of arbitration, including through conciliation conducted by the arbitrator, are recognized and enforceable as consent awards.[539]

Criticism has been raised against the hesitant attitude of Brazilian arbitrators toward settlement facilitation, particularly when the law considers the mandate as one of their fundamental duties,[540] which, according to Brazil's Supreme Court, may even

529. Stipanowich, 2021a, pp. 318-319; Costa Braga de Oliveira, 2009, p. 89.
530. Costa Braga de Oliveira, 2009, 89.
531. Stipanowich, 2021a, pp. 318-319; Netto, 2005, pp. 587-588; Costa Braga de Oliveira, 2009, p. 89.
532. Brazil Arbitration Act, 1996, Article 21§4; Aragaki, 2021, pp. 45-46; Costa Braga de Oliveira, 2009, p. 89; Netto, 2005, p. 583.
533. Brazil Arbitration Act, 1996, Article 28.
534. Costa Braga de Oliveira, 2009, p. 90; Aragaki, 2021, pp. 62-63.
535. According to the literature, the absolute prohibition of Med-Arb procedures in Brazil may stem from widespread skepticism toward mediation, which has only recently been recognized as a legitimate mechanism for resolving commercial disputes. Alternatively, it may reflect a desire to protect parties with limited negotiating leverage, such as employees, consumers, or unrepresented individuals. *See* Stipanowich, 2021a, p. 319.
536. Brazil Mediation Act, 2015, Article 7.
537. Stipanowich, 2021a, p. 317; Netto, 2005, p. 584.
538. Ross, 2013, pp. 362-363; Nigmatullina, 2018, p. 108; Costa Braga de Oliveira, 2009, p. 90; Stipanowich, 2021a, p. 319.
539. Brazil Arbitration Act, 1996, Article 28; Nigmatullina, 2018, p. 108; Costa Braga de Oliveira, 2009, p. 90; Aragaki, 2021, p. 63; Stipanowich, 2021a, p. 319.
540. Costa Braga de Oliveira, 2009, p. 89; Netto, 2005, p. 583.

possess constitutional significance.[541] Since the current legal environment in Brazil does not support the more active involvement of arbitrators in the settlement negotiations, some scholars suggest promoting the role "on a case-by-case basis, as another way to accelerate the rendering of justice ... provided the panel or the sole arbitrator attains the professional level indispensable for such a delicate task."[542] Most criticism has been raised against the Brazilian dual approach toward hybrid procedures. According to some commentators, "it is difficult to comprehend why a state would take such diametrically opposite positions on the same basic combination of arbitration and mediation, based solely on which process preceded the other."[543] Other scholars contend that the absolute prohibition on Med-Arb imposes an excessive limitation on the freedom of business parties to customize the dispute-resolution process to suit their specific needs, let alone the concerns it creates regarding the enforcement of international awards arising from Med-Arb procedures in Brazil.[544] While prohibiting Med-Arb procedures certainly reduces the parties' freedom to design the dispute-resolution process according to their needs, this approach of the Brazilian legislator is still logical. As discussed in Chapter 3, the provisions of the New York Convention apply to the recognition and enforcement of arbitral awards "arising out of differences" between the disputants.[545] When a dispute is settled through mediation before the commencement of the arbitration, it can be argued that there is no longer a dispute to submit to arbitration, so the settlement cannot be recorded as an arbitral award since it was concluded in a process other than arbitration.[546] Therefore, in terms of enforceability, it seems much safer to initiate settlement efforts only after the arbitration commences.[547] It can be assumed that the Brazilian legislator considered these enforcement concerns when instituting the prohibition on Med-Arb proceedings. At the same time, Brazil's prohibition on Med-Arb, akin to Australia's complete ban on arbitrators' direct involvement in settlement negotiations within international proceedings,[548] underscores the critical importance of the forum and the governing law in ICA processes that empower arbitrators to facilitate settlements—particularly within hybrid processes—while ensuring the enforceability of their outcomes.

541. *MBV v. Resil, STF (Supreme Federal Court of Brazil), SE. No. 5.206-7*, 2001. In this landmark decision, the Supreme Court in the country upheld the constitutionality of the Brazilian Arbitration Act, rejecting the argument that arbitration clauses—which require parties to submit their disputes to arbitration—undermine their constitutional right to have the dispute heard and decided by Brazilian courts.
542. Netto, 2005, pp. 587-588.
543. Aragaki, 2021, pp. 62-63.
544. Stipanowich, 2021a, p. 319. This criticism finds partial support in the decision of the Superior Court of Justice of Brazil in *REsp No. 1.543.903/DF, STJ*, 2015, which, although not directly addressing the arbitrator's dual role, confirmed the validity and enforceability of a multi-tiered dispute resolution clause stipulating "mediation or arbitration" without a mandatory sequence. The court held that, as mediation is a voluntary procedure, its inclusion in the clause does not invalidate the agreement to arbitrate. Accordingly, if mediation fails or is not pursued, arbitration remains a binding and enforceable option.
545. New York Convention, 1958, Article I(1). *See* the discussion in section 3.6.3.
546. Ortolani, 2025, §21.4-21.5(a); Kryvoi & Davydenko, 2015, p. 866; Alexander, 2009, p. 28.
547. Kryvoi & Davydenko, 2015, p. 867; Yip, 2021, p. 196; Ortolani, 2025, §21.4-21.5(a).
548. *See* the discussion in section 5.3.1.3.

5.4 CONCLUSIONS

The legal traditions and practices of the judiciary and arbitral tribunals in the home jurisdictions of ICA practitioners and parties have shaped the divergent views regarding the role of arbitrators as settlement facilitators. Broadly speaking, Eastern legal cultures have traditionally favored conciliatory approaches, so procedures prioritizing compromise, such as mediation, are deeply rooted in their dispute-resolution frameworks. Historically, these cultures have preferred mediation over court proceedings, which has led to the widespread acceptance and encouragement of adjudicators' involvement in facilitating settlements. In contrast, Western legal cultures, which emphasize legal certainty and individualism, have traditionally been more litigious. Nonetheless, attitudes in the West regarding adjudicators' roles as settlement facilitators remain divided. While Common Law systems have historically confined adjudicators to the role of dispute-deciders, Civil Law systems have adopted more liberal approaches that view adjudicators as dispute-resolvers while tolerating their proactive involvement in settlement efforts.

As demonstrated in this chapter, while these classifications hold some validity, they are generalized and fail to capture the nuanced realities across jurisdictions within the same legal culture. Moreover, they neglect the varied individual approaches and preferences of arbitration practitioners and users. For example, East Asian countries, despite sharing common cultural dimensions, exhibit diverse approaches to the arbitrator's role as a settlement facilitator. Chinese arbitrators often engage in settlement negotiations and mediation without safeguards to address due process concerns. Conversely, arbitrators in Singapore and Hong Kong, influenced by Common Law traditions, are more reluctant to adopt this role despite explicit legislative frameworks acknowledging it and implementing safeguards for due process. Similarly, attitudes toward the arbitrator's involvement in settlement negotiations vary significantly within Western Civil Law systems. Germanic legal traditions encourage and expect arbitrators to engage proactively in settlement efforts, while jurisdictions such as France and Italy display greater hesitancy, even when domestic laws permit such roles.

Furthermore, traditional categorizations by the legal culture overlook the cross-cultural nature of ICA, which fosters mutual influence among legal traditions. This interaction has contributed to the development of transnational standards that not only transcend local norms but, in some cases, also diminish their influence. For instance, China's leading arbitral institutions and the CICC under the BRI initiative have recently aligned their procedures with Western trends to attract international users. Hence, China has established a distinct legal regime for "foreign-related arbitrations" by moving away from domestic practices that rely heavily on hybrid procedures conducted by the same neutral without addressing due process concerns. Similarly, Western Common Law jurisdictions, traditionally resistant to arbitrator involvement in settlement processes, have begun adopting more pragmatic approaches regarding this dual role. These shifts prioritize parties' autonomy to design arbitration processes suited to their needs by empowering arbitrators to facilitate settlements—including through hybrid processes allowing caucusing—subject to safeguards that ensure due process, impartiality, and independence.[549] However, Common Law jurisdictions appear more amenable to this role in international rather than domestic proceedings, as evidenced by practices in the UK and, to some extent, the US. These developments in Eastern and Western contexts reflect the mutual influence of legal traditions competing in a "marketplace of ideas" regarding best practices for the arbitrator's role as a settlement facilitator.[550] This dynamic has fostered a broader consensus on the arbitrator's dual role, particularly in international arbitral proceedings. Examples of these influences are discussed in the next chapter, which examines international rules and guidelines for cross-border commercial arbitration, some of which aim to reconcile diverse approaches rooted in differing legal traditions.

Despite the trends supporting arbitrators' roles as settlement facilitators and the diminishing relevance of traditional binary divisions,[551] certain aspects of this role remain contentious. While a broad consensus exists on the "managerial role" of arbitrators and their ability to employ procedural tools to promote settlements, practices such as case evaluation and caucusing continue to create divisions. These practices distinguish Eastern and Western positions and differentiate jurisdictions within the West.[552] For instance, Germanic legal traditions accept case evaluation, whereas other Western jurisdictions remain skeptical despite its growing acceptance. Additionally, Western jurisdictions' cautious stance on ex parte communications fuels their hesitancy toward hybrid procedures involving the same neutral. This skepticism is evident in Australia, where legislative provisions authorize arbitrators to mediate in domestic arbitrations under due process safeguards, yet these provisions are rarely utilized. Similarly, jurisdictions like Austria impose legal restrictions on hybrid procedures that reflect broader concerns. However, a recent study reviewing arbitration and mediation legislation across 195 jurisdictions (2021 Aragaki Study) revealed that most regulations addressing arbitrators' settlement facilitation roles pertain solely to hybrid procedures, primarily those involving mediation followed by arbitration, with only a few jurisdictions outright prohibiting such procedures.[553] Against this backdrop, Australia's choice to prevent arbitrators in international proceedings from engaging in settlement negotiations appears exceptional. Nonetheless, this prohibition does not extend to arbitrators' managerial role in procedural aspects, which can still serve as valuable tools for promoting settlements.

While the emerging trend of supporting arbitrators' roles as settlement facilitators—particularly in ICA processes—transcends the borders of diverse legal cultures, the stances of local jurisdictions remain crucial for two key reasons. *First*, national laws govern most aspects of the ICA process and play a pivotal role in

549. Sussman & Berger, 2021b, p. 37; Marriott, 2005, pp. 537-538.
550. Kun, 2013b, p. 180.
551. Berger, 2019, pp. 311-312; Nigmatullina, 2018, p. 78; Berger & Jensen, 2017, p. 916.
552. Hwang, 2005, pp. 573-576.
553. Aragaki, 2021, pp. 40-41, 42-49. According to the collected data, of 59 jurisdictions that regulate the use of the same neutral for Med-Arb, only 16 prohibit its use, 13 of which are Civil Law jurisdictions. Additionally, among the 31 jurisdictions that regulate the use of the same neutral for Arb-Med, only 3 jurisdictions (including Austria and Liechtenstein) prohibit its use, while 6 jurisdictions (none of which are Civil Law jurisdictions) impose conditions for allowing the arbitrator to resume their adjudicative role following a failed mediation.

enforcing arbitration outcomes. Thus, the attitudes of relevant jurisdictions—especially those where enforcement may be sought—should be carefully considered when designing international arbitral agreements or applying existing institutional rules that permit arbitrators to promote settlements. *Second*, local jurisdictions contribute to the harmonization of ICA. Their experiences with arbitrators' roles as settlement facilitators, including strategies to address related concerns, provide valuable insights for shaping its transnational legal regime.[554] As explored in the next chapter, these considerations are partly reflected in previous transnational efforts to harmonize the arbitrator's role as a settlement facilitator in ICA.

554. Kun, 2013b, p. 177.

CHAPTER 6

Transnational Harmonization Trends in the Arbitrator's Role as a Settlement Facilitator in ICA

6.1 INTRODUCTION

The growing transnational trend that encourages neutrals, practitioners, and users of ICA worldwide to broaden their perspectives on the arbitrator's mandate and embrace their role as settlement facilitators, even in hybrid processes incorporating arbitration, mediation, and caucusing, is supported by recent and compelling empirical data presented in this chapter. This updated empirical evidence, alongside the extensive data presented in the previous chapter covering various jurisdictions from Eastern and Western regions, illustrates that traditional binary views regarding the arbitrator's dual role between East and West and among Civil and Common Law traditions are diminishing.[1] Instead, practitioners and users of ICA have favored more flexible processes that facilitate amicable dispute resolution, driven by pragmatic considerations such as efficiency and a focus on future business relations.[2] As part of this trend that underscores the consensual nature of arbitration and the parties' "freedom to tailor the proceedings to their specific needs and to select arbitrators accordingly,"[3] an increasing demand exists among ICA users for neutrals with settlement facilitation skills.

1. Sussman & Berger, 2021a, p. 28; Sussman & Berger, 2021b, p. 37.
2. Berger, 2019, p. 313; Berger & Jensen, 2017, p. 890; Jemielniak, 2014, p. 331; Plant, 2000, p. 143; Lew & Shore, 1999, p. 38, suggesting while relating to allegations about Americanization and formalization of the arbitral process, that "as long as pragmatism prevails, ... the harmonization of cultural differences in international arbitral practice should proceed with relative ease."
3. Berger & Jensen, 2017, p. 895. *See also* Naughton, 2007, p. 33; Mayer, 2016, p. 3; Cremades, 1998, p. 163.

The growing interest in procedures that enable and encourage international arbitrators to facilitate settlements and act as mediators in the same dispute is further highlighted by past initiatives aimed at enhancing the harmonization and codification of norms related to this role at the transnational level. Promoted over the last two decades by different stakeholders in the domain, these various initiatives reflect the aforementioned growing call of ICA users to abandon the traditional perception observing the arbitrator's role as a "decision-maker" in favor of a more liberal and pragmatic one that views that role in broader terms as a "dispute manager" and a "proactive problem solver."[4] These previous initiatives have played a significant role in increasing awareness among users of ICA regarding the dual role of arbitrators, including in hybrid processes involving arbitration and mediation, while promoting its harmonization. However, unlike the broader transnational harmonization process of norms, standards, and practices related to ICA, which encompasses hard and soft norms introduced by various stakeholders, including official domestic actors and state-related international organizations,[5] previous efforts to standardize the practice and legal framework of the arbitrator's dual role in ICA have been relatively limited in scope. *First*, as discussed in this chapter, these initiatives have been primarily driven by non-governmental or private actors within the "global arbitration community" and have relied solely on soft norms, such as arbitral rules and guidelines suggesting "best practices" and safeguards associated with the conduct of the dual role.[6] Consequently, these attempts have mainly focused on internal issues within the arbitral process, with little attention given to external measures that could be undertaken by these actors and other official stakeholders in ICA, including state-related actors,[7] to potentially improve the regulation and acceptance of the arbitrator's dual role among users from various legal traditions and further enhance the harmonization of its practice and normative regime worldwide. *Second*, most previous harmonization attempts were influenced by the legal culture of their promoters,[8] with only a few initiatives making efforts to address users of ICA widely and across various jurisdictions and legal backgrounds.[9]

This chapter presents and critically examines most former harmonization initiatives connected with the arbitrator's role as a settlement facilitator in ICA. However, before delving into these initiatives, it is important to explore the current perspectives of ICA users and practitioners regarding the dual role, as reflected in recent empirical data.

4. Berger & Jensen, 2017, p. 889; Sussman & Berger, 2021a, p. 26; Marzolini, 2016, p. 99; Berger, 2018b, p. 509.
5. *See* the discussion in section 1.2.
6. Ali, 2021, pp. 12-14, 20, 27; Bermann, 2017, p. 58; Kaufmann-Kohler, 2010, pp. 285, 295.
7. Nigmatullina, 2019, pp. 13, 21; Najar, 2009, pp. 522-526.
8. Stipanowich & Mironi, 2021, p. 30; Stipanowich, 2021a, pp. 312, 327-330; Berger & Jensen, 2017, p. 911; Stipanowich & Ulrich, 2014b, p. 14; Kun, 2013b, p. 218; CEDR Report on Settlement in ICA, 2009, section 2(2)-(3). Examples for such initiatives are discussed in sections 6.3.3.1-6.3.3.3 below.
9. Such as some initiatives undertaken by leading practitioners and scholars in international arbitration, along with the ongoing efforts of the International Task Force on Mixed Mode Dispute Resolution, as discussed in sections 6.3.3.4 & 6.3.4 below. *See also Mixed Mode Task Force: About*, n.d.; Stipanowich & Fraser, 2017, pp. 844-846.

6.2 CURRENT PERSPECTIVES OF ICA USERS

Recent surveys and empirical studies confirm a clear trend among users of ICA from various legal cultures in acknowledging the arbitrator's role as a settlement facilitator in these processes. When asked whether the arbitrator has a role in fostering a settlement, approximately 78% of respondents to the 2020 Mixed Mode Task Force Survey, which surveyed 75 arbitration practitioners from jurisdictions globally about the role of arbitrators in the settlement and various settlement facilitation techniques,[10] answered positively.[11] The respondents based their supportive attitude on various responsibilities they designated to arbitrators in the settlement process, starting with educating the parties about procedural options related to settlement, continuing with designing the procedural framework to support settlement as well as encouraging the parties to settle, and ending with playing an active and substantial role in the settlement process, subject to the parties' consent.[12] Based on the collected data, the survey concluded that:

> While legal and geographical culture still has influence, it should not be viewed as limiting the arbitrator's choice in crafting a process most suitable for the dispute at issue as long as care is taken to ensure that there is no breach of any governing ethical, legal or rule-based principle and the parties are consulted and have confirmed their agreement to the process.[13]

These results align with earlier studies indicating an increasing harmonization across cultures regarding the arbitrator's role in the settlement process. In the 2016-2017 GPC Survey,[14] the respondents were asked various questions about their preferences regarding dispute resolution processes related to cross-border commercial contracts.[15] When asked to describe the most effective commercial dispute resolution process, a clear majority stated that it should usually combine adjudicative and non-adjudicative processes, such as arbitration and mediation.[16] In addition, when asked to select the most influential trends in the future of commercial dispute resolution, most respondents specified a greater emphasis on collaborative instead of adversarial processes for resolving disputes, enhanced approaches of business players toward conflict prevention, and the harmonization of transnational legal instruments and standards related to mechanisms of dispute resolution.[17] According to some scholars, these results indicate that parties to cross-border commercial adjudication, including international arbitration, show a growing interest in settling their disputes amicably and more openness to the direct involvement of the adjudicator in the

10. *See* the discussion in section 2.2.3.
11. Sussman & Berger, 2021a, p. 26; Sussman & Berger, 2021b, p. 7; ICC Report on Facilitating Settlement in ICA, 2023, p. 5.
12. Sussman & Berger, 2021a, p. 26; Sussman & Berger, 2021b, p. 7; ICC Report on Facilitating Settlement in ICA, 2023, p. 5.
13. Sussman & Berger, 2021a, p. 28; Sussman & Berger, 2021b, p. 11.
14. *See* the discussion in section 1.3.
15. GPC Series, 2016-2017; GPC Series, 2018, p. 2; Lack, 2021, p. 12; Chua, 2018, p. 1.
16. GPC Series, 2016-2017, Question 2(5). *See also* Lack, 2021, p. 12; Chua, 2018, p. 1.
17. GPC Series, 2016-2017, Question 4(5).

settlement negotiations throughout proceedings that combine "adjudicatory with non-adjudicatory mechanisms."[18] Another significant survey regarding the arbitrator's role in the settlement of cross-border commercial disputes is the 2007 Ali Survey conducted among 115 highly experienced arbitration practitioners from over 18 Eastern and Western jurisdictions.[19] Although the survey revealed regional variations concerning the actual role of arbitrators in the settlement, with a higher tendency of arbitrators working in the East to encourage settlements compared to their counterparts in the West,[20] still approximately 74% of practitioners from Eastern and Western jurisdictions agreed that arbitrators could suggest settlement negotiations to the parties. Additionally, 58% agreed that arbitrators could actively engage in the settlement negotiations if requested by the disputants.[21] Interestingly, all participants who functioned as arbitrators, regardless of jurisdiction, agreed that arbitrators could suggest settlement negotiations in their cases and take an active part in their course, subject to the disputants' request.[22] These survey findings were explained by international guidelines' role in harmonizing practitioners' perspectives regarding the arbitrator's role as a settlement facilitator.[23] This conclusion corresponds with other opinions expressed in the literature about the need to develop further guidelines and rules connected with the arbitrator's dual role to enhance harmonization between different legal cultures:

> The development of more effective guidance should be a welcome step. ... A set of non-binding guidelines providing a comprehensive and specific framework for choice-making in consensual commercial dispute resolution is the logical starting point for the development (or refinement) of norms and practices for and by business users and in-house counsel, advocates, arbitrators, mediators, and policymakers. This foundation may eventually facilitate the development of better rules and procedures for med-arb, arb-med, and arbitral facilitation of settlement, along with ethical standards governing the arena of "mixed-mode" practice for neutrals. It may also assist in the promulgation or refinement of relevant statutes and judicial decisions affecting domestic and international arbitration and dispute resolution, as well as interpretations of international conventions and treaties.[24]

6.3 PREVIOUS HARMONIZATION EFFORTS

Over the past two decades, various initiatives have emerged from different stakeholders in ICA aimed at enhancing the harmonization and codification process of norms

18. Berger & Jensen, 2017, pp. 897-898. *See also* Lack, 2021, p. 12; Chua, 2018, p. 2; Ruckteschler & Wendelstein, 2021, p. 771, holding that "there seems to be a growing trend towards arb-med-arb proceedings where the mediator is the same person as the arbitrator and is allowed to return to his/her role of arbitrator if the mediation fails."
19. *See* the discussion in sections 2.3.3 & 5.2.2.
20. *See* the discussion in section 5.2.2. *See also* Ali, 2011b, p. 17.
21. Ali, 2011b, p. 18.
22. Ali, 2011b, p. 17.
23. Ali, 2011b, p. 17.
24. Stipanowich, 2021a, p. 339. *See also* Sussman & Berger, 2021b, pp. 37-38; Kaufmann-Kohler, 2009, pp. 204-205; Stipanowich & Ulrich, 2014b, pp. 29-31; Nigmatullina, 2019, p. 45; Guo, 2020, p. 224; Kaufmann-Kohler, 2010, pp. 295-297; Lüth & Wagner, 2012, p. 416.

and practices related to the arbitrator's role as a settlement facilitator in ICA. As mentioned earlier, these efforts have primarily been led by non-governmental or private actors in the domain while relying exclusively on soft norms, which currently play a pivotal role in the transnational legal regime of ICA and serve as the main vehicle for facilitating its harmonization process.[25] According to the literature, the undisputed dominance of soft norms in the transnational legal framework of ICA and their key role in its harmonization are attributed to several reasons. *First*, compared to any other area of private international law or commercial law, conventions, treaties, and domestic legislation related to ICA intentionally leave many subjects unregulated[26] to maintain the flexibility of the arbitral process and uphold the principle of party autonomy.[27] In this reality, soft norms have come to fill the gaps left by these normative sources to enhance the regulation, effectiveness, and predictability of the arbitral process,[28] particularly due to the continuous growth in the number and complexity of ICA proceedings[29] and the inability of unpublished and hardly reviewed arbitral awards to provide guidance and reference for users.[30] *Second*, compared to conventions and treaties, soft law instruments are easier and faster to agree on.[31] Conventions and treaties with binding components require consensus among participating parties, which often leads to a prolonged and complex negotiation process that may result in compromises and a race to the bottom in terms of harmonization.[32] While soft norms may also necessitate compromises during negotiation and drafting,[33] reaching an agreement about their content is generally easier and quicker due to their non-binding nature and the ability to apply them selectively.[34] Therefore, compared to binding norms, soft norms are more likely to accommodate progressive and innovative legal approaches and practices that have not yet gained wide recognition among users of international arbitration.[35] *Third*, unlike national laws and regional treaties confined to specific geographical boundaries, soft norms generally emerge directly in the global

25. Ali, 2021, pp. 12-14, 20, 27; Berger, 2019, pp. 303-304; Park, 2017, pp. 1-2; Bermann, 2017, p. 58; Tschanz, 2016, p. 82; Draetta, 2015, p. 331; Bantekas, 2015, p. 66; Karrer, 2011; Pate, 2010, p. 144; Kaufmann-Kohler, 2010, pp. 285, 295; Park, 2006, p. 141.
26. Bermann, 2017, p. 66; Bantekas, 2015, p. 58; Abbott & Snidal, 2000, p. 421; Kaufmann-Kohler, 2010, p. 298.
27. Bantekas, 2015, pp. 4-5; Ali, 2021, p. 30; Hrnčiříková, 2016, p. 97; Berger & Jensen, 2016, pp. 4-5; Pate, 2010, p. 161; Kaufmann-Kohler, 2010, p. 298.
28. Guo, 2020, p. 224; Bermann, 2017, p. 66; Ali, 2021, p. 13; Cordero-Moss, 2012, p. 112; Pate, 2010, p. 146; Park, 2006, p. 142; Berger, 2019, pp. 303-305; Kaufmann-Kohler, 2010, p. 298; Stephan, 1999, p. 745; Stipanowich, 2021b, p. 272; Gomez, 2015, p. 154; Brekoulakis, 2016b, p. 15; Bantekas, 2015, p. 66; Carter, 1994, pp. 785-786.
29. Horvath, 2011, pp. 254, 258-259; Dasser, 2021, pp. 57-58, arguing that following this growth "arbitration morphed from an art into an industry. Industrial production requires standards. The arbitration community responded to this new challenge by churning out guidelines, notes, rules, lists of best practices, and conferences devoted to arbitration procedure."
30. Gojkovic, 2021, p. 69; Pate, 2010, p. 160; Kaufmann-Kohler, 2010, p. 296.
31. Pate, 2010, p. 161; Kaufmann-Kohler, 2010, p. 285; Kaufmann-Kohler, 2005, p. 348; Cordero-Moss, 2012, p. 143.
32. Cordero-Moss, 2012, pp. 132, 143; Pate, 2010, pp. 151, 155, 161.
33. Ali, 2021, pp. 29-30; Abbott & Snidal, 2000, p. 455.
34. Cordero-Moss, 2012, pp. 143, 147; Ali, 2021, p. 22.
35. Cordero-Moss, 2012, p. 143; Bermann, 2017, p. 60; Pate, 2010, pp. 147-148; CEDR Report on Settlement in ICA, 2009, section 4(5)(4).

arena as transnational legal instruments detached from specific jurisdictions and drafted to apply in all arbitration seats.[36] This detachment is particularly true when these norms relate to common subjects in arbitral proceedings, such as accepted international commercial practices, ethical considerations, and the interpretation of basic principles or widely accepted arbitration rules.[37] *Fourth*, soft norms exhibit a significant degree of normativity. When incorporated into contractual relations, domestic laws, or conventions, they effectively transform into hard law.[38] Nevertheless, their normativity is also derived from their codification process, which organizes them into a coherent and logical structure, thereby enhancing their accessibility, comprehensibility, and practical application.[39] Through this codification process, which can involve both compilation and innovation,[40] soft norms acquire a self-contained normative existence. Their addressees may recognize them as binding[41] or intentionally choose to apply them for various reasons, including respect for their authors, the need for predictability and certainty, or their enhanced accessibility.[42] In the context of ICA, which is largely self-regulated by its global community[43]—and, according to some drastic views in legal theory, has undergone complete privatization resulting in an *autonomous* or *delocalized legal order* independent of any national legal system[44]—the members of this community increasingly participate in the creation and consultation processes preceding the formation of soft norms.[45] This involvement strengthens their

36. Kun, 2013b, p. 177.
37. Hrnčiříková, 2016, p. 106; Kaufmann-Kohler, 2005, p. 347; Born, 2015, p. 3504; Kaufmann-Kohler, 2010, p. 285; Draetta, 2015, p. 331.
38. Ali, 2021, p. 13; Bantekas, 2015, pp. 63-64, 66; Tschanz, 2016, p. 83; Kaufmann-Kohler, 2010, pp. 288, 295; Cordero-Moss, 2012, p. 113; Pate, 2010, p. 147.
39. Kaufmann-Kohler, 2010, pp. 286-287, 297-298; Ali, 2021, p. 14; Lüth & Wagner, 2012, p. 410.
40. Cordero-Moss, 2012, p. 139; Kaufmann-Kohler, 2010, pp. 286-287, 294-295.
41. Berger, 2019, pp. 303-304; Kaufmann-Kohler, 2010, p. 284. Concerns about possible misunderstandings regarding the statutory nature of soft norms were particularly raised in connection with the UNCITRAL Notes on Arbitration and IBA Guidelines on Conflicts of Interest, given the prestigious status of their authors and their considerable legitimacy among the arbitration community. As a result, the UNCITRAL Notes on Arbitration deliberately use the terms "notes" and "planning checklist" and refrain from using the terms "guidelines" or "code," to avoid any misunderstanding that they have a statutory nature. Similarly, the IBA Guidelines on Conflicts of Interest emphasize their non-statutory nature. *See* Holtzmann, 1996, p. 178; IBA Guidelines on Conflicts of Interest in International Arbitration, 2024, Introduction (para. 6); Berger, 2019, p. 304.
42. Ali, 2021, p. 20; Draetta, 2015, p. 331; Kaufmann-Kohler, 2010, pp. 284-285; Jansen, 2010, p. 43; Cordero-Moss, 2012, p. 143; Lüth & Wagner, 2012, p. 416; Hrnčiříková, 2016, p. 109.
43. Bantekas, 2015, p. 66; Kaufmann-Kohler, 2010, p. 295; Ali, 2021, p. 14; Bermann, 2015, p. 76.
44. Gaillard, 2023, p. 35; Blackaby et al., 2022, §§1.85-1.91 & §§3.86-3.95; Bantekas, 2015, pp. 48, 52; Jemielniak, 2014, pp. 319, 327; Jemielniak, 2017, p. 171; Draetta, 2015, p. 327; Tschanz, 2016, pp. 83-84; Kun, 2013b, p. 184; Kun & Jemielniak, 2016, p. 582; Von Schlabrendorff, 2009, p. 114; Karton, 2014, p. 24; Cordero-Moss, 2012, p. 134; Nazzini, 2016, p. 693; Derains, 1995, pp. 10, 14.
45. Such as the consultation process that preceded the UNCITRAL Notes on Arbitration, as discussed in section 1.2. Another example is the consultation process of UNCITRAL WGII, which oversees dispute settlement and regularly invites arbitral institutes and organizations to submit their perspectives on various issues. Additionally, the special working group of the IBA, comprising 51 specialists and practitioners from 28 countries, including arbitrators, has been actively assisting UNIDROIT in promoting awareness of its principles in international contracts and dispute resolution practices worldwide. *See UNCITRAL WGII*, n.d., at Working Documents;

sense of shared ownership over these norms.[46] Consequently, soft norms have gained recognition and legitimacy within the global arbitration community, influencing the conduct of arbitral proceedings and occasionally prompting amendments to laws relating to international and domestic arbitration.[47] The growing status of instruments such as the IBA Guidelines on Conflicts of Interest and the IBA Rules on the Taking of Evidence illustrates this recognition. These soft law instruments serve to harmonize the interpretation of arbitration rules and national arbitration laws with accepted international practices. Furthermore, frequent amendments to arbitration rules and domestic laws often draw upon the legal principles and frameworks established in these instruments, further solidifying their role in shaping the evolution of arbitration practices.[48]

The extensive use of soft norms in ICA has been criticized for contributing to the "modern disease of overregulation" within ICA,[49] which arguably results in losing the flexibility of this process and potentially restricting parties' autonomy.[50] Despite this criticism, empirical data suggests that soft norms enjoy high recognition among ICA users. Most respondents in the 2015 Queen Mary International Arbitration Survey voiced high satisfaction with guidelines and soft norms in ICA as an effective instrument that supplements existing rules and law, codifies existing widespread practices, and provides guidance where little or none exists.[51] Additionally, 70% of those surveyed expressed contentment with the current amount of soft law regulations in ICA.[52] These results align with repeated opinions expressed in the literature that solutions suggested and promoted by the arbitration community are made possible mainly due to the reliance of the domain on soft norms, which indicates that ICA has a flexible normative regime that can "change, adapt, and be refined by common sense" to remain relevant in the ever-changing international business reality.[53]

This section presents and critically debates the primary previous efforts to codify and harmonize practices and norms related to the arbitrator's role as a settlement

IBA Working Group on the practice of the UNIDROIT Principles, 2019; Stipanowich, 2021a, p. 339; Bantekas, 2015, p. 64; Ali, 2021, pp. 27-28, 32-33; Kaufmann-Kohler, 2010, p. 299.

46. Karmel & Kelly, 2009, p. 897; Abbott & Snidal, 2010, p. 327; Ali, 2021, pp. 26-27, 30.
47. Stipanowich, 2021a, p. 339; Sussman & Berger, 2021b, pp. 37-38; Pate, 2010, p. 160; Kaufmann-Kohler, 2010, pp. 296, 298; Ali, 2021, pp. 27, 30; Ellis, 2012, p. 325.
48. Hrnčiříková, 2016, p. 106; Park, 2006, p. 142; Gunter, 2005, p. 129; Lüth & Wagner, 2012, p. 417; Draetta, 2015, p. 331; Bermann, 2017, p. 60; Bantekas, 2015, pp. 64, 66-67; Kaufmann-Kohler, 2010, pp. 296-297, relating to various court decisions that granted significant weight to the IBA Guidelines on Conflicts of Interest.
49. Lalive, 1998, p. 484. *See also* Draetta, 2015, p. 342; Hrnčiříková, 2016, p. 109; Park, 2009, p. 693; Berger, 2019, p. 306.
50. Draetta, 2015, p. 341; Bermann, 2017, p. 71; Berger, 2019, pp. 305-306; Kaufmann-Kohler, 2010, p. 298; Pate, 2010, p. 163; Park, 2006, p. 141.
51. Queen Mary University of London and White & Case LLP, 2015, p. 33; Bermann, 2017, p. 71; Hrnčiříková, 2016, p. 109.
52. Queen Mary University of London and White & Case LLP, 2015, p. 9; Hrnčiříková, 2016, p. 109.
53. Pate, 2010, p. 161. *See also* Berger, 2016b; Marriott, 1996, p. 72, suggesting that "after all, we must ensure that rules or guidelines do not constitute a straitjacket which fetters our innovative ideas and abilities to change. As a very distinguished Law Lord has said, there are no permanent solutions to the problems of commercial dispute resolution and each generation must think again."

facilitator in ICA, divided into four categories: (a) institutional rules that refer to the role, including the ICC Arbitration Rules, the Swiss Arbitration Rules, the NAI Arbitration and Mediation Rules, and the ADRIC Arbitration and Med-Arb Rules; (b) international arbitration guidelines connected with its conduct, including those embedded in the UNCITRAL Notes on Arbitration, the IBA Rules and Guidelines, the AAA Code of Ethics, the Rules and Guidelines of the Chartered Institute of Arbitrators (CIArb), and indirectly in the Model Law on ICA; (c) efforts made by professional organizations intended to enhance the efficiency of international arbitration while addressing practical and ethical issues, those are the CPR and the CEDR initiatives, the Prague Rules and the International Task Force on Mixed Mode Dispute Resolution; and (d) efforts promoted by leading practitioners and scholars in international arbitration. As demonstrated below, in addition to their exclusive reliance on soft norms and, in most cases, their alignment with the legal culture of their promoters, most of these attempts "do not provide indications and/or suggestions as to how an arbitrator should actually exercise such a role,"[54] as proposed in detail in Chapter 2. Moreover, only a few of these initiatives offer comprehensive safeguards that address the various concerns associated with the practice of the arbitrator's dual role in ICA.

6.3.1 Institutional Rules

Several institutional rules concerning the arbitrator's role as a settlement facilitator were discussed in previous chapters. Chapter 4 addressed the UNCITRAL Arbitration Rules that recognize the arbitrator's proactive mandate, the ICSID Arbitration Rules that authorize the arbitral tribunal to facilitate settlements and, subject to the parties' consent to mediate in the same dispute, and the SIAC Investment Arbitration Rules, which empower the tribunal to act proactively and engage in the settlement process.[55] Chapter 5 reviewed the CIETAC, BAC, and SCIA Arbitration Rules of China that allow arbitrators to facilitate settlements and mediate disputes before them subject to the parties' consent,[56] the JAMS Arbitration Rules in the US that authorize arbitrators to act as settlement facilitators and subject to the parties' agreement to act as mediators in the same disputes,[57] and the DIS Arbitration Rules of Germany, which impose a duty on arbitrators to facilitate settlements throughout the arbitral process except when the parties object to the application of that role.[58] Similar authorization to that of the DIS rules is anchored in the arbitration rules of the Milan Chamber of Arbitration, stipulating that:

54. Marzolini, 2016, p. 99. *See also* Stipanowich, 2021a, p. 334.
55. *See* the discussion in section 4.4.2.3.
56. CIETAC Arbitration Rules, 2024, Article 47; BAC Arbitration Rules, 2022, Article 43; SCIA Arbitration Rules, 2022, Article 48; Cao, 2020, pp. 2-5; Gu, 2021, pp. 69-72; Ruckteschler & Wendelstein, 2021, pp. 765-766; Kun & Kaufmann-Kohler, 2008, pp. 485-486.
57. JAMS Comprehensive Arbitration Rules and Procedures, 2021, Rule 28(a)-(b); Stipanowich, 2021a, p. 303.
58. DIS Arbitration Rules, 2018, Article 26; Berger, 2018b, p. 505; Nigmatullina, 2018, p. 66; Stipanowich, 2021a, pp. 314-315; Marzolini, 2016, pp. 103-104.

> At any time in the proceedings, the Arbitral Tribunal may attempt to settle the dispute between the parties, including by inviting the parties to refer the case to the Mediation Service of the Milan Chamber of Arbitration.[59]

Having these rules debated in earlier sections, the discussion below examines additional institutional rules that provide valuable insights into the arbitrator's role as a settlement facilitator, namely the ICC Arbitration Rules, the Swiss Arbitration Rules, the NAI Arbitration and Mediation Rules, and the ADRIC Arbitration and Med-Arb Rules.

6.3.1.1 ICC Arbitration Rules

A significant set of arbitration rules to consider concerning the arbitrator's role in the settlement process are those of the ICC.[60] Revised in 2012 following a report on controlling time and costs in ICA,[61] these rules oblige the arbitral tribunal to conduct arbitration expeditiously and efficiently.[62] Hence, the tribunal is authorized to hold case management conferences with the parties[63] and, where it does not conflict with the arbitration agreement, to implement any or all of the case management techniques outlined in the rules' appendices.[64] These techniques include organizing a pre-hearing conference, bifurcating the proceedings, issuing partial awards, and identifying subjects suitable for settlement.[65] Additionally, the tribunal is explicitly empowered to facilitate a settlement of the dispute:

> Where agreed between the parties and the arbitral tribunal, the arbitral tribunal may take steps to facilitate settlement of the dispute, provided that every effort is made to ensure that any subsequent award is enforceable at law.[66]

Some scholars have commended the ICC rules' proactive stance in endorsing a more liberal approach to the arbitrator's role in facilitating settlements, marking a departure from the cautious attitude traditionally associated with most rules and standards governing transnational arbitral proceedings.[67] Certain commentators argue that the general wording of this provision grants arbitrators broad discretion in facilitating settlements, including direct involvement in the settlement negotiations, delivering preliminary views on some or all issues in dispute, and drafting settlement

59. Milan Chamber Arbitration Rules, 2023, Article 25(3); Marzolini, 2016, p. 104.
60. *ICC: About ICC dispute resolution*, 2023; ICC Arbitration Rules, 2021.
61. ICC Commission on Arbitration and ADR, 2018; Stipanowich & Ulrich, 2014b, pp. 11-12; Berger, 2019, p. 299. For further discussion, *see* ICC Guide on Effective Management of Arbitration, 2018.
62. ICC Arbitration Rules, 2021, Article 22.
63. ICC Arbitration Rules, 2021, Article 24; Webster & Bühler, 2018, §24-6.
64. ICC Arbitration Rules, 2021, Article 22(2) & Appendix IV; Marzolini, 2016, p. 101.
65. ICC Arbitration Rules, 2021, Appendix IV, paras. (a)-(b) & (g).
66. ICC Arbitration Rules, 2021, Appendix IV, para. (h)(ii). *See also* Ortolani, 2025, §21.3; ICC Report on Facilitating Settlement in ICA, 2023, p. 5; ICC Guide on Effective Conflict Management, 2023, p. 35; Born, 2021, §13.04[D]; Berger & Jensen, 2017, p. 893; Marzolini, 2016, pp. 101-102; Nigmatullina, 2018, pp. 192-193.
67. Berger, 2019, p. 308; Stipanowich & Ulrich, 2014b, p. 12.

agreements to be submitted to the parties.[68] However, other commentators criticize this general language for failing to indicate concrete methods to facilitate settlements,[69] provide clearer guidelines for conducting case management conferences,[70] or suggest specific provisions dedicated to hybrid procedures.[71]

6.3.1.2 Swiss Arbitration Rules

The Swiss Arbitration Rules exemplify another innovative approach acknowledging arbitrators' role as settlement facilitators.[72] Under the rules, the tribunal is authorized to apply procedures it deems appropriate[73] to uphold its general duty to conduct the proceedings efficiently while avoiding excessive expenses and delays.[74] Moreover, with the parties' consent, the tribunal is explicitly authorized to facilitate the settlement of the dispute:

> With the agreement of each of the parties, the arbitral tribunal may take steps to facilitate the settlement of the dispute before it. Any such agreement by a party shall constitute a waiver of its right to challenge an arbitrator's impartiality based on the arbitrator's participation and knowledge acquired in taking the agreed steps.[75]

Despite its similarity to the corresponding provision in the ICC rules, this provision differs in two essential aspects. *First*, it does not explicitly link the arbitrators' facilitation of settlements to their duty to deliver enforceable awards. *Second*, it mandates that this role is contingent upon the parties waiving their right to challenge the arbitrators based on their involvement in the settlement process or any information acquired during its course.[76] Judging by the wording of the provision, the protection afforded to arbitrators facilitating settlements appears both unconditional and extensive. It does not subordinate the initiatives arbitrators are allowed to implement to the parties' consent or agreement, fails to address scenarios where the parties withdraw their consent before the settlement process concludes, and does not emphasize the arbitrators' duty to deliver an enforceable award.

---

68. Marzolini, 2016, p. 102; Berger, 2018b, pp. 508-509. This broad interpretation is supported by section 34 of the ICC Mediation Guidance Notes, 2014, allowing parties to arbitral proceedings to authorize the arbitrator to mediate the dispute under the Guidance Notes and retain their adjudicative role after failed efforts to settle amicably. *See also* Ruckteschler & Wendelstein, 2021, p. 764.
69. Berger & Jensen, 2017, p. 893.
70. Berger, 2019, p. 308.
71. Benzidi, 2017, p. 28; Ruckteschler & Wendelstein, 2021, p. 765.
72. Kozmenko & Groselj, 2021; Marzolini, 2016, pp. 102-103; Swiss Arbitration Rules, 2021.
73. Swiss Arbitration Rules, 2021, Article 19(1); Marzolini, 2016, pp. 102-103; Gamba, 2013, pp. 192-194; Mayer, 2016, p. 2.
74. Swiss Arbitration Rules, 2021, Article 16(1).
75. Swiss Arbitration Rules, 2021, Article 19(5). *See also* Sussman & Berger, 2021a, p. 26; Marzolini, 2016, p. 103.
76. Gamba, 2013, pp. 194-195; Marzolini, 2016, p. 103.

6.3.1.3 *NAI Arbitration and Mediation Rules*

The arbitration and mediation rules of the NAI, applicable to both domestic and cross-border proceedings, adopt a proactive approach that acknowledges and promotes the arbitrator's role as a settlement facilitator. Similar to the ICC and Swiss rules, the NAI Arbitration Rules emphasize the tribunal's obligation to conduct the arbitral process efficiently.[77] To fulfill this duty, and subject to the provisions of applicable law and the parties' agreement, the tribunal is granted significant discretion in determining procedures and timetables for the proceedings.[78] The rules further mandate the tribunal to convene a case management conference with the parties to establish the procedural framework and address measures to streamline the process, including limiting document production and submissions, tailoring procedures for taking evidence, and considering the necessity of expedited arbitration.[79] Additionally, the rules empower the tribunal to undertake a variety of measures aimed at enhancing efficiency and resolution, including the early determination of legal and factual issues,[80] the issuance of partial final awards,[81] the rendering of decisions on an equitable basis,[82] and the recording of settlements as awards on agreed terms.[83] Importantly, the rules also require the tribunal to hold a midstream conference with the parties—preferably conducted by its chair—to explore the possibility of a settlement.[84] However, the rules provide no specific guidance on the settlement exploration aspect of the midstream conference, as they remain silent on whether the tribunal is permitted to address substantive elements of the settlement or directly engage in settlement negotiations. A more explicit recognition of the arbitrator's direct involvement in the settlement process is anchored in the NAI Mediation Rules, which acknowledge the arbitrator's role as a mediator in the same dispute. According to these rules:

> If the parties wish to terminate ongoing mediation in whole or in part in order to have all or part of their dispute resolved by means of arbitration ... the mediator will not be permitted to act as the arbitrator ... in such arbitral proceedings ... unless all the parties explicitly accept the mediator's intended role in the arbitral proceedings.[85]

Although the NAI Mediation Rules by default prohibit mediators from acting as arbitrators in the same proceedings, the fact that the parties can agree otherwise reflects a de facto recognition of Med-Arb conducted by the same neutral. According to these rules, the parties should principally suspend any ongoing proceedings between

77. NAI Arbitration Rules, 2024, Article 25(3).
78. NAI Arbitration Rules, 2024, Article 25(1).
79. NAI Arbitration Rules, 2024, Article 26.
80. NAI Arbitration Rules, 2024, Article 45.
81. NAI Arbitration Rules, 2024, Article 47.
82. NAI Arbitration Rules, 2024, Article 48(3).
83. NAI Arbitration Rules, 2024, Articles 47 & 51.
84. NAI Arbitration Rules, 2024, Article 30. For further discussion about the midstream conference under these rules, *see* the discussion in section 2.2.7.
85. NAI Mediation Rules, 2017, Article 6(6).

them during the mediation.[86] Furthermore, once its "purpose has been discussed with and agreed to by all the parties," the neutral is permitted to conduct ex parte communications and receive confidential information from one or more parties.[87] When later disclosure of such information is necessary to facilitate the implementation of a settlement agreement, the parties are allowed to waive confidentiality.[88] The rules further stipulate that if a settlement agreement is concluded during mediation, the parties and the mediator can agree to incorporate it as an arbitral award on agreed terms under the NAI Arbitration Rules.[89] However, this option raises potential enforcement difficulties. According to the NAI Arbitration Rules, the tribunal may only record a settlement as an arbitral award when it is "reached between the parties during the course of the [arbitral] proceedings."[90] This provision, consistent with the New York Convention's requirements regarding a "difference" submitted to arbitration,[91] suggests that initiating mediation after the commencement of arbitration is advisable. Otherwise, challenges may arise asserting that the settlement was not reached during arbitration or that, following the settlement's conclusion during mediation, no "difference" remains to submit to arbitration.[92] Since both the mediation and arbitration rules of the NAI grant parties significant discretion regarding procedural frameworks,[93] while neither explicitly prohibits an arbitrator from acting as a mediator in the same dispute, this Arb-Med-Arb process appears to be compatible with both sets of rules.

6.3.1.4 ADRIC Arbitration and Med-Arb Rules

Another explicit recognition of the arbitrator's role as a settlement facilitator is embedded in both ADRIC's Arbitration and Med-Arb Rules, which apply to domestic and international proceedings.[94] According to the ADRIC Arbitration Rules:

> (a) The Tribunal may encourage settlement of the dispute and recommend that the parties use mediation, conciliation, or other dispute resolution procedures at any time during the arbitration proceedings.
> (b) The Tribunal must not act as a mediator, conciliator, or other facilitator of the settlement of the dispute except under a written agreement to that effect.
> (c) If the parties agree to continue the arbitration as a Med-Arb and unless the parties agree otherwise, the ADRIC Med-Arb Rules apply ...[95]

86. NAI Mediation Rules, 2017, Article 6(5).
87. NAI Mediation Rules, 2017, Article 6(4).
88. NAI Mediation Rules, 2017, Article 10(b) & (g).
89. NAI Mediation Rules, 2017, Article 8.
90. NAI Arbitration Rules, 2024, Article 51(1).
91. *See* the discussion in section 3.6.3.
92. Ortolani, 2025, §21.4-21.5(a). This approach is also supported by the Dutch Arbitration Act, 2015, Article 1069, which requires that a settlement be concluded during the arbitral proceedings in order to be recorded as a consent award.
93. NAI Arbitration Rules, 2024, Article 25(1); NAI Mediation Rules, 2017, Article 6(1).
94. ADRIC Arbitration Rules, 2025, Article 1(3); ADRIC Med-Arb Rules, 2020, Introduction, Part II.
95. ADRIC Arbitration Rules, 2025, Article 4(20).

While this provision clearly authorizes the tribunal to promote settlement—including by mediating the dispute—subject to the parties' written consent, it offers limited guidance on the practical implementation and regulation of the arbitrator's dual role. The ADRIC Med-Arb Rules, however, provide a more detailed framework specifically designed for proceedings conducted by the same neutral. Under these rules, the neutral first attempts to resolve the dispute through mediation and then proceeds to binding arbitration for any unresolved issues.[96] According to the Med-Arb Rules, the mediation stage concludes when all issues in dispute are settled, the agreed mediation timeframe ends, or the parties or the Med-Arbitrator decide to terminate the mediation and proceed to arbitration.[97] At this juncture, parties are not required to provide renewed consent for the arbitration to be conducted by the same neutral unless mandated by applicable law.[98] If a party seeks to challenge the neutral based on the mediation stage, they must raise such a challenge at the outset of the arbitration phase, and the neutral is tasked with deciding the challenge promptly. Failure of the parties to raise the challenge at that point results in a waiver of the right to challenge on this basis.[99] By agreeing to the Med-Arb Rules, parties also waive their right to assert procedural unfairness or loss of jurisdiction solely based on the grounds of the arbitrator's involvement in mediation. This waiver extends to the neutral's conduct of ex parte communications, expression of evaluative opinions on the parties' positions, and reliance on confidential information disclosed during mediation, provided the parties have consented to its use.[100] The Med-Arb Rules further stipulate that the arbitration stage is governed by the ADRIC Arbitration Rules to ensure that any final award—whether based on mediation or arbitration—is regulated by these arbitration rules.[101] However, this arrangement raises potential enforcement challenges for awards or portions thereof that rely exclusively on the mediation phase. According to the ADRIC Arbitration Rules, a tribunal may record a settlement as an award on agreed terms only if the settlement is reached "during the arbitration proceedings."[102] Consequently, because the Med-Arb Rules are subordinate to the ADRIC Arbitration Rules and cannot contradict them,[103] initiating mediation under the Med-Arb Rules only after the commencement of arbitration—effectively conducting an Arb-Med-Arb process—may mitigate enforcement risks. Since both the Arbitration and the Med-Arb Rules explicitly permit an arbitrator to also serve as a mediator in the same dispute, this configuration appears feasible under the ADRIC framework.

It is evident that the ADRIC Med-Arb Rules aim to establish a more structured framework for the arbitrator's dual role, allowing the neutral to caucus with the parties during mediation, offer evaluative opinions, and rely on confidential information that

96. ADRIC Med-Arb Rules, 2020, Articles 1(1) & 4.
97. ADRIC Med-Arb Rules, 2020, Article 6(3).
98. ADRIC Med-Arb Rules, 2020, Article 6(4)(c). In domestic proceedings conducted under these rules, such consent prior to the initiation of arbitration is mandated by section 620 of Quebec Arbitration Act, 2014.
99. ADRIC Med-Arb Rules, 2020, Article 6(5)(a)-(b).
100. ADRIC Med-Arb Rules, 2020, Articles 5(2) & 6(6).
101. ADRIC Med-Arb Rules, 2020, Article 6(2).
102. ADRIC Arbitration Rules, 2025, Article 5(5)(2).
103. ADRIC Med-Arb Rules, 2020, Article 2(7).

parties agreed to its use. However, the requirement for renewed consent to arbitration after failed mediation only where legally mandated—and the inflexible provisions authorizing caucusing and evaluative opinions while preemptively waiving challenges based on such conduct—may unnecessarily restrict party autonomy and discourage parties from adopting the Med-Arb Rules at the outset.

As the analysis in this section demonstrates, despite differences in language and criticisms of their frameworks, the institutional rules discussed—most from leading arbitration institutes—alongside those examined in previous chapters, empower and encourage arbitrators to adopt a proactive approach to settlement, including direct engagement in settlement processes. This trend reflects the increasing recognition of the arbitrator's dual role in ICA, which is progressively evolving into a standard practice rather than an exception. Nonetheless, these rules generally provide limited guidance on the practical execution of this role, and most are reluctant to implement comprehensive regulations to safeguard its use and outcomes.

6.3.2 International Arbitration Guidelines

Similar to institutional arbitration rules, an increasing number of international arbitration guidelines have explicitly acknowledged the arbitrator's role as a settlement facilitator.[104] However, these guidelines vary considerably. While all require the parties' express consent for arbitrators to fulfill this role, they establish different terms and boundaries for this involvement. As presented below, while some guidelines prioritize party autonomy, others focus on protecting the arbitrators following their involvement in the settlement process, often by imposing mandatory waivers or prohibiting caucusing, when only a handful of guidelines tend to comprehensively regulate the dual role of arbitrators.

6.3.2.1 UNCITRAL Notes on Organizing Arbitral Proceedings

The UNCITRAL Notes on Arbitration serve as an essential guide for conducting proceedings in institutional and ad hoc international arbitration,[105] so they are significant in delineating common and innovative ICA practices.[106] A notable evolution in recognizing the arbitrator's role as settlement facilitator in ICA is evident in the substantial differences between the 1996 version and the current 2023 version of the Notes.[107] While the 1996 version allowed arbitrators to only "bring up the possibility of settlement" and "suggest settlement negotiations with caution" without direct involvement in the process,[108] the updated version of the Notes applies a more liberal

104. Marzolini, 2016, p. 106.
105. UNCITRAL Notes on Arbitration, 2023, para. 1; Dasser, 2021, p. 76; Born, 2021, §1.04[D][5]; Berger & Jensen, 2017, p. 905.
106. Ali, 2021, p. 13; Berger & Jensen, 2017, p. 905; Helmer, 2003, pp. 60-61; Uzelac, 1997, p. 154.
107. Sussman & Berger, 2021a, p. 26; Berger & Jensen, 2017, pp. 905-906; Nigmatullina, 2018, p. 78.
108. UNCITRAL Notes on Arbitration, 1996, Article 12; Marzolini, 2016, p. 107.

approach by acknowledging the role of arbitrators in the settlement process, albeit subject to certain preconditions:

> In appropriate circumstances, the arbitral tribunal may raise the possibility of a settlement between the parties. In some jurisdictions, the arbitration law permits facilitation of a settlement by the arbitral tribunal with the agreement of the parties. In other jurisdictions, it is not permissible for the arbitral tribunal to do more than raise the prospect of a settlement that would not involve the arbitral tribunal. Where the applicable arbitration law permits the arbitral tribunal to facilitate a settlement, it may, if so requested by the parties, guide or assist the parties in their negotiations. Certain sets of arbitration rules provide for facilitation of a settlement by the arbitral tribunal.[109]

Despite highlighting the controversy surrounding the dual role of arbitrators—stemming from varying legal approaches in its regard[110]—this provision clearly acknowledges this role, contingent on the parties' agreement and permission by applicable law.[111] However, the Notes do not prescribe specific settlement techniques or provide guidelines for this dual role, whether in standalone arbitrations or hybrid procedures. Additionally, the Notes are vague about the nature of permission required from the applicable law, which leaves the question of whether implied permission or the absence of prohibition is sufficient. Proper interpretation suggests that if the applicable law allows parties to agree on arbitration procedures and lacks an absolute prohibition on this role, this should qualify as adequate permission to utilize the arbitrator's dual role.[112]

6.3.2.2 IBA Rules and Guidelines

Despite being a private association of professionals,[113] the IBA is considered by many practitioners and scholars as the most influential formulating agency in the field of ICA worldwide, with generally accepted practice standards on various issues, including conflict of interests, counsel conduct, drafting of arbitration clauses, and the taking of evidence.[114] By presenting the role of arbitrators in the settlement process as "an internationally recognised possibility,"[115] the IBA soft norms constitute an important driving force behind the convergence of standards connected with that role. The IBA Rules on the Taking of Evidence encourage the arbitrator to take a proactive role in arbitral proceedings by authorizing them to deliver preliminary determination of legal issues and identify and discuss with the parties any issue that may streamline the proceedings or lead to an agreement about disputed subjects.[116] Additionally, the IBA

109. UNCITRAL Notes on Arbitration, 2023, Article 12. *See also* Berger, 2018b, p. 508.
110. Marzolini, 2016, p. 107.
111. Sussman & Berger, 2021a, p. 26; Berger & Jensen, 2017, p. 906; Nigmatullina, 2018, p. 78.
112. *See* the discussion in section 6.3.2.5 below about the interpretation of the Model Law on ICA.
113. Kaufmann-Kohler, 2010, p. 292.
114. Dasser, 2021, p. 82; Berger, 2019, p. 302; Bermann, 2017, pp. 66-67; Ali, 2011b, p. 9.
115. Von Schlabrendorff, 2009, p. 98.
116. IBA Rules on Evidence in International Arbitration, 2020, Article 2(3); Berger, 2018b, pp. 508, 510; Berger & Jensen, 2017, p. 893.

Guidelines on Conflicts of Interest have established the arbitrator's role in settlement facilitation as a best practice, provided the parties involved grant express consent:

> An arbitrator may assist the parties in reaching a settlement of the dispute, through conciliation, mediation, or otherwise, at any stage of the proceedings. However, before doing so, the arbitrator should receive an express agreement by the parties that acting in such a manner shall not disqualify the arbitrator from continuing to serve as arbitrator. Such express agreement shall be considered to be an effective waiver of any potential conflict of interest that may arise from the arbitrator's participation in such a process, or from information that the arbitrator may learn in the process. If the assistance by the arbitrator does not lead to the final settlement of the case, the parties remain bound by their waiver. However, ... the arbitrator shall resign if, as a consequence of the arbitrator's involvement in the settlement process, the arbitrator develops doubts as to the arbitrator's ability to remain impartial or independent in the future course of the arbitration.[117]

Unlike its older version,[118] this practice standard seems to refrain from imposing limitations on arbitrators while facilitating settlements, as they can mediate the dispute or use any other ADR method at any stage of the proceedings. Moreover, this standard grants comprehensive protection to arbitrators following their involvement in the settlement process,[119] as the prerequisite of the parties' informed consent, which should not necessarily be in writing,[120] is bundled with the waiver of any potential claim about information received by the arbitrators during the settlement efforts or against their qualification to resume their arbitral role if those efforts fail.[121] Although the standard requires arbitrators to resign if they have doubts about remaining impartial or independent in the renewed arbitration, according to the provision's language, this decision is subject to the mere discretion of the arbitrators and supposedly not influenced by the parties' position.[122]

Despite their innovative and liberal approach regarding the role of arbitrators as settlement facilitators, the IBA guidelines fail to address critical issues connected with the settlement process. For example, the guidelines do not regulate the handling of confidential information disclosed to arbitrators during settlement negotiations, whether in the presence of all parties or through caucusing. In addition, the irrevocable waiver of claims against that information or the qualification of arbitrators to continue

117. IBA Guidelines on Conflicts of Interest in International Arbitration, 2024, General Standard 4(d). *See also* Sussman & Berger, 2021a, p. 26; Ruckteschler & Wendelstein, 2021, p. 770; Berger, 2019, p. 309; Berger & Jensen, 2017, p. 904; Nigmatullina, 2018, p. 178; Von Schlabrendorff, 2009, p. 98.
118. IBA Rules of Ethics for International Arbitrators, 1987, Article 8, allowing the tribunal to make settlement proposals to all parties simultaneously, subject to their consent. Additionally, the rules advised arbitrators to avoid ex parte communications to prevent any risk of disqualification from further participation in the arbitration. *See also* Nigmatullina, 2018, p. 192; Sussman, 2010a, p. 386; Marriott, 2005, p. 539.
119. Marzolini, 2016, p. 106; Berger, 2018b, p. 514.
120. IBA Guidelines on Conflicts of Interest in International Arbitration, 2024, Explanation to General Standard 4(d); Berger, 2018b, p. 514.
121. Ruckteschler & Wendelstein, 2021, p. 770; Berger & Jensen, 2017, p. 913. On the other hand, *see* Sussman & Berger, 2021a, p. 26, holding that if parties lose their faith in the arbitrator, they may still attempt to challenge them despite that waiver.
122. Nigmatullina, 2018, p. 183.

the arbitration following failed efforts to settle seems far-reaching and unnecessary. This arrangement, which appears indispensable, narrows the parties' autonomy as it may leave them "trapped" in their previous consent even following unexpected developments or undesired behavior of the tribunal during the settlement negotiations. Consequently, it may rationalize claims regarding breach of due process, which can risk the enforceability of the arbitral award[123] and deter parties from engaging with procedures acknowledging the arbitrator's dual role.

6.3.2.3 CIArb Rules and Guidelines

Based in London, the CIArb is another leading international organization that has made significant contributions to the production of soft norms and the promotion of best practices in the field of international arbitration.[124] The CIArb provides education, training, and advice in the practice and profession of ADR for thousands of members across 149 countries.[125] Thus, its professional guidelines are addressed to its members and the global arbitration community, aiming to promote harmonized solutions that reflect best practices for effectively avoiding, managing, and resolving commercial disputes worldwide.[126] One practice relates to the role of arbitrators as settlement facilitators. While CIArb refrains from explicit recommendations on the role of arbitrators, it acknowledges that there are significant benefits to parties from its exercise, as it fits well with the modern business landscape and party autonomy as a pivotal principle in arbitration.[127] The CIArb Arbitration Rules grant arbitrators the discretion to conduct the proceedings in a way that avoids unnecessary delays and expenses and provides a fair and efficient resolution of the dispute.[128] Hence, they are authorized to hold case management conferences to address the possibility of bifurcating the proceedings or resolving the dispute through any other ADR mechanism.[129] When requested by the parties, they are further empowered to decide the dispute as *amiable compositeur* or *ex aequo et bono*[130] or record concluded settlements as arbitral awards on agreed terms.[131]

In addition, the 2021 CIArb Professional Practice Guideline on the Use of Mediation in Arbitration appears as one of the most comprehensive soft norms

123. Ruckteschler & Wendelstein, 2021, p. 772.
124. Bermann, 2017, pp. 66-67; Dasser, 2021, pp. 83-84.
125. *CIArb: About us*, n.d.
126. *CIArb: What we do*, n.d.; Dasser, 2021, p. 84; Von Schlabrendorff, 2009, p. 95; Ross, 2015. According to CIArb, to ensure that the Guidelines reflect international best practices and consider different legal backgrounds and cultures, they are drafted by a committee that includes members from 13 different jurisdictions and reviewed by over 60 scholars and practitioners from the CIArb's teaching faculty and international branches. *See* CIArb Introduction to Practice Guidelines, 2015, pp. 1-2.
127. CIArb Practice Guideline on the Use of Mediation in Arbitration, 2021, Articles 2(1)-(2) & 8(2).
128. CIArb Arbitration Rules, 2015, Article 17. *See also* CIArb Guidelines on Managing Arbitrations, 2016, Article 1.
129. CIArb Arbitration Rules, 2015, Appendix II(15)-(16). *See also* CIArb Guidelines on Managing Arbitrations, 2016, Article 2.
130. CIArb Arbitration Rules, 2015, Article 35.
131. CIArb Arbitration Rules, 2015, Article 36(1).

suggested so far to address the dual role of arbitrators. Despite focusing on hybrid procedures that combine arbitration with mediation, the guideline still suggests a few settlement techniques to implement within standalone arbitral proceedings, including: (a) settlement conferences designed to narrow the controversies and enable partial or full settlement of the dispute; and (b) evaluative techniques, including preliminary views on disputed issues and opinions on the merits, which are recommended for use only subject to these safeguards: the express consent of the parties in writing, a clear explanation of the tribunal that these views are not final, so the tribunal's mind remains open, and the ability to replace the tribunal if attempts to settle fail and one or more parties have concerns about the tribunal's ability to continue the arbitration.[132]

When relating to hybrid procedures combining arbitration and mediation by the same neutral, the guideline emphasizes the voluntariness of such process and the tribunal's duty to avoid any pressure on the parties to agree to mediation or other arrangements that employ part of its elements.[133] Moreover, the guideline specifies two preliminary cautions for the parties to consider before participating in such procedures: (a) no assurance exists that all jurisdictions relevant to the arbitration will consider an explicit waiver of the right to challenge the tribunal for its involvement in mediation as valid, even if it embodies party autonomy;[134] and (b) settlements concluded during mediation before the arbitral proceedings have commenced may face enforcement challenges as at that stage there is arguably no "dispute" to decide, so parties should consider attempting mediation during arbitration.[135] According to the guideline, when the parties are nevertheless willing to authorize the arbitrator to mediate the dispute, the following cumulative safeguards are advised to mitigate enforceability risks to the arbitration's outcome: the arbitrator may proceed with mediation only following the consent of all parties; before accepting to fulfill the dual role, the arbitrator should clarify the risks associated with this role while verifying the parties' understanding in writing;[136] the arbitrator should familiarize themselves with the legal attitudes regarding the dual role in all relevant jurisdictions to the arbitration, including the seat and enforcement jurisdictions; before mediation starts, parties should formulate clear agreement on whether ex parte meetings are permitted, and if so whether information communicated in their course should be disclosed in the resumed arbitration or stay confidential;[137] before the conduct of mediation, parties should also agree if and to

132. CIArb Practice Guideline on the Use of Mediation in Arbitration, 2021, Articles 2(3) & 5.
133. CIArb Practice Guideline on the Use of Mediation in Arbitration, 2021, Article 6(2).
134. CIArb Practice Guideline on the Use of Mediation in Arbitration, 2021, Article 8(3).
135. CIArb Practice Guideline on the Use of Mediation in Arbitration, 2021, Article 9(3). *See* the discussion in section 3.6.3 regarding enforceability challenges associated with settlements concluded prior to initiating arbitration and ways to address them.
136. Interestingly, although it is recommended to obtain written verification of the parties' understanding of the associated risks, there is no requirement for the initial agreement authorizing arbitrators to mediate to be in writing. This interpretation is further reinforced by another guideline article, discussed below, which addresses the necessity of renewed consent from the parties for the arbitrator to resume arbitration following an unsuccessful mediation.
137. This liberal approach, which allows the parties to decide on caucusing and the use of confidential information, represents a departure from the more hesitant attitude of previous version of the guideline relating to arbitrators' use of ADR procedures. While not prohibiting these techniques when the parties agree to their use and waive their right to challenge, the

what extent arbitrators are authorized to implement evaluative methods and express to the parties, jointly or individually, opinions on the merits;[138] before the commencement of mediation, parties should waive—clearly and in writing—any objection to the award solely on the ground that arbitrators have acted as mediators according to the agreement between the parties; if mediation fails, only renewed consent of the parties, in writing,[139] allows arbitrators to retain their adjudicative role in the continued arbitration.[140] In addition to the above-suggested safeguards, the guideline outlines several options for incorporating mediated settlements: concluding the settlement as a regular contract, recording it as an arbitral award on agreed terms,[141] or, as recommended by the guideline as "a good practice," recording and enforcing the mediated settlement under the Singapore Convention, provided that "the place of mediation is a signatory to the Convention" and all parties agree.[142]

As observed, in contrast to the IBA soft norms discussed earlier, the modernized CIArb guideline on hybrid procedures seeks to address various concerns associated with the arbitrator's dual role. In this effort, party autonomy—while recognized as a core principle in arbitration—is not treated as an absolute but rather as a relative principle that must be balanced against other considerations. For instance, unlike provisions mandating arbitrators to disclose confidential information obtained during caucusing if arbitration resumes following unsuccessful mediation,[143] the guideline deliberately defers this issue to the parties' discretion while recognizing that a strict disclosure requirement may limit party autonomy and discourage parties from agreeing to the arbitrator's dual role.[144] Simultaneously, the guideline emphasizes the importance of aligning party autonomy with the legal expectations of all relevant jurisdictions regarding the dual role to mitigate enforcement risks. In addressing these issues, the guideline adopts an innovative and pragmatic approach that precedes other soft norms and suggests safeguards for dual-role arbitrators. However, the updated CIArb guideline seems to have three main shortcomings. *First*, as previously mentioned, the guideline is inconsistent regarding the written consent requirement for authorizing

earlier guideline recommended refraining from their utilization. *See* CIArb Guidelines for Arbitrators on the use of ADR procedures, 2011, Article 7(1); Nigmatullina, 2018, p. 192; Marzolini, 2016, pp. 106-107.

138. Unlike the use of evaluative techniques in standalone arbitration, which, according to the guideline, requires the parties' written consent, their application within hybrid procedures does not necessitate such written consent. This inconsistency—extending to the initial agreement authorizing arbitrators to mediate, where written consent is not required, and the subsequent renewed consent for the arbitrator to resume their role, which must be in writing—can lead to varied interpretations. This lack of clarity may create confusion and potentially jeopardize the outcome of the process.

139. CIArb Practice Guideline on the Use of Mediation in Arbitration, 2021, Article 10(4), requiring renewed consent in writing, even if the earlier agreement concerning the arbitrator's dual role was in written form. This suggests that the initial agreement authorizing the arbitrator to mediate the dispute need not necessarily be in writing.

140. CIArb Practice Guideline on the Use of Mediation in Arbitration, 2021, Articles 8-10.

141. CIArb Practice Guideline on the Use of Mediation in Arbitration, 2021, Article 9(1).

142. CIArb Practice Guideline on the Use of Mediation in Arbitration, 2021, Article 9(4).

143. Such as those adopted in Singapore and Hong Kong, and for domestic arbitrations also in Australia. *See* the discussion in sections 5.2.2.2-5.2.2.3 & 5.3.1.3.

144. CIArb Practice Guideline on the Use of Mediation in Arbitration, 2021, Article 8(4)-(5).

arbitrators to fulfill the dual role and implement evaluative techniques during the process, which may create confusion and challenge its outcome. *Second*, although the guideline addresses a few settlement techniques that can be implemented within standalone arbitration, it primarily focuses on hybrid procedures and fails to address other initiatives on the continuum of settlement facilitation. *Third*, the recommendation to record mediated settlements under the Singapore Convention if the seat of arbitration is a signatory to that convention does not guarantee enforceability because few jurisdictions have ratified the convention. Crucially, for enforcement under the Singapore Convention, the jurisdiction where enforcement is sought must be a party to the convention, irrespective of its applicability in the jurisdiction where the mediation occurred or the settlement agreement was concluded.[145]

6.3.2.4 AAA Code of Ethics

The American Arbitration Association (AAA), the largest and longest-standing provider of commercial arbitration services in the US, has, through its International Centre for Dispute Resolution (ICDR),[146] become a leading international arbitration institution globally and a significant driving force behind the harmonization of arbitration rules and practices.[147] The AAA Code of Ethics for Arbitrators in Commercial Disputes acknowledges the arbitrator's role as a settlement facilitator, including the possibility to act as a mediator in the same dispute:

> Although it is not improper for an arbitrator to suggest to the parties that they discuss the possibility of settlement or the use of mediation, or other dispute resolution processes, an arbitrator should not exert pressure on any party to settle or to utilize other dispute resolution processes. An arbitrator should not be present or otherwise participate in settlement discussions or act as a mediator unless requested to do so by all parties.[148]

Despite implementing a cautious approach toward the arbitrator's direct involvement in the settlement process, according to this rule, parties may nevertheless opt out and empower them with the mandate.[149] Additionally, the AAA practical guide on the drafting of dispute resolution clauses, despite its reservation from scenarios allowing arbitrators to resume their adjudicative role following failed mediation—which, according to the guide, should be commended only in rare circumstances—still offers a sample clause regarding hybrid procedures to parties willing to empower arbitrators with the dual role.[150] However, according to the AAA Code of Ethics, even when

145. *See* the discussion in section 3.6.2.
146. *See ICDR: Who we are*, n.d.
147. Dasser, 2021, p. 89; Stipanowich, 2010, p. 6; McLean, 2009, pp. 1092-1093; Helmer, 2003, pp. 41-42; Kaufmann-Kohler, 2005, pp. 340, 348; Garnett, 2002, p. 409. For an overview of the comprehensive list of the AAA rules and guidelines on commercial dispute resolution, *see AAA: Active rules*, n.d.
148. AAA Code of Ethics, 2004, Canon IV(F). *See also* Berger & Jensen, 2017, p. 905; Marriott, 2005, p. 539.
149. Marzolini, 2016, p. 107; Benzidi, 2017, pp. 10-11.
150. AAA Drafting Dispute Resolution Clauses, 2013, section V(S); Benzidi, 2017, p. 11.

authorized to facilitate settlement, arbitrators should refrain from ex parte communications during the settlement process.[151]

Although the AAA acknowledges the dual role of arbitrators, including hybrid procedures, its soft law instruments lack substantive guidance on implementing this role. Furthermore, its Code of Ethics does not establish safeguards for the appropriate exercise of the dual role, apart from a blanket prohibition on caucusing. This prohibition seems to be an overly restrictive response to the concerns associated with this practice. As demonstrated earlier, more balanced solutions exist to effectively address these concerns while preserving party autonomy.

6.3.2.5 *Model Law on ICA*

Although the Model Law on ICA does not directly relate to the arbitrator's role as a settlement facilitator,[152] it is highly relevant to the discussion since the literature is divided over whether the role can be inferred from its provisions. According to the Model Law, parties can determine their arbitration procedures by mutual agreement. Otherwise, the tribunal is empowered to implement the procedures it deems appropriate for the arbitration.[153] Additionally, when expressly authorized by the parties, the tribunal shall decide the case "*ex aequo et bono* or as *amiable compositeur*."[154] According to one approach, these authorizations only address how arbitrators adjudicate the dispute but do not relate to settlement facilitation. Therefore, in the absence of express authorization in the text, it can be concluded that the Model Law on ICA is agnostic about the dual role of arbitrators. Hence, by its adoption, states ostensibly declare that they do not recognize this role.[155]

According to a different approach, since the aforementioned authorizations grant parties extensive freedom to design arbitration procedures, they implicitly recognize the arbitrator's dual role. This position emphasizes the identity between the above authorizations under the Model Law on ICA and those embedded in the English Arbitration Act, which several commentators have interpreted as permitting arbitrators to facilitate settlements and engage in hybrid processes.[156] Furthermore, this position relies on the arbitrator's authority under the Model Law on ICA to record settlements as consent awards, which carry the same legal effect as regular awards.[157] While these justifications provide strong support for construing the aforementioned arrangements under the Model Law on ICA as allowing arbitrators to assume a dual role subject to the parties' consent, this position is further reinforced by the language of the Model Law on ICM and its compelling legislative history. According to the Model Law on ICM:

151. AAA Code of Ethics, 2004, Canon III(B); Stipanowich, 2021a, p. 302; Marriott, 2005, p. 539.
152. Aragaki, 2021, p. 31; Ali, 2011b, p. 12; *UNCITRAL WGII*, n.d., at Report of the Working Group on Arbitration on the work of its thirty-fifth session (A/CN.9/506), para. 132.
153. Model Law on ICA, 2006, Article 19.
154. Model Law on ICA, 2006, Article 28.
155. Aragaki, 2021, p. 31.
156. U.K. Arbitration Act, 1996, section 1(b); Houzhi, 2005, p. 549; Scherpe & Marten, 2013, p. 375; Aragaki, 2021, p. 31. For further discussion, *see* section 5.3.1.2.
157. Model Law on ICA, 2006, Article 30; Berger, 2018b, p. 513; Aragaki, 2021, p. 31.

> Unless otherwise agreed by the parties, the mediator shall not act as an arbitrator in respect of a dispute that was or is the subject of the mediation proceedings or in respect of another dispute that has arisen from the same contract or legal relationship or any related contract or legal relationship.[158]

While this rule generally directs mediators to avoid serving as arbitrators in the same proceedings, it permits this dual role if the parties agree.[159] The official guide of the Model Law on ICM explains that this default rule aims to bolster trust in the mediator, as parties may be hesitant to engage in mediation when failed settlement attempts could result in the mediator acting as the arbitrator.[160] Nonetheless, the guide underscores that party autonomy remains the primary consideration when determining the mediator's role:

> In some legal systems, mediators are permitted to act as arbitrators if parties so agree and, in other legal systems, that is subject to rules embedded in professional codes of conduct. The Model Law provides a default rule subject to party autonomy: The agreement of the parties and the mediator may be able to override any limitation on that point, even where the matter is subject to rules embedded in codes of conduct. ... The provision poses no obstacle to the appointment of the former mediator provided that the parties depart from the rule by agreement—for example, by a joint appointment of the mediator to serve as an arbitrator.[161]

Furthermore, the legislative history of the Model Law on ICM provides remarkably interesting and noticeable insights into the opposite situations where arbitrators act as mediators in the same dispute. Indeed, an early draft of the Model Law on International Commercial Conciliation, which was later replaced by the Model Law on ICM,[162] contained the following provision explicitly aimed at regulating these situations:

> It is not incompatible with the function of an arbitrator if the arbitrator raises the question of a possible conciliation and, to the extent agreed to by the parties, participates in efforts to reach an agreed settlement.[163]

According to the Report of WGII on Arbitration, this provision was disputed while discussing the final text of the Model Law. Its supporters, mainly representing East Asian jurisdictions,[164] raised the following justifications for its inclusion: (a) this provision would be useful for jurisdictions demonstrating little experience with

158. Model Law on ICM, 2018, Article 13. The same arrangement was anchored in former version of this model law, *see* Model Law on International Commercial Conciliation, 2002, Article 12. Additionally, similar provision is anchored in the UNCITRAL Mediation Rules, 2021, Article 12 (*see* the discussion in section 4.4.2.3).
159. Ruckteschler & Wendelstein, 2021, p. 769; Stipanowich, 2021a, p. 273.
160. Model Law on ICM, 2018, at Guide to Enactment and Use, paras. 87-88; Stipanowich, 2021a, pp. 288-289.
161. Model Law on ICM, 2018, at Guide to Enactment and Use, paras. 87-88.
162. Model Law on International Commercial Conciliation, 2002.
163. *UNCITRAL WGII*, n.d., at Report of the Working Group on Arbitration on the work of its thirty-fifth session (A/CN.9/506), para. 130. *See also UNCITRAL WGII*, n.d., at Settlement of commercial disputes—Model legislative provisions on international commercial conciliation (A/CN.9/WG.II/WP.115), p. 24.
164. Ali, 2011b, pp. 11-12.

mediation, (b) it endorses the already accepted principle by WGII that arbitrators can mediate the same dispute, and (c) this provision is required since the Model Law on ICA does not relate to this issue at all.[165] Its opponents called for its exclusion from the final draft based on the following reasons: (a) given that this provision pertains to the competence and functions of arbitrators, its appropriate placement should be within legislation related to arbitration to avoid any confusion[166] and (b) as arbitration practices, particularly those relating to arbitrators acting as mediators, vary from one jurisdiction to another based on legal and social traditions, uniform legislation is not the appropriate means to unify them.[167] Although after discussions, the opponents' view prevailed and WGII omitted the provision from the final draft, the following important explanation was still included in the final draft to emphasize the primary status of party autonomy in arbitral proceedings and clarify that the abrogation was not aimed at prohibiting arbitrators from fulfilling the dual role:

> The draft Model Law was not intended to indicate whether or not an arbitrator could act or participate in a conciliation relating to the dispute, a matter that was to the discretion of the parties acting within the context of applicable law.[168]

Although the Model Law on ICA does not explicitly mention the role of arbitrators as mediators, its "legislator" expressed a clear position, albeit during discussions on a different model law, that no obstacle exists in allowing the role, subject to the parties' agreement. In addition, at no point during the discussions did the "legislator" suggest that the role was inconsistent with the provisions of the Model Law on ICA. Hence, like the aforementioned guidelines, the Model Law on ICA also recognizes the dual role of arbitrators. Any contrary interpretation would create an unreasoned and undesirable inconsistency between the model laws regarding the arbitrators' ability to conduct hybrid procedures involving arbitration and mediation. Furthermore, if both model laws recognize hybrid procedures, it follows *per a fortiori* that other moderate steps within the spectrum of settlement initiatives should also be acknowledged. Additionally, the "legislator" of the model laws, which plays a significant role in harmonization, has expressed a clear position that party autonomy, as the cornerstone principle in international arbitration, takes precedence over other procedural limitations, even those embedded in arbitral rules or codes of conduct, provided compliance with the applicable law is maintained. If these significant recognitions (i.e., the arbitrator's

165. *UNCITRAL WGII*, n.d., at Report of the Working Group on Arbitration on the work of its thirty-fifth session (A/CN.9/506), para. 132. *See also* Model Law on ICM, 2018, at Guide to Enactment and Use, para. 90.
166. *UNCITRAL WGII*, n.d., at Report of the Working Group on Arbitration on the work of its thirty-fifth session (A/CN.9/506), paras. 131-132. *See also UNCITRAL WGII*, n.d., at Settlement of commercial disputes—Model legislative provisions on international commercial conciliation (A/CN.9/WG.II/WP.115), para. 44.
167. Model Law on ICM, 2018, at Guide to Enactment and Use, para. 90. For a critical discussion on the race to the bottom in terms of harmonization during the legislation process of the Model Law, *see* Kaufmann-Kohler, 2010, p. 293; Cordero-Moss, 2012, pp. 132, 143; Pate, 2010, pp. 151, 155, 161.
168. *UNCITRAL WGII*, n.d., at Report of the Working Group on Arbitration on the work of its thirty-fifth session (A/CN.9/506), para. 132. *See also* Model Law on ICM, 2018, at Guide to Enactment and Use, para. 90.

mandate to facilitate settlement subject to the parties' agreement and the paramount status of party autonomy, which supersedes other procedural provisions embedded in arbitral rules or codes of conduct) extend to domestic jurisdictions that currently exhibit hesitancy toward the dual role of arbitrators, they may play a pivotal role in reshaping attitudes toward this practice and dispelling lingering taboos about its implementation. This objective can be most effectively achieved if, alongside reflection in the Model Law on ICM and its supplementary extra-legislative documents, the "legislator" explicitly codifies these acknowledgments within the Model Law on ICA itself, as recommended in a subsequent section.[169]

6.3.3 Initiatives by Professional Organizations

Moreover, professional organizations have undertaken significant initiatives in recent years to promote the harmonization of the arbitrator's role as a settlement facilitator at the transnational level. These initiatives involve proposing guidelines related to its practice to reconcile differing approaches stemming from various legal cultures and addressing due process concerns associated with its fulfillment.[170] However, like arbitral rules and guidelines, these organizational initiatives vary considerably, and most of them reflect the legal traditions of their promoters.[171]

6.3.3.1 CPR Commission on the Future of Arbitration

The CPR, an independent international organization dedicated to promoting the prevention and resolution of conflicts,[172] introduced the first established institutional initiative to provide practice guidance for arbitrators involved in the settlement process within hybrid procedures combining arbitration and mediation.[173] This effort, led by more than 50 leading arbitrators and practitioners, culminated in the 2001 Final Report on the Future of Arbitration.[174] While the report acknowledged the dual role of arbitrators and provided guidance on its implementation, it generally reflected the traditionally cautious stance of U.S. practice toward hybrid procedures and advised against its use in arbitral proceedings.[175] This attitude was based on several concerns, including fundamental incompatibility of the neutral with mediative and arbitral skills,

169. *See* the discussion in section 8.3.2.
170. Ali, 2021, p. 14; Bermann, 2017, pp. 65-66; Jemielniak, 2014, p. 333; Kaufmann-Kohler, 2010, p. 295; Kaufmann-Kohler, 2003, pp. 1323-1324; Lynch, 2003, pp. 96-100.
171. A notable exception in this regard is the International Task Force on Mixed Mode Dispute Resolution, which appears to transcend the influence of specific legal traditions and aims to address a broad spectrum of ICA users.
172. *CPR: About us*, n.d.
173. Stipanowich, 2021a, p. 327.
174. The Report the CPR was published in Stipanowich & Kaskell, 2001, pp. 20-33. *See also* Stipanowich, 2021a, pp. 327-330.
175. Stipanowich & Kaskell, 2001, p. 22; Stipanowich & Mironi, 2021, p. 30; Stipanowich, 2021a, pp. 295, 327-328. This approach is evident in the CPR rules for both domestic and international arbitration, which stipulate that unless otherwise agreed by the parties, mediation should be conducted by a neutral party separate from the arbitrator and kept confidential from the

the fear of coercion during settlement negotiations, the fear of uncandid communication of the parties knowing that the neutral may decide the case following failed settlement efforts, due process concerns resulting from ex parte communication and exposure to confidential information that may affect the neutral's impartiality, and potential risks to the enforcement of the arbitral award.[176] Nonetheless, recognizing that potential parties and neutrals would express willingness to engage with such procedures,[177] the report advocated limiting the dual role through the following measures: (a) during the settlement process, the arbitrator should refrain from expressing any evaluative views on the dispute or its outcome, and (b) the arbitrator should avoid caucusing or engaging in ex parte communications with the parties.[178] According to the commission, despite their potential contribution to the effectiveness of mediation processes, these techniques may "be challenging even for a highly sophisticated arbitrator" and, therefore, should not be permitted even when parties granted informed consent in their regard.[179]

In addition to these restrictions, the CPR report proposed several safeguards for exercising the dual role. *First*, the parties should grant informed consent to the arbitrator's dual role within a written agreement, which includes a waiver of grounds for disqualifying the arbitrator or challenging the award based on that dual role. *Second*, before authorizing the arbitrator with the dual role, parties should ensure that the arbitrator is fully qualified for both roles. *Third*, the arbitrator should not coerce the parties to agree to the dual role and should only accept a joint invitation of all parties embedded in an explicit agreement. *Fourth*, the arbitrator should respect the confidentiality of the settlement negotiations and be capable of deciding the case based only on the formal record. *Fifth*, if, during the settlement negotiations, the arbitrator receives confidential information—whether during caucusing or other circumstances—that compromises their ability to render an impartial decision based on the formal record, the arbitrator should resign from the resumed arbitration.[180]

Despite its attempt to promote practical guidance about the role of arbitrators as settlement facilitators, the CPR commission failed to address critical issues connected with that role. *First*, as aforementioned, the report focuses on hybrid procedures and says little about other initiatives arbitrators can take to promote settlements in standalone arbitration. It could be expected that, due to its hesitant approach toward hybrid procedures, the commission would expand the discussion on those initiatives and promote guidelines for their implementation. *Second*, as stated above regarding other rules and guidelines, the absolute prohibition on caucusing and evaluative

arbitrator. *See* CPR Rules for International Arbitration, 2019, Rule 21; CPR Rules for Non-Administered Arbitration, 2018, Rule 19; Stipanowich & Ulrich, 2014b, p. 11.

176. Stipanowich & Kaskell, 2001, pp. 21-22.
177. Stipanowich & Kaskell, 2001, p. 30; Stipanowich, 2021a, p. 328; Stipanowich, 2010, p. 51.
178. Stipanowich & Kaskell, 2001, pp. 30, 32-33; Stipanowich, 2021a, pp. 329-330. This approach is reflected in the CPR Code of Ethics for Arbitrators, 2005, Canons III(B) & IV(F), which, while recognizing the role of arbitrators as settlement facilitators (subject to the parties' consent), explicitly prohibits caucusing and other ex parte communications with the parties, except for discussions on technical or logistical matters.
179. Stipanowich & Kaskell, 2001, p. 30. *See also* Stipanowich, 2021a, p. 330.
180. Stipanowich & Kaskell, 2001, pp. 23-24, 32-33; Stipanowich, 2021a, pp. 328-329.

techniques undermines party autonomy and prevents the disputants from shaping the arbitral process according to their needs and interests. The same applies to the disregard rule concerning confidential information disclosed to the arbitrator during settlement negotiations, which does not allow for any deviation from its application. *Third*, the report places the decision regarding the arbitrator's competence to continue the resumed arbitration solely in the hands of the arbitrator. Given the strong opposition to ex parte communications and exposure to confidential information, it would have been reasonable for the report to recommend precluding the arbitrator from resuming their adjudicative role following unsuccessful settlement efforts. Alternatively, the report could have suggested conditioning the arbitrator's continuation on renewed consent from the parties and a clear agreement on the handling of confidential information disclosed during the settlement process.

6.3.3.2 CEDR Commission on Settlement in International Arbitration

Another organizational initiative aimed at suggesting practice guidance for the role of arbitrators in the settlement process was taken by the CEDR. This London-based independent international organization provides ADR services and training, including mediation and arbitration. The CEDR constitutes an important catalysator for developing global consent on transnational procedures in international arbitration.[181] In 2009, the CEDR formed a commission of 80 leading arbitrators and practitioners from various jurisdictions. It consulted with more than 45 leading arbitration institutes worldwide[182] to examine existing practices related to ICA settlement facilitation and recommend how to enhance their utilization by practitioners and users.[183] After considering different approaches for the encouragement of settlement within arbitral proceedings, mainly those of China, Hong Kong, Germany, and Switzerland,[184] the commission set the following three principles as the starting point for elaborating the arbitrator's role as a settlement facilitator in ICA: (a) the main task of the arbitral tribunal is to render a binding and enforceable award regarding the dispute, (b) unless the parties specify otherwise, the tribunal should facilitate the amicable resolution of the dispute or any portion of it, and (c) while facilitating a settlement, the tribunal should avoid actions that could undermine its award, particularly caucusing or obtaining information through ex parte communications, unless such actions are permitted in all jurisdictions relevant to enforceability or are conducted following the express consent of the parties after they have considered the potential consequences.[185] Based on these principles, the commission's final report included recommendations

181. *CEDR: About us*, 2024; Berger, 2019, p. 301; Stipanowich & Ulrich, 2014b, p. 14; Berger & Jensen, 2017, p. 893; Kun, 2013b, p. 217.
182. CEDR Report on Settlement in ICA, 2009, Appendix 5.
183. CEDR Report on Settlement in ICA, 2009, section 1(5).
184. CEDR Report on Settlement in ICA, 2009, section 2(2)-(3); Stipanowich & Mironi, 2021, p. 30; Stipanowich & Ulrich, 2014b, p. 14; Stipanowich, 2021a, p. 327; Kun, 2013b, p. 218.
185. CEDR Report on Settlement in ICA, 2009, section 2(4); Stipanowich, 2021a, pp. 331, 333; Sussman, 2010a, p. 386.

incorporated into the supplementary Rules for the Facilitation of Settlement in International Arbitration,[186] which was designed to provide tools for ICA users worldwide.[187]

Unlike the CPR report, which focused mainly on hybrid procedures, the CEDR report recommended several initiatives that arbitrators may undertake within standalone arbitral proceedings. *First*, enforcing multi-tiered dispute resolution clauses that incorporate a pre-arbitration settlement phase. *Second*, using the first procedural conference to encourage the parties to explore settlement opportunities. *Third*, exploring with parties and counsels the status of settlement discussions and suggesting different ADR processes or techniques, such as mediation windows, to promote amicable resolutions throughout the arbitration process. *Fourth*, unless otherwise agreed by the parties in writing, providing preliminary findings on legal and factual matters as well as preliminary views on the merits, including indications of which evidence is expected to prevail. *Fifth*, upon receiving a written request from all disputants, presenting settlement offers for further negotiation or convening settlement conferences to explore additional settlement options. *Sixth*, when allocating arbitration costs, considering rejected settlement offers relative to the final decision, as well as any unreasonable refusal to permit a mediation window or other pre-arbitration procedures outlined in the contract, such as negotiation or mediation.[188]

However, given the above principles dominating the role of arbitrators in the settlement process, the report and its supplementary rules set the following conditions for taking these initiatives: (a) their use should not result in a successful challenge of the arbitrator or jeopardize the enforceability of the final award,[189] (b) mandatory provisions shall take precedence if there is a conflict between any of these initiatives and the mandatory provisions of the applicable law,[190] (c) the implementation of these initiatives should align with and support the objectives of the arbitral rules governing the dispute,[191] (d) the use of these initiatives shall not establish any ground for disqualifying the arbitrator or challenging the award,[192] (e) nothing said or communicated during the settlement discussions shall affect the arbitral award unless it has already been formally presented in the arbitration,[193] (f) the arbitrator shall refrain from caucusing or obtaining information through ex parte communications during the

186. CEDR Rules for Settlement Facilitation, 2009. For a critical discussion of the rules, *see* Masood, 2010.
187. CEDR Report on Settlement in ICA, 2009, section 2(1). According to section 3, these rules may be applied through mechanisms such as contractual agreement, incorporation into the existing rules of arbitral institutions, or the adoption of other procedural alternatives.
188. CEDR Report on Settlement in ICA, 2009, section 4; CEDR Rules for Settlement Facilitation, 2009, Articles 4-6; Stipanowich, 2021a, pp. 331-333; Stipanowich & Ulrich, 2014b, pp. 14-15; Berger & Jensen, 2017, pp. 895, 908, 911, 916; Berger, 2018b, pp. 510-513; Kun, 2011b, pp. 554-555; Nigmatullina, 2018, p. 219.
189. CEDR Report on Settlement in ICA, 2009, section 2(7)(2); CEDR Rules for Settlement Facilitation, 2009, Article 3(1).
190. CEDR Rules for Settlement Facilitation, 2009, Article 2(2).
191. CEDR Rules for Settlement Facilitation, 2009, Article 2(3).
192. CEDR Rules for Settlement Facilitation, 2009, Article 3(3).
193. CEDR Rules for Settlement Facilitation, 2009, Article 3(4)-(5).

settlement negotiations,[194] and (g) if, after engaging in unsuccessful settlement attempts, the arbitrator has doubts about their impartiality or independence in the resumed arbitration, they should resign.[195]

Despite the aversion of the CEDR commission to hybrid procedures[196] and recognizing that such procedures are accepted in some jurisdictions and that business parties may be willing to accept the associated risks,[197] the final report recommended the following safeguards for arbitrators who engage in caucusing with the parties, typically within hybrid processes. *First*, parties should grant written consent to the hybrid process before mediation commences. *Second*, this consent should explicitly allow the arbitrator to caucus with the parties and resume their adjudicative role following the mediation. *Third*, the consent should include an agreement about the treatment of information disclosed to the arbitrator during mediation. *Fourth*, the consent should encompass a waiver of any right to challenge the arbitrator or the award solely on the grounds that the arbitrator had previously mediated the dispute. *Fifth*, if the arbitrator has doubts about their impartiality or independence in the resumed arbitration after engaging in an unsuccessful mediation, they should resign. *Sixth*, if the parties seek to enhance protection against the risks associated with caucusing, they may agree to implement a safeguard requiring renewed consent following the mediation phase before allowing the arbitrator to resume their adjudicative role.[198]

Undeniably, unlike other initiatives, including that of the CPR, the CEDR commission successfully presented a wide range of measures arbitrators can take to facilitate settlements during arbitration. While some steps are indirect and can only set the stage for settlements, others are more liberal and include direct and assertive[199] participation in the settlement negotiations. In addition, compared to other efforts to address concerns related to ex parte communications and exposure to confidential information, the CEDR report offers a more comprehensive discussion of these issues. Nonetheless, three principal difficulties exist with the outcome of the CEDR commission. *First*, the CEDR report and its supplementary rules stipulate that the arbitrator's settlement initiatives must comply with the mandatory provisions of applicable law and, seemingly, with the arbitral rules governing the dispute, without providing further guidance on the implications of this requirement. As previously discussed regarding the UNCITRAL Notes on Arbitration, this gap raises questions about whether implied

194. CEDR Report on Settlement in ICA, 2009, section 2(4)(3); CEDR Rules for Settlement Facilitation, 2009, Article 5(2); Berger, 2018b, pp. 512-513; Sussman, 2010a, p. 386; Nigmatullina, 2018, p. 192.
195. CEDR Report on Settlement in ICA, 2009, section 4(3); CEDR Rules for Settlement Facilitation, 2009, Article 7.
196. According to the commission, hybrid procedures raise potential challenges to the arbitration's outcome, the qualifications of arbitrators to resume their adjudicative role after failed settlement discussions, and the parties' willingness to negotiate openly and frankly knowing that the arbitrator may decide the dispute if no settlement is reached. *See* CEDR Safeguards for Caucusing, 2009, Articles 4-5.
197. CEDR Safeguards for Caucusing, 2009, Articles 7-8.
198. CEDR Safeguards for Caucusing, 2009, Article 7(1)-(6); Stipanowich, 2021a, pp. 333-334; Aragaki, 2021, p. 48; Kun, 2011b, p. 553; Nigmatullina, 2018, pp. 170-171.
199. Stipanowich & Ulrich, 2014b, p. 8; Stipanowich, 2021a, p. 333.

permission or the absence of prohibition in the applicable law or governing rules concerning the arbitrator's dual role is sufficient to justify its utilization. Furthermore, by adopting a cautious approach that automatically subordinates these initiatives to the arbitration rules governing the dispute, the commission missed an opportunity to thoroughly explore and provide recommendations on the relationship between party autonomy—recognized as the cornerstone principle in ICA—and procedural limitations embedded in arbitral rules or codes of conduct that govern the arbitral process. This contrasts with the in-depth discussions on this matter that preceded the introduction of the former version of the Model Law on ICM.[200] *Second*, despite proposing safeguards for arbitrators engaging in caucusing, the CEDR report adopted a remarkably hesitant stance on hybrid procedures, refrained from presenting or discussing the diverse options for accommodating arbitration within their framework, and expressly advised end-users to avoid them. Given the multiple safeguards suggested by the commission for caucusing, greater efforts could have been made to enhance the accessibility of hybrid procedures for users. These efforts are particularly important given the commission's mandate to provide tools that may be utilized by ICA users worldwide, including in jurisdictions that permit hybrid procedures or are open to considering their use under appropriate guidance. *Third*, according to the CEDR report and its supplementary rules, arbitrators are permitted to provide evaluative views about the disputed issues without the parties' prior consent.[201] As discussed below in the context of the Prague Rules, this arrangement seems to undermine party autonomy. Like any other form of direct involvement in settlement negotiations, case evaluation should, by default, require the parties' prior consent to preserve the foundational principle of party autonomy in arbitration.

6.3.3.3 The Prague Rules

Further efforts to provide practical guidance on the arbitrator's role as a settlement facilitator in ICA were undertaken as part of a broader initiative to enhance arbitration efficiency by encouraging arbitrators to adopt a more active role as procedural managers.[202] This initiative, led by a working group of prominent arbitration practitioners from approximately 30 jurisdictions—primarily civil law countries in Continental Europe, Latin America, and Asia—examined procedural traditions in ICA. Drawing on these findings, the 2018 Prague Rules were introduced.[203] These soft law guidelines, developed to address concerns about the Americanization of ICA and the traditionally passive approach of arbitrators within its framework,[204] were primarily influenced by

200. *See* the discussion in section 6.3.2.5 above.
201. According to the rules, this is the default arrangement, and if the parties wish to establish a different approach, they must formalize it in a written agreement. *See* CEDR Rules for Settlement Facilitation, 2009, Article 5(1).
202. Prague Rules, 2018, p. 3.
203. Prague Rules, 2018, p. 2; Panov & Krapoutski, 2018, p. 42; Born, 2021, §1.04[D][4].
204. Blackaby et al., 2022, §6.106; Rombach & Shalbanava, 2019, p. 54; *Prague Rules on taking of evidence to launch in December 2018*, 2018; Stipanowich, 2023, p. 693.

German and Chinese legal traditions.[205] The rules empower arbitrators to proactively manage each aspect of the arbitral proceedings, including the authority to express evaluative views on various aspects of the dispute, encourage amicable outcomes through direct involvement in the settlement negotiations, and, subject to the parties' consent, through mediation.[206] As stipulated by the rules, the tribunal may express its perspectives on the parties' positions during the case management conference or at any point in the proceedings by addressing factual and legal issues, the relief requested, the burden of proof required, and the significance and pertinence of the evidence presented.[207] These initial evaluations do not require the parties' consent[208] and cannot furnish any grounds for disqualifying the tribunal or challenging its impartiality or independence.[209] Moreover, the rules expressly empower the tribunal to take an active and direct role in the settlement efforts:

> (1) Unless one of the parties objects, the arbitral tribunal may assist the parties in reaching an amicable settlement of the dispute at any stage of the arbitration.
> (2) Upon the prior written consent of all parties, any member of the arbitral tribunal may also act as a mediator to assist in the amicable settlement of the case.
> (3) If the mediation does not result in a settlement within an agreed period of time, the member of the arbitral tribunal who has acted as mediator: (a) may continue to act as an arbitrator in the arbitration proceedings after obtaining written consent from all parties at the end of the mediation; or (b) shall terminate his/her mandate in accordance with the applicable arbitration rules if such written consent is not obtained.[210]

As noted, the tribunal's general authority to assist the parties in settlement negotiations, akin to the provisions of the German Arbitration Act and the DIS Arbitration Rules,[211] does not require the parties' consent by default.[212] However, mediating the dispute requires prior written consent from all parties, and following a failed mediation, an identical renewed consent is necessary for the tribunal to resume its arbitral role.[213] At the same time, unlike the tribunal's expression of preliminary views, which enjoys absolute protection from challenge and disqualification under the

205. Stipanowich & Mironi, 2021, p. 30; Stipanowich, 2021a, p. 274; Berger, 2019, pp. 308-309.
206. Prague Rules, 2018, Articles 2 & 9; Lew, 2020, pp. 180-181; Sussman & Berger, 2021a, p. 27; Berger, 2019, pp. 306-307; Stipanowich, 2021a, p. 336.
207. Prague Rules, 2018, Article 2(1) & 2(4).
208. According to the rules, the tribunal's discretion in their application is only subject to the principle of fair and equal treatment of the parties. *See* Prague Rules, 2018, Article 1(2) & 1(4).
209. Prague Rules, 2018, Article 2; Berger, 2019, pp. 307-308; Stipanowich, 2021a, p. 336; Lew, 2020, p. 181.
210. Prague Rules, 2018, Article 9. *See also* Sussman & Berger, 2021a, p. 27; Henriques, 2018, pp. 356, 360-361; Panov & Krapoutski, 2018, p. 45; Stipanowich, 2021a, pp. 336-337; Berger, 2019, pp. 308-309; Berger, 2018b, pp. 514-515; Lew, 2020, pp. 184-185; Ruckteschler & Wendelstein, 2021, p. 770.
211. Berger, 2019, p. 309.
212. According to the rules, this general authority can be excluded only following an objection of at least one party. *See* Prague Rules, 2018, Article 9(1); Lew, 2020, p. 184; Stipanowich, 2021a, pp. 337-338.
213. Ruckteschler & Wendelstein, 2021, p. 770; Lew, 2020, pp. 184-185; Stipanowich, 2021a, pp. 337-338; Berger, 2019, p. 308.

rules, the tribunal's direct engagement in the settlement process, including mediation, does not benefit from such protection. In this respect, the Prague Rules implement a more restrictive stance than the IBA Guidelines, which consider the parties' consent to the arbitrator's dual role as an effective waiver of their right to challenge.[214]

The Prague Rules should be praised for the highly assertive and proactive role they assign to the tribunal, which, alongside the authority to sanction the parties for unreasonable procedural conduct when deciding the arbitration costs,[215] may secure more efficient and cost-effective proceedings. By recognizing and promoting the role of arbitrators as settlement facilitators and mediators to a best-practice standard, the Prague Rules offer an innovative approach that surpasses many existing soft norms regulating the dual role of arbitrators.[216] However, compared to other initiatives, such as the CEDR, the Prague Rules are not detailed. Apart from specifying the issues on which preliminary views may be expressed, they do not provide guidance on how and when the tribunal may promote settlement or mediate the case.[217] Moreover, the rules exhibit several fundamental drawbacks. *First*, authorizing the tribunal to deliver preliminary evaluative views on various aspects of the dispute without prior party consent, while granting absolute protection from challenge, may discourage disputants—particularly those with legal backgrounds that disallow such methods or have little experience with their practice—from applying the rules, thereby hindering their global acceptance. A similar concern arises regarding the tribunal's general authority to facilitate amicable settlement of the dispute, which does not generally require prior party consent, except in the case of mediation. The absence of a consent requirement for direct tribunal involvement in settlement efforts may lead to enforcement challenges.[218] If the rules mandate consent for mediation, they should similarly require it for any direct tribunal involvement in settlement facilitation. *Second*, as with other rules and guidelines, the Prague Rules are silent on caucusing and the handling of confidential information disclosed to the tribunal during the settlement process. While the requirement for renewed consent following failed mediation partially addresses concerns about the tribunal's impartiality, it offers only a limited remedy. Confidential information may still be revealed during joint settlement meetings, which, under the rules, do not require renewed consent. This omission could deter parties from agreeing to mediation. Therefore, this requirement for renewed consent cannot preclude the need to introduce more comprehensive safeguards to address all concerns connected with the arbitrator's dual role. *Third*, the rules are ambiguous about whether all members of the tribunal can participate in mediation or only one member. Unlike general involvement in the settlement process for which "the arbitral tribunal may assist the parties,"[219] mediation is described as an activity that "any member of the arbitral tribunal" can conduct.[220] This ambiguity could jeopardize the outcome of the

214. Berger, 2019, p. 309; Ruckteschler & Wendelstein, 2021, p. 770.
215. Prague Rules, 2018, Article 11; Berger, 2019, p. 306.
216. Berger, 2019, p. 309.
217. Stipanowich, 2021a, p. 338.
218. Rombach & Shalbanava, 2019, pp. 55-56; Stipanowich, 2021a, p. 337; McIlwrath, 2018.
219. Prague Rules, 2018, Article 9(1).
220. Prague Rules, 2018, Article 9(2).

arbitration if multiple tribunal members participate in mediation.[221] It also constitutes a missed opportunity to provide clear guidance on how the involvement of select tribunal members in settlement efforts could balance the tribunal's duty to promote settlement with the need to mitigate risks associated with this role.[222]

6.3.3.4 *The International Task Force on Mixed Mode Dispute Resolution*

Another significant effort, although not yet completed, in suggesting guidelines for the arbitrator's role as a settlement facilitator is that of the International Task Force on Mixed Mode Dispute Resolution, a collaborative initiative involving the IMI, the CCA, and the Straus Institute.[223] Organized into seven working groups comprising over 60 scholars, arbitrators, mediators, and experienced lawyers worldwide,[224] the Task Force has examined the interactions between different dispute resolution methods, including arbitration and mediation, to provide professional guidance on their concurrent, sequential, or combined use.[225] In addition to academic discussions on these mixed-mode scenarios from diverse cultural and legal perspectives,[226] the Task Force's final work is anticipated to propose practical guidelines for their implementation, which will target business users, practitioners, and dispute resolution professionals.[227] Working Group 5 of the Task Force has examined and elaborated on scenarios involving different dispute resolution procedures conducted by the same neutral. However, the guidelines in their regard have not yet been announced.[228]

Nevertheless, based on recent publications of the Task Force, the current working draft of the guidelines relating to these scenarios seems to include the following key elements. *First*, the decision to employ neutrals with dual roles or allow the direct engagement of arbitrators in the settlement process should result from a cautious and informed agreement between all parties. *Second*, given the diversity of expectations regarding these roles stemming from different legal cultures and traditions, parties to cross-border business disputes should coordinate expectations regarding their utilization. *Third*, neutrals may shift between dual roles only when the parties are confident of their fitness and qualifications for both roles. Additionally, given the arbitrator's duty to maintain impartiality and independence, which may be undermined following mediating the same dispute, parties should consider limiting the

221. Stipanowich, 2021a, pp. 337-338. On the other hand, *see* Lew, 2020, p. 184, holding that under the rules either one or all members of the tribunal may mediate the case.
222. *See* the recommendations regarding this outline in section 7.4.5.
223. *Mixed Mode Task Force: About*, n.d.; Stipanowich & Fraser, 2017, pp. 844-846; Stipanowich, 2021a, pp. 274-275. For further discussion about the task force and its various missions, *see* Mixed Mode Task Force, 2016; Lack, 2021.
224. Stipanowich & Fraser, 2017, p. 845; Lack, 2021, p. 11; Nigmatullina, 2019, p. 21.
225. Mixed Mode Task Force, 2016; Lack, 2021, p. 11; *Mixed Mode Task Force: About*, n.d.; Nigmatullina, 2019, p. 20; Stipanowich & Fraser, 2017, p. 846.
226. Lack, 2021, p. 11. For the full list of articles published by the task force, *see Mixed Mode Task Force: About*, n.d.
227. *Mixed Mode Task Force: About*, n.d.; Nigmatullina, 2019, p. 21.
228. Stipanowich & Mironi, 2021, pp. 30-31, stating that the Practice Guidelines are "now in working-draft stage."

arbitrator's mandate when reverting to arbitration after a failed mediation, as customary in MEDALOA and similar alternatives, restraining the arbitrator's discretion when deciding the dispute.[229] *Fourth*, any agreement about the dual role, whether ex ante or ad hoc, should be integrated into a written contract that clearly demarcates between the arbitration and mediation phases, includes a precise description of how and when the neutral may shift between the roles, and states whether they are authorized to caucus with the parties, engage in case evaluation, and offer settlement proposals. As part of this agreement, parties should waive their right to challenge the award or disqualify the neutral following their engagement in settlement discussions, ex parte communication, case evaluation, or after exposure to confidential information. *Fifth*, the possibility of avoiding private caucuses should be considered when the neutral is allowed to arbitrate the dispute following failed attempts to settle. However, if the parties agree to caucusing, they should also agree on various questions, including whether the arbitral award should depend solely on the formal recorded or consider information received during ex parte communications, whether, following failed mediation, the neutral should disclose to the parties any confidential information revealed in its course, whether following failed negotiations the parties should grant separate written consent regarding the continued service of the neutral to guarantee that they can opt out of the process at that stage, and whether in these circumstances they should permit the neutral to recuse from the resumed arbitral role. *Sixth*, when the tribunal includes more than one arbitrator, parties may consider allowing only the panel chair to engage in the settlement efforts or agree on engaging the two wing arbitrators in the role.[230]

Since the guidelines relating to the arbitrator's dual role have not yet been declared, it would be unrealistic to stimulate a comprehensive discussion about them. However, when judging according to the aforementioned key elements of their draft, it appears that the guidelines are expected to grant a more comprehensive regulation of the dual role than previous initiatives in the matter. Moreover, the guidelines emphasize party autonomy and grant much freedom to the parties in designing the proceedings according to their interests and wishes. However, the initial draft does not include guidance about the manner and timing of settlement facilitation or enforcement considerations, which in certain jurisdictions may become crucial for awards resulting from facilitated or mediated settlements. In the interest of harmonization, it would be prudent to establish specific mandatory safeguards for the dual role that are not subject to party negotiation, as the current draft potentially allows. That said, other published articles and documents from the Task Force address methods employed by arbitrators to facilitate settlements[231] and the impact of enforceability on the design of dispute resolution processes.[232] This suggests that Working Group 5 is likely to address these important issues in the final, detailed version of the guidelines.

229. *See* the discussion in section 2.4.1 regarding different alternatives to limit the arbitrator's mandate when deciding the dispute.
230. Stipanowich & Mironi, 2021, pp. 31-32; Stipanowich, 2021a, pp. 341-361.
231. Sussman & Berger, 2021a.
232. Paisley & Player, 2021.

6.3.4 Initiatives by Leading Practitioners and Scholars

Being remarkably regulated by its professional community,[233] the legal literature of international arbitration is filled with attempts by leading practitioners and scholars to advocate for and sometimes challenge the role of arbitrators as settlement facilitators. These endeavors often involve proposing ad hoc rules and safeguards to address procedural and ethical challenges that may arise during implementation.[234] Due to practical limitations, this section cannot cover all of these initiatives,[235] which frequently present pragmatic attitudes toward the dual role while seeking to reconcile the differing approaches of legal cultures and backgrounds.[236] Instead, this section focuses on a few pioneering initiatives by practitioners and scholars that, upon presentation, diverged from the prevailing approaches taken by their home jurisdictions regarding the arbitrator's role as a settlement facilitator. This departure may be explained by the influence of harmonization trends in ICA, including those related to the arbitrator's dual role, on members of its global community from various legal traditions.

One of the first initiatives intended to encourage the arbitrator's role as a settlement facilitator in ICA was presented by Prof. Harold Abramson, a leading American mediator and arbitrator. In 1999, Prof. Abramson introduced the Protocols for International Arbitrators Who Dare to Settle Cases,[237] which demonstrated a highly innovative approach when the academic literature and U.S. legal practice hesitated about arbitrators' role in the settlement process.[238] Along with detailing the benefits arising from the dual role of the arbitrator, the protocols suggested the following

233. Bantekas, 2015, p. 66; Kaufmann-Kohler, 2010, p. 295; Ali, 2021, p. 14; Bermann, 2015, p. 76.
234. Ali, 2021, p. 14; Kaufmann-Kohler, 2010, p. 295; Jemielniak, 2014, p. 333; Kaufmann-Kohler, 2003, p. 1325; Vilaça, 2016, pp. 502-503; Helmer, 2003, p. 60; Lynch, 2003, pp. 96-100; Jemielniak, 2017, p. 170.
235. Prominent examples of such initiatives include: Stipanowich, 2021a (one of the main scholars behind the International Task Force on Mixed Mode Dispute Resolution, suggesting practical solutions and common cross-border ground for neutrals fulfilling dual roles in resolving international commercial disputes, while considering the influence of diverse legal cultures and traditions on this role and previous efforts to regulate its practice); Kaufmann-Kohler, 2009, pp. 204-205 (proposing preliminary guidelines for the evolving transnational standard regarding the arbitrator's role as a settlement facilitator, which include the following safeguards: informed consent of the parties to the process, refraining from caucusing, refraining from facilitating settlements in disputes involving strong public interests, and resignation of the arbitrator following failed settlement efforts if resuming the arbitral role may affect their impartiality); Nigmatullina, 2019 (proposing substantial solutions to enhance the use of hybrid procedures combining arbitration and mediation, including adopting supportive legislation, developing international guidelines for their implementation, increasing the involvement of dispute resolution institutions in promoting their use, and improving training for professionals engaged with hybrid procedures); Berger, 2018b, pp. 509-514 (suggesting various initiatives for the arbitrator's proactive role in settlement, with a focus on ensuring the parties' informed and uncoerced consent); Berger & Jensen, 2017, pp. 906-916 (proposing various tools for arbitrators seeking to facilitate settlements in their cases, regardless of their cultural background).
236. Berger & Jensen, 2017, p. 916; Berger, 2018b, p. 516; Jemielniak, 2017, p. 167; Nariman, 2000, p. 267; Craig et al., 2000, §23.04; Kaufmann-Kohler, 2003, p. 1325; Rau, 2005, p. 450; Berger, 2019, p. 304.
237. Abramson, 1999.
238. Blankley, 2011, p. 337; Donahey, 1995, pp. 76-77; Ehle, 2010, p. 79; Stipanowich, 2021a, p. 302; Favalli & Hasenclever, 2008, p. 2.

safeguards for its fulfillment within international proceedings. *First*, neutrals serving as settlers and arbitrators should be trained in both roles' techniques, norms, and ethics. *Second*, the arbitrator should take no settlement initiatives without the parties' consent. *Third*, neutrals facilitating settlements should respect the principle of party autonomy and refrain from coercive conduct while attempting to settle the case. *Fourth*, clients with settlement authority should actively participate in the settlement negotiations to improve the settlement chances. *Fifth*, all communications during the settlement phase, including statements and documents, should be confidential and not influence the arbitral award. *Sixth*, neutrals should refrain from expressing evaluative opinions during the settlement negotiations. *Seventh*, neutrals should refrain from caucusing unless the parties agree otherwise. *Eighth*, parties should waive later objections to the neutral or the award merely based on the neutral's engagement in the settlement process.[239] Indeed, some of the criticisms raised earlier regarding other rules and guidelines are equally applicable to these protocols. For example, the protocols fail to specify the form in which the parties' consent should be provided, including whether it must be in writing or whether renewed consent is required after unsuccessful settlement negotiations. Furthermore, despite emphasizing party autonomy, the protocols do not permit parties to opt out of provisions that restrict arbitrators from expressing evaluative opinions or the disregard rule concerning confidential information disclosed during the settlement phase. Additionally, although the protocols address international arbitration, they remain silent on enforcement considerations for facilitated awards, which can be critical in cross-border contexts. Nevertheless, the protocols should be commended for their innovative approach, which diverged from the prevailing U.S. practice of the time regarding the arbitrator's role as a settlement facilitator.

Other initiatives to mention are those of Edna Sussman and John Blankenship. These leading international arbitrators and mediators from the US advocated hybrid procedures combining arbitration with mediation to settle international commercial disputes[240] and using ex parte communications[241] despite skepticism among most U.S. practitioners and scholars about hybrid procedures[242] and ex parte communications of the arbitrator with the parties.[243] To encourage the use of hybrid procedures within international arbitration, Blankenship suggested implementing an "adoptive ADR" attitude, which emphasizes party autonomy and calls practitioners to abandon categorical thinking and insistence on existing and recognized procedures in favor of creative thinking that is only bound to the parties' needs and interests, and therefore welcomes "adaptable, combinable, reversible and even discardable" methods to settle commercial disputes.[244] Similarly, Sussman praised hybrid procedures for offering

239. Abramson, 1999, pp. 7-15.
240. Blankenship, 2006; Sussman, 2009a; Sussman, 2010a.
241. Sussman, 2013, pp. 10-11; Blankenship, 2006, p. 35.
242. Ehle, 2010, p. 79; Favalli & Hasenclever, 2008, p. 6; Donahey, 1995, pp. 76-77; Stipanowich, 2021a, pp. 299, 302; Lemley, 2004, pp. 307-309.
243. Pappas, 2015, pp. 177-178; Stipanowich, 2021a, p. 302; Deason, 2013, pp. 228-229; Blankley, 2011, pp. 332-337; De Vera, 2004, pp. 192-194; Donahey, 1995, pp. 76-77.
244. Blankenship, 2006, pp. 38-41.

reduced costs, increased efficiency, and enhanced chances to resolve disputes in a "win-win" manner.[245] Thus, Sussman suggested the following solutions aimed at creating a more effective process and reducing the tension between the adjudicative and mediative functions of the neutral: (a) ensuring party self-determination, mutual understanding about the arbitrator's dual role, and informed consent of the parties to the process to overcome later challenges to the arbitral award;[246] (b) selecting the right neutral who is trained and skilled in both processes;[247] (c) when parties agree to allow caucusing, considering whether only part of the tribunal should engage in the settlement negotiations and whether following failed efforts to settle the arbitrator should disclose classified information received ex parte and whether the parties are permitted to opt out of the process;[248] and (d) adopting procedural solutions to secure enforcement under the New York Convention, for example by appointing the neutral as an arbitrator before mediation is commenced.[249]

Initiatives that deviate from the legal traditions of their promoters are not exclusive to Western jurisdictions. Weixia Gu, a Chinese arbitrator and professor of private international law, critiqued the dichotomy observed in China between arbitration proceedings under leading institutions that adopt Western standards to attract international users and those conducted by domestic institutes, which prioritize efficiency over due process standards through traditional "Chinese-styled arb-med" practices.[250] Prof. Gu called for reforms to China's domestic arb-med practices, advocating the adoption of contemporary procedures and regulations that "comply with international due process standards."[251] Prof. Fan Kun, a prominent international scholar and arbitrator from China, echoed these sentiments, particularly following the *Gao Haiyan* case,[252] and suggested rethinking the use of certain initiatives (e.g., caucusing, expressing opinions on the merits, and presenting settlement proposals to parties) in a way that may jeopardize arbitration outcomes, although these initiatives are widely accepted in China.[253]

6.4 CONCLUSIONS

The evolving trend recognizing the arbitrator's role as a settlement facilitator is apparent at the domestic and transnational levels. In addition to the domestic trends highlighted in the previous chapter, which demonstrate the growing acceptance of this role in jurisdictions with different legal backgrounds while blurring traditional binary divisions associated with its practice and legal framework, various empirical data and

245. Sussman, 2009a, p. 73.
246. Sussman, 2009a, p. 73; Sussman, 2010a, p. 384.
247. Sussman, 2010a, pp. 390-391; Sussman, 2009a, p. 73.
248. Sussman, 2010a, pp. 384-385; Sussman, 2009a, p. 71.
249. Sussman, 2010a, pp. 394-395.
250. Gu, 2019, pp. 142, 169-170. According to the author, the vast majority of proceedings in China involve neither foreign parties nor foreign subject matters and are therefore conducted within domestic institutions.
251. Gu, 2019, p. 169.
252. *See* the discussion in section 5.2.2.1.
253. Kun, 2011b, pp. 552-555.

past codification initiatives discussed in this chapter further affirm the transnational nature of this harmonization trend. Recent surveys and empirical studies have confirmed that ICA users worldwide increasingly prefer more flexible arbitral processes, prioritizing amicable resolutions of their cross-border disputes. These preferences are driven by pragmatic approaches emphasizing efficiency, the preservation of business relations, party autonomy, and the contractual freedom inherent in the arbitral process. Consequently, a discernible demand exists for international arbitrators with settlement facilitation skills since parties are increasingly willing to employ them in standalone proceedings and hybrid processes that incorporate arbitration, mediation, and caucusing. As part of this clear trend, over the past two decades, various stakeholders in ICA have introduced different initiatives to enhance the harmonization of the arbitrator's dual role among ICA users worldwide. These initiatives include suggestions for rules, guidelines, and "best practices" concerning this role. Despite variations in their approaches and levels of detail, these initiatives consistently emphasize the consensual nature of arbitration and the parties' freedom to tailor the process to suit their dispute. This focus marks a shift from traditional views of the arbitral process and the arbitrator's duties, prioritizing adaptability and customization over strict adherence to established norms.

Given these notable developments regarding the acceptance of the arbitrator's dual role in ICA and its current supportive transnational legal framework, it can be concluded that subject to express consent, appropriate safeguards, and enforcement considerations, parties to ICA processes can expand the arbitrator's mandate to include the role of a settlement facilitator to the extent and manner that aligns with their interests and needs.[254] Consequently, today:

> The question is not *whether* arbitrators should or should not facilitate settlement from a conceptual point of view. It is *how* they can best assist the parties to resolve their dispute: either by rendering a final award or assisting them in achieving a negotiated settlement if and to the extent that they so wish. Hence, techniques to facilitate settlement of the dispute should belong to the arsenal of every international arbitrator.[255]

To ensure access to such techniques and practices, promote their harmonization, and safeguard the admissibility and enforceability of their outcome, an undeniable need exists to develop and codify further normative instruments.[256] Given that the

254. Berger, 2018b, p. 516; Marzolini, 2016, p. 117; Karton, 2013, pp. 106-107; Blankenship, 2006, pp. 39-40; Blankley, 2011, p. 329; Plant, 2000, p. 146; Berger & Jensen, 2017, p. 904.
255. Berger & Jensen, 2017, pp. 916-917. *See also* Baysal & Cevik, 2021; Nariman, 2000, p. 267, holding that "an arbitrator, is an arbitrator, is an arbitrator, whose function it is, not merely to adjudicate the dispute, but also to help resolve it amicably with the co-operation of the parties. ... 'Arbitration' must never be considered as excluding from its purview the settlement of a dispute before the arbitrator because this is of the essence of *the spirit* of arbitration."
256. Stipanowich, 2021a, p. 339; Sussman & Berger, 2021b, pp. 37-38; Stipanowich & Mironi, 2021, pp. 30-31; Guo, 2020, p. 224; Kaufmann-Kohler, 2009, pp. 204-205; Stipanowich & Ulrich, 2014b, pp. 29-31; Nigmatullina, 2019, p. 45; Kaufmann-Kohler, 2010, pp. 295-297; Lüth & Wagner, 2012, p. 416.

transnational legal regime of ICA has increasingly been shaped by its global community, this responsibility should significantly rely on stakeholders from this community.[257] Indeed, as demonstrated in this chapter, previous initiatives promoted over the last two decades by these stakeholders have significantly raised awareness among ICA users regarding the arbitrator's role as a settlement facilitator, including in hybrid processes involving arbitration, mediation, and caucusing, thus contributing to its transnational standardization. Furthermore, reliance on soft norms in these efforts appears highly satisfactory to those users, as supported by the empirical data presented in this chapter. This satisfaction stems from the ability of soft norms to introduce and codify innovative practices, such as the arbitrator's dual role, while serving as a cornerstone of the transnational legal regime of ICA, for reasons elaborated in this chapter. Consequently, soft norms currently play a central role in harmonizing global perspectives on the arbitrator's role.

Despite significant strides toward transnational standardization, most prior attempts to harmonize the arbitrator's dual role have fallen short of providing a comprehensive set of available initiatives for arbitrators to facilitate settlements in ICA, as detailed in Chapter 2. Furthermore, these efforts have often lacked comprehensive guidance on the various aspects of the dual role and corresponding safeguards. Two fundamental factors have constrained these previous harmonization efforts. *First*, they have been largely influenced by the legal culture of their promoters, with few initiatives catering to users of ICA across diverse legal cultures. *Second*, these initiatives, primarily driven by non-governmental or private actors within the global arbitration community and reliant solely on soft norms, have tended to focus on internal aspects of the arbitral process. They have paid insufficient attention to external measures that these actors and other stakeholders in ICA could adopt to foster broader acceptance of the arbitrator's dual role among users from different legal cultures and to further harmonize its practice and normative framework globally.

Building on the comparative analysis presented in Chapters 5 and 6—and in light of the gaps identified in previous harmonization efforts, as well as the findings discussed throughout this and earlier chapters—the next part of the book introduces a comprehensive set of normative recommendations aimed at enhancing the harmonization of the arbitrator's role as a settlement facilitator in ICA. Chapter 7 presents internal solutions within the arbitral process that ICA users can implement under the current legal framework to ensure this role aligns with fundamental principles of arbitration and mitigates enforcement risks arising from its use. Chapter 8 then proposes external solutions that integrate with ICA's multifaceted legal regime, emphasizing the responsibilities of various stakeholders—including arbitral institutions, lawmakers, and practitioners—in advancing the harmonization of this role across diverse legal traditions and perspectives.

257. Draetta, 2015, p. 328; Bermann, 2015, p. 76, arguing that "we must recognize that in virtually ... the direction in which international arbitration moves and the pace at which it does so is also largely in the hands of its practitioners themselves."

Part IV Ways to Enhance the Harmonization of the Arbitrator's Role as a Settlement Facilitator in ICA

CHAPTER 7
Internal Solutions to the Arbitral Process

7.1 INTRODUCTION

Despite the clear trend acknowledging the arbitrator's role as a settlement facilitator in ICA, which, as demonstrated in previous chapters, has been accompanied by various harmonization efforts regarding its practice and legal framework at the domestic and transnational levels, the existing manifold legal regime of ICA—comprising treaties, domestic arbitration laws, and multiple soft norms—still presents divergent approaches regarding different aspects of this role. These unaligned approaches—often reflecting concerns of the legal tradition about the adherence of different components of this role to fundamental principles of arbitration and the potential violation of parties' autonomy and due process rights—constitute barriers to harmonization by influencing the attitudes of practitioners and users toward the arbitrator's dual role within ICA proceedings while impacting the recognition and enforcement of awards resulting from processes that endorsed it. These barriers, in turn, can further deter ICA parties from employing the arbitrator as a settlement facilitator.

Given that formal and authoritative changes in the multilayer legal regime of ICA, including those related to the arbitrator's role in settlement, often require extended timeframes and gradual socialization within its different normative levels,[1] and considering the growing acceptance of this role among parties to cross-border business relations—who, as supported by various empirical data presented throughout previous chapters, are increasingly willing to employ the arbitrator with this mandate due to practical considerations prioritizing flexibility, the preservation of business relations, and amicable outcomes—there is a need for pragmatic, voluntarily adopted solutions intended to enhance the implementation of this role within the current legal framework of ICA. These solutions should aim to mitigate the potential risks associated with the arbitrator's role as a settlement facilitator, thereby fostering its broader recognition

1. Kun, 2013b, p. 218; Alkoby, 2008, pp. 184-187.

among ICA practitioners and users from various legal backgrounds and contributing to its global harmonization.

This chapter concentrates on internal solutions within the arbitral process, primarily suggesting various safeguards that ICA parties can implement to enhance the regulation and safe utilization of the arbitrator's role as a settlement facilitator. Alongside mandatory party autonomy safeguards—intended to ensure that the parties' desire to employ the arbitrator in the dual role is respected and implemented only according to their agreement, without undermining their control over the process or depriving them of their basic right to self-determination—various due process safeguards are also suggested. These safeguards include mandatory ones, such as the possibility of opting out from the arbitral process under agreed terms following unsuccessful settlement efforts or continuing arbitration with the same arbitrator, subject to renewed consent of the parties and agreement about the handling of settlement-stage information. Voluntary due process safeguards are also suggested, such as limiting the arbitrator's mandate following futile settlement attempts and involving only a subset of the tribunal in the settlement process when it consists of several members.

In addition to their immediate applicability within the parties' agreement, these safeguards, together with the continuum of the arbitrator's settlement initiatives suggested in Chapter 2 and summarized in Appendix A, can form the basis for the formal regulation of this role, as proposed in the next chapter addressing external solutions to the arbitral process. Designed to provide maximum flexibility and adaptability regarding the components of the arbitrator's dual role and, to some extent, their application, these safeguards aim to address the needs and align with the expectations of users, practitioners, and stakeholders from various legal traditions, thereby enhancing the recognition of the role and contributing to its global harmonization. However, given the current diverse approaches among jurisdictions regarding certain aspects of the arbitrator's dual role, these safeguards cannot entirely eliminate the risks associated with its use. Ultimately, they strive to balance considerations of party autonomy and flexibility with the need to ensure procedural fairness and enforceability of the process outcome. This limitation is particularly pronounced when the arbitrator is directly involved in settlement negotiations or hybrid procedures combining arbitration and mediation.

7.2 ENFORCEMENT AS THE COMPASS FOR SETTLEMENT FACILITATION

When considering the arbitrator's role as a settlement facilitator in ICA, it is essential to emphasize that the arbitrator's prime duty is to render a final and enforceable decision on the controversies between the parties:

> Making certain the award is enforceable is one of the most central duties of the arbitral tribunal. If the arbitral tribunal wants to issue an enforceable award, the process has to meet certain quality standards. These minimum quality standards are, of course, procedural. They can be called due process requirements just like

> the minimum standards in ordinary court procedure. In the same way, they establish the minimum procedural safeguards necessary for someone to be deprived of his property or other rights. As such, they can be considered aspects of such elements as procedural fairness, opportunity to be heard, and equal treatment as well as access to justice.[2]

This primary duty of the arbitrator is based on foundational legal sources in international arbitration, including the New York and ICSID Conventions and the Model Law on ICA, which place recognition and enforcement of arbitral awards as their main concern.[3] In addition, the arbitrator's primary duty is explicitly anchored in various arbitration rules and guidelines, including those related to the arbitrator's role as a settlement facilitator, such as the UNCITRAL Notes on Arbitration, the CEDR Rules for Settlement Facilitation, and the ICC Arbitration Rules.[4] The importance of enforcement considerations for ICA users is also reflected in the 2015 and 2018 Queen Mary International Arbitration Surveys, where enforcement was ranked as the most valuable characteristic for users of this dispute-resolution mechanism.[5] Hence, the cornerstone of any harmonization effort regarding the arbitrator's role as a settlement facilitator is securing the enforceability of awards resulting from processes incorporating this role or, at the very least, mitigating the risks associated with enforceability.[6]

Based on previous conclusions drawn in this book, three underlying and cumulative principles should guide any effort to harmonize the arbitrator's dual role within the existing legal regime of ICA. *First*, since enforcement under the New York and ICSID Conventions is reserved for arbitral awards arising from "differences" between the parties, settlement efforts should only begin after the formal initiation of arbitration. Otherwise, enforceability risks may arise, as a settlement reached before the tribunal's constitution arguably eliminates the existence of a "difference" to submit to arbitration, potentially depriving the tribunal of jurisdiction.[7] Consequently, Med-Arb hybrid processes—in their literal sense—may be inadvisable as a mechanism for settlement facilitation by the arbitrator[8] unless (a) the legal framework governing the arbitration and the enforcement of its outcome explicitly permits settlement or

2. Kurkela & Turunen, 2010, pp. 1-2. *See also* Marzolini, 2016, p. 117; Stipanowich, 2021a, p. 344; Nigmatullina, 2018, p. 67; Berger & Jensen, 2016, p. 6; Kryvoi & Davydenko, 2015, p. 868; Lew, 2005, p. 425; CEDR Report on Settlement in ICA, 2009, section 2(4)(1); Horvath, 2001, pp. 135-136.
3. New York Convention, 1958, Article III; ICSID Convention, 1966, Article 54; Model Law on ICA, 2006, Article 35.
4. UNCITRAL Notes on Arbitration, 2023, Article 3(b); CEDR Rules for Settlement Facilitation, 2009, Article 3(1); ICC Arbitration Rules, 2021, Appendix IV, para. (h)(ii).
5. Queen Mary University of London and White & Case LLP, 2018, p. 7; Queen Mary University of London and White & Case LLP, 2015, p. 6.
6. Kaufmann-Kohler, 2009, p. 200; Marriott, 2005, p. 546; Nigmatullina, 2018, p. 183; CIArb Practice Guideline on the Use of Mediation in Arbitration, 2021, Article 8(3).
7. *See* the discussion in sections 3.6.3 & 4.4.2.3.
8. Ortolani, 2025, §21.5(f); Stipanowich, 2021a, p. 287; Kaster, 2018, p. 50; Nigmatullina, 2018, p. 41; Ross, 2013, p. 362; Nottage & Garnett, 2010, p. 35; Paisley & Player, 2021, p. 33; Chua, 2018, p. 13.

mediation processes to precede arbitration,[9] (b) the parties intend to rely on enforcement mechanisms other than the New York or ICSID Conventions (e.g., the Singapore Convention or the Hague Judgments Convention),[10] or (c) the parties wish to anchor their mediated settlement through contractual arrangements.[11]

Second, as demonstrated in Chapter 5, while a broad consensus exists among various jurisdictions regarding settlement initiatives falling within the "managerial role" of the arbitrator, gaps persist regarding other aspects of the dual role, including case evaluation, caucusing, and the treatment of confidential information disclosed during the settlement process.[12] Additionally, in some jurisdictions, the conditions or authority allowing the same neutral to engage in hybrid processes involving arbitration and mediation remain contentious.[13] Since attitudes toward these components may impact the enforceability of arbitral awards resulting from processes that endorse them, parties—guided by their counsel and, where applicable, the arbitrator—should carefully examine the legal stance regarding the role in the seat of arbitration and potential enforcement jurisdictions prior to any agreement about the arbitrator's dual role in a particular ICA process.[14] This examination is crucial for making an informed decision about the concrete design of the process to follow and, when faced with multiple jurisdictions for the seat and enforcement, for selecting the most appropriate jurisdictions to fulfill the role.[15] Similar considerations should be given to the applicable arbitration rules and guidelines, as these—irrespective of the legal attitudes in the seat or enforcement jurisdictions—may restrict the arbitrator from fulfilling the dual role or certain components thereof, such as caucusing or offering evaluative views on disputed issues, without providing the parties the flexibility to agree otherwise.[16]

Third, since challenges to the arbitral process may arise in the seat and the jurisdiction of enforcement due to violations of party autonomy and due process

9. Ross, 2013, pp. 362-363; Sussman, 2010a, pp. 386-387; ADRIC Med-Arb Rules, 2020, Introduction, Part II.
10. *See* the discussion in sections 3.6.1-3.6.2.
11. CIArb Practice Guideline on the Use of Mediation in Arbitration, 2021, Article 9(4).
12. Stipanowich, 2021a, pp. 347, 349, 352-354; Benzidi, 2017, pp. 21, 26; Stipanowich & Mironi, 2021, p. 30; Baysal & Cevik, 2021; Nigmatullina, 2018, p. 168; Stipanowich & Kaskell, 2001, pp. 30-32; Abramson, 1999, p. 7; CIArb Practice Guideline on the Use of Mediation in Arbitration, 2021, Article 8(1)-(3); Hopt & Steffek, 2013, p. 58.
13. However, according to the 2021 Aragaki Study that reviewed arbitration and mediation legislation in 195 jurisdictions worldwide, of 59 jurisdictions that regulate the use of the same neutral for Med-Arb, only 16 prohibit its use. Additionally, among the 31 jurisdictions that regulate the use of the same neutral for Arb-Med, only 3 prohibit its use and 6 impose conditions for allowing the arbitrator to resume their adjudicative role following a failed mediation. *See* Aragaki, 2021, pp. 40-41, 42-49; section 5.4.
14. Ross, 2013, p. 365.
15. Stipanowich, 2021a, pp. 341, 347; Nigmatullina, 2018, p. 168; Sussman, 2010a, pp. 386-387; Kun, 2011b, p. 553; Ross, 2013, pp. 362-363, 365; Bartel, 1991, p. 691; CIArb Practice Guideline on the Use of Mediation in Arbitration, 2021, Article 8(6).
16. *See*, for example, HKIAC Mediation Rules (discussed in section 5.2.2.2) and LMAA Mediation Rules (discussed in section 5.3.1.2), both of which implement indispensable arrangements prohibiting the mediator from serving as an arbitrator in the same dispute. Additionally, *see* CPR Code of Ethics for Arbitrators, 2005, Canon III(B), stipulating that even when arbitrators are authorized by the parties to act as settlement facilitators, they are prohibited from engaging in caucusing with the parties.

rights,[17] arbitral processes utilizing the arbitrator's dual role should implement safeguards to protect the parties' self-determination rights and ensure procedural fairness, thereby adhering to fundamental principles of arbitration.[18] While the first and second underlying principles are relatively easier to fulfill, realizing this third principle is more challenging[19] for the following reasons: (a) arguments concerning the violation of due process and party autonomy often pertain to the components of the dual role that have not yet achieved consensus across different jurisdictions and legal traditions, so they complicate efforts to address them uniformly; (b) as presented below, even when parties are willing to waive their right to challenge the award or disqualify the neutral following their engagement in the settlement process, uncertainties remain regarding the acceptance and effectiveness of such waivers due to differing attitudes among jurisdictions regarding the capability of ICA parties to waive their procedural rights, particularly those related to due process and equal treatment by the tribunal; (c) as demonstrated in Chapter 5, courts in jurisdictions where enforcement is sought may evaluate claims of violating party autonomy and due process rights based on public policy considerations[20] and deny enforcement on these grounds.[21] This approach is significant because, according to the New York Convention and the Model Law on ICA, enforcement may be denied at the court's discretion if it contradicts public policy, irrespective of any agreement between the parties concerning their due process rights.[22] This outcome contrasts with the common route outlined in the Convention and the Model Law, which permits the refusal of enforcement following a violation of the parties' procedural rights only if arguments are raised and evidence is presented by the interested party, often taking into account prior agreements made by the disputants on such matters.[23] Given these challenges, the internal solutions suggested in this

17. Nicholas & Partasides, 2007, pp. 39-40. The court's authority to refuse enforcement on the grounds of a violation of the parties' due process rights is rooted in the New York Convention, 1958, Introduction and Article V(1), as well as in the Model Law on ICA, 2006, Articles 18 & 36(1)(a).
18. Paisley & Player, 2021, pp. 35-36; Benzidi, 2017, p. 22; Stipanowich & Fraser, 2017, pp. 861-862; Kryvoi & Davydenko, 2015, pp. 856, 860; Jemielniak, 2014, pp. 319, 327; Kun, 2011b, p. 550; Kurkela & Turunen, 2010, pp. 1-2; Horvath, 2001, pp. 143-144; Mayer, 1986, p. 284; Cordero-Moss, 2012, p. 134; Berger & Jensen, 2017, p. 904.
19. Ali, 2021, p. 21; Paisley & Player, 2021, pp. 34-35; Nigmatullina, 2018, p. 59.
20. Benzidi, 2017, pp. 23-24; Bernardini, 2004, pp. 118-119. Additionally, *see* the discussion in section 5.2.2.1 regarding the *Gao Haiyan* case and its implications on due process and public policy considerations.
21. The authority to do so is anchored in the New York Convention, 1958, Article V(2)(b), and the Model Law on ICA, 2006, Article 36(1)(b)(ii). *See also* Paisley & Player, 2021, p. 36; Kryvoi & Davydenko, 2015, pp. 856, 860; Stipanowich & Fraser, 2017, pp. 861-862; Horvath, 2001, pp. 143-144; Ortolani, 2025, §21.5(a),(g); Cordero-Moss, 2012, p. 134, suggesting that since enforceability is constrained by national public policy considerations, "soft law instruments must refer to or comply with principles of the various legal systems, if the contract or arbitral award based on them is to be effective." Additionally, *see* the discussion in section 2.2.10 regarding various arbitration rules that authorize arbitrators to decline recording settlement agreements as consent awards due to public policy considerations.
22. New York Convention, 1958, Introduction and Article V(2)(b); Model Law on ICA, 2006, Article 36(1)(b)(ii).
23. New York Convention, 1958, Introduction and Article V(1); Model Law on ICA, 2006, Articles 18 & 36(1)(a). *See also* Paisley & Player, 2021, p. 36; Kryvoi & Davydenko, 2015, pp. 856, 860; Stipanowich & Fraser, 2017, pp. 861-862; Horvath, 2001, pp. 143-144.

chapter focus on safeguarding various aspects related to the arbitrator's role as a settlement facilitator. These safeguards aim to improve compliance with fundamental principles of arbitration, including the procedural fairness of the process, while mitigating the enforceability risks associated with its practice. Empirical data indicates that addressing these concerns is vital to alleviating reservations about the arbitrator's dual role and improving its acceptance among ICA users from diverse legal traditions and perspectives.[24]

7.3 PARTY AUTONOMY SAFEGUARDS

Given the consensual nature of arbitration, which grants the parties procedural and substantive freedom over the proceedings,[25] it is imperative that casting the arbitrator as a settlement facilitator should not infringe upon the parties' right to self-determination. Otherwise, the award and the arbitrator may face challenges for violating the principle of party autonomy.[26] In the context of assigning a dual-role arbitrator, this principle is generally secured through the following combined requirement: (a) the *express consent* of the parties concerning the arbitrator's dual role, which is deemed vital and indispensable since the parties constitute the optimal safeguard of the arbitral process,[27] and (b) an *explicit waiver of the right to challenge the arbitrator or the award* following the fulfillment of the role, which is needed to ensure that the parties' agreement to employ the arbitrator as a settlement facilitator is respected by the tribunal and the court.[28] These safeguards of the principle of party autonomy are discussed in the following sections.

7.3.1 Express Consent to the Arbitrator's Dual Role

Consent is the primary prerequisite in almost all arbitration rules and guidelines that acknowledge the arbitrator's role in promoting settlement and in most national laws granting the arbitrator this authority.[29] The notable exception is China's Arbitration

24. According to the data collected in the 2010 Condliffe and Zeleznikow Study (discussed in section 3.4), users of processes permitting the arbitrator's dual role are more concerned about aspects of procedural justice than efficiency. Therefore, the concept of justice, particularly in its procedural dimensions, shapes their preferences regarding such processes. *See* Condliffe & Zeleznikow, 2014, pp. 338-339. For additional discussion on the importance of ensuring procedural fairness in arbitral processes employing the dual role, *see* Stipanowich, 2021a, p. 339.
25. Kaufmann-Kohler, 2003, p. 1321; Nigmatullina, 2018, p. 166; Bernardini, 2004, pp. 114-115.
26. Ruckteschler & Wendelstein, 2021, p. 771; Nigmatullina, 2018, p. 166; Mayer, 2016, p. 3; Almoguera, 2010, p. 130; Marriott, 2005, p. 538; Stipanowich & Kaskell, 2001, pp. 24, 32; Bartel, 1991, pp. 689-691.
27. Abramson, 1999, p. 15; Stipanowich, 2021a, p. 341; Marriott, 2005, p. 544, holding that "the consent of the parties will clearly obviate many of the worries about an arbitrator's role in facilitating settlement and potentially reverting to the role of arbitrator."
28. Stipanowich, 2021a, p. 352; Baysal & Cevik, 2021; Nigmatullina, 2018, p. 181; Berger & Jensen, 2017, p. 913; Marzolini, 2016, p. 116.
29. In addition to the arbitration rules, guidelines, and domestic provisions discussed in Chapters 5 and 6, *see* CEDR Report on Settlement in ICA, 2009, Appendix 4, reviewing various provisions of domestic arbitration and mediation acts that condition this role in the parties' consent.

Law, which empowers the arbitrator to facilitate a settlement and conduct full mediation without the parties' consent.[30] However, as exemplified in Chapter 5, this arrangement does not align with the standards set by leading arbitration institutes in China hosting most ICA processes, which require clear consent from the parties for the arbitrator to assume the role.[31]

Some commentators hold that as long as the parties mutually agree to empower the arbitrator to act as a settlement facilitator, with neither party coerced into the particular procedure allowing the role, a formal or express agreement is not necessarily needed.[32] However, according to the prevailing approach, to repel enforcement challenges for alleged violation of party autonomy, parties should be able to demonstrate *express consent* regarding any involvement of the arbitrator in the settlement process that goes beyond the permitted initiatives under the arbitration rules or domestic laws.[33] Drawing on the collective experience with the requirement of consent, as demonstrated in Chapters 5 and 6 concerning various domestic arbitration laws and court decisions, as well as local and international arbitration rules and guidelines,[34] the parties' consent regarding the arbitrator's role as a settlement facilitator should encompass the following key features: (a) it should be *written, advance, and revocable*—anchored in written form before any involvement of the arbitrator in the settlement efforts, with parties retaining the right to withdraw their consent subject to agreed terms; (b) *detailed*, by specifying the permitted initiatives on the continuum of settlement facilitation, including general terms regarding their timing during the arbitral proceedings, as well as the mandatory and voluntary due process safeguards discussed below; and (c) *informed*, meaning it should be granted only after the parties have a clear understanding of the risks associated with the arbitrator's dual role. This section further explores these features of consent, but first examines whether consent is required for every available initiative of the arbitrator to facilitate a settlement.

7.3.1.1 Is Consent Always Needed?

Not every initiative of the arbitrator on the continuum of settlement facilitation requires direct engagement in its course or details. As exhibited in Chapter 2, several

30. Arbitration Law of the People's Republic of China, 1994, Article 51; Gu, 2021, p. 80; Gu, 2019, p. 140.
31. *See* the discussion in section 5.2.2.1. *See also* CIETAC Arbitration Rules, 2024, Article 47(1)-(3); BAC Arbitration Rules, 2022, Article 43(1); SCIA Arbitration Rules, 2022, Article 48(1)-(4).
32. Berger, 2003, p. 393; Koch & Schäfer, 1999, p. 171; Nigmatullina, 2018, p. 168.
33. Nigmatullina, 2018, p. 168; Benzidi, 2017, p. 19; Mayer, 2016, p. 3; Kun, 2011b, p. 551. *See*, for example, IBA Guidelines on Conflicts of Interest in International Arbitration, 2024, General Standard 4(d), relating explicitly to "expressed agreement" as a prerequisite for allowing the arbitrator's role as a settlement facilitator.
34. *See*, in particular, Hong Kong Arbitration Ordinance, 2011, Article 33(1)-(4); Singapore International Arbitration Act, 1994, Article 17(1) & (3); Singapore Arbitration Act, 2001, Article 63(1) & (3); Australia Commercial Arbitration Act, 2010, Part 5, section 27D; JAMS Comprehensive Arbitration Rules and Procedures, 2021, Rule 28(b); the Hong Kong court decisions in the *Gao Haiyan* case discussed in section 5.2.2.1; the U.S. court decisions discussed in section 5.3.1.1.

initiatives entail minimal or indirect participation by the arbitrator in the settlement process and are often regarded as integral to their duty to conduct the proceedings efficiently.[35] In contrast to direct involvement in settlement endeavors, indirect initiatives typically should not warrant successful challenges to the arbitrator or the award, especially when permitted by the ad hoc or institutional arbitration rules.[36] Consequently, the threshold for requiring consent should primarily be crossed when the arbitrator becomes directly engaged in the settlement efforts:

> The requirement of the parties' consent relates solely to concrete steps towards the settlement of the dispute which the arbitrators may consider taking during the proceedings. This would imply that, for instance, the simple question put by the arbitrators to the parties whether the parties have considered talking to each other with a view to exploring settlement opportunities, or the suggestion that the parties should consider such course of action, does not amount to such a concrete "step" and does therefore not require any prior consent by the parties.[37]

Considering the proposed guideline, the following initiatives—categorized in Chapter 2 as "indirect initiatives" aimed at only setting the stage for settlement—should not inherently require the parties' consent unless explicitly mandated by the governing law, arbitration rules, or stipulated by the parties: (a) managing the first organizational conference proactively, (b) asking the parties targeted questions on procedural and substantive issues related to the dispute, (c) raising abstract proposals to consider settlement, (d) bifurcating the arbitral process, and (e) initiating a mid-term arbitration review.[38] The same applies to offering to formalize the parties' settlement as a consent award or encouraging them to empower the tribunal to resolve the dispute as an *amiable compositeur*, although their implementation depends on the parties' consent, with deciding the case as an *amiable compositeur* also subject to recognition by the governing law or arbitration rules.[39] Nonetheless, given the divergent perspectives across jurisdictions and the requirement for the parties' cooperation or authorization under the governing law or arbitration rules, the following initiatives should be undertaken only with the parties' consent, despite not involving the arbitrator's direct participation in the settlement negotiations or its details: (a) the determination of preliminary issues, (b) providing early neutral evaluation of the case,

35. Sachs, 2020, p. 232; Carrara, 2019, p. 43; Marzolini, 2016, p. 112; Ehle, 2010, p. 85; Stipanowich & Ulrich, 2014b, p. 29; Kaufmann-Kohler, 2009, p. 197. Additionally, *see* the following arbitration rules imposing an obligation on the arbitrator to conduct the arbitration efficiently and cost-effectively: IBA Rules on Evidence in International Arbitration, 2020, Article 2; UNCITRAL Arbitration Rules, 2021, Article 17; ICC Arbitration Rules, 2021, Article 22; NAI Arbitration Rules, 2024, Article 25(3).
36. Berger & Jensen, 2016, p. 15; Gill, 2006, p. 158. Additionally, *see* the discussion in section 2.2.7 about various arbitration laws and rules granting discretion to the arbitrator in applying the appropriate procedures for the particular dispute when those are not agreed by the parties.
37. Marzolini, 2016, p. 103. *See also* Gill, 2006, p. 158; Plant, 2000, p. 145.
38. *See* the discussion in sections 2.2.1-2.2.4 & 2.2.7 about the recognition of these initiatives in various arbitration rules and guidelines. Additionally, *see* Gill, 2006, p. 158, holding that "there is no objection to the arbitrator seeking to encourage the parties to become involved in a settlement process nor to his taking steps within the procedural framework of the arbitration in an effort to ... reach agreement."
39. *See* the discussion in sections 2.2.9-2.2.10.

(c) designing mediation windows throughout the proceedings and (d) using sealed offers to allocate costs and legal fees.[40] A detailed and comprehensive reference regarding the necessity of parties' consent for each settlement facilitation initiative on the continuum is provided in Appendix A.

Although most of the aforementioned indirect initiatives do not inherently demand parties' consent, recent empirical data presented in Chapter 2 implies that arbitrators in ICA do not widely embrace them.[41] This reluctance to implement these legitimate managerial tools may stem from a misinterpretation of the general obligation to render an enforceable award as "an obligation to safeguard due process by making every effort to let the parties present their case in any way they want."[42] This attitude, described by most respondents of the 2015 Queen Mary International Arbitration Survey as the "due process paranoia" of arbitrators,[43] can result in increased costs and delays due to inefficient proceeding management while leading to missed opportunities for settlement in ICA, as evidenced by the empirical data presented earlier.[44] Therefore, arbitral institutes, arbitrators, and practitioners should recognize these indirect initiatives, emphasize their non-necessity for parties' consent, and promote their utilization in ICA since they can significantly contribute to amicable dispute resolution outcomes. Hence, the scale between the arbitrator's duty to safeguard parties' due process rights and the responsibility for efficient and cost-effective proceedings should not automatically tilt in favor of the former:

> An instinct to protect the parties' due process rights is, and should be, a vital part of any successful arbitrator's DNA. However, it is also important not to blindly follow this instinct in any given case. An over-emphasis on due process is the root cause for arbitrators' inhibitions to conduct streamlined proceedings when faced with delicate procedural requests from the parties, even in scenarios in which due process concerns are unjustified. Procedural management that is dominated by such inhibitions can prove detrimental to both the parties in the specific arbitration and the arbitration process as a whole.[45]

40. *See* the discussion in sections 2.2.3, 2.2.5-2.2.6 & 2.2.8. *See also* Stipanowich, 2021a, pp. 290, 301; Gu, 2019, p. 136; Love, 1997, pp. 940, 942; Stipanowich & Kaskell, 2001, pp. 30-32; Abramson, 1999, pp. 7, 10-11; Hopt & Steffek, 2013, p. 58; Berger & Jensen, 2017, p. 908. Additionally, *see* CEDR Rules for Settlement Facilitation, 2009, Article 5(3)(1), imposing a duty on the arbitrator to insert a mediation window only when requested by all parties; CEDR Report on Settlement in ICA, 2009, section 4(2)(6), clarifying that sealed offers should only be used following consent of all parties. On the other hand, *see* Stipanowich, 2021a, pp. 345-346, relating to the designing of mediation windows and allocation of the arbitration's costs to promote settlement as instruments that fall within the arbitral mandate.
41. *See* the discussion in section 2.2.
42. Berger & Jensen, 2016, p. 6. *See also* Rivkin, 2008, p. 380; Sussman & Berger, 2021b, p. 26; Harris, 2016, pp. 96-97; Howes & Stowell, 2020, p. 52; section 2.2.5.
43. Queen Mary University of London and White & Case LLP, 2015, p. 10; Berger & Jensen, 2016, p. 6.
44. *See* the discussion in section 2.2. Additionally, *see* Sussman & Berger, 2021a, p. 28; Stipanowich, 2021a, p. 345; Berger & Jensen, 2016, p. 6; Stipanowich & Ulrich, 2014a, pp. 445-451, 458-461.
45. Berger & Jensen, 2016, p. 4. For further discussion on the arbitrator's reluctance to facilitate settlements and the potential underling reasons for this hesitance, *see* the discussion in section 4.3.3.

7.3.1.2 Written, Advance, and Revocable Consent

Stipulating the arbitrator's dual role in written consent from all parties aligns with the prevailing opinion in the literature, which views written form as the appropriate means of implementing the requirement for express consent.[46] As demonstrated in previous chapters, this requirement is enshrined in several arbitration laws, rules, and guidelines regulating the arbitrator's role as a settlement facilitator, including the arbitration acts of Singapore and Hong Kong,[47] the CEDR Safeguards for Caucusing,[48] the JAMS Arbitration Rules,[49] and, to some extent, the Prague Rules.[50] Furthermore, the necessity for written consent finds support in the language of the New York Convention and the Model Law on ICA, which empower the court to decline recognition or enforcement if one party provides evidence of the following:

> The arbitral procedure was not in accordance with the agreement of the parties or, failing such agreement, was not in accordance with the law of the country where the arbitration took place.[51]

Considering this provision, written consent is a prerequisite for employing the arbitrator as a settlement facilitator, which serves a dual purpose. *First*, it reinforces the voluntariness of the parties to agree to this role and prevents misunderstandings about their intentions regarding its scope and characteristics.[52] Consequently, it can repel arguments against enforcement on the grounds that this role was implemented contrary to the parties' intentions or agreement.[53] *Second*, written consent appears necessary if the parties wish to deviate from the arrangement established by the applicable law at the seat regarding the arbitrator's dual role, which, given the hesitant attitude taken by various jurisdictions, may challenge the parties' desire to employ it. On a practical level, written consent allows for better coordination of expectations between the parties and the arbitrator regarding the arbitrator's exact mandate in the settlement process. It also allows an examination of whether the arbitrator has the necessary qualifications to fulfill the role.[54] For these reasons, the written form is

46. Ludington, 2017, p. 321; Benzidi, 2017, p. 19; Marzolini, 2016, pp. 116-117; Baysal & Cevik, 2021; Nigmatullina, 2018, p. 169; Stipanowich, 2021a, pp. 350-351; Berger, 2018b, p. 516; Ross, 2013, pp. 363-364; Stipanowich & Mironi, 2021, p. 31; Goodrich, 2012, p. 8; Kun, 2011b, p. 551; Ehle, 2010, p. 88; Wenger, 2006, p. 148; Lew, 2005, p. 428; Hwang, 2005, p. 578; Sawada, 2003, p. 36; Stipanowich & Kaskell, 2001, p. 23; Plant, 2000, p. 146; Brewer & Mills, 1999, pp. 36-38; Schneider, 1998, p. 87.
47. Singapore International Arbitration Act, 1994, Article 17(1); Singapore Arbitration Act, 2001, Article 63(1); Hong Kong Arbitration Ordinance, 2011, Article 33(1). Additionally, *see* IBA Guidelines on Conflicts of Interest in International Arbitration, 2024, Explanation to General Standard 4(d), noting that in various jurisdictions, parties are required to provide written and signed consent for the arbitrator's involvement in the settlement process.
48. CEDR Safeguards for Caucusing, 2009, Article 7(2).
49. JAMS Comprehensive Arbitration Rules and Procedures, 2021, Rule 28(b).
50. Prague Rules, 2018, Article 9(2), in relation to the arbitrator's authority to act as a mediator.
51. New York Convention, 1958, Article V(1)(d); Model Law on ICA, 2006, Article 36(1)(a)(iv). *See also* Rosoff, 2009, p. 98.
52. Nigmatullina, 2018, p. 172; Almoguera, 2010, p. 130; Bartel, 1991, pp. 689-691.
53. Ludington, 2017, p. 321.
54. Stipanowich, 2021a, pp. 342, 344, 348-349; Ludington, 2017, p. 321.

suggested for any renewed consent during the arbitral process,[55] which, as discussed below, may constitute an important safeguard for the parties' due process rights when the arbitrator returns to their adjudicative role following futile efforts to settle the dispute amicably.

Next, consent regarding the arbitrator's dual role should be obtained before the arbitrator takes any direct steps to facilitate a dispute settlement.[56] This requirement for advance consent serves several purposes. *First*, per the empirical data presented earlier, advance consent regarding the arbitrator's dual role may help the parties overcome one of the barriers to settlement—hesitation to propose or make the first move toward a settlement—as it normalizes this role of the arbitrator in the particular arbitral process, which alleviates the fear of appearing weak when suggesting or agreeing to this role in real time.[57] *Second*, advance consent provides the parties sufficient time to design the process after considering the various available initiatives the arbitrator can take as a settlement facilitator and the possible safeguards for their due process rights. These considerations reduce the chances of agreeing to a process that does not meet their wishes and needs.[58] *Third*, advance consent may prevent the possibility of compelling parties to agree to the arbitrator's dual role or part of its components.[59] When parties are asked to agree to the engagement of the arbitrator in the settlement process during arbitration, whether at the arbitrator's initiative or following a proposal of the other party in the attendance of the arbitrator, they may feel coerced into the process, as refusal to do so could upset the arbitrator who will eventually decide the dispute.[60] For these reasons, parties should ideally agree on the process authorizing the arbitrator to facilitate a settlement while negotiating their dispute-resolution clause as part of their business relations or in the early stages of the dispute, preferably not later than the pre-hearing management conference.[61]

However, these possibilities are not always available. For instance, parties may consider employing the arbitrator with the dual role only after the arbitral process has commenced, particularly if this option is raised for the first time by the arbitrator or one of the parties during the proceedings. Alternatively, the parties may prefer to avoid an advance commitment to this arrangement until sufficient trust has been established among all participants in the proceedings, including the arbitrator.[62] Furthermore, even when the parties have reached a prior agreement regarding the arbitrator's dual role, they may choose to modify or adjust this agreement during the arbitration, for

55. Ruckteschler & Wendelstein, 2021, p. 771.
56. Ludington, 2017, p. 321; Stipanowich, 2021a, p. 342; Nigmatullina, 2018, p. 170; Berger, 2018b, p. 516; Berger & Jensen, 2017, p. 904; Elsing, 2015, p. 690; Kun, 2011b, p. 551; Kaufmann-Kohler, 2009, p. 204; CEDR Safeguards for Caucusing, 2009, Article 7(3).
57. *See* the discussion in section 3.2.
58. Ludington, 2017, p. 321; Stipanowich, 2021a, p. 342.
59. Berger, 2018b, p. 513.
60. *See* the discussion in section 4.2.2. *See also* Nigmatullina, 2018, p. 172; Bartel, 1991, p. 689.
61. Ludington, 2017, p. 321; Nigmatullina, 2018, pp. 169-170; Stipanowich, 2021a, p. 342. For a discussion on the significance of the first organizational meeting in designing the arbitral process to accommodate the arbitrator's dual role, *see* section 2.2.1.
62. Berger, 2018b, pp. 513-514; Nigmatullina, 2018, pp. 169-170; Elsing, 2015, p. 690; Plant, 2000, p. 146; Stipanowich, 2021a, p. 349.

example, in response to suggestions made by the arbitrator or to address unforeseen developments in the arbitral process.[63] Regardless of the reason, when the arbitrator's dual role becomes a point of discussion after the commencement of the arbitral process, the proceedings should be paused to allow the parties to independently reach a written agreement on the matter, free from the arbitrator's involvement.[64]

Given the voluntary nature of the process that employs the arbitrator as a settlement facilitator, another important aspect of consent is the parties' ability to withdraw from the settlement phase to avoid being trapped by previous consent in a manner that undermines their right to self-determination.[65] Unlike the opt-out safeguard discussed below that may result in replacing the arbitrator or terminating the arbitration, the right to revoke consent to the arbitrator's involvement in the settlement process allows for the resumption of the formal arbitral proceedings with the same arbitrator. Most arbitration laws, rules, and guidelines regulating the arbitrator's dual role, in concurrence with the prevailing opinion in the literature, support the parties' right to revoke their consent at *any time*.[66] However, this approach has faced criticism because it may enable tactical manipulation of the settlement phase[67] or render agreements to employ the arbitrator in a dual role impractical, as parties may find it difficult to rely on such arrangements with reasonable certainty.[68] Additionally, it may discourage parties from considering more effective arrangements that strengthen their incentive to settle without depriving them of the right to self-determination, such as agreeing to a time-limited settlement phase during which withdrawal from negotiations is not permitted.[69] Therefore, in light of the additional due process safeguards presented below—including the right to opt out of arbitration, particularly after the implementation of direct settlement facilitation initiatives—it is proposed that the right to withdraw from the settlement phase at any time be established as a default rule rather than an absolute one. This default approach would allow parties to adopt alternative arrangements that condition the right to withdraw on specific agreed terms, thereby providing flexibility while safeguarding their rights and interests.

63. Stipanowich, 2021a, p. 348.
64. Stipanowich, 2021a, p. 348; Nigmatullina, 2018, p. 170; Berger, 2018b, pp. 513-514; Stipanowich & Kaskell, 2001, p. 23.
65. Fullerton, 2009, p. 34; Nigmatullina, 2018, p. 52.
66. Stipanowich, 2021a, p. 304; Nigmatullina, 2018, p. 201. Additionally, *see* the following arbitration laws and rules endorsing this attitude: Japan Arbitration law, 2003, Article 38(4)-(5); Australia Commercial Arbitration Act, 2010, Part 5, section 27D; Hong Kong Arbitration Ordinance, 2011, Article 33(1); Singapore International Arbitration Act, 1994, Article 17(1); Singapore Arbitration Act, 2001, Article 63(1); CIETAC Arbitration Rules, 2024, Article 47(3); SCIA Arbitration Rules, 2022, Article 48(4).
67. *See* the discussion of this issue in section 5.2.2.3.
68. Nigmatullina, 2018, p. 183.
69. Marriott, 2005, p. 543; Nigmatullina, 2018, p. 201. Additionally, *see* Goodrich, 2012, p. 7, suggesting that if the disputants "wish to engage in mediation over a set period such as a day with an unambiguous waiver for that mediation followed by a return to arbitration if the matter cannot be settled, ... it would be undesirable to allow a party to withdraw the mediation power during the day."

7.3.1.3 *Detailed Consent*

Undertaking the drafting of a comprehensive and well-considered agreement that encompasses all aspects concerning the arbitrator's capacity as a settlement facilitator is another vital prerequisite for preserving the parties' autonomy:

> Spending the time and energies that may be necessary to negotiate these terms may be well worth the effort. Although it may seem easier to simply avoid these discussions until, and if, an issue arises during [the process], ... these issues may be more difficult to resolve, and the ramifications may be greater, than if they are dealt with up front. ... Addressing these issues at the outset, and memorializing these details in the parties' agreement, may avoid a later problem and allow the neutral to complete the [process].[70]

As demonstrated in Chapters 5 and 6, legislative provisions and rules regulating the arbitrator's role as a settlement facilitator often lack sufficient guidance on conducting this role and guaranteeing its compliance with the parties' due process rights.[71] As controversies regarding the arbitrator's dual role usually arise during the proceedings due to different expectations about its scope and boundaries or following the arbitral process when one or more parties express dissatisfaction with its outcome, it is advisable to have a detailed agreement in place even when the applicable law or arbitration rules acknowledge that role of the arbitrator, as, in these scenarios, resorting to a detailed agreement may become necessary to resolve these differences. Furthermore, considering the diverse perceptions among legal cultures regarding different components of the arbitrator's dual role, drafting a detailed agreement allows parties to take a balanced approach that ensures a meeting of the minds.[72] These measures may, in turn, enhance the enforceability of the arbitration's outcome, particularly for the following reasons: (a) similar to the aforementioned impact of the written feature, a detailed agreement may reduce the chances of challenging the arbitrator's dual role or the arbitral award, especially when the role was executed precisely according to the agreement between the parties,[73] and (b) a detailed agreement that coordinates expectations among all participants in the settlement process may increase the parties' trust in the dual-role arbitrator and the process and diminish the likelihood of challenging the arbitrator or the award, even when the parties had hoped for a better outcome.[74] While the parties should independently finalize any agreement regarding the arbitrator's dual role, free from any pressure

70. Ludington, 2017, p. 316. *See also* Stipanowich, 2021a, pp. 342, 351; Marzolini, 2016, p. 117; Brewer & Mills, 1999, pp. 36-38; ICC Guide on Effective Conflict Management, 2023, pp. 9-12.
71. *See also* Ruckteschler & Wendelstein, 2021, pp. 768-769, 771; Stipanowich, 2021a, p. 273; Berger & Jensen, 2017, p. 891; Plant, 2000, p. 143.
72. Stipanowich, 2021a, pp. 340, 344, 351; Stipanowich & Mironi, 2021, p. 31; Abramson, 1999, p. 7.
73. Ludington, 2017, p. 321; Marriott, 2005, p. 545, recommending that "whatever guidelines the parties and/or arbitrators decide to use, they should be clearly disclosed and understood by all involved to reduce the likelihood that the award will be susceptible to challenge."
74. Baysal & Cevik, 2021; Stipanowich, 2021a, p. 349; Nigmatullina, 2018, p. 168; Ludington, 2017, p. 321; Raeschke-Kessler, 2005, p. 531; Marriott, 2005, p. 544; Bartel, 1991, p. 691. Additionally, *see* the discussion in section 7.3.1.4 below on another feature of express consent—informed

exerted by the arbitrator, receiving input from the arbitrator or the arbitration institute at the earliest possible stage can be beneficial. Such input facilitates necessary adjustments before the arbitrator initiates the settlement process, ensuring that the arrangement aligns with the parties' expectations and minimizing the risk of potential disaccords between the parties and the arbitrator during its implementation.[75]

Therefore, the agreement between the parties should detail any direct initiatives the arbitrator is authorized to undertake, as well as indirect initiatives that require the parties' cooperation or consent under the governing law or arbitration rules.[76] Hence, the spectrum of settlement facilitation initiatives proposed in Chapter 2 and summarized in Appendix A can provide a template for further development and modifications by potential parties seeking to engage the arbitrator in a dual role. In particular, the agreement should address the following components of the role, which, as previously discussed, tend to provoke the most controversy: (a) whether and to what extent the arbitrator is authorized to grant *evaluative views* about the disputed issues and the outcome of the process; (b) whether the arbitrator is authorized to provide *settlement proposals*, including how detailed those proposals can be and whether they are limited only to the disputed issues; (c) whether the arbitrator is permitted to *mediate the dispute*; and (d) whether the arbitrator is allowed to *caucus with the parties*, and if so, whether those meetings are limited to the presence of the party and its counsel or can be conducted with one of them.[77]

Additionally, since decisions regarding the initiatives permitted for the arbitrator to facilitate a settlement often influence the selection of corresponding due process safeguards, it is beneficial to explicitly outline in the agreement the relevant mandatory safeguards and any voluntary safeguards chosen to supplement them, as discussed in section 7.4 below. Clear safeguards addressing the most challenging aspects of the arbitrator's dual role—such as the conditions under which the arbitrator may resume their adjudicative authority following unsuccessful settlement attempts and the treatment of settlement-stage information in the resumed arbitration—can help mitigate risks to the process and the arbitral award.[78] Another important aspect to incorporate

---

consent—which may further reduce the parties' inclination to challenge the award or the arbitrator, even in cases of less favorable outcomes than anticipated.

75. Ludington, 2017, pp. 316, 321; Stipanowich, 2021a, pp. 342, 347-348; Stipanowich & Mironi, 2021, p. 31; Pair, 2002, p. 73; Stipanowich & Kaskell, 2001, p. 23; CIArb Practice Guideline on the Use of Mediation in Arbitration, 2021, Article 8(6).
76. Ruckteschler & Wendelstein, 2021, p. 771; Abramson, 1999, p. 7; Stipanowich, 2021a, pp. 349, 351; Kaufmann-Kohler, 2009, p. 204; Marzolini, 2016, p. 117, suggesting that "the settlement attempts should be conducted in accordance with the parties' agreement," which "should contain a clear indication of what is expected of the arbitrators." Since parties are typically invested in a detailed agreement, they may choose to include specific indirect initiatives, even those that do not principally necessitate consent, to ensure clarity and certainty in the process.
77. Stipanowich & Mironi, 2021, p. 31; Marzolini, 2016, pp. 116-118; Benzidi, 2017, pp. 23, 30; Ross, 2013, p. 364; Kun, 2011b, p. 552; Stipanowich, 2021a, pp. 344, 347-349, 352-354; Nigmatullina, 2018, p. 190; CEDR Safeguards for Caucusing, 2009, Article 7(4); CIArb Practice Guideline on the Use of Mediation in Arbitration, 2021, Article 8(1) & (6).
78. Nigmatullina, 2018, p. 170; Ross, 2013, p. 364; Stipanowich & Mironi, 2021, pp. 31-32; Marriott, 2005, p. 545; Goodrich, 2012, p. 8; Schneider, 1998, p. 87; Cremades, 1998, p. 164. Additionally, *see* the following arbitration guidelines that advocate for including explicit arrangements in the parties' agreement regarding the handling of confidential information disclosed during the

into the agreement pertains to the timing of the settlement efforts. While designing a flexible process that grants sufficient discretion to the arbitrator regarding the timing of settlement attempts is important for successfully fulfilling the dual role,[79] the agreement should broadly specify when these efforts are expected to commence to allow adequate and advanced preparations.[80] Similarly, the agreement should establish a clear demarcation between the formal arbitration and the settlement phases to help prevent confusion among the parties regarding the nature of each phase and the capacity of the arbitrator during these stages. Additionally, where applicable, the agreement should delineate issues that are amenable to settlement efforts from those that must remain subject to adjudication.[81]

7.3.1.4 Informed Consent

Furthermore, the parties' consent to engage the arbitrator in a dual role should be grounded in a clear understanding of the concerns and legal implications associated with its implementation.[82] While some commentators argue that detailed and written consent from the parties is sufficient to ensure informed consent,[83] the prevailing view among scholars advocates for dedicated and active counseling regarding the dual role's benefits, risks, and legal ramifications. This counseling should ideally be provided by the parties' respective counsel or the arbitrator, preferably by both. Additionally, this counseling should be documented in writing before the arbitrator undertakes any active steps to facilitate a settlement in the dispute.[84] This recommended requirement for informed consent protects the parties' right to self-determination while also safeguarding the arbitrator and the resulting award from potential challenges that may arise after the arbitrator resumes their adjudicative role following unsuccessful settlement efforts. Documenting informed consent provides substantial evidence that the parties clearly understood the potential consequences of the dual role.[85] The necessity

settlement process if the arbitrator resumes their arbitral role following unsuccessful settlement attempts: CIArb Practice Guideline on the Use of Mediation in Arbitration, 2021, Article 8(6); CEDR Safeguards for Caucusing, 2009, Article 7(1).

79. Kaufmann-Kohler, 2009, p. 197; Berger, 2018b, pp. 515-516; Nigmatullina, 2018, p. 44; Berger & Jensen, 2017, p. 899; Ehle, 2010, pp. 85-86; Phillips, G. F., 2009, p. 76; Kun, 2011b, p. 537; Abramson, 1999, p. 7. For further exploration of the benefits associated with flexibility in the timing of the arbitrator's initiatives, *see* section 3.2.
80. Marriott, 2005, p. 543; Stipanowich, 2021a, p. 351.
81. Stipanowich & Mironi, 2021, p. 31; Stipanowich, 2021a, p. 351; Ross, 2013, p. 364; Benzidi, 2017, pp. 9-10; Marriott, 2005, p. 543.
82. Stipanowich, 2021a, p. 342; Berger, 2018b, pp. 513-514, 516; Berger & Jensen, 2017, p. 904; Nigmatullina, 2018, p. 174; Kun, 2011b, p. 551; Sussman, 2010a, p. 384; Ehle, 2010, p. 89; Kaufmann-Kohler, 2009, pp. 198, 204; Sussman, 2009a, p. 73; Stipanowich & Kaskell, 2001, p. 31; Brewer & Mills, 1999, p. 36; Phillips, G. F., 2009, p. 76; Abramson, 1999, p. 15; Bartel, 1991, p. 691.
83. Ludington, 2017, p. 321; Flake, 2016, p. 4; Burr, 2005, p. 64; Talbot, 2001, p. 229.
84. Benzidi, 2017, p. 31; Nigmatullina, 2018, p. 176; Goodrich, 2012, p. 8; Stipanowich & Kaskell, 2001, p. 32; Brewer & Mills, 1999, pp. 36-38; Abramson, 1999, p. 15. Additionally, *see* Phillips, G. F., 2009, pp. 77-79, offering a sample form of informed consent for parties opting to engage an arbitrator in a dual role.
85. Berger, 2018b, pp. 513-514, 516; Weisman, 2013, p. 40.

for written informed consent is supported by key professional guidelines, including the CIArb Professional Practice Guideline on the Use of Mediation in Arbitration,[86] the CPR Final Report on the Future of Arbitration,[87] and the IBA Guidelines on Conflicts of Interest.[88] Additionally, the JAMS Arbitrators Ethics Guidelines, while not requiring written documentation of informed consent, oblige the arbitrator to inform the parties about the characteristics of the dual-role process and its potential implications.[89]

7.3.2 Explicit Waiver of the Right to Challenge the Arbitrator or the Award

The question arises of whether written informed consent to the process also entails a waiver of the parties' right to disqualify the arbitrator or challenge the award due to fulfilling the dual role. According to one approach, informed consent implies a waiver of the right of challenge on this ground.[90] This approach is embedded in several arbitration rules and guidelines discussed in previous chapters, including the IBA Guidelines on Conflicts of Interest,[91] the CEDR Rules for Settlement Facilitation,[92] the Swiss Arbitration Rules,[93] and the DIS Arbitration Rules, which, as supported by several decisions of the German court, consider informed consent as an effective waiver.[94] However, the prevailing approach suggests that relying merely on the parties' informed consent may leave unnecessary risks regarding the enforcement of the award or the ability of the arbitrator to retain their adjudicative role following futile settlement efforts. Hence, an additional express and written waiver is deemed necessary.[95] This cautious approach is supported by various arbitration rules and guidelines that regulate the arbitrator's dual role, including the CIArb Professional Practice Guideline on the

86. CIArb Practice Guideline on the Use of Mediation in Arbitration, 2021, Article 8(6).
87. Stipanowich & Kaskell, 2001, pp. 23-24, 32-33; Stipanowich, 2021a, pp. 328-329.
88. IBA Guidelines on Conflicts of Interest in International Arbitration, 2024, Explanation to General Standard 4(d); Berger, 2018b, p. 514.
89. JAMS Arbitrators Ethics Guidelines, 2021, Article III(B). A comparable responsibility, albeit as a recommendation, is anchored in the CEDR Safeguards for Caucusing, 2009, Article 6. *See also* Stipanowich, 2021a, p. 347.
90. Kaufmann-Kohler, 2009, p. 204; Nigmatullina, 2018, p. 177; Ross, 2013, p. 363; Kun, 2011b, p. 551; Rosoff, 2009, p. 94; Pitkowitz & Richter, 2009, pp. 228-229; Lew, 2005, p. 428.
91. IBA Guidelines on Conflicts of Interest in International Arbitration, 2024, General Standard 4(d). *See also* the discussion in section 6.3.2.2; Sussman & Berger, 2021a, p. 26; Ruckteschler & Wendelstein, 2021, p. 770; Berger, 2019, p. 309; Berger & Jensen, 2017, p. 904; Nigmatullina, 2018, p. 178.
92. CEDR Rules for Settlement Facilitation, 2009, Article 3(3). *See also* the discussion in section 6.3.3.2.
93. Swiss Arbitration Rules, 2021, Article 19(5). *See also* the discussion in section 6.3.1.
94. DIS Arbitration Rules, 2018, Article 26. *See also* the discussion and presented cases in section 5.3.2.1.
95. Stipanowich, 2021a, p. 352; Baysal & Cevik, 2021; Stipanowich & Mironi, 2021, p. 31; Nigmatullina, 2018, p. 181; Berger & Jensen, 2017, p. 913; Marzolini, 2016, p. 116; Ross, 2013, p. 364; Goodrich, 2012, p. 8; Ehle, 2010, p. 93; Rosoff, 2009, pp. 93-95; Burr, 2005, p. 64; Stipanowich & Kaskell, 2001, pp. 23, 32; Plant, 2000, p. 146; Koch & Schäfer, 1999, p. 173; Abramson, 1999, p. 15; Schneider, 1998, p. 87.

Use of Mediation in Arbitration,[96] the JAMS Arbitrators Ethics Guidelines,[97] the CPR Final Report on the Future of Arbitration,[98] the CEDR Safeguards for Caucusing,[99] and the draft guidelines of the International Task Force on Mixed Mode Dispute Resolution.[100] As demonstrated in Chapter 5, this approach has been implemented in various court decisions in the US[101] and *Smith v. Kvaerner Cementation* in the UK.[102]

Enforcement risks following the absence of an express waiver stem from the unresolved controversy in the literature and in case law in various jurisdictions regarding the broader question of whether parties to ICA are permitted to waive the right for due process and impartial tribunal and under what conditions. One viewpoint posits that waiver of the parties' procedural rights should not be accepted in principle, as it may contravene public policy and violate Article 18 of the Model Law on ICA, which imposes an unconditional obligation on the tribunal to act impartially and grant each party the full opportunity to present its case.[103] Consequently, even if the parties waive their procedural rights, evidence of a breach of due process or an apparent or real bias, as exemplified by the U.K. cases of *Glencot Development & Design Ltd v. Ben Barrett & Son Ltd* and *R v. Gough*,[104] would allow parties to challenge the arbitrator or the award and leave the waiver potentially ineffective.[105] According to the prevailing view, while core procedural rights cannot be completely waived, the principle of party autonomy—which distinguishes arbitration from standard adjudicative processes and, according to the "legislator" of the Model Law on ICA, should override other limitations on the arbitral procedure subject to compliance with the applicable law[106]—grants parties broad discretion over their application, including the possibility of waiving "certain issues and rights pertaining to the realm of fair trial."[107] However, given the

96. CIArb Practice Guideline on the Use of Mediation in Arbitration, 2021, Article 8(6). *See also* the discussion in section 6.3.2.3.
97. JAMS Arbitrators Ethics Guidelines, 2021, Article III(B).
98. Stipanowich & Kaskell, 2001, p. 23; Stipanowich, 2021a, p. 328. *See also* the discussion in section 6.3.3.1.
99. CEDR Safeguards for Caucusing, 2009, Article 7(2) & (5). Interestingly, this requirement for explicit waiver applies only to caucuses. In contrast, for other settlement facilitation initiatives, the CEDR Rules establish a general arrangement where consent is deemed to imply waiver. *See* CEDR Rules for Settlement Facilitation, 2009, Article 3(3).
100. Stipanowich & Mironi, 2021, pp. 31-32.
101. *See* the discussion of these cases in section 5.3.1.1.
102. *See* the discussion of this case in section 5.3.1.2.
103. Kryvoi & Davydenko, 2015, p. 849; Nigmatullina, 2018, p. 187; Aall, 2011, pp. 210, 222; Leon & Peterson, 2009, p. 93; Bühring-Uhle et al., 2006, p. 264; Pryles, 2007, p. 329; Holtzmann & Neuhaus, 1989, p. 583; Model Law on ICA, 2006, Article 18. This attitude is supported by section 33(1)(a) of the U.K. Arbitration Act, 1996, which as discussed in section 5.3.1.2, imposes a mandatory and nonwaivable duty on the tribunal to act fairly and impartially, while ensuring that the parties are given a reasonable opportunity to present their case and respond to their opponents.
104. *See* the discussion of these cases in section 5.3.1.2.
105. Ortolani, 2025, §21.5(f); Nigmatullina, 2018, p. 183; McIlwrath, 2018; Berger & Jensen, 2017, p. 914; Lack, 2010, p. 376; Rosoff, 2009, p. 98. *See also* CIArb Practice Guideline on the Use of Mediation in Arbitration, 2021, Article 8(3), warning that relevant jurisdictions to the arbitration may not consider an express waiver to be effective.
106. *See* the discussion in section 6.3.2.5.
107. Seatzu & Vargiu, 2022, pp. 213-214. *See also* Blackaby et al., 2022, §10.25-10.29; Born, 2021, §15.05; Benzidi, 2017, p. 24; Aall, 2011, pp. 210-211, 222-224; Berger & Jensen, 2017, p. 915,

magnitude of these rights and the lack of determination or regulation regarding the possibility and conditions for their waiver in many jurisdictions,[108] any waiver arrangement should be expressed and ensure the parties' clear understanding of its significance and implications, while not violating their fundamental access to justice.[109] This approach, which has gained increasing acceptance among scholars, practitioners, and jurisdictions with diverse legal traditions, emphasizes that, alongside a detailed agreement regarding any process involving the arbitrator in a dual role, parties should also expressly waive their right to challenge the arbitral process or the award solely on the basis of the arbitrator's involvement in settlement negotiations. Such a requirement is particularly relevant when this involvement includes participation in ex parte communications or exposure to confidential information. This framework, designed to mitigate the risk of successful challenges to the award or the arbitrator arising from their dual-role activities,[110] is reflected in several case law examples discussed in Chapter 5, including (a) the decision of the U.S. court in *Conkle and Olesten v. Goodrich Goodyear and Hinds*, where a challenge to the award based on the arbitrator's previous mediation of a closely related case was rejected because the parties waived confidentiality in a direct and unequivocal manner;[111] (b) the decision of the U.S. court in *U.S. Steel Mining Company v. Wilson Downhole Services*, where an objection to enforcement based on a partiality argument was dismissed since the parties' written agreement expressly authorized the arbitrator to "rely on information which he deems relevant, whether obtained in ex parte communication or otherwise;"[112] (c) the decision of the Australian court in *The Duke Group Ltd v. Alamain*

holding that the principle of party autonomy places ICA parties in the best position "to determine the specific impact of a waiver of their right to be heard in exchange for the increased possibility that they achieve a settlement."; Elliott, 1995, p. 169, arguing that although the dual role arbitrator "has pitted 'natural justice' concerns ... against 'party autonomy' concepts ... increasingly, although certainly not universally, the party autonomy view seems to be gaining the upper hand." Additionally, *see* Nigmatullina, 2018, pp. 181, 187, referencing some views in the literature that distinguish, for waiver purposes, between the right to an impartial tribunal—which may be waived subject to adequate safeguards—and other due process rights, particularly the right to be heard, which cannot be waived. However, this differentiation is not supported by the language of Article 18 of the Model Law, which treats the right to be heard and the right to an impartial tribunal uniformly, nor by Article 6 of the ECHR and the decisions of the ECtHR, as discussed below.

108. Berger & Jensen, 2017, pp. 914-915; Ortolani, 2025, §21.5(f); McIlwrath, 2018; Nigmatullina, 2018, pp. 183, 189; Bühring-Uhle et al., 2006, p. 264.
109. Blackaby et al., 2022, §10.26; Seatzu & Vargiu, 2022, p. 213; Nigmatullina, 2018, pp. 181, 188; Berger & Jensen, 2017, p. 914; Kryvoi & Davydenko, 2015, p. 849; Almoguera, 2010, p. 121; Lack, 2010, p. 374; Limbury, 2009b, p. 9; Steele, 2007, p. 1407; Blankenship, 2006, p. 36; Sawada, 2003, p. 30; Talbot, 2001, p. 228; Schneider, 1998, p. 94. Additionally, *see* Aall, 2011, p. 210, holding that "even in an arbitration context there is a presumption that the parties have agreed on no less than a fair procedure."
110. Kryvoi & Davydenko, 2015, p. 849; Rosoff, 2009, p. 91.
111. *See* the discussion of this case in section 5.3.1.1.
112. *U.S. Steel Mining Company v. Wilson Downhole Services*, 2006, §5. Additionally, *see* the discussion of this case in section 5.3.1.1. For a review of additional U.S. cases where parties successfully waived their right to impartial tribunal after employing the arbitrator in a dual role, *see* Kaufmann-Kohler, 2009, p. 198; Rosoff, 2009, p. 93.

Investments Ltd, which, by approving ex parte communications between the adjudicator and the parties based on their consent and clear understanding of the implications, recognized a broader concept wherein party autonomy should prevail over procedural fairness when the right safeguards are maintained;[113] and (d) the decision of the U.K. court in *Smith v. Kvaerner Cementation* that acknowledged the parties' liberty to waive the right to challenge the award or object to the arbitrator on grounds of apparent bias, provided that the waiver was clear, unequivocal, and made with full knowledge regarding its consequences.[114] Beyond recognizing the parties' authority to waive their right of challenge, domestic court rulings have also established important time limitations for initiating such challenges. For instance, in *ASM Shipping Ltd of India v. TTMI Ltd of England*, the U.K. court ruled that a party's failure to raise bias claims immediately or within the permitted time limit frame could result in losing the right to do so.[115] Similarly, in the case of *Gao Haiyan*, the Hong Kong court ruled that bias claims should be raised promptly and within the arbitral proceedings; otherwise, the parties may be considered to have waived their right to challenge on that basis.[116]

In addition to domestic court decisions, the capability of ICA parties to waive their procedural rights has been confirmed in a series of decisions by the European Court of Human Rights (ECtHR). In *Osmo Suovaniemi and others v. Finland*, the parties consented to the appointment of an arbitrator despite a disclosed conflict of interest. Subsequently, one of the parties challenged the final award, alleging that the arbitrator's conflict of interest compromised their impartiality, thereby violating Article 6 of the European Convention on Human Rights (ECHR), which stipulates that every litigant "is entitled to a fair ... hearing ... by an independent and impartial tribunal established by law."[117] Despite reservations in the literature regarding the classification of a voluntary arbitral tribunal as "established by law" for the convention's purposes,[118] the ECtHR aligned with previous decisions in the matter and applied Article 6 on voluntary arbitral proceedings.[119] However, this application was a "mild" version that still acknowledged the principle of voluntary waiver of procedural rights by parties

113. *See* the discussion of this case in section 5.3.1.3. *See also* Limbury, 2010b, pp. 3-4; Croft, 2014, pp. 3-4; Limbury, 2009a, p. 85; Nigmatullina, 2018, pp. 188-189; Limbury, 2009b, p. 9; Lack, 2010, p. 374.
114. *See* the discussion of this case in section 5.3.1.2.
115. *See* the discussion of this case in section 5.3.1.2.
116. *See* the discussion of this case in section 5.2.2.1.
117. European Convention on Human Rights, 1950, Article 6.
118. Trakman & Montgomery, 2017, p. 421; Horvath, 2011, p. 258. Additionally, *see* Seatzu & Vargiu, 2022, p. 215, arguing that arbitration tribunals "can hardly be regarded as 'established by law' in cases of voluntary arbitrations. Arbitral tribunals are neither governed nor regulated according to the rules of the judiciary: not only they are not state organs, but it is questionable whether they could even be considered as legal entities."
119. *See*, for example, *Lithgow and Others v. The United Kingdom*, 1986, paras. 201-202, stating that for the purpose of Article 6 of the ECHR, the expression "tribunal" incorporates any adjudicative body established to handle a limited number of matters according to principles of fair trial, when the term "established by law" relates not only to the legal source of the tribunal's activity but also to its compliance with any particular rules that govern it. *See also* Seatzu & Vargiu, 2022, p. 212.

to the ICA.[120] After finding that the parties were represented by counsel and had granted unequivocal consent to waive the requirement of impartiality, which "was accompanied by sufficient guarantees commensurate to its importance," the ECtHR held that the waiver should be enforced. Consequently, the national court's decision refusing to set aside the award was confirmed.[121] The ECtHR adopted a comparable stance in its final judgment in *Deweer v. Belgium*:

> In the Contracting States' domestic legal systems a waiver of this kind is frequently encountered ... in civil matters, notably in the shape of arbitration clauses in contracts. ... The waiver, which has undeniable advantages for the individual concerned as well as for the administration of justice, does not in principle offend against the Convention [on Human Rights].[122]

These ECtHR determinations were reaffirmed in the very recent judgment in *Beg S.p.A. v. Italy*. Despite its failure to clarify the scope of the permissible waiver of procedural rights or provide detailed guidance to guarantee its successful and safe implementation in ICA proceedings, the court nonetheless prioritized considerations of party autonomy and process flexibility over the parties' procedural rights, subject to maintaining certain safeguards:

> A distinction must be drawn between voluntary arbitration and compulsory arbitration. In the case of voluntary arbitration, to which consent has been freely given, no real issue arises under Article 6. The parties to a dispute are free to take certain disagreements arising under a contract to a body other than an ordinary court of law. By signing an arbitration clause the parties voluntarily waive certain rights secured by the Convention. Such a waiver is not incompatible with the Convention provided it is established in a free, lawful and unequivocal manner. In addition, in the case of certain Convention rights, a waiver, in order to be effective for Convention purposes, requires minimum guarantees commensurate to its importance.[123]

Based on the above-discussed domestic and ECtHR cases, the likelihood of successfully challenging an award or disqualifying an arbitrator solely for undertaking a dual role diminishes when parties provide a clear and detailed waiver in addition to their informed consent.[124] Consequently, empowering an arbitrator to assume a dual role should go beyond merely securing the parties' informed consent and include an express waiver of their right to challenge the award or disqualify the arbitrator on the grounds of performing that role in accordance with their agreement. In line with several domestic court rulings, this waiver arrangement can also impose time limits for raising objections regarding the arbitrator's impartiality or alleged violations of due

120. At the same time, the scope of that waiver, and whether all procedural rights can be completely waived by parties to arbitral proceedings, remained unresolved.
121. *Osmo Suovaniemi and others v. Finland*, 1999. *See also* Seatzu & Vargiu, 2022, pp. 215-216; Nigmatullina, 2018, p. 182; Kaufmann-Kohler, 2009, p. 198.
122. *Deweer v. Belgium*, 1980, para. 49.
123. *Beg S.p.A. v. Italy*, 2021, para. 127. *See also* Seatzu & Vargiu, 2022, pp. 212-213.
124. Berger & Jensen, 2017, p. 913; Ross, 2013, p. 364; Limbury, 2009b, p. 13; Kaufmann-Kohler, 2009, p. 198. Additionally, *see Nordström-Janzon v. Netherlands*, 1996, where the ECtHR explicitly stated that a deviation by parties in arbitral proceedings from the principles outlined in Article 6 of the ECHR should not necessarily lead to the setting aside of the arbitral award.

process stemming from the implementation of the dual role. These time limitations seem possible according to the language of the Model Law on ICA, which permits parties "to agree on a procedure for challenging an arbitrator"[125] and further provides:

> A party who knows that any provision of this Law from which the parties may derogate or any requirement under the arbitration agreement has not been complied with and yet proceeds with the arbitration without stating his objection to such non-compliance without undue delay or, if a time-limit is provided therefor, within such period of time, shall be deemed to have waived his right to object.[126]

The remaining question is whether an express waiver is necessary when the applicable arbitration law, rules, or guidelines apply an approach that treats informed consent as a waiver, as demonstrated above in relation to certain arbitration rules and guidelines. Some commentators hold that in these situations, the parties' informed consent to the dual role suffices, rendering an additional express waiver unnecessary.[127] While the logic behind this approach is understandable, every agreement to engage an arbitrator in a dual role should include an express written waiver, irrespective of the stance taken by the applicable law, rules, or guidelines. *First*, not all arbitration laws, rules, and guidelines explicitly address waivers, which leaves the parties' agreement as the simplest and most secure mechanism to guarantee that a matter with significant enforceability implications is properly regulated. This risk is particularly pronounced when an award is enforceable in jurisdictions other than the seat of arbitration, where multiple legal systems may apply. *Second*, arbitration laws, rules, and guidelines addressing waivers often apply unequal arrangements. For example, while some rules and guidelines, such as the IBA Guidelines on Conflicts of Interest, establish a broad waiver relating to any involvement of the arbitrator in the settlement efforts,[128] others, such as the Prague Rules and the CEDR Rules for Settlement Facilitation, apply a waiver only for certain initiatives of settlement facilitation.[129] Furthermore, while some rules and guidelines, including the IBA

125. Model Law on ICA, 2006, Article 13(1). According to the subsequent Article 13(2), if the parties' agreement does not specify a timeframe for challenging the arbitrator, the challenge must be initiated within 15 days of becoming aware of the circumstances justifying it.
126. Model Law on ICA, 2006, Article 4. Similar arrangements are anchored in the U.K. Arbitration Act, 1996, section 73(1), as well as in the IBA Guidelines on Conflicts of Interest in International Arbitration, 2024, General Standard 4(a). Additionally, *see* Article 23(3) of the NAI Arbitration Rules, 2024, and Article 3(6)(2) of the ADRIC Arbitration Rules, 2025, which stipulate that a party to arbitration may not challenge the impartiality or independence of an arbitrator more than 14 days and 15 days, respectively, after becoming aware of the grounds for such a challenge. Article 6(5) of the ADRIC Med-Arb Rules, 2020, further specifies that a challenge based on the arbitrator's prior role as a mediator must be raised at the commencement of the arbitration; otherwise, the relevant party is deemed to have waived "any challenge to the Med-Arbitrator based on the mediation phase." For further discussion, *see* Blackaby et al., 2022, §4.159-4.164 & §10.27-10.29; Ross, 2013, p. 364.
127. Nigmatullina, 2018, p. 181.
128. IBA Guidelines on Conflicts of Interest in International Arbitration, 2024, General Standard 4(d).
129. Prague Rules, 2018, Article 2, setting waiver only for preliminary views expressed by the tribunal; CEDR Rules for Settlement Facilitation, 2009, Article 3(3), limiting the waiver to initiatives that do not involve caucusing.

Guidelines on Conflicts of Interest, set an irrevocable waiver,[130] others, like the Australian Arbitration Act, the CIArb Professional Practice Guideline on the Use of Mediation in Arbitration, the CEDR Safeguards for Caucusing, and the Prague Rules regarding the arbitrator's role as a mediator, limit that waiver by requiring renewed consent of the parties before arbitration resumes following failed efforts to settle.[131] Given these disparities, parties are better positioned to design an alternative arrangement tailored to their specific needs. For instance, they may opt to unconditionally waive their right to challenge the arbitrator's dual role[132] or, alternatively, condition the waiver on the precise fulfillment of all agreed terms, including those governing permissible settlement initiatives and safeguards. This customized arrangement, deemed permissible under the language of the Model Law on ICA, can incentivize the arbitrator to adhere strictly to the agreement while deviating only with the parties' explicit prior approval[133] and generally approaching the settlement process with caution while maintaining the appearance of justice.[134] *Third*, given the remaining uncertainties regarding the admissibility and effectiveness of waivers in different jurisdictions, when parties agree about waiver in an *active, express, detailed, and written manner* and condition it on the exact implementation of the dual role according to their agreement, the chances of deeming such waiver effective appear much higher because this approach indicates that the parties reached a comprehensive agreement covering all aspects related to the involvement of the arbitrator in the settlement process.[135] *Fourth*, while the Model Law on ICA grants parties the freedom to agree on arbitration procedures, it does not clarify whether this freedom is temporally restricted.[136] Some scholars contend that, once the tribunal is constituted, parties cannot agree on new procedures, including those concerning waivers, without the arbitrator's consent because the arbitrator either becomes a party to the agreement or cannot be compelled to accept new procedures.[137] Consequently, agreeing on a waiver as early as

130. IBA Guidelines on Conflicts of Interest in International Arbitration, 2024, General Standard 4(d), specifying that parties remain bound by their initial waiver, even if settlement efforts are unsuccessful.
131. Australia Commercial Arbitration Act, 2010, Part 5, section 27D; CIArb Practice Guideline on the Use of Mediation in Arbitration, 2021, Article 10(4); CEDR Safeguards for Caucusing, 2009, Article 7(1)-(6); Prague Rules, 2018, Article 9(3).
132. *See*, for example, Phillips, G. F., 2009, p. 78, proposing an unrestricted waiver form for parties engaging in hybrid processes that combine arbitration with mediation.
133. Marriott, 2005, pp. 540, 542; Stipanowich & Kaskell, 2001, p. 32; Bernardini, 2004, p. 121, holding that once agreed, the arbitration rules and agreement "should remain fixed unless there are good and objective reasons to modify them. Changing the rules in midgame may be felt by the parties to be unfair or a breach of due process." The implication of the arbitrator's failure to fulfill in precise manner the agreed or mandatory safeguards regarding the dual role is exemplified by the recent decision of the Australian court in *Ku-ring-gai Council v. Ichor Constructions Pty Ltd* (discussed in section 5.3.1.3), where resuming the arbitration by the neutral following failed efforts to settle without receiving a renewed written consent from the parties led to their mandate being terminated and the award revoked.
134. Seatzu & Vargiu, 2022, p. 209; Kun, 2011b, pp. 549-556; Lang, 2009, p. 99.
135. Nigmatullina, 2018, p. 184; Kryvoi & Davydenko, 2015, p. 849; Rosoff, 2009, p. 91.
136. Model Law on ICA, 2006, Article 19(1).
137. Pryles, 2007, pp. 330-333; Fouchard et al., 1999, pp. 601-602; Holtzmann & Neuhaus, 1989, pp. 556-557.

possible—preferably before arbitration commences—minimizes the risk of the arbitrator rejecting it during the proceedings and preserves the ability to implement the dual role effectively.[138]

7.4 DUE PROCESS SAFEGUARDS

Ensuring the parties' autonomy when authorizing the arbitrator as a settlement facilitator is essential yet insufficient. Additional safeguards are necessary to prevent consent to this role from becoming a "trap" that undermines participants' fundamental right to access justice and protect their due process rights. As demonstrated throughout this book, most arbitration laws, rules, and guidelines primarily address due process concerns in the context of ex parte communications, whether in standalone arbitrations or hybrid processes involving arbitration and mediation, and suggest safeguards accordingly. While the potential risks to due process resulting from caucusing are acknowledged, and a *no-caucus approach* can mitigate serious risks associated with the dual role,[139] as discussed in previous sections, caucusing, an integral part of mediation processes in various jurisdictions that has gained popularity across various legal backgrounds, can significantly contribute to a settlement.[140] Therefore, categorically excluding caucusing from the settlement facilitator's toolbox is not advisable, especially when parties are willing to utilize it, and the applicable arbitration laws and rules do not prohibit its use.

Moreover, due process concerns may arise from settlement efforts carried out in the presence of all parties, whether in standalone arbitration or hybrid processes that exclude ex parte communications. For instance, concerns may arise when the arbitrator coerces parties into a settlement, decisively promotes settlement offers, expresses evaluative views, or relies on settlement-stage information—including prior settlement negotiations between the parties and compromise positions—revealed to the arbitrator

---

138. Pryles, 2007, p. 332; Holtzmann & Neuhaus, 1989, p. 583. Conversely, *see* Benzidi, 2017, p. 24, and Berger & Jensen, 2017, pp. 914-915, noting that, based on public policy considerations, some jurisdictions may prohibit parties from preemptively waiving their procedural rights in the arbitral agreement before a dispute arises.
139. Stipanowich, 2021a, pp. 354-356; Benzidi, 2017, pp. 16-17, 30; Berger & Jensen, 2017, p. 915; Nigmatullina, 2018, p. 191; Deekshitha & Saha, 2014, p. 95; Ross, 2013, p. 363; Pappas, 2013, pp. 43-44; Ehle, 2010, pp. 92-93; Kaufmann-Kohler, 2009, p. 204; Sussman, 2009a, p. 71; Rosoff, 2009, p. 92; Gill, 2006, p. 164; Stipanowich & Kaskell, 2001, p. 30; Abramson, 1999, pp. 11-12.
140. *See* the discussion in sections 2.3.3 & 2.4. *See also* Benzidi, 2017, pp. 13, 16-17; Deekshitha & Saha, 2014, pp. 95-96; Thevenin, 2013, pp. 369-379; Ross, 2013, p. 360; Kun, 2011b, p. 553; Nigmatullina, 2018, p. 195; Blankley, 2011, p. 335; Rosoff, 2009, p. 92; Leon & Peterson, 2009, p. 93; Stipanowich & Kaskell, 2001, p. 30; Abramson, 1999, pp. 11-12; Bartel, 1991, p. 687; Stipanowich, 2021a, p. 354. Additionally, *see* Ruckteschler & Wendelstein, 2021, p. 772, arguing that preventing the arbitrator from caucusing with the parties in hybrid processes involving arbitration and mediation "would constitute serious obstacles against a successful mediation and result in no more than settlement talks with the assistance of the arbitral tribunal. ... The parties will not really open up to a mediator and not participate seriously in the mediation if there are no confidential conversations between each of the parties and the mediator."

in the presence of all parties but not part of the formal record.[141] In light of the above and per the guideline proposed earlier regarding initiatives requiring parties' consent,[142] it is inadvisable to restrict due process safeguards solely to caucuses or hybrid processes involving arbitration with mediation. Instead, their application should be extended to other forms of direct arbitrator involvement in the settlement process, such as holding settlement conferences and presenting settlement offers to the parties. Additionally, applying these safeguards to indirect initiatives that necessitate parties' consent or tend to provoke controversies among legal backgrounds and practitioners should be considered, such as providing evaluative views on the merits.

This section suggests two categories of due process safeguards. The first includes the following *mandatory safeguards* to be implemented after unsuccessful attempts by the arbitrator to settle the dispute amicably: (a) the parties' option to opt out of arbitration with the same neutral to employ a different arbitrator in the resumed proceedings, commence the arbitration afresh, or pursue ADR methods *or alternatively* (b) reverting to formal arbitration with the same arbitrator, contingent upon renewed consent and agreed arrangement regarding the treatment of settlement-stage information that is not part of the formal record; *and cumulatively* (c) the arbitrator's option to opt out of the resumed arbitration if, following their involvement in the settlement process, they develop doubts regarding their ability to remain independent and impartial. The second group comprises the following *voluntary safeguards*, which can complement the mandatory ones: (a) limiting the arbitrator's adjudicative mandate during the resumed arbitral proceedings following futile settlement attempts and (b) involving a portion of the tribunal in the settlement efforts when it comprises several arbitrators.

7.4.1 Parties' Opt-Out of the Arbitral Process

Allowing each party to opt out of the arbitral proceedings with the same neutral engaged in unsuccessful settlement efforts enforces the parties' control over the process and confirms their right to self-determination[143] while enhancing the protection of their due process rights.[144] *First*, if following this engagement, the parties develop concerns regarding the arbitrator's capability to remain impartial in the continued arbitration—such as when sensitive information is revealed during the settlement negotiations, conflicts with the arbitrator arise, or significant pressure is exerted by the arbitrator—they may prefer to employ a different neutral for the resumed arbitration to remove these concerns and eliminate potential challenges to the

141. *See* the discussion in section 4.2.
142. *See* the discussion in section 7.3.1.1. Additionally, *see* Appendix A, which provides an overview of the continuum of settlement facilitation initiatives and indicates whether parties' consent is required for each.
143. Pappas, 2013, p. 44; Nigmatullina, 2018, p. 142; Blankenship, 2006, p. 37; Stipanowich, 2021a, p. 356.
144. Stipanowich, 2021a, p. 325; Stipanowich & Mironi, 2021, p. 32; Chua, 2018, p. 11; Nigmatullina, 2018, p. 142; Gu, 2016, p. 102; Sussman, 2009a, p. 71; Gu, 2014, p. 119; Blankenship, 2006, p. 37; Limbury, 2009b, p. 15; Peter, 2005, p. 164; Berger, 2003, p. 394.

award in the future.[145] Alternatively, subject to their agreement and likely only in exceptional circumstances, the parties may terminate the proceeding and start arbitration anew or resort to other dispute-resolution methods.[146] *Second*, knowing that parties are authorized to revoke the mandate after the settlement stage incentivizes the arbitrator to implement the parties' agreement precisely and refrain from coercive behavior during the settlement negotiations or compelling the parties into a settlement agreement they are not interested in. Additionally, the right of termination encourages the parties to engage more openly in the settlement negotiations, thereby increasing the likelihood of amicably resolving the dispute.[147]

Replacing the arbitrator or terminating the process could undoubtedly undermine one of the key benefits of the arbitrator's dual role—the efficiency it brings to the process—due to the additional costs and time required to educate a new neutral with evidence, arguments, and submissions already presented during the initial arbitral process.[148] However, parties can consider implementing one or more of the following measures to mitigate these concerns. *First*, the parties may opt to schedule the settlement efforts relatively early in the arbitration process or, at least, not too late during the proceedings to strike a fair balance between cost-effectiveness and due process.[149] *Second*, if the arbitrator is replaced within the same arbitral process, the parties can agree to continue the arbitration from the point it ceased with the initial arbitrator.[150] If arbitration commences anew, the parties may leverage previously

145. Chua, 2018, p. 11; Ross, 2013, pp. 364-365; Limbury, 2009b, p. 15; Stipanowich & Mironi, 2021, p. 32; Nigmatullina, 2018, p. 143; Bühring-Uhle et al., 2006, pp. 253-254; Blankenship, 2006, p. 37. According to most arbitration laws and rules, the new arbitrator should be appointed according to the same procedures as the replaced one. *See*, for example, Model Law on ICA, 2006, Article 15; UNCITRAL Arbitration Rules, 2021, Article 14; NAI Arbitration Rules, 2024, Article 22(1); DIS Arbitration Rules, 2018, Article 16(5); Swiss Arbitration Rules, 2021, Article 15(1).
146. However, the possibility of terminating arbitral proceedings before rendering an award is not always feasible and generally requires the consent of all parties. For instance, the Model Law on ICA, 2006, Article 32, stipulates that early termination of arbitration requires the consent of all parties. Additionally, the following arbitration rules restrict the termination of arbitral proceedings before an award is issued to cases where continuation becomes unnecessary or impossible, subject to the tribunal's discretion: UNCITRAL Arbitration Rules, 2021, Article 36(2); Swiss Arbitration Rules, 2021, Article 36(2); ICDR International Arbitration Rules, 2021, Article 35(3).
147. Nigmatullina, 2018, p. 143; Kun, 2011b, pp. 551-552; Blankenship, 2006, p. 37; Peter, 1997, pp. 99-100; Bühring-Uhle et al., 2006, p. 254; CEDR Safeguards for Caucusing, 2009, Article 7(3).
148. Ruckteschler & Wendelstein, 2021, pp. 771-772; Kaufmann-Kohler, 2009, pp. 204-205; Limbury, 2009b, p. 15; Rosoff, 2009, p. 98; Stipanowich, 2021a, p. 325; Nigmatullina, 2018, p. 143; Ross, 2013, p. 365; Peter, 1997, p. 100.
149. Gu, 2014, p. 119; Stipanowich, 2021a, p. 325. For further discussion on the interplay between efficiency and the timing of the settlement efforts, *see* section 3.3.
150. Many arbitration rules state as a default that when an arbitrator is replaced, the proceedings must continue from the stage at which they were suspended, unless the tribunal, not the parties, decides otherwise. *See*, for example, UNCITRAL Arbitration Rules, 2021, Article 15; NAI Arbitration Rules, 2024, Article 22(2); Swiss Arbitration Rules, 2021, Article 15(3). Other rules, such as the LCIA Arbitration Rules, 2020, Article 11(3), grant the tribunal complete discretion over this issue. In contrast, the DIS Arbitration Rules, 2018, Article 16(6), adopt an exceptional approach, permitting the parties to make this decision.

agreed-upon issues, submissions, and collected evidence from the terminated arbitration. Moreover, in both scenarios, the parties should have the flexibility to exclude issues agreed upon during the settlement process from those to be addressed by the substitute arbitrator or the neutral in the new process to which the parties revert.[151] *Third*, despite the proposed scope of due process safeguards, the parties may still choose to limit the application of the opt-out safeguard to specific initiatives that raise their greatest concerns. In doing so, they can consider various aspects, including the nature of the dispute, the quality of their business relationship, the level of trust among them and possibly between them and the arbitrator, the acceptance of the dual role's relevant components in the seat of arbitration and enforcement jurisdictions, and whether additional due process safeguards, including the voluntary ones presented below, are implemented in the particular process. This attitude also appears possible in light of the parties' right to revoke consent to the arbitrator's dual role at any time or subject to agreed terms, which results in reverting to the formal arbitral process with the same arbitrator.[152] In this context, the right to withdraw consent to the arbitrator's dual role and the option to opt out of arbitration with the same arbitrator can serve as supplementary safeguards, which delineate the spectrum of settlement facilitation between initiatives allowing the arbitrator to retain their adjudicative role following unsuccessful settlement attempts and those justifying opting-out of arbitration. Such a targeted approach to the opt-out safeguard is endorsed by Australia's Domestic Arbitration Act, the CIArb Practice Guideline on the Use of Mediation in Arbitration, and the Prague Rules. These frameworks allow parties to opt out, primarily to appoint a substitute arbitrator within the same proceedings, only when the arbitrator has acted as a mediator in hybrid processes involving arbitration and mediation—irrespective of whether caucusing with the parties occurred during mediation—and failed to achieve an amicable settlement.[153] A more limited approach is reflected in the CEDR Safeguards for Caucusing, which recommend this safeguard only if the arbitrator conducted ex parte communications with the parties during the settlement stage.[154] Despite the parties' discretion in determining the precise demarcation point between initiatives allowing opting out from arbitration and others that are only subject to withdrawing consent, the cross-cultural nature of ICA and the differing attitudes of legal backgrounds and practitioners regarding specific aspects of the arbitrator's dual role suggest a broader application of the opt-out safeguard than implemented by the aforementioned frameworks. Therefore, it is advisable to extend this safeguard beyond processes involving arbitration and mediation or permitting caucusing to at least encompass clear, direct initiatives of the arbitrator to facilitate settlement, such as holding settlement conferences and presenting settlement offers to the parties.

151. For further discussion about this alternative, *see* section 3.3.
152. *See* the discussion in section 7.3.1.2 above.
153. Australia Commercial Arbitration Act, 2010, Part 5, section 27D(4); CIArb Practice Guideline on the Use of Mediation in Arbitration, 2021, Article 10(4); Prague Rules, 2018, Article 9(3).
154. CEDR Safeguards for Caucusing, 2009, Article 7(3).

7.4.2 Renewed Consent and Agreement Regarding Settlement-Stage Information

If the opt-out safeguard allows parties to terminate the proceedings or appoint a different neutral to handle the dispute after unsuccessful settlement attempts by the initial arbitrator, renewed consent permits arbitration to continue with the same arbitrator. Despite being alternatives, these safeguards engage identical considerations because they represent opposite sides of the same coin: the parties' right to retain self-determination over the process.[155] However, unlike the opt-out safeguard, which addresses concerns stemming from the arbitrator's involvement in the settlement efforts by removing the arbitrator, renewed consent, allowing the same arbitrator to retain their adjudicative role in the resumed arbitration, does not inherently alleviate these concerns. Therefore, it is advisable to implement the requirement for renewed consent in conjunction with another safeguard that addresses settlement-stage information disclosed to the arbitrator during the settlement negotiations but not part of the formal record to safeguard the parties' due process rights.[156]

Interestingly, most arbitration laws, rules, and guidelines concerning these safeguards typically implement only one,[157] with Australia's Domestic Arbitration Act being the exception by incorporating both.[158] Moreover, existing safeguards often have narrow scopes. Usually regulated by the same provisions allowing opting out from arbitration, the requirement for renewed consent following failed settlement efforts typically applies only to hybrid processes where the arbitrator also serves as a mediator or processes involving caucuses. Similarly, current safeguards related to settlement-stage information solely focus on confidential disclosures made to the arbitrator during ex parte communications without sufficient attention to other settlement-related information, the regulation of which is important for protecting the parties' due process rights. These safeguards are presented below, along with recommendations for broadening their scope and enhancing their implementation.

155. Stipanowich & Mironi, 2021, p. 32; Stipanowich, 2021a, pp. 325, 356; Nigmatullina, 2018, pp. 142, 171.
156. Stipanowich, 2021a, p. 356; Weisman, 2013, p. 41; Ross, 2013, p. 364; Blankley, 2011, pp. 362-363. When parties opt out of arbitration, they remain bound by the confidentiality of the settlement stage. No further actions are typically required regarding off-record settlement-stage information, such as disclosure, since the initial arbitrator will be excused from any further involvement in the dispute. *See* Rosoff, 2009, p. 98.
157. As discussed in Chapter 5, Singapore's and Hong Kong's arbitration acts incorporate a safeguard regarding confidential information disclosed to the arbitrator during mediation. However, they do not require renewed consent from the parties for the arbitrator to resume their initial role following unsuccessful settlement efforts. In contrast, as discussed in Chapter 6, the Prague Rules require renewed consent after the arbitrator's involvement in mediation but do not address the regulation of settlement-stage information. Moreover, the CIArb Professional Practice Guideline on the Use of Mediation in Arbitration mandates renewed consent and delegates the regulation of disclosed confidential information to the parties. Similarly the CEDR Safeguards for Caucusing place both the necessity for renewed consent and the regulation of confidential information within the parties' decision-making process. *See* the discussion in sections 5.2.2.2-5.2.2.3, 6.3.2.3 & 6.3.3.2-6.3.3.3.
158. Australia Commercial Arbitration Act, 2010, Part 5, section 27D(4) & (7). Additionally, *see* the discussion in section 5.3.1.3.

7.4.2.1 *Renewed Consent*

The requirement for parties to provide renewed written consent following failed settlement efforts, as a prerequisite for the arbitrator to retain their adjudicative role in the resumed arbitration, has been introduced by Australia's Domestic Arbitration Act,[159] Quebec's arbitration act,[160] the Prague Rules,[161] the CIArb Practice Guideline on the Use of Mediation in Arbitration,[162] and the CEDR Safeguards for Caucusing.[163] Given their equal considerations, much of the discussion above regarding the opt-out safeguard is also applicable to the renewed consent safeguard, including its impact on bolstering the parties' due process rights, the potential for its implementation alongside the right to revoke consent as complementary safeguards, and the recommendations about the desired scope of its application. Renewed consent should be deemed essential following particular settlement initiatives to ensure that parties are not unduly bound by their initial consent and waiver to the arbitrator's dual role—as stipulated in the IBA Guidelines on Conflicts of Interest[164]—and mitigate the risk of procedural rights being compromised due to developments in the settlement process or concerns about the arbitrator's ability to maintain impartiality and independence post-settlement negotiations.[165] While the scope of its application can be subject to agreement, it should not be confined solely to hybrid processes involving arbitration and mediation or processes allowing ex parte communications, as mandated in the aforementioned frameworks. Instead, it should at least encompass any clear, direct involvement of the arbitrator in settlement efforts, as recommended above concerning the opt-out safeguard.

The benefits of requiring second consent are evident. Unlike parties' initial consent, renewed consent before reverting to formal arbitration enables parties to reassess their stance toward the arbitrator after considering all concerns raised during the settlement negotiations, including those related to the disclosure of confidential information and their vested interests.[166] This requirement undoubtedly contributes to mitigating the risks of bias and violations of due process rights.[167] Consequently, some scholars suggest that if attempts are made throughout the process to address separate issues at different intervals, renewed consent should be sought after each interval.[168]

159. Australia Commercial Arbitration Act, 2010, Part 5, section 27D(4).
160. Quebec Arbitration Act, 2014, section 620.
161. Prague Rules, 2018, Article 9(3), only in relation to the arbitrator's role as a mediator.
162. CIArb Practice Guideline on the Use of Mediation in Arbitration, 2021, Article 10(4).
163. CEDR Safeguards for Caucusing, 2009, Article 7(3).
164. IBA Guidelines on Conflicts of Interest in International Arbitration, 2024, General Standard 4(d). For criticism about this arrangement, *see* section 6.3.2.2.
165. Ruckteschler & Wendelstein, 2021, pp. 771-772; Gu, 2016, p. 102; Ross, 2013, p. 364; Nigmatullina, 2018, p. 170; Limbury, 2009b, p. 15; Stipanowich & Mironi, 2021, p. 32; Naughton, 2007, p. 37.
166. Limbury, 2009b, p. 15; Deekshitha & Saha, 2014, pp. 96-97; Ross, 2013, p. 364; Nigmatullina, 2018, p. 171. Additionally, *see* CEDR Safeguards for Caucusing, 2009, Article 7(3), considering consent granted post-settlement stage more effective, as it allows parties to incorporate insights from the settlement negotiations.
167. Deekshitha & Saha, 2014, pp. 96-97; Nigmatullina, 2018, p. 201.
168. Ross, 2013, p. 364; Nigmatullina, 2018, p. 170.

Furthermore, since second consent, as proposed above, should be accompanied by an express waiver of the right of challenge, it may offer better protection to the award against future challenges. The timing of the renewed consent and waiver demonstrates that the parties are fully informed about the process and have chosen to proceed in alignment with their interests and needs after reevaluating the developments and reconsidering the consequences of the arbitrator reverting to the adjudicative role.

7.4.2.2 Agreement Regarding Settlement-Stage Information

Based on the literature and current legal instruments concerning the arbitrator's role as a settlement facilitator, two opposing approaches can be adopted for handling information disclosed to the arbitrator during the settlement process that is not part of the formal record. According to one approach, when the arbitrator retains the adjudicative role following unsuccessful settlement attempts, they should refrain from relying on that information and instead base the award solely on the formal arbitration record.[169] This *disregard approach*, employed by some arbitration rules and guidelines,[170] underscores the confidential nature of the settlement stage, which is frequently mandated as an explicit legal obligation of the parties and the neutral by mediation and arbitration statutes,[171] rules, and guidelines.[172] Arguably, by preserving confidentiality during the settlement stage and respecting the need to base the arbitral award solely on the formal record, this regulatory arrangement aligns with the fundamental features of each dispute resolution method when conducted independently.[173] Although the arbitrator may not be able to completely "forget" off-record information shared during the settlement negotiations, as a professional adjudicator, they should be capable of excluding that information while deciding the dispute, just as judges do when inadmissible submissions or classified information are accidentally or unlawfully presented before them:

169. Ruckteschler & Wendelstein, 2021, p. 772; Stipanowich, 2021a, p. 355; Nigmatullina, 2018, p. 202; Benzidi, 2017, pp. 14-15, 17-18; Goodrich, 2012, p. 7; Leon & Peterson, 2009, p. 93; Burr, 2005, p. 68; Abramson, 1999, p. 14; Plant, 2000, p. 146; Marriott, 2005, p. 545; Limbury, 2009b, p. 15.
170. CEDR Rules for Settlement Facilitation, 2009, Article 3(4)-(5); CEDR Safeguards for Caucusing, 2009, Article 7(1); Stipanowich & Kaskell, 2001, pp. 24, 32-33, relating to this approach as adopted by the CPR Final Report on the Future of Arbitration; Abramson, 1999, p. 14, advocating for this approach in the Protocols for International Arbitrators Who Dare to Settle Cases.
171. Such as U.S. Uniform Mediation Act, 2010, sections 4-5; Singapore International Arbitration Act, 1994, Article 17(2)(b); Hong Kong Arbitration Ordinance, 2011, Article 33(3)(b); Australia Commercial Arbitration Act, 2010, Part 5, section 27D(2)(b).
172. Such as UNCITRAL Mediation Rules, 2021, Articles 5-7; LCIA Mediation Rules, 2020, Article 12; CIETAC Guidelines on Evidence, 2024, Article 19(1); NAI Mediation Rules, 2017, Article 10; Stipanowich & Kaskell, 2001, p. 24, in relation to the CPR Final Report on the Future of Arbitration. On the other hand, as discussed in section 5.2.2.1, leading arbitration rules in China impose statutory confidentiality of the settlement stage only on the parties, leaving uncertainties regarding its application to the arbitrator.
173. Benzidi, 2017, p. 14.

> It will, of course, be difficult for the arbitrator to completely disregard and "forget" any confidential information received during the mediation. However, this is not a completely unusual situation for an arbitrator. The same mental exercise is required of an arbitrator when he/she gains knowledge from documents which were submitted without the prior permission of the arbitral tribunal and which the arbitral tribunal does not accept, or in situations where the arbitrator needs to make sure that he/she does not rule with hindsight knowledge because only the information which was available at an earlier point in time is relevant.[174]

Consequently, concerns regarding bias and due process are mitigated,[175] with the assurance that information shared during the settlement stage will neither be disclosed to other parties nor used by the arbitrator as a basis for the award.[176] This assurance may encourage parties to consent to the arbitrator's role as a settlement facilitator and engage candidly and openly during the settlement stage. Such openness, in turn, increases the likelihood of reaching an amicable resolution to the dispute.[177]

According to another approach, despite being a professional adjudicator, it is unrealistic to expect the arbitrator to mentally disregard inadmissible settlement-stage information while deciding the dispute,[178] a task professional judges struggle to successfully accomplish, per the empirical data.[179] Therefore, by agreeing to employ the arbitrator with the dual role, the parties opt for a "different process"[180] with a unique regime that allows the arbitrator to knowingly consider confidential information and other in-depth knowledge acquired during the settlement phase when deciding the dispute.[181] Therefore, to ensure enhanced transparency of this process, secure the parties' right to be heard and answer their opponents' claims, minimize bias

174. Ruckteschler & Wendelstein, 2021, pp. 772-773. *See also* Kun, 2020a, p. 156; Nigmatullina, 2018, pp. 207-208; Ross, 2013, p. 360; Weisman, 2013, p. 41; Goodrich, 2012, p. 7; Blankley, 2011, pp. 365-366; Kun & Kaufmann-Kohler, 2008, p. 491; Schneider, 1998, p. 94; Marriott, 2005, pp. 544-545, arguing that basing the award solely on the formal record should not be difficult for arbitrators, who "are all taught to make decisions only on the basis of applicable evidence properly admitted." Additionally, *see* the discussion in section 5.2.2.1 concerning the disregard of settlement-stage information by Chinese arbitrators, as well as the 2006 Robinson Survey, discussed in section 5.3.1.1, where 95% of the respondent judges expressed a lack of concern after being exposed to inadmissible or confidential information during the pre-trial conference, when, following unsuccessful settlement attempts, they had to decide the dispute.
175. Nigmatullina, 2018, pp. 202, 207.
176. Deason, 2013, p. 227; Nigmatullina, 2018, p. 203; Stipanowich & Mironi, 2021, p. 31; Stipanowich, 2021a, p. 301. *See also* Rosoff, 2009, p. 96, holding that waiving the right of challenge after employing the arbitrator in a dual role "necessarily contain a waiver of the arbitrator's duty to disclose confidential information obtained" during the settlement stage.
177. *See* the discussion in sections 2.3.3 & 3.4 regarding the parties' incentive to settle.
178. Ludington, 2017, p. 320; Benzidi, 2017, pp. 14-15, 18; Harris, 2016, p. 94; Nigmatullina, 2018, pp. 206, 208-210; Lew, 2005, p. 426; Pappas, 2013, p. 42; Peter, 1997, p. 94; Cremades, 1998, p. 163; Ross, 2013, p. 360; Elliott, 1995, p. 167.
179. *See* the discussion in section 4.2.1 regarding the 2002-2004 Andrew Study and the 2008 Wissler Survey, which demonstrate that judges may be susceptible to bias after being exposed to inadmissible information, potentially impairing their ability to handle the case impartially following failed settlement attempts.
180. Blankenship, 2006, p. 37.
181. Gu, 2021, p. 75; Kun, 2020a, p. 154; Gu, 2019, p. 135; Benzidi, 2017, pp. 18-19; Nigmatullina, 2018, pp. 208, 210; Stipanowich, 2021a, p. 356; Stipanowich & Mironi, 2021, p. 31; Rosoff, 2009, p. 100; Kun & Kaufmann-Kohler, 2008, p. 492; Marriott, 2005, p. 545; De Vera, 2004, p. 186.

and due process concerns,[182] and consequently diminish future enforceability risks,[183] the arbitrator should disclose that information to all parties before reverting to their adjudicative role:

> A natural advantage of this process is that arbitrator-mediators are allowed to be influenced by mediation and the problems associated with the combination of arbitration and mediation proceedings are mostly resolved. Since the arbitrator-mediator can merely disclose information received during mediation for the purposes of resuming arbitration, there is no need to question whether or not such information affected his decisions in arbitration. In fact, mediation under this system may provide an alternative way to introduce or obtain evidence to be used in arbitration.[184]

Although the settlement stage is typically subject to statutory confidentiality, disclosure of settlement-stage information should be permissible given the parties' recognized right to waive privilege in proceedings covered by confidentiality.[185] As evidenced in earlier sections, this right is supported by mediation laws,[186] as well as mediation and arbitration rules and guidelines.[187] This *disclosure approach* is further affirmed by court decisions discussed in Chapter 5, including the court-developed waiver doctrine in the US, which permits waiver subject to express agreement among all relevant parties.[188] Additionally, a recent precedent in the UK has recognized the waiver of confidentiality within arbitral proceedings, even when based on the parties' implicit consent.[189] In the context of arbitral proceedings, disclosure of settlement-stage information can be legitimized under Article 24(3) of the Model Law on ICA,

182. Yip, 2021, pp. 193-194; Stipanowich, 2021a, p. 321; Ludington, 2017, p. 318; Rosoff, 2009, p. 100; Nigmatullina, 2018, p. 198.
183. Nigmatullina, 2018, p. 198; Schneider, 1998, p. 96; Marriott, 2005, p. 545.
184. Rosoff, 2009, p. 100. *See also* Stipanowich, 2021a, p. 355; Harris, 2016, p. 94, arguing that "disclosure of confidential information received is perhaps a more realistic approach than expecting an arbitrator to forget what he or she has heard." Additionally, *see* the CEDR Safeguards for Caucusing, 2009, Article 7(1), acknowledging that returning to arbitration after mediation may impose a disclosure duty on the arbitrator.
185. Benzidi, 2017, pp. 11-12, 20; Nigmatullina, 2018, pp. 204-206; Blankley, 2011, pp. 322, 338-339, 351-354; Deekshitha & Saha, 2014, p. 90.
186. Such as the Model Law on ICA, 2006, Articles 9-10, and the U.S. Uniform Mediation Act, 2010, sections 4-5 & 7A, which permit parties involved in mediation and settlement proceedings covered by confidentiality to waive privilege, subject to their consent or agreement.
187. Such as UNCITRAL Mediation Rules, 2021, Article 6; ICSID Mediation Rules, 2022, Article 10; DIS Conciliation Rules, 2002, Article 14; LCIA Mediation Rules, 2020, Article 12(3); CEDR Safeguards for Caucusing, 2009, Article 7(4); CIArb Practice Guideline on the Use of Mediation in Arbitration, 2021, Article 3(4); NAI Mediation Rules, 2017, Article 10(b) & (g); ADRIC Med-Arb Rules, 2020, Article 6(6); ADRIC Mediation Rules, 2012, Article 15(3); Stipanowich & Kaskell, 2001, p. 32, in relation to the Protocol for Arbitrators Who Participate in Settlement Discussions, Protocol 6, which allows parties to waive settlement-stage confidentiality subject to express written agreement.
188. *See* the discussion in section 5.3.1.1, particularly regarding the following cases: *Bowden v. Weickert*, 2003; *Gaskin v. Gaskin*, 2006; *Town of Clinton v. Geological Services Corp.*, 2006.
189. *Halliburton Company v. Chubb Bermuda Insurance Ltd*, 2020, discussed in section 5.3.1.2. The court stated (in para. 88) that, where disclosure of confidential information is required, the parties' necessary consent need not always be expressly stated but may "be inferred from the arbitration agreement itself." Despite the said, given the court's indication in this case that the test for impartiality may be enforced more strictly in ICA proceedings, it appears significantly

which specifies that "all statements, documents or other information supplied to the arbitral tribunal by one party shall be communicated to the other party."[190] This duty of disclosure also arises from the arbitrator's obligation to reveal any circumstances that may cause reasonable concerns about their impartiality or independence—a statutory obligation recognized in many arbitration laws and rules and applicable throughout the arbitral process.[191] Arguably, if the arbitrator is exposed to information during the settlement stage that may influence their discretion when rendering the award, they are obliged to disclose that information to all parties before resuming their adjudicative role,[192] as stipulated in the arbitration laws of jurisdictions such as Singapore, Hong Kong, and Australia that authorize arbitrators to act as settlement facilitators.[193]

Admittedly, the practical choice between the two competing approaches to handling settlement-stage information is far from straightforward, as both struggle to fully mitigate the risks to parties' due process rights arising from the arbitrator's exposure to such information.[194] *First*, neither approach can inherently guarantee that the arbitrator remains entirely uninfluenced by settlement-stage information when deciding the dispute. The aforementioned empirical data regarding judges demonstrates that even when adjudicators attempt to avoid off-record information, they may still be subject to its influence, at least unconsciously.[195] Nevertheless, the same can be said about the disclosure approach, as the mere fact that irrelevant or inadmissible information revealed to the arbitrator during the settlement negotiations is disclosed to the parties and excluded from the award does not guarantee that it did not subtly influence the arbitrator's reasoning or decision-making process.[196] *Second*, both approaches are accompanied by notable implementation difficulties. The disregard approach, which prohibits any disclosure of settlement-stage information regardless of the arbitrator's obligation to avoid it, may practically hinder the ability to examine whether and how the information has improperly influenced the arbitrator's discretion while rendering the award. In the context of information shared with the arbitrator during caucusing, the comparison to the duty of judges to disregard inadmissible

safer to rely on an explicit written agreement to waive confidentiality, even when the regulatory framework of the applicable law or rules adopts a disclosure-based approach. For further discussion, *see* Nigmatullina, 2018, p. 206; Blankley, 2011, p. 366.

190. Model Law on ICA, 2006, Article 24(3).
191. Gojkovic, 2021, p. 70; Stipanowich, 2021a, p. 350; Benzidi, 2017, p. 26. For instance, this continuing duty of disclosure is established in the following arbitration laws and rules: Model Law on ICA, 2006, Article 12; U.K. Arbitration Act, 1996, Article 24(1)(a); UNCITRAL Arbitration Rules, 2021, Article 11; NAI Arbitration Rules, 2024, Article 13(2)-(4); Swiss Arbitration Rules, 2021, Article 12; LCIA Arbitration Rules, 2020, Article 5(5).
192. Stipanowich, 2021a, p. 350. Conversely, *see* Rosoff, 2009, p. 96, suggesting that disclosure should not necessarily relate to the information received during the settlement stage but rather to the circumstances that may create a risk of bias.
193. Singapore International Arbitration Act, 1994, Article 17(2)(b); Hong Kong Arbitration Ordinance, 2011, Article 33(3)(b); Australia Commercial Arbitration Act, 2010, Part 5, section 27D(2)(b).
194. Harris, 2016, p. 94; Kun, 2011b, p. 554; Blankley, 2011, pp. 366-367.
195. Nigmatullina, 2018, p. 208; Deekshitha & Saha, 2014, p. 96; Lang, 2009, p. 100; Kaufmann-Kohler, 2009, pp. 198-199.
196. Harris, 2016, p. 94; Blankley, 2011, pp. 334-335.

submissions may not be entirely accurate. Unlike judicial proceedings where inadmissible submissions are often known to all parties or documented in the formal record, information shared with the arbitrator ex parte is known only to the disclosing party and the arbitrator, with no formal documentation, which makes future review challenging.[197] The disclosure approach also presents significant implementation difficulties. In addition to its general downsides (e.g., deterring parties from engaging the arbitrator with the dual role, inhibiting candidness during the settlement process, and tactically using the settlement stage to avoid disclosure or, contrarily, to allow disclosure related to other parties),[198] the decision about the scope of disclosure can be challenging. While full disclosure may be seen as far-reaching, leaving the scope of disclosure to the arbitrator's discretion—as implemented in the regulatory arrangements in Singapore, Hong Kong, and Australia, which oblige the arbitrator to disclose settlement-stage information "material to the arbitral proceedings"[199]—introduces uncertainties regarding handling the information and may further discourage parties from engaging the arbitrator as a settlement facilitator.[200] Moreover, current regulatory arrangements implementing the disclosure approach focus solely on information shared with the arbitrator during caucusing[201] without regulating settlement-related information disclosed during joint settlement sessions, which should also be addressed, as recommended below. *Third*, strict and inflexible regulation of settlement-stage information through either of these diametrically opposed approaches risks undermining party autonomy and may affect parties' decision on whether to engage the arbitrator in a dual role and share relevant information during the settlement stage.[202]

For these reasons, and considering the contractual nature of arbitration—which should respect "the parties' intent regarding the use of information shared with the neutral" during the settlement process[203]—the precise regulatory framework for this

197. Limbury, 2009a, p. 85; Nigmatullina, 2018, pp. 208-209; Peter, 1997, pp. 93-94.
198. *See* the discussion in sections 5.2.2.3 & 5.3.1.3. *See also* Ruckteschler & Wendelstein, 2021, p. 773; Monichino, 2010, p. 46; Harris, 2016, p. 94; CIArb Practice Guideline on the Use of Mediation in Arbitration, 2021, Article 8(5).
199. Singapore International Arbitration Act, 1994, Article 17(3); Hong Kong Arbitration Ordinance, 2011, Article 33(4); Australia Commercial Arbitration Act, 2010, Part 5, section 27D(7).
200. *See* the discussion in section 5.2.2.3. *See also* Ruckteschler & Wendelstein, 2021, p. 773, arguing that this obligation is more challenging for the arbitrator than simply disregarding any confidential information disclosed during the settlement phase "as the evaluation of which information is material to the arbitration proceedings may well differ from his/her point of view and from the point of view of the respective other party."
201. Singapore International Arbitration Act, 1994, Article 17(3); Hong Kong Arbitration Ordinance, 2011, Article 33(4); Australia Commercial Arbitration Act, 2010, Part 5, section 27D(7); CEDR Safeguards for Caucusing, 2009, Article 7(1); CIArb Practice Guideline on the Use of Mediation in Arbitration, 2021, Article 8(6); Stipanowich & Mironi, 2021, pp. 31-32, discussing the draft guidelines of the International Task Force on Mixed Mode Dispute Resolution, which regulate only the disclosure of information shared with the arbitrator ex parte. *See also* Stipanowich, 2021a, p. 355; Nigmatullina, 2018, p. 190.
202. Gojkovic, 2021, p. 71; Nigmatullina, 2018, p. 202; Ludington, 2017, pp. 320-321; Goodrich, 2012, pp. 6-8.
203. Ludington, 2017, pp. 320-321. *See also* Gojkovic, 2021, p. 71, holding that, given the contractual nature of arbitration, the approach to handling information disclosed to the arbitrator during the settlement stage should be determined "from the eyes of the parties.";

matter should be left to the parties' discretion, as proposed by certain guidelines addressing settlement-stage information.[204] However, to enable parties to explore more flexible and adaptable regulatory options, this book proposes a roadmap for addressing settlement-stage information from a broader perspective than current approaches, drawing on two key insights derived from the discussions in previous chapters. *First*, confidential discussions and settlement-related information can affect the parties' due process rights, whether shared with the arbitrator ex parte or during joint settlement sessions. As discussed in Chapter 4, joint settlement sessions often provide the arbitrator with valuable and sensitive off-record information that may significantly influence their discretion when deciding the dispute, which typically would not have been disclosed to a "pure arbitrator" in formal arbitral proceedings. This information may include the parties' personal histories, business relationships, underlying conflicts and interests, and possibly information about previous settlement negotiations. Additionally, the arbitrator's behavior and remarks during these joint sessions regarding the parties' arguments, evidence, and the discussed settlement elements are crucial for assessing the effect of the arbitrator's involvement in the settlement negotiations on the final award.[205] Therefore, instead of confining the regulation of confidentiality and related safeguards solely to information shared and discussions made during caucusing, extending its application to each of the following levels is suggested, depending on several considerations presented below: (a) *joint-sessions confidentiality*, which applies to settlement-related discussions and information shared with the arbitrator in the presence of all parties but not part of the formal record, and (b) *ex parte confidentiality*, which covers settlement-related discussions and information shared with the arbitrator during caucusing that is obviously not part of the formal record.[206] *Second*, while disclosure of confidential information is typically required when the arbitrator is authorized to rely on it to formulate the award, limiting disclosure solely to this scenario may not align with reality. In practice, some disclosure may also be required regarding settlement-stage information that cannot be used to formulate the award. For

Blankley, 2011, p. 366, claiming that the decision regarding "what mediation communications, if any, can be considered for the purpose of the arbitration award" should stem from a carefully detailed, contractually agreed arrangement between the parties.

204. *See*, for example, the following guidelines that delegate decisions on handling settlement-stage information in renewed arbitration to the parties: CEDR Safeguards for Caucusing, 2009, Article 7(1); CIArb Practice Guideline on the Use of Mediation in Arbitration, 2021, Article 8(6); Stipanowich & Mironi, 2021, pp. 31-32, referring to the draft guidelines of the International Task Force on Mixed Mode Dispute Resolution, which stipulate that parties should decide whether information shared with the arbitrator ex parte during the settlement stage should be disclosed when arbitration resumes and whether the award can be based on this information or solely on the formal record. Additionally, *see* ADRIC Mediation Rules, 2012, Article 15(7), requiring the mediator, before engaging in any ex parte communication or obtaining confidential information, to discuss the nature of such interactions with the parties, reach an agreement regarding disclosure, and inform them of any limitations to confidentiality.

205. *See* the discussion in sections 4.2.1-4.2.2.

206. Benzidi, 2017, pp. 12, 17-18, identifying two levels of confidentiality in hybrid processes involving arbitration and mediation: the first pertains to joint sessions where the neutral meets with all parties, and the second to caucuses involving only one party. *See also* Blankley, 2011, p. 334, relating to both joint and ex parte settlement sessions as involving confidential communications with the arbitrator.

instance, parties may prefer to permit enhanced judicial review concerning the influence of the arbitrator's involvement in the settlement process on the final award, particularly if the arbitrator coerces parties into a settlement or violates the agreed terms of the dual role.[207] In this context, just as confidentiality of the settlement process serves the interests of the parties involved in the specific dispute and aligns with wider public policy considerations aimed at protecting classified information from unauthorized discovery,[208] disclosure can be viewed more broadly as a mechanism to enhance the limited judicial review of arbitral proceedings and strengthen the protection of the parties' due process rights.[209] However, when disclosure is needed merely to allow enhanced future review, it may not need to be made directly to all parties. Instead, it may be carried out through classified records attached to the file, accessible only to the relevant parties. Indeed, this arrangement may invite objections to the enforceability of the final award from losing parties—who earlier waived their right of challenge—while relating to those classified records. However, when this arrangement, which strives to enable a fair trade-off between the need to educate the arbitrator with information necessary for settlement facilitation and the legitimate desire to maintain confidentiality, is implemented only related to one of the aforementioned levels of confidentiality, the risk for future challenge is mitigated. Additionally, the possibility of enhanced future review, even if eventually not executed, may incentivize the arbitrator to approach the settlement process cautiously while adhering to the parties' agreement precisely and avoiding behavior and discussions that could undermine due process rights and, consequently, the enforcement of the award.

Considering the above, parties may agree on the approach to be applied to settlement-stage information corresponding to each level of confidentiality. If parties permit the arbitrator to rely on such information when deciding the dispute following unsuccessful settlement attempts, they should explicitly waive confidentiality for that level.[210] Hence, classified records can document the relevant parts of the settlement stage, and before the arbitrator resumes their adjudicative role, these records can be disclosed to all parties. If parties opt not to allow the arbitrator to rely on settlement-stage information when formulating the award, they can choose between implementing the disregard approach, maintaining the relevant parts of the settlement stage both confidential and without any documentation,[211] or keeping them confidential but documenting them within classified records accessible only to the relevant parties and possible future review. In addition to offering a more flexible framework for regulating settlement-stage information, this roadmap provides a clear solution regarding the scope of disclosure—precisely, the information documented in classified records in real time—thereby reducing the likelihood of future discords with the arbitrator on this matter.

207. Blankley, 2011, p. 336.
208. Blankley, 2011, p. 359.
209. Houzhi, 2005, 554.
210. Benzidi, 2017, pp. 19-20; Ross, 2013, p. 364; Blankley, 2011, pp. 365-366.
211. *See*, in this regard, LCIA Mediation Rules, 2020, Article 12(5), which prohibit maintaining any formal record or transcript of the mediation.

As part of their discretion in applying these regulatory options, the parties can permit the arbitrator to rely on information disclosed during joint settlement sessions while implementing the disregard approach for information revealed during caucuses.[212] This middle-way approach offers two main advantages. *First*, it only waives confidentiality for joint sessions, making it potentially less deterrent to the parties than a complete waiver of confidentiality. *Second*, it allows the parties to decide during the settlement process itself, based on the forum in which the information is shared—joint or ex parte sessions—how the arbitrator should handle the information. This decision of the parties can rely on practical considerations, such as the nature of the dispute, the sensitivity of the information, the main setting of the settlement stage (i.e., joint sessions or caucusing),[213] the level of trust between parties and with the arbitrator, potential future business relationships, the likelihood of amicable settlement, and the stance of applicable arbitration laws and rules on settlement-stage information.[214] As part of this outline, settlement-stage information shared during joint sessions, although already known to all parties, should formally be disclosed by the arbitrator since they are authorized to rely on it while deciding the dispute.

Although this roadmap provides more regulatory options for settlement-stage information than current approaches, none can guarantee complete protection of parties' due process rights following the arbitrator's involvement in the settlement negotiations and exposure to such information. Therefore, the decision on the exact regulatory architecture can be made from an even broader perspective by considering additional possible configurations of the tribunal during and following the settlement stage.[215] This expansive approach can include limiting the arbitrator's decision authority after futile settlement attempts and involving only some tribunal members in the settlement efforts, which, as discussed below, can further mitigate potential risks to parties' due process rights.

212. *See*, in this regard, Blankley, 2011, p. 334, emphasizing that while both sessions are confidential, "parties may have different expectations of privacy in a joint session than they do in a caucus. For example, parties who may be comfortable with the neutral relying on joint session communications in fashioning an award may not be comfortable with the arbitrator relying on caucus communications to fashion the same award. Information shared in a caucus is meant to be 'extra' confidential, and it usually cannot be disclosed to the opposing party without the speaking party's consent." *See also* Benzidi, 2017, pp. 20-21, 29, suggesting that when the arbitrator is authorized to engage in the settlement process, the default rule should include a waiver of confidentiality over joint settlement sessions unless the parties agree otherwise.
213. Blankley, 2011, pp. 366-367.
214. For example, Chinese arbitration law, applicable to both domestic and international arbitral proceedings, is silent on the possibility of utilizing settlement-stage information in rendering an award. However, as noted earlier, leading arbitration institutes in the country explicitly prohibit parties (but interestingly not arbitrators) from using such information during resumed arbitration, which may indicate that the disregard approach is the only applicable one under their rules. *See* CIETAC Arbitration Rules, 2024, Article 47(9); BAC Arbitration Rules, 2022, Article 43(5); SCIA Arbitration Rules, 2022, Article 48(6).
215. Kun, 2011b, p. 554.

7.4.3 Arbitrator's Opt-Out of the Arbitral Process

Another recommended mandatory safeguard for parties' due process rights is allowing the arbitrator to resign from the resumed arbitration if, following their engagement in unsuccessful settlement attempts, they develop doubts regarding their ability to remain independent and impartial in its course:

> There's no litmus test that can be applied in such a situation because everything depends upon the particular circumstances and the personalities involved. ... You will have to consider the nature of what had been imparted to you confidentially, ... the extent to which it related to the issues for determination in the arbitration phase and whether it is likely to affect the way in which you would perceive relevant witnesses and their credibility or has otherwise left you feeling uncomfortable about the prospect of ensuring a fair hearing and providing an unbiased award.[216]

This opt-out alternative for the arbitrator is anchored in certain rules and guidelines concerning the arbitrator's role as a settlement facilitator, all of which entrust the decision to the arbitrator.[217] The question is whether the arbitrator should exercise this opt-out option after failed settlement efforts if parties grant a second consent accompanied by a renewed waiver of the right of challenge based on such involvement in the settlement. According to one view, since the arbitrator is obliged to carry out the dual role according to the specific terms and conditions of the parties' agreement,[218] so long as these conditions are met, opting out of arbitration should typically be subordinated to the parties' will. If, after failed settlement efforts, the parties have reevaluated their attitudes toward the continuing services of the arbitrator and granted a renewed consent and waiver, then, considering the timing of these renewed consent and waiver, the chances to challenge the award or the arbitrator are quite low. Therefore, the arbitrator should not necessarily withdraw from the resumed arbitration despite any doubts about the ability to remain impartial and independent.[219] However, according to the prevailing view in the literature, if, following their engagement in the settlement process and exposure to settlement-stage information, the arbitrator develops doubts, then resignation is mandatory, even when parties are willing for the arbitrator to maintain their adjudicative role.[220]

216. Limbury, 2009b, p. 17.
217. *See*, for example, IBA Guidelines on Conflicts of Interest in International Arbitration, 2024, General Standard 4(d); CEDR Rules for Settlement Facilitation, 2009, Article 7; CEDR Safeguards for Caucusing, 2009, Article 7(6); Stipanowich & Kaskell, 2001, p. 24, referring to the CPR Final Report on the Future of Arbitration; Stipanowich & Mironi, 2021, p. 32, referring to the draft guidelines of the International Task Force on Mixed Mode Dispute Resolution.
218. Stipanowich & Kaskell, 2001, p. 32; Plant, 2000, p. 146.
219. Nigmatullina, 2018, p. 208; Ludington, 2017, p. 320, holding that parties may waive the arbitrator's obligation to withdraw from arbitration despite concerns about impartiality after participating in the settlement process.
220. Baysal & Cevik, 2021; Stipanowich, 2021a, p. 357; Chua, 2018, p. 11; Marzolini, 2016, p. 118; Ross, 2013, p. 365; Kaufmann-Kohler, 2009, pp. 204-205; Rosoff, 2009, pp. 96-97.

Indeed, the arbitrator's obligation to act impartially and independently is a continuous and self-contained commitment that applies throughout the arbitral proceedings.[221] The fact that parties have waived their right of challenge cannot grant the arbitrator the right to act partially during the arbitral process or while deciding the dispute.[222] Therefore, although starting the arbitration anew or replacing the arbitrator is counterproductive in terms of efficiency—which, as mentioned, constitutes an important consideration for initially allowing the arbitrator's dual role[223]—it is advisable to keep this mandatory safeguard subject to the sole decision of the arbitrator. Hence, the arbitrator's independent duty to remain impartial is better expressed, while the parties' due process rights can potentially be better served. Granting this power to the arbitrator allows them "to act as gatekeepers and help to establish safeguards to ensure that these single-neutral hybrid processes remain more efficient, ethical and afford finality."[224] Knowing that the arbitrator can recuse themselves from arbitration if, following their engagement in the settlement efforts, they have lingering doubts regarding their impartiality and independence, the parties are incentivized to precisely adhere to the agreed terms of the settlement process and refrain from involving the arbitrator in the conflict in a way that undermines their impartiality and independent discretion. Consequently, when similar to the parties' opt-out option, the application of this safeguard is limited only to direct settlement initiatives of the arbitrator or indirect initiatives that necessitate express consent or tend to provoke controversies among legal backgrounds and practitioners, the chances for the arbitrator's resignation to occur in practice become significantly exceptional.[225]

At the same time, since the arbitrator is a party to the agreement allowing the dual role or, at least, is responsible for its implementation,[226] they should refrain from surprising the parties with a resignation, even when doubts arise following their involvement in the settlement process. Therefore, a default rule is recommended: when the arbitrator considers resigning, they should first announce their intention to the parties and inquire about their positions.[227] If at least one party agrees that the doubts justify resignation, the arbitrator can exercise the opt-out option immediately.

---

221. For example, this duty of the arbitrator is anchored in the following arbitration laws, rules and guidelines: Model Law on ICA, 2006, Article 12; UNCITRAL Arbitration Rules, 2021, Articles 11 & 12(1); NAI Arbitration Rules, 2024, Article 13(2); Swiss Arbitration Rules, 2021, Article 12(1); ICC Arbitration Rules, 2021, Article 14(1); ICDR International Arbitration Rules, 2021, Article 14; IBA Guidelines on Conflicts of Interest in International Arbitration, 2024, General Standard 4(d); U.K. Arbitration Act, 1996, section 33(1)(a). *See also* Gu, 2019, p. 143; Benzidi, 2017, p. 26; Rosoff, 2009, p. 96.
222. Rosoff, 2009, p. 96.
223. Ruckteschler & Wendelstein, 2021, pp. 771-772; Kaufmann-Kohler, 2009, pp. 204-205; Limbury, 2009b, p. 15; Stipanowich, 2021a, p. 325; Nigmatullina, 2018, p. 143; Ross, 2013, p. 365; Peter, 1997, p. 100.
224. Ross, 2013, p. 352.
225. Kaufmann-Kohler, 2009, p. 205; Rosoff, 2009, p. 97.
226. Pryles, 2007, pp. 330-333; Fouchard et al., 1999, pp. 601-602; Holtzmann & Neuhaus, 1989, pp. 556-557.
227. Nigmatullina, 2018, p. 207; Limbury, 2009b, p. 17; Limbury, 2009a, p. 85. This approach is reflected in Article 21(6) of the NAI Arbitration Rules, 2024, stipulating that the release of an arbitrator, even at the arbitrator's own request, must be preceded by consultation with the parties to hear their positions.

However, if all parties express a clear preference for the arbitrator to resume the adjudicative role, the arbitrator can use this opportunity to address the factors underlying the doubts regarding impartiality. For example, if these doubts stem from particular information shared by one party during caucusing that remained confidential, the arbitrator may seek permission from that party to disclose the information to the other parties, thereby allowing them to assess its impact on the arbitrator's ability to resume their role. If permission is granted, which enables the arbitrator to "come clean" with that burdensome information, the subsequent second consent and waiver from the parties are reinforced, thus nullifying the need for resignation from the arbitrator's perspective.

7.4.4 Limiting the Arbitrator's Mandate Following Futile Attempts to Settle

If the parties are willing to further enhance the protection of their due process rights following the arbitrator's return to their adjudicative role after unsuccessful settlement attempts, they can agree on a complementary arrangement that limits the subjects to be adjudicated during the renewed arbitration. This arrangement can exclude matters that raise most of their concerns regarding the arbitrator's ability to remain independent and impartial due to their involvement in the settlement process and exposure to confidential information. However, this option, which de facto implements the aforementioned parties' opt out of arbitration on a partial basis, may not always be practical and may also result in additional costs and delays, as excluded issues from the scope of the renewed arbitration must be resolved via an alternative method to arbitration. Therefore, in addition to limiting the issues to be adjudicated within the renewed arbitration—or as an alternative measure—the parties can narrow the arbitrator's decision-making authority on the case's merits.[228] Several methods exist to implement this voluntary safeguard, which were originally designed as variations of Med-Arb processes. Nonetheless, these variations can equally apply to all scenarios, allowing the arbitrator to facilitate a settlement, whether as part of a standalone arbitration or within hybrid processes involving arbitration and mediation.[229] As discussed in Chapter 2, following unsuccessful settlement attempts, parties can implement a "baseball arbitration" or an analogous version to MEDALOA, where each party presents a final offer, and the arbitrator is limited to adopting one of them based on equity standards or other agreed criteria. Alternatively, parties can agree on High-Low Arbitration, where they exchange written final offers or agree on a range for the award. If these offers or agreed ranges are disclosed to the arbitrator, the arbitrator is obliged to issue the final award within their limits. If they are not disclosed to the arbitrator, an award falling within the agreed limits becomes final and binding; otherwise, the award is automatically corrected to the nearest edge of the agreed range.[230]

228. Kun, 2011b, p. 554.
229. Stipanowich, 2021a, p. 357; Stipanowich & Mironi, 2021, p. 32; Nigmatullina, 2018, pp. 149-150.
230. *See* the discussion about these alternatives in section 2.4.1.

Indeed, these limitations on the arbitrator's decision authority cannot eliminate all due process concerns stemming from the arbitrator's involvement in the settlement process and the resulting exposure to confidential information.[231] Additionally, these arrangements still require considerable trust from the parties in the arbitrator,[232] the erosion of which, following engagement with the settlement attempts, was the reason for limiting their decision authority. Furthermore, such arrangements seem suitable primarily for monetary disputes and less for disputes involving multiple issues that require non-monetary decisions.[233] Nevertheless, limiting the arbitrator's decision authority following direct involvement in the settlement negotiations can suggest a partial remedy to due process concerns, as such futile involvement and the confidential information learned in its course are expected to have less influence on the final award given the arbitrator's obligation to choose between the parties' offers or to establish the award within the agreed range as set by the parties.[234] Consequently, the need to replace the arbitrator following failed settlement attempts decreases, while the risk of future challenges to the final award diminishes, as the outcome is more anticipated and more accepted by all parties, including the losing one. Furthermore, this outline incentivizes each of the parties to submit a reasonable and realistic offer to increase the chances of its selection by the arbitrator,[235] which by itself may encourage parties to move closer, enhance the chances for an amicable outcome, and further decrease the risks of a successful future challenge to the final award.[236] However, as discussed in the previous section,[237] limiting the arbitrator's discretion to the parties' offers or ranges while deciding the dispute can raise enforceability concerns under the New York Convention, as this limited mandate may arguably undermine the arbitrator's real authority as a decision-maker.[238] Therefore, implementing these arrangements places significant responsibility on the arbitrator to deliver a well-founded award that thoroughly explains the choice between the parties' offers or the chosen figure within their agreed ranges while also corresponding with fundamental principles of the law.[239]

7.4.5 Involving Part of the Tribunal in the Settlement Efforts

When the tribunal comprises three members, which is customary in many ICA and investor-state arbitral proceedings,[240] involving all of them as settlement facilitators

231. Stipanowich & Kaskell, 2001, p. 26; Nigmatullina, 2018, p. 150.
232. Stipanowich, 2021a, p. 358.
233. Sussman & Gleason, 2019, p. 20; Rivkin, 2008, p. 383; Flake, 2016, p. 9; Stipanowich, 2021a, pp. 357-358; Stipanowich & Kaskell, 2001, pp. 25-26; Nigmatullina, 2018, p. 152; Peter, 1997, p. 102.
234. Stipanowich & Kaskell, 2001, p. 26; Nigmatullina, 2018, pp. 149-151; Flake, 2016, pp. 8-9; Ross, 2013, pp. 361-362; Kun, 2011b, p. 554.
235. Ross, 2013, pp. 361-362; Nigmatullina, 2018, pp. 151-152.
236. Flake, 2016, p. 9; Stipanowich & Kaskell, 2001, p. 26; Nigmatullina, 2018, pp. 151-152.
237. *See* the discussion in section 3.6.3.
238. Dendorfer & Lack, 2007, pp. 92-94; Benzidi, 2017, p. 27; Stipanowich & Kaskell, 2001, p. 26.
239. Sussman & Gleason, 2019, pp. 20-21; Benzidi, 2017, p. 27.
240. Blackaby et al., 2022, §4.22; Abramson, 1999, p. 12. For instance, under the UNCITRAL Arbitration Rules, 2021, Article, 7(1), the tribunal should consist of three arbitrators unless the

may result in an overly cumbersome settlement process[241] and a missed opportunity to further mitigate due process risks associated with the arbitrator's dual role by employing only part of the panel members in this role.[242] When all arbitrators are involved in the settlement process as a team, the risks for due process in the renewed arbitration following futile settlement efforts and exposure to settlement-stage information are identical to those associated with the return of a sole arbitrator to their adjudicative role when settlement attempts are unsuccessfully tried. Consequently, in both situations, arbitrators may limit themselves to comparatively safe initiatives that exclude direct involvement in the settlement negotiations to avoid future challenges to the arbitral award.[243] However, when only part of the panel is authorized to participate in the settlement stage, as acknowledged by the Final Report of the CEDR Commission on Settlement in International Arbitration,[244] the Prague Rules,[245] the NAI Arbitration Rules,[246] and both the CPR International and Non-Administered Arbitration Rules,[247] more far-reaching initiatives, including those allowing direct involvement in the settlement negotiations such as caucusing, may be considered. With the proper arrangements concerning settlement-stage information implemented, the nonparticipating arbitrators remain uncontaminated by these attempts, leaving their discretion completely uninfluenced and concerns about the parties' due process rights reduced.[248]

Given the flexibility offered by an arbitral panel consisting of three members, different ways exist to implement this voluntary safeguard.[249] When the panel includes a neutral chair, usually appointed by the arbitration institute, and two party-appointed arbitrators, parties can agree on one of two alternative options. *First*, the chair can act as a settlement facilitator without sharing settlement-stage information with the party-appointed arbitrators to preserve their impartiality. Following unsuccessful settlement attempts, arbitration can resume before the same panel or, in rare cases, with the chair being replaced by the arbitral institution. If parties wish to take a safer route following the chair's return to their adjudicative role, they can agree that only the

parties agree otherwise. Similarly, under the ICSID Arbitration Rules, 2022, Article 15(2), the parties should agree on any uneven number of arbitrators, otherwise according to Article 37(2)(b) of the ICSID Convention, 1966, the tribunal should consist of three arbitrators. Additionally, the following arbitration rules grant parties the discretion to determine the number of arbitrators: Model Law on ICA, 2006, Article 10(1); NAI Arbitration Rules, 2024, Article 14; DIS Arbitration Rules, 2018, Article 10; ICC Arbitration Rules, 2021, Article 12; ICDR International Arbitration Rules, 2021, Article 12; LCIA Arbitration Rules, 2020, Article 5(8); Swiss Arbitration Rules, 2021, Article 9(1).

241. Stipanowich & Mironi, 2021, p. 32; Stipanowich, 2021a, p. 360.
242. Kun, 2011b, p. 554; Abramson, 1999, p. 12; Nigmatullina, 2018, p. 157.
243. Abramson, 1999, p. 14.
244. CEDR Report on Settlement in ICA, 2009, section 4(6)(4).
245. Prague Rules, 2018, Article 9(2).
246. NAI Arbitration Rules, 2024, Article 30, authorizing the tribunal, unless otherwise agreed by the parties, to designate its chair to conduct a midstream conference, which may explore settlement possibilities.
247. CPR Rules for International Arbitration, 2019, Rule 19(2); CPR Rules for Non-Administered Arbitration, 2018, Rule 19(2).
248. Kun, 2011b, p. 554; Abramson, 1999, pp. 12-14; Stipanowich & Mironi, 2021, p. 32; Stipanowich, 2021a, p. 360.
249. Stipanowich, 2021a, p. 360; Stipanowich & Mironi, 2021, p. 32; Nigmatullina, 2018, p. 157; Kun, 2011b, p. 554; Rosoff, 2009, p. 89; Abramson, 1999, p. 12.

two party-appointed arbitrators will render the award, with the chair acting as a tiebreaker if needed.[250] *Second*, both party-appointed arbitrators can collectively act as settlement facilitators without sharing settlement-stage information with the chair. If ex parte communications are conducted during the settlement stage, the parties can agree whether both arbitrators are authorized to caucus together with each of the parties or whether each party-appointed arbitrator may caucus solely with the appointing party or with the opposing party. Following unsuccessful efforts to settle, arbitration can resume before the chair as a sole arbitrator, before the same panel, or, in rare cases, with the party-appointed arbitrators being replaced.[251] When the arbitral institution or the parties appoint the whole panel, the parties can opt for a *third* option that allows each of the arbitrators to engage in the settlement efforts without sharing settlement-stage information with the remaining arbitrators to preserve their impartiality. Following futile settlement attempts, arbitration can resume before the same panel or, in rare cases, with the arbitrator involved with the settlement being replaced. If parties wish to take a safer route, they can agree that following the settlement facilitator's return to their adjudicative role, only the remaining two arbitrators will render the award, with the settlement facilitator acting as a tiebreaker if needed.[252]

7.5 CONCLUSIONS

Despite the clear trend toward recognizing and promoting the arbitrator's role as a settlement facilitator in ICA—including hybrid processes that combine arbitration, mediation, and caucusing—gaps persist in different aspects of this role. Driven by pragmatic considerations and supported by efforts to harmonize its practice and legal framework at both domestic and transnational levels, this trend faces challenges rooted in differing legal traditions and attitudes. These challenges arise from concerns about the compatibility of certain components of the arbitrator's dual role to fundamental principles of arbitration and their potential risks to party autonomy and due process. Such gaps may affect the recognition and enforcement of awards resulting from processes endorsing this dual role, thereby acting as counterforces to its global harmonization.

Given that formal and authoritative changes in the multifaceted legal regime of ICA often require extended timeframes and gradual socialization, and considering the growing acceptance of the arbitrator's dual role among parties to cross-border business relations, this chapter recommends various safeguards ICA parties can implement within their contractual relations to improve the regulation and utilization of this role under the domain's existing legal regime. Subject to fulfilling the cornerstone of any attempt by the arbitrator to facilitate a settlement—ensuring the enforceability of the

250. Abramson, 1999, p. 13; Stipanowich & Mironi, 2021, p. 32; Nigmatullina, 2018, p. 157. *See also* Mayer, 2016, p. 5, arguing that "given a certain distrust that parties feel vis-à-vis the co-arbitrator appointed by the other party, it is preferable that the initiative be taken by the president, even if it has been suggested by a co-arbitrator."
251. Abramson, 1999, pp. 12-13; Kun, 2011b, p. 554; Stipanowich, 2021a, p. 360; Nigmatullina, 2018, p. 157; Sussman, 2010a, p. 385; Sussman, 2009a, p. 71.
252. Abramson, 1999, pp. 13-14; Nigmatullina, 2018, p. 157; Rosoff, 2009, p. 89.

arbitral award or at least mitigating enforceability risks—these safeguards, summarized in Appendices B and C, strive to provide maximum flexibility and adaptability regarding the components of the arbitrator's dual role and, to some extent, their application. This pragmatic approach aims to align with the attitudes of users, practitioners, and stakeholders from different legal backgrounds, thus contributing to the global harmonization of its practice and legal framework.

The safeguards proposed in this chapter—which, together with the continuum of settlement initiatives suggested in Chapter 2 and summarized in Appendix A, can form the basis for the formal regulation of this role as offered in the next chapter—are divided into two groups. *The first group* is designed to protect two different aspects of *party autonomy*: ensuring that the parties' decision to employ the arbitrator as a settlement facilitator is respected by the arbitrator and the court, whether for enforcement purposes or while reviewing the arbitral process, and guaranteeing that the dual role is implemented only in accordance with the parties' agreement while maintaining their control over the process and their right to self-determination. To achieve these goals, this group includes the following *cumulative and mandatory safeguards* intended to guarantee *express consent* to the arbitrator's dual role, although—as suggested in this chapter—such consent may not be needed for every initiative by the arbitrator on the continuum of settlement facilitation: (a) written, advance, and revocable consent; (b) detailed consent; and (c) informed consent. This group of safeguards also includes the *explicit waiver of the right to challenge the arbitrator or the award* after fulfilling the role according to the parties' agreement.

The second group of safeguards aims to protect the parties' *due process* rights when employing the arbitrator as a settlement facilitator. It includes the following *mandatory safeguards* to be implemented following unsuccessful settlement attempts: (a) the parties' option to opt out of arbitration with the same arbitrator to employ a different arbitrator in the resumed proceedings, commence the arbitration afresh, or pursue ADR methods; *or alternatively* (b) reverting to formal arbitration with the same arbitrator, subject to renewed consent and agreement regarding the treatment of settlement-stage information that is not part of the formal record; *and cumulatively* (c) the arbitrator's option to opt out of the resumed arbitration if, following their involvement in the settlement negotiations, they develop doubts regarding their ability to remain independent and impartial. Additionally, this group includes the following *voluntary safeguards*, which can complement the mandatory ones: (a) limiting the arbitrator's adjudicative mandate during the resumed arbitral proceedings following futile settlement attempts and (b) involving only part of the tribunal in the settlement efforts when it comprises several arbitrators.

While these safeguards aim to suggest flexibility, adaptability, and solutions for controversial aspects connected to the arbitrator's dual role, they cannot entirely eliminate risks associated with its utilization in ICA.[253] This limitation is primarily due to diverse approaches among legal traditions regarding certain components of the arbitrator's dual role and their compliance—together with part of the suggested

253. Kaufmann-Kohler, 2009, p. 200; Nigmatullina, 2018, p. 183; CIArb Practice Guideline on the Use of Mediation in Arbitration, 2021, Article 8(3).

safeguards, such as waivers of the right to challenge—with fundamental principles of arbitration or public policy considerations. Additionally, this restraint derives from the relative nature of the suggested solutions, which attempt to balance considerations of party autonomy and flexibility with the need to secure procedural fairness and enforceability. Nevertheless, in this regard, these solutions are not exceptional, as no dispute-resolution method—particularly one assigning the neutral different and sometimes contradicting responsibilities, as seen in the arbitrator's role as a settlement facilitator—is expected to be risk-free for its users:

> The resolution of disputes is not an exact science; indeed, it is not a science at all. It involves a complex blend of facts, human impulse, and pragmatism, looking for solutions, notwithstanding apparent difficulties and conceptual objections, which will work in practice. ... We ought to be encouraging arbitrators to promote settlement in all sorts of ways, both in the public interest of resolving disputes and private interest in enabling private parties to get on with their commercial activities. ... We run a serious risk of becoming irrelevant if, as arbitrators and practitioners, we do not adapt to the challenges of our time. ... We may think that there is no alternative to the existing system, but we are mistaken, for as the courts have learnt, parties will vote with their feet. Let us adopt the maxim: "Blessed are the peacemakers."[254]

Implementing the solutions suggested in this chapter requires advanced and detailed planning by ICA parties, necessitating additional time and effort in designing their dispute-resolution agreements. Moreover, insisting on safeguards such as informed consent and waivers of the right to challenge may deter some parties from engaging the arbitrator in dual roles. Hence, these processes seem suitable for innovative and subtle parties who understand the advantages and risks associated with this role and, as the "owners" of the process, prefer to maintain control over the arbitrator's responsibilities to resolve their dispute.[255] For these parties, the "transnational paradigm for the conduct of international arbitrations is not carved in stone." Instead, it implements a pragmatic and flexible approach that "requires thinking outside the box" and adopting a "menu approach,"[256] which allows parties to design the arbitral process according to their needs and interests within the constantly evolving landscape of transnational commercial dispute resolution.[257] Based on recent and compelling empirical data presented throughout the book, which confirms a clear growing interest among parties to cross-border commercial adjudication—including international arbitration—in amicable dispute resolution facilitated by the adjudicator, it is evident that ICA users are well-positioned to endorse the arbitrator's dual role and reap its benefits.

254. Marriott, 2005, p. 546.
255. Ross, 2013, p. 363; Nigmatullina, 2018, p. 176.
256. Berger, 2019, pp. 311-312. *See also* McIlwrath, 2018; Marriott, 1996, p. 72.
257. Stipanowich, 2021a, p. 268; Guo, 2020, p. 225; Berger, 2016b.

CHAPTER 8
External Solutions to the Arbitral Process

8.1 INTRODUCTION

The internal solutions discussed in the previous chapter aim to enhance the global recognition and regulation of the arbitrator's role as a settlement facilitator within the existing legal regime of ICA. These solutions primarily focus on suggesting party autonomy and due process safeguards, which, when implemented by parties to ICA processes as part of their contractual relations, can mitigate potential risks associated with the arbitrator's dual role. This chapter extends the scope of the parties' contractual relations to recommend external solutions to the arbitral process aimed at harmonizing the perspectives toward the arbitrator's dual role worldwide. Considering the manifold legal regime of the domain, which allocates the responsibility for harmonizing its practice and legal framework to various stakeholders—including arbitration institutes and organizations, state-related forces, practitioners, and users[1]—this chapter outlines various actions these stakeholders can implement to enhance the global recognition of this role, standardize its legal regime across jurisdictions and legal traditions, and reduce legal risks associated with its practice. These actions, in turn, can contribute to the security of cross-border commercial relations for the benefit of specific parties, the broader business community, and states.[2]

External solutions recommended in this chapter include amending the Model Law on ICA, domestic arbitration laws, and international arbitration rules and guidelines to better accommodate and regulate the arbitrator's mandate to facilitate settlement. The safeguards suggested in the previous chapter and summarized in Appendices B and C, along with the continuum of the arbitrator's settlement initiatives suggested in Chapter 2 and summarized in Appendix A, can constitute the basis for

1. Stipanowich & Ulrich, 2014b, pp. 29-30; Najar, 2009, pp. 522, 527.
2. Bernardini, 2004, p. 118; Pate, 2010, p. 146.

such formal regulation. While the idea of regulating the arbitrator's dual role may run counter to the contractual nature of arbitration and the flexibility it grants to users,[3] as demonstrated in the previous chapter, some limitations on flexibility and party autonomy are unavoidable to guarantee the parties' procedural rights alongside the recognition and enforcement of awards resulting from processes that endorse this role.[4] Moreover, as discussed below, regulation and codification may be indispensable to the effective application of the arbitrator's dual role and to enhancing its global acceptance. Subject to these considerations, the regulatory framework associated with this role should aim to provide ICA users with maximum flexibility and adaptability regarding its components and, as demonstrated in the previous chapter, to some extent also regarding the safeguards to be implemented. This flexibility could facilitate greater acceptance of the arbitrator's dual role across jurisdictions, arbitration institutions, practitioners, and users from diverse legal traditions, thereby promoting the harmonization of its practice and legal regime on a global scale.[5]

The contribution of amendments to different legal frameworks connected with the practice of the arbitrator's dual role in ICA toward its global harmonization is undeniable. Nevertheless, given the influence of legal traditions on approaches to the arbitral process in general and the role of the arbitrator in particular, achieving a global consensus on all aspects of the arbitrator's dual role among stakeholders is less probable despite notable strides toward the general harmonization of arbitration laws and rules worldwide. Recognizing this limitation is important for managing expectations about the impact of such amendments on harmonization—acknowledging that some degree of cultural or regional divergence regarding the arbitrator's role in settlement may persist—and highlighting the responsibilities of other stakeholders in achieving harmonization. These responsibilities include developing adequate training for the practice of the arbitrator's dual role, enhancing the selection process for qualified arbitrators suited to this role, and improving user involvement in arbitral processes that endorse it.

8.2 ARBITRATION INSTITUTIONS AND ORGANIZATIONS

Given that ICA is largely self-regulated by its global community,[6] international arbitration institutions and organizations—often regarded as the domain's "market operators"[7]—bear significant responsibility for standardizing and harmonizing the practice and legal framework of ICA. As demonstrated in Chapter 6, this framework has

3. Benzidi, 2017, p. 31; Ross, 2013, p. 363.
4. Berger, 2019, p. 311; Benzidi, 2017, p. 31; Ross, 2013, p. 363, arguing that "the formalities required to provide adequate safeguards are inversely proportionate to the flexibility of the process itself."
5. Berger & Jensen, 2017, p. 904; Berger, 2018b, p. 516; Benzidi, 2017, p. 31; Marzolini, 2016, p. 117; Karton, 2013, pp. 106-107; Blankenship, 2006, pp. 39-40; Blankley, 2011, p. 329; Plant, 2000, p. 146; Smit, 1986, pp. 20-21; Bernardini, 2004, p. 122.
6. Ali, 2021, p. 14; Bantekas, 2015, p. 66; Kaufmann-Kohler, 2010, p. 295; Bermann, 2015, p. 76.
7. Kronke, 2000, p. 20.

increasingly extended to include the arbitrator's role as a settlement facilitator.[8] In this context, these institutions' responsibility encompasses various aspects, including the development and refinement of arbitration rules and guidelines to recognize and regulate the arbitrator's dual role, the enhancement of selection processes for arbitrators qualified for this role, and the provision of adequate training for arbitrators and practitioners at both academic and professional levels, as further elaborated below.

8.2.1 Developing and Refining Arbitration Rules and Guidelines

Among the various obligations of arbitral institutions, the most crucial for enhancing the harmonization of the arbitrator's dual role across different legal traditions and attitudes in ICA is the refinement of arbitration rules and the development of detailed guidelines to recognize and regulate its utilization.[9] This step is essential because codification is a prerequisite for the effective application of such norms.[10] Moreover, the non-binding nature of these rules and guidelines as soft norms makes them a highly effective channel for transferring innovative practices and normative instruments—including those related to the arbitrator's role in settlement—across different levels of the transnational and multilayered normative regime of ICA.[11] This harmonization process encompasses several dimensions, including the localization of global norms, standards, and practices within specific jurisdictions, the exportation of such instruments from the local level to other jurisdictions and the global stage, and the emergence of new instruments directly within the global arena.[12] This interactive process of "legal transplantation"[13] relies heavily on soft norms and is routinely led by "legal agents"[14] within the global arbitration community. These agents, leveraging shared expectations derived from repeated cross-border interactions over time, as well as common training, practice, and expertise in ICA beyond the realm of specific jurisdictions,[15] facilitate the direct assimilation of these instruments at one normative level or their gradual socialization across different levels and professional circles within the domain.[16] Consequently, codified rules and guidelines acknowledging and

8. *See* the discussion regarding these initiatives in sections 6.3.1-6.3.3.
9. Ruckteschler & Wendelstein, 2021, p. 773; Stipanowich, 2021a, pp. 339, 360-361; Sussman & Berger, 2021b, pp. 37-38; Kaufmann-Kohler, 2009, pp. 204-205; Benzidi, 2017, pp. 20-21; Stipanowich & Ulrich, 2014b, pp. 29-31; Guo, 2020, p. 224; Nigmatullina, 2019, p. 18; Nigmatullina, 2018, pp. 218-219; Kaufmann-Kohler, 2010, pp. 295-297; Lüth & Wagner, 2012, p. 416; Goodrich, 2012, p. 8; CEDR Report on Settlement in ICA, 2009, section 4(7)(1).
10. Ali, 2021, p. 14; Kaufmann-Kohler, 2010, pp. 286-287, 297-298; Lüth & Wagner, 2012, p. 410; Nazzini, 2016, p. 703.
11. *See* the discussion in section 6.3 regarding the reasons contributing to the prevalence of soft norms in the transnational legal framework of ICA and their pivotal role in promoting its harmonization.
12. Kun, 2013b, pp. 177, 186-187; Gillespie, 2009, p. 209; Koh, 1996, p. 184; Kun, 2016a, p. 245; Karton, 2014, pp. 21-22.
13. Carvalho, 2019, p. 22; Kun, 2013b, pp. 178-182; Teubner, 2001, p. 418; Kahn-Freund, 1974, p. 7.
14. Alkoby, 2008, pp. 184-185.
15. Ginsburg, 2003, p. 1337; Kun, 2016a, p. 287; Dezalay & Garth, 1996, p. 18.
16. Kun, 2013b, p. 218; Alkoby, 2008, pp. 184-187.

regulating the arbitrator's role in settlement facilitation can attract parties to endorse this role in their dispute-resolution clauses.[17] This effect is particularly pronounced when these instruments introduce a range of settlement facilitation initiatives and safeguards, as suggested in this book, while allowing parties to apply them selectively and flexibly according to their needs and interests, whether by direct reference or as a source of inspiration.[18] Additionally, codified rules and guidelines may encourage policymakers to amend arbitration laws and treaties in alignment with their principles and objectives, and prompt domestic judicial systems to accept or accommodate the dual role when interpreting arbitration laws and conventions or reviewing ICA proceedings that endorsed it. Furthermore, they may encourage other arbitration institutes and organizations, alongside additional stakeholders in the domain, to develop further rules, guidelines, and ethical standards regarding the arbitrator's dual role, thereby contributing to the harmonization of its practice and legal regime.[19] Even if initially such rules and guidelines are endorsed by only a few institutions and organizations, the continuous expansion of arbitration institutions worldwide—operating in cooperative and competitive dynamics on geographical or sectoral bases[20]—suggests that broader adoption is likely over time:

> International arbitral institutions constitute a remarkably open and vibrant market for competition for the rendition of arbitration services. While market mechanisms undoubtedly foster innovation that, in the short term, produces differences among institutions, those differences tend to fade as institutions respond to competitive pressures by adopting those practices of other arbitral institutions that have proved popular in the marketplace. If anything, formally localized arbitral institutions have contributed powerfully to the migration of arbitration practices and ideas.[21]

To guarantee that rules and guidelines related to the arbitrator's dual role are widely adopted by users of ICA, it is advisable to avoid narrowing their content and orientation to specific legal traditions, as implemented by most codification initiatives

17. Stipanowich & Ulrich, 2014b, p. 30.
18. CEDR Report on Settlement in ICA, 2009, section 4(5)(1). Empirical data supports this approach. When respondents to the 2016-2017 GPC Survey were asked about their expectations from dispute resolution service providers, a clear majority across all stakeholder groups pointed to receiving guidance on the optimal methods for resolving disputes, as parties frequently lack a definitive preference for a specific process. *See* GPC Series, 2016-2017, Question 1(4); Lack, 2021, p. 12.
19. Stipanowich, 2021a, p. 339; Ruckteschler & Wendelstein, 2021, p. 773; Stipanowich & Ulrich, 2014b, pp. 29-31; Smit, 1986, p. 14. For empirical data supporting the role of international arbitration rules and guidelines in harmonizing the perspectives of ICA stakeholders globally on the arbitrator's role as a settlement facilitator, *see* the discussion in section 6.2.
20. Berger, 2018a, p. 474; Bermann, 2017, pp. 59-60; Gerbay, 2016, §2.01[A]-[B]; Bantekas, 2015, p. 64; Draetta, 2015, p. 330; Ali, 2021, p. 34; Abbott & Snidal, 2009, p. 526; Smit, 1986, p. 13.
21. Bermann, 2017, p. 60. *See also* Kaufmann-Kohler, 2010, p. 295; Ali, 2021, p. 34; Pate, 2010, pp. 147-148; Abbott & Snidal, 2009, p. 526; Lynch, 2003, pp. 96-100; CEDR Report on Settlement in ICA, 2009, section 4(5)(4); Draetta, 2015, p. 330, arguing that "beyond any differences among them, there is a tendency towards the harmonization of the arbitration procedural rules of the various arbitration institutions. There are regular contacts among such institutions, which periodically review their regulations taking into consideration each other's rules. Thus, a significant level of uniformity and universality is reached."

discussed in Chapter 6, which were shaped by the legal traditions of their promoters. Instead, these rules and guidelines should allow for maximum flexibility and adaptability regarding the components of the arbitrator's dual role and, to some extent, the safeguards to be applied. This approach would enable ICA users to design arbitration procedures tailored to their specific needs and preferences.[22] To achieve this objective, arbitration institutions and organizations should engage stakeholders from diverse legal traditions in the consultation processes preceding the promulgation of these rules and guidelines. This inclusive strategy should ensure representation from jurisdictions with established experience in utilizing and regulating the arbitrator's dual role, facilitating the collection of a broad range of ideas and insights. Such an approach would ultimately enhance the acceptance and applicability of these rules and guidelines across different legal cultures.[23]

If explicit acknowledgment and regulation of this role within arbitration rules and guidelines is unfeasible to promote, these institutions and organizations can alternatively recognize party autonomy as the cornerstone principle guiding arbitral proceedings under their purview. Institutional rules often restrict party autonomy by defining certain provisions as mandatory, thereby preventing parties from excluding their arrangements even when they contradict their arbitration agreement.[24] As presented in Chapter 6, some of these mandatory articles impose various restrictions on the arbitrator's role as a settlement facilitator, including the absolute prohibition on its use. In such scenarios, parties opting for institutional rules[25]—or ad hoc arbitration governed by such rules[26]—may encounter a "party autonomy paradox" since, by exercising their autonomy to select institutional rules, they simultaneously restrict their autonomy to modify those rules according to their preferences, as constrained by the institution's mandatory provisions.[27] This paradox is further reinforced by the

22. Berger & Jensen, 2017, p. 904; Berger, 2018b, p. 516; Benzidi, 2017, p. 31; Marzolini, 2016, p. 117; Karton, 2013, pp. 106-107; Blankenship, 2006, pp. 39-40; Blankley, 2011, p. 329; Plant, 2000, p. 146; Bernardini, 2004, p. 122.
23. Ali, 2021, pp. 31-32; Alvarez, 2007, pp. 159-163; Ellis, 2012, p. 325; Najar, 2009, pp. 520-521; Cremades, 1998, p. 160; Kaufmann-Kohler, 2009, p. 204; Stewart, 2014, pp. 211-212, advocating for a transnational regulation process that affords "equal respect and regard for all relevant individuals and groups and their interests and concerns." For instance, the establishment of the UNCITRAL Regional Centre for Asia and the Pacific (RCAP) in 2012 aims to enhance the formation process of transnational soft law in cross-border trade and dispute resolution. The RCAP facilitates knowledge transfer from UNCITRAL to private and national actors in the Asia-Pacific region while gathering information, feedback, and regional practices from these actors to improve UNCITRAL's legislative efforts. *See UNCITRAL Regional Centre for Asia and the Pacific (RCAP)*, n.d.; Ali, 2021, pp. 2-4; O'Brien, 2011.
24. Hrnčiříková, 2016, p. 105; Berger, 2018a, pp. 474, 486-492; Scherer & Gerbay, 2015, p. 206; Smit, 1986, p. 21. *See*, for example, LCIA Arbitration Rules, 2020, Article 14(5)-(6), authorizing the tribunal to deviate from the parties' agreement if adherence would compromise the efficiency of the proceedings.
25. Blackaby et al., 2022, §1.155; Warwas, 2017, pp. 19-20; Berger, 2018a, pp. 475-476.
26. *See*, in this regard, Queen Mary University of London and White & Case LLP, 2021, p. 9, affirming that the vast majority of ad hoc arbitrations continue to apply institutional rules, with UNCITRAL and LMAA rules being the most commonly utilized.
27. Berger, 2018a, p. 477. *See also* Kaufmann-Kohler, 2003, p. 1323.

general reluctance of domestic courts to intervene in mandatory institutional provisions, often under the guise of respecting party autonomy.[28] While parties may principally select an arbitral institution or rules that better align with their desire to employ the arbitrator in a dual role,[29] this option may not always be available due to practical, legal, or contractual limitations.[30] Therefore, alongside recognizing the primacy of party autonomy, arbitration institutions and organizations should refrain from overtly prohibiting the arbitrator's role as a settlement facilitator or different aspects thereof. Similarly, they should refrain from imposing rigid due process safeguards that deviate from the balanced framework proposed in the previous chapter. By adopting such an approach, institutions and organizations can better accommodate the diverse needs and expectations of ICA users while fostering broader acceptance and harmonization of this practice.

8.2.2 Enhanced Selection Process of Qualified Arbitrators

Apart from developing rules and guidelines that recognize and safeguard the arbitrator's dual role, arbitration institutes, given their experience in the field and their involvement in the selection process of arbitrators, are usually best positioned to ensure the appointment of neutrals with the optimal skills and experience for successfully and effectively fulfilling their arbitral role given the nature of the dispute and the parties' interests and needs.[31] Therefore, these institutes should be attentive to parties who wish to employ the arbitrator with a dual role and facilitate the appointment of a qualified neutral who can gain the trust of parties and their counsel, thus increasing the chances of settling the dispute amicably while enhancing the overall credibility and attractiveness of these processes among ICA users.[32] As previously discussed, the skills required for an arbitrator to successfully implement the adjudicative and settlement-facilitating roles are different and sometimes even opposing. The lack of adequate training in both roles, as well as in the cross-cultural context of international business disputes, exacerbates the challenges and reluctance faced by arbitrators in fulfilling the dual role and, more broadly, in identifying suitable candidates for this demanding

28. Paulsson, 2013, p. 2; Berger, 2018a, p. 483, along with the cases discussed therein.
29. In certain instances, parties may agree for one institution to administer their arbitration while applying the rules of another institution. Domestic courts in various jurisdictions have examined and upheld such agreements, emphasizing party autonomy considerations. *See* Gerbay, 2016, §1.02[B][3]; Schroeter, 2017, p. 182; Smit, 1986, p. 20; Berger, 2018a, pp. 478-483, along with the cases discussed therein.
30. For example, geographical restrictions, legal considerations aimed at protecting third parties' rights, or situations involving one of the arbitration parties being part of a "weaker" category within the business community. *See* Lüth & Wagner, 2012, p. 419; Pate, 2010, pp. 162-163; Kaufmann-Kohler, 2010, p. 299; Stipanowich, 2023, p. 689.
31. Najar, 2009, pp. 523-524; Smit, 1986, pp. 14, 17.
32. Yip, 2021, p. 194; Stipanowich & Mironi, 2021, pp. 30-31; Stipanowich, 2021a, p. 349; Nigmatullina, 2018, p. 60; Benzidi, 2017, p. 31; Ross, 2013, p. 366; Weisman, 2013, p. 41; Kun, 2011b, pp. 550-551; Blankley, 2011, p. 337; Phillips, G. F., 2009, p. 78; Rosoff, 2009, p. 97; Costa Braga de Oliveira, 2009, p. 90; Blankenship, 2006, p. 34; Marriott, 2005, p. 544; Bartel, 1991, pp. 687-688; Sussman, 2010a, p. 391; CEDR Report on Settlement in ICA, 2009, section 4(5)(2) & 4(6)(4).

mandate.[33] Therefore, arbitration institutes and organizations should enhance their training programs to accommodate the necessary knowledge and skills essential for the effective utilization of the arbitrator's dual role.

8.2.3 Adequate Training in the Arbitrator's Dual Role

Given their intensive involvement in training, arbitration institutes and organizations are the most suitable stakeholders for promoting adequate training for neutrals and practitioners willing to engage in processes that allow the arbitrator to act as a settlement facilitator. This training should include the necessary knowledge about various ways of facilitating settlement,[34] the ethical standards and guidelines for implementing the arbitrator's dual role,[35] the flexible design of dispute resolution processes relating to international commercial relations,[36] the transitory skills between domestic and international arbitration and between adversary and consensual attitudes,[37] and education about cross-cultural differences and their impact on the resolution process of international business disputes.[38] Since these organizations are also involved in the academic development of the domain, they can contribute to the acceptance of this role through the early academic education of "those who will conduct international arbitration proceedings in the future" or become part of the business community.[39] When such training is offered to potential neutrals and practitioners of ICA from different legal backgrounds, it can significantly contribute to harmonizing perspectives regarding the arbitrator's dual role globally:

> An American lawyer, a Chinese lawyer, and a Japanese lawyer, all having taken the arbitration courses at one of the arbitration master's programs, gone through the arbitration training at one of the professional organizations, and having worked in the arbitration practice group in one of the multinational law firms, may indeed produce a common set of expectations, norms, and behaviors.[40]

---

33. *See* the discussion in section 4.4.1.
34. CEDR Report on Settlement in ICA, 2009, section 4(6)(6)-4(6)(7); Abramson, 1999, p. 8; Nigmatullina, 2019, pp. 27-31; Stipanowich, 2021a, p. 349.
35. Stipanowich & Ulrich, 2014b, p. 31.
36. Stipanowich, 2021a, p. 340; Nigmatullina, 2019, pp. 37-38; Bühring-Uhle et al., 2006, p. 247.
37. *See* the discussion in section 8.5 below.
38. Stipanowich, 2021a, pp. 340-341, 361; Thevenin, 2013, p. 374; CEDR Report on Settlement in ICA, 2009, section 4(9)(4); Nigmatullina, 2019, pp. 31-37.
39. Horvath, 2011, p. 271. Empirical data supports the impact of early education on the acceptance of the arbitrator's dual role. In the 2016-2017 GPC Survey, a clear majority of respondents identified better education in law schools and the business community about adjudicative and non-adjudicative dispute resolution options as the most effective way to improve parties' understanding of their choices in resolving commercial disputes. *See* GPC Series, 2016-2017, Question 4(2). For further discussion on the importance of early legal education on negotiation, mediation, and other dispute resolution methods, *see* Stipanowich, 2023, p. 693; Nigmatullina, 2019, pp. 30-31, 37-39.
40. Kun, 2016a, p. 287. *See also* Dezalay & Garth, 1996, p. 18, referring to common training, practice, and expertise as a "symbolic capital" force that plays a pivotal role in shaping an international culture of arbitration; UNCITRAL Guidelines on Mediation of Investment Disputes, 2024, section M (at para. 47), emphasizing the importance of adequate training and capacity-building in raising awareness of methods designed to facilitate amicable dispute resolution.

8.3 STATE-RELATED STAKEHOLDERS

The transnationalization of ICA practice and its legal framework has challenged the traditional dominance of domestic law in such proceedings.[41] However, despite the prevailing trend toward globalization, "the present world order is still founded on the traditional concept of the national state."[42] Without the support and freedom provided by national legal systems in fostering the development of practices, rules, and standards, the current transnational status of ICA could not have been achieved.[43] Nonetheless, the existing multilayered legal regime governing ICA accords significant importance to domestic legal systems that interact with arbitral proceedings, whether as the seat of arbitration, the applicable substantive law, or the jurisdiction for enforcement.[44] This central role of domestic legal systems is evident in the field's primary harmonization instruments—the New York Convention and the Model Law on ICA. *First*, while the New York Convention focuses on the recognition and enforcement of foreign arbitral awards, it primarily defers to domestic legal systems for regulating most aspects of ICA proceedings[45] and subjects the enforcement of awards to public policy considerations defined by national jurisdictions.[46] *Second*, although the Model Law on ICA ostensibly allows parties to select transnational principles over domestic laws to govern the substance of their dispute,[47] since the arbitral tribunal extracts its authority from the parties, who remain bound by the laws and principles of the relevant national legal system, it remains unclear whether these transnational principles can contradict or entirely supersede domestic laws. Moreover, potential gaps in the content of transnational principles may necessitate recourse to domestic legal systems to address unresolved issues.[48] *Third*, the Model Law on ICA applies its provisions only when the place of arbitration falls within its geographical scope, thus implementing a territorial test that precludes a distinction between the seat of arbitration—legally

41. Blackaby et al., 2022, §7.04; Alvarez, 2006, p. xvii; Bermann, 2017, p. 59.
42. Pate, 2010, p. 151, citing Schmitthoff, 1968, p. 105.
43. Blackaby et al., 2022, §3.88 & §3.97; Draetta, 2015, p. 327; Tschanz, 2016, p. 82; Kaufmann-Kohler, 2003, p. 1323; Cremades, 1998, pp. 170-172; Bernardini, 2004, p. 118, claiming that states "have overcome their historical mistrust of arbitration, viewed as a derogation from the natural jurisdiction of their courts, to consider that it represents an important factor of stability and development in transnational economic relations."
44. Bantekas, 2015, p. 37; Jemielniak, 2014, p. 325; Blackaby et al., 2022, §7.05-7.06.
45. Bantekas, 2015, p. 37; Jemielniak, 2014, pp. 322-323.
46. Horvath, 2001, pp. 143-144; Cordero-Moss, 2012, p. 134; Mayer, 1986, p. 284; Jemielniak, 2014, pp. 319, 327; New York Convention, 1958, Article V(2)(b).
47. This increasingly accepted practice among ICA parties appears to be permitted under Article 28(1) of the Model Law on ICA, which states that "the arbitral tribunal shall decide the dispute in accordance with such rules of law as are chosen by the parties as applicable to the substance of the dispute." The use of the term "rules of law," as opposed to simply "law," is generally interpreted as granting parties the freedom to apply soft norms, rather than just national laws, to govern their dispute. This approach has been adopted in various arbitration laws and rules, including the Quebec Arbitration Act, 2014, section 620; Swiss Domestic Arbitration Law, 2008, Article 381(1)(a); Swiss International Arbitration Law, 1987, Article 187(1); and NAI Arbitration Rules, 2024, Article 48(1)-(2). For further discussion, *see* Blackaby et al., 2022, §3.212-3.215; Model Law on ICA, 2006, para. 39 to Explanatory Note (part two); Cordero-Moss, 2012, p. 134; Bantekas, 2015, p. 48.
48. Cordero-Moss, 2012, p. 134; Tschanz, 2016, pp. 83-84.

speaking—and the applicable procedural law.[49] Subsequently, in most ICA processes, institutional rules and guidelines regulating arbitral proceedings cannot override the obligatory provisions of the procedural law of the seat, including those designed to guarantee due process and the right to challenge the award.[50] *Fourth*, under the New York Convention, arbitral proceedings must be localized in the specific jurisdiction where the award is issued.[51] This requirement extends to online arbitration, where concerns regarding recognition and enforcement necessitate designating the place of award issuance.[52]

Thus, the "the idea that arbitral proceedings may somehow be 'floating' or 'delocalised' by reason of the parties' consent ... is probably best reserved for the realms of imagination."[53] While the harmonization of ICA—including aspects related to the arbitrator's dual role—has been primarily advanced through soft norms developed by the arbitration community, given the significant role of domestic law within the current transnational normative regime of the domain, it would be unrealistic to assume that any comprehensive effort to enhance the harmonization of ICA practices and legal frameworks across diverse legal systems and traditions, including those related to the arbitrator's dual role, could avoid extending to the domestic level.[54]

8.3.1 Amending Domestic Arbitration Laws

Considering the central role of domestic law within the normative regime of ICA, the arbitrator's role as a settlement facilitator should be formally recognized through explicit provisions incorporated into domestic arbitration laws pertaining to ICA proceedings. Alongside granting freedom regarding the components of the role to be

49. Model Law on ICA, 2006, Article 1(2); Dasser, 2021, p. 72; Jemielniak, 2014, p. 325. The territorial test has been followed by the vast majority of jurisdictions that have adopted the Model Law on ICA, as well as many others that have not adopted its regulations. *See* Kaufmann-Kohler, 2003, pp. 1315-1317.
50. Bantekas, 2015, p. 64; Nazzini, 2016, p. 692; Blackaby et al., 2022, §7.06; Jemielniak, 2014, p. 325; Kaufmann-Kohler, 2003, p. 1319. Additionally, *see* the New York Convention, 1958, Article V(1)(a), and the Model Law on ICA, 2006, Articles 34(2)(a)(i) & 36(1)(a)(i), empowering courts to refuse recognition and enforcement of arbitral awards if the arbitral agreement is deemed void under the law of the seat.
51. Jemielniak, 2014, p. 319.
52. Morek, 2006, p. 186; Lynch, 2003, p. 391; Jemielniak, 2014, p. 319; *UNCITRAL WGII*, n.d., at Access to Justice and the Role of Online Dispute Resolution (A/CN.9/WG.II/WP.223), p. 5.
53. Bantekas, 2015, p. 37. *See also* Blackaby et al., 2022, §1.91 & §3.87; Hrnčiříková, 2016, p. 99; Gaillard, 2023, pp. 42-46, holding that while the current transnational legal order of ICA operates with a degree of "autonomy" from specific national legal systems, it remains inherently interconnected with and not entirely independent of those systems.
54. Ali, 2021, p. 24; Kaufmann-Kohler, 2010, p. 299; Kronke, 2000, p. 20, stating that it would be a "misconception to envisage a future of harmonization and unification of commercial law solely driven by the market operators and loosely framed by soft law instruments." Empirical data supports this view. The 2016-2017 GPC Survey asked respondents which stakeholders hold the most influence in shaping the future of commercial dispute resolution practices. The majority cited domestic legislators and adjudicative providers such as arbitrators and arbitral institutes equally. However, when asked who bears the greatest responsibility for action, national legislators were ranked first, with adjudicative providers second. *See* GPC Series, 2016-2017, Questions 3(5) & 4(1).

applied by the parties within the particular process, these provisions can implement the safeguards suggested in the previous chapter to enhance its regulation.[55] Nevertheless, given that domestic legislation relating to ICA, akin to conventions and treaties, often intentionally employs general formulations and leaves various subjects unregulated to maintain party autonomy and the flexibility of the process,[56] these legislative amendments should at least expressly recognize party autonomy as the guiding principle in arbitration. As verified in Chapter 6, the "legislator" of the Model Law on ICA acknowledges party autonomy as the leading principle in ICA and accepts the attitude that, subject to compliance with the applicable law, party autonomy should override any limitation on the arbitral procedure, even if embedded in arbitral rules or codes of conduct.[57] This moderate legislative approach, while not providing a complete solution in terms of harmonization, may nevertheless allow for better convergence of approaches regarding the arbitrator's dual role, thus contributing to its harmonization among different legal traditions.[58] Additionally, when implemented alongside influential guidelines acknowledging the arbitrator's dual role within ICA proceedings—such as the IBA Guidelines on Conflicts of Interest, which are often referred to by domestic courts for the uniform interpretation of arbitration laws, rules, and agreements according to accepted international practices[59]—these legislative amendments may encourage local judges to perceive that "arbitrators and judges are in reality partners in the effective administration of justice as desired by the parties in their legitimate use of contractual autonomy" and that ICA should be approached with an increased international mentality.[60] Consequently, when reviewing ICA proceedings endorsing the arbitrator's role as a settlement facilitator, domestic courts could be encouraged to adopt broader perspectives on this role and accord "equal dignity" to all relevant national laws and legal traditions applicable to the particular process. Such an approach would mitigate the legal risks associated with the utilization of this role in ICA and further enhance its transnational harmonization.

The advocacy for domestic legislative amendments can be championed by "agents" within the global arbitration community who also operate within domestic and state-related international spheres.[61] They contribute to harmonizing hard norms (e.g., state legislation, regional treaties, and international conventions) through their involvement in various local and international initiatives and participation in consultation processes offered by domestic legislators and international organizations before their endorsement.[62] Even if these legislative amendments are initially adopted in only a select few jurisdictions that serve as prominent hubs for ICA proceedings or

55. Ruckteschler & Wendelstein, 2021, p. 773; Benzidi, 2017, pp. 20-21; Nigmatullina, 2019, pp. 13-17; Nigmatullina, 2018, pp. 215-218; Goodrich, 2012, pp. 5-8.
56. *See* the discussion in section 6.3.
57. *See* the discussion in section 6.3.2.5.
58. Nazzini, 2016, pp. 702-703; Draetta, 2015, p. 341; Tschanz, 2016, p. 82; Kaufmann-Kohler, 2003, p. 1323.
59. *See* the discussion in sections 6.3 & 6.3.2.2.
60. Cremades, 1998, pp. 170-172.
61. Jemielniak, 2017, p. 170; Kauppi & Madsen, 2013, p. 5.
62. Stipanowich, 2021a, p. 339; Bantekas, 2015, p. 64; Ali, 2021, pp. 27-28, 32; Kaufmann-Kohler, 2010, p. 299.

implement hesitant attitudes toward different aspects of this role,[63] they may ultimately inspire other jurisdictions to follow suit. In this context, while institutional arbitration rules foster competition among arbitral institutions in overseeing ICA proceedings, domestic laws drive competition between jurisdictions by promoting arbitration-friendly and non-interventionist approaches.[64] This competition influences the parties' choice of law governing the substance of the dispute, the procedural rules, and the enforcement of the arbitral award:

> Account is then to be taken of the rules of procedural law in force in the place of arbitration, inasmuch as the latter may in various ways limit or enlarge the powers of the international arbitrator. The rules governing the merits of the dispute also have a bearing, to the extent that they may confer specific powers on the arbitrator or he or she may enjoy a measure of flexibility in their application. ... As a matter of practice, the measure of autonomy enjoyed by the arbitrator derives from the particular mission entrusted to him or her, which is to resolve the dispute between the parties in their interest.[65]

8.3.2 Amending the Model Law on ICA

Among all possible paths to encourage the recognition of the arbitrator's role as a settlement facilitator across domestic legal systems, the most effective one is to incorporate a dedicated amendment to the Model Law on ICA, which, alongside acknowledging the dual role, can implement safeguards for its utilization according to the outline suggested in the previous chapter. Given the Model Law's high recognition and wide influence on designing and amending domestic arbitration laws worldwide,[66] and since it serves "as a 'transnational benchmark' to evaluate the user-friendliness of domestic statutes for international arbitrations around the globe,"[67] its endorsement of the arbitrator's dual role may carry substantial weight in encouraging global adoption, including in jurisdictions that have not fully incorporated its text into their legislation, thereby significantly contributing to the harmonization of this role.[68] As demonstrated in the previous chapter, an early draft of the Model Law on International Commercial Conciliation, which was later replaced by the Model Law on ICM,[69] included the following clause recognizing the arbitrator's dual role:

63. *See* the 2021 Aragaki Study, discussed in section 5.4, regarding jurisdictions that regulate the arbitrator's dual role in hybrid processes involving arbitration and mediation, some of which prohibit its use.
64. Blackaby et al., 2022, §3.87-3.88; Tschanz, 2016, p. 85; Jemielniak, 2014, p. 328; Carducci, 2021, p. 80; Berger, 2019, p. 300.
65. Bernardini, 2004, pp. 114-118.
66. *See* the discussion in section 1.2 on the central role of the Model Law in the harmonization of ICA.
67. Berger, 2019, p. 300.
68. *See* the discussion in section 6.2 on empirical data confirming that the harmonization of international laws and standards related to the arbitrator's dual role constitutes a key factor in its acceptance among practitioners and users of ICA worldwide.
69. Model Law on International Commercial Conciliation, 2002.

> It is not incompatible with the function of an arbitrator if the arbitrator raises the question of a possible conciliation and, to the extent agreed to by the parties, participates in efforts to reach an agreed settlement.[70]

Nonetheless, this provision was not included in the final draft, partly because it relates to the competence and functions of arbitrators, which are more appropriately addressed in legislation specific to arbitration. However, the "legislator" of the model laws clarified that this omission was not intended to indicate that arbitrators are prohibited from acting as settlement facilitators. Rather, it emphasized that empowering arbitrators with this mandate should be left to the parties' discretion, subject to the applicable law.[71] Given the growing transnational trend of recognizing and encouraging the arbitrator's dual role and its clear acknowledgment by the "legislator" of the model laws, it is essential to incorporate this recognition into an explicit and detailed provision within the Model Law on ICA. If promoting a detailed provision proves unfeasible, an alternative amendment could adapt the above provision originally proposed for the Model Law on International Commercial Conciliation and its successor, the Model Law on ICM. Such a provision would still acknowledge the arbitrator's role and, equally importantly, convey the principle that party autonomy should take precedence when considering or reviewing the utilization of this role. Additionally, the promoted provision should ideally clarify its relationship with Article 24(3) of the Model Law, which mandates the arbitrator to disclose to all parties any information received from one party to the arbitration.[72] According to some scholars, this article is indispensable and prohibits parties from implementing alternative arrangements regarding the handling of confidential information communicated during the settlement process, such as partial disclosure.[73] Instead of removing this article from domestic arbitration laws that adopt a provision recognizing the arbitrator's role as a settlement facilitator—an approach taken by the Australian legislator in its Domestic Arbitration Act[74]—it seems sufficient to clarify that the arrangement anchored in Article 24(3) applies by default unless the parties agree otherwise or to exclude its application to provisions addressing the arbitrator's dual role.

8.4 LEGAL TRADITIONS AS A LIMITING FACTOR TO HARMONIZATION

While amendments to arbitration laws, rules, and guidelines recognizing and regulating the arbitrator's role in the settlement process can significantly impact the global harmonization of the practice and legal framework related to this role, this approach has limitations. As demonstrated in Chapter 5, despite explicit amendments to

70. *UNCITRAL WGII*, n.d., at Report of the Working Group on Arbitration on the work of its thirty-fifth session (A/CN.9/506), para. 130. *See also UNCITRAL WGII*, n.d., at Settlement of commercial disputes—Model legislative provisions on international commercial conciliation (A/CN.9/WG.II/WP.115), p. 24.
71. *See* the discussion in section 6.3.2.5.
72. Model Law on ICA, 2006, Article 24(3).
73. Nigmatullina, 2018, pp. 198-200, along with the references listed therein.
74. *See* the discussion in section 5.3.1.3.

arbitration laws in Australia, Singapore, and Hong Kong acknowledging the role of the arbitrator and regulating various aspects of party autonomy and due process, the legal practice in these jurisdictions has remained hesitant to fully embrace it. This hesitancy is attributed to criticisms of various aspects of these arrangements, which impact their attractiveness and implementation.[75] However, it is mainly influenced by the prevailing legal traditions in these jurisdictions, which act as a limiting factor in adopting external dispute resolution models imported from different legal cultures.[76] Indeed, legal theory acknowledges that despite globalization, "legal institutions cannot be easily moved from one context to another, like the 'transfer' of a part from one machine into another," but should instead be implanted and cultivated carefully in the new environment to adapt to its cultural context.[77] When significant differences exist between external and internal legal traditions, they can "unleash an evolutionary dynamics in which the external rule's meaning will be reconstructed and the internal context will undergo fundamental change."[78] Given the clashes between legal traditions regarding the methodology of the arbitral process in general and the arbitrator's role in particular,[79] the aspiration to reach complete uniformity among all legal traditions regarding every aspect of the arbitrator's mandate may be seen as an ideal,[80] when in practice, some degree of divergence regarding these aspects is unavoidable.[81]

This conclusion should not undermine the harmonization efforts related to the practice and legal framework of ICA. Instead, it aligns with the consensual nature of the domain, which prioritizes party autonomy and flexibility while granting parties the freedom to selectively apply norms and rules.[82] Indeed, constructing the normative regime of ICA without insisting on homogeneity acknowledges divergence as an inherent feature from the outset.[83] Nevertheless, through the selective application of practices and legal instruments offered in the "marketplace" of ICA, users can balance various interests relevant to dispute resolution, including their specific commercial needs, legal traditions, and the enforceability of the arbitral award.[84] While such

75. *See* the discussion in sections 5.2.2.2-5.2.2.3 & 5.3.1.3.
76. Link & Haftel, 2021, pp. 562-563; Kun, 2016a, p. 251; Chase & Bruner, 2005, p. 49; Lazareff, 1999, p. 1.
77. Teubner, 2001, p. 418. *See also* Kun, 2016a, p. 282; Kun, 2013b, p. 179.
78. Teubner, 2001, p. 441. This process is illustrated in section 5.2.2.1 concerning the introduction of the modern arbitration concept into China, where it was adapted to the local tradition by combining arbitration with mediation. *See also* Kun, 2016b, p. 448; Kun, 2016a, pp. 253-254, discussing the complex interplay between global and local norms in ICA, coined as the "glocalization of arbitration," to emphasize the process through which global norms and practices are assimilated into local contexts while local norms are projected onto the global stage.
79. Cremades, 1998, p. 159; Kun & Jemielniak, 2016, p. 584.
80. Cole, 2007, p. 55; Dasser, 2021, p. 87; Stipanowich, 2021a, pp. 361-362.
81. Pate, 2010, p. 160; Gillespie, 2009, p. 209; Kun, 2016a, p. 290. Additionally, *see* Kaufmann-Kohler, 2003, p. 1322, arguing that "consensus on principles does not mean agreement on details. Due process provides an illustration of this proposition. Even though there is consensus on the core principle, the exact parameters of due process may fluctuate from one legal system to another."
82. Ali, 2011b, p. 30.
83. Pate, 2010, p. 156; Stipanowich, 2021a, p. 361.
84. Ali, 2021, p. 21; Paisley & Player, 2021, pp. 34-35.

freedom may not result in full uniformity, it can foster convergence and harmonization over time,[85] as successful practices that gain widespread acceptance among stakeholders may eventually integrate into the normative mainstream of ICA.[86]

Hence, harmonization efforts in the law and practice of the arbitrator's role as a settlement facilitator are unlikely to produce a universal and uniform approach that eliminates all differences between legal traditions.[87] Since these traditions influence practitioners even when they operate at the transnational level,[88] the same can be said for transnational legal instruments relating to the arbitrator's dual role in ICA, as demonstrated in Chapter 6. Harmonization efforts relating to this role of the arbitrator should, therefore, aim for unification and standardization in its legal regime and practice worldwide, while tolerating "homeward trends"[89] and regional or cultural variations,[90] which may diminish over time in the "continuing melting pot of ideas, concepts and approaches across jurisdictions."[91] This conclusion underscores the aforementioned responsibility of arbitration organizations and institutes to promote adequate training—including in cross-cultural differences and their impact on the resolution of international business disputes—for neutrals and practitioners willing to engage in processes authorizing the arbitrator to act as a settlement facilitator. Additionally, it highlights the responsibility of practitioners and parties participating in ICA proceedings to abandon local legal patterns and attitudes associated with adjudicative processes,[92] which, as discussed below, is essential when the arbitral process employs the arbitrator with a dual role.

8.5 PRACTITIONERS OF ICA

In addition to being educated and trained in the techniques, norms, and ethics related to the arbitrator's role as a settlement facilitator, given the diversity among ICA practitioners, who represent a "global mix of national origin, legal qualification, and place of practice,"[93] practitioners in general, and arbitrators in particular, should refrain from relying solely on their own attitudes or approaches accepted in their legal traditions or home jurisdictions when considering this role of the arbitrator.[94] Instead,

85. Mistelis, 2001, p. 9; Pate, 2010, p. 156.
86. Bermann, 2017, p. 60; Draetta, 2015, p. 330.
87. Kun, 2013b, p. 219.
88. Stipanowich, 2021a, p. 361.
89. Pate, 2010, p. 157.
90. Ali, 2011b, p. 17; Kun, 2016a, p. 283; Stipanowich, 2021a, p. 361. This openness to different approaches in the concept and practice of international arbitration is exemplified by the current efforts of the Swiss Arbitration Association, in cooperation with UNCITRAL, to develop an Arbitration Toolbox. This tool aims to explains the various procedural options available for users of ICA, without recommending any particular procedures as best practices. *See ASA: Arbitration Toolbox*, n.d.; Dasser, 2021, p. 87.
91. Sussman & Berger, 2021a, p. 28.
92. Berger, 2019, p. 312.
93. Sussman & Berger, 2021a, pp. 27-28.
94. Berger, 2018b, p. 516; Blackaby et al., 2022, §6.01. *See also* Gaillard, 2023, pp. 44-45, emphasizing that in ICA, arbitrators "do not administer justice on behalf of any given state, but... act for the benefit of the international community."

as exemplified in Chapter 6 by some innovative initiatives promoted by leading practitioners and scholars,[95] they should adopt a dispute resolution mechanism that, subject to enforcement considerations, prioritizes the preferences, needs, and interests of the specific parties:

> Arbitration practitioners active in cross-cultural cases must navigate between the perils of legal parochialism on one side and excessive use of comparative analysis and transnationalizing trends on the other. The ability of leaving preconceptions, interpretive patterns, drafting mannerisms and procedural habits of one's domestic background is highly important, as one of the most frequently indicated reasons for selecting arbitration rather than domestic litigation is precisely the need for a neutral forum, free from the municipal particularities, which do not befit [the] international character of the case.[96]

To successfully implement such a transnational mindset that transcends the barriers of domestic legal cultures and approaches,[97] and allows for the application of tailored procedural solutions empowering the arbitrator with effective tools to facilitate settlement according to the parties' wishes and needs,[98] ICA practitioners are challenged to adapt advanced transitory skills. These skills enable them to move elegantly between the national and international contexts of arbitral proceedings,[99] as well as between adversarial and settlement-oriented approaches.[100]

8.6 USERS OF ICA

As the real target audience of ICA,[101] parties can insist on dispute resolution approaches that prioritize party autonomy, problem prevention, time and cost savings, preserving business relationships, and amicable outcomes.[102] Ultimately, the basic

95. *See* the discussion in section 6.3.4.
96. Jemielniak, 2014, p. 332. *See also* ICC Guide on Effective Conflict Management, 2023, pp. 35-36; Berger, 2018b, p. 516, holding that the mandate of international arbitrators "to engage in proactive facilitation of an amicable settlement of a dispute should not depend on the stance taken in the arbitrators' home jurisdiction, but only on the will of the parties." Some scholars argue that today the choice of most practitioners regarding the methodology of the ICA process is more pragmatic and case-driven than ideological, so they may move from one methodology to another depending on considerations connected with the case. *See* Sussman & Berger, 2021a, p. 28; Berger, 2019, p. 313; Lew & Shore, 1999, p. 38; Donovan, 2013, p. 198. Additionally, *see* Model Law on ICA, 2006, para. 6 to Explanatory Note (part two), warning against the "unfortunate consequence ... [when] traditional local concepts are imposed on international cases and the needs of modern practice are not met."
97. Bermann, 2010, p. 336; Jemielniak, 2014, p. 326.
98. Donovan, 2013, p. 198; Berger, 2018b, p. 516.
99. Jemielniak, 2014, p. 332; Cremades, 1998, p. 170.
100. Stipanowich, 2021a, p. 340; Limbury, 2010b, p. 6; Ross, 2013, p. 366; Weisman, 2013, p. 41. *See also* UNCITRAL Guidelines on Mediation of Investment Disputes, 2024, section I (at para. 27), highlighting the distinct role that legal representatives should adopt during the settlement process, in contrast to adversarial proceedings, with an emphasis on collaborative approaches, a focus on business interests, and the pursuit of future-oriented solutions.
101. Najar, 2009, p. 521.
102. Blackaby et al., 2022, §1.191; Stipanowich & Kaskell, 2001, p. 7. Empirical data supports the pragmatic attitude of ICA users toward dispute resolution. When respondents to the 2016-2017 GPC Survey were asked to select the most influential trends shaping the future of commercial

concept of arbitration involves "two business people taking their dispute to a wise business person in whom they both trusted, describing their respective claims, and then asking the arbitrator to provide them with the best solution to their dispute."[103] If parties, who likely seek a rapid resolution to return their focus to business affairs,[104] are interested in involving the arbitrator in the settlement process—including in a hybrid procedure combining arbitration with mediation and allowing the arbitrator to caucus with them—why insist on a different approach when all necessary safeguards are in place, and the process is not anticipated to face enforcement challenges due to a violation of public policy at the seat of arbitration or in enforcement jurisdictions?[105] To achieve this end, parties should not automatically rely on their counsel's advice regarding the methodology to be applied during ICA processes. Instead, they should raise questions to understand their alternatives and become actively involved in deciding the methods and procedures that align with their approaches to dispute resolution.[106] Additionally, to enhance the chances of successful settlement efforts led by the arbitrator, parties should ensure that senior members of their management, who have decision-making authority, are present or available on short notice during the settlement stage to approve or comment on settlement directions and offers, which is often crucial to maintaining the momentum of settlement negotiations and preventing missed settlement opportunities.[107]

Furthermore, in-house counsel are usually responsible for negotiating and drafting dispute-resolution clauses, advising parties on their options, and selecting arbitrators and external counsel. Thus, they can ensure that the agreed dispute-resolution arrangements empower the arbitrator to facilitate settlement while implementing the necessary safeguards. They can also help select the right external counsel and

---

dispute resolution, the majority cited changes in corporate attitudes toward conflict prevention and a greater focus on collaborative rather than adversarial processes as among the most influential trends. *See* GPC Series, 2016-2017, Question 4(5).

103. Rivkin, 2008, p. 378. *See also* Berger, 2016b; Najar, 2009, p. 527.

104. Blackaby et al., 2022, §1.01, holding that "no sensible businessperson, corporation, or state wants to spend time and money on legal proceedings if this can be avoided."; Najar, 2009, p. 526, arguing that "businesses make decisions extremely rapidly. ... Early alternative dispute mechanisms, including arbitration, are cornerstones of dispute management. Just as importantly, resolving disputes without letting animosity overtake rationality can result in mutually beneficial outcomes. The use of alternative dispute resolution techniques allows businesses to preserve relationships for future dealing."

105. Naughton, 2007, p. 33; Sussman & Berger, 2021b, pp. 37-38; Stipanowich, 2021a, p. 362; Mayer, 2016, p. 4; Draetta, 2015, p. 328; Cremades, 1998, pp. 164-165. This proposed approach aligns with the contemporary theoretical characterization of ICA as a "mixed nature" mechanism that integrates two historically contrasting authorities: the contractual authority, which emphasizes the arbitrator's role in enforcing the parties' will, and the jurisdictional authority, which underscores the arbitrator's adjudicative mandate and their responsibility to render a final decision on the dispute. *See* Gaillard, 2023, pp. 28-35; Mayer, 2016, pp. 3-7, discussing these authorities in the context of independent initiatives taken by the arbitrator during the arbitral process. Additionally, for further discussion on the arbitration community's duty to consider users' expectations and preferences regarding the arbitral process to ensure ICA remains a relevant and competitive mechanism for resolving cross-border disputes, *see* Blackaby et al., 2022, §1.191; Berger, 2016b.

106. Stipanowich, 2023, pp. 692-693; ICC Guide on Effective Conflict Management, 2023, p. 36.

107. Stipanowich & Kaskell, 2001, p. 32; CEDR Report on Settlement in ICA, 2009, section 4(9)(3); Abramson, 1999, pp. 9-10.

arbitrators with the skills, knowledge, and attitude needed to successfully utilize the arbitrator's dual role.[108] Even after authorizing external counsel to represent the business in arbitral proceedings, in-house counsel should remain involved in the resolution process. They should help develop the arbitration strategy, encourage decision-makers in the business to engage in the process, and, while applying a problem-solving mindset, emphasize the merits of the arbitrator's role in settlement for enhancing corporate governance, saving time and costs, and improving business relationships. By doing so, in-house counsel can prevent or mitigate possible conflicts of interest between the business and external counsel concerning the optimal procedures and resolution strategies that align with the business's actual interests and needs.[109]

8.7 CONCLUSIONS

In addition to the internal solutions recommended in the previous chapter, which aim to enhance the recognition of the arbitrator's role as a settlement facilitator in ICA by improving its regulation and mitigating risks associated with its practice under the current legal regime of the domain, this chapter proposes external solutions to harmonize perspectives on this role globally. Various actions were outlined for implementation by key stakeholders, including arbitration institutes and organizations, state-related entities, practitioners, and users. External solutions include amending the Model Law on ICA, domestic arbitration laws, and international arbitration rules and guidelines to better accommodate and regulate the arbitrator's dual role. The proposed amendments should strive to maintain maximum flexibility and adaptability regarding the components of this role and the safeguards to be applied. This approach provides ICA users the freedom to design procedures according to their specific needs, thus accommodating diverse attitudes rooted in different legal traditions and contributing to the global recognition of this role. The safeguards suggested in the previous chapter and summarized in Appendices B and C, along with the continuum of the arbitrator's settlement initiatives outlined in Chapter 2 and summarized in Appendix A, can form the basis for such formal regulation. Even if these recommended normative amendments are initially adopted only by leading arbitration institutes and a select number of jurisdictions serving as prominent hubs for ICA proceedings, the dynamic nature of the domain and the ongoing competition among jurisdictions and arbitral institutions on international arbitration services may encourage broader adoption over time. This outcome may contribute to standardizing the practice and legal regime associated with this role, reducing legal risks, and enhancing global harmonization.

108. Phillips, G. F., 2009, p. 78; CEDR Report on Settlement in ICA, 2009, section 4(9)(1); Nigmatullina, 2019, p. 39; Stipanowich, 2021a, p. 349; ICC Guide on Effective Conflict Management, 2023, pp. 35-36.
109. Najar, 2009, pp. 521-522, 524-526; CEDR Report on Settlement in ICA, 2009, section 4(9)(3) & 4(9)(5). For further discussion on the role of in-house counsel in drafting dispute resolution clauses and designing effective dispute resolution processes, *see* ICC Guide on Effective Conflict Management, 2023, pp. 9-11.

Future research on the arbitrator's role as a settlement facilitator can focus on establishing a comprehensive database that collects information about the recognition and regulation of this role by legislators and courts across domestic legal systems worldwide. This database should include information on limitations regarding particular settlement facilitation initiatives, mandatory safeguards, and considerations related to the recognition and enforcement of awards resulting from processes employing this role. Additionally, it should encompass information on the recognition and regulation of this role in the rules and guidelines of leading arbitration institutes and organizations.[110] The necessity of such a database stems from the shortcomings of previous attempts to systematically compile information on the regulation of the arbitrator's role in settlement. These earlier efforts were constrained in their scope, focusing either on a limited range of jurisdictions or addressing only specific aspects of the arbitrator's role. Notable examples include the Final Report of the CEDR Commission on Settlement in International Arbitration, which collected data on legislative provisions in 16 jurisdictions concerning settlement in arbitration,[111] and the 2021 Aragaki Study, which reviewed national legislation in 195 jurisdictions regarding hybrid processes involving arbitration and mediation,[112] along with similar initiatives by other scholars.[113] The potential contribution of such a comprehensive database to harmonization is clear:

> Only by collecting and sharing meaningfully detailed accounts of our experiences—good and bad—with med-arb, arb-med, and arbitrator engagement with settlement will we be in a position to overcome our varied predispositions in favor of more deliberate and functional approaches. Only by this means may we come to appreciate the potentialities and limits of different forms of third-party engagement during the settlement process, including the use of private caucusing, forms of evaluation, putting forth specific proposals for settlement, and other formats that are now subjects of controversy.[114]

A frequently updated database can provide valuable insights to ICA practitioners and parties about available alternatives for employing the arbitrator in a dual role while identifying the most appropriate arbitration rules and guidelines, as well as the suitable arbitration laws—whether to govern the substance of the dispute, the procedural rules, or the enforcement of the arbitral award. These insights can help mitigate enforcement risks arising from the use of the arbitrator's dual role. By embodying the aforementioned "marketplace" and "menu approach" to practices and regulation relating to the arbitrator's role as a settlement facilitator, such a database may also encourage legislators of soft and hard norms to recognize and optimally regulate this role to

110. The Queen Mary International Arbitration Survey, which regularly ranks the most preferred seats, arbitration institutes, and arbitration rules for ICA proceedings worldwide, serves as a valuable starting point for selecting the arbitration rules and guidelines to be reviewed.
111. CEDR Report on Settlement in ICA, 2009, Appendix 4.
112. *See* the discussion in section 5.4.
113. *See*, for example, Gu, 2016, pp. 95-99, reviewing and comparing the acceptance and regulation of Med-Arb processes in various jurisdictions, including the procedural safeguards implemented to prevent actual or apparent bias.
114. Stipanowich, 2021a, p. 361.

remain relevant in the ongoing competition for ICA proceedings. Moreover, future research can lay the foundation for ethical guidelines for neutrals and practitioners engaged in settlement facilitation within ICA proceedings.[115]

While amendments to arbitration laws, rules, and guidelines that recognize and regulate the arbitrator's role as a settlement facilitator significantly contribute to the global harmonization of its practice and legal framework, divergent approaches among legal traditions and the considerable influence of these traditions on the transnational legal regime of ICA render full consensus on all aspects of this role unlikely. This limitation underscores the importance of additional solutions recommended in this chapter to enhance the harmonization process for the arbitrator's dual role. These solutions include developing adequate training programs for the role, improving the selection process for qualified arbitrators who can transcend local legal patterns and attitudes rooted in adjudicative processes, and improving user involvement in arbitral proceedings that endorse this role.

115. Gu, 2016, p. 102; Stipanowich & Ulrich, 2014b, p. 31, recommending the development of specific ethical guidelines concerning the arbitrator's role in the settlement process, either through standalone guidelines or by revising the IBA Rules of Ethics for International Arbitrators.

Summary

THE ARBITRATOR'S ROLE AS A SETTLEMENT FACILITATOR IN INTERNATIONAL COMMERCIAL ARBITRATION

Toward Harmonized Transnational Standards

International commercial arbitration (ICA), a time-honored method of peaceful dispute resolution, has become the foremost approach to resolving cross-border business conflicts worldwide. Its rise to prominence is attributed to a constellation of advantages that have set it apart from national court proceedings and other alternative dispute resolution (ADR) mechanisms, including the impartiality of the tribunal, the adaptable and flexible nature of the process, and the emphasis on party autonomy. Parties can stipulate the seat of arbitration, applicable laws and rules, and the composition of the arbitral panel. Moreover, arbitration ensures confidentiality, fosters the preservation of business relationships, and is cost-effective, saving time and resources. Arbitration crucially provides a conclusive resolution to disputes, with the assurance that outcomes are subject to the enforcement mechanism of the New York Convention. In the wake of globalization, marked by a dramatic expansion in the scale, scope, and complexity of international business relationships, ICA has undergone significant harmonization of numerous areas of the domain and its overriding principles. This transformation aims to meet the unified needs of global merchants and business entities for a reliable dispute resolution mechanism operating on standardized principles.

However, ICA's rise has not been without challenges. In recent decades, users have criticized the "judicialization" of the domain, characterized by the assimilation of judicial-style regulations and procedures. This trend has increased costs and delays and has shifted the focus from business considerations toward formal, narrow legal rights-based approaches akin to traditional court proceedings. Consequently, ICA has faced mounting competition from other methods of dispute resolution, particularly international mediation, which has recently been bolstered by the introduction of an international enforcement mechanism for mediated settlement agreements (i.e., the

Singapore Convention). Moreover, ICA has encountered evolving competition from litigation before national courts, particularly with the expansion of international commercial courts that, despite being seated in specific jurisdictions, strive to operate in accordance with transnational legal standards. In addition to existing bilateral, multilateral, and regional enforcement frameworks for transnational litigation—such as the EU Regulation on the Recognition and Enforcement of Judgments in Civil and Commercial Matters, which facilitates the seamless enforcement of judgments across EU Member States—a new international enforcement mechanism for foreign judgments in civil and commercial matters has recently been introduced (i.e., the Hague Judgments Convention), which may enhance the appeal of court litigation for resolving cross-border commercial disputes. Additionally, broader shifts in the transnational dispute-resolution landscape have necessitated a recalibration of traditional adjudicative methods in favor of approaches that integrate adjudicative and non-adjudicative methods and prioritize flexibility, party autonomy, enhanced efficiency, the preservation of business relations, and early settlements with the assistance of an adjudicator.

In response to these challenges that can potentially undermine the established status of ICA as the primary method for resolving cross-border commercial disputes, stakeholders in the domain—ranging from states and arbitral institutions to practitioners and scholars—have promoted various initiatives to address user needs. Alongside initiatives focusing on improving the efficiency of ICA as a standalone adversarial process and others combining arbitration with ADR methods while assigning different neutrals for each dispute-resolution method, few innovative initiatives have advanced the role of the arbitrator as a settlement facilitator. This book focuses on this mandate in international arbitration, which, alongside adjudicating the dispute, empowers the arbitrator to facilitate amicable resolutions by conducting various possible initiatives, whether during a standalone arbitration or within a hybrid process involving arbitration and mediation. Recent, compelling empirical data alongside various domestic and transnational regulative efforts relating to this dual role have highlighted its growing recognition worldwide, including in legal traditions and jurisdictions that historically showed hesitant attitudes in its regard. Nevertheless, established transnational standards regarding the practice and normative framework of this dual role have not yet been achieved, which is not desirable considering its clear acceptance, alongside the transnational nature of the domain and the general harmonization of its practice and legal regime.

The book identifies three main obstacles to the global harmonization of the arbitrator's role as a settlement facilitator: (a) ambiguity regarding the specific components of this role; (b) divergent approaches among legal traditions regarding its practice, particularly between Eastern and Western legal cultures and between Common law and Civil law legal systems; and (c) controversy about the compatibility of this role (or aspects of it) with fundamental principles of arbitration. To effectively address these barriers to harmonization and realize the full potential of this role in ICA, the book poses several key questions outlined in section 1.5: What are the specific components of the arbitrator's role as a settlement facilitator in ICA? What are the associated advantages and risks of this role? How do various jurisdictions approach this role or components thereof in both domestic and international arbitral proceed ings? What are the prevailing perspectives of ICA users regarding this role? What progress has been achieved toward harmonizing its practice and legal framework on the transnational level? What solutions could further promote the global harmonization of this role?

Part I, Chapter 1, introduces the current trends in the harmonization of ICA, the driving forces behind these trends, and the present challenges confronting the domain. Chapter 2 provides a comprehensive definition of the arbitrator's role as a settlement facilitator, categorizing the spectrum of initiatives available for its implementation. These initiatives, summarized in Appendix A, are grouped into three levels based on the arbitrator's degree of involvement in the settlement process. The first category involves minimal or indirect involvement, aimed at setting the stage for settlement through party-led negotiations. These initiatives (e.g., the proactive management of the first organizational conference, designing mediation windows, bifurcating the arbitral proceedings, deciding preliminary issues, and offering to decide the dispute on equitable considerations or issuing consent awards) have been widely recognized in international arbitration rules and guidelines as integral to the arbitrator's procedural role. Typically, these actions do not require prior party consent and involve minimal risk of challenges to the arbitrator or the arbitral award. The second category involves direct initiatives within standalone arbitration to promote settlement by integrating mediation techniques into the arbitral process. Examples include arbitrators making settlement proposals, convening settlement conferences to explore settlement terms in detail, and engaging in ex parte communications (i.e., caucusing) to better understand the parties' positions and underlying interests. The third category pertains to direct involvement in hybrid processes, where the arbitrator "switches hats" between the roles of arbitrator and mediator within the same dispute. These processes—addressed in this book according to the literal sequence in which the mediation and arbitration phases occur—include Med-Arb and its variations (e.g., MEDALOA and High-Low Arbitration), Arb-Med, and Arb-Med-Arb. The mediation phase may include or exclude caucusing in these hybrid processes, depending on the approach adopted.

Subsequently, Part II of the book delves into the advantages and drawbacks of implementing this role in ICA. Chapter 3 highlights the main advantages of the arbitrator's dual role by examining it from the contractual prism of the arbitral process, which provides parties with the autonomy to tailor the proceedings to their needs and interests, as well as the broader mandate of the arbitrator as a dispute-resolver, emphasizing the role's contribution to the administration of justice. The analysis demonstrates that the dual role offers significant benefits, including flexibility, adaptability, and cost and time savings. Additionally, it can enhance parties' commitment to the dispute resolution process by addressing key barriers to settlement, including hesitation in suggesting negotiations or making the first move toward settlement. This role further incentivizes settlement by allowing parties to maintain control over the process, avoid uncertainties associated with an arbitral award, and leverage their trust in the arbitrator's authority and expertise. Moreover, the dual role can improve the quality and variety of potential solutions by shifting the focus from rigid legal rights to broader underlying interests, facilitating creative, equitable, and business-oriented resolutions. Even when settlement efforts fail to achieve a comprehensive resolution, the arbitrator can assist in narrowing the disputed issues, leading to a more predictable, informed, and acceptable binding award. Other notable advantages are the finality of the dispute and international enforceability of the outcomes under the New York Convention, which offers a safer and more effective enforcement mechanism compared to alternatives saved for national judgments or settlements resulting from international mediation.

However, the chapter also underscores that these advantages are not absolute and vary across the continuum of settlement facilitation initiatives. Their effectiveness depends on the timing of the implementation and, in hybrid processes involving arbitration and mediation, the sequence in which these phases are conducted. Notably, for hybrid processes, the advantage of international enforceability under the New York Convention is only assured if settlement efforts commence after establishing the arbitral tribunal. This limitation effectively excludes Med-Arb and its variations from the recommended initiatives for arbitrators serving in a dual role.

Chapter 4 examines the concerns associated with the arbitrator's role as a settlement facilitator by focusing on the inherent tension between the arbitrator's authority as a dispute-decider and the mandate to promote amicable resolution. These concerns, which typically arise when the arbitrator directly engages in settlement efforts, are classified into three primary categories. The first category involves fundamental concerns related to due process rights, including party autonomy, impartiality, and the right to be heard. Any violation of these principles risks undermining the arbitral process and jeopardizing the enforcement of its outcome. These risks are often associated with the practice of caucusing, exposure to confidential information, coercive behavior by the arbitrator, and, in some jurisdictions, the expression of evaluative views by the arbitrator. The second category pertains to hesitant attitudes toward the settlement process, which include the parties' tactical use of the settlement stage and their reluctance to negotiate openly, as well as the arbitrator's hesitation to engage in settlement efforts, whether for personal preferences, a lack of confidence in their ability to balance dual roles, or the influence of their legal background. The third category encompasses concerns external to the arbitral process, such as the arbitrator's competence in managing the dual role, which requires a unique and sometimes contradictory skill set for successful implementation. Additionally, there are questions about the appropriateness of settlements when public interests are at stake, as is often the case in investor-state disputes. In this context, while the empirical data indicates that arbitrators rarely facilitate settlements in investor-state disputes, the chapter advocates for the equal application of the arbitrator's dual role in these cases. This advocacy is grounded in recognizing the dual role under various rules and guidelines related to investment arbitration and its significant advantages, including enhanced enforceability and stronger protection of public interests—benefits that the current investment mediation framework cannot guarantee. However, as with ICA proceedings under the New York Convention, enforcement of facilitated or mediated investor-state settlements under the ICSID Convention requires that settlement efforts begin only after the arbitral tribunal is established.

After weighing the concerns associated with the arbitrator's dual role against the advantages discussed in Chapter 3, the chapter concludes that the most effective and balanced approach to employing this role in both cross-border commercial and investor-state disputes is within the framework of standalone arbitration or Arb-Med-Arb hybrid process. This flexible setting addresses enforceability concerns by initiating settlement efforts only after the arbitration process has commenced. Early settlement efforts in this framework can save money and time while preserving business relationships. Furthermore, by incorporating party autonomy and due process safeguards for direct settlement initiatives—as suggested below and summarized in Appendices B and C—this setting mitigates many of the concerns associated with the arbitrator's dual role.

Having mapped the advantages and concerns associated with the arbitrator's role as a settlement facilitator, Part III of this book examines the evolution of this role from diverse local practices rooted in normative frameworks and legal traditions toward more standardized approaches supported by a developing transnational legal regime. Chapter 5 undertakes a comprehensive comparative analysis of traditional and contemporary perspectives from various Eastern and Western legal traditions regarding the arbitrator's dual role by emphasizing two key jurisdictional groups. The first group includes jurisdictions with distinctive practices or legal frameworks concerning the arbitrator's mandate as a settlement facilitator, such as Islamic and Arab countries, China, Australia, Germany, and Brazil. The second group comprises jurisdictions recognized as prominent hubs for international arbitration, including the US, the UK, Hong Kong, and Singapore. Analyzing these jurisdictions' experiences with the practice and regulation of this role and their strategies for addressing associated concerns offers critical insights into global efforts to harmonize the arbitrator's dual role. The findings reveal that traditional attitudes of ICA practitioners and parties toward the arbitrator's settlement facilitation role are strongly shaped by the legal traditions and practices of the judiciary and arbitral tribunals in their home jurisdictions. Broadly, Eastern legal cultures, which historically emphasize conciliation, are more accepting of arbitrator-led settlement facilitation. In contrast, Western legal systems display varying tolerance levels, with Civil Law traditions generally more permissive than Common Law systems. Nonetheless, significant intra-regional differences exist, such as the varied approaches within East Asia and among Western Civil Law jurisdictions.

Despite the persistence of these traditional views, an updated perspective based on contemporary regulatory developments, court decisions, and extensive empirical data reveals that pragmatic considerations and mutual jurisdictional influences lead to the erosion of traditional binary distinctions. This shift reflects a growing cross-cultural acceptance of the arbitrator's dual role, particularly in ICA proceedings, which are inherently transnational and cross-cultural. For example, China has adopted Western practices to attract international users, while historically skeptical Western Common Law jurisdictions—including those now permitting hybrid processes with ex parte communications—have gradually embraced the dual role. However, even amid this convergence, certain components of the dual role remain controversial and are unevenly regulated across jurisdictions. These contentious components include case evaluation, the presentation of settlement proposals, and ex parte communications involving exposure to confidential information. The chapter concludes that given the pivotal role of national laws in ICA processes—especially in the enforcement of arbitral outcomes—these divergent components warrant careful attention in efforts to advance the harmonization of the arbitrator's dual role and its associated legal framework. Solutions aimed at harmonization must account for these differences to ensure effective implementation within the legal landscapes governing ICA.

Chapter 6 reaffirms that the evolving recognition of the arbitrator's role as a settlement facilitator has transcended the domestic sphere and gained significant traction at the transnational level. Recent surveys and empirical studies discussed in this chapter confirm that users of ICA increasingly favor flexible arbitral processes that emphasize amicable resolutions for cross-border disputes. This growing preference is driven by pragmatic considerations such as efficiency, the preservation of business relationships, party autonomy, and the contractual freedom that underpins arbitration. As a result, a notable demand exists for arbitrators skilled in settlement facilitation, with parties showing greater willingness to engage such arbitrators in standalone proceedings and hybrid processes integrating arbitration, mediation, and caucusing. This trend is further evidenced by past initiatives aimed at harmonizing and codifying norms related to this role at the transnational level. Over the past two decades, various stakeholders in ICA—including leading arbitration institutions, organizations, practitioners, and scholars—have promoted suggestions for rules, guidelines, and best practices concerning the arbitrator's dual role. While these initiatives have varied in their approaches and levels of detail, they have shared a common emphasis on prioritizing the consensual nature of arbitration and the parties' freedom to tailor the process to their specific disputes. This emphasis marks a departure from traditional views of arbitration and the arbitrator's duties in favor of adaptability and customization over rigid adherence to established norms. Given these developments, and in light of the growing domestic acceptance of this role outlined in Chapter 5, this chapter concludes that—subject to party consent, appropriate safeguards, and enforcement considerations—parties in ICA proceedings should have the ability to expand the arbitrator's mandate to include the role of a settlement facilitator. This expansion may encompass processes that combine arbitration with mediation, caucusing, and exposure to confidential information structured in a manner that aligns with the parties' interests and needs.

A critical examination of previous codification efforts at the transnational level reveals that, while these initiatives have played a significant role in raising awareness of the arbitrator's dual role among ICA users, they have notable shortcomings. Most prior efforts have failed to provide a comprehensive framework outlining the available initiatives for arbitrators to facilitate settlements in ICA disputes, as proposed in this book. Furthermore, these initiatives have often lacked detailed guidance on controversial components of this role, such as caucusing, exposure to confidential information, and presenting settlement proposals, as well as safeguards to mitigate associated risks. Another limitation of these earlier harmonization efforts is their narrow focus, primarily driven by non-governmental or private actors within the global arbitration community. These efforts mostly reflected the legal cultures of their promoters, relied overtly on soft norms, and centered on internal procedural issues within arbitration. Moreover, they paid insufficient attention to external measures that arbitration stake holders could undertake to harmonize the dual role's practice and legal framework globally. Consequently, this chapter highlights the need to develop and codify more detailed normative instruments regarding the arbitrator's role as a settlement facilitator in ICA. These instruments can provide greater access to the practices and techniques of settlement facilitation while offering a clearer understanding of potential risks and corresponding safeguards to enhance the global acceptance of the dual role among practitioners and users from diverse legal traditions. Additionally, the chapter underscores the importance of complementary measures external to the arbitral process, aimed at harmonizing perspectives on this role and further standardizing its legal regime at both domestic and transnational levels.

Acknowledging the remaining gaps among legal traditions and attitudes regarding different aspects of the arbitrator's role as a settlement facilitator in ICA and building on the experiences gained from past regulatory efforts at the domestic and transnational levels, this book culminates in Part IV with a comprehensive set of recommendations aimed at enhancing harmonization in the practice and legal frameworks associated with this role, while also highlighting their limitations and suggesting future research in the subject. Recognizing that formal changes in the multifaceted legal regime of ICA often require gradual socialization and extended timeframes, Chapter 7 focuses on internal solutions that ICA users can adopt contractually within the existing legal regime of the domain. These internal solutions are grounded in safeguards designed to align the arbitrator's dual role with the fundamental principles of arbitration. Subject to fulfilling the cornerstone of any attempt by the arbitrator to facilitate a settlement within the arbitral process—that is, ensuring the enforceability of the arbitral award or at least mitigating enforceability risks—these safeguards, summarized in Appendixes B and C and outlined briefly below, emphasize maximum flexibility and adaptability regarding the components of the arbitrator's dual role and their application, accommodating the diverse attitudes of users, practitioners, and stakeholders from various legal traditions. This approach seeks to foster global harmonization of the arbitrator's dual role in practice and legal frameworks.

The proposed safeguards are divided into two categories. The first focuses on protecting party autonomy, addressing two key aspects: (a) ensuring that the parties' desire to employ the arbitrator as a settlement facilitator is respected by both the arbitrator and the courts, whether for enforcement purposes or for reviewing the arbitral process, and (b) ensuring that this dual role is implemented strictly according to the parties' agreement while maintaining their control over the process and their fundamental right to self-determination. Hence, the following *cumulative* safeguards are recommended to guarantee express consent to the arbitrator's dual role, although this consent is not necessarily needed for indirect initiatives implemented within the procedural framework of the arbitration or while exercising the arbitrator's procedural authority over the arbitral process: (a) written, advance, and revocable consent, to guarantee that parties provide clear consent before the arbitrator initiates settlement efforts, with the option to revoke it under agreed terms; (b) detailed consent, which should specify the scope and boundaries of the arbitrator's role in facilitating settlement and the safeguards to be implemented to ensure clarity and mutual understanding; and (c) informed consent to ensure that parties fully understand the implications and potential risks associated with the arbitrator's dual role before granting consent. Additionally, this group includes a safeguard requiring (d) an explicit waiver of the right to challenge the arbitrator or the award based on their settlement facilitation role, provided the arbitrator acted in accordance with the parties' agreement.

The second group of safeguards aims at protecting the parties' due process rights when employing the arbitrator with a dual role. It includes the following mandatory safeguards to be implemented after unsuccessful settlement attempts: (a) an opt-out option for the parties to discontinue arbitration with the same arbitrator under agreed terms, allowing them to appoint a new arbitrator for the resumed proceedings, commence arbitration afresh, or pursue ADR methods; *or alternatively* (b) a reversion to formal arbitration with the same arbitrator, subject to renewed consent, which must include an agreement on handling any settlement-stage information not part of the formal record—whether disclosed during ex parte or joint sessions—in accordance with a recommended roadmap; *and cumulatively* (c) an opt-out option for the arbitrator to recuse themselves from the resumed arbitration if, following their settlement facilitation role, they developed doubts regarding their ability to remain independent and impartial during the renewed arbitration. Additionally, this group embraces the following voluntary safeguards, which can complement the mandatory ones: (a) limiting the arbitrator's mandate in the resumed proceedings by excluding certain issues from adjudication or restricting their decision-making scope, such as adopting one of the parties' final offers or deciding within a pre-agreed range, and (b) in tribunals comprising several arbitrators, involving only a subset of arbitrators in the settlement efforts, according to some recommended configurations.

Despite the flexibility and adaptability of these safeguards, they cannot guarantee absolute protection against all risks associated with the arbitrator's dual role in ICA. This limitation stems from the inherently relative nature of these measures, which strive to balance party autonomy and flexibility with procedural fairness and enforceability considerations. Additionally, the application and effectiveness of these safeguards may vary across jurisdictions due to differences in legal traditions, fundamental principles, and public policy concerns. In this respect, these solutions are not exceptional. Indeed, no dispute-resolution method—particularly one that assigns the neutral dual and potentially conflicting responsibilities—can be entirely risk-free for its users. This conclusion highlights the need for external measures to complement the internal safeguards. These measures should aim to harmonize global perspectives on the arbitrator's dual role and strengthen its regulatory framework.

Chapter 8 extends the discussion beyond the scope of parties' contractual relations by proposing external solutions to address the harmonization of the arbitrator's dual role in ICA. Acknowledging the multifaceted legal regime of ICA, which assigns responsibility for standardizing practices and legal frameworks to various stakeholders—including arbitration institutions, state-related actors, practitioners, and users—this chapter identifies actions these stakeholders can undertake to enhance global recognition of the arbitrator's dual role. These measures aim to standardize its legal framework across jurisdictions and legal traditions, mitigate associated legal risks, and bolster the security of cross-border commercial relations to benefit individual parties, the broader business community, and states. External solutions include amending the Model Law on ICA, domestic arbitration laws, and international arbitration rules and guidelines to better accommodate and regulate the arbitrator's dual role. These amendments should strive to preserve maximum flexibility and adaptability regarding the components of this role and the safeguards to be applied. Hence, ICA users can be free to design procedures tailored to their needs and aligned with diverse legal traditions while promoting global recognition. The safeguards proposed in this book and detailed in Appendices B and C, along with the continuum of settlement facilitation initiatives outlined in Chapter 2 and summarized in Appendix A, can serve as foundational elements for such formal regulation. Even if these normative amendments are initially embraced by a limited number of leading arbitration institutions and jurisdictions prominent in ICA, the dynamic nature of the field and the competitive environment among jurisdictions and arbitral institutions vying for international arbitration services will likely encourage broader adoption. This expansion can enhance global harmonization, reduce legal risks, and contribute to standardizing practice and legal frameworks associated with the arbitrator's dual role.

However, given the contrasting approaches rooted in various legal traditions regarding aspects of this role and the significant influence of these traditions within the current transnational legal regime of ICA, achieving a universal consensus on all aspects of the arbitrator's dual role is improbable. Efforts toward harmonization should aim for unification and standardization while tolerating "homeward trends" and regional or cultural variations, which will likely diminish over time as convergence increases. Therefore, complementary measures are needed to foster harmonization and align global attitudes toward the arbitrator's dual role. These additional measures include developing comprehensive training programs to equip arbitrators with the necessary skills for settlement facilitation, refining the selection process to identify qualified arbitrators capable of transcending local legal patterns and adjudicative attitudes, and encouraging greater user involvement in arbitral processes that endorse this role. Thus, future research can focus on creating a comprehensive, frequently updated database documenting the recognition and regulation of the arbitrator's dual role across jurisdictions and arbitration rules worldwide. Furthermore, developing ethical guidelines for neutrals and practitioners engaged in settlement facilitation within ICA proceedings can provide essential guidance to ensure consistency and ethical integrity in this evolving role.

Appendix A

The Continuum of Settlement Facilitation Initiatives and Parties' Consent

Setting the Stage for Settlement Indirect Involvement of the Arbitrator in the Settlement Efforts		
Initiative	*Characteristics and Variations of the Initiative*	*Consent Needed?*
Proactive Case Management Conference	In addition to setting timetables for submissions, disclosure, and hearings, handling key procedural issues and tailoring the procedural framework to support efficiency and promote full or partial settlement of the dispute, for instance, by narrowing disputed issues, examining early submissions and initial merits, offering and designing mediation windows and pre-hearing conference, and suggesting early resolution of issues, bifurcation of the proceedings, and early neutral evaluation of legal or factual issues.	NO, unless otherwise agreed upon by the parties or required by the governing law or arbitration rules.
Targeted Questions on Procedural and Substantive Issues	Pointing, through targeted questions, to the strengths and weaknesses in the parties' arguments and positions, creating a psychological effect that motivates the disputants to settle or opens the door for informal examination of whether they are willing to explore settlement possibilities.	NO, unless otherwise agreed upon by the parties or required by the governing law or arbitration rules.
Abstract Proposals to Settle	Raising the prospect of reaching a full or partial settlement regarding the disputed issues; encouraging the parties to negotiate directly with each other (with or without the presence of their counsels) while allowing for "cooling-off periods" during the proceedings for that purpose.	NO, unless otherwise agreed upon by the parties or required by the governing law or arbitration rules.

Setting the Stage for Settlement
Indirect Involvement of the Arbitrator in the Settlement Efforts

Initiative	*Characteristics and Variations of the Initiative*	*Consent Needed?*
Bifurcation of the Arbitral Process	Dividing the proceedings between the liability and the quantum of damages phases, usually by deciding liability first, but sometimes through reverse bifurcation where liability is addressed only regarding issues that have already been decided to bear damages. Other options for bifurcation include addressing jurisdiction before the merits or deciding the highest monetary value claim through a partial or interim award to streamline discussions on overlapping factual and legal issues concerning the remaining claims.	NO, unless otherwise agreed upon by the parties or required by the governing law or arbitration rules.
Mid-Term Arbitration Review	During the early stage of the proceedings, preferably after the initial round of submissions and witness statements, parties and their counsel convene before the tribunal for a comprehensive discussion. This discussion covers key legal and factual issues that may necessitate further submissions or evidence, sets limitations on replies to written submissions, identifies issues suitable for accelerated determination, assesses document disclosure and the relevance of requested documents, facilitates proceedings to narrow disputed issues between the experts, organizes documents for the main hearing, and addresses issues related to damages. Expert witnesses may also attend this meeting to elucidate their findings and highlight areas of disagreement with other experts. Such discussions can significantly enhance efficiency and bolster the prospects of amicably settling the disputed issues, either fully or partly.	NO, unless otherwise agreed upon by the parties or required by the governing law or arbitration rules.
Offer to Render a Consent Award Following a Concluded Settlement	Reminding the parties about the option to convert settlement agreements into arbitral awards on agreed terms and offering the arbitrator's cautious guidance in this process to ensure the award's compliance with the necessary legal principles, thereby enhancing its enforceability under the New York Convention.	NO, but rendering a consent award is contingent upon the parties' consent and prior settlement agreement.
Offer to Decide the Dispute, in Whole or in Part, *Ex aequo et bono* or as *Amiable Compositeur*	Encouraging the parties to authorize the arbitrator to decide the case, or part of it, based on equitable grounds, essentially fairness, justice, and good conscience, rather than on principles of law. When the equitable decision relates to "stumbling block" issues, whose	NO, but deciding the case on equitable grounds is subject to the parties' request and authorization

Setting the Stage for Settlement ***Indirect Involvement of the Arbitrator in the Settlement Efforts***		
Initiative	*Characteristics and Variations of the Initiative*	*Consent Needed?*
	resolution opens the door for agreement between the parties regarding the others, this may increase the chances of settling the dispute amicably.	by the governing law or arbitration rules.
Determination of Preliminary Issues	Deciding claims on jurisdiction, discovery (including limitations on the discovery process), and key legal points, as well as granting dispositive motions that allow early dismissal of claims or defenses that clearly lack legal merit or exceed the tribunal's jurisdiction, thus narrowing the disputed issues and potentially opening the door for settlement.	YES, unless otherwise agreed by the parties or authorized by the governing law or arbitration rules.
Providing Early Neutral Evaluation of the Case	Non-final and non-binding evaluation by the arbitrator on preliminary findings of facts, conclusions of law, and the level of proof required to establish the issues in dispute. Despite their "early" nature, these preliminary evaluations can be delivered by the arbitrator at various stages of the proceedings and may be supported by "decision-tree" analysis to assist the parties in approaching the dispute more realistically and potentially enhancing the chances for settlement.	YES, unless otherwise agreed by the parties or authorized by the governing law or arbitration rules.
Designing of Mediation Windows	Alongside permitting spontaneous mediation windows following developments that create momentum to promote settlement, scheduling those windows in advance to allow better preparations by the parties and help them overcome one of the main barriers to settlement—the fear of showing weakness by agreeing to settlement discussions after the initiation of the arbitral process. Mediation windows can be carried out simultaneously with the arbitral process or while staying it to allow undisturbed attempts to settle. The arbitrator may assist in determining the issues to be negotiated between the parties during the mediation window, and possibly selecting the mediator when this window involves mediation in front of a separate neutral.	YES
Using Sealed Offers to Allocate Costs and Legal Fees	Following a final decision on liability and quantum, rather than determining the process costs and legal fees according to the basic rule of "costs follow the event," considering the parties' responses to sealed settlement offers	YES

Setting the Stage for Settlement Indirect Involvement of the Arbitrator in the Settlement Efforts		
Initiative	*Characteristics and Variations of the Initiative*	*Consent Needed?*
	made by one or more parties during the arbitral process on a "without prejudice save as to costs" basis. Unjustified refusals of offers may lead to bearing those costs, either fully or partly, irrespective of the outcome of the process. Sealed offers may increase the parties' incentive to settle because these costs can represent a significant percentage of the amount in dispute.	

Direct Involvement of the Arbitrator in the Settlement Efforts		
Initiative	*Characteristics and Variations of the Initiative*	*Consent Needed?*
Settlement Proposals by the Arbitrator	Provide oral or written settlement proposals to the parties, with the nature and scope varying depending on the arbitrator's stance, the parties' requests, and the circumstances of the disputed issues. These proposals can range from a general outline for agreement to a specific range of possibilities or amounts, serving as a basis for direct negotiations between the parties. Alternatively, they may consist of detailed and comprehensive suggestions regarding concrete actions and figures, including cost allocations. In ongoing or long-term contractual disputes, settlement proposals may also involve revising disputed clauses to avoid future disagreements between the parties.	YES
Settlement Conferences with the Parties	Chair one or more designated settlement conferences intended to allow thorough discussions between the arbitrator and the parties regarding settlement options and possible contents of the settlement. It can conclude with a detailed settlement proposal by the arbitrator or, ideally, with a finalized settlement agreement. Typically, settlement conferences are intended to allow a careful relaxation of the trial-like atmosphere and, therefore, are conducted in the presence of all parties and exclude caucusing.	YES
Caucusing	Holding separate meetings with the parties to the arbitral process to better understand the dispute's background and the parties' underlying interests and desires. Those ex parte meetings facilitate the exploration of possible settlement avenues through reality checks and ways to overcome barriers to an amicable	YES

Direct Involvement of the Arbitrator in the Settlement Efforts		
Initiative	*Characteristics and Variations of the Initiative*	*Consent Needed?*
	outcome of the dispute. Usually, caucusing relies on either *facilitative techniques*—wherein the arbitrator assists the parties to formulate a settlement without expressing views on the merits or the appropriate terms of settlement—or *evaluative techniques*—wherein the arbitrator takes an active and interventionist role by expressing views on the merits and making suggestions regarding the settlement. Sometimes, a combination of both techniques is used.	

Arbitrator "Switching Hats" Dual Role as an Arbitrator and Mediator in the Same Dispute		
Initiative	*Characteristics and Variations of the Initiative*	*Consent Needed?*
Med-Arb	The neutral is appointed first as a mediator who assists the parties in settling the dispute amicably before arbitration commences. After the mediation phase, the parties appoint the same neutral as an arbitrator for the same dispute to render a consent award on agreed issues and decide the remaining after their adjudication. The process may involve or exclude caucusing and allow for one or more mediation attempts. Variations of this process: Mediation followed by Last-Offer Arbitration (MEDALOA, also known as baseball arbitration); Mediation followed by High-Low Arbitration; Med-Arb Show Cause; and Med-Arb-Opt-Out (where, following unsuccessful attempts to fully resolve the dispute during mediation, the parties can opt out of the arbitral process and engage a different neutral to resolve the dispute).	YES
Arb-Med	The neutral is initially appointed as an arbitrator. After the full arbitral process is concluded but before rendering the award (which, if written at this stage, must be kept sealed), the neutral is appointed as a mediator to assist the parties in resolving their dispute amicably. If mediation is successful, the arbitrator drafts a new award based on the settlement agreement. Otherwise, the neutral renders the sealed award, and if it has not been written yet, then writes it based on the arbitration phase and publishes it to the parties. The process can include or exclude caucusing and allow for one or more mediation attempts.	YES

Arbitrator "Switching Hats" ***Dual Role as an Arbitrator and Mediator in the Same Dispute***		
Initiative	*Characteristics and Variations of the Initiative*	*Consent Needed?*
Arb-Med-Arb	After arbitration commences, the arbitrator attempts to settle the dispute by acting as a mediator. The arbitration proceedings are renewed upon successful mediation to record the settlement as a consent award. Otherwise, substantive arbitration hearings resume for the unsettled matters, which will eventually be decided through a binding award. The process may include or exclude caucusing and allow for one or more mediation attempts. Another variant of this process is Arb-Med-Arb-Opt-Out, wherein, following unsuccessful mediation attempts, the parties can opt out of the arbitral process and engage a different neutral to resolve the dispute.	YES

Appendix B

Party Autonomy Safeguards

Safeguard		*Characteristics of the Safeguard*
Express Consent to the Arbitrator's Dual Role	**Written**	All parties involved in the arbitral process should provide their consent to the arbitrator's dual role in written form. Any renewed consent during the arbitral process must also be in written form.
	Advance	Consent to the arbitrator's dual role should be obtained from the parties before the arbitrator initiates any direct steps to facilitate a settlement, ideally within their dispute resolution clause or during the early stages of the dispute. If consent is required on one or more additional occasions after the arbitration has commenced, such as when the parties decide to deviate from the initial agreement regarding the arbitrator's dual role, the proceedings should be temporarily halted to allow the parties to shape and finalize those additional or renewed consents before the arbitrator further engages in the settlement process.
	Revocable	Each party retains the right to withdraw consent to the arbitrator's dual role, subject to agreed terms. Consequently, the arbitrator resumes their adjudicative role in the proceedings. While many arbitration laws, rules, and guidelines permit parties to revoke their consent to the arbitrator's dual role at *any time*, considering the additional mandatory and voluntary due process safeguards, parties may contemplate alternative arrangements that *condition this right with specific terms*. For example, parties may agree to a limited phase during which they cannot withdraw from the settlement negotiations and, therefore, cannot revoke their consent to the arbitrator's dual role within that timeframe.

Safeguard		*Characteristics of the Safeguard*
	Detailed	Consent to the arbitrator's dual role should encompass detailed provisions regarding *all direct initiatives* the arbitrator is entitled to take and any *indirect initiatives requiring the parties' consent*. The continuum of initiatives, outlined in Chapter 2 and summarized in Appendix A, can serve as a template for further refinement and adjustment by potential ICA parties considering employing the arbitrator in a dual role. Consent should particularly address the following initiatives, which have not yet achieved consensus across various legal backgrounds: (a) whether and to what extent the arbitrator is authorized to *express evaluative views*; (b) whether the arbitrator is empowered to *provide settlement proposals*, including how detailed those proposals can be and whether they are limited only to the disputed issues; (c) whether the arbitrator is permitted to *mediate the dispute*; (d) whether the arbitrator is allowed to *caucus with the parties*, and if so, whether those meetings are limited to the presence of both party and its counsel, or can also be carried out with one of them. Consent should outline, at least in general terms, the *timing of the settlement efforts*. It should also establish a clear *demarcation between these efforts and the formal arbitral process*. Additionally, where relevant, consent should demarcate between issues suitable for settlement and those exclusively adjudicated. Consent should specify both the *mandatory and agreed voluntary due process safeguards*, as outlined in Chapter 7 and summarized in Appendix C. A detailed agreement is advisable even when applicable law or arbitration rules acknowledge the arbitrator's dual role because these regulations often offer limited guidance on the scope and conduct of this role and how to ensure its compliance with parties' due process rights.
	Informed	Consent to the arbitrator's dual role should be granted only after dedicated, clear, and active counseling about the role's advantages, risks, and legal implications. This counseling should be conducted by the parties' counsel or the arbitrator, preferably by both. It is imperative that this counseling be documented in writing before the arbitrator takes any active step to facilitate a settlement of the dispute.

Safeguard	Characteristics of the Safeguard
Explicit Waiver of the Right to Challenge the Arbitrator or the Award	In addition to their informed consent, parties willing to engage the arbitrator in a dual role should explicitly waive their right to challenge the award or disqualify the arbitrator exclusively on the basis of fulfilling that role. This waiver arrangement can also include time limits regarding the possibility of raising arguments against the arbitrator's partiality or violation of the parties' due process rights resulting from the arbitrator's dual role. To better protect party autonomy and due process rights, parties may consider applying the waiver only when their agreement regarding the dual role has been fully and accurately implemented by the arbitrator, including its parts relating to the settlement initiatives the arbitrator is allowed to carry out and the obligatory and agreed safeguards. An express waiver is recommended even when the applicable arbitration law, rules, or guidelines apply an approach that observes the parties' informed consent as a waiver of their right of challenge.

Appendix C

Due Process Safeguards

Mandatory Due Process Safeguards		
Parties' Opt Out of the Arbitral Process	If, following the arbitrator's engagement in the unsuccessful settlement process and exposure to settlement-stage information, parties develop concerns regarding the arbitrator remaining impartial in the resumed arbitration, each party is allowed to opt out of arbitration. They can choose to employ a different arbitrator in the resumed proceedings or, in exceptional circumstances, may opt to commence the arbitration afresh or pursue ADR methods. Parties' ability to opt out of arbitration can encompass any direct involvement of the arbitrator in the settlement process, including through hybrid processes involving arbitration with mediation or processes allowing caucusing. It can also extend to indirect initiatives requiring parties' consent or may provoke controversies among legal backgrounds and practitioners. Alternatively, the opt-out option can be tailored to specific initiatives that raise the parties' most significant concerns, considering the level of trust among them and with the arbitrator, the nature of the dispute, enforceability considerations, and the implementation of other safeguards, such as the right to withdraw consent to the arbitrator's dual role, which can serve as a supplementary safeguard alongside parties' opting out from arbitration.	
Or alternatively		
Renewed Consent and Agreement regarding Settlement-Stage Information	**Renewed Consent**	To ensure that parties are not unduly bound by their initial consent and waiver to the arbitrator's dual role and to mitigate the risk of procedural rights being compromised due to developments in the settlement process or concerns about the arbitrator's ability to maintain impartiality and independence post-settlement negotiations, renewed consent and waiver should be deemed essential following particular settlement initiatives.

	Similar to the parties' opt-out option, the scope of application for renewed consent can be broad or confined solely to initiatives that raise the parties' most significant concerns. Additionally, renewed consent can be implemented in conjunction with the right to withdraw consent to the arbitrator's dual role as supplementary safeguards.
	AND
Agreement regarding Settlement-Stage Information	Due process concerns arise not only during caucusing but also during joint settlement sessions. Therefore, the confidentiality of settlement-stage information should be regulated at two levels: (a) *Joint-session confidentiality* applies to settlement-related discussions and information shared with the arbitrator in the presence of all parties but not part of the formal record. (b) *Ex parte confidentiality* covers settlement-related discussions and information shared with the arbitrator during caucusing, which is obviously not part of the formal record. While disclosure of confidential information is typically required when the arbitrator is authorized to rely on it to formulate the award, some disclosure may also be required regarding settlement-stage information that cannot be used to formulate the award. For example, when parties prefer to allow enhanced judicial review concerning the influence of the arbitrator's involvement in the settlement process on the final award, particularly if the arbitrator coerces parties into a settlement or violates the agreed terms of their role as a settlement facilitator. For each level of confidentiality, parties should agree on whether to permit the arbitrator to rely on settlement-stage information while deciding the dispute after unsuccessful settlement attempts. If the arbitrator is authorized to rely on that information, parties should explicitly waive confidentiality for the relevant level(s). For this purpose, classified records can document the relevant parts of the settlement stage, and before the arbitrator resumes their adjudicative role, these records can be disclosed to all parties.

	If parties opt not to allow the arbitrator to rely on settlement-stage information when formulating the award, they can choose between implementing the disregard approach, maintaining the relevant parts of the settlement stage both confidential and undocumented, or keeping them confidential but documenting them within classified records accessible only to the relevant parties and for possible future review.
AND cumulatively	
Arbitrator's Opt Out of the Arbitral Process	If, after engaging in unsuccessful settlement attempts and being exposed to settlement-stage information, the arbitrator doubts their ability to remain independent and impartial in the resumed arbitration, they may resign from the case—even if the parties wish them to continue. This option exists even when the parties reaffirm their consent and waive their right of challenge based on such involvement in the settlement process. Given the significant impact of an arbitrator's resignation on the proceedings, this safeguard can be limited to direct settlement initiatives or indirect ones requiring explicit consent or likely to generate controversy among legal backgrounds. In any case, the arbitrator should first inform the parties of their intention to resign and seek their views. If all parties prefer the arbitrator to continue, the arbitrator can discuss the concerns underlying their doubts to determine whether resignation is necessary or avoidable.
	Voluntary Due Process Safeguards
Limiting the Arbitrator's Mandate Following Futile Attempts to Settle	Parties can limit the arbitrator's mandate by excluding certain matters from being adjudicated during the renewed arbitration if these matters raise most of their concerns regarding the arbitrator remaining independent and impartial following their involvement in the settlement process and exposure to confidential information.
	In addition to this partial opt-out of the parties from arbitration on a subject basis, or completely instead of such limitation, in monetary disputes, parties can opt to narrow the arbitrator's decision authority on the merits of the dispute, primarily by implementing one of the following methods: (a) *"Baseball arbitration" or an analogous version to MEDALOA*, where each party presents a final offer, and the arbitrator is limited to adopting one of them based on equity standards or other agreed criteria. (b) *High-Low Arbitration*, where parties exchange written final offers or agree on a range for the award. If these offers or agreed range are disclosed to the arbitrator, they must issue the final award within their limits. When they are not disclosed to the arbitrator, if the final award falls within the agreed limits, it becomes final and binding; otherwise, it is automatically corrected to the nearest edge of the agreed range.

Involving Part of the three-member Tribunal in the Settlement Efforts	When the tribunal consists of a neutral chair, usually appointed by the arbitration institute, and two party-appointed arbitrators, parties can agree on one of the following outlines: (a) *The chair acts as a settlement facilitator* without sharing settlement-stage information with the party-appointed arbitrators to preserve their impartiality. Following unsuccessful settlement attempts, arbitration can resume before the same panel or, in rare cases, with the chair being replaced by the arbitral institution. If parties wish to take a safer route following the chair's return to their adjudicative role, they can agree that only the two party-appointed arbitrators will render the award, with the chair acting as a tiebreaker if needed. (b) *Both party-appointed arbitrators collaborate as settlement facilitators* without sharing settlement-stage information with the chair to preserve their impartiality. If ex parte communications are carried out during the settlement stage, parties can agree whether both arbitrators are authorized to caucus together with each of the parties or whether each party-appointed arbitrator may caucus solely with the appointing party or with the opposing party. Following unsuccessful efforts to settle, arbitration can resume before the chair as a sole arbitrator, before the same panel, or, in rare cases, with the party-appointed arbitrators being replaced. When the parties or the arbitral institution appoint the whole panel, the parties can agree that (c) *each of the arbitrators may engage in the settlement efforts* without sharing settlement-stage information with the remaining arbitrators to preserve their impartiality. Following futile settlement attempts, arbitration can resume before the same panel or, in rare cases, with the arbitrator involved with the settlement being replaced. If parties wish to take a safer route, they can agree that following the settlement facilitator returning to their adjudicative role, only the remaining two arbitrators will render the award, with the settlement facilitator acting as a tiebreaker if needed.

Bibliography

Books, Book Chapters, and Articles

Aall, J. (2011). Waiver of human rights: Waiver of procedural rights according to ECHR Article 6. *Nordic Journal of Human Rights, 29*(2-3), 206-252 https://doi.org/10.18261/issn1891-814x-2011-02-03-04.

Abbott, K. W. & Snidal, D. (2000). Hard and soft law in international governance. *International Organization, 54*(3), 421-456 https://doi.org/10.1162/002081800551280.

Abbott, K. W. & Snidal, D. (2009). Strengthening international regulation through transnational new governance: Overcoming the orchestration deficit. *Vanderbilt Journal of Transnational Law, 42*, 501.

Abbott, K. W. & Snidal, D. (2010). International regulation without international government: Improving IO performance through orchestration. *Review of International Organizations, 5*(3), 315-344 https://doi.org/10.1007/s11558-010-9092-3.

Abou Youssef, K. (2012). The present: Commercial arbitration as a transnational system of justice—Universal arbitration between freedom and constraint: The challenges of jurisdiction in multiparty, multi-contract arbitration. In Jan Van den Berg, A. (Ed.), *Arbitration: The next fifty years, ICCA congress series* (Volume 16, pp. 103-132). Kluwer Law International.

Abramson, H. I. (1999). Protocols for international arbitrators who dare to settle cases. *The American Review of International Arbitration, 10*, 1-17.

Abu Sadah, M. & Norton, S. (2008). The application of UNCITRAL Model Law principles in the Middle East Region. *Arab Law Quarterly, 22*(3), 219-269 https://doi.org/10.1163/157302508x336601.

Alexander, N. (2009). *International and Comparative Mediation*. Kluwer Law International.

Alexander, N. (2017). Global trends in mediation. In Trenzcek, T. et al. (Eds.), *Mediation und Konfliktmanagement Praxishandbook* (2nd ed., pp. 1-16). Nomos-Verlag.

Alexander, N., Hussin, A. & Kück, C. (2018). SIAC-SIMC's Arb-Med-Arb Protocol. *New York Dispute Resolution Lawyer, 11*(2), 85-87.

Ali, S. F. (2010). Barricades and checkered flags: An empirical examination of the perceptions of roadblocks and facilitators of settlement among arbitration practitioners in East Asia and the West. *Pacific Rim Law & Policy Journal, 19*(2), 243.

Ali, S. F. (2011a). *Resolving disputes in the Asia-Pacific region: International arbitration and mediation in East Asia and the West.* Routledge.

Ali, S. F. (2011b). The morality of conciliation: An empirical examination of arbitrator "role moralities" in East Asia and the West. *Harvard Negotiation Law Review, 16*, 1.

Ali, S. F. (2015). Prospects of utilizing Investor-state mediation and UNCITRAL Rules on Transparency for polycentric environmental disaster-related disputes: The case of Vattenfall v. Germany. In Ramaswamy, M. P. & Ribeiro, J. (Eds.), *Trade development through harmonization of commercial law.* New Zealand Association of Comparative Law.

Ali, S. F. (2020). Cultural issues in international arbitration. In Naon, H. G. & Mason, P. E. (Eds.), *International Commercial Arbitration Practice: 21st Century Perspectives.* (Chapter 6). LexisNexis.

Ali, S. F. (2021). *Forming transnational dispute settlement norms: Soft Law and the role of UNCITRAL's Regional Centre for Asia and the Pacific.* Edward Elgar Publishing.

Ali, S. F. & Repousis, O. G. (2017). Investor-state mediation and the rise of transparency in international investment law: Opportunity or threat? *Denver Journal of International Law and Policy, 45*(2), 225.

Alkoby, A. (2008). Theories of compliance with international law and the challenge of cultural difference. *Journal of International Law & International Relations, 4*(1), 151-198.

Almoguera, J. (2010). Arbitration and mediation combined: The independence and impartiality of arbitrators. In Fernández-Ballesteros, M. A. & Arias, D. (Eds.), *Liber Amicorum Bernardo Cremades* (pp. 101-130). La Ley.

Almutawa, A. M. & Maniruzzaman, M. (2014). The UAE's pilgrimage to international arbitration stardom. *The Journal of World Investment & Trade, 15*(1-2), 193-244 https://doi.org/10.1163/22129000-01502006.

Alvarez, J. E. (2006). *International organizations as lawmakers.* Oxford University Press.

Alvarez, J. E. (2007). Introducing the themes. *Victoria University of Wellington Law Review, 38*, 159 https://doi.org/10.26686/vuwlr.v38i2.5525.

Ames, R. T. & Rosemont Jr., H. (1999). *The analects of Confucius: A philosophical translation.* Ballantine Books.

Anders, G. (2004). Lawyers and anthropologists: A legal pluralist approach to global governance. In Dekker, I.F. & Werner, W.G. (Eds.), *Governance and International Legal Theory* (pp. 37-58). Brill.

Anderson, V. A. (2003). Alternative dispute resolution and professional responsibility in South Carolina: A changing landscape. *South Carolina Law Review, 55*(1), 191.

Andrew J. W., Guthrie, C. & Rachlinski, J. J. (2005). Can judges ignore inadmissible information? The difficulty of deliberately disregarding. *University of Pennsylvania Law Review, 153*(4), 1251-1345 https://doi.org/10.2307/4150614.

Antaki, N. N. (2009). Muslims' and Arabs' practice of ADR. *New York Dispute Resolution Lawyer 2*(1), 113-116.

Aragaki, H. N. (2021). A snapshot of national legislation on same neutral Med-arb and Arb-med around the globe. In Reyes, A. & Gu, W. (Eds.), *Multi-Tier approaches to the resolution of international disputes: A global and comparative study* (pp. 25-66). Cambridge University Press.

Astor, H. & Chinkin, C. (2002). *Dispute resolution in Australia.* LexisNexis Butterworths.

Atik, J. (2004). Legitimacy, transparency and NGO participation in the NAFTA Chapter 11 process. In Weiler, T. (Ed.), *NAFTA investment law and arbitration: Past issues, current practice, future prospects* (pp. 135-150). Brill Nijhoff.

Badr, G. M. (1978). Islamic law: Its relation to other legal systems. *The American Journal of Comparative Law, 26*(2), 187-198 https://doi.org/10.2307/839667.

Baer, H. (2001). History, process, and a role for judges in mediating their own cases. *New York University Annual Survey of American Law, 58*(2), 131.

Baldwin, E., Kantor, M. & Nolan, M. (2006). Limits to enforcement of ICSID awards. *Journal of International Arbitration, 23*(1), 1-24 https://doi.org/10.54648/joia2006001.

Bantekas, I. (2015). *An introduction to international arbitration.* Cambridge University Press.

Barker, J. (1996). International mediation: A better alternative for the resolution of commercial disputes—Guidelines for a U.S. negotiator involved in an international commercial mediation with Mexicans. *Loyola of Los Angeles International and Comparative Law Journal, 19*(1), 1.

Bartel, B. C. (1991). Med-Arb as a distinct method of dispute resolution: History, analysis, and potential. *Willamette Law Review, 27*(3), 661.

Baum, A. (2001). Reconciling Anglo-Saxon and Civil law procedure: The path to a procedural Lex Arbitrationis. In Briner, R. & Boöckstiegel, K. H. (Eds.), *Law of international business and dispute settlement in the 21st century* (pp. 21-30). Heymann.

Benedettelli, M. V. (2013). To bifurcate or not to bifurcate? That is the (ambiguous) question. *Arbitration International, 29*(3), 493-506 https://doi.org/10.1093/arbitration/29.3.493.

Benzidi, S. (2017). Med-Arb: How to mitigate the risk of setting aside or refusal of recognition and enforcement of a Med-Arb award. *American Journal of Mediation, 10*, 1.

Berger, K. P. (2003). Integration of mediation elements into arbitration: "Hybrid" procedures and "intuitive" mediation by international arbitrators. *Arbitration International, 19*(3), 387-403 https://doi.org/10.1093/arbitration/19.3.387.

Berger, K. P. (2009). The international arbitrator's dilemma: Transnational procedure versus home jurisdiction—A German perspective. *Arbitration International, 25*(2), 217-238 https://doi.org/10.1093/arbitration/25.2.217.

Berger, K. P. (2015). *Private dispute resolution in international business: Negotiation, mediation, arbitration*. Kluwer Law International.

Berger, K. P. (2016a). Promoting settlements in arbitration: Is the "German Approach" really incompatible with the role of the arbitrator? *New York Dispute Resolution Lawyer, 9*(2), 46.

Berger, K. P. (2018a). Institutional arbitration: Harmony, disharmony and the "Party Autonomy Paradox." *Arbitration International, 34*(4), 473-493 https://doi.org/10.1093/arbint/aiy028.

Berger, K. P. (2018b). The direct involvement of the arbitrator in the amicable settlement of the dispute: Offering preliminary views, discussing settlement options, suggesting solutions, caucusing. *Journal of International Arbitration, 35*(5), 501-516 https://doi.org/10.54648/joia2018027.

Berger, K. P. (2019). Common Law v. Civil Law in international arbitration: The beginning or the end? *Journal of International Arbitration, 36*(3), 295-313 https://doi.org/10.54648/joia2019014.

Berger, K. P. & Jensen, J. O. (2016). Due process paranoia and the procedural judgment rule: A safe harbour for procedural management decisions by international arbitrators. *Arbitration International, 32*(3), 1-21 https://doi.org/10.1093/arbint/aiw020.

Berger, K. P. & Jensen, J. O. (2017). The arbitrator's mandate to facilitate settlement. *Fordham International Law Journal, 40*(3), 887.

Berger, B. & Kellerhals, F. (2015). *International and domestic arbitration in Switzerland* (3rd ed.). Stämpfli.

Berman, P. (2005). From international law to law and globalization. *The Columbia Journal of Transnational Law, 43*(2), 485-556.

Bermann, G. A. (2010). Mandatory rules of law in international arbitration. In Ferrari, F. & Kröll, S. (Eds.), *Conflict of laws in international arbitration* (pp. 325-340). Sellier-De Gruyter.

Bermann, G. A. (2015). International commercial arbitration: Past, present, future. *Alternatives to the High Cost of Litigation (2001), 33*(5), 65-76 https://doi.org/10.1002/alt.21580.

Bermann, G. A. (2017). *International arbitration and private international law*. Brill Nijhoff.

Bernardini, P. (2004). The role of the international arbitrator. *Arbitration International, 20*(2), 113-122 https://doi.org/10.1093/arbitration/20.2.113.

Bernini, G. (2007). The future of arbitration: Flexibility or rigidity. In Lew, J. D. M. & Mistelis, L. A. (Eds.), *Arbitration insights: Twenty years of the Annual Lecture of the School of International Arbitration, sponsored by Freshfields Bruckhaus Deringer, International Arbitration Law Library*, (Volume 16, pp. 47-62). Kluwer Law International.

Beviglia-Zampetti, A. (2003). Democratic legitimacy in the World Trade Organization: The justice dimension. *Journal of World Trade, 37*(1), 105-126 https://doi.org/10.54648/trad2003012.

Blackaby, N., Partasides, C. & Redfern, A. (2022). *Redfern and Hunter on international arbitration*. (7th ed.). Oxford University Press.

Blackaby, N. & Richard, C. (2010). Amicus Curiae: A panacea for legitimacy in investment arbitration?. In Waibel, M. et al. (Eds.), *The backlash against investment arbitration* (pp. 253-274). Kluwer Law International.

Blankenship, J. T. (2006). Developing your ADR attitude: Med-Arb, a template for adaptive ADR. *Tennessee Bar Journal, 42*(11), 28-44.

Blankley, K. M. (2011). Keeping a secret from yourself? Confidentiality when the same neutral serves both as mediator and as arbitrator in the same case. *Baylor Law Review, 63*(2), 317.

Böckstiegel, K. H. (2009). Past, present, and future perspectives of arbitration. *Arbitration International, 25*(3), 293-302 https://doi.org/10.1093/arbitration/25.3.293.

Boisson de Chazoumes, L. (2005). Making the proceedings public and allowing third party interventions: Are the new generation bilateral investment treaties (U.S., Canada) bifurcating investment arbitration from international commercial arbitration? *The Journal of World Investment & Trade, 6*(1), 105-112.

Boog, C. (2015). The new SIAC/SIMC AMA protocol: A seamless Multi-Tiered dispute resolution process tailored to the user's needs. *Asian Dispute Review, 17*(2), 91-96.

Born, G. B. (2015). *International arbitration: Cases and materials.* Wolters Kluwer.

Born, G. B. (2021). *International commercial arbitration* (3rd ed.). Kluwer Law International.

Braun, T. R. (2010). Investor-State mediation: Is there a future?. In Rovine, A. W. (Ed.), *Contemporary issues in international arbitration and mediation: The Fordham Papers (2009)* (pp. 374-388). Brill Nijhoff.

Brekoulakis, S. (2016a). Parties in international arbitration: Consent v. commercial reality. In Brekoulakis, S. & Lew, J. D. M. (Eds.), *The evolution and future of international arbitration* (pp. 119-160). Kluwer Law International.

Brekoulakis, S. (2016b). The evolution and future of international arbitration. In Brekoulakis, S. & Lew, J. D. M. (Eds.), *The evolution and future of international arbitration* (pp. 1-20). Kluwer Law International.

Brewer, T. J. & Mills, L. R. (1999). Combining mediation and arbitration. *Dispute Resolution Journal, 54*(4), 32.

Brower, C. N. & Blanchard, S. (2014). What's in a Meme? The truth about Investor-State arbitration: Why it need not, and must not, be repossessed by states. *The Columbia Journal of Transnational Law, 52*(3), 689-779.

Brown, H. J. & Marriott, A. L. (1999). *ADR principles and practice* (2nd ed.). Sweet & Maxwell.

Brunet, E. J. (2003). Judicial mediation and signaling. *Nevada Law Journal, 3*, 232.

Bühring-Uhle, C. (1996). *Arbitration and mediation in international business: Designing procedures for effective conflict management.* Kluwer Law International.

Bühring-Uhle, C. et al. (2006). *Arbitration and mediation in international business* (2nd ed.). Wolters Kluwer Law & Business.

Bühring-Uhle, C., Scherer, G. & Kirchhoff, L. (2003). The Arbitrator as Mediator-Some Recent Empirical Insights. *Journal of International Arbitration, 20*(1), 81-88 https://doi.org/10.54648/joia2003017.

Burdick, F. M. (1902). What is the Law Merchant? *Columbia Law Review, 2*(7), 470-485 https://doi.org/10.2307/1109926.

Burr, A. (2005). Med-Arb: A viable hybrid solution?. *Les Arbitres Internationaux, 8*, 57.

Calamita, N. J. (2014). Dispute settlement transparency in Europe's evolving investment treaty policy. *The Journal of World Investment & Trade, 15*(3-4), 645-678 https://doi.org/10.1163/22119000-01504014.

Calliess, G. P. (2007). The making of transnational contract law. *Indiana Journal of Global Legal Studies, 14*(2), 469-483 https://doi.org/10.2979/gls.2007.14.2.469.

Calliess, G. P. & Renner, M. (2009). Transnationalizing private law: The public and the private dimensions of transnational commercial law. *German Law Journal, 10*(10), 1341-1355 https://doi.org/10.1017/s2071832200018253.

Cao, L. (2006). Combining conciliation and arbitration in China: Overview and latest developments. *International Arbitration Law Review, 9*, 84.

Cao, L. (2020). Harmony in dispute: Influence of Chinese culture on Chinese arbitration. In Kaplan, N. et al. (Eds.), *International arbitration: When East Meets West—Liber Amicorum Michael Moser* (pp. 1-12). Kluwer Law International.

Carducci, G. (2021). Mandatory rules, court litigation and arbitration (domestic and international disputes). *New York Dispute Resolution Lawyer, 14*(1), 78-81.

Carrara, C. (2019). How to productively conduct a case management conference: Well begun is half done. *New York Dispute Resolution Lawyer, 12*(1), 43-45.

Carter, J. H. (1994). The international commercial arbitration explosion: More rules, more laws, more books, so what?. *Michigan Journal of International Law, 15*(3), 785-796.

Carvalho, J. (2019). Law, language, and knowledge: Legal transplants from a cultural perspective. *German Law Journal, 20*(1), 21-45 https://doi.org/10.1017/glj.2019.4.

Chaisse, J. & Shang, C. S. (2021). The resolution of international commercial and financial disputes: Hybrid dispute resolution in Hong Kong. In Reyes, A. & Gu, W. (Eds.), *Multi-Tier approaches to the resolution of international disputes: A global and comparative Study* (pp. 92-109). Cambridge University Press.

Chase, O. G. & Bruner, J. S. (2005). *Law, culture, and ritual: Disputing systems in cross-cultural context*. NYU Press.

Checkley, J. C. (2020). Cross-border enforcement of mediated settlement agreements and potential impact on the practice of international arbitration. In Meskić, Z. et al. (Eds.), *Balkan Yearbook of European and International Law 2019* (pp. 23-40). Springer International Publishing.

Cheng, T. H. (2010). Reflections on culture in Med-Arb. In Rovine, A. W. (Ed.), *Contemporary issues in international arbitration and mediation: The Fordham Papers (2009)* (pp. 419-428). Brill Nijhoff.

Cheng, T. H. (2011). International mediation, arbitration, and innovation. In Rovine, A. W. (Ed.), *Contemporary issues in international arbitration and mediation: The Fordham Papers (2010)* (pp. 434-440). Brill Nijhoff.

Cheng, T. H. & Kohtio, A. (2009). Some limits to applying Chinese Med-Arb internationally. *New York Dispute Resolution Lawyer, 2*(1), 95-97.

Chew, S., Reed, L. & Thomas, J. C. (2018). Report: Survey on obstacles to settlement of investor-state disputes. *NUS Centre for International Law Research Paper Nr. 18/01* (pp. 1-41).

Choudhury, B. (2008). Recapturing public power: Is investment arbitration's engagement of the public interest contributing to the democratic deficit?. *Vanderbilt Journal of Transnational Law, 41*, 755.

Chua, E. (2018). A contribution to the conversation on mixing the modes of mediation and arbitration: Of definitional consistency and process structure. *Transnational Dispute Management, 5*, 1.

Chung, Y. (2016). Combining arbitration with mediation: Two cultures of China and Malaysia. *Journal of Arbitration Studies, 26*(3), 149-174 https://doi.org/10.16998/jas.2016.26.3.149.

Coe, J. J. (2010). Should mediation of investment disputes be encouraged, and, if so, by whom and how?. In Rovine, A. W. (Ed.), *Contemporary issues in international arbitration and mediation: The Fordham Papers (2009)* (pp. 339-357). Brill Nijhoff.

Cohen, J. A. (1966). Chinese mediation on the eve of modernization. *California Law Review, 54*(3), 1201-1226 https://doi.org/10.2307/3479280.

Cohen, R. (1991). Negotiating across cultures: Communication obstacles in international diplomacy. In *Policy File*. United States Institute of Peace.

Cole, T. (2007). Commercial arbitration in Japan: Contributions to the debate on Japanese non-litigiousness. *New York University Journal of International Law & Politics, 40*(1), 29-114.

Collins, M. (2003). Do international arbitral tribunals have any obligations to encourage settlement of the disputes before them? *Arbitration International, 19*(3), 333-343 https://doi.org/10.1093/arbitration/19.3.333.

Condliffe, P. & Zeleznikow, J. (2014). What process do disputants want? An experiment in disputant preferences. *Monash University Law Review, 40*(2), 305-339.

Conlon, D. E., Moon, H. & Ng, K. Y. (2002). Putting the cart before the horse. *Journal of Applied Psychology, 87*(5), 978-984 https://doi.org/10.1037//0021-9010.87.5.978.

Cordero-Moss, G. (2012). Soft law codifications in the area of commercial law. In *International investment law and soft Law* (pp. 109-147). Edward Elgar Publishing.

Costa Braga de Oliveira, P. A. (2009). Designing effective Med-Arb and Arb-Med processes in Brazil. *New York Dispute Resolution Lawyer 2*(1), 89-91.

Cotterrell, R. (2012). What is transnational law?. *Law & Social Inquiry, 37*(2), 500-524 https://doi.org/10.1111/j.1747-4469.2012.01306.x.

Craig, W. L., Park, W. W. & Paulsson, J. (2000). *International Chamber of Commerce arbitration* (3rd ed.). Oceana Publications.

Cratsley, J. C. (2011). Judges and settlement: So little regulation with so much at stake. *Dispute Resolution Magazine, 17*(3), 4.

Cremades, B. M. (1998). Overcoming the clash of legal cultures: The role of interactive arbitration. *Arbitration International, 14*(2), 157-172 https://doi.org/10.1093/arbitration/14.2.157.

Dasser, F. (2021). *"Soft law" in international commercial arbitration*. Brill Nijhoff.

De Brabandere, E. (2014). The role, function and qualifications of arbitrators in investment treaty arbitration. In *Investment Treaty arbitration as Public International Law: Procedural aspects and implications* (pp. 73-121). Cambridge University Press.

De Gramont, A. (2017). Open and shut: The innovative use of opening arguments in international arbitration. *New York Dispute Resolution Lawyer 10*(1), 55-57.

De Gramont, A., Igyarto, M. D. & Sainati, T. (2017). Divergent paths: Settlement in US litigation and international arbitration. *Fordham International Law Journal, 40*(3), 953.

De Vera, C. (2004). Arbitrating harmony: "med-arb" and the confluence of culture and rule of law in the resolution of international commercial disputes in China. *Columbia Journal of Asian Law, 18*(1), 149.

Deason, E. E. (2001). The quest for uniformity in mediation confidentiality: Foolish consistency or crucial predictability? *Marquette Law Review, 85*(1), 79.

Deason, E. E. (2013). Combinations of mediation and arbitration with the same neutral: A framework for judicial review. *Arbitration Law Review, Yearbook on Arbitration & Mediation 5*, 219-249.

Deekshitha, S. & Saha, A. (2014). Amalgamating the conciliatory and the adjudicative: Hybrid process and Asian arbitral institutions. *Indian Journal of Arbitration Law, III*(1), 76-100.

Dendorfer, R. & Lack, J. (2007). The interaction between arbitration and mediation: Vision v reality. *Dispute Resolution International, 1*(1), 73-98.

Derains, Y. (1995). The ICC arbitral process. Part VIII. Choice of the law applicable to the contract and international arbitration. *ICC Bulletin, 6*(1), 6.

Dezalay, Y. & Garth, B. G. (1996). *Dealing in virtue: International commercial arbitration and the construction of a transnational legal order*. The University of Chicago Press.

Donahey, M. S. (1995). Seeking harmony: Is the Asian concept of the conciliator/arbitrator applicable in the West? *Dispute Resolution Journal, 50*(2), 74.

Donovan, D. F. (2013). The international arbitrator as transnational judge. *World Arbitration and Mediation Review 7*, 193.

Draetta, U. (2009). Leveraging the arbitral process to encourage settlement: Some practical and legal issues. *International Business Law Journal*, 487-496.

Draetta, U. (2015). The transnational procedural rules for arbitration and the risks of overregulation and bureaucratization. *ASA Bulletin (Association Suisse de L'arbitrage), 33*(2), 327-342 https://doi.org/10.54648/asab2015025.

Dress, T. P. (1988). International commercial mediation and conciliation. *Loyola of Los Angeles International and Comparative Law Journal, 10*(3), 569.

Ehle, B. (2006). Nouvelles de l'arbitrage en Suisse: ASA conference on best practices in international arbitration, Zurich, January 27, 2006. *ASA Bulletin (Association Suisse de L'arbitrage), 24*(2), 255-259 https://doi.org/10.54648/asab2006030.

Ehle, B. (2010). The arbitrator as a settlement facilitator. In Caprasse, O. et al., (Eds.), *Walking a thin line: What an arbitrator can do, must do or must not do: Recent developments and trends* (pp. 79-95). Bruylant.

Eiseman, N. M., Bulman, J. E. & Dunn, R. T. (2013). A tale of two lawyers: How arbitrators and advocates can avoid the dangerous convergence of arbitration and litigation. *Cardozo Journal of Conflict Resolution, 14*, 683.

El-Ahdab, A. H. & El-Ahdab, J. (2011). *Arbitration with the Arab countries* (3rd ed.). Kluwer Law International.

El-Ahdab, J. & Stackpool-Moore, R. (2008). Arab arbitration v. International arbitration? The case for a reconciliation. *Journal of International Arbitration, 25*(2), 275-288 https://doi.org/10.54648/joia2008019.

Elliott, D. C. (1995). Med/Arb: Fraught with danger or ripe with opportunity. *Alberta Law Review, 34*(1), 163 https://doi.org/10.29173/alr1104.

Ellis, J. (2012). Shades of grey: Soft law and the validity of public international law. *Leiden Journal of International Law, 25*(2), 313-334. https://doi.org/10.1017/s0922156512000052.

Elsing, S. H. (2011). Procedural efficiency in international arbitration: Choosing the best of both legal worlds. *German Arbitration Journal (SchiedsVZ), 3*, 114-123.

Elsing, S. H. (2015). Commentary on the arbitration rules of the German Institution of Arbitration (DIS Rules), section 32: Settlement. In Nacimiento, P. et al. (Eds.), *Arbitration in Germany: The Model Law in Practice (Second Edition)* (pp. 690-692). Kluwer Law International.

Faleck, D. (2021). Opening mediation windows: Role of parties, contracts and institutions. *New York Dispute Resolution Lawyer 14*(1), 51-54.

Farina, A. J. (1989). "Talking disputes into harmony": China approaches international commercial arbitration. *The American University Journal of International Law and Policy, 4*(1), 137.

Ferrari, F. (2014). The judicial attempt at conciliation: The new section 185-bis of the Italian Code of Civil Procedure. *Russian Law Journal, 2*(3), 80-95.

Fiechter, E. W. (2008). Mediation: Casting issues—Can or should the same person be mediator, or conciliator and arbitrator?. *Croatian Arbitration Yearbook, 15*, 255.

Floyd, D. H. (1994). Can the judge do that? The need for a clearer judicial role in settlement. *Arizona State Law Journal, 26*(1), 45.

Folberg, J. (2016). *Resolving disputes: Theory, practice, and law* (3rd ed.). Wolters Kluwer.

Footer, M. E. (2010). The (re)turn to "soft law" in reconciling the antinomies in WTO law. *Melbourne Journal of International Law, 11*(2), 241-276.

Foster, D. & Barratt, J. (2013). Challenge to and replacement of arbitrators. In Lew, J. D.M. et al. (Eds.), *Arbitration in England, with chapters on Scotland and Ireland* (pp. 319-338). Kluwer Law International.

Fouchard, P., Gaillard, E. & Savage, J. (1999). *Fouchard, Gaillard, Goldman on international commercial arbitration*. Kluwer Law International.

Fraser, V. & Kun, F. (2021). Mediators using non-binding evaluations and making settlement proposals. *New York Dispute Resolution Lawyer 14*(1), 21-24.

Friedman, L. M. (1975). *The legal system: A social science perspective* (1st ed.). Russell Sage Foundation.

Fu, H. (2003). The politics of mediation in a Chinese county: The case of Luo Lianxi. *The Australian Journal of Asian Law, 5*(2), 107-127.

Fu, H. & Cullen, R. (2011). From mediatory to adjudicatory justice: The limits of Civil Justice Reform in China. In Woo, M. Y. K. & Gallagher, M. E. (Eds.), *Chinese justice: Civil dispute resolution in contemporary China* (pp. 25-57). Cambridge University Press.

Fuller, L. L. (1970). Mediation: Its forms and functions. *Southern California Law Review, 44*, 305.

Fullerton, R. (2009). The ethics of mediation-arbitration. *Colorado Lawyer, 38*(5), 31.

Gaillard, E. (2023). Theories of international arbitration. In Kröll, S., Bjorklund, A. K. & Ferrari, F. (Eds.), *Cambridge Compendium of International Commercial and Investment Arbitration* (pp. 27-46). Cambridge University Press.

Galanter, M. (1985). "A settlement judge, not a trial judge:" Judicial mediation in the United States. *Journal of Law and Society, 12*(1), 1-18 https://doi.org/10.2307/1410244.

Gamba, A. (2013). Arbitral proceedings: General provisions (Art. 15). In Zuberbühler, T. et al. (Eds.), *Swiss Rules of International Arbitration: Commentary* (2nd ed.) (pp. 185-195). Schulthess Juristische Medien AG.

Garnett, R. (2002). International arbitration law: Progress towards harmonisation. *Melbourne Journal of International Law, 3*(2), 400-413.

Garnett, R. (2015). Australia's international and domestic arbitration framework. In Moens, G. A. & Philip, E. (Eds.), *Arbitration and dispute resolution in the resources sector: An Australian perspective* (pp. 7-21). Springer International Publishing.

Garnett, R. & Nottage, L. (2011). The 2010 amendments to the International Arbitration Act: A new dawn for Australia? *Asian International Arbitration Journal, 7*(1), 29-53 https://doi.org/10.54648/aiaj2011002.

Gerbay, R. (2016). *The functions of arbitral institutions*. Kluwer Law International.

Gill, J. (2006). The arbitrator's role in bringing about a settlement: An English view. In Wirth, M. (Ed.), *Best Practices in International Arbitration: ASA Special Series No. 26* (pp. 155-165). ASA Association Suisse de l'Arbitrage.

Gillespie, J. (2009). Developing a framework for understanding the localisation of global scripts in East Asia. In Halpin, A. & Roeben, V. (Eds.), *Theorising Legal Globalization* (pp. 209-232). Hart Publishing.

Ginsburg, T. (2003). The culture of arbitration. *Vanderbilt Journal of Transnational Law, 36*(4), 1335.

Ginsburg, T. (2011). Lawrence M. Friedman's Comparative Law. In Gordon, R. W. & Horwitz, M. J. (Eds.), *Law, society, and history: Themes in the legal sociology and legal history of Lawrence M. Friedman* (pp. 52-64). Cambridge University Press.

Giovannini, T. (2010). The continental European perspective and practice of advocacy. In Bishop, D. & Kehoe, E. G. (Eds.), *The art of advocacy in international arbitration* (2nd. ed., pp. 499-518). JurisNet.

Glenn, H. P. (2009). Cosmopolitan legal orders. In Halpin, A. & Roeben, W. (eds.) *Theorising the global legal order*. Hart Publishing.

Goh, B. C. (2002). *Law without Lawyers, Justice without Courts*. Routledge.

Gojkovic, E. V. (2021). UK Supreme Court delivers landmark judgment on arbitrator bias and duty of disclosure. *New York Dispute Resolution Lawyer 14*(1), 68-71.

Goldberg, S. B., Sander, F. & Rogers, N. H. (1992). *Dispute resolution: Negotiation, mediation, and other processes* (2nd ed.). Little Brown.

Gomez, M. A. (2015). A sour battle in Lago Agrio and beyond: The metamorphosis of transnational litigation and the protection of collective rights in Ecuador. *The University of Miami Inter-American Law Review, 46*(2), 153-177.

Goode, R. et al. (2007). *Transnational commercial law: Text, cases, and materials*. Oxford University Press.

Greenwood, L. (2011a). A window of opportunity? Building a short period of time into arbitral rules in order for parties to explore settlement. *Arbitration International, 27*(2), 199-210 https://doi.org/10.1093/arbitration/27.2.199.

Greenwood, L. (2011b). Does bifurcation really promote efficiency? *Journal of International Arbitration, 28*(2), 105-111 https://doi.org/10.54648/joia2011009.

Greenwood, L. (2019). Revisiting bifurcation and efficiency in international arbitration proceedings. *Journal of International Arbitration, 36*(4), 421-429 https://doi.org /10.54648/joia2019021.

Gregory, D. L. (2001). The internationalization of employment dispute mediation. *New York International Law Review, 14*(1), 2-32.

Gu, W. (2014). The delicate art of Med-Arb and its future institutionalisation in China. *UCLA Pacific Basin Law Journal, 31*(2), 97 https://doi.org/10.5070/p8312024 963.

Gu, W. (2016). When local meets international: Mediation combined with arbitration in China and its prospective reform in a comparative context. *The Journal of Comparative Law, 10*(2), 84-105.

Gu, W. (2017). Piercing the veil of arbitration reform in China: Promises, pitfalls, patterns, prognoses, and prospects. *The American Journal of Comparative Law, 65*(4), 799-840 https://doi.org/10.1093/ajcl/avx040.

Gu, W. (2019). Hybrid dispute resolution beyond the belt and road: Toward a new design of Chinese arb-med(-arb) and its global implications. *Washington International Law Journal, 29*(1), 117-172.

Gu, W. (2021). Combinations of mediation and arbitration: The case of China. In Reyes, A. & Gu, W. (Eds.), *Multi-Tier approaches to the resolution of international disputes: A global and comparative study* (pp. 69-91). Cambridge University Press.

Gu, W. & Zhang, X. (2012). The Keeneye case: Rethinking the content of public policy in cross-border arbitration between Hong Kong and Mainland China. *Hong Kong Law Journal, 42*, 1001-1029.

Gunter, P. Y. (2005). Transnational rules on the taking of evidence. In Schlaepfer, A. V., Pinsolle, P. & Degos, L. (Eds.), *Towards a uniform international arbitration law?* (pp. 129-148). Juris Publishing.

Guo, Y. (2020). From conventions to protocols: Conceptualizing changes to the international dispute resolution landscape. *Journal of International Dispute Settlement, 11*(2), 217-241 https://doi.org/10.1093/jnlids/idz023.

Hacking, D. (2011). Arbitration is only as good as its arbitrators. In Kröll, S. M., Mistelis, L. A. et al. (Eds.), *International arbitration and international commercial law: Synergy, convergence and evolution* (pp. 223-229). Kluwer Law International.

Hanis, W. (2015). Sulh: Its applications in Malaysia. *IOSR Journal of Humanities and Social Science, 20*(6), 71-79.

Harpole, S. A. (2007). The combination of conciliation with arbitration in the People's Republic of China. *Journal of International Arbitration, 24*(6), 623-633 https://doi.org/10.54648/joia2007046.

Harris, C. (2016). Arbitrators and settlement: A Common Law perspective. In Baizeau, D. & Spoorenberg, F. (Eds.), *The arbitrators' initiative: When, why, and how should it be used?—ASA Special Series No. 45* (pp. 89-98). JurisNet.

Harvard Law Review. (2014). Mediation of investor-state conflicts. *Harvard Law Review, 127*(8), 2543-2564.

Hatzistergos, J. (2010). Arbitration reform must continue. *Financial Review, 18*, 33.

Hazard, G. (1998). Discovery and the role of the judge in civil law jurisdictions. *The Notre Dame Law Review, 73*(4), 1017-1028.

Helmer, E. V. (2003). International commercial arbitration: Americanized, "civilized," or harmonized? *Ohio State Journal on Dispute Resolution, 19*(1), 35.

Henriques, D. G. (2018). The Prague rules: Competitor, alternative or addition to the IBA rules on the taking of evidence in international arbitration?. *ASA Bulletin, 36*(2), 351 https://doi.org/10.54648/asab2018030.

Henry, K. C. (1988). Med-Arb: An alternative to interest arbitration in the resolution of contract negotiation disputes. *Ohio State Journal on Dispute Resolution, 3*(2), 385.

Herrmann, G. (1998). UNCITRAL's basic contribution to the international arbitration culture. In Jan van den Berg, A. (Ed.), *International dispute resolution: Towards an international arbitration culture, ICCA congress series* (Volume 8, pp. 49-52). Kluwer Law International.

Hess, B. & Pelzer, N. (2015). Mediation in Germany: Finding the right balance between regulation and self-regulation. In Esplugues, C. & Marquis, L. (Eds.), *New developments in civil and commercial mediation: Global comparative perspectives* (pp. 291-312). Springer International Publishing.

Hioureas, C. G. (2019). The Singapore Convention on International Settlement Agreements resulting from mediation: A new way forward? *Berkeley Journal of International Law, 46*(1), 61.

Hodges, P. & Greenaway, J. (2013). Duties of arbitrators. In Lew, J. D. M. et al. (Eds.), *Arbitration in England, with chapters on Scotland and Ireland* (pp. 293-318). Kluwer Law International.

Hofstede, G. (2001). *Culture's consequences: Comparing values, behaviors, institutions, and organizations across nations* (2nd ed.). Sage Publications.

Hofstede, G., Hofstede, G. J. & Minkov, M. (2010). *Cultures and organizations: Software of the mind—Intercultural cooperation and its importance for survival.* (3rd ed.). McGraw-Hill.

Hofstede, G. & McRae, R. (2004). Personality and culture revisited: Linking traits and dimensions of culture. *Cross-Cultural Research, 38*(1), 52-88 https://doi.org/10.1177/1069397103259443.

Holtzmann, H. M. (1996). Questions concerning the desirability and text of the UNCITRAL project to improve planning of arbitral proceedings. In Jan Van den Berg, A. (Ed.), *Planning efficient arbitration proceedings: The law applicable in international arbitration, ICCA congress series* (Volume 7, pp. 173-195). Kluwer Law International.

Holtzmann, H. M. & Neuhaus, J. (1989). *A guide to the UNCITRAL Model Law on International Commercial Arbitration: Legislative history and commentary.* Kluwer Law International.

Honka, H. (1996). Harmonization of contract law through international trade: A Nordic perspective. *Tulane European and Civil Law Forum 11*, 111-184.

Hopt, K. J. & Steffek, F. (2013). *Mediation: Principles and regulation in comparative perspective.* Oxford University Press.

Horvath, G. J. (2001). The duty of the tribunal to render an enforceable award. *Journal of International Arbitration, 18*(2), 135-158 https://doi.org/10.54648/317806.

Horvath, G. J. (2011). The judicialization of international arbitration: Does the increasing introduction of litigation-style practices, regulations, norms and structures into international arbitration risk a denial of justice in international business disputes?. In Kröll, S. M. et al. (Eds.), *International arbitration and international commercial law: Synergy, convergence and evolution* (pp. 251-271). Kluwer Law International.

Houzhi, T. (2005). Combination of arbitration with conciliation: Arb-Med. In Jan Van den Berg, A. (Ed.), *New horizons in international commercial arbitration and beyond, ICCA congress series* (Volume 12, pp. 547-555). Kluwer Law International.

Howes, B. T. & Stowell, A. (2020). The impact of summary disposition on international arbitration: A quantitative analysis. *New York Dispute Resolution Lawyer 13*(1), 52-42.

Hrnčiříková, M. (2016). The meaning of soft law in international commercial arbitration. *International and Comparative Law Review, 16*(1), 97-109 https://doi.org/10.1515/iclr-2016-0007.

Huang, Z. (1990). Negotiation in China: Cultural and practical characteristics. *China Law Reporter, VI(2)*, 139.

Hwang, M. (2005). The role of arbitrators as settlement facilitators: Commentary. In Jan Van den Berg, A. (Ed.), *New horizons for international commercial arbitration and beyond* (pp. 571-581). Kluwer Law International.

Hwang, M. (2015). Commercial courts and international arbitration: Competitors or partners? *Arbitration International, 31*(2), 193-212 https://doi.org/10.1093/arbint/aiv038.

Hyman, D. A. & Kovacic, W. E. (2019). State enforcement in a polycentric world. *Brigham Young University Law Review, 2019*(6), 1447-1470.

Iqbal, W. (2001). Dialogue and the practice of law and spiritual values: Courts, lawyering, and ADR: Glimpses into the Islamic tradition. *Fordham Urban Law Journal, 28*(4), 1035-1045.

Irani, G. E. & Funk, N. C. (1998). Rituals of reconciliation: Arab-Islamic perspectives. *Arab Studies Quarterly, 20*(4), 53-73.

James, R. & Morris, P. (2003). The new Financial Ombudsman Service in the United Kingdom: Has the second generation got it right? In Rickett, C. E. F. & Telfer, T. G. W. (Eds.), *International perspectives on consumers' access to justice* (pp. 167-195). Cambridge University Press.

Jandt, F. E. (2013). *An introduction to intercultural communication: Identities in a global community* (7th ed.). Sage Publications.

Jansen, N. (2010). *The making of legal authority: Non-legislative codifications in historical and comparative perspective.* Oxford University Press.

Javits, J. M. (2017). Better process, better results: Integrating mediation and arbitration to resolve collective bargaining disputes. *ABA Journal of Labor & Employment Law, 32*(2), 167-187.

Jemielniak, J. (2014). Transnationalization of domestic law in international commercial arbitration through comparative analysis: Challenges for legal profession. *Contemporary Asia Arbitration Journal, 7*(2), 309-340.

Jemielniak, J. (2017). Comparative analysis as an autonomization strategy in international commercial arbitration. *International Journal for the Semiotics of Law—Revue Internationale de Sémiotique Juridique, 31*(1), 155-173.

Jessup, P. C. (1956). *Transnational Law.* Yale University Press.

Johnson, L. & Sachs, L. (2016). The outsized costs of Investor-State dispute settlement. *AIB Insights (Acad. of Int'l Bus.), 16*(1), 10 https://doi.org/10.46697/001c.16894.

Jones, D. S. (2005). Various non-binding (ADR) processes. In Jan Van den Berg, A. (Ed.), *New horizons in international commercial arbitration and beyond, ICCA congress series* (Volume 12, pp. 367-414). Kluwer Law International.

Jordaan, B. (2009). Hybrid ADR processes in South Africa. *New York Dispute Resolution Lawyer 2*(1), 117-119.

Kagel, S. (1973). Combining mediation and arbitration. *Monthly Labor Review, 96*(9), 62-63.

Kahn-Freund, O. (1974). On uses and misuses of comparative law. *Modern Law Review, 37*(1), 1-27 https://doi.org/10.1111/j.1468-2230.1974.tb02366.x.

Kaplan, N. (2014). If it ain't broke, don't change it. *CIArb Arbitration, 80*(2), 172-175.

Karmel, R. S. & Kelly, C. R. (2009). The hardening of soft law in securities regulation. *Brooklyn Journal of International Law, 34*(3), 883.

Karrer, P. A. (2011). Law, para-regulatory texts and people in international arbitration: Predictability or Fureur Reglementaire?. In Kröll, S. M. et al. (Eds.), *International arbitration and international commercial law: Synergy, convergence and evolution* (pp. 291-299). Kluwer Law International.

Karton, J. (2013). *The culture of international arbitration and the evolution of contract law*. Oxford University Press.

Karton, J. (2014). International arbitration culture and global governance. In Mattli, W. & Dietz, T. (Eds.), *International arbitration and global governance: Contending theories and evidence* (pp. 1-45). Oxford University Press.

Kaster, L.A. (2018). Consent or agreed awards and the New York Convention—What is the status?. *New York Dispute Resolution Lawyer 11*(2), 48-50.

Kaufmann-Kohler, G. (2003). Globalization of arbitral procedure. *Vanderbilt Journal of Transnational Law, 36*(4), 1313.

Kaufmann-Kohler, G. (2004). Beyond gadgetry: Substantive new concepts to improve arbitral efficiency. *The Journal of World Investment & Trade, 5*(1), 69-72.

Kaufmann-Kohler, G. (2005). Global implications of the U.S. Federal Arbitration Act: The role of legislation in international arbitration. *ICSID Review, 20*(2), 339-356 https://doi.org/10.1093/icsidreview/20.2.339.

Kaufmann-Kohler, G. (2009). When arbitrators facilitate settlement: Towards a transnational standard: Clayton Utz/University of Sydney International Arbitration Lecture. *Arbitration International, 25*(2), 187-206 https://doi.org/10.1093/arbitration/25.2.187.

Kaufmann-Kohler, G. (2010). Soft law in international arbitration: Codification and normativity. *Journal of International Dispute Settlement, 1*(2), 283-299 https://doi.org/10.1093/jnlids/idq009.

Kaufmann-Kohler G. & Bonnin, V. (2007). Arbitrators as conciliators: A statistical study of the relation between an arbitrator's role and legal background. *ICC Bulletin 18*(2), 79-85.

Kauppi, N. & Madsen, M. R. (2013). *Transnational power elites: The new professionals of governance, law and security*. Routledge.

Kellor, F. & Angell, J. R. (1948). *American arbitration: Its history, functions and achievements*. Harper & Brothers.

Kerr, M. (1997). Concord and conflict in international arbitration. *Arbitration International, 13*(2), 121-143 https://doi.org/10.1093/arbitration/13.2.121.

Kichaven, J. (2009). Med-Arb should be dead. *New York Dispute Resolution Lawyer 2*(1), 80-82.

Kim, G. L. (2007). East Asian cultural influences. In Pryles, M. & Moser, M. J. (Eds.), *Asian leading arbitrators' guide to international arbitration* (pp. 17-52). JurisNet.

Koch, C. & Schäfer, E. (1999). Can it be sinful for an arbitrator actively to promote settlement?. *The Arbitration and Dispute Resolution Law Journal, 3*, 153-184.

Koh, H. H. (1996). Transnational legal process. *Nebraska Law Review, 75*(1), 181-207.

Kronke, H. (2000). International uniform commercial law conventions: Advantages, disadvantages, criteria for choice. *Revue de Droit Uniforme, 5*(1), 13-21 https://doi.org/10.1093/ulr/5.1.13.

Kryvoi, Y. & Davydenko, D. (2015). Consent awards in international arbitration: From settlement to enforcement. *Brooklyn Journal of International Law, 40*(3), 827.

Kun, F. (2011a). Mediation and Civil Justice Reform in Hong Kong. *The International Litigation Quarterly, 27*(2), 11-14.

Kun, F. (2011b). The risks of apparent bias when an arbitrator acts as a mediator: Remarks on Hong Kong court's decision in Gao Haiyan. In Romano, G. P. et al. (Eds.), *Yearbook of Private International Law (2011)*: *Vol. XIII* (pp. 535-556). De Gruyter.

Kun, F. (2012). The new Arbitration Ordinance in Hong Kong. *Journal of International Arbitration, 29*(6), 715-722 https://doi.org/10.54648/joia2012044.

Kun, F. (2013a). *Arbitration in China: A legal and cultural analysis*. Bloomsbury Publishing.

Kun, F. (2013b). Glocalization of arbitration: Transnational standards struggling with local norms through the lens of arbitration transplantation in China. *Harvard Negotiation Law Review, 18*, 175.

Kun, F. (2013c). International dispute resolution trends in Asia. *Transnational Dispute Management 10*(4), 1.

Kun, F. (2014). An empirical study on arbitrators facilitating settlement in China. *Cardozo Journal of Conflict Resolution 15, 777*.

Kun, F. (2016a). "Glocalization" of international arbitration: Rethinking tradition—Modernity and East-West binaries through examples of China and Japan. *University of Pennsylvania East Asia Law Review, 11*(2), 243-292.

Kun, F. (2016b). Salient features of international commercial arbitration in East Asia: A comparative study of China and Japan. *American University Business Law Review, 5*(3), 447-483.

Kun F. (2020a). Can you leave your hat on? An empirical study of Med-Arb/Arb-Med in China. In Campbell, C. (Ed.), *Comparative Law Yearbook of International Business, Volume 41a* (pp. 129-157). Kluwer Law International.

Kun, F. (2020b). Mediation of Investor-State disputes: A treaty survey. *Journal of Dispute Resolution, 2*, pp. 327-342.

Kun, F. & Jemielniak, J. (2016). Ethnographic methods in the study of hybrid processes in arbitration: The Chinese and Western perspectives. *European Business Law Review, 27*(4), 555-585 https://doi.org/10.54648/eulr2016025.

Kun, F. & Kaufmann-Kohler, G. (2008). Integrating mediation into arbitration: Why it works in China. *Journal of International Arbitration, 25*(4), 479-492 https://doi.org/10.54648/joia2008035.

Kurkela, M. S. & Turunen, S. (2010). *Due process in international commercial arbitration*. Oxford University Press.

Lack, J. (2010). Appropriate dispute resolution (ADR): The spectrum of hybrid techniques available to the parties. In Ingen-Housz, A. (Ed.), *ADR in business: Practice and issues across countries and cultures II* (pp. 339-379). Kluwer Law International.

Lack, J. (2021). Introduction to the series of articles on the Mixed Mode Task Force. *New York Dispute Resolution Lawyer 14*(1), 11-13.

Lalive, P. (1998). Arbitration: The civilized solution. *ASA Bulletin (Association Suisse de l'Arbitrage), 16*(3), 483-497.

Landry, S. (1996). Med-arb: Mediation with a bite and an effective ADR model. *Defense Counsel Journal, 63*(2), 263.

Lang, J. (2009). Med-Arb: An English perspective. *New York Dispute Resolution Lawyer 2*(1), 98-102.

Langbein, J. H. (1985). The German advantage in civil procedure. *The University of Chicago Law Review, 52*(4), 823-866 https://doi.org/10.2307/1599518.

Langford, M. et al. (2020). Special issue: UNCITRAL and investment arbitration reform: Matching concerns and solutions. *The Journal of World Investment & Trade, 21*(2-3), 167-187 https://doi.org/10.1163/22119000-12340171.

Lazareff, S. (1999). International arbitration: Towards a common procedural approach. In Frommel, S. & Rider, B. (Eds.), *Conflicting legal cultures in commercial arbitration: Old issues and new trends* (pp. 1-5). Kluwer Law International.

Lee, J. S. (2001). No "double-dipping" allowed: An analysis of Waste Management, Inc. v. United Mexican states and the Article 1121 waiver requirement for arbitration under Chapter 11 of NAFTA. *Fordham Law Review, 69*(6), 2655.

Lemley, K. M. (2004). I'll make him an offer he can't refuse: A proposed model for alternative dispute resolution in intellectual property disputes. *Akron Law Review, 37*(2), 287.

Leon, B. & Peterson, A. (2009). Med-Arb in Ontario: Enforceability of Med-Arb agreement confirmed by Court of Appeal. *New York Dispute Resolution Lawyer 2*(1), 92-94.

Levit, J. K. (2005). A bottom-up approach to international lawmaking: The tale of three trade finance instruments. *The Yale Journal of International Law, 30*(1), 125 https://doi.org/10.4324/9781315086392-36.

Lew, J. D. M. (2005). Multi-Institutionals conciliation and the reconciliation of different legal cultures. In Jan Van den Berg, A. (Ed.), *New horizons in international commercial arbitration and beyond, ICCA congress series* (Volume 12, pp. 421-429). Kluwer Law International.

Lew, J. D. M. (2007). Achieving the dream: Autonomous arbitration?. In Lew, J. D. M. & Mistelis, L. A. (Eds.), *Arbitration insights: Twenty years of the Annual Lecture of the School of International Arbitration, sponsored by Freshfields Bruckhaus Deringer, International Arbitration Law Library* (Volume 16, pp. 455-485). Kluwer Law International.

Lew, J. D. M. (2020). Procedural efficiency: Prague rules applicable for the particular case. In Kaplan, N. et al. (Eds.), *International arbitration: When East meets West—Liber Amicorum Michael Moser* (pp. 175-186). Kluwer Law International.

Lew, J. D. M. & Shore, L. (1999). International commercial arbitration: Harmonizing cultural differences. *Dispute Resolution Journal, 54*(3), 32.

Limbury, A. L. (2009a). Making Med-Arb work in Australia. *New York Dispute Resolution Lawyer 2*(1), 84-86.

Limbury, A. L. (2010a). ADR in Australia. In Ingen-Housz, A. (Ed.), *ADR in business: Practice and issues across countries and cultures II* (pp. 429-456). Kluwer Law International.

Limbury, A. L. (2010b). Med-Arb: Getting the best of both worlds. *Law Society Journal: The Official Journal of the Law Society of New South Wales, 48*(8), 1-7.

Lincoln, A. (2008). Notes for a Law Lecture. In Stowell, D. W. & Krause, S. (Eds.), *The papers of Abraham Lincoln: Legal documents and cases*. University of Virginia Press.

Link, M. & Haftel, Y. Z. (2021). Islamic legal tradition and the choice of investment arbitration forums. *Review of International Political Economy*, *28*(3), 559-583 https://doi.org/10.1080/09692290.2019.1679223.

Lombardi, C. B. (2006). *State law as Islamic law in modern Egypt: The incorporation of the Sharīa into Egyptian constitutional law*. Brill.

Lopez-Rodriguez, A. M. (2003). *Lex Mercatoria and harmonization of contract law in the EU*. Djøf Publishing.

Lopez-Rodriguez, A. M. (2017). Investor-State dispute settlement in the EU: Certainties and uncertainties. *Houston Journal of International Law*, *40*(1), 139.

Love, L. P. (1997). The top ten reasons why mediators should not evaluate. *Florida State University Law Review*, *24*(4), 937.

Lu, H. (2011). State channeling of social grievances: Theory and evidence in China. *Hong Kong Law Journal*, *41*(2), 231-256.

Ludington, C. A. (2017). Med-Arb: If the parties agree. *Yearbook on International Arbitration*, *5*, 313.

Lurie, P. M. & Lack, J. (2014). Guided choice dispute resolution processes: Reducing the time and expense to settlement. *Dispute Resolution International*, *8*(2), 167-178.

Lynch, K. A. (2003). *The forces of economic globalization: Challenges to the regime of international commercial arbitration*. Kluwer Law International.

Ma, G. & Brock, D. (2017). *Arbitration in Hong Kong: A practical guide*. Sweet & Maxwell.

Marriott, A. L. (1996). Pros and cons of more detailed arbitration laws and rules. In Jan Van den Berg, A. (Ed.), *Planning efficient arbitration proceedings: The law applicable in international arbitration, ICCA congress series* (Volume 7, pp. 65-72). Kluwer Law International.

Marriott, A. L. (1997). England's new Arbitration Law. *ICC Bulletin*, *8*(1), 28-36.

Marriott, A. L. (2005). Arbitrators and settlement. In Jan Van den Berg, A. (Ed.), *New horizons in international commercial arbitration and beyond, ICCA congress series* (Volume 12, pp. 533-546). Kluwer Law International.

Marzolini, P. (2016). The arbitrator as a dispute manager: The exercise of the arbitrator's powers to act as settlement facilitator. In Baizeau, D. & Spoorenberg, F. (Eds.), *The arbitrators' initiative: When, why, and how should it be used?—ASA Special Series No. 45* (pp. 99-119). JurisNet.

Mason, P. E. (2011). The arbitrator as mediator, and mediator as arbitrator. *Journal of International Arbitration*, *28*(6), 541-551 https://doi.org/10.54648/joia2011043.

Masood, A. (2010). Settlement in international arbitration: Comments on the CEDR Settlement Rules. *Arbitration: The International Journal of Arbitration, Mediation and Dispute Management*, *76*(2), 269.

Masucci, D. (2018). The 2016-2017 Global Pound Conference events, like those before them, looked to the future. *Dispute Resolution Magazine*, *24*(3), 6-8.

Mayer, P. (1986). Mandatory rules of law in international arbitration. *Arbitration International, 2*, 274-293 https://doi.org/10.1093/arbitration/2.4.274.

Mayer, P. (2016). The arbitrator's initiative: Its foundation and its limits. In Baizeau, D. & Spoorenberg, F. (Eds.), *The arbitrators' initiative: When, why, and how should it be used?—ASA Special Series No. 45* (pp. 1-7). JurisNet.

McFadden, D. (2013). *Mediation in Greater China: The new frontier for commercial mediation*. CCH Hong Kong, Wolters Kluwer law & business.

McGillicuddy, N. B., Welton, G. L. & Pruitt, D. G. (1987). Third-party intervention: A field experiment comparing three different models. *Journal of Personality and Social Psychology, 53*(1), 104-112 https://doi.org/10.1037//0022-3514.53.1.104.

McLaren, R. H. & Sanderson, J. P. (1994). *Innovative dispute resolution: The alternative*. Carswell.

McLean, D. J. (2009). Toward a new international dispute resolution paradigm: Assessing the congruent evolution of globalization and international arbitration. *University of Pennsylvania Journal of International Economic Law, 30*(4), 1087-1097.

McIlwrath, M. & Alvarez, H. (2020). Common and Civil Law approaches to procedure: Party and arbitrator perspectives. In Naon, H. G. & Mason, P. E. (Eds.), *International commercial arbitration practice: 21st century perspectives*. (Chapter 2). LexisNexis.

Menkel-Meadow, C. J. (1985). For and against settlement: Uses and abuses of the mandatory settlement conference. *UCLA Law Review, 33*(2), 485.

Menkel-Meadow, C. J. (2013). Regulation of dispute resolution in the United States of America: From the formal to the informal to the "semi-formal." In Steffek, F., et al. (Eds.), *Regulating dispute resolution: ADR and access to justice at the crossroads* (pp. 419-491). Hart Publishing.

Michaels, R. (2007). The true Lex Mercatoria: Law beyond the state. *Indiana Journal of Global Legal Studies, 14*(2), 447-468 https://doi.org/10.2979/gls.2007.14.2.447.

Michaels, R. (2013). Dreaming law without a state: Scholarship on autonomous international arbitration as utopian literature. *London Review of International Law, 1*(1), 35-62 https://doi.org/10.1093/lril/lrt008.

Miller, A. R. (1984). The August 1983 amendments to the federal rules of civil procedure: Promoting effective case management and lawyer responsibility. *Federal Judicial Center Workshop, 84*(2), 1. Federal Judicial Center.

Minzner, C. F. (2011). China's turn against law. *The American Journal of Comparative Law, 59*(4), 935-984 https://doi.org/10.5131/ajcl.2011.0006.

Mironi, M. M. (2007). From mediation to settlement and from settlement to final offer arbitration: An analysis of transnational business dispute mediation. *Arbitration: The International Journal of Arbitration, Mediation and Dispute Management, 73*(1), 52-59.

Mistelis, L. A. (2001). Is harmonisation a necessary evil?: The future of harmonisation and new sources of international trade law. In Fletcher, I., Mistelis, L. A. & Marise, C. (Eds.), *Foundations and perspectives of international trade law* (pp. 3-27). Sweet & Maxwell.

Mitchell, S. M. & Powell, E. J. (2011). Major legal traditions of the world. In *Domestic law goes global: Legal traditions and international courts* (pp. 20-67). Cambridge University Press.

Monichino, A. (2010). Arbitration reform in Australia: Striving for international best practice. *The Arbitrator & Mediator, 29*(1), 29-47.

Morek, R. (2006). The regulatory framework for online dispute resolution: A critical view. *The University of Toledo Law Review, 38*(1), 163.

Morresi, R. M. (2009). The use of Med-Arb-like mechanisms in Italy and other European countries. *New York Dispute Resolution Lawyer 2*(1), 106-109.

Myers, J. J. (1996). 10 techniques for managing arbitration hearings. *Dispute Resolution Journal, 51*(1), 28.

Nadar, A. (2009). Islamic finance and dispute resolution: Part 2. *Arab Law Quarterly, 23*(2), 181-193 https://doi.org/10.1163/157302509x415701.

Najar, J. C. (2009). Inside out: A user's perspective on challenges in international arbitration. *Arbitration International, 25*(4), 515-527 https://doi.org/10.1093/arbitration/25.4.515.

Nappert, S. & Flader, D. (2011). A psychological perspective on the facilitation of settlement in international arbitration: Examining the CEDR Rules. *Journal of International Dispute Settlement, 2*(2), 459-470 https://doi.org/10.1093/jnlids/idr008.

Nariman, F. S. (2000). The spirit of arbitration: The Tenth Annual Goff Lecture. *Arbitration International, 16*(3), 261-278.

Nariman, F. S. (2005). The role of arbitrators as settlement facilitators: Introduction. In Jan Van den Berg, A. (Ed.), *New horizons for international commercial arbitration and beyond* (pp. 531-532). Kluwer Law International.

Nater-Bass, G. (2016). The initial discussion with the parties: How should it be done? Which topics must be or may be addressed?. In Baizeau, D. & Spoorenberg, F. (Eds.), *The arbitrators' initiative: When, why, and how should it be used?: ASA Special Series No. 45* (pp. 9-29). JurisNet.

Naughton, P. (2007). The role of arbitrators and arbitration institutions in the use of alternatives for the settlement of disputes. *Arbitration: The Journal of International Arbitration, Mediation, and Dispute Management (CIArb), 73*(1), 31-37.

Nazzini, R. (2016). The law applicable to the arbitration agreement: Towards transnational principles. *The International and Comparative Law Quarterly, 65*(3), 681-703 https://doi.org/10.1017/s0020589316000233.

Nelken, D. (2011). Towards a sociology of legal adaptation. In Nelken, D. & Feest, J. (Eds.), *Adapting legal cultures* (pp. 7-54). Hart Publishing.

Netto, C. N. (2005). The Brazilian approach to arbitrators as settlement facilitators. In Jan Van den Berg, A. (Ed.), *New horizons in international commercial arbitration and beyond, ICCA congress series* (Volume 12, pp. 582-588). Kluwer Law International.

Newmark, C. (2002). Is mediation effective for resolving sports disputes?. In Blackshaw, I. (Ed.), *Mediating sports disputes, national and international perspectives* (pp. 78-91). Asser Press.

Newmark, C. (2008). Controlling time and costs in arbitration. In Newman, L. W. & Hill, R. D. (Eds.), *The leading arbitrators' guide to international arbitration* (2nd ed., pp. 81-96). Juris Publishing.

Nicholas, G. & Partasides, C. (2007). LCIA Court decisions on challenges to arbitrators: A proposal to publish. *Arbitration International, 23*(1), 1-42 https://doi.org/10.1093/arbitration/23.1.1.

Nigmatullina, D. (2018). *Combining mediation and arbitration in international commercial dispute resolution* (1st ed.). Routledge.

Nigmatullina, D. (2019). Aligning dispute resolution processes with global demands for change: Enhancing the use of mediation and arbitration in combination. *b-Arbitra, 2019*(1), 7-51.

Nitschke, F. (2014). The IBA's investor-State mediation rules and the ICSID dispute settlement framework. *ICSID Review, 29*(1), 112-132 https://doi.org/10.1093/icsidreview/sit049.

Nitschke, F. (2019). The ICSID conciliation rules in practice. In Titi, C. & Gomez, K. F. (Eds.), *Mediation in international commercial and investment disputes* (pp. 121-143). Oxford University Press.

Nobles, K. C. (2012). Emerging issues and trends in international arbitration. *California Western International Law Journal, 43*(1), 77.

Nolan-Haley, J. M. (2012). Mediation: The "new arbitration." *Harvard Negotiation Law Review, 17*, 61-96.

Nolan-Haley, J. M. (2020). Mediators in arbitration. In Schultz, T. & Ortino, F. (Eds.), *The Oxford Handbook of International Arbitration* (1st ed., pp. 283-303). Oxford University Press.

Nottage, L. (2002). Is (international commercial) arbitration ADR?. *The Arbitrator & Mediator, 21*(1), 83.

Nottage, L. (2004). Japan's new arbitration law: Domestication reinforcing Internationalisation?. *International Arbitration Law Review, 7*, 54-60.

Nottage, L. (2012). Drafting arbitration clauses to minimise costs and delays in ICA: An Asia-Pacific perspective. *The Australian ADR Reporter, 16*, 1-8.

Nottage, L. (2013). International commercial arbitration in Australia: What's new and what's next? *Journal of International Arbitration, 30*(5), 465 https://doi.org/10.54648/joia2013031.

Nottage, L. (2014). In/formalisation and Glocalisation of international commercial arbitration and investment treaty arbitration in Asia. In Zekoll, J., Bälz, M. & Amelung, I. (Eds.), *Formalisation and Flexibilisation in dispute resolution* (pp. 211-249). Brill Nijhoff.

Nottage, L. & Garnett, R. (2010). Top 20 things to change in or around Australia's International Arbitration Act. *Asian International Arbitration Journal, 6*(1), 1-43 https://doi.org/10.54648/aiaj2010001.

Nurmohamed, R. (2020). Shari'a law and its impact on the development of Muslim and non-Muslim business relations in the United Arab Emirates. *Law and Development Review (Berkeley, Calif.), 13*(2), 443-472 https://doi.org/10.1515/ldr-2020-0052.

Oghigian, H. (2003). The mediation/arbitration hybrid. *Journal of International Arbitration, 20*(1), 75-80 https://doi.org/10.54648/joia2003016.

Ortolani, P. (2025). From settlement to award: Challenges and opportunities of consent awards. In Klaassen, C. J. M. et al. (Eds.), *Arbitration in the Netherlands, in particular NAI arbitration* (pp. 511-532). Wolters Kluwer.

Othman, A. (2007). "And amicable settlement is best": Sulh and dispute resolution in Islamic Law. *Arab Law Quarterly, 21*(1), 64-90 https://doi.org/10.1163/026805507x197857.

Pair, L. M. (2002). Cross-cultural arbitration: Do the differences between cultures still influence international commercial arbitration despite harmonization? *ILSA Journal of International & Comparative Law, 9*(1), 57.

Paisley, K. & Player, J. (2021). The impact of enforcement on dispute resolution methodology. *New York Dispute Resolution Lawyer 14*(1), 33-36.

Palmer, M. (2010). Compromising courts and harmonizing ideologies: Mediation in the administrative chambers of the people's courts in the people's Republic of China. In Harding, A. & Nicholson, P. (Eds.), *New Courts in Asia* (pp. 251-276). Routledge.

Pappas, B. A. (2013). Med-Arb: The best of both worlds may be too good to be true—A response to Weisman. *Dispute resolution magazine (American Bar Association), 19*(3), 42.

Pappas, B. A. (2015). Med-arb and the legalization of alternative dispute resolution. *Harvard Negotiation Law Review, 20*, 157.

Park, W. W. (2006). The procedural soft law of international arbitration: Non-governmental instruments. In Mistelis, L. A. & Lew, J. D. M. (Eds.), *Pervasive problems in international arbitration* (pp. 141-154). Kluwer Law International.

Park, W. W. (2009). Arbitrator integrity: The transient and the permanent. *The San Diego Law Review, 46*(3), 629.

Park, W. W. (2017). Soft law and transnational standards in arbitration: The challenges of res judicata. *Boston University School of LawPublic Law Research Paper No. 17-26*, 1-21.

Pate, R. A. (2010). The future of harmonization: Soft law instruments and the principled advance of international lawmaking. *Touro International Law Review, 13*(2), 142-164.

Paulsson, J. (1995). Arbitration without privity. *ICSID Review, 10*(2), 232-257 https://doi.org/10.1093/icsidreview/10.2.232.

Paulsson J. (2008). International arbitration is not arbitration. *Stockholm International Arbitration Review, 2*, 1.

Paulsson, J. (2013). *The idea of arbitration.* Oxford University Press.

Peter, J. T. (1997). Note & comment: Med-Arb in international arbitration. *The American Review of International Arbitration, 8*, 83.

Peter, J. T. (2005). Med-Arb in international arbitration. *Revista de Arbitragem e Mediação, 4*, 155.

Phillips, F. P. (2009). Commercial mediation in China: Challenge of shifting paradigms. *Contemporary issues in international arbitration and mediation: The Fordham Papers, 2(2008)*, 319-329. https://doi.org/10.1163/ej.9789004175556.i-382.110.

Phillips, G. F. (2009). Same-Neutral Med-Arb: What does the future hold?. *New York Dispute Resolution Lawyer 2*(1), 75-79.

Pitkowitz, M. M. & Richter, M. T. (2009). May a neutral third person serve as arbitrator and mediator in the same dispute?. *German Arbitration Journal (SchiedsVZ), 4,* 225-230.

Plant, D. W. (2000). The arbitrator as settlement facilitator. *Journal of International Arbitration, 17*(1), 143-146 https://doi.org/10.54648/267919.

Power, J. (2007). The role of arbitrators as settlement facilitators. In American Arbitration Association (AAA), *ADR and the Law* (21st ed., pp. 246-258). JurisNet.

Pruitt, D. G. et al. (1989). Process of mediation in dispute settlement centres. In Kressel, K., Pruitt, D. G. & Associates (Eds.), *Mediation research: The process and effectiveness of third-party intervention* (pp. 368-393). Jossey Bass Publishers.

Pryles, M. (2007). Limits to party autonomy in arbitral procedure. *Journal of International Arbitration, 24*(3), 327-339 https://doi.org/10.54648/joia2007023.

Qouteshat, O. H. (2017). The enforceability of the unfair arbitration agreement in consumer disputes before Dubai courts. *Arab Law Quarterly, 31*(1), 1-29 https://doi.org/10.1163/15730255-12341330.

Raeschke-Kessler, H. (2005). The arbitrator as settlement facilitator. *Arbitration International, 21*(4), 523-536 https://doi.org/10.1093/arbitration/21.4.523.

Rashid, S. K. (2004). Alternative dispute resolution in the context of Islamic law. *The Vindobona Journal of International Commercial Law and Arbitration, 8*(1), 95-118.

Rau, A. S. (2005). The culture of American arbitration and the lessons of ADR. *Texas International Law Journal, 40*(3), 449.

Raviv, A. (2012). No more excuses: Toward a workable system of dispositive motions in international arbitration. *Arbitration International, 28*(3), 487-510 https://doi.org/10.1093/arbitration/28.3.487.

Rawding, N., Fullelove, G. R. & Martin, P. (2013). International arbitration in England: A procedural overview. In Lew, J. D. M. et al. (Eds.), *Arbitration in England, with chapters on Scotland and Ireland* (pp. 361-398). Kluwer Law International.

Rayner, S. E. (1991). *The theory of contracts in Islamic law: A comparative analysis with particular reference to the modern legislation in Kuwait, Bahrain and the United Arab Emirates*. Graham & Trotman.

Rees, P. J. (2007). The conduct of international arbitration in England: The challenge has still to be met. *Arbitration International, 23*(3), 505-510 https://doi.org/10.1093/arbitration/23.3.505.

Resnik, J. (1982). Managerial judges. *Harvard Law Review, 96*(2), 374-448 https://doi.org/10.2307/1340797.

Respondek, A. (2014). Five proposals to further increase the efficiency of international arbitration proceedings. *Journal of International Arbitration, 31*(4), 507-513 https://doi.org/10.54648/joia2014024.

Risse, J. (2013). Ten drastic proposals for saving time and costs in arbitral proceedings. *Arbitration International, 29*(3), 453-466 https://doi.org/10.1093/arbitration/29.3.453.

Rivkin, D. W. (2008). Towards a new paradigm in international arbitration: The Town Elder model revisited. *Arbitration International, 24*(3), 375-386 https://doi.org/10.1093/arbitration/24.3.375.

Roebuck, D. (2007). The myth of modern mediation. *Arbitration: The International Journal of Arbitration, Mediation and Dispute Management, 73*(1), 105.

Rogers, C. A. & Jeng, J. C. (2014). The ethics of international arbitrators. In Newman, L. W. & Hill, R. D. (Eds.), *The leading arbitrators' guide to international arbitration* (3rd. ed., pp. 175-206). JurisNet.

Rombach, A. & Shalbanava, H. (2019). The Prague Rules: A new era of procedure in arbitration or much ado about nothing? *German Arbitration Journal (SchiedsVZ), 17*(2), 53-60.

Rosoff, J. (2009). Hybrid efficiency in arbitration: Waiving potential conflicts for dual role arbitrators in Med-Arb and Arb-Med proceedings. *Journal of International Arbitration, 26*(1), 89-100 https://doi.org/10.54648/joia2009004.

Ross, D. (2013). Med-Arb/Arb-Med: A more efficient ADR process or an invitation to a potential ethical disaster?. In Rovine, A. W. (Ed.), *Contemporary issues in international arbitration and mediation: The Fordham Papers (2012)* (pp. 352-366). Brill Nijhoff.

Roth, B. J., Wulff, R. W. & Cooper, C. A. (2021). *Alternative dispute resolution practice guide*. Thomson Reuters.

Ruckteschler, D. & Wendelstein, A. (2021). Efficient Arb-Med-Arb proceedings: Should the arbitrator also be the mediator? *Journal of International Arbitration, 38*(6), 761-774 https://doi.org/10.54648/joia2021035.

Ruggie, J. G. (2014). Global governance and "new governance theory": Lessons from business and human Rights. *Global Governance, 20*(1), 5-17 https://doi.org/10.1163/19426720-02001002.

Sachs, K. (2020). Do we deliver: How to make international arbitration more efficient. In Kaplan, N. et al. (Eds.), *International arbitration: When East meets West—Liber Amicorum Michael Moser* (pp. 221-234). Kluwer Law International.

Sachs, K. & Weiler, M. (2020). A comparison of the recognition and enforcement of foreign decisions under the 1958 New York Convention and the 2019 Hague Judgments Convention. In Gebauer, M., Klötzel, T. & Schütze, R. (Eds), *Festschrift für Roderich C. Thümmel zum 65. Geburtstag am 23.10.2020* (pp. 763-780). De Gruyter.

Sanders, P. (1996). The 1996 Alexander Lecture: Cross-border arbitration—A view on the future. *Arbitration-London,* 62, 168-174.

Sanders, P. (1999). *Quo vadis arbitration?: Sixty years of arbitration practice—A comparative study*. Kluwer Law International.

Saville, L. J. (1997). Departmental advisory committee on arbitration law 1996 report on the arbitration bill. *Arbitration International, 13*(3), 275-316 https://doi.org/10.1093/arbitration/13.3.275.

Sawada, T. (2003). Hybrid Arb-Med: Will West and East never meet? *ICC International Court of Arbitration Bulletin, 14(2)*, 29.

Scherer, M. & Gerbay, R. (2015). *Arbitrating under the 2014 LCIA Rules: A user's guide.* Kluwer Law International.

Scherpe, J. M. & Marten, B. (2013). Mediation in England and Wales: Regulation and practice. In Hopt, K. J. & Steffek, F. (Eds.), *Mediation: Principles and regulation in comparative perspective*. Oxford University Press.

Scheu, J. & Nikolov, P. (2021). Jurisdiction of tribunals to settle intra-EU investment treaty disputes. *ICSID Review, 36*(1), 171-188 https://doi.org/10.1093/icsidreview/siaa048.

Scheuerman, W. (1999). Globalization and the fate of law. In Dyzenhaus, D. (Ed.), *Recrafting the Rule of Law* (pp. 243-266). Bloomsbury Publishing.

Schill, S. W. (2011). Enhancing international investment law's legitimacy: Conceptual and methodological foundations of a new public law approach. *Virginia Journal of International Law, 52*(1), 57.

Schill, S. W. (2014). Editorial: Five times transparency in international investment law. *The Journal of World Investment & Trade, 15*(3-4), 363-374 https://doi.org/10.1163/22119000-01504001.

Schill, S. W. (2015). Editorial: The Mauritius convention on transparency. *The Journal of World Investment & Trade, 16*(2), 201-204 https://doi.org/10.1163/22119000-01602009.

Schmitthoff, C. M. (1968). The unification of the law of international trade. *The Journal of Business Law, 4*, 105-119 https://doi.org/10.1093/iclqaj/17.3.551.

Schnabel, T. (2019). The Singapore convention on mediation: A framework for the cross-border recognition and enforcement of mediated settlements. *Pepperdine Dispute Resolution Law Journal, 19*(1), 1.

Schneider, M. E. (1998). Combining arbitration with conciliation. In Jan Van den Berg, A. (Ed.), *International dispute resolution: Towards an international arbitration culture, ICCA congress series* (Volume 8, pp. 57-97). Kluwer Law International.

Schneider, M. E. (2007). Combining arbitration with conciliation. *Transnational Dispute Management, 1*, 9.

Schneider, M. E. (2010). The art of blending arbitration and other ADR methods: Some examples from international practice. In Ingen-Housz, A. (Ed.), *ADR in business: Practice and issues across countries and cultures II* (pp. 313-325). Kluwer Law International.

Schroeter, U. G. (2017). Ad Hoc or institutional arbitration: A clear-cut distinction?—A closer look at borderline cases. *Contemporary Asia arbitration journal, 10*, 141.

Seatzu, F. & Vargiu, P. (2022). Three views of a secret: Missed opportunities in the ECHR's recent case-law on international commercial arbitration. *The Italian Review of International and Comparative Law, 1*(2), 203-223 https://doi.org/10.1163/27725650-01020001.

Seidl-Hohenveldern, I. (1979). *International economic "soft law": Collected courses of the Hague Academy of International Law* (Volume 163). Brill.

Shihata, I. (1986). Obstacles facing ICSID's proceedings and international law in general. *News from ICSID, 3*(1), 8.

Shihata, I. (1995). Chapter Eleven ICSID's role in the resolution of investment disputes. In Shihata, I. et al. (Eds.), *The World Bank in a Changing World* (pp. 425-454). Brill Nijhoff. https://doi-org.leidenuniv.idm.oclc.org/10.1163/9789004639041_013.

Silberberg, R. H. & Badaracco, A. P. (2019). Arb-Med: Workable or worrisome?. *New York Dispute Resolution Lawyer, 12*(2), 33-36.

Smit, H. (1986). The future of international commercial arbitration: A single transnational institution? *The Columbia Journal of Transnational Law, 25*(1), 9-34.

Stallard, A. (2002). Joining the culture club: Examining cultural context when implementing international dispute resolution. *Ohio State Journal on Dispute Resolution, 17*(2), 463.

Steele, B. L. (2007). Enforcing international commercial mediation agreements as arbitral awards under the New York Convention. *UCLA Law Review, 54*(5), 1385-1412.

Stephan, P. B. (1999). The futility of unification and harmonization in international commercial law. *Virginia Journal of International Law, 39*(3), 743.

Stevens, M. & Love, B. (2010). Investor-State mediation: Observations on the role of institutions. In Rovine, A. W. (Ed.), *Contemporary issues in international arbitration and mediation: The Fordham Papers (2009)* (pp. 389-417). Brill Nijhoff.

Stewart, R. B. (2014). Remedying disregard in global regulatory governance: Accountability, participation, and responsiveness. *The American Journal of International Law, 108*(2), 211-270 https://doi.org/10.5305/amerjintelaw.108.2.0211.

Stipanowich, T. J. (2004). ADR and the "Vanishing Trial": The growth and impact of "Alternative Dispute Resolution." *Journal of Empirical Legal Studies, 1*(3), 843-912 https://doi.org/10.1111/j.1740-1461.2004.00025.x.

Stipanowich, T. J. (2009). East meets West: An international dialogue on mediation and med-arb in the United States and China. *Pepperdine Dispute Resolution Law Journal, 9*(2), 379.

Stipanowich, T. J. (2010). Arbitration: The "new litigation." *University of Illinois Law Review, 2010*(1), 1-59.

Stipanowich, T. J. (2014). Reflections on the state and future of commercial arbitration: Challenges, opportunities, proposals. *The American Review of International Arbitration, 25*(3-4), 297.

Stipanowich, T. J. (2015). The international evolution of mediation: A call for dialogue and deliberation. *Law Review (Wellington), 46*(4), 1191-1243 https://doi.org/10.26686/vuwlr.v46i4.4889.

Stipanowich, T. J. (2021a). Arbitration, mediation, and mixed modes: Seeking workable solutions and common ground on Med-Arb, Arb-Med, and settlement-orientated activities by arbitrators. *Harvard Negotiation Law Review, 26*, 265.

Stipanowich, T. J. (2021b). Multi-tier commercial dispute resolution processes in the United States. In A. Reyes & W. Gu (Eds.), *Multi-Tier approaches to the resolution of international disputes: A global and comparative study* (pp. 271-293). Cambridge University Press.

Stipanowich, T. J. (2023). Of time and tide. *Texas A&M Law Review, 10*(4), 685-696 https://doi.org/10.37419/lr.v10.i4.8.

Stipanowich, T. J. & Fraser, V. (2017). The international task force on mixed mode dispute resolution: Exploring the interplay between mediation, evaluation and arbitration in commercial cases. *Fordham International Law Journal, 40*(3), 839.

Stipanowich, T. J. & Kaskell, P. H. (2001). *Commercial arbitration at its best: Successful strategies for business users: A report of the cpr commission on the future of arbitration*. CPR Institute for Dispute Resolution.

Stipanowich, T. J. & Lamare, J. R. (2014). Living with ADR: Evolving perceptions and use of mediation, arbitration, and conflict management in fortune 1000 corporations. *Harvard Negotiation Law Review, 19*, 1.

Stipanowich, T. J. & Mironi, M. M. (2021). "Switching hats": Developing international practice guidance for single-neutral Med-Arb, Arb-Med, and Arb-Med-Arb. *New York Dispute Resolution Lawyer 14*(1), 29-32.

Stipanowich, T. J. & Ulrich, Z. P. (2014a). Arbitration in evolution: Current practices and perspectives of experienced commercial arbitrators. *The American Review of International Arbitration, 25*(3-4), 395.

Stipanowich, T. J. & Ulrich, Z. P. (2014b). Commercial arbitration and settlement: Empirical insights into the roles arbitrators play. *Penn State Yearbook on Arbitration and Mediation, 6*, 1-31.

Strong, S.I. (2013). Increasing legalism in international commercial arbitration: A new theory of causes, a new approach to cures. *World Arbitration and Mediation Review, 7*(2), 117.

Strong, S. I. (2014a). Beyond international commercial arbitration? The promise of international commercial mediation. *Washington University Journal of Law and Policy, 45*, 11.

Stulberg, J. B. (1989). A mediator's responsibility for fairness. *Selected SPIDR Proc. 1987-1988*, 40.

Stulberg, J. B. (1998). Fairness and mediation. *Ohio State Journal on Dispute Resolution, 13*(3), 909-946.

Stulberg, J. B. & Montgomery, B. R. (1986). Design requirements for mediator development programs. *Hofstra Law Review, 15*, 499.

Stutzer, H. (2017). Settlement facilitation: Does the arbitrator have a role? The "Referentenaudienz"—The "Zurich-Way" of settling the case. *ASA Bulletin (Association Suisse de L'arbitrage), 35*(3), 589-608 https://doi.org/10.54648/asab2017052.

Sun, X. (2020). A Chinese approach to international commercial dispute resolution: The China International Commercial Court. *The Chinese Journal of Comparative Law, 8*(1), 45-54 https://doi.org/10.1093/cjcl/cxaa015.

Sussman, E. (2009a). Developing an effective Med-Arb/Arb-Med process. *New York Dispute Resolution Lawyer 2*(1), 71-74.

Sussman, E. (2009b). The New York Convention through a mediation prism. *Dispute Resolution Magazine, 15*(4), 10.

Sussman, E. (2010a). Combinations and permutations of arbitration and mediation: Issues and solutions. In Ingen-Housz, A. (Ed.), *ADR in business: Practice and issues across countries and cultures II* (pp. 381-398). Kluwer Law International.

Sussman, E. (2010b). Investor-State dispute mediation: The benefits and obstacles. *Contemporary issues in international arbitration and mediation: The Fordham Papers, 3(2009)*, 321-338. https://doi.org/10.1163/ej.9789004182912.i-452.96.

Sussman, E. (2013). Med-Arb: An argument for favoring ex parte communications in the mediation phase. *World Arbitration and Mediation Review, 7*(2), 1-14.

Sussman, E. (2020). The mediation window: An arbitration process measure to facilitate settlement. *New York Dispute Resolution Lawyer 13*(1), 20-22.

Sussman, E. & Berger, K. P. (2021a). Arbitrator techniques and their (direct or potential) effect on settlement. *New York Dispute Resolution Lawyer 14*(1), 25-28.

Sussman, E. & Gleason, E. (2019). Putting final offer/baseball arbitration to use. *Alternatives to the High Cost of Litigation (2001), 37*(2), 19-21 https://doi.org/10.1002/alt.21772.

Talbot, P. (2001). Should an arbitrator or adjudicator act as a mediator in the same dispute?. *Arbitration: The International Journal of Arbitration, Mediation and Dispute Management, 67*(3), 221.

Tang, Z. S. (2019). "The belt and road" and cross-border judicial cooperation. *Hong Kong Law Journal, 49*(1), 121-152.

Taniguchi, Y. (1998). Is there a growing international arbitration culture?: An observation from Asia. In Jan van den Berg, A. (Ed.), *International dispute resolution: Towards an international arbitration culture, ICCA congress series* (Volume 8, pp. 31-40). Kluwer Law International.

Taylor, V. L. & Pryles, M. (2006). The cultures of dispute resolution in Asia. In Pryles, M. (Ed.), *Dispute resolution in Asia* (3rd. ed., pp. 1-33). Kluwer Law International.

Teramura, N. (2020). *Ex Aequo et Bono as a response to the "over-judicialisation" of international commercial arbitration*. Kluwer Law International.

Teubner, G. (2001). Legal irritants: How unifying law ends up in new divergences. In Hall, P. A. & Soskice, D. (Eds.), *Varieties of capitalism: The institutional foundations of comparative advantage* (pp. 417-441). Oxford University.

Teubner, G., Van de Kerdrove, M. & Oss, F. (1997). Breaking frames: The global interplay of legal and social systems. *The American Journal of Comparative Law, 45*(1), 149-169 https://doi.org/10.2307/840962.

Tezuka, H. (2020). Rise of hybrid arbitration/mediation in the era of the Singapore mediation convention. In Kaplan, N. et al. (Eds.), *International arbitration: When East meets West: Liber Amicorum Michael Moser* (pp. 277-290). Kluwer Law International.

Thevenin, N. M. (2013). Caucusing and the cross-cultural divide. In Rovine, A. W. (Ed.), *Contemporary issues in international arbitration and mediation: The Fordham Papers* (pp. 367-375). Brill Nijhoff.

Thomas, J. C. (1999). Investor-state arbitration under NAFTA Chapter 11. *Canadian Yearbook of International Law, 37*, 99 https://doi.org/10.1017/s006900580000713x.

Tienhaara, K. (2011). Regulatory chill and the threat of arbitration: A view from political science. In Brown, C. & Miles, K. (Eds.), *Evolution in investment treaty law and arbitration* (pp. 606-628). Cambridge University Press.

Tietje, C. & Nowrot, K. (2004). Forming the centre of a transnational economic legal order? Thoughts on the current and future position of non-state actors in WTO

Law. *European Business Organization Law Review, 5*(2), 321-351 https://doi.org/10.1017/s1566752904003210.

Trakman, L. (2006). "Legal traditions" and international commercial arbitration. *The American Review of International Arbitration, 17*(1), 1.

Trakman, L. (2007). Ex Aequo et Bono: Demystifying an ancient concept. *Chicago Journal of International Law, 8*(2), 621-642.

Trakman, L. & Montgomery, H. (2017). The "Judicialization" of international commercial arbitration: Pitfall or virtue? *Leiden Journal of International Law, 30*(2), 405-434 https://doi.org/10.1017/s0922156517000024.

Tschanz, P. Y. (2016). Selected questions regarding arbitrator's initiatives. In Baizeau, D. & Spoorenberg, F. (Eds.), *The arbitrators' initiative: When, why, and how should it be used?: ASA Special Series No. 45* (pp. 77-88). JurisNet.

Twining, W. (2009). Implications of "Globalisation" for law as a discipline. In Halpin, A. & Roeben, W. (Eds.), *Theorising the global legal order*. Hart Publishing.

Uzelac, A. (1997). UNCITRAL notes on organizing arbitral proceedings: A regional view. *Croat. Arb. Y.B., 4*, 135.

Van Harten, G. & Loughlin, M. (2006). Investment treaty arbitration as a species of global administrative law. *European Journal of International Law, 17*(1), 121-150 https://doi.org/10.1093/ejil/chi159.

Vesting, T. (2004). The network economy as a challenge to create new public law (beyond the state). In Ladeur, K. H. (Ed.), *Public governance in the age of globalization (1st ed.)* (pp. 247-287). Routledge.

Vilaça, G. V. (2016). Why a theory of international arbitration and transnational legality? *The Canadian Journal of Law and Jurisprudence, 29*(2), 495-520 https://doi.org/10.1017/cjlj.2016.21.

Von Kann, C. E. (2009). A report card on the quality of commercial arbitration: Assessing and improving delivery of the benefits customers seek. *DePaul Business & Commercial Law Journal, 7*(3), 499.

Von Schlabrendorff, F. (2009). Ethical standards for arbitrators, hybrid proceedings, rules of transnational law: Are we moving towards a uniform law of international arbitration? *Anali Pravnog Fakulteta u Beogradu, 57*(3), 90-115.

Wang, M. (2000). Are alternative dispute resolution methods superior to litigation in resolving disputes in international commerce? *Arbitration International, 16*(2), 189-211.

Wang, G., Lee, Y. L. & Leung, P. M. (2020). *Dispute resolution mechanism for the Belt and Road Initiative*. Springer.

Warwas, B. A. (2017). *The liability of arbitral institutions: Legitimacy challenges and functional responses*. Asser Press & Springer.

Webster, T. H. & Bühler, M. W. (2018). *Handbook of ICC arbitration: Commentary and materials*. Sweet & Maxwell.

Weisman, M. (2013). Med-Arb: The best of both worlds. *Dispute Resolution Magazine (American Bar Association), 19*(3), 40.

Wenger, W. (2006). The role of the arbitrator in bringing about a settlement: A Swiss perspective. In Wirth, M. (Ed.), *Best practices in international arbitration: ASA Special Series No. 26* (pp. 139-154). ASA Association Suisse de l'Arbitrage.

Wissler, R. L. (2011). Court-connected settlement procedures: Mediation and judicial settlement conferences. *Ohio State Journal on Dispute Resolution, 26*(2-3), 271.

Wistrich, A., Guthrie, C. & Rachlinski, J. (2005). Can judges ignore inadmissible information? The difficulty of deliberately disregarding. *University of Pennsylvania Law Review, 153*(4), 1251-1345 https://doi.org/10.2307/4150614.

Wolf, B. J.C. (2006). On-line but out of touch: Analyzing international dispute resolution through the lens of the Internet. *New Europe Law Review, 14*(1), 281.

Wolski, B. (2013). Arb-Med-Arb (and MSAs): A whole which is less than, not greater than, the sum of its parts? *Contemporary Asia Arbitration Journal, 6*(2), 249-274.

Wong, B. (2000). Traditional Chinese philosophy and dispute resolution. *Hong Kong Law Journal, 30*(2), 304-319.

Woolf, H. K. (1996). *Access to justice: Final report to the Lord Chancellor on the civil justice system in England and Wales.* HM Stationery Office.

Woolf, H. K. (2008). *The pursuit of justice.* Oxford University Press.

Xingzhong, Y. (1989). Legal pragmatism in the People's Republic of China. *Journal of Chinese Law, 3*(1), 29.

Xu, X. & Wilson, G. D. (2000). One country, two-international commercial arbitration-systems. *Journal of International Arbitration, 17*(6), 47-105 https://doi.org/10.54648/313897.

Yip, M. (2021). Combinations of mediation and arbitration: The Singapore perspective. In Reyes, A. & Gu, W. (Eds.), *Multi-Tier approaches to the resolution of international disputes: A global and comparative study* (pp. 182-202). Cambridge University Press.

Zhang, X. (2015). Rethinking the mediation campaign. *The Journal of Comparative Law, 10*(2), 44-64.

Zweigert, K. & Koötz, H. (1987). *Introduction to comparative law* (2nd. ed.). Clarendon Press.

Internet Sources

AAA: Active rules. (n.d.). American Arbitration Association. https://www.adr.org/active-rules.

Al Houti, D. (December 18, 2018). *Dubai arbitration week recap: New frontiers in arbitration—The MENA region.* Kluwer Arbitration Blog. http://arbitrationblog.kluwerarbitration.com/2018/12/18/dubai-arbitration-week-recap-new-frontiers-in-arbitration-the-mena-region/.

ASA: Arbitration Toolbox. (n.d.). Swiss Arbitration Association. https://toolbox.swissarbitration.org/toolbox/case-overview.

ASA: Swiss Arbitration Academy. (October 16, 2024). Swiss Arbitration Association. https://www.swissarbitration.org/academy/.

Baysal, P. & Cevik, B. K. (September 29, 2021). *Arbitrator as a settlement facilitator: An illusory divide?.* Mondaq. https://www.mondaq.com/turkey/arbitration-dispute-resolution/1116356/arbitrator-as-a-settlement-facilitator-an-illusory-divide-.

Berger, K. P. (May 23, 2016b). *It takes pressure to form diamonds: The changing landscape of dispute resolution and its implications for international arbitration.* Kluwer Arbitration Blog. https://arbitrationblog.kluwerarbitration.com/2016/05/23/the-changing-landscape-of-dispute-resolution-and-its-implications-for-international-arbitration/.

Böckstiegel, K. H. (2010). Assumptions regarding common law versus civil law in the practice of international commercial arbitration. *The conference of the German Institution of Arbitration (DIS), (21/22 October 2010).* https://cdn.arbitration-icca.org/s3fs-public/document/media_document/media113194214157020l-common_law_versus_civil_law_.pdf.

Borrasso, A. (April 6, 2018). *U.S. district courts rule consent awards fall within New York Convention.* Kluwer Arbitration Blog. http://arbitrationblog.kluwerarbitration.com/2018/04/06/u-s-district-courts-rule-consent-awards-fall-within-new-york-convention/.

Burgsdorff, C. & Burkert, R. (March 26, 2020). *The Hague convention on the enforcement and recognition of foreign judgments in civil or commercial matters: Game changer or non-starter?.* Luther. https://www.luther-lawfirm.com/en/newsroom/blog/detail/the-hague-convention-on-the-enforcement-and-recognition-of-foreign-judgments-in-civil-or-commercial-matters-game-changer-or-non-starter.

CEDR: About us. (July 31, 2024). Centre for Effective Dispute Resolution. https://www.cedr.com/aboutus/.

CIArb: About us. (n.d.). Chartered Institute of Arbitrators. https://www.ciarb.org/about-us/.

CIArb: What we do. (n.d.). Chartered Institute of Arbitrators. https://www.ciarb.org/about-us/what-we-do/.

Coe, J. J. (February 1, 2007). *Toward a complementary use of conciliation in Investor-State disputes: A preliminary sketch.* Transnational Dispute Management (TDM). https://www.transnational-dispute-management.com/article.asp?key = 960

CPR: About us. (n.d.). International Institute for Conflict Prevention & Resolution. https://www.cpradr.org/about-us.

Croft, C. (2014). Alternative dispute resolution in arbitration: Is Arb-med really an option?. *The 2014 International Arbitration Conference: Sydney,* 1-14. https://docsbay.net/alternative-dispute-resolution-in-arbitration-is-arb-med-really-an-option

D'Agostino, J. (February 15, 2011a). *Mediator-Arbitrators: The perfect match or no love lost?.* Kluwer Arbitration Blog. http://arbitrationblog.kluwerarbitration.com/2011/02/15/mediator-arbitrators-the-perfect-match-or-no-love-lost-a-valentines-day-blog/?print = pdf.

D'Agostino, J. (June 1, 2011b). *New Hong Kong Arbitration ordinance comes into effect.* Kluwer Arbitration Blog. http://arbitrationblog.kluwerarbitration.com/2011/06/01/new-hong-kong-arbitration-ordinance-comes-into-effect/.

Emmerson, A. (June 8, 2016). *Should the use of sealed offers be encouraged in international arbitration?.* Mondaq. https://www.mondaq.com/courtprocedure/498768/should-the-use-of-sealed-offers-be-encouraged-in-internationalarbitratio.

Favalli, D. & Hasenclever, M. K. (2008). The role of arbitrators in settlement proceedings. *Mealey's International Arbitration Report (Lexis Nexis) 23*(7), 1-10. https://www.vischer.com/fileadmin/uploads/vischer/Documents/Activities/Daniele.arb072308cm2.pdf.

FDRC: Dispute resolution process. (n.d.). Hong Kong Financial Dispute Resolution Centre. https://fdrc.org.hk/en/html/resolvingdisputes/resolvingdisputes_fdrsprocess.php.

FDRC: Objectives. (n.d.). Hong Kong Financial Dispute Resolution Centre. https://fdrc.org.hk/en/html/resolvingdisputes/resolvingdisputes_fdrs.php?lang = en.

Firth, A. (July 19, 2018). *All right, stop! mediate and listen: Guidance on the use of Med-Arb in Australia.* Conventus Law. https://conventuslaw.com/report/all-right-stop-mediate-and-listen-guidance-on-the/.

Flake, R. P. (2016). Nuances of Med/Arb: A neutral's perspective. *AAA Handbook on Mediation (Chapter 59)*, 1-10. ArbitrationLaw.com. https://arbitrationlaw.com/library/nuances-medarb-neutrals-perspective-chapter-59-aaa-handbook-mediation-third-edition.

Freehills, H. S. (November 12, 2001). *Can adjudicators get involved?.* Mondaq. https://www.mondaq.com/uk/property-litigation/14136/can-adjudicators-get-involved.

Georgiou, P. & Seow, I. C. L. (September 7, 2014). *Hong Kong strengthens position as leading jurisdiction for international arbitration with major overhaul of legislative framework.* ViewHK. https://viewhk.blogspot.com/2014/09/hong-kong-strengthens-position-as.html.

Global Pound Conference Series: Overview. (n.d.). International Mediation Institute. https://imimediation.org/research/gpc/.

Goodrich, M. (2012). Arb-med: Ideal solution or dangerous heresy?. *White & Case, March 2012*, 1-8. https://www.whitecase.com/sites/whitecase/files/files/download/publications/articles-IALR-2012-Arb-med-solution-or-dangerous-heresay.pdf.

GPC Series. (2016-2017). *Global pound conference series: Cumulated data results.* International Mediation Institute. https://www.imimediation.org/wp-content/uploads/2017/07/Aggregated-Data-Report-GPC_28Dec.pdf.

GPC Series. (2018). *Global pound conference series report: Global data trends and regional differences.* International Mediation Institute. https://www.pwc.com/gx/en/forensics/gpc-2018-pwc.pdf.

Guide to international arbitration law and rules in England and Wales. (2022). CMS Law Tax. https://cms.law/en/int/expert-guides/cms-expert-guide-to-international-arbitration/england-and-wales.

Henderson, A. & Chua, E. (December 11, 2014). *Singapore international mediation centre is launched, offering parties an "Arb-med-arb" process in partnership with SIAC.* Herbert Smith Freehills. https://www.hsfkramer.com/notes/arbitration/2014-12/singapore-international-mediation-centre-is-launched-offering-parties-an-arb-med-arb-process-in-partnership-with-siac/.

IBA Working Group on the practice of the UNIDROIT Principles. (2019). *Perspectives in practice of the UNIDROIT Principles*. International Bar Association. https://www.ibanet.org/MediaHandler?id = D266F2AF-3E0B-4DC0-AFCE-662E5D49BB7E.

ICC: About ICC dispute resolution. (November 9, 2023). International Chamber of Commerce. https://iccwbo.org/dispute-resolution/about-icc-dispute-resolution-services/.

ICC Commission on Arbitration and ADR. (2018). *Techniques for controlling time and costs in arbitration* (2nd ed.). International Chamber of Commerce. https://iccwbo.org/wp-content/uploads/sites/3/2018/03/861-2-ENG-Controlling-Time-and-Costs-in-Arbitration.pdf.

ICDR: Who we are. (n.d.). International Centre for Dispute Resolution. https://www.icdr.org/about_icdr.

ICSID: Caseload Statistics. (2022). International Centre for Settlement of Investment Disputes. https://icsid.worldbank.org/sites/default/files/publications/The_ICSID_Caseload_Statistics_2022-2_ENG.pdf.

ICSID rules and regulations: Mediation. (n.d.). International Centre for Settlement of Investment Disputes. https://icsid.worldbank.org/rules-regulations/mediation.

Johnson, L. (2014). The transparency rules and transparency convention: A good start and model for broader reform in investor-state arbitration. *Columbia FDI Perspectives No. 126 (2014, July 21)*, 1-3. https://academiccommons.columbia.edu/doi/10.7916/D8Q5461Q

Kadhim, N. (October 23, 2021). *Upheaval of dispute resolution centres in the Gulf: Recent developments in Qatar and Dubai.* Kluwer Arbitration Blog. http://arbitrationblog.kluwerarbitration.com/2021/10/23/upheaval-of-dispute-resolution-centres-in-the-gulf-recent-developments-in-qatar-and-dubai/.

Kaplan, N. (2011). Introduction. In Sanders, P. (Ed.), *ICCA's guide to the interpretation of the 1958 New York convention: A handbook for judges.* International Council for Commercial Arbitration (ICCA). https://www.academia.edu/50839333/Judges_guide_english_composite_final_revised_may.

Kozmenko, A. & Groselj, L. (February 1, 2021). *Settlement facilitation by the arbitral tribunal: A Swiss perspective.* Arbitration Journal. https://journal.arbitration.ru/analytics/settlement-facilitation-by-the-arbitral-tribunal-a-swiss-perspective/.

Kryvoi, Y. (November 25, 2015). *Enforcement of settlement agreements reached in arbitration and mediation.* Kluwer Arbitration Blog. http://arbitrationblog.kluwerarbitration.com/2015/11/25/enforcement-of-settlement-agreements-reached-in-arbitration-and-mediation/.

Lauren, M. (2019). The New Jersey International Arbitration, Mediation, and Conciliation Act: Closing the gap in international commercial ADR proceedings. *Law School Student Scholarship*, 965, pp. 1-25. Seton Hall University. https://scholarship.shu.edu/cgi/viewcontent.cgi?article = 1984&context = student_scholarship.

Limbury, A. L. (2009b). Hybrid dispute resolution processes: Getting the best while avoiding the worst of both worlds?. *Second CIArb's Mediation Symposium (London: 2009, October 29)*. https://www.imimediation.org/wp-content/uploads/2017/11/AlanLimbury-HybridDisputeResolutionProcessesArticle.pdf.

Lüth, F. & Wagner, P. K. (2012). Soft law in international arbitration: Some thoughts on legitimacy. *Studentische Zeitschrift für Rechtswissenschaft 3/2012*, pp. 409-422. https://studzr.de/medien/beitraege/2012/3/pdf/StudZR_2012-3_Lueth-Wagner_international_arbitration.pdf.

Majid, S. & Lenzen, F. (March 25, 2011). *Application of Islamic law in the Middle East*. Mondaq. https://www.mondaq.com/international-trade-investment/52976/application-of-islamic-law-in-the-middle-east.

Maniruzzaman, M. (May 30, 2013). *A rethink of Investor-State dispute settlement*. Kluwer Arbitration Blog. https://arbitrationblog.kluwerarbitration.com/2013/05/30/a-rethink-of-investor-state-dispute-settlement/.

McIlwrath, M. (December 12, 2018). *The prague rules: The real cultural war isn't over civil vs common law*. Kluwer Arbitration Blog. http://arbitrationblog.kluwerarbitration.com/2018/12/12/the-prague-rules-the-real-cultural-war-isnt-over-civil-vs-common-law/.

Mediation statistics for Civil Justice Reform related cases. (n.d.). Hong Kong Judiciary. https://mediation.judiciary.hk/en/figures_and_statistics.html.

Miller, S., Hicks, G. & Nadeau, P. (March 24, 2015). *Investor-State dispute settlement*. Center for Strategic & International Studies. https://www.csis.org/analysis/investor-state-dispute-settlement.

Mixed Mode Task Force (April 5, 2016). *International task force on mixed mode dispute resolution: Memo on the task force and project*. College of Commercial Arbitrators, International Mediation Institute, and the Straus Institute. http://www.imimediation.org/wp-content/uploads/2017/11/Memo_on_the_Mixed_Modes_Task_Force_and_Project_April_5_2016.pdf.

Mixed Mode Task Force: About. (n.d.). College of Commercial Arbitrators, International Mediation Institute, and the Straus Institute. https://imimediation.org/about/who-are-imi/mixed-mode-task-force/.

Obadia, E. M. (1999). How proactive arbitrators really are in conducting arbitral proceedings: An ICSID perspective. *News from ICSID, 16*(2), 8-10. https://icsid.worldbank.org/sites/default/files/publications/1999%20Fall%20Volume%2016%20%28No.%202%29%20%E2%80%93%20Download.pdf.

O'Brien, P. (January 10, 2011). *Enhancing international trade and development in the Asia-Pacific region: Opining speech*. UNCITRAL Regional Centre for Asia and the Pacific. https://legal.un.org/ola/media/info_from_lc/POB%20Incheon-Welcome%20Address.pdf.

Panov, A. & Krapoutski, A. (2018). The Prague Rules: An alternative way of conducting international arbitration?. *Arbitration.ru 1*(1), 41-46. https://journal.arbitration.ru/upload/iblock/849/Arbitration.ru_N1_1_August_2018_2.pdf.

PCA: Application of UNCITRAL rules. (n.d.). Permanent Court of Arbitration. https://pca-cpa.org/en/services/arbitration-services/uncitral-arbitration-rules/.

Prague Rules on taking of evidence to launch in December 2018. (April 4, 2018). Practical Law Arbitration. https://praguerules.com/upload/iblock/856/8563f3faf4c2236098577bedb329bdf8.pdf.

Queen Mary University of London and White & Case LLP. (2015). *International arbitration survey: Improvements and innovations in international arbitration*. https://www.qmul.ac.uk/arbitration/media/arbitration/docs/2015_International_Arbitration_Survey.pdf.

Queen Mary University of London and White & Case LLP. (2018). *International arbitration survey: The evolution of international arbitration*. https://www.qmul.ac.uk/arbitration/media/arbitration/docs/2018-International-Arbitration-Survey---The-Evolution-of-International-Arbitration-(2).PDF.

Queen Mary University of London and White & Case LLP. (2021). *International arbitration survey: Adapting arbitration to a changing world*. https://www.qmul.ac.uk/arbitration/media/arbitration/docs/LON0320037-QMUL-International-Arbitration-Survey-2021_19_WEB.pdf.

Rewald, R. & Jachimek, K. (July 18, 2014). *Expanding ADR in Poland: Mediation and arbitration together*. Lexology. https://www.lexology.com/library/detail.aspx?g=c8a459d3-8c59-4633-9b6d-276c3f4e269e.

Ross, A. (October 14, 2015). *CIArb updates guidelines on practice*. Global Arbitration Review. https://globalarbitrationreview.com/article/ciarb-updates-guidelines-practice.

Samberg, G. A. (May 22, 2018). *Arbitration jujitsu: "Sealed settlement offer" add leverage*. LAW360. https://www.law360.com/articles/1045886/arbitration-jujitsu-sealed-settlement-offers-add-leverage.

SIMC: Arb-Med-Arb. (n.d.). Singapore International Mediation Centre. https://simc.com.sg/arb-med-arb.

Sperow, J. L. (September 24, 2020). *Dispositive motions in arbitration: Authority, rules and practical tips*. CPR Speaks Blog. https://blog.cpradr.org/2020/09/24/dispositive-motions-in-arbitration-authority-rules-practical-tips/.

Status: Hague Judgments Convention. (n.d.). Hague Conference on Private International Law. Retrieved June 1, 2025, from https://www.hcch.net/en/instruments/conventions/status-table/?cid=137.

Status: Model Law on ICA. (n.d.). UN Commission on International Trade Law. Retrieved June 1, 2025, from https://uncitral.un.org/en/texts/arbitration/modellaw/commercial_arbitration/status.

Status: Model Law on ICM. (n.d.). UN Commission on International Trade Law. Retrieved June 1, 2025, from https://uncitral.un.org/en/texts/arbitration/modellaw/commercial_conciliation/status.

Status: New York Convention. (n.d.). UN Commission on International Trade Law. Retrieved June 1, 2025, from https://uncitral.un.org/en/texts/arbitration/conventions/foreign_arbitral_awards/status2.

Status: Singapore Convention. (n.d.). UN Commission on International Trade Law. Retrieved June 1, 2025, from https://uncitral.un.org/en/texts/mediation/conventions/international_settlement_agreements/status.

Status: UNCITRAL Arbitration Rules. (n.d.). UN Commission on International Trade Law. Retrieved June 1, 2025, from https://uncitral.un.org/en/texts/arbitration/contractualtexts/arbitration/centres.

Stipanowich, T. J., Von Kann, C. & Rothman, D. (2010). *Protocols for expeditious, cost-effective commercial arbitration: Key action steps for business users, counsel, arbitrators & arbitration provider institutions.* College of Commercial Arbitrators. https://ssrn.com/abstract=1982169.

Strong, S. I. (2014b). Use and perception of international commercial mediation and conciliation: A preliminary report on issues relating to the proposed UNCITRAL Convention on International Commercial Mediation and Conciliation. *University of Missouri School of Law Legal Studies Research Paper No. 2014-28,* 1-53. https://ssrn.com/abstract=2526302.

Sussman, E. & Berger, K. P. (November 16, 2021b). *Mixed mode task force: Working group 4—Arbitrator techniques and their (direct or potential) effect on settlement.* College of Commercial Arbitrators, International Mediation Institute, and the Straus Institute. https://imimediation.org/wp-content/uploads/2021/11/WG-4-Arbitrators-and-settlement-16-Nov-2021.pdf.

Tannous, S. & Omran, A. (May 11, 2018). *The Middle Eastern and African arbitration review 2018: Middle East.* Global Arbitration Review. https://globalarbitrationreview.com/review/the-middle-eastern-and-african-arbitration-review/2018/article/middle-east.

Telford, M. E. (2000). *Med-Arb: A viable dispute resolution alternative.* Queen's University IRC Press. https://irc.queensu.ca/wp-content/uploads/2013/04/articles_med-arb-a-viable-dispute-resolution-alternative.pdf.

The Singapore Mediation Convention: An update on developments in enforcing mediated settlement agreements. (September, 2019). Norton Rose Fulbright. https://www.nortonrosefulbright.com/en-mh/knowledge/publications/b5906716/the-singapore-mediation-convention.

Tietje, C. & Nowrot, K. (2006). Laying conceptual ghosts of the past to rest: The rise of Philip C. Jessup's "Transnational Law" in the regulatory governance of the international economic system. In Tietje, C., Brouder, A. & Nowrot, K. (Eds.), *Philip C. Jessup's transnational law revisited: On the occasion of the 50th anniversary of its publication* (pp. 17-43). Institut für Wirtschaftsrecht. https://docslib.org/doc/12733348/philip-c-jessups-transnational-law-revisited.

Timothy, G. (November 30, 2015). *Investor-State mediations/conciliation in India.* Mediate.com. https://mediate.com/investor-state-mediations-conciliation-in-india/.

UN Conference on Trade and Development. (2014). *Series on international investment agreements II: Investor-State dispute settlement.* United Nations. https://unctad.org/system/files/official-document/diaeia2013d2_en.pdf.

UNCITRAL Regional Centre for Asia and the Pacific (RCAP). (n.d.). UN Commission on International Trade Law. https://uncitral.un.org/en/TA/regionalcentre_asia_pacific.

UNCITRAL WGII. (n.d.). UN Commission on International Trade Law. https://uncitral.un.org/en/working_groups/2/arbitration.

UNCITRAL WGIII. (n.d.). UN Commission on International Trade Law. https://uncitral.un.org/en/working_groups/3/investor-state.

UNIDROIT: Overview. (May 30, 2023). International Institute for the Unification of Private Law. https://www.unidroit.org/about-unidroit/overview/.

Weisman, M. (October 10, 2011). *Med/Arb: A time and cost-effective hybrid for dispute resolution.* Michigan Lawyer's Weekly. https://wyrpc.com/files/med-arb_-_a_cost_effective_hybrid_for_dispute_resolution.pdf.

Wilson, C. (February 1, 2012). *The Arb-Med hybrid in Hong Kong: Much ado about nothing?.* Kluwer Mediation Blog. http://mediationblog.kluwerarbitration.com/2012/02/01/the-arb-med-hybrid-in-hong-kong-much-ado-about-nothing/.

Winnington-Ingram. L. M. & Kim, J. W. (March 29, 2021). *Investment Court System under EU trade and investment agreements: Enforcement issues.* Reed Smith LLP. https://www.reedsmith.com/en/perspectives/2021/03/investment-court-system-under-eu-trade-and-investment-agreements.

World Bank Group. (March 29, 2018). *Belt and Road initiative.* World Bank Brief https://www.worldbank.org/en/topic/regional-integration/brief/belt-and-road-initiative.

WTO: Overview. (n.d.). World Trade Organization. https://www.wto.org/english/thewto_e/thewto_e.htm.

Yan, S. & Woo, E. (September 30, 2014). *Opposing the enforcement of PRC arbitral award on public policy ground? Not as easy as you think!.* ONC Lawyers. https://www.onc.hk/en_US/publication/opposing-the-enforcement-of-prc-arbitral-award-on-public-policy-ground-not-as-easy-as-you-think.

Table of Cases

Australia

Ku-ring-gai Council v. Ichor Constructions Pty Ltd, NSWLR 610 (2018)
The Duke Group Ltd v. Alamain Investments Ltd, SASC 272 (2003)

Brazil

MBV v. Resil, STF (Supreme Federal Court of Brazil), SE. No. 5.206-7 (2001, December 12)
REsp No. 1.543.903/DF, STJ (Superior Court of Justice of Brazil) (2015, June 18)

European Court of Human Rights

Beg S.p.A. v. Italy, Application No. 5312/11, ECtHR (2021, May 20)
Deweer v. Belgium, Application No. 6903/75, ECtHR (1980, February 27)
Lithgow and Others v. The United Kingdom, Applications No. 9006/80, 9262/81, 9263/81, 9265/81, 9266/81, 9313/81, 9405/81, ECtHR (1986, July 8)
Nordström-Janzon v. Netherlands, Application No. 28101/95, ECtHR (1996, November 27)
Osmo Suovaniemi and others v. Finland, Application No. 31737/96, ECtHR (1999, February 23)

Germany

Bayerisches Oberstes Landesgericht, 102 SchH 135/24e (2024, November 7)
BVerfG, 1 BvR 1351/01 (2007, February 14)
Oberlandesgericht Berlin, 13 SchH 2/17, MDR 2018 (2018, February 12)
Oberlandesgericht Bremen, 1 U 35/12, NJW-RR 2013 (2012, November 19)
Oberlandesgericht Dresden, 3 Sch 3/12 (2012, July 26)
Oberlandesgericht Frankfurt, 26 SchII 1/06, SchiedsVZ 2006 (2006, April 27)
Oberlandesgericht Köln, 9 Sch (H) 22/03 (2004, April 2)
Oberlandesgericht Munich, 34 SchH 3/07, SchiedsVZ (2008, January 1)
Oberlandesgericht Munich, 34 SchH 5/15, NJW 2016 (2015, November 24)

Hong Kong

Gao Haiyan and Xie Heping v. Keeneye Holdings Ltd and New Purple Golden Resources Development Ltd, HKEC (CFI) 514 (2011)
Gao Haiyan and Xie Heping v. Keeneye Holdings Ltd and New Purple Golden Resources Development Ltd, CACV (CA) 79 (2011)

United Kingdom

ASM Shipping Ltd of India v. TTMI Ltd of England, [2006] EWCA Civ 1341 (2006, October 16)
Glencot Development & Design Ltd v. Ben Barrett & Son Ltd, [2001] EWHC Technology 15 (2001, February 13)
Halliburton Company v. Chubb Bermuda Insurance Ltd, [2020] UKSC 48 (2020, November 27)
Halsey v. Milton Keynes General NHS Trust, [2004] EWCA Civ 576 (2004, May 11)
Jacqueline Anne Calderbank v. John Thomas Calderbank, [1975] EWCA Civ J0605-1 (1975, June 5)
North Range Shipping Ltd v. Seatrans Shipping Corp., [2002] EWCA Civ 405 (2002, March 14)
R v. Gough, [1993] UKHL 1 (1993, May 20)
Smith v. Kvaerner Cementation, [2006] EWCA Civ 242 (2006, March 21)

United States

Actors' Equity Ass'n v. Paradise Square Prod. Servs. Inc., No. 22 Civ. 7325, 2023 WL 3293577, S.D.N.Y. (2023, May 5)
Albtelecom SH.A v. UNIFI Communs. Inc., Case No. 16 Civ. 9001, 2017 U.S. Dist. LEXIS 82154, S.D.N.Y. (2017, May 30)
Ballantine Books Inc. v. Capital Distributing Co., 302 F.2d 17, 2d Cir. (1962)
Bell v. Johnson, 404 F.3d 997, 6th Cir. (2005)
Bowden v. Weickert, No. S-02-017, 2003 WL 21419175, Ohio App. 6 Dist. (2003, June 20)
Castro v. Tri Marine Fish Co. LLC, 921 F.3d 766, 772-76, 9th. Cir. (2019)
Conkle and Olesten v. Goodrich Goodyear and Hinds, Nos. G033972, G034063, 2006 WL 3095964, Cal. App. 4 Dist. (2006, November 1)
Gaskin v. Gaskin, No. 2-06-039-CV, 2006 WL 2507319, Tex. App.-Fort Worth (2006, September 21)
John Eisendrath v. Superior Court, DJDAR 5849 (2003)
Johnson v. Shaker Heights City School District, U.S. Dist. LEXIS 17963, N.D. Ohio (2007)
Lindsay v. Lewandowski, 139 Cal. App. 4th 1618, 43 Cal. Reptr. 3d 846. Ct. Appeals, 4th Dist. Div. 3 (2006)
Logan v. Logan, No. F051606, 2007 WL 2994640, Cal. App. 5 Dist. (2007, October 16)
McGuire v. Safeguard Metals, LLC, No. 23-CV-05874-SVW-MRW, 2023 WL 6386497, C.D. Cal. (2023, September 28)
New York City & Vicinity Dist. Council of Carpenters v. J.M.R. Concrete Corp., No. 16-CV-711 (ENV) (ST), 2018 WL 2078476, E.D.N.Y. (2018, February 26)

Spector v. Torenberg, 825 F.Supp. 201, S.D.N.Y. (1994)
Teamsters Loc. 630 v. W. Cent. Produce, No. 221CV09294MWFJPRX, 2022 WL 3636167, C.D. Cal. (2022, May 26)
Town of Clinton v. Geological Services Corp., No. 04-0462A, 2006 WL 3246464, Mass. Super. (2006, November 8)
Transocean Offshore Gulf of Guinea Vii v. Erin Energy Corp., Case No. H-17-2623, S.D. Tex. (2018, March 12)
Trustees for Mason Tenders Dist. Council Welfare Fund v. Golden Dev. & Constr. Corp., No. 15 CIV. 769 (GBD), 2018 L 2316632, S.D.N.Y. (2018, May 7)
U.S. Steel Mining Company v. Wilson Downhole Services, No 02:00CV1758, 2006 WL 2869535, W.D. Pa. (2006, October 5)
Wiley v. United Parcel Service Inc., 11 Fed. Appx. 181, 4th Cir. (2001)

Table of Conventions and Treaties

CETA EU-Canada. (January 14, 2017). *The Comprehensive Economic and Trade Agreement (CETA) between Canada and the European Union and its Member States*. Council of the European Union. https://eur-lex.europa.eu/legal-content/EN/TXT/?uri = CELEX%3A22017A0114%2801%29

Convention on Transparency in Investor-State Arbitration. (December 10, 2014). *United Nations Convention on Transparency in Treaty-based Investor-State Arbitration* (Res. 69/116, U.N. Doc. A/69/496). United Nations. https://uncitral.un.org/sites/uncitral.un.org/files/media-documents/uncitral/en/transparency-convention-e.pdf

EU Mediation Directive. (May 21, 2008). *Directive 2008/52/EC of the European Parliament and of the Council on certain aspects of mediation in civil and commercial matters*. Official Journal of the European Union, L 136, 3-8. https://eur-lex.europa.eu/legal-content/EN/TXT/?uri = CELEX:32008L0052.

EU Regulation on Jurisdiction and the Recognition and Enforcement of Judgments in Civil and Commercial Matters. (December 12, 2012). *Regulation (EU) No 1215/2012 of the European Parliament and of the Council on jurisdiction and the recognition and enforcement of judgments in civil and commercial matters*. Official Journal of the European Union, L 351, 1-32. https://eur-lex.europa.eu/legal-content/EN/TXT/HTML/?uri = OJ:L:2012:351:FULL

European Convention on Human Rights. (November 4, 1950). *Convention for the protection of human rights and fundamental freedoms* (ETS No. 005). Council of Europe. https://www.coe.int/en/web/conventions/full-list?module = treaty-detail&treatynum = 005

Hague Judgments Convention. (July 2, 2019). *Convention on the recognition and enforcement of foreign judgments in civil or commercial matters* (No. 013672). Hague Conference on Private International Law. https://www.hcch.net/en/instruments/conventions/full-text/?cid = 137

ICSID Convention. (October 14, 1966). *Convention on the settlement of investment disputes between states and nationals of other states* (No. 8359). Washington, D.C.: International Centre for Settlement of Investment Disputes. https://icsid.worldbank.org/sites/default/files/ICSID_Convention_EN.pdf

New York Convention. (June 10, 1958). *Convention on the recognition and enforcement of foreign arbitral awards* (No. 4739, United Nations Treaty Series, 330, 3). United Nations. https://uncitral.un.org/sites/uncitral.un.org/files/media-documents/uncitral/en/new-york-convention-e.pdf

Riyadh Arab Agreement for Judicial Cooperation (April 6, 1983). *The Riyadh Arab agreement for judicial cooperation*. League of Arab States. https://www.refworld.org/docid/3ae6b38d8.html

Singapore Convention. (December 20, 2018). *Convention on international settlement agreements resulting from mediation* (No. 56376, United Nations Treaty Series, XXII-4). United Nations. https://uncitral.un.org/sites/uncitral.un.org/files/media-documents/EN/Texts/UNCITRAL/Arbitration/mediation_convention_v1900316_eng.pdf

Table of Legislation

Australia

Australia Commercial Arbitration Act No. 160 (1984)
Australia Commercial Arbitration Act No. 61 (2010)
Australia International Arbitration Act No. 136 (1974)

Austria

Austrian Law on Mediation in Civil Law Matters No. 26 (2003)

Brazil

Brazil Arbitration Act No. 9.307 (1996)
Brazil Code of Civil Procedure No. 13.105 (2015)
Brazil Mediation Act No. 13140 (2015)

Canada

British Columbia International Commercial Arbitration Act, R.S.B.C. c. 233 (1996)
Quebec Arbitration Act, CCP C-25.01 (2014)

China

Arbitration Law of the People's Republic of China (1994)
Civil Procedure Law of the People's Republic of China (1991)

France

French Arbitration Act (2011)
French Code of Civil Procedure NCPC (2011)

Georgia

Law of Georgia on Mediation (2019)

Germany

German Arbitration Law (2005)

German Code of Civil Procedure ZPO (2005)

Hong Kong

Hong Kong Arbitration Ordinance (Cap. 609) L.N. 38 (2011)

India

India Arbitration and Conciliation Act No. 26 (1996)

Italy

Italian Arbitration Law (2013)
Italian Code of Civil Procedures (2013)

Japan

Japan Arbitration law No.138 (2003)

Netherlands

Dutch Arbitration Act (2015)
Dutch Code of Civil Procedure (2011)

Singapore

Singapore Arbitration Act (2001)
Singapore International Arbitration Act (1994)

South Korea

Republic of Korea Arbitration Act No. 14176 (2016)

Switzerland

Swiss Code of Best Practice for Corporate Governance (2002)
Swiss Domestic Arbitration Law (2008)
Swiss International Arbitration Law (1987)

United Kingdom

U.K. Arbitration Act c. 23 (1996)
U.K. Civil Procedure Rules (1998)
U.K. Human Rights Act c. 42 (1998)

United States

California International Commercial Arbitration and Conciliation Act (2016)
New Jersey International Arbitration Mediation and Conciliation Act (2017)
North Carolina International Commercial Arbitration and Conciliation Act (2013)
Ohio International Commercial Arbitration and Conciliation Act (2015)
Oregon Mediation and Arbitration Act (2021)
Texas International Commercial Arbitration and Conciliation Act (2008)
U.S. Alternative Dispute Resolution Act 28 U.S.C. (1998)
U.S. Civil Justice Reform Act 28 U.S.C. (1990)

U.S. Federal Arbitration Act, 9 U.S.C. Ch. 1 (1925)
U.S. Federal Rules of Civil Procedure (1938)
U.S. Federal Rules of Civil Procedure (1983)
U.S. Federal Rules of Civil Procedure (1993)
U.S. Uniform Mediation Act U.L.A. 117 (2010)

Table of Rules and Guidelines

AAA Arbitration Rules. (2022). *Commercial arbitration rules*. American Arbitration Association. https://www.adr.org/sites/default/files/Commercial_Rules_Web.pdf

AAA Code of Ethics. (2004). *Code of ethics for arbitrators in commercial disputes*. American Arbitration Association. https://www.arias-us.org/wp-content/uploads/2016/11/3.-AAA-Code-of-Ethics.pdf

AAA Drafting Dispute Resolution Clauses. (2013). *Drafting dispute resolution clauses: A practical guide*. American Arbitration Association. https://www.scribd.com/document/697189974/Guide-for-Drafting-ADR-Clauses-1

ABA Model Code of Judicial Conduct. (2020). *Model code of judicial conduct*. American Bar Association. https://www.americanbar.org/groups/professional_responsibility/publications/model_code_of_judicial_conduct/

ACICA Arbitration Rules. (2021). *Arbitration rules*. Australian Centre for International Commercial Arbitration. https://acica.org.au/acica-rules-2021/

ADRIC Arbitration Rules. (2025). *Arbitration rules*. ADR Institute of Canada. https://adric.ca/rules/ADRIC-Arbitration-Rules-2025.pdf

ADRIC Med-Arb Rules. (2020). *Med-Arb rules*. ADR Institute of Canada. https://adric.ca/wp-content/uploads/2023/12/ADRIC_Med_Arb_Rules_2020_booklet-p.12.pdf

ADRIC Mediation Rules. (2012). *National mediation rules*. ADR Institute of Canada. https://adric.ca/pdf/ADRMEDIATIONRULES2014.pdf

BAC Arbitration Rules. (2022). *Arbitration rules*. Beijing Arbitration Commission. https://eng.bjac.org.cn/english/page/zc/guize_en2022.html

BAC Mediation Rules. (2011). *Mediation rules*. Beijing Arbitration Commission. https://eng.bjac.org.cn/english/page/data_dl/tjgz_en.pdf

CEDR Report on Settlement in ICA. (2009). *Final report of the CEDR commission on settlement in international arbitration*. Centre for Effective Dispute Resolution. https://www.cedr.com/wp-content/uploads/2021/04/Arbitration-Commission-Document-April-2021.pdf

CEDR Rules for Settlement Facilitation. (2009). *Rules for the facilitation of settlement in international arbitration*. Centre for Effective Dispute Resolution. https://www.cedr.com/wp-content/uploads/2021/03/Rules-Settlement-Arbitration.pdf

CEDR Safeguards for Caucusing. (2009). *Safeguards for arbitrators who use private meetings with each party as a means of facilitating settlement (Appendix 2)*. Centre for Effective Dispute Resolution. https://www.cedr.com/wp-content/uploads/2021/04/Arbitration-Commission-Document-April-2021.pdf

CIArb Arbitration Rules. (2015). *Arbitration rules*. Chartered Institute of Arbitrators. https://www.ciarb.org/media/v1lpnacq/1-ciarb-arbitration-rules.pdf

CIArb Guidelines for Arbitrators on the use of ADR procedures. (2011). *Guidelines for arbitrators on the use of ADR procedures*. Chartered Institute of Arbitrators. https://acica.org.au/wp-content/uploads/2020/04/2011-adr-procedures-in-arb itration.pdf

CIArb Guidelines on Managing Arbitrations. (2016). *Guidelines on managing arbitrations and procedural orders*. Chartered Institute of Arbitrators. https://www.ciarb.org/media/0v2ldpbw/6-managing-arbitrations-and-procedural-orders-201 5.pdf

CIArb Introduction to Practice Guidelines. (2015). *Introduction to the international arbitration practice guidelines*. Chartered Institute of Arbitrators. https://www.ciarb.org/media/g4bhetey/introduction-to-the-international-arbitration-practice -guidelines.pdf

CIArb Practice Guideline on the Use of Mediation in Arbitration. (2021). *Professional practice guideline on the use of mediation in arbitration*. Chartered Institute of Arbitrators. https://www.ciarb.org/media/qgndw1eo/14-professional-practice-guideline-on-the-use-of-mediation-in-arbitration-2021.pdf

CIETAC Arbitration Rules. (2024). *Arbitration rules*. China International Economic and Trade Arbitration Commission. https://www.cietac.org/en/articles/32216

CIETAC Guidelines on Evidence. (2024). *Guidelines on evidence*. China International Economic and Trade Arbitration Commission. https://www.cietac.org/en/articles/25113

Code of Sports-Related Arbitration. (2023). *Code of Sports-Related arbitration*. Court of Arbitration for Sport. https://www.tas-cas.org/fileadmin/user_upload/CAS_Code_2023__EN_.pdf

CPR Code of Ethics for Arbitrators. (2005). *Code of ethics for arbitrators in commercial disputes*. International Institute for Conflict Prevention & Resolution. https://drs .cpradr.org/rules/protocols-guidelines/ethics-codes/code-of-ethics-for-arbitrato rs-in-commercial-disputes

CPR Rules for International Arbitration. (2019). *Rules for administered arbitration of international disputes*. International Institute for Conflict Prevention & Resolution. https://drs.cpradr.org/rules/international/arbitration/2019-international-administered-arbitration-rules

CPR Rules for Non-Administered Arbitration. (2018). *Non-administered arbitration rules*. International Institute for Conflict Prevention & Resolution. https://drs.cpradr.org/rules/arbitration/non-administered/2018-cpr-non-administered-arbi tration-rules

DIS Arbitration Rules. (2018). *Arbitration rules*. German Arbitration Institute. https://www.disarb.org/en/tools-for-dis-proceedings/dis-rules

DIS Conciliation Rules. (2002). *Conciliation rules*. German Arbitration Institute. https://www.disarb.org/en/tools-for-dis-proceedings/dis-rules

DIS Mediation Rules. (2010). *Mediation rules*. German Arbitration Institute. https://www.disarb.org/en/tools-for-dis-proceedings/dis-rules

HKIAC Arbitration Rules. (2024). *Administered arbitration rules*. Hong Kong International Arbitration Centre. https://www.hkiac.org/arbitration/rules-practice-notes/hkiac-administered-2024

HKIAC Mediation Rules. (1999). *Mediation rules*. Hong Kong International Arbitration Centre. https://www.hkiac.org/mediation/rules/hkiac-mediation-rules

Hong Kong Judiciary Practice Direction on Mediation. (2010). *General guide to Practice Direction 31: Mediation*. Hong Kong Judiciary. https://mediation.judiciary.hk/en/doc/GeneralGuide_PD31-Eng.pdf

IAMA Arbitration Rules. (2014). *Arbitration rules*. Institute of Arbitrators and Mediators Australia. https://www.resolution.institute/web/public-in-dispute/rules-and-regulations/iama-arbitration-rules-2014.aspx?ss360SearchTerm = arbitratio n%20rules

IBA Guidelines on Conflicts of Interest in International Arbitration. (2024). *Guidelines on conflicts of interest in international arbitration*. International Bar Association. https://www.ibanet.org/document?id = Guidelines-on-Conflicts-of-Interest-in-International-Arbitration-2024

IBA Rules for Investor-State Mediation. (2012). *Rules for Investor-State mediation*. International Bar Association. https://www.ibanet.org/MediaHandler?id = C74 CE2C9-7E9E-4BCA-8988-2A4DF573192C

IBA Rules of Ethics for International Arbitrators. (1987). *Rules of ethics for international arbitrators*. International Bar Association. https://www.ibanet.org/document?id = Rules-of-ethics-for-international-arbitrators

IBA Rules on Evidence in International Arbitration. (2020). *Rules on the taking of evidence in international arbitration*. International Bar Association. https://www.ibanet.org/MediaHandler?id = def0807b-9fec-43ef-b624-f2cb2af7cf7b

ICC Arbitration Rules. (2021). *Arbitration rules*. International Chamber of Commerce. https://iccwbo.org/dispute-resolution/dispute-resolution-services/arbitration/rules-procedure/2021-arbitration-rules/

ICC Guide on Effective Conflict Management. (2023). *Guide: Effective conflict management*. International Chamber of Commerce. https://iccwbo.org/wp-content/uploads/sites/3/2023/09/2023_Effective-Conflict-Management-901-1.pdf

ICC Guide on Effective Management of Arbitration. (2018). *Effective management of arbitration: A guide for in-house counsel and other party representatives*. International Chamber of Commerce. https://iccwbo.org/wp-content/uploads/sites/3/2017/05/866-3-ENG-Effective-Management-of-Arbitration.pdf

ICC Mediation Guidance Notes. (2014). *Mediation guidance notes*. International Chamber of Commerce. https://iccwbo.org/wp-content/uploads/sites/3/2014/12/icc-mediation-guidance-notes-english.pdf

ICC Note on the Conduct of Arbitration. (2021). *Note to parties and arbitral tribunals on the conduct of the arbitration under the ICC Rules of Arbitration*. International Chamber of Commerce. https://iccwbo.org/content/uploads/sites/3/2020/12/icc-note-to-parties-and-arbitral-tribunals-on-the-conduct-of-arbitration-english-2021.pdf

ICC Report on Facilitating Settlement in ICA. (2023). *Report on facilitating settlement in international arbitration*. International Chamber of Commerce. https://iccwbo.org/wp-content/uploads/sites/3/2023/09/2023_Facilitating-Settlement-in-International-Arbitration-900-1.pdf

ICDR Final Offer Arbitration Rules. (2015). *ICDR final offer arbitration supplementary rules*. International Centre for Dispute Resolution of the AAA. https://icdr.org/sites/default/files/document_repository/Final_Offer_Supplementary_Arbitration_Procedures.pdf

ICDR International Arbitration Rules. (2021). *ICDR international arbitration rules*. International Centre for Dispute Resolution of the AAA. https://www.icdr.org/sites/default/files/document_repository/ICDR_Rules_1.pdf?utm_source = icdr-website&utm_medium = rules-page&utm_campaign = rules-intl-update-1mar

ICSID Arbitration Rules. (2022). *Arbitration rules*. International Centre for Settlement of Investment Disputes. https://icsid.worldbank.org/sites/default/files/documents/ICSID_Convention.pdf

ICSID Mediation Rules. (2022). *Mediation rules*. International Centre for Settlement of Investment Disputes. https://icsid.worldbank.org/sites/default/files/documents/ICSID_Mediation.pdf

JAMS Arbitrators Ethics Guidelines. (2021). *Arbitrators ethics guidelines*. Judicial Arbitration and Mediation Services. https://www.jamsadr.com/arbitrators-ethics/

JAMS Comprehensive Arbitration Rules and Procedures. (2021). *Comprehensive arbitration rules and procedures*. Judicial Arbitration and Mediation Services. https://www.jamsadr.com/rules-comprehensive-arbitration/

JAMS International Arbitration Rules and Procedures. (2021). *International arbitration rules and procedures*. Judicial Arbitration and Mediation Services. https://www.jamsadr.com/international-arbitration-rules/english

LCIA Arbitration Rules. (2020). *Arbitration rules*. London Court for International Arbitration. https://www.lcia.org/Dispute_Resolution_Services/lcia-arbitration-rules-2020.aspx

LCIA Mediation Rules. (2020). *Mediation rules*. London Court for International Arbitration. https://www.lcia.org/Dispute_Resolution_Services/lcia_mediation_rules_2020.aspx

LMAA Arbitration Rules. (2021). *The LMAA terms*. London Maritime Arbitrators Association. https://lmaa.london/wp-content/uploads/2022/11/LMAA-Terms-2021.pdf

LMAA Early Neutral Evaluation Guidance Note. (2022). *LMAA early neutral evaluation: Guidance note*. London Maritime Arbitrators Association. https://lmaa.london/wp-content/uploads/2022/01/LMAA-EARLY-NEUTRAL-EVALUATION-Guidelines.pdf

LMAA Mediation Rules. (2002). *LMAA mediation terms*. London Maritime Arbitrators Association. https://lmaa.london/wp-content/uploads/2020/08/mediationterms.pdf

Milan Chamber Arbitration Rules. (2023). *Arbitration rules*. Milan Chamber of Arbitration. https://www.camera-arbitrale.it/upload/documenti/arbitrato/CAM%20arbitration%20rules%202023.pdf

Model Law on ICA (2006). *Model law on international commercial arbitration*. Sales No. E.08.V.4. UN Commission on International Trade Law. https://uncitral.un.org/sites/uncitral.un.org/files/media-documents/uncitral/en/19-09955_e_ebook.pdf

Model Law on ICM. (2018). *Model law on international commercial mediation and international settlement agreements resulting from mediation*. Sales No. E.22.V.25. UN Commission on International Trade Law. https://uncitral.un.org/sites/uncitral.un.org/files/media-documents/uncitral/en/22-01363_mediation_guide_e_ebook_rev.pdf

Model Law on International Commercial Conciliation. (2002). *Model law on international commercial conciliation*. Sales No. E.05.V.4. UN Commission on International Trade Law. https://uncitral.un.org/sites/uncitral.un.org/files/media-documents/uncitral/en/03-90953_ebook.pdf

NAI Arbitration Rules. (2024). *Arbitration rules*. Netherlands Arbitration Institute. https://nai.nl/2024-nai-arbitration-rules/

NAI Mediation Rules. (2017). *Mediation rules*. Netherlands Arbitration Institute. https://nai.nl/nai-mediation-rules/

PCA Arbitration Rules. (2012). *Arbitration rules*. Permanent Court of Arbitration. https://docs.pca-cpa.org/2015/11/PCA-Arbitration-Rules-2012.pdf

Prague Rules. (2018). *Rules on the efficient conduct of proceedings in international arbitration (Prague Rules)*. Working Group on increasing the efficiency of arbitral proceedings. https://praguerules.com/upload/medialibrary/9dc/9dc31ba7799e26473d92961d926948c9.pdf

SCC Arbitration Rules. (2023). *Arbitration rules*. Stockholm Chamber of Commerce. https://sccarbitrationinstitute.se/wp-content/uploads/2024/12/SCC_Arbitration_Rules_2023_English.pdf

SCIA Arbitration Rules. (2022). *Arbitration rules*. Shenzhen Court of International Arbitration. https://en.scia.com.cn/ArbitrationRules.html

SIAC Arbitration Rules. (2025). *Arbitration rules*. Singapore International Arbitration Centre. https://siac.org.sg/wp-content/uploads/2025/04/SIAC-Rules-7th-Edition_250825.pdf

SIAC Investment Arbitration Rules. (2017). *Investment arbitration rules*. Singapore International Arbitration Centre. https://siac.org.sg/wp-content/uploads/2022/06/SIAC-Investment-Rules-2017.pdf

SIAC-SIMC AMA Protocol. (2014). *SIAC-SIMC Arb-Med-Arb protocol*. Singapore International Arbitration Centre & Singapore International Mediation Centre. https://siac.org.sg/arb-med-arb-ama-protocol

Swiss Arbitration Rules. (2021). *Swiss rules of international arbitration*. Swiss Arbitration Association. https://www.swissarbitration.org/centre/arbitration/arbitration-rules/

UNCITRAL Arbitration Rules. (2021). *Arbitration rules*. UN Commission on International Trade Law. https://uncitral.un.org/sites/uncitral.un.org/files/media-documents/uncitral/en/21-07996_expedited-arbitration-e-ebook.pdf

UNCITRAL Code of Conduct for Arbitrators in Investment Arbitration. (2024). *Code of conduct for arbitrators in international investment dispute resolution*. UN Commission on International Trade Law. https://uncitral.un.org/sites/uncitral.un.org/files/media-documents/uncitral/en/2318824e-coc_arbitrators_ebook_11june.pdf

UNCITRAL Expedited Arbitration Rules. (2021). *Expedited arbitration rules*. UN Commission on International Trade Law. https://uncitral.un.org/sites/uncitral.un.org/files/media-documents/uncitral/en/21-07996_expedited-arbitration-e-ebook.pdf

UNCITRAL Guidelines on Mediation of Investment Disputes. (2024). *Guidelines on mediation for international investment disputes*. UN Commission on International Trade Law. https://uncitral.un.org/sites/uncitral.un.org/files/media-documents/uncitral/en/2401497e_mediation_guidelines_-ebook_eng.pdf

UNCITRAL Mediation Rules. (2021). *Mediation rules*. UN Commission on International Trade Law. https://uncitral.un.org/sites/uncitral.un.org/files/media-documents/uncitral/en/22-01369_mediation_rules_ebook_1.pdf

UNCITRAL Model Clauses on SPEDR. (2024). *Model clauses on specialised express dispute resolution*. UN Commission on International Trade Law. https://uncitral.un.org/sites/uncitral.un.org/files/media-documents/uncitral/en/mc-spedr_en.pdf

UNCITRAL Model Provisions on Mediation of Investment Disputes. (2024). *Model provisions on mediation for international investment disputes (Annex)*. UN Commission on International Trade Law. https://uncitral.un.org/sites/uncitral.un.org/files/media-documents/uncitral/en/2401497e_mediation_guidelines_-ebook_eng.pdf

UNCITRAL Notes on Arbitration. (1996). *Notes on organizing arbitral proceedings*. UN Commission on International Trade Law. https://www.un-ilibrary.org/content/books/9789210450720s007-c003/read

UNCITRAL Notes on Arbitration. (2023). *Notes on organizing arbitral proceedings (with an additional note on early dismissal and preliminary determination adopted in 2023)*. UN Commission on International Trade Law. https://uncitral.un.org/sites/uncitral.un.org/files/media-documents/uncitral/en/notes-on-organizing-arbitral-proceedings-2023.pdf

UNCITRAL Rules on Transparency in Investor-State Arbitration. (2014). *Rules on transparency in treaty-based Investor-State arbitration*. UN Commission on International Trade Law. https://uncitral.un.org/sites/uncitral.un.org/files/media-documents/uncitral/en/rules-on-transparency-e.pdf

Table of Surveys and Empirical Studies

1987 McGillicuddy Field Experiment
2001-2004 Bühring-Uhle Study
2002 Conlon Study
2002-2004 Andrew Study
2002-2005 Kaufmann-Kohler and Bonnin Study
2006 Robinson Survey
2007 Ali Survey
2007 Kun and Kaufmann-Kohler Study
2008 Wissler Survey
2010 Condliffe and Zeleznikow Study
2011 Cornell University Survey
2011-2012 Kun and Kaufmann-Kohler Survey
2013 Straus Institute Survey
2013 Sussman Survey
2014 Nigmatullina Study
2014 Straus Institute Survey
2015 Queen Mary International Arbitration Survey
2016 National University of Singapore Survey
2016-2017 GPC Survey
2018 Queen Mary International Arbitration Survey
2020 Mixed Mode Task Force Survey
2020 UNCTAD Study
2021 Aragaki Study
2021 Queen Mary International Arbitration Survey

Table of UN Resolutions

UN General Assembly. (1966, December 17). *Establishment of the United Nations Commission on International Trade Law* (Resolution 2205 [XXI]). https://undocs.org/en/A/RES/2205(XXI)

UN General Assembly. (1985, December 11). *Model Law on international commercial arbitration of the United Nations Commission on International Trade Law* (Resolution 40/72). https://digitallibrary.un.org/record/196028?ln=en&v=pdf

UN General Assembly. (2016, December 19). *2016 notes on organizing arbitral proceedings of the United Nations Commission on International Trade Law* (Resolution 71/137). https://digitallibrary.un.org/record/845611?ln=en&v=pdf

www.ingramcontent.com/pod-product-compliance
Lightning Source LLC
LaVergne TN
LVHW020002031026
849161LV00023B/816
9789403538099